Advance Praise for DEEP FREEZE

"Dian Belanger has written an exciting and thought-provoking account of the U.S. Navy Seabees, flyers, and scientists who lived through and made the transition from the 'heroic' age to the 'scientific' age of Antarctic exploration. These mostly young men (no women were allowed on 'the Ice') risked lives and endured both cold and dark Antarctic winters and un-imaginable isolation from the world to provide a U.S. presence on the vast, remote, ice-covered continent. *Deep Freeze,* based on countless interviews and painstaking research, is a timely and gripping account."

—JOHN C. BEHRENDT, president of the American Polar Society and
author of *The Ninth Circle* and *Innocents on the Ice*

"With its well-timed arrival on the eve of the International Polar Year 2007–2008, *Deep Freeze* offers a welcome and thorough new examination of America's involvement in Antarctica during the IGY, often told through the words of the participants themselves."

—JEFF RUBIN, author of *Lonely Planet Antarctica*

"An excellent historical chronology of the United States Antarctic Program and the first establishment of permanent scientific research facilities on the continent of Antarctica. Those who brought this program to life are heroes by every definition of the word. The truly amazing stories of pioneers are chronicled in this detailed and entertaining read. Dian Belanger's count-less hours interviewing living heroes who accomplished Herculean tasks give us pause to remember where this all began."

—JERRY W. MARTY, National Science Foundation Representative,
South Pole Station, Antarctica

"With the fifty-year anniversary of the International Geophysical Year approaching, the author has done a remarkable job in researching the IGY through archival materials and interviews with some of the major individu-als involved. Writing for a wide audience, she offers in-depth discussions of U.S. preparations for stations, their construction, scientific research, winterover experiences, and the formulation of the Antarctic Treaty, the glue that holds it all together."

—JOHN SPLETTSTOESSER, Advisor to the International
Association of Antarctica Tour Operators

"The story of the beginning of Operation Deep Freeze has finally been told by a dynamic writer and historian."

—RMC BILLY-ACE PENGUIN BAKER, USN (retired)
Vice Chairman, Antarctic Deep Freeze Association

"*Deep Freeze* provides a wealth of hitherto unreported history. The use of oral history accounts, diary-based material, and quotations from literature of the era is a particular strength in this major recapturing of the heady days of 1957–59. Very little comprehensive historical scholarship has been devoted to IGY since the popular preliminary accounts that appeared (by Dufek, Sullivan, Wilson, Chapman, Eklund and Beckman, etc.) in the late 1950s and early 1960s."

—PETER-NOEL WEBB, geologist for U.S. and New Zealand IGY
expeditions and Trans-Antarctic Expedition

"In *Deep Freeze* Dian Belanger has written an important book, fine and well-researched, focusing on the IGY in Antarctica (1957–1958), which led to the Antarctic Treaty."

—J. MERTON ENGLAND, NSF historian (retired) and
author of *A Patron for Pure Science*

"This is a comprehensive and lively book about the people and events that transformed Antarctica into an international laboratory for science. Through their vision, courage, and willingness to work together, the people of Deep Freeze and the IGY brought about a legacy of discovery that continues today and that helps us to understand both Antarctica and the forces of global change. To tell this fascinating and important story, Dian Belanger not only used existing historical records but also added to that documentation with extensive interviews."

—RAIMUND E. GOERLER, Chief Archivist/Byrd Polar
Research Center of The Ohio State University

"Dian Belanger's account of the historical development of the early infrastructure for the American Antarctic science operation is superb. Compellingly told, the book incorporates significant research from new sources and unused collections. A must read for anyone with an interest in Antarctica and the early science it provided."

—GEORGE T. MAZUZAN, NSF historian (retired)

"Dian Belanger's *Deep Freeze* presents science in Antarctica with fascinating perspective, present and past, all rewarding. Well documented."

—DICK BOWERS, CDR CEC USN (retired), Officer in charge of construction,
McMurdo and Pole Stations, Deep Freeze I and II

DEEP FREEZE

DEEP

DEEP FREEZE

The United States,
the International Geophysical Year,
and the Origins of Antarctica's Age of Science

Dian Olson Belanger

UNIVERSITY PRESS OF COLORADO

© 2006 by the University Press of Colorado

Published by the University Press of Colorado
5589 Arapahoe Avenue, Suite 206C
Boulder, Colorado 80303

 The University Press of Colorado is a proud member of
the Association of American University Presses.

The University Press of Colorado is a cooperative publishing enterprise supported, in part, by Adams State College, Colorado State University, Fort Lewis College, Mesa State College, Metropolitan State College of Denver, University of Colorado, University of Northern Colorado, and Western State College of Colorado.

∞ The paper used in this publication meets the minimum requirements of the American National Standard for Information Sciences—Permanence of Paper for Printed Library Materials. ANSI Z39.48-1992

Library of Congress Cataloging-in-Publication Data

Belanger, Dian Olson, 1941–
 Deep freeze : the United States, the International Geophysical Year, and the origins of Antarctica's age of science / Dian Olson Belanger.
    p. cm.
 Includes bibliographical references and index.
  ISBN: 978-0-87081-830-1 (hardcover : alk. paper) — ISBN: 978-1-60732-066-1 (pbk. : alk. paper) 1. Antarctica—Discovery and exploration—American. 2. Antarctica—Discovery and exploration. 3. United States. Navy. Task Force 43—History. 4. International Geophysical Year, 1957–1958. I. Title.
  G872.A46B45 2006
  919.8'9—dc22

                                                                            2006017263

Design by Daniel Pratt

15   14   13   12   11   10   09   08   07   06   10   9   8   7   6   5   4   3   2   1

A National Science Foundation grant, No. OPP-9810431 through the Office of Polar Programs, supported the research, including a visit to McMurdo and South Pole Stations, Antarctica, and the writing of this book. The interpretations are the author's and do not necessarily reflect the views of the National Science Foundation.

To
the Antarctic pioneers
of the landmark 1950s
who lived this story
and had to wait too long to have it told

CONTENTS

CONTENTS

MAPS AND FIGURES

ILLUSTRATIONS

Antarctic Convergence   The region where the colder, denser polar
waters flowing north meet and dip below the warmer seas flowing south. A marked surface temperature change occurs.

ATCM   Antarctic Treaty Consultative Meeting.

ATCP   Antarctic Treaty Consultative Parties.

ATS   Antarctic Treaty System.

aurora australis   Colorful, moving displays of light in the Antarctic
night sky. Atomic particles from the sun, channeled by the earth's
magnetic field, collide with oxygen and nitrogen molecules in
the upper atmosphere, releasing visible energy.

austral Southern; pertaining to the Southern Hemisphere.

BAS British Antarctic Survey, formerly Falkland Islands Dependencies Survey (FIDS).

beset Situation of a ship surrounded by and stuck in the ice.

Big Eye Insomnia caused by the twenty-four-hour sunlight of austral summer. Also occurs in the continuous dark of winter.

calving The breaking off of a piece of ice from an ice shelf or glacier to form an iceberg. Tabular (flat-topped) bergs born of ice shelves are unique to the Antarctic.

CCAMLR Convention on the Conservation of Antarctic Marine Living Resources, a legally separate treaty within the ATS.

Clements hut A box-shaped modular building constructed by connecting identical insulated 4' x 8' plywood panels. Used for IGY housing.

CO Commanding officer.

COMNAP Council of Managers of National Antarctic Programs.

CPO, CWO Chief petty officer, chief warrant officer; U.S. Navy enlisted leaders.

CRAMRA Convention on the Regulation of Antarctic Mineral Resource Activities. Never ratified, it was superseded by the Environmental Protocol.

crevasse A steep fissure in a glacier that can vary greatly in all dimensions, sometimes dangerously hidden by a wind-formed snow bridge.

CSAGI Comité Spécial de l'Année Géophysique Internationale, the special committee created by ICSU to plan and implement the IGY.

Deep Freeze, Operation Code name of the U.S. Naval Support Force, Antarctica, Task Force 43.

firn Old snow that has become dense but retains tiny pockets of air; a transitional substance between snow and ice.

floe A relatively flat piece of floating sea ice. The U.S. Navy Hydrographic Office, in 1956, suggested that small floes be thought of as about the size of a city block; medium floes, a golf course; giant floes, a small town.

geodesy The study of the earth's shape and size and the precise location of points on its surface.

geomagnetic poles Theoretical points on the earth's surface visualized as the ends of a bar magnet through its center if all the earth's magnetic fields were caused by that magnet.

geomagnetism The study of the magnetic phenomena exhibited by the earth; also called terrestrial magnetism.

geophysics The application of the principles of physics to the study of the earth as a planet.

glacier A mass of snow and ice continuously moving like a frozen river from higher to lower ground.

glaciology The study of all forms of glaciers, their characteristics and processes; broadly, the study of all aspects of ice and snow.

Gondwanaland Vast proto-continent of the Southern Hemisphere.

GPS Global Positioning System, a satellite-based triangulation method that determines geographic location on earth within a few meters.

Grid A coordinate system used for navigating near the Pole, where the lines of longitude converge and all directions are north. The Prime Meridian (0°) is arbitrarily designated Grid North, making 180° Grid South, and so on.

ham An amateur shortwave-radio operator.

hamgram A message transmitted from Antarctica in Morse code, translated and typed out by the receiving U.S. ham and mailed to the addressee. Hamgrams were also sent from the States.

heavy swing, or swing Another name for the tractor trains that supplied inland Byrd Station from Little America.

Hercules A C-130, a four-engine transport plane denoted LC-130 when ski-equipped; popularly called a "Herc."

iceberg A large mass of floating or stranded freshwater ice broken away from a glacier or ice shelf—by definition, about the size of a ship or larger. Smaller bergy bits are about the size of a small cottage; hazardous, difficult-to-see growlers, a grand piano; brash ice, loose fragments of wrecked ice forms, small pool-table size.

ice sheet A mass of snow and glacier ice of considerable breadth and thickness overlying a large land area (rock) or floating. An ice cap is similar but smaller in extent.

ice shelf The floating extension of a continental ice sheet beyond the coastline. Its seaward edge is called an ice front.

ICSU International Council of Scientific Unions, parent organization for the IGY.

IGY International Geophysical Year, 1 July 1957 through 31 December 1958.

Jamesway   An easily assembled prefabricated hut made of wooden arches covered with insulated canvas. Of Korean War vintage, used by the military in cold climates.

JATO   Jet-assisted takeoff, achieved by exploding gases in canisters strapped to aircraft.

katabatic   Fierce, gravity-driven winds caused by cold, dense air rushing down from the polar plateau toward the coast.

knot   A nautical unit of speed. One nautical or geographical mile equals 1.15 statute miles (1.85 km).

lead   A ribbon or path of open water within floes of pack ice that enable a ship to move through.

LGP   Low ground pressure, obtained by widening the tracks of a tractor to distribute its weight over the snow.

magnetic poles   The migrating points on the earth's surface to which the poles of a compass needle point, where the earth's magnetic lines of force are vertical.

NAS   National Academy of Sciences, a private organization to which distinguished scientists are elected. By federal charter (1863) it advises the government on scientific and technological matters.

NBS   National Bureau of Standards, a federal agency devoted to establishing accurate measurement standards for U.S. science, industry, and commerce.

névé   Literally, "last year's snow." Hard, granular, consolidated snow on the upper part of a glacier that has not yet turned to solid glacial ice.

NRC   National Research Council, the research arm of the National Academy of Sciences.

NSB   National Science Board, the NSF board of directors.

NSC   National Security Council, an interdepartmental, interagency group advising the president on military and foreign policy issues.

NSF   National Science Foundation, an independent federal agency promoting the progress of science by support of research through grants and contracts.

NSFA   Naval Support Force, Antarctica. Designated Task Force 43.

nunatak   "Lonely rock" in Inuit; the top of a mountain or large rock projecting up through an ice sheet.

OAE   Old Antarctic explorer.

OCB   Operations Coordinating Board, an interagency body of the National Security Council charged to uphold national interests during the IGY. Admiral Dufek chaired its working group on Antarctica.

pack ice   An area of drifting sea ice, whether loose floes or consolidated (frozen together), covering the sea surface with little or no open water.

phone patch   A way of talking with someone at home. The Antarctic station radio operator contacted a U.S. "ham," who would telephone the desired person. The callee would pay any U.S. phone charges.

polynya   A "lake" (area of open water) within the pack ice.

PRB   Polar Research Board of the National Academy of Sciences, an advisory body on scientific programs. From its origins in 1958 until 1975, it was called the Committee on Polar Research.

pressure ice   Floating ice that has been squeezed together by wind or currents, often forced upward into rafted (overriding) ice, hummocks (mounds), or ridges.

SAR   Search and rescue.

sastrugi   Wind- and erosion-formed "dunes" of snow. The irregular ridges, parallel to the direction of the prevailing wind, can be high, sharp, and very hard.

SCAR   Scientific (until 1961, Special) Committee on Antarctic Research, an international group charged to recommend scientific programs to participating governments within the ATS.

Seabees   Members of the construction battalions of the U.S. Navy's Civil Engineer Corps, founded in World War II.

seismology   The study of earthquakes and the vibrations (seismic waves) they produce in the earth. During the IGY, seismic waves were produced by explosives to study ice depth and materials beneath it.

serac   A pointed ice ridge in a crevassed area.

SIPRE   Snow, Ice and Permafrost Research Establishment of the U.S. Army Corps of Engineers.

SITREP   Situation report.

synoptic   Occurring simultaneously in numerous locations.

TAE   The British Commonwealth Transantarctic Expedition.

the ice   Antarctica.

USAP   United States Antarctic Program, the successor to USARP in 1971 when NSF assumed responsibility for all U.S. Antarctic activities, including support operations purchased from the Navy.

USARP   United States Antarctic Research Program, established by NSF in March 1959 to coordinate the overall U.S. Antarctic program and manage its budget.

USCG   United States Coast Guard.

USGS   United States Geological Survey.

USN   United States Navy.

USNC or **USNC-IGY**   United States National Committee for the IGY.

VX-6   Air Development Squadron SIX, the Navy's air arm for Operation Deep Freeze.

VXE-6   Antarctic Development Squadron SIX, successor to VX-6, established in 1969.

wanigan   A small hut mounted on a tractor-pulled sled for use by a field party.

whiteout   A disorienting condition in which light is diffused by multiple reflections between a low overcast sky and the snow surface so that shadows vanish, making it impossible to distinguish the horizon or surface features.

WMO   World Meteorological Organization.

Zulu   Phonetic for "z," the zero meridian of longitude, which runs through Greenwich, England. Zulu Time, or Greenwich Mean Time (GMT), was used for recording scientific observations.

FOREWORD

This book began as a wish to tell the story of the men—military and civilian—who planned, built, and helped operate the network of facilities in Antarctica that were established to support scientists during the International Geophysical Year (IGY), scheduled to begin in mid-1957. The initial concept began in Christchurch, New Zealand, in late 1995 at the fortieth anniversary celebration of the Navy's Operation Deep Freeze program. Dick Bowers, who as a young engineering officer in Deep Freeze I and II had charge of constructing both McMurdo and South Pole stations, expressed concern to Erick Chiang of the National Science Foundation (NSF) that so many of the early veterans were no longer living. He hoped their collective experiences and accomplishments could be documented by those remaining before it was too late. Chiang, who heads the Office of Polar Programs' Polar Research Support Section, thought an oral history program might be the answer.

Several months later, Bowers's Deep Freeze teammate Jim Bergstrom, executive officer at the McMurdo Air Operations Facility, met with Chiang and Guy Guthridge, Polar Information Program Manager, at NSF headquarters in Arlington, Virginia, to discuss the matter further. He spoke on behalf of the Antarctic Deep Freeze Association (ADFA), an organization composed primarily of veterans of the early Deep Freeze years, who heartily supported the idea of an oral history project. They remained enthusiastic when the NSF representatives later proposed a history whose scope was enlarged to provide not only a more complete background of activities preceding the IGY but also the scientific pursuits of the IGY itself and the political aspects of the pre- and post-IGY period that led to the Antarctic Treaty and a continuous stream of important scientific endeavor for nearly fifty years.

With the guidance of the NSF officials, historian Dian Belanger was asked to participate. She agreed to prepare a request for a grant from the NSF and, upon grant approval, to conduct and record oral history interviews, perform related research, and write a book based on her findings. A committee of ADFA members, including Bill Stroup as financial officer, agreed to administer the grant and assist her in any way possible, using the full resources of the ADFA. A grant was awarded in August 1998. This book is the culmination of her effort. The dozens of oral histories, besides being sources for the book, are separately preserved in polar archives.

The ADFA is extremely proud of the work Dian Belanger has accomplished and is delighted with the way she captured both events and the mood with color and realism. The ADFA is also greatly indebted to the National Science Foundation for its support during the life of the grant.

James H. Bergstrom, CAPT, USN (Ret.), Project CEO
Richard A. Bowers, CDR, CEC USN (Ret.), Project Asst. CEO
William E. Stroup, CWO4, CEC USN (Ret.), Project CFO

PREFACE AND ACKNOWLEDGMENTS

My partners tell the story of the origins of this history in their gener-
ous Foreword. They left out but one important name—that of George
Mazuzan, National Science Foundation (NSF) historian. George, who
had earlier overseen the writing of my history of NSF support of engi-
neering research and remained an advocate, sat in on James
Bergstrom's meeting with Guy Guthridge and Erick Chiang in NSF's
Office of Polar Programs. He recommended me to carry forward the
Antarctic oral history idea launched by Richard Bowers's musings in
New Zealand. Would I be interested, George called to ask? "Sure, that
sounds cool," I said, with no conscious pun and no inkling whatever

of the transformative journey that lay ahead. After I met with Jim and absorbed the magnitude and excitement of the Deep Freeze story, I gladly drafted a proposal for NSF funding and then another when Guy and George suggested that I also write a history that would include all that had happened because of the International Geophysical Year (IGY) in Antarctica—the Navy's essential enabling role, the IGY scientists' coordinated quest for polar knowledge, and politicians' and statesmen's bold pursuit of a treaty to preserve the IGY ideal on the polar continent.

At length the grant came through and, with that, my relationship with the Antarctic Deep Freeze Association grew beyond any of our imaginings. Jim, as CEO, managed our administrative affairs with meticulous attention, keeping me aware of requirements and ahead of deadlines. Dick suggested interview subjects and made introductory contacts for me. He found answers to my never-ending stream of questions. William (Bill) Stroup, also a DF I veteran, handled all financial matters with NSF. They all faithfully stayed with me even when the project expanded beyond their own polar involvement and the time and effort they thought they had committed. They plied me with research materials, personal insights, and encouragement, especially when barriers were encountered. An unusual partnership perhaps, it has been a warm and fruitful one. Once-yeoman Bob Chaudoin, on his own, spent months retyping, and annotating, for my use, the thick McMurdo and South Pole narratives and transcribing Navy officer-in-charge David Canham's diary.

More than forty south-polar pioneers scattered around the United States, and one in Antarctica, enthusiastically agreed to talk with me about their experiences in widely varying roles. Identified formally in the Notes on Sources, they shared memories and interpretations that illuminated every phase of the history. Please visit their names. My former colleague, Darlene Wilt, beautifully transcribed the interview tapes. Ben Koether of the Glacier Society kindly helped me set up interviews with former crew members of the icebreaker *Glacier.*

In addition, I was fortunate to use many oral history interviews conducted for the Byrd Polar Research Center's Polar Oral History Archival Program, headed by Capt. Brian Shoemaker, USN (Ret.), of the American Polar Society, and Dr. Raimund Goerler of the Ohio State University Libraries. While their NSF-funded project encompassed both polar regions and a broader time frame, Brian coordinated his interview lists with mine, intentionally including subjects relevant to my study. He expedited the transcription of those tapes and forwarded the first drafts to me. We conducted three interviews together. These worthy human resources are also named in the Notes on Sources.

Family members of deceased participants generously came forward to help. I welcomed Mildred Rodgers Crary's offer of several valuable documents pertaining to the Antarctic career of her late husband, among them a copy of Albert P. Crary's unpublished memoir, his work on an uncompleted history of the IGY, his near-transcription notes on Chief Scientist Harry Wexler's diary, copies of papers, and eulogies following his death in 1987. Carole Anderson, widow of IGY glaciologist Vernon Anderson, offered his diary, lovingly transcribed by their daughter Suzanne. A photocopy of David Canham's handwritten diary came to me with the permission of his son and namesake via Dave Grisez. Susan Wexler Schneider and Libby Wexler Novotny warmly supported my using their father's Antarctic diary, and Susan has given support and friendship ever since. Sharon Boyer lent the Antarctic correspondence of her late husband, *National Geographic* photographer David Boyer. Frank Hudman provided information on the P2V crash that claimed his father, Rayburn Hudman. Joanne Loomis offered her late husband, Raymond Loomis's, engineering report on Hallett Station. Edward Slagle shared a taped narration made by his father, Capt. T. D. Slagle, chief medical officer in 1958; and Marc Swadener sent a CD of a slide talk given by his late brother, J. R. (Dick) Swadener, on the first Pole landing, and more.

Dozens of Antarcticans and others lent or gave me valuable personal material, some in quantity, for my research—books, magazines, articles, official documents, memoranda, private memoirs, diaries, personal papers, newsletters, maps and navigation charts, personal photographs in albums and on CDs, official Navy photographs, newspaper clippings, scrapbooks, tapes, videos (professional and personal), and information and advice by telephone, correspondence, conversation, and e-mail. It is not enough to simply name them, but it is all that space will allow. Despite my best efforts, the list undoubtedly misses someone, for which I am sorry: Ken Aldrich, Bob Allen, Ed Anderson, Ernest Angino, Billy-Ace Baker, John Behrendt, Jim Bergstrom, Charlie Bevilacqua, Dick Bowers, John (Jack) Brown, Lynn Cavendish, Bob Chaudoin, Dan Derkics, Cliff and Jean Dickey, Earl (Buz) Dryfoose, Forrest Durnell, Dave Grisez, Pembroke Hart, Glen and Gwen Hartong, James Hoenig, Con Jaburg, Bill Littlewood, Philip Mange, Ed Marolda, Ken Meyer, William Mills, George and Eunice Moss, Paul Noonan, Crystal Polis, Al Raithel Jr., John Randall, Kathleen Reedy, Colon Roberts, Gail Ross, Stanley Ruttenberg, Don Scott, Dan Secrest, Bernard (Bud) Singer, Paula Smith, Bill Spindler, Hank Stephens, Frank Stokes, Bill Stroup, Charles Swithinbank, Robert Thomson, George Toney, Jim Waldron, Ken Waldron, Ed Ward, Vic Young.

Early on, my collaborators decided that I must see Antarctica for myself. Guy Guthridge, who for four years provided guidance and encouragement, made it happen, in January 2001. My polar education, which took on extraordinary new meaning, was enhanced at McMurdo Station by CWO Pat Calpin, USCG, Ted Dettmar, Bob Fleming, Irma Hale, Sharon Heilman, Kristan Hutchison, Wade Jeffrey, Curt LaBombard, Kay Lawson, Donal Manahan, John Nicoletti, David Oliver, Col. Richard Saburro, USAF, Sara Smolenack, Brian Stone, Michelle Waknitz, Buck Wilson, Peter Cleary and Chris Cochran at Scott Base, and, especially, Ed Anderson, resident historian of the 1950s who did all he could to make my visit historically meaningful and personally special. I hope all those others who shared their awesome stories, helped me with heavy loads, answered my questions, and wanted to know about my work will forgive me for missing their names.

At the South Pole, NSF's Jerry Marty devoted an unaffordable afternoon to making mine memorable and informative, along with Carlton Walker, Scott Smith, and the crews of both Hercs who honored me with spectacular flights in the cockpit. Jerry's support before and since has been exceptional. In Christchurch, John and Noela Claydon showed me extraordinary hospitality and New Zealand's appreciation of Admiral Dufek. Curator Baden Norris personally guided me through the splendid Antarctic hall of the Canterbury Museum.

During my documentary research, archivists Janice Goldblum and Daniel Barbiero at the National Academies were unfailingly helpful, as were Barry Zerby, Marjorie Ciarlante, and others at the National Archives and Laura Kissel at the Byrd Polar Research Center. Dean Allard, Jim Bergstrom, Dick Bowers, Bill Stroup, Vic Young, John Behrendt, and Kim Malville helpfully read all or pertinent parts of the manuscript in draft. George Mazuzan gave helpful advice at many points. At the University Press of Colorado, Director Darrin Pratt and Sandy Crooms, Laura Furney, Dan Pratt, Ann Wendland, and Cheryl Carnahan of his staff were encouraging, understanding, and helpful throughout.

For all this assistance and for getting to know these special people I am grateful beyond words. It is, of course, my fault and regret, not theirs, if I still failed to get something right, although I hope they understand that their "truth" might not be the whole of it. I hope they will forgive me for the great stories that could not make the final cut and for the favors and material help I have inadvertently neglected to mention.

Finally, my inadequate thanks to my family, who embraced this history almost as keenly as I have. I could not begin to enumerate everything my husband, Brian, contributed to its completion. For his and our children's and grandchildren's love and support, indulgence and understanding, Antarctic books and penguin mementos, I shall ever feel graced.

DEEP FREEZE

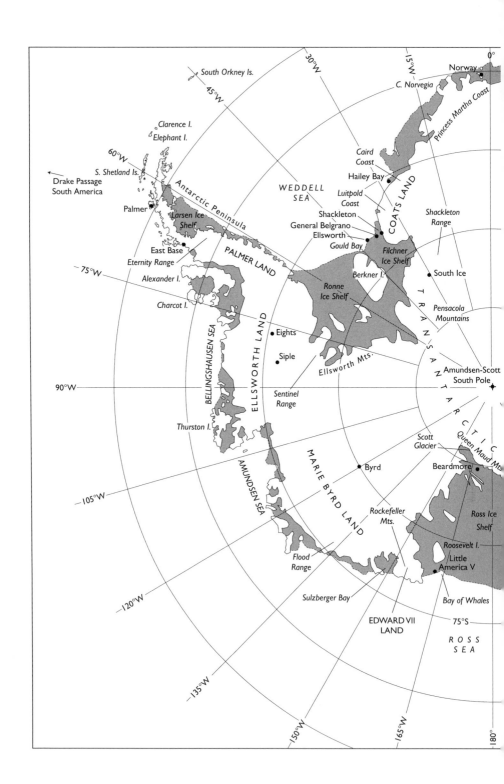

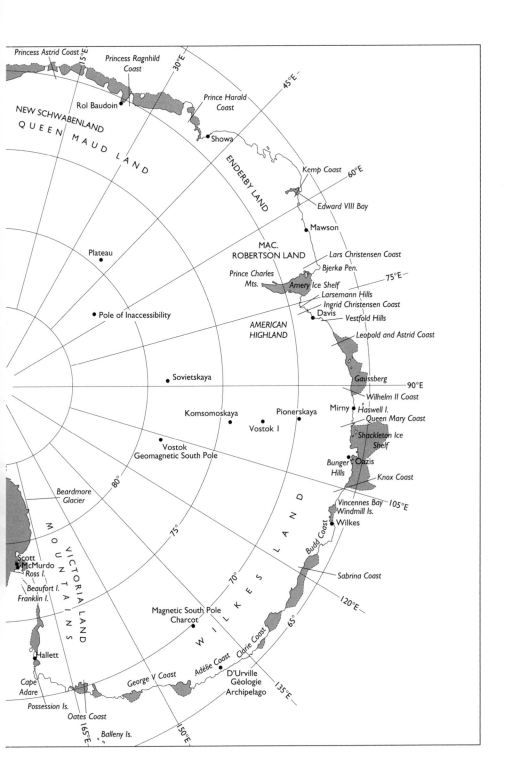

INTRODUCTION

The giants of Antarctica's so-called Heroic Age—Scott, Shackleton, Amundsen, Mawson, later Byrd—are familiar figures, even among the many who know little about the desolate desert of ice at the bottom of the globe. But after the handful of larger-than-life pre–World War I heroes came the pioneers. It was they who, in mid-century, mostly anonymously, built the Antarctica of today.

Their story centers on the International Geophysical Year (IGY), 1 July 1957 through 31 December 1958—a coordinated, cooperative worldwide effort to understand the earth and its environment. Of the earth's two great unknowns at the time, one was Antarctica. (The other was space. The Soviets' orbiting of Sputnik in October 1957 marked the achievement of a shared IGY goal, though few would remember that connection.) The IGY focus on otherworldly Antarctica was fed by irresistible scientific curiosity. Just how vast and deep was the continental ice sheet? What lay beneath it? How much did frigid Antarctica influence hemispheric, if not global, weather patterns? How did the proximity of the magnetic and geomagnetic poles affect solar and atmospheric phenomena such as cosmic rays and the aurora australis?

Scientific interest in Antarctica was not new. Qualified scientists accompanied many of the earliest expeditions, whose primary impellers were wealth or glory. For some leaders, the quest for knowledge enjoyed high priority in its own right; for all, it was recognized as a way to add stature to the venture. Given that virtually nothing was known of the immense whiteness, every finding was significant no matter how limited the scope of effort. Even international polar science had precedent. The IGY began as the *Third* International Polar Year. Two earlier modest, yet remarkable, international scientific surveys—in 1882–1883 and 1932–1933—concentrated on the more accessible, more germane polar North, but they established the effectiveness and value of numerous nations making the same kinds of scientific observations simultaneously over a broad area and sharing the results. Even as the polar-year concept of the 1950s blossomed into an ambitious global endeavor, the poles remained anchor points, now especially the mystical high-latitude South. The Norwegian-British-Swedish Antarctic Expedition of 1949–1952 offered a timely model of a multinational scientific (not geographic) pursuit that employed the latest technologies for work and travel. The IGY would borrow from all of these forerunners, but its unprecedented scope, scale, and outcomes would make it something new.

The IGY fathers took their idea and enthusiasm directly to the international scientific community, embodied in the International Council of Scientific Unions (ICSU), which in turn sought the support of the dozens of national academies of science that comprised its membership. ICSU also formed a special organizing and coordinating committee, the Comité Spécial de l'Année Géophysique Internationale. But each participating country's "national program" would be planned by its own national committee, according to its own means and interests, and would be financed and implemented by its government, the only possible source of sufficient support.

The need for government funding, of course, inevitably introduced politics. Fortunately, the key science leaders, starting with American Lloyd Berkner and Britisher Sydney Chapman who conceived the IGY in the spring of 1950, were savvy and influential players in that milieu. They had the political acumen to promote a studiously "apolitical" program. They would welcome all nations wishing to join in without regard to political philosophy. They deliberately excluded "controversial" sciences like geology and mapping, disciplines of an obviously geophysical nature, lest they reveal valuable mineral resources—and thus set off a "rush" for territorial advantage. (Americans would not be alone in quietly pursuing these activities anyway.) The planners attempted neither financial nor program management at the international level, thus avoiding hopeless accounting complexities, not to mention political quagmires. (Their approach also minimized international overhead.) Yet concepts such as World Days and World Data Centers would demonstrate international collaboration at its best. Finally, they astutely waited to approach their respective governments until the science plans were sufficiently advanced to present a persuasive case on scientific merits. It did not hurt that they could then use other countries' commitments as levers to pry more generous funding from potentially parsimonious legislators.

At home, the United States National Committee for the IGY was born a creature of the prestigious National Academy of Sciences (NAS), which provided much of the expertise through technical panels and special committees. It also created and housed a small bureaucracy to run the U.S. program. But only a government agency could request and dispense congressional appropriations; the private NAS could not. So the cub National Science Foundation (NSF) took on the funding management role. It was a leap: NSF's initial IGY budget submission, though technically separate, doubled its own. These two voices of science would sometimes find it hard to harmonize their approaches and methods, while other agencies, especially the defense and diplomatic establishments, sang their own songs—ever seeking to link IGY activity to the protection and enhancement of U.S. security and strategic interests. Always, behind the facade of cooperative science lurked gut-felt fears that the Russians would preempt the polar continent if the "Free World" did not act first.

The staggering logistical challenges of mounting an ambitious, far-flung scientific enterprise in Antarctica demanded exacting care. In the United States, unlike the far-northern, ice-wise Soviet Union, no civilian entity possessed either the equipment or the expertise to fulfill a mission so large and complex under conditions so harsh. The American IGY, by necessity, turned to the U.S. Navy and other military services to identify, assemble, and transport every volunteer, every tractor, roof truss, and frozen turkey and to plan, site, construct, and maintain an infrastructure so that scientists could pursue the science they came to do. Besides technical capability, the Navy brought to the task a history of two Antarctic expeditions, a century apart—the Wilkes Expedition of exploration and national prestige building, 1838–1842, and Operation Highjump in the austral summer of 1946–1947, the largest extreme-cold-weather naval training exercise ever. A then-classified but primary goal was to establish a basis for claiming sovereignty over as much of the polar continent as possible.

In the following decade, the Navy's Operation Deep Freeze, set up specifically to provide logistical support for the IGY in Antarctica, faced a huge charge—frenzied by a truncated time frame, the world's longest supply line, the need to provision for two years in case impenetrable ice thwarted resupply efforts, and the certain knowledge that anything left behind would be done without. But the men would come through—with diligent planning, ingenious improvisation, plenty of brute force, and "can do" spirit. Their ships negotiated hummocky pack ice, their planes soupy whiteouts. Naval Construction Battalions (the Seabees) built six scientific stations and a logistics base, each with its own problems of access, terrain, and weather. Byrd Station, deep in the so-called American sector, would owe its existence to heavy, sled-hauling tractor trains whose tortuous route through deadly crevasses was laid out and made safe by U.S. Army crevasse experts. Air Force cargo planes would airdrop onto the South Pole every great and small thing essential for life there. Admiral Dufek, the Navy man, seized ability where he found it. Wintering-over Navy support personnel would melt snow for water, cook meals of renowned quality, nurse along overworked equipment, run cranky generators, provide radio contact with the outside world, and much more. They would mourn a few dead. Their practical triumphs made possible the scientific successes that followed.

The American scientists, mostly young and inexperienced, were themselves pathfinders. With IGY leaders sometimes dismissive of their ability to perform beyond "cookbook" instrument reading and their mentors a world away, they mastered the use, maintenance, and repair of complicated equipment and conducted preliminary analyses of tons of data. They calculated the thickness of ice shelves and ice sheets and measured rates of snow accumulation and glacial flow. A few dozen of them crawled thousands of miles over the unknown continent in grumbling tracked Sno-Cats to push back the frontiers of knowledge. Some of their findings even they had trouble believing.

The Navy and IGY-science community made an odd couple; tension marked their relations from the start. Navy leaders, straining to make a home for nearly 300 men at widespread locations within the space of two short polar summers, felt little regard for scientists who set unseen sites on paper in the comfort of temperate conference halls with no idea of the actual conditions or appreciation for the costs of prevailing over them. IGY leaders, focused on their own performance requirements and frantic to begin on time, seemed to find in every setback evidence of Navy indifference. On the ice, sailors and scientists viewed one another across divergent goals, social and educational cleavages, and differences in tastes and habits. Yet, wintering over in intimate proximity, they adjusted remarkably well to each other overall. Cultural clashes were exceptions. A dual command system, a reluctant compromise both civilian and military leaders deplored, proved generally workable and effective in the reality of polar camp life. Indeed, the most conspicuous leadership failure accompanied the one case where a single commander had charge of an entire station.

This history bears an American emphasis, an American point of view. But the story cannot be told without interfaces with the people and politics of the eleven other nations that sent IGY teams to the polar continent. The United States operated one station bilaterally. All the others feared and distrusted the Soviet Union; ongoing territorial rivalries also threatened the cooperative enterprise. One outstanding achievement of the IGY, therefore, was an international exchange of Antarctic scientists. In particular, Russian meteorologists (and those of several other countries) lived and worked at Little America's Antarctic Weather Central facility while U.S. counterparts wintered over at USSR Station Mirny, giving both sides a chance to find friendly humanity beyond the ideological walls. On the ice, distant Cold War machinations mattered little, and that fact gave one more nudge to what followed.

In fact, even before the IGY officially opened, U.S. IGY leaders proposed that the barely begun scientific work in Antarctica continue when the "Year" was over. Congress countered with reminders of a promised "one-shot" expenditure. The Navy had ambivalent feelings about continuing to pour resources into a nonmilitary effort in an area of questionable strategic importance, and the State Department was wary as always about allowing an inadvertent Communist advantage. The international response was also mixed, but when the Russians announced they were staying on, that decided it for everyone else. In the end, the participating countries agreed to extend the program for one additional year, to be called the International Geophysical Cooperation–1959, to buy time to work out more permanent arrangements.

The prickliest issue had to do with "ownership" of the polar continent. Seven nations, all of them friendly to the United States, had made pie-shaped territorial claims terminating at the Pole, some conflicting. While over the years American explorers had deposited claim sheets all over Antarctica, the government had never formally acted on them—to the consternation of many politicians and political activists—although it retained the "right" to do so. At the same time, it did not recognize any claims of others. The Soviets, inactive since Bellingshausen's early-nineteenth-century circumnavigations of the continent, echoed that policy. If the United States could boast the strongest "basis for a claim," the consequences of asserting one began to appear ever more problematic, the value ever more uncertain.

Finally, after years of agonizing, U.S. policy makers found in the IGY an opportune moment and a possible path to institutionalize the scientific cooperation while putting aside the treacherous political issue of claims. Painstaking negotiations among the twelve Antarctic IGY nations at length yielded the compromises, controls, and acts of faith that became the Antarctic Treaty of 1959. A determined band of U.S. senators, passionately anti-Communist and pro–American "rights," did their best to prevent ratification. But this small, imperfect, rather miraculous bond of peace and purposefulness in a troubled world still holds today.

It was an extraordinary time. The period in question was remarkably short. From the time the Navy ships of Operation Deep Freeze I met the ice of the Southern Ocean to the signing of the Antarctic Treaty was a scant four years. From the emergence of the IGY concept to the indefinite extension of the IGY in Antarctica was less than a decade. It was a dangerous time in history, with atomic weapons poised between two implacable adversaries—both major Antarctic players. Perhaps that backdrop of Cold War terror somehow inspired the peaceable scientific quest—a way to stay nuclear annihilation.

Altogether, this is a story of how an uncommon mix of people, representing cultures, agencies, organizations, and countries from all the inhabited continents, came together to study the last continent and then to reserve it as a continuing haven for science and peace. It is a story of how science was brought to serve politics, national interests, and humankind. Fifty years after the human and material resources of the United States and eleven other nations moved in on the puzzled penguins, it is time to take a look at their historic experience and its significance.

THE CALL OF THE ICE

*To the south of Magellan Strait there is a supposed continent,
twice the size of the United States, which is justly called the
most mysterious land in the world.*

—*National Geographic*, 1907[1]

The pioneers of today's Antarctica followed a handful of predecessors who, over the previous 180 years, approached and pricked the polar continent seeking riches, knowledge, or glory. A few highlights from what went before help illuminate and anticipate the extraordinary developments of the 1950s, when the context, scale, and character of Antarctic activity changed profoundly.

Those who have been there—anywhere on the Antarctic continent—call it, simply, the ice. The term is a sort of privileged shorthand for the small circle who know firsthand the look and feel of the coldest, windiest, highest (on average), driest, emptiest, most remote place on earth. Those few have, over time, determined that the ice sheet that covers and joins the geologically distinct regions known as East and West Antarctica is as thick as three miles, averaging more than half of that. It contains 90 percent of the earth's total ice volume and 70 percent of its fresh water. Weather is both extreme and volatile. Blizzards can appear in a moment; at least once the recorded temperature dropped sixty-five degrees in twelve minutes. In much of the interior new snow is scant—the equivalent of about two inches of rain per year. Antarctica boasts no native peoples, no plants save scarce mosses and lichens, no terrestrial animal life more complex than wingless insects. Four species each of seals and penguins come ashore to breed but nourish themselves from the teeming sea.[2]

Historically, it was called *Terra Australis Incognita*—unknown southern land. With no evidence beyond reason, ancient Greeks argued the existence of a continent to balance those known in the Northern Hemisphere. The large void at the bottom of world maps remained for centuries a mystery, although belief in a temperate, possibly populated, land in the southern high latitudes persisted. Captain James Cook, the great English navigator, disproved that notion by circumnavigating the ice-shrouded continent between 1772 and 1775, sometimes south of the Antarctic Circle (67°S). That put him below the Antarctic Convergence, where colder, denser polar waters flowing northward sink beneath warmer, saltier, less dense sub-Antarctic waters. That line, which circles the earth between about 50 and 60 degrees south latitude, shifts some from season to season but defines the Antarctic as well as any boundary, since winter ice almost doubles the size of the continent and summer melting can vary significantly by year.[3]

Cook did not see land, but his reports of abundant seals and whales soon brought the first surge of European and American explorers to the Antarctic. They faced their wooden ships into the icy spray of the Southern (merging Atlantic, Pacific, and Indian) Ocean, the world's angriest, not to discover but to make money. The "fabulous prices" commanded by fur seal pelts in China made some of them fortunes—but not for long. They slaughtered so greedily that fur seals were almost extinct by 1820. Waves of similarly heedless exploitation of elephant seals (for their oil) and of whales had similar results later in the century. Unfortunately for history, to protect their profits from potential competitors, the hunters typically kept their geographic findings secret.[4]

Continental land was sighted, but by whom first is still debated. If Britons Edward Bransfield and William Smith saw what they thought they saw in January 1820, they were first to glimpse the northernmost tip. Some Americans contended it was Nathaniel Palmer, twenty-year-old captain of the sloop *Hero*, part of a sealing fleet in late 1820. It could well have been Captain Thaddeus

Bellingshausen, commanding the Russian naval vessels *Vostok* and *Mirnyy*, who made an easterly continental circumnavigation, 1819–1821. Improbably, on 6 February 1821, as a thick fog lifted, these latter two found themselves staring at each another at close range somewhere near the South Shetland Islands. Palmer later wrote that the Russian leader, acknowledging his discovery of land, had named it Palmers Land (now Antarctic Peninsula), but contemporary records do not decide the issue.[5]

Competing for strategic advantage and national prestige, three other navies followed the Russians south. A French naval exploratory expedition, 1837–1840, commanded by Admiral J.S.C. Dumont d'Urville, landed near the Adélie Coast south of Australia. In January 1841 Sir James Clark Ross led two ice-strengthened British Admiralty ships, *Erebus* and *Terror*, through the pack ice surrounding the continent to open water in what would become known as the Ross Sea and cruised in amazement along the towering "Great Icy Barrier," now called the Ross Ice Shelf. The next year he tried, but failed, to penetrate the thicker, more pressure-driven ice of the Weddell Sea.[6]

The fourth naval expedition of the period, third to embark, was American—the United States Exploring Expedition, 1838–1842, with Lieutenant Charles Wilkes in command of four small ships, none ideal for the job. Nor, apparently, was the hot-tempered, second-choice leader. The four-year, wide-ranging Wilkes Expedition accomplished a remarkable program, however—not least boldly waving the flag of the young republic where the great powers, Britain and France, were simultaneously sailing. Twice Wilkes pushed into the Southern Ocean for long cruises that skirted the pack ice along the stormy coast south of Australia, sighting land several times. On 30 January 1840 he reported "dark, volcanic rocks" and high, snow-covered land extending east to west "fully sixty miles." And then, "[N]ow that all were convinced of its existence, I gave the land the name of the Antarctic Continent." Ross and others would discredit some of Wilkes's claims of discovery, to which he held fast. Later investigators have shown that some of his "impossible" sightings resulted from exceptionally clear Antarctic air, which shrinks visual distances, and to mirages, an optical phenomenon whereby objects below the horizon are seen in reflection, sometimes righted by re-reflection.[7]

Wilkes, an excellent mathematician and physical scientist, established the expedition as "a milestone in American science." Geologist James Eights, who as the first American scientist in the Antarctic in 1829–1830 had discovered a new species of "sea spider," collected fossils, and concluded from observing rocks embedded in icebergs that land (unseen) lay not far to the south, was unfortunately bumped from this voyage at the last minute. But seven scientists did work in "practically all phases of the physical and natural sciences of the day," and that work, like Eights's perceptive and prolific output, was of sufficient scope and rigor to be admired by scientists a century later. To support their primary mission of promoting navigation and commerce, the eighty-three officers aboard made observations in geography, hydrography, meteorology, astronomy, and terrestrial magnetism.[8]

Following this flurry of international naval activity, however, Antarctica slept more or less undisturbed for almost half a century. As historian of Antarctic science G. E. Fogg wrote, there were "no tangible prospects of colonization nor commercial incentives to attract governments to further ventures south." For the moment, whales could be found in friendlier waters. Would-be European explorers could find "ample excitement" in the nearer Arctic and Africa, while Americans endured the Civil War and plumbed their own vast West.[9]

A conspicuous activist in this quiescent period was Matthew Fontaine Maury, superintendent of the U.S. Navy's Depot of Charts and Instruments from 1842 to 1861. Maury systematically compiled a series of *Wind and Current Charts* with explanatory *Sailing Directions*, tabulating data from the logbooks of naval ships and any commercial vessels that would oblige in exchange for a copy of his latest revision. When varying a ship's track according to his recommendations proved to save days of sailing, Maury gained respect and cooperation worldwide. He had little information, however, on the southern high latitudes, which he believed "held the key" to the weather of the Southern Hemisphere. When Civil War preoccupations deflected his appeals for U.S. Antarctic exploration to fill such knowledge gaps, he urged the help of "fellow-laborers under all flags." He did not succeed. Yet two International Polar Years and the International Geophysical Year itself would owe much to Maury's vision and persuasive powers.[10]

The first cooperative international polar studies grew from the mind of Austrian naval lieutenant Karl Weyprecht, a member of the Austro-Hungarian North Pole Expedition of 1872–1874. With time to ponder after his ship was beset, he came to believe polar expeditions should focus on increasing scientific knowledge rather than discovering new geographic features whose purpose was merely "to confer honour upon this flag or the other." At a meeting of the Association of German Naturalists and Physicists in Graz in 1875, he proposed that a ring of scientific stations be established around the Arctic Circle where synchronous observations of weather, terrestrial magnetism, and other geophysical phenomena would be made over the span of a year. Weyprecht's idea saw fruition (sadly, after his death at age forty-one) in the First International Polar Year, 1882–1883, when scientists from ten European nations and the United States operated fourteen such polar stations, obtaining, for example, the "first orderly picture" of the aurora borealis. While the program focused north, a French station at Cape Horn and a German base on South Georgia Island furnished comparative data from sub-Antarctic latitudes.[11]

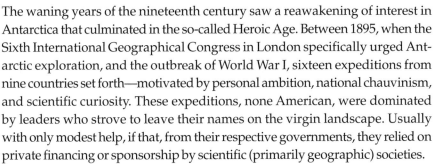

The waning years of the nineteenth century saw a reawakening of interest in Antarctica that culminated in the so-called Heroic Age. Between 1895, when the Sixth International Geographical Congress in London specifically urged Antarctic exploration, and the outbreak of World War I, sixteen expeditions from nine countries set forth—motivated by personal ambition, national chauvinism, and scientific curiosity. These expeditions, none American, were dominated by leaders who strove to leave their names on the virgin landscape. Usually with only modest help, if that, from their respective governments, they relied on private financing or sponsorship by scientific (primarily geographic) societies.

The thrilling, oft-told stories of the heroes' triumphs and failures offered the few direct lessons that could be applied by those who would follow in mid-century. Irish-born Ernest Shackleton, for example, who had tramped 400 miles south from McMurdo Sound with Robert Falcon Scott in 1902, earned British knighthood for his own audacious push to the South Pole in 1908–1909. Forced by insufficient food, he turned back 97 miles from his goal—a crushing, courageous, almost-too-late decision. In 1914–1916 he braved the treacherous Weddell Sea in an attempt to sledge across the entire continent. But pressure ice trapped his ship, as it had those of at least three other contemporary explorers—including the *Belgica* of Adrien de Gerlache, which in 1898, without choice, became the first to winter over, in the pack ice of the Bellingshausen Sea. The ice eventually freed the Belgian party, but, horrifically, it crushed and sank Shackleton's *Endurance*. An inspired natural leader, Shackleton succored and saved every man of his stranded crew of twenty-eight—in the end, by a superhuman 800-mile sea journey in a 22-foot open boat.[12]

If the largely inexperienced officers and young men of Operation Deep Freeze could name only one explorer from the Heroic Age, it would likely be Britain's Scott, who staggered to the South Pole on foot on 17 January 1912, only to discover that Roald Amundsen had planted the Norwegian flag there a month earlier, on 14 December 1911. Scott's company of five, man-hauling their sledges, all died of the cold and starvation on the return trek. Amundsen and his four companions, on skis, with dogs pulling their sleds, returned to their ice-shelf base camp fatter than when they set out. Scott, whose diaries painted compelling pictures of travail and bad luck, became an almost mythical hero in "noble" death while the taciturn Amundsen's success was brushed aside. His straightforward tale of miles covered, beacon cairns built, food depots laid, and more sounded too easy for "adventure."[13]

But Amundsen got it right, as Roland Huntford made clear in his harsh but persuasive comparative biography and as their own accounts confirm. Amundsen took pains to acquire every relevant experience and skill. As first mate on the *Belgica*, he had gleaned insights on leadership and preparedness from the mostly negative example of that unhappy ship. He perfected every piece of equipment, every article of clothing. He calculated every detail, especially food (to suffice between depots with a generous surplus), leaving nothing to chance. Scott had motorized sledges and Siberian ponies to Amundsen's sled dogs, but the "motors" failed after a few miles and the ponies, copied from Shackleton, were a disastrous choice. They were herbivores on a barren landscape. Hoofed, they had no footing on ice. With enormous weight concentrated on each footfall, they floundered belly-deep in soft snow. There was no saving one fallen into a crevasse. Dogs ate available seal, and Amundsen sacrificed the weakest ones to sustain their harness mates. Scott calculated provisions "too fine," relied on improvisation, and championed the patriotic "manliness" of human labor. He used the word "hope" noticeably often; his party's march became, as Huntford has said, one of "witless valor." By the 1950s, dogs were anachronistic, but Amundsen's meticulous, clear-eyed approach and tested methods were the models to adopt.[14]

World War I effectively put an end to the heroic expeditions.[15] But the war stimulated technological advances, which later explorers, as outlined by geographer Kenneth Bertrand, lost no time in adapting to polar use—especially the airplane, motorized land vehicle, aerial camera, and radio. A new, mechanized age was born. Although all of these innovations had in some form been previously introduced, their systematic use changed the nature of Antarctic operations. Sir Hubert Wilkins, an Australian with American financing, made the first south-polar flights in November and December 1928, from Deception Island south over the Antarctic Peninsula. Thwarted by unusually warm weather that made the remnant volcano's frozen caldera unsafe for takeoff on skis, the party had to smooth a runway on a spit of volcanic ash and switch to wheels. That made field landings—and thus Wilkins's planned trans-Antarctic flight—impossible.[16]

Americans were foremost in the new polar era. By far the most important and renowned Antarctic explorer in the first half of the twentieth century was Richard Evelyn Byrd who, from the first of his five expeditions, 1928–1930, embraced every technology. A naval aviator trained in the Great War, he was but narrowly beaten by Wilkins in flying over the continent (his first such flight was in January 1929), and he used aircraft as a centerpiece of his program thereafter—as has every "serious expedition" since. The wide-tracked motorized vehicles of his second expedition, 1933–1935, were the first that were reliable enough to be called practical. The photographs of Scott's Herbert Ponting and Frank Hurley, who wintered with both Shackleton and Douglas Mawson of Australia, were breathtakingly beautiful as well as priceless records, but Byrd's Ashley McKinley took his cameras to the air, thus introducing a new artistic and documentary perspective and the new practice of aerial mapping. Mawson set up the first radio station at his base in East Antarctica's Commonwealth Bay, 1911–1914, but range was limited and contact required exceptional weather conditions. By his time, Byrd could routinely facilitate the work, safety, and movement of trail and airborne parties by radio. During his second expedition, he set up voice broadcasts to U.S. radio stations, reaping their inestimable publicity value. Bertrand wrote, "Marie Byrd Land became, in the popular mind, peculiarly American."[17]

Byrd brought much to his polar ambitions. Well connected through his old Virginia family, he was, historian Lisle Rose wrote, handsome, charming, charismatic. He was, moreover, singularly talented at "what he called 'the hero business,'" according to scientist-writer David Campbell. Perhaps that helped explain why he quirkily clung to fur suits and dog teams long after contemporaries had discarded them. Professing to hate it, he "hustle[d]" the rich and influential for their patronage while creating an adoring personal following and generating broad interest in the polar South. A superb organizer, Byrd set up a main base camp for each expedition (the previous one by then buried in drift) near the Bay of Whales site of Amundsen's "Framheim" on the Ross Ice Shelf. Ships could usually get through the pack ice there and moor against sheltered bay ice, and planes could take off from the smooth barrier surface. He named them all Little America, numbered consecutively—Little America II, then III, IV, and V (the latter two substantially the work of others).[18]

Byrd sent out both aerial and overland parties in complementary and coordinated programs of exploration. Among his discoveries were the Rockefeller and Edsel Ford mountain ranges (named for backers) and Marie Byrd Land (honoring his wife). His maiden expedition forged its right to remembrance by his flight over the South Pole on 28–29 November 1929. It took jettisoning over 200 pounds of emergency food to climb over the "Hump" of the Transantarctic Mountains onto the high polar plateau, but it was that or dump critical gasoline. Only "white desolation and solitude" greeted them, Byrd wrote: "It is the effort to get there that counts." His claimed overflight of the North Pole in May 1926 has since been questioned, as has this one, but not his planning, determination, or courage.[19]

Byrd mentored a cadre of young men who later played major Antarctic roles. His first expedition science leader, University of Michigan geology professor Laurence Gould, led the longest scientific dog-sledging trek in Antarctic history, studying ice-shelf movement and the composition of the Queen Maud Mountains. He later chaired the U.S. IGY Antarctic Committee. Paul Siple, a nineteen-year-old Eagle Scout who won a national competition to accompany Byrd, would find his life's work on the ice, capped by leading the first wintering at the South Pole. Lloyd Berkner, a radio engineer with Byrd in 1928 who became an influential figure in U.S. science policy, would father the IGY idea.

The success of the first Polar Year had spurred similar scientific organizations and national committees in thirty-three countries to plan a Second International Polar Year for 1932–1933, exactly fifty years later, with a similar but more extensive scientific program. Much would be learned, especially about the burgeoning field of radio communications, although the global economic depression of the time "severely curtailed" the effort. Byrd, made rear admiral by act of Congress, was eager to return south. While he did not emphasize it, the timing of his second expedition allowed him to take advantage of the fundraising and public relations potential of the Polar Year as well as contribute (a bit late) some meteorological, ice-depth, upper-air physics, and oceanographic observations. Byrd's team also generated Antarctica's first electricity for light and power and discovered the southernmost fossil-bearing coal deposits to date.[20]

But this expedition will ever be known for Byrd's solitary winter at Bolling Advance Weather Base, a tiny "shack" buried in drift 100 miles south of Little America. Why he chose to remain there alone, in defiance of polar survival wisdom, still perplexes. He wrote that time ran out to provision the camp for the intended three persons; two he viewed as a potential psychological nightmare, and so there would be one—himself. Besides making weather and auroral observations, he had "no important purposes" except to "taste peace and quiet and solitude long enough to find out how good they really are." He claimed self-revelations about harmony, values, and human meaning but nearly died of carbon-monoxide poisoning from an improperly ventilated stove. A tractor party bravely journeyed out to him in the dark, caring for him until he could withstand a flight out. Charles J.V. Murphy, *New York World* reporter on the expedition, wrote later in private correspondence that Byrd grew "old before his time. . . . The ordeal at the Barrier had sapped his strength and, I suspect, unsettled his mind. He was not the same afterwards."[21]

Perhaps the most courageous—surely the most rash—American to leave his name on the interwar Antarctic map was the millionaire Lincoln Ellsworth, who had flown in the Arctic with Amundsen. His self-financed ambition, managed and advised by Wilkins, was to fly across the polar continent. It took him three tries in three successive seasons. Ellsworth chose an outstanding pilot, Herbert Hollick-Kenyon, and a custom-made single-engine aircraft with low-mounted wings that could be dug in flush with the snow for wind protection. He was also helped by thorough preparation, his excellent navigational skills, and—especially—luck. The map beneath him was mostly blank. He had no backup plane, no rescue team, no fuel to retrace his steps. The pair took off from Dundee Island on the tip of the Antarctic Peninsula on 23 November 1935, and after about 2,200 miles and four intermediate ski landings on the ice—some for days because of blizzards—they came down on 5 December, out of gas, about 16 miles from Little America. It took them ten days to find the empty base.[22]

Admiral Byrd went back once more in 1939, this time to lead a government operation called the United States Antarctic Service (USAS). A civilian program organized by the State, Treasury, Navy, and Interior departments, the USAS was run by the Navy. Franklin Roosevelt, long fascinated by Byrd's exploits, renewed his interest when he learned of Nazi polar activity. The two already shared a wish to establish a permanent American presence on the ice. With Roosevelt's personal involvement, the USAS became an amalgam of two proposed expeditions—one by Finn Ronne and Richard Black, both veterans of Byrd's second expedition, and a private foray Byrd was planning. The president's friendship won Byrd the command. Ronne, already upstaged by Black on a polar plan he called his own, was galled to find himself in shadow. The USAS set up two stations—West Base (Little America III, again at the Bay of Whales) headed by Paul Siple, and East Base on Stonington Island off the west coast of the Antarctic Peninsula, where Black had charge, with Ronne as second-in-command. Sledge journeys and aerial reconnaissance once more added to geographical, geological, meteorological, and biological knowledge. But as war loomed in 1941, the bases were evacuated, not relieved with new personnel as planned.[23]

By Byrd's final two journeys to the frozen continent, the times had changed dramatically, and the luster of his name was more valued than his leadership.

Indeed, he spent little time on the ice with the USAS. This and later expeditions were too large, too complex, and too expensive to be dominated by one larger-than-life hero whose polar operations were personally planned. As in corporate and political America, the organization came to overshadow the mark of the individual.

Politics inevitably followed exploration and discovery. By World War II, seven countries—Great Britain, Argentina, Chile, France, Norway, Australia, and New Zealand—had laid formal claim "based on discovery, adjacency, or decree" to various parts of Antarctica. Except for Norway's undefined inner and outer boundaries, these were designated in pie-shaped "sectors" that terminated at the South Pole. The British had, in fact, since about 1920, planned secretly to acquire the entire continent. They offered Byrd friendly assistance but suggested he was trespassing on imperial territory and sent Mawson out to lead a British-Australian–New Zealand expedition (BANZARE, 1929–1931), ostensibly for research but certainly to wave the Union Jack. Argentina and Chile considered the Antarctic Peninsula an extension of their homelands; their claims and Britain's overlapped, causing friction and occasional skirmishes. One sector remained unclaimed. Fortunately, all the claimant states were friendly to the United States. Germany's 1939 Neu-Schwabenland Expedition, however, and its wartime threats to allied shipping in the Southern Hemisphere caused great concern, and after the war the Soviet Union's designs came under intensified suspicion, though it never asserted a claim.[24]

The United States, nervous yet chronically indecisive on the matter, pressed no claims and recognized none. In 1924 Secretary of State Charles Evans Hughes argued from international law that discovery did "not support a valid claim of sovereignty" unless it was followed by "actual settlement." Ten years later the government amended Hughes's policy to "reserve all rights," meaning that it could, if it wished, act on a legitimate basis for a claim at some future time. George Toney, IGY staff member and then scientific leader at Byrd Station, thought later that one reason for that camp's inland location was that it was "spang in the middle of a huge unclaimed wedge of Antarctica where the United States might well launch a claim later on, if it came to that." Meanwhile, American explorers strewed claim sheets over the ice on their travels, with highly placed if hushed encouragement. Roosevelt, for example, told Byrd in 1939 to keep "careful records" of claims dropped from aircraft or left in cairns; such "might assist in supporting a sovereignty claim." He should

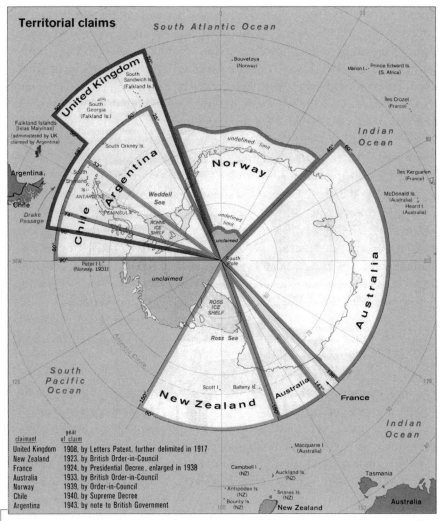

Seven nations, all friendly to the United States, maintained territorial claims in Antarctica. Some overlapped. One pie-shaped sector remained unclaimed. Antarctic Information Map, adapted. Courtesy, the International Antarctic Centre, Christchurch, New Zealand.

make "no public announcement," however, "without specific authority in each case from the Secretary of State." But official policy and action were still years away.[25]

Except for Britain's secret expedition called Operation Tabarin, 1943–1945, which challenged the claims of neutral but Nazi-leaning Argentina by establishing its own permanent facility on the Antarctic Peninsula, the continent lay quiet during World War II after the Germans and Americans departed. But after the war, the United States military renewed its strategic interest after more than a century (since the Wilkes Expedition) of thinking that Antarctica, cold and lifeless, was too distant from the world's centers of population and political power to bother about. That attitude changed—not for reasons intrinsic to Antarctica but in response to perceived dangers at the other pole.[26]

Japanese incursions in Alaska were a recent memory, and fears of a Soviet air attack over the North Pole gained strength as the Cold War—personified by Europe's "iron curtain," the nuclear arms race, and Russian designs in the Middle East and Asia—overtook a shaky peace. To prepare for threats in the polar north, the Navy created Task Force 68, Operation Nanook, to train personnel, evaluate equipment, and test ships in the ice floes between Greenland and Canada during the summer of 1946. The need for more extensive training in frigid conditions was early agreed, but the long, dark winter was rapidly approaching. Besides, diplomatic considerations discouraged conducting large-scale military operations in the Arctic, where no U.S. land went far enough north to be a suitable proving ground.[27]

So the Antarctic emerged as a surrogate Arctic test site. Thanks to the reversed seasons of the Southern Hemisphere, the same ships and personnel could train in twenty-four-hour daylight first in one polar region and then the other. The south's huge landmass made it appreciably colder, which offered the punishing benefit that operations conducted successfully there could surely promise reliability in the relatively less harsh north. Antarctica's isolation and emptiness ensured maximum security—that is, secrecy—and minimum political complications. The sparsity of knowledge about the polar continent, coupled with a desire to challenge task-force members with interesting problems under battle-worthy conditions, led Byrd to propose a concomitant program of exploration and scientific research. Where did the observed mountain ranges originate? What did the vast stretches of still-unseen coastline look like? How extensive were the known Antarctic coal deposits? Postwar thinkers seemed hopeful, if not confident, of finding mineral resources in economically viable quantities, and the United States did not want to miss out on their exploitation. The added cost of a science program would be almost incidental. Some American planners naively thought the countries closest to Antarctica would "welcome an international approach" to its "scientific unveiling."[28]

Thus it was that the U.S. Navy Antarctic Developments Project, code-named Operation Highjump,[29] was established on 26 August 1946 and hastily organized that fall as Nanook wound down. Its primary purpose was to train personnel and test equipment in frigid zones. Tellingly, number two on its list of goals was to extend the basis for U.S. claims in the Antarctic. The then-classified Navy report put this sound-bite phrase more baldly—to "consolidate and extend US sovereignty over the largest practicable area of the Antarctic continent." Territorial ambition, however ambiguously acknowledged, would underlie a great deal of U.S. interest and activity in Antarctica for many years, always colored by fear of Soviet machination. So the State Department maintained a bulging file of U.S. explorers' duplicate claim sheets, listened as some claimant countries hinted that they would welcome a U.S. claim (to buttress the legitimacy of their own claims and forestall Soviet designs), and did little to discourage domestic political pressure for asserting a claim. Highjump's other plans, practical and predictable, were to investigate potential base sites, perfect cold-weather flying techniques, increase scientific knowledge, and generally supplement the Arctic objectives of Operation Nanook.[30]

Byrd was named officer in charge, to exercise technical control while on the ice. Rear Adm. Richard Cruzen, who as a lieutenant commander had skippered Byrd's *The Bear of Oakland* on the USAS expedition, commanded Task Force 68 and one of the three ship groups deployed around the continent. Capt. George Dufek, who had served with Cruzen both on the *Bear* and in Nanook, had charge of the Eastern Group's three ships. He would be back. Cmdr. William ("Trigger") Hawkes headed the air squadron, impressing Dufek enough to assure himself future polar duty. Thus, the top leadership was nominally shared, but as would be illustrated even more starkly in 1955, by command authority this was a Navy operation. Cruzen would call the shots. Renowned himself by then, Siple awkwardly served as both the War Department's senior representative on the flagship *Mount Olympus* and Byrd's personal representative. He and Byrd were kept from the planning details, he complained to Cruzen, not for the last time smarting that proven polar expertise got little respect.[31]

The first thing to be said about Operation Highjump is that it was huge—by far the largest Antarctic expedition ever. Four thousand seven hundred naval and marine personnel participated, with thirteen ships—including an aircraft carrier and a submarine—nineteen fixed-wing aircraft, and four helicopters. Forty-four observers from the Army (there had been some talk of a joint Army-Navy task force), government agencies, and the press also went along. The nucleus of this force came from Nanook, but its great size necessitated many new faces, another obvious characteristic of the exercise noted by Rose. Ice experience was rare among the leader corps and practically nonexistent in the lower ranks. The intrepid Seabees of the wartime construction battalions were now nearly bereft of experienced builders.[32]

Inexperience also marked the all-important air operations. No pilot or flight crew member had ever flown in Antarctic skies, and few had flown from carriers. Navigation with the distortions of a grid system overlying the disorienting convergence of longitudinal lines near the Pole—not to mention the absence of stars or reliable charts or weather stations or airfields—would shake the confidence of the most cocky. There was practically no time to design, fabricate, and test skis for the aircraft, essential for landing on snow. Conrad ("Gus") Shinn, then a twenty-four-year-old Navy pilot, remembered Hawkes telling him—in November, the eve of deployment—to "take an airplane and get a set of skis and go up someplace and test these skis and see if they'll work." So he flew to Edmonton, Alberta, tried a few ski landings, and reported back, "Yes, they'll work." That thin experience gave Shinn Highjump's margin of ski expertise; for every other pilot, his ski landing on the Ross Ice Shelf was his first.[33]

It was not much different for the ships, which sailed on 2 December 1946 for their month-long journey south. The aircraft carrier *Philippine Sea*, from which the largest planes yet would be launched, had just completed its shakedown cruise. Of the two icebreakers, the Navy's *Burton Island* was brand new and just undergoing sea trials. The smaller, older *Northwind* of the Coast Guard was severely tested in ice that was unusually thick and difficult that year. Despite helicopter searches for leads (fingers of open water), all of the unprotected vessels suffered damage to hulls, rudders, or propellers. The submarine *Sennet* never made it through and had to be towed back out. Once into the open waters of the Ross Sea beyond, the mariners discovered that the ice shelf forming the Bay of Whales—historic haven for expeditions—had shifted, leaving only a narrow entrance. The bay itself was choked with ice, which, fortunately, the *Northwind* managed to clear.[34]

Off-loading began immediately, and the Seabees hurriedly constructed a temporary base, Little America IV, about two and a half miles from Byrd's now-buried Little America III. Fifty-four pyramidal tents for quarters, neatly arranged in rows and columns like polka dots on the snow, joined various other structures housing the necessary functions—communications, power generation, food service, aviation maintenance, sanitation. But the season was short, the officers reluctant to risk the thin-skinned ships in the menacing ice. So only personnel who could be evacuated by icebreaker—fewer than 200—would remain ashore to conduct the aerial surveys and scientific work. The upshot was the rather ludicrous necessity of some crews reloading cargo aboard ship even as others were still unloading material for use at the base. The *Burton Island* would evacuate everyone left in camp on 23 February 1947.[35]

Air exploration was a top Highjump goal, to be conducted primarily by six twin-engine R4Ds (the equivalent of civilian DC-3s). With insufficient range (800 miles) to fly in directly from New Zealand, they were toted south, some partially dismantled to save space, on the *Philippine Sea*. On the plus side, R4Ds were economical and simple to maintain, their landing-gear configurations suitable for skis. Canadians had already used them effectively in the Arctic. But to take off from the carrier, the planes required wheels; to land on the ice, skis were necessary. So slots were cut in the wide, stubby skis, through which the wheels would protrude—but the distance felt safe for takeoff was too far for safe landing. Byrd and Hawkes finally settled on a slim three inches of clearance from deck to skis. Moreover, carriers were built for swept-wing fighters. The R4Ds' wide-span wings would not clear the superstructure; they could use only the forward half of the flight deck. Rightly concerned, Byrd invited Shinn to his stateroom for dinner, pressing him with, "You really think you're going to get off? You really think so?"[36]

When the moment came, the *Philippine Sea* held on station 700 miles out, beyond the pack ice. Byrd, his leadership instinct intact, climbed aboard the first plane. Hawkes took the pilot's seat, chewing on his habitual unlit cigar. With blasts of JATO—canisters of propellant strapped to the belly for a short-lived but powerful jet-assisted takeoff—the plane shot off the deck, dipped, wobbled, and fought to remain airborne. When it did so, the relief was palpable, though Shinn described it nonchalantly: the planes "took off in a couple hundred feet—a couple of fuselage lengths maybe. No problem." All six eventually landed safely on the Little America snow strip. With their wheels then removed, the R4Ds operated effectively on the ice, but with recovery impossible, they had to be abandoned when the exercise was over. Not until Deep Freeze II, 1956, would an R4D—augmented with a huge fuel tank in the fuselage—manage a direct flight from New Zealand. Highjump saw the first and last use of an aircraft carrier in the Antarctic. The giant platforms were too valuable to be risked in the ice and were needed elsewhere.[37]

Byrd had hoped to photograph and map all of Antarctica's 16,000-mile coastline with the R4Ds and long-range PBM (Patrol Bomber, Martin) flying boats carrying three-lensed "trimetrogon" cameras that would take simultaneous pictures straight ahead and off to the left and right at specified angles. If the planes flew at the same constant altitude, mapmakers could then supply contour and elevation lines. The pilots, however, were not used to precision flying and knew neither the continent nor aerial mapping techniques. Foul weather stole visibility. With no time to establish ground-control points, they did what they could with overlapping photos and tying in with old fixes and geographic features, using the Astro-compass and sun lines plotted across the flight track. In truth, the navigation was iffy. "We didn't really know where we were most of the time," said Shinn. Yet they saw a lot. Lt. W. R. Kreitzer, pilot of the Western Group, overflew a rocky, open-water area of East Antarctica's Budd Coast, now called the Windmill Islands, in Vincennes Bay. His favorable report would help site Wilkes IGY Station in 1957. Pilot David Bunger discovered another unusual rocky, ice-free zone with pools of meltwater variously colored by algae. It became known as Bunger Hills, after initial fame as "Bunger's Oasis" when the press sent out overblown descriptions suggesting some "mysterious heat source."[38]

Antarctica doled out its famed adversity. On 30 December 1946 the Eastern Group, working along the "phantom coast" of the Antarctic Peninsula (so-called for the effect its incessant storminess had on visibility), suffered a tragic loss when a PBM crashed, killing three crew members. Thick weather delayed rescue of the survivors for thirteen days. One would lose both feet. Dufek himself went into the icy drink when his helicopter crashed into the sea and again while transferring between ships in a breeches buoy (an airborne chair traveling on cables between pulleys). He survived both dunkings without ill effect. The Eastern and Western groups intended to explore around the continent from opposite directions until they met, but difficult pack ice hampered ship movements, and persistent fog, sleet, and snow prevented the launching of seaplanes. Dufek ordered, "Let's get out of here," and Highjump was over.[39]

Measured against the rushed planning, glaring inexperience, and brief operating season (three scant months, only thirty-six days ashore), Highjump could claim a creditable showing despite the losses and disappointments. For Rose, the "most discouraging" result was that the estimated 300,000 square miles "photomapped" was only about a quarter of the original objective. About half of the almost 70,000 hard-won aerial photographs lacked adequate ground control. Still, thousands of miles, including mountains and glaciers, were visually documented, and the first nearly complete map of the coastline was produced. Rose also cited the submarine failure, tracked-vehicle shortcomings, and the loss of lives to judge Highjump but a "limited success." Yet most of the types of transport introduced that summer would serve in every future expedition. This first Antarctic use of icebreakers and helicopters established the indispensability of the one, the potential of the other. Ski-wheel landing gear and JATO extended flying options. Low-ground-pressure tracked vehicles, clothing improved by wartime research, and shortwave radio increased human reach and endurance. The naval forces learned about polar operations and the continent itself, concluding that they could live and work on it for extended periods. And they affirmed and extended U.S. presence in Antarctica.[40]

Almost a decade later, when the Navy leaders of Operation Deep Freeze pored over the three-volume Highjump report, they would profit from such observations as: Winds and currents can, and will, change ice conditions radically over a short period of time. Parking a plane on the ice "for even one second" can mean sticking fast to it; placing plywood under the wheels helps. Icebreaker channels cut as straight as possible help prevent ships following in convoy from scraping their sides on jagged ice. Polar living requires a 30 percent increase in the normal ration allowance, and good food boosts morale. And, if anyone needed reminding: the Antarctic is "relentlessly unforgiving of mistakes and slipshod work."[41]

As for Highjump's science program, it was clearly a secondary consideration. Siple wrote that some of the scientists aboard grew so frustrated with Admiral Cruzen's disregard for their needs in his focus on exploration that they vowed never to return to Antarctica with a Navy expedition. (They did, of course.) On the other hand, Father William Menster, the Navy chaplain who did not know where he was going until he reported aboard the *Mount Olympus*, wrote in his memoir that Highjump was to be a scientific expedition; the function of those who were not scientists was to assist those who were. Whether the innocence was his or his to convey is not clear. Regardless, significant scientific accomplishments included synoptic weather and magnetic observations, surveys of whales and other fauna, radar and sonar testing on ice targets, ionospheric measurements and studies of radio-wave propagation, and air sampling for chemical analysis.[42]

The Army observers who accompanied Highjump later prepared a "Plan for Antarctic Scientific Exploration," an unattributed document that undoubtedly bore Siple's hand. First among its observations was that the historic Heroic Age had run its course. It was time to "cease classical or adventurous exploration" and begin a scientific exploitation, made possible by new methods and tools of science and engineering. Also, the scientific answers to be wrested from the ice "belonged to the world" and would be best obtained by the world's scientists systematically working together from many locations—a wishful, if not prescient, anticipation of the IGY. Recognizing the obstacle of territorial claims, the plan suggested that the United Nations provide governance (later acknowledging that the then-infant organization was unready for such a responsibility) or that an English-speaking joint-sovereignty arrangement be concluded. At least an agreement could specify that scientific work would not be used to promote claims—here prefiguring future diplomatic developments.[43]

One last privately financed exploring expedition, the Ronne Antarctic Research Expedition (RARE), steamed southward on 26 January 1947, two months after Highjump. Its leader, Norwegian-born Finn Ronne, could trace his polar passions to his father, Martin Ronne, who had gone to the Antarctic with both Amundsen and Byrd. Ronne, an expert skier and dog driver, had previously wintered over with Byrd and with the USAS at East Base, to which he was now returning. Ronne managed to cadge a Navy ship, three Air Force planes, war-surplus clothing, and other help from various government agencies. In return, he promised to test materials and conduct certain research. Some private institutions contributed scientific instruments or sponsored scientists for specific studies.[44]

For its small size, just twenty-one men, the Ronne expedition contributed significantly to knowledge of both sides of the southern half of the Antarctic Peninsula and adjacent areas along the coast of the Weddell Sea. By his account, Ronne explored and mapped new territory two and a half times the size of Texas. The area west of the ice shelf described in 1912 by German explorer Wilhelm Filchner, he named Edith Ronne Land for his wife. Later, it would become the Ronne Ice Shelf. He had proposed to determine if the Weddell and Ross seas were connected and surmised from the lay of the land that they were not, a conclusion also reached by two Byrd expeditions and by Operation Highjump, operating from the Ross Sea side.[45]

Astonishing in its time was the presence of women on this expedition, the first known to winter over in Antarctica. Edith Ronne, called Jackie, had accompanied her husband as far as Chile, where he proposed that she continue on south—to the intense opposition of the men, including pilot Harry Darlington, who protested that "there are some things women don't do. They don't become Pope or President or go down to the Antarctic!" This he directed to his bride, Jennie, also still aboard, when the others grudgingly decided that two women would be less intolerable than one. Sadly, this historic first was stained with discord. When Ronne grounded Darlington after an irreparable falling out, the loyal young women lost each other's companionship, too.[46]

An irony of the RARE effort was that the British Falkland Islands Dependencies Survey (FIDS) had in the interim also set up a base on Stonington Island, not a quarter of a mile from East Base, where Ronne expected to use leftover equipment, supplies, and living quarters. The two leaders testily accused each other of trespass. As Ronne wrote, "It was incongruous that the only two expeditions on the more than 5 million sq. m. Antarctic continent had to be sitting practically on top of one another and arguing about who claimed the land." Indeed, the American base sat on disputed ground, and the British Base "E" was clearly aimed at shoring up the validity of the UK claim against those of Chile and Argentina. For his part, Ronne scattered U.S. claim sheets, firmed up U.S. presence in the region, and laid groundwork for U.S. interest in a Weddell Sea station for the IGY. Eventually, the two parties did some joint exploring, combining American airplanes and British dogs to mutual advantage.[47]

A year after Highjump, the U.S. Navy established a Second Antarctic Developments Project, its mission similar. Lacking an official code name, it came to be dubbed "Operation Windmill," apparently for its whirling helicopters. Commander Gerald L. Ketchum, who had captained the *Burton Island* in Highjump, was put in charge of the new, much smaller Task Force 39—only 500 men, two icebreakers, and no press. They arrived at Little America on 1 February 1948, already late in the season. The Windmill investigators revisited distant Wilkes Land, finding difficult pack ice, the Bunger Lakes area unsuitable for a base (the Russians would later build one there), and the water in most of its "lakes" bitterly saline. They did locate a site in the Windmill Islands where boats could land, a point later recalled by IGY planners. They also established more geodetic ground-control points for the Highjump trimetrogon photographs, essential for mapping. Several scientists aboard made tidal, magnetic, and biological observations. They were limited by time and bad weather but did not report the fierce winds characteristic of the area. The project was basically a "footnote to Highjump," wrote Rose.[48]

The task force also operated in the Ross Sea and off the coast of West Antarctica. On 20 February 1948 the *Burton Island* detoured to break out the *Port of Beaumont*, Ronne's expedition ship, which remained stuck in Marguerite Bay. The previous autumn it had been deliberately frozen in, but now the short summer was neither stormy nor warm enough to dissipate the ice. The rescue was critical; Jennie Darlington was pregnant. Ronne made it sound like a social call from Captain Ketchum, "an old friend."[49]

At the same time, in Washington, D.C., those who both celebrated the massive Highjump project and lamented its limitations began to push for a large-scale Highjump II, to be deployed in the austral summer 1949–1950. A new Task Force 66—seven ships, 3,500 men—would ambitiously train, test, and explore as before, emphasizing aerial photomapping of "vast virgin areas." It amounted to a "very definite and aggressive plan" to strengthen the U.S. claims posture. When a special National Academy of Sciences committee reported that "every square mile of unexplored territory must be assumed to have potential value at some time in the future, if not now," military planners were further spurred. Byrd, Dufek, and Siple would all serve in familiar roles. Ronne quickly proposed a scientific expedition at Gould Bay in the Weddell Sea, an area "unknown geographically, geologically and geophysically." Stressing U.S. glory and knowledge to be shared with the world, he outlined geographical goals— his own—and a multifaceted science program whose details would clearly be left to others. What is interesting beyond Ronne's tireless pursuit of expedition support is how often copies of his proposal were appended to Highjump II planning documents. It is unclear whether or how the Navy intended to use Ronne or his plans, although Gould Bay came to be one of the three proposed base sites.[50]

But Highjump II was not to be. Staff studies were finding the cost ($6.5 million, later nearly halved) too high, the time frame too tight, and the benefits (claims, resources) too iffy. By February 1949 the newly created Department of Defense, struggling over priorities in a time of extreme austerity even as the Navy was seeking its place within the unified organization, concluded that the "continuing unsettled international situation" spoke against costly deployments into "distant and nonstrategic areas." The State Department's "somewhat qualified" approval damned the plan with faint praise. On 25 August 1949 the chief of Naval Operations canceled the exercise, for "compelling reasons of economy." Byrd was appalled—at the waste of $1.3 million already spent, the missed opportunity to acquire "vast areas of Antarctica," the loss of cold-weather training. "We go South to learn how to conquer the North polar areas," he fumed. Siple, sharing Byrd's view, laid the blame to "political considerations": Secretary of Defense Louis Johnson "wanted to seize upon something spectacular to eliminate so that his postwar economy drive would appear politically significant." Like others, Siple also fingered Harry Truman: newspapers reported that the president, who was "engaged in a completely unrelated squabble" with the explorer's brother, Senator Harry F.

Byrd of Virginia, allegedly complained of "too many birds (Byrds)." His target unattainable, he shot at the one he could.[51]

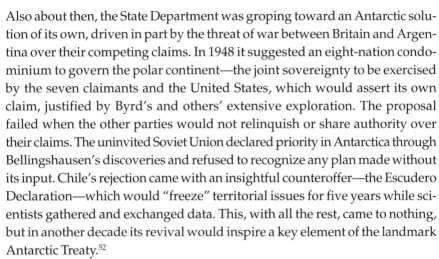

Also about then, the State Department was groping toward an Antarctic solution of its own, driven in part by the threat of war between Britain and Argentina over their competing claims. In 1948 it suggested an eight-nation condominium to govern the polar continent—the joint sovereignty to be exercised by the seven claimants and the United States, which would assert its own claim, justified by Byrd's and others' extensive exploration. The proposal failed when the other parties would not relinquish or share authority over their claims. The uninvited Soviet Union declared priority in Antarctica through Bellingshausen's discoveries and refused to recognize any plan made without its input. Chile's rejection came with an insightful counteroffer—the Escudero Declaration—which would "freeze" territorial issues for five years while scientists gathered and exchanged data. This, with all the rest, came to nothing, but in another decade its revival would inspire a key element of the landmark Antarctic Treaty.[52]

For now, the United States would cling to its "right" to make territorial claims while avoiding the military and diplomatic messiness of actually pressing them. Mineral resources, if any, seemed locked too deeply under the ice for economical development, while living resources could be exploited from ships without land bases. The Navy would not return to Antarctica until 1955, still unsure whether the cold continent offered strategic value beyond denying access to potential enemies. In any case, the armed forces were soon swept up in the Korean conflict and the worsening Cold War. Any polar energy was directed toward North Pole dangers from the now-nuclear USSR and implementing the DEW (Distant Early Warning) Line of radars along the 70th parallel, which would eventually stretch from Alaska to Greenland.

While U.S. exploratory, military, and diplomatic initiatives receded for a time, the Norwegian-British-Swedish expedition to Queen Maud Land, 1949–1952, marked a substantive transition in Antarctica. This international party focused on systematic scientific observations, not methodological "firsts" or "making as long a journey as possible into new territory." Its logistical and scientific approaches would be directly transferable to the Scientific Age about to be born.[53] Indeed, the scientific community was about to burst with an idea that would change forever the history of the polar continent.

THE INTERNATIONAL GEOPHYSICAL YEAR
Idea to Reality

The IGY is the world studying itself. It is seldom that this world of ours acts together. . . . Yet, for the next 18 months, east and west, north and south, will unite in the greatest assault in history on the secrets of the earth. . . . At the same time, it may well help to solve the real problem—the conflict of ideas.

—Prince Philip, Duke of Edinburgh, 1957[1]

Early Antarctic explorers often used scientific research to legitimize and attract support for their expensive expeditions. The disappointed Shackleton brought back coal, fossil plants, and petrified wood from his near-conquest of the South Pole, proof of a temperate past. Sometimes there was genuine interest, as with Scott who supported a broad science program besides famously man-hauling thirty-five pounds of rock specimens to the last. Byrd showcased science on his own expeditions and promoted it as a worthy context for Operation Highjump. Now, in mid-century, science was enjoying unprecedented respect and popularity, having been widely credited with winning World War II with such breakthroughs as radar, the proximity fuse, and the atomic bomb. The establishment of the Office of Naval Research in 1946 and the National Science Foundation (NSF) in 1950 were but two governmental responses to the increasing glorification of science. For scientists, expectations were high, opportunities great. So perhaps it is not surprising that a small cadre of influential scientists would audaciously propose a worldwide commitment to probe the secrets of the earth. But could they pull it off in a world teetering over a nuclear abyss?

In this pregnant atmosphere, internationally renowned British geophysicist Sydney Chapman of Oxford visited the Johns Hopkins University Applied Physics Laboratory in the spring of 1950. One scientist he called on was James Van Allen who, after critical wartime work, was leading early research on guided missiles. Van Allen invited Chapman to his home in nearby Silver Spring, Maryland, on 5 April, along with a few other American scientists similarly making careers of bringing science to bear on U.S. military and security interests. Among them was Lloyd V. Berkner, a leading ionospheric physicist, telecommunications expert, and veteran of the first Byrd expedition, who headed a unit called Exploratory Geophysics of the Atmosphere at the Carnegie Institution of Washington and whose presence was said to fill any room. Sometime during that evening of spirited conversation, mellowed by Abigail Van Allen's "splendid" dinner, Berkner proposed, "Well, Sydney, don't you think it's about time for another Polar Year?"[2]

The others knew Berkner was referring to those previous periods of cooperative scientific observation in the high latitudes. By the timing of the first two, a third Polar Year should occur in 1982. But fifty years seemed too long a wait for enthusiasts who were also well aware of the rapid advances being made in the research tools of geophysics—radiosonde balloons to transmit weather data, radar to track them, rockets to lift scientific instruments even above the atmosphere, cosmic ray recorders, improved spectroscopes, and electronic (albeit room-sized) computers. Berkner suggested a twenty-five-year interval. "Good idea, Lloyd! Why don't we get together on that?" Chapman replied—so immediately and specifically that Van Allen believed the Britisher had already thought all this out for himself. It was Chapman who pointed out that the twenty-five-year mark, 1957–1958, would coincide with a period of maximum solar activity. Berkner later called his words "spur of the moment," but he came superbly prepared for that moment. In 1949 he had contributed the ionosphere proposal for a National Academy of Sciences (NAS) study, "Antarctic Research: Elements of a Coordinated Program," a paper requested by the State Department in a renewal of polar interest. His newest report, "Science and Foreign Relations," linked international scientific cooperation and national security, with emphasis on the poles. Virtually every aspect of what was to come had precedent in his work.[3]

Thus crystallized the concept of what would become the International Geophysical Year (IGY). Chapman's international prestige and personal initiative would go far to make the IGY a reality. Berkner, more of an "idea man," was a gifted promoter. For example, at an NAS symposium designed to "sell" the IGY to the press, government, and popular audiences, geographer Paul Siple, who by then had wintered over three times, could not reply with certainty to queries about alternate routes from the ice shelf to the polar plateau. Berkner, presiding, exclaimed, "It is an extraordinary matter that we who are living in 1954, sitting in the National Academy of Sciences, in which some knowledge of the earth presumably should be present, should discuss one of the continents, having 6 million square miles, and not know whether there are some high mountains in an area or a gentle slope available for a cat [Caterpillar tractor] train." It was a quotable plug for polar science.[4]

These leaders' efforts brought the still-named Third Polar Year through subsidiary groups to the International Council of Scientific Unions (ICSU), a nongovernmental umbrella organization made up of thirteen international scientific societies and forty-five countries, acting through their national academies of science. The ICSU executive board, meeting in Washington, D.C., in October 1951, enthusiastically endorsed the proposal, and the ICSU Bureau, its operating body, invited its members to join the effort. It also included the Soviet Academy of Sciences, not then an adhering group but obviously, for the country's size if nothing else, important to any worldwide scientific data gathering. When the World Meteorological Organization agreed to join in planning the "Year," it felt the polar focus was too narrow. Chapman then suggested an International Geophysical Year. The ICSU General Assembly approved this expanded scope in October 1952 and formed a special committee, the Comité Spécial de l'Année Géophysique Internationale (CSAGI—called Ca-Soggy), to coordinate it. The CSAGI elected Chapman president, Berkner vice president, and Marcel Nicolet—an authority on the chemistry of the upper air at Belgium's Royal Meteorological Institute—secretary-general. Nicolet's office in suburban Brussels became the IGY headquarters. At first anticipated to run from August to August, the IGY became an eighteen-month "year," 1 July 1957 to 31 December 1958, to allow completion of all planned programs and encompass the entire period of maximum sunspot activity. That period also provided a fuller span of seasons in both polar regions, where access might be difficult.[5]

Planning for the IGY was a huge undertaking, with little precedent to guide it. The special committee urged the ICSU member nations (and others) to form national IGY committees to develop their own national programs. Naturally varying in scope according to means and interest, these programs would be coordinated for consistency and overall geographic and disciplinary coverage through ongoing efforts of the pertinent scientific unions and annual CSAGI meetings. By the time of the first CSAGI meeting in Brussels, 30 June to 3 July 1953, twenty-two nations had committees working on "specific planetary problems of the earth." By the second meeting in Rome, 30 September to 4 October 1954, thirty-six nations had detailed plans. (There would eventually be sixty-six.) About 100 of the world's leading scientists met to hammer out an integrated IGY program from the various components. Among them was a small delegation from the Soviet Union, apparently a little freer to participate internationally after Stalin's death in 1953. Their leader, Vladimir Beloussov, pushed hard to include seismology and gravity, areas of Russian strength. Numerous disciplinary, technical, and regional working groups labored throughout the conference to draft recommendations on scientific activities and stations, uniform experimental methods, and information-coordination mechanisms. By its end, Berkner recalled, the delegates had a "rather thoroughly complete" IGY program in place.[6]

An important criterion for justifying a global effort was that the national projects require simultaneous observations over a broad area. To facilitate and amplify these synoptic measurements, an international panel with Berkner as rapporteur worked out dates and other details for concentrated scientific observations—three so-called World Days per month and periodic ten-day World Intervals for intensive data taking, especially in meteorology. The International Scientific Radio Union (URSI in French transliteration) helped set up a communications network so that last-minute World Days could be quickly implemented if, say, a solar flare or major storm suddenly developed.[7]

A regional focus also emerged at the Rome meeting—to create geophysical profiles of the Arctic, the equatorial belt, and three pole-to-pole meridians chosen to include all the continents. Trumping these in glamour and attention were bold reaches to the earth's two profoundest unknowns. One was space, to be probed by rocket in the upper atmosphere and by earth-orbiting artificial satellite—an idea Van Allen had promoted since 1948. Five months later, NAS and NSF officials shared their anticipation that sending up a U.S. satellite (code-named LPR—long-playing rocket) would, beyond expanding geophysical knowledge, provide useful military and diplomatic leverage and "display American scientific leadership." They noted that *Pravda* had "publicized the Soviet intention to launch an artificial satellite," but when was not clear—

during the IGY they thought "unlikely." The other great mystery was the frozen continent of Antarctica.[8]

In Washington in March 1953, the NAS Office of International Relations, headed by Wallace Atwood, established the United States National Committee for the International Geophysical Year (USNC-IGY, or USNC). In addition to a core of leading geophysicists, it also named subsidiary technical panels for each of the IGY scientific disciplines to review proposals from public and private institutions such as laboratories and universities and formulate their respective programs. The national committee met two or three times a year, its executive committee about monthly. Joseph Kaplan, professor of physics at UCLA, director of its Institute of Geophysics, and an authority on upper-atmospheric spectra (aurora), was tapped to chair the USNC. Berkner used his influence to have Alan Shapley, a radio propagation specialist who forecasted ionospheric disturbances at the National Bureau of Standards (NBS), appointed vice chair. The self-styled "quite junior" Shapley had helped map out the World Days, and Berkner, impressed, maneuvered him into leadership of that effort and even membership on the CSAGI. In Shapley's mind, the distinguished Kaplan served effectively as the "front man"; he was the "working stiff." He must have earned high regard, as very little USNC activity occurred without his involvement. In fact, it was he whom the committee dispatched to NBS in late 1953 to lure away the much more senior Hugh Odishaw, then assistant to the director, to become executive director of the USNC-IGY. A former Westinghouse radar expert, Odishaw would eventually lead a staff of forty-eight to provide administrative services and programmatic leadership for the US IGY.[9]

Berkner, unsurprisingly, "had Antarctica on his mind" from the beginning, remembered Shapley, "and he made sure it was on our minds, too." In the fall of 1954 the USNC appointed a U.S. Antarctic Committee, though not before spirited discussion about the risk of committing to an expense so great that it might sink other programs with it if Congress balked. Siple, winning the day, called it unthinkable to leave to other countries such a vast and potentially valuable area. This committee, chaired by Laurence Gould and more often meeting in ad hoc groups, considered logistics, policies, technical planning, and leader and personnel selection. President of Carleton College, the suave Gould enjoyed friendships with senators and entrée to the White House. Prominent, constructive, and influential, he was a "wonderful, wonderful guy," according to Shapley, who also served on his committee.[10]

Energetic, avid Harry Wexler, director of Meteorological Services at the U.S. Weather Bureau, became vice chair of the Antarctic Committee, which also included Odishaw and John Hanessian Jr., who headed the IGY Regional Programs [Antarctic] Office; Admiral Byrd; Air Force colonel and veteran polar pilot Bernt Balchen; Paul Siple, representing the Army and non-IGY Defense interests; Antarctic explorer Richard B. Black, from the Office of Naval Research; Lincoln Washburn, who headed SIPRE—the Army Corps of Engineers' Snow, Ice and Permafrost Research Establishment; Grant Hilliker of the State Department; and a few others. Finn Ronne was listed as a consultant. Admiral George Dufek was a "visitor" at first, by summer a member. Siple, who with Byrd understandably chafed at having their "Antarctic authority" snubbed by "untried newcomers," sniffed that Gould had "last been" in the Antarctic twenty-five years earlier and Wexler had never been there. For Atwood, building the Antarctic Committee was a "delicate procedure," there being "very definite factions among the Antarctic experts."[11]

In late April 1955 Wexler was summoned to IGY headquarters and invited to be chief scientist for Antarctica. He consented, but at "gray dawn," after a sleepless night, he worried to his new diary, "what am I getting into? Am I losing 5 years of my scientific life with global meteorological problems to concentrate on a small area, to act as father-confessor to frustrated Antarctic scientists, to battle with the Navy for scientific program priorities?" Occasionally indulging in private peevishness but to others an open, hearty colleague and mentor, Wexler vowed he would "not be swallowed up by IGY"—and he never did devote himself full-time, to Odishaw's dismay. Hardworking Albert Crary, infectious science enthusiast behind what *Newsweek* called a "mournful moustache," later agreed to be deputy chief scientist, as well as chief scientist for Antarctic glaciology. In his mind this meant being the chief "in all but name as soon and as long as I am in Antarctica." There was nothing he wanted more, he wrote home, though he added his belief that Wexler had gotten the senior title through politics and self-promotion. Crary would spend more than two years, spanning more than the IGY, on the ice.[12]

Significant Antarctic decisions had already been made. At its second meeting, on 1 May 1953, the U.S. National Committee had agreed to one primary and three satellite stations to sustain the IGY in Antarctica. But they needed specific locations so that detailed scientific, logistical, and financial planning could begin. USNC members met at the fledgling National Science Foundation, then in the old Cosmos Club on Lafayette Square, where they spread out a map of the polar continent on an ample conference table. A return to Little America seemed a given, in deference to the venerated Byrd and to extend the history of weather data there that went back to Amundsen. But there had never been a year-round station in the forbidding, unrevealed interior, an obvious need for geographic coverage of the globe. By now, such coverage seemed technically feasible and, thus, tempting.

Seeking scientific justification for a site, Wexler remembered that George Simpson, meteorologist on Scott's last expedition, had reported "pressure surges" that seemed to emanate from the area around latitude 80° South, longitude 120° West. Investigating that phenomenon could be defended (though it was later found baseless). Maximum auroral activity was also expected there. Nor was it lost on anyone that this region of Marie Byrd Land lay in territory unclaimed but broadly viewed as the "American sector." Observing this, Shapley, who knew the importance of the angle of the sun in ionospheric measurements, pointed to the geographic South Pole, where the zenith angle would be constant. Well, he later chuckled, if others saw strategic considerations there, too, he had first claimed the spot. Later, the Navy refused to use the advancing ice shelf at Little America as a staging area for the South Pole, since compacted snow runways could not support heavy wheeled aircraft. So the logistics base was moved to McMurdo Sound, in New Zealand's claim, where because of the nearness of Scott Base no science was planned (a policy later modified). Odishaw and Shapley helped NSF prepare the first IGY budgets for Congress based on these four U.S. Antarctic stations.[13]

As the national polar programs rapidly developed, IGY leaders recognized the need for international consultation on Antarctic planning. Berkner, pressing this point in a letter to Nicolet in February 1955, suggested Paris as a site neutral to political differences and Colonel Georges Laclavère of France, secretary-general of the International Union of Geodesy and Geophysics, as convener. The able and astute Laclavère duly organized the first CSAGI Antarctic Conference, which was held in early July 1955. He was elected president, Gould vice president, and Odishaw one of the secretaries. Eleven countries sent altogether forty-eight delegates (Argentina, Australia, Belgium, Chile, Federal Republic of Germany, France, Great Britain, New Zealand, Norway, the Soviet Union, and the United States). Japan, newly freed from postwar occupation, sought "international moral support" (which Chapman urged) for its planned south polar expedition but could not send a delegate. The interested Union of South Africa was also absent.[14]

The savvy Laclavère opened the conference by urging that discussion be confined to technical (scientific) concerns and, specifically, not financial or political matters. He soon demonstrated his meaning. Argentina's representative, a diplomat, objected to the large map hanging behind the lectern because it showed Antarctica's pie-shaped claims, in particular those conflicting with its own. CSAGI staff member Philip Mange recalled, "With a dramatic gesture, the IGY convener strode to the wall and ripped down the offending sheet." No politics meant no politics, even though the map innocently served scientific planning. In Crary's view, this first meeting "set the stage for open discussion of science in an area where political rights of the claimants and political ambitions of the U.S. (for one) might easily have jeopardized fruitful discussions of the IGY sciences." Wexler came away "strongly impressed" with a sense that the Antarctic countries were "trying to out-do each other—scientifically, logistically, in mutual aid and in general trying to build up goodwill." The delegates planned reciprocal support in areas such as communications, weather forecasting, search-and-rescue operations, and coordination to avoid duplication of scientific effort. Admiral Dufek had charge of a working group on mutual logistics support, to include anticipated and unforeseen emergency assistance.[15]

The national Antarctic committees came to Paris prepared with the locations of their proposed stations and descriptions of their scientific programs, facilities, equipment, technical personnel, and operational timetables. They shared a hope that their stations (ultimately around sixty, of twelve nations) would be "adequately distributed" over the continent to maximize the data return, and much conference attention went to siting stations to fill geographic gaps. The U.S. Antarctic Committee had already agreed internally on the scientific value of a station (later Ellsworth) at Vahsel Bay on the Weddell Sea, for example, even though the Weddell ice had historically resisted penetration. Moreover, supporting this distant location would require a separate risky expedition that could threaten the budget of more desirable stations. Of course, political needs factored in as well. The State and Defense departments and the CIA wanted the United States or a "friendly" nation there for their own reasons—to monitor, perhaps mediate, the rival claims of the established Argentines and the British, who would build their own scientific station and support Vivian Fuchs's proposed Commonwealth Trans-Antarctic Expedition. Some skepticism over the quality of Argentine science was also apparent. This "gap" was getting a bit crowded, but in the end the delegates justified "clusters" with the rationale that proximity would permit a "detailed study of phenomena."[16]

As other countries shared their plans, pressure increased on the United States to establish additional bases. Some of this could be explained by an assumption that the Americans had the deepest pockets, as evidenced by many requests for icebreaker service and other assistance, but much could be laid to disquiet over Soviet designs. On 8 July, Beloussov arrived and announced his country's intent to place a station on the Knox Coast, one "near" the geographic pole, and a third at an intermediate site. While U.S. planners had long eyed the Pole, Siple, at least, believed there was as yet no firm commitment on it. But when the Soviet "bombshell" dropped and everyone turned to the stunned Americans, the smooth Laclavère, with an "air of regret," told the Russians, "I'm sorry, but we have accepted the offer of the United States to erect and man a South Pole Station." He then adroitly suggested that the USSR put stations in the still-empty quadrant south of Africa, which came to mean the Geomagnetic Pole and the Pole of Inaccessibility (remotest from any coast). Thus, the Soviets would get two "Poles," though everyone knew where the glamour lay. Did the Russians really not know of the rival plans? They seemed to be pushing beyond their expectations to test how far they could go. Beloussov readily agreed to the compromise.[17]

The other Antarctic nations feared in common the "danger of Soviet penetration," suspicious that the Russians' IGY activity was "motivated by long term strategic considerations" (as if that of others was not). Australia was particularly nervous about the extensive Soviet program scheduled within its claim. The United States, also wary, firmed its decision to build a station on the Knox Coast of East Antarctica (later named for explorer Charles Wilkes, in emphasis of U.S. historical precedent there), to keep an eye on the Russians. When Alan Shapley was asked years later if this base was sited for political reasons, he whispered, "Ssh-h-h!" But even friendly nations grew tense over the claims issue. In August 1955 the Australian chargé d'affaires ad interim wrote to the secretary of state welcoming U.S. interest in "conducting scientific research in the Australian sector of the Antarctic" and offering to "render any assistance in its power to this end." The secretary's polite but terse reply reiterated his country's have-it-both-ways position: "This kind offer is appreciated although the Government of the United States does not, of course, recognize any claims so far advanced in the Antarctic and reserves all rights accruing to the United States out of activities of its nationals in the Antarctic."[18]

For all that, the world's scientists did amazingly well in steering the IGY clear of political whitewater to accomplish what their respective governments could not. They simply agreed, with the tacit approval of those governments, that during the IGY all political issues, especially claims, were off the table.

Only once did politics threaten the entire enterprise. Communist China selected scientists to participate but protested when CSAGI also agreed to accept scientists from rival Taiwan. The Nationalist Chinese, belatedly showing interest in the IGY, demanded in turn (with U.S. support) that the mainland group be excluded. Treading carefully, CSAGI reminded all parties of the IGY's nonpolitical character. As ICSU later emphasized, welcoming scientists from anywhere held "no implication whatsoever" for political recognition of their country. The CSAGI Bureau even proposed to not list committees as "national," since they were supposed to be nongovernmental anyway, but neither side was satisfied. U.S. policy makers debated pulling out of the IGY if "CHICOM" participated but in the end decided that such a move would be "unthinkable"—contrary to U.S. interests, damaging to its prestige, a setback to scientific progress. Red China did finally withdraw, the only one of sixty-seven nations to do so. It apparently carried out a good part of its planned program, but the official loss of so large an area was unfortunate.[19]

Mostly, the IGY negotiators stuck to scientific concerns. Rewarding Wexler's vision and tireless persuasion, the Paris conferees asked the United States to operate an Antarctic Weather Central facility at Little America—to assemble and analyze weather observations sent in by all stations, conduct research, and aid in search and rescue. Immediate tasks were to figure out how to get all the weather information to Weather Central, including that from over-snow traveling parties, ships, and aircraft; establish schedules and forms for uniform data recording; and ensure effective communication of the information and forecasts within Antarctica and with cooperating Southern Hemisphere countries. Shapley helped work out a bottleneck-reducing relay system in which certain "mother" stations would each receive data from several "daughter" stations and then transmit the combined information to Weather Central. Arranging the reporting pattern to take advantage of easier communication across the auroral zone rather than along it made scientific sense, but in truth a key goal was to concentrate transmissions among "politically friendly" colleagues. Chile, Shapley remembered, "would be damned if it would report back through Argentina," for example, and "nobody trusted the Russians." Weather Central optimistically planned to issue two synoptic maps per day, up to four in summer, with the analyses no more than six hours old (to serve air operations). Obviously, Weather Central could not operate without radio, and the Antarctic Radio Transmission Working Group, chaired by Shapley, turned itself to such obstinate, never fully solved problems as interference caused by electrical generators, auroral conditions, and stations using similar frequencies.[20]

Beloussov endorsed the Weather Central concept but only if it were "truly international," that is, if it included representatives of other nations. Only a "working meteorologist," not someone in a "liaison" capacity, could be accommodated in the limited facilities, replied Wexler, sounding suspicious of spy activity. He shrewdly countered by suggesting a broader international exchange of scientists. While he thought Russian meteorologists could learn much from the Americans, he reasoned that a U.S. scientist assigned with the Soviets would profit from their geophysical techniques, especially in glaciology. So, over the course of this and two more Antarctic conferences, the planners worked out the details of including meteorologists from several countries at Weather Central and an American to winter over at the Soviets' Mirny Station. Weather Central would prove a scientific success and a model of international cooperation.[21]

The Soviets were not finished causing anxiety, however. At the second Antarctic Conference, which took place just a few months later in Brussels, 8–14 September 1955, in conjunction with the third CSAGI meeting, the Soviet Academy of Sciences confirmed it would establish stations at the Pole of Inaccessibility, at the South Geomagnetic Pole, and on the Knox Coast between the proposed Australian and American bases—but asked, twice, if the United States was planning on the geographic pole, "attesting to their eagerness to go in, I suppose," wrote Wexler. Cmdr. Edward Ward, then Dufek's staff officer for the Antarctic air squadron, repeated a story the admiral told about that meeting. With no others present at the close of a session, the Russian leader motioned Dufek over to a wall map of Antarctica. He pointed to the site of Mirny Station and to himself and smiled; this was a Russian base. He pointed in turn to McMurdo Sound, Little America, and Dufek. Another smile. Then he thumped the geographic South Pole and stamped both feet! Dufek got the message and never shook the worry that the Russians might still claim the South Pole first.[22]

Moreover, the Soviets' detailed presentations on their Antarctic program left no doubt of their technical and scientific capability. Kaplan foresaw serious competition for the United States, perhaps for years, especially in oceanography, glaciology, and seismology. Crary was more blunt. In a letter to Odishaw in July 1956 he wrote that despite overall scientific leadership in the IGY and far greater outlay of manpower and funds, the United States was "very apt not only to be second to USSR, but a very poor second" in both polar regions. The "plain" reason was the polar experience of the giant far-north country. Its nonmilitary Northern Sea Route Administration employed 12 icebreakers, 1,500 planes, and "an abundance" of specialized scientific and logistical personnel.

Its ship *Ob* was an oceanographic laboratory that, on its way to build its base, Mirny, had "in all probabilities" already accomplished more research than the United States had in the last thirty years. One hundred Russian scientists at Mirny would be a year ahead before their American counterparts even got to the ice, and their program went beyond the IGY sciences to work in marine biology, geology, and mapping. U.S. scientists had to rely on military ships where, "to put it bluntly, scientists are 'in the way,'" and on military operational support "because we are not capable of operating without them." Crary understood and accepted that support, but it did not dull his respectful envy of the rival system.[23]

By the time of the third Antarctic Conference, in Paris, 30 July to 4 August 1956, a number of polar expeditions were well under way, among them the U.S. Navy's Operation Deep Freeze I. Those ships and planes had returned, and the men who built the first two bases at McMurdo Sound and Little America were more than halfway through the long night of the first winter-over. In Paris, ten working groups met to finalize programs and arrangements in meteorology, radio communications, logistic support (under Dufek), Antarctic mapping, publications, gravity, seismology (under Beloussov), glaciology, coordination, and a combined group for the ionosphere, cosmic rays, aurorae, and geomagnetism (under J. W. Joyce of the National Science Foundation). Weather Central details emerged.

Final decisions on bases were also made in Paris, with a good deal of more-or-less friendly horse trading. Laclavère repeated a request first raised at Brussels: Would the United States and New Zealand consider jointly operating a station at Cape Adare, the first landfall on the flight path from New Zealand to McMurdo Sound and a desirable location for several sciences? Odishaw, who understood that most of the money and men would be American, promised to take the idea back to the U.S. National Committee, and by November it was agreed. So now there were seven U.S. Antarctic facilities to finance, build, and run. At home, Wexler reported the Paris conference "notably successful" in completing the earlier negotiations and in "advancing mutual understanding and good-will." Dufek's multilingual aerologist [meteorologist], Lt. Cmdr. John Mirabito, agreed, also suggesting that whenever a new facility or equipment was needed, there was an expectation (apparently justified) that the Americans would supply it.[24]

The IGY organizers assumed from the start, and formally agreed at the 1955 Brussels CSAGI conference, that all IGY data would be available to scientists from all countries. To that end, they appointed international rapporteurs to coordinate the work by discipline; the latter wrote guides to ensure parallel

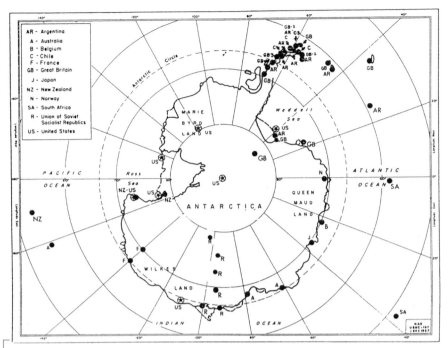

The locations of IGY scientific stations were chosen for scientific and strategic reasons, but in the end access and terrain determined specific sites. NAS USNC-IGY map, June 1957.

goals and comparable measurements in formats suitable for machine process-ing, if possible. Meeting in Uccle, Belgium, in April 1957, they drafted ground rules for sharing scientific information via three World Data Centers—Center A in the United States, B in the Soviet Union, and C in Western Europe, with branches later in Japan and Australia. By duplicating and sharing all data submitted, each center would eventually hold a complete set as well as pub-lished reports for the use of future researchers.[25]

Two other CSAGI conferences, in Barcelona in 1956 and Moscow in 1957, would complete the international planning, but there was still much technical, logistical, and personnel work to do within the United States, many political and financial challenges to meet. First, the U.S. IGY organizational structure was a complicated mix of private and public interests. The nongovernmental National Academy of Sciences might lend its prestige and design and oversee a scientific program, but it could neither fund the effort nor carry it out without massive governmental assistance requiring a complex web of cooperation and coordination. Congress would, if it chose, appropriate the money, but it could do so only through a federal agency. Nothing could happen without the blessing of the defense, security, budgetary, and foreign policy establishments, who all pushed their own objectives within overall administration policy. Scientific and technical agencies and institutions also brought their views and voices. Fortunately, President Eisenhower gave glad support. He called the IGY a "unique opportunity to advance science," pursue technological gains, and promote global cooperation.[26]

Paying for the IGY was the first hurdle. A USNC finance working group first met in early 1953 but could do little until a "reasonably firm" technical program emerged. The technical planners, in turn, had difficulty because they did not know how much money would be available—although they no doubt considered a range from what Crary called "cautionness to recklessness." The exact financial and logistical role of the military was also still unclear. The working group debated going for a single special congressional appropriation, asking participating agencies to request their own additional funds, and seeking private sources, eventually using all three approaches in varying degrees. They agreed that housing the IGY within the academy's National Research Council structure would permit the handling of private monies, and the NAS willingly provided the secretariat. They knew the new National Science Foundation could disburse federal funds (also private, they learned later), but its annual budget was still limited by statute to a modest $15 million. NSF gave the USNC a $5,000 grant for early work in 1953, another $22,000 for 1954, and then almost $2 million for IGY scientific equipment through its regular grants program, but at first "no one really expected" it to be able to produce "the millions that IGY would need."[27]

Nevertheless, Kaplan and others of the USNC brought the IGY's first $10.5 million budget request to NSF's National Science Board (NSB) on 29 January 1954. They found NSF keen to become the IGY fiscal authority—even though the huge collaborative effort was a departure from its usual pattern of funding individual scientists in academic laboratories and a serious stretch for its limited infrastructure. While IGY monies remained independent of the agency's own budget, they almost doubled it. Following through, NSF director Alan Waterman appealed to the Bureau of the Budget to put national interest before costs and be mindful that the IGY was a "special, non-recurring" expenditure, although before it was over there would be several such supplications. By the time the USNC presented its supplemental budget request to the NSB for fiscal

1956, the figure had grown to $27.6 million, two-thirds of which was for satellites. "In a rare expansive mood," Crary wrote, the NSB gave its approval "not to exceed $29,000,000." The year before, the science board had "viewed with extreme concern" the $2.5 million (a quarter of Kaplan's total) that went forward as the president's supplemental to "permit preparations to begin."[28]

When the budget requests got to Congress, a phalanx of USNC and NSF witnesses testified in fervent support of what Odishaw called a "minimal" IGY budget. Any less for any part of the program would, in his words, "vitiate the whole project." Gould cited the great scientific potential of Antarctica, and others spoke of the promise of international cooperation for world peace at a frightening time of Cold War friction. They all played to a fierce national competitiveness, highlighting the Soviet Union's formidable scientific plans and the opportunity for visible U.S. leadership. The combination lured Congress into increasing receptivity. As time went on, NSF historian J. Merton England saw these congressional budget encounters becoming "love feasts," the legislators exhibiting "a childlike curiosity in questioning the IGY wizards." Congress would eventually appropriate $43 million for the U.S. IGY, growing NSF's potency in the bargain.[29]

For Antarctica, the USNC had to deal, above all, with the Department of Defense (DOD), primarily the Navy, for its critical logistics role. Defense figured that its share of the cost of an Antarctic operation could range from $8 million up to $60 million, which its own priorities did not justify. But DOD officials agreed to seek the funds if "broader considerations" could be "reasonably demonstrated." Defense itself had to work within the apparatus of the president's National Security Council (NSC) and the NSC's interagency Operations Coordinating Board (OCB), whose working group on Antarctica was chaired by Admiral Dufek. By formal policy (NSC 5421/1 of July 1954), the NSC approved military support for IGY Antarctic operations—but for its own national-interests reasons: exploration, mapping, and resource evaluation. The IGY leaders understandably chafed at such Navy priorities, which made IGY goals secondary at best. Dufek, as noted by Crary, had written to Odishaw outlining plans for a "base to support military operations" at McMurdo Sound, air operations to establish the inland stations, and "the performance of other aircraft missions" (clearly military) while also later complaining about the "magnitude of the USNC-IGY requirements," which far exceeded original estimates. The USNC also felt its programmatic role entitled it to a seat on the OCB Antarctic Working Group, but because it was not a government body, it was never included. When NSF was invited to join this board, Hanessian fumed to Odishaw that its representatives had "wrongly pretended" that the

USNC had appointed them the official voice of the IGY and were evasive about providing requested information, too.[30]

Thus, many relationships promised tension, but none more than the scientific-military marriage for the IGY. The people involved were high level, with egos to match, and there was jockeying for position as well as divergence of goals. For example, in his diary Wexler noted with some heat a Navy proposal to have "Siple as DOD Chief Scientist with (presumably) IGY Chief Scientist under him. A vigorous roll-back of this will be made & Gould will reiterate IGY Chief Scientist in charge [of] *all* scientific work in AA [Antarctica]." A few days later he wrote that Siple, as the task force commander's science adviser, would be "in charge of all non-IGY science programs," a happy clarification. The same day Wexler recorded that "TF 43 (Mirabito) doesn't want too many IGY 'inspectors' around during Pre-IGY period 55–56. . . . It's important that two go down." Wexler sparred with Siple over the latter's promotion of additional stations to strengthen national policy; he wanted only as many as could support good science. If the NSC tried to "mesh" the IGY into its own "national objectives" without being open about it, the IGY people preferred to ignore the defense establishment's strategic concerns for Antarctica. Leaders like Berkner, who operated effectively in both cultures, were useful exceptions. He wisely strove to keep security aspects of the IGY separate from the scientific, with attention on the latter, even as he discreetly served both interests. "The more we can keep the IGY on the plane of pure knowledge the better," Berkner wrote, quoting Chapman, hoping to quiet Soviet jitters over U.S. military support.[31]

A difficult and fundamentally important IGY-military policy issue was that of the command structure at the IGY stations. The problem was the presence of naval support personnel in a civilian scientific operation. The scientists, correctly viewing the IGY as their show, insisted that a scientist be in charge at all stations. The Navy countered that military personnel could not take orders from a civilian, so a naval officer must have the final word. Neither side would yield, and a stream of marked-up memoranda and draft procedures flowed between the Pentagon and the NAS. Siple made a passionate case for civilian control, arguing that the structure must reflect the nonmilitary nature of the international endeavor. Station leaders must be chosen for their proven leadership, scientific prestige, and polar experience, he wrote, and senior military personnel lacked these qualifications. Moreover, success in "extreme isolation" would depend upon cooperation, self-discipline, and peer pressure, not military orders and disciplinary action. Split authority was as "impractical as command by remote control." Siple's solution was a civilian station leader who would appoint a deputy leader from the station's advisory "council" made up of the scientific coordinator, the military executive, and the medical officer.[32]

Siple was not alone in positing that "discipline and morale could not be stable under two heads," but the compromise reached after great exertion did indeed feature split command. Each station's scientific leader would be responsible for the scientific program, including fieldwork, and its personnel, including foreign guest workers. He would be assisted by the senior leaders in each scientific discipline, wherever they individually resided on the continent. The senior military officer would be in charge of the military personnel, responsible for their safety, well-being, and performance. The two leaders would "work closely" to "plan out the operating characteristics of the station." Housekeeping, for example, would be equitably shared by all. They would refer any unresolvable disagreements between them to the deputy chief scientist and commander of the Naval Support Units Antarctica at Little America. Any differences at this level would be radioed to Washington for resolution. The agreement expressly permitted a single station leader, if mutually agreeable to the scientific and military interests.[33]

Byrd, obliged to react after the fact, objected strenuously to dual command, which could only breed division. In winter isolation, "local leadership" was "more important than any chain of command." Attempts to settle petty disputes "by absentee judges over the radio" would be "impractical and fanciful." He would place the stations under a "single, clearly defined leadership," whether civilian (preferred) or military, and safeguard minority interests by naming a deputy from the other side. For Byrd it would be neither just nor effective to use "my Deputy, Dr. Paul Siple," as the "chairman of a half-dozen scientific observers to make known their logistic needs to some junior officer or non-com logistician over whom he would have no authority and who could not possibly have the polar living experience of Dr. Siple."[34] Ironically, Siple and his counterpart junior officer, who both resisted dual command, would lead together superbly at America's most challenging station, while never-ending difficulties, great and small, would threaten the one station that had a single leader.

———

Other agencies and institutions also became part of the IGY mosaic. The Department of Defense, apart from its logistics role, had a strategic interest in new knowledge of radio propagation, weather forecasting, and the properties of the upper atmosphere. The Commerce Department's Weather Bureau became the USNC contractor for detailed plans, central files, and equipment inspection, while its National Bureau of Standards developed equipment and lent expertise, especially in ionospheric physics. Other agencies similarly supported programs relevant to their missions. An early NAS study concluded that foundations and universities could not solely fund the huge national IGY program, but they could contribute to the support of scientists planning and advising operations; the purchase of astronomical and oceanographic facilities; the implementation of special projects, such as biology, not in the IGY budget; and the analysis and publication of data. If industry had no immediate commercial interest in the IGY, it might supply technical assistance and perhaps experimental supplies and materials.[35]

The Department of State early made it known that it "traditionally fostered international cooperation" and found the IGY "consistent with the objectives of our foreign policy." Its role would be mostly behind the scenes, however, as foreign policy makers recognized that the "quasi-formal" network of scientists could accomplish an international détente that would be impossible to achieve officially. All of the IGY players solicited State's views, and it was a member of the OCB Antarctic Working Group. Dufek invited a department representative, along with others having a "policy interest" in Antarctica, to accompany the Deep Freeze I expedition of 1955–1956, to provide press briefings and political advice and to obtain firsthand observations.[36]

Aside from such Cold War conundrums as divided China, the State Department's primary concern was the perennially sensitive issue of territorial claims. National Security Council policy in 1955 (NSC 5424/1) called for a reassertion of "rights" in the Antarctic, which were "ours as the inherent result of discovery, exploration, and unofficial claims." That really meant formalizing a claim. But where? How much? When? What were the prime areas economically or strategically, if any? What would the current claimants say? What would the Soviets do? Foreign policy analysts would wrestle with such questions throughout the IGY period even as the passage of time eroded negotiating space and every conceivable option carried risks of great consequence. When the ships sailed for Antarctica in late 1955 to make ready for the IGY, the United States continued its default policy of not recognizing others' claims while reserving its own right to make one.[37]

Thus intersected historic expeditionary groundwork, military capability, strategic interest, and scientific opportunity. As the talk continued, the Navy was rushing to cast off for the ice.

CHAPTER TWO

ALL HANDS ON DECK
Logistics for the High Latitudes

The Seabees go now and build camps, the stargazers come later.

—Seabee, Deep Freeze I, 1955[1]

When Captain George Dufek reported for command of the U.S. Naval Support Force, Antarctica (Task Force 43), on 16 August 1954, charged to ensure all logistical support for the International Geophysical Year, he knew the Navy had "exactly two years and ten months to lay out the red carpet for the scientists." The scientific community might continue its Antarctic IGY planning right to the eve of departure, but Dufek could lose no time in marshaling the necessary personnel, ships, aircraft, land transport, equipment, materials, and supplies. To have seven stations built and fully functioning by 1 July 1957, the first expedition would have to be en route by early November 1955. This would allow one season to establish the first two bases, at McMurdo

Sound and Little America. From these footholds there would be but one more short austral summer to build the two incomparably more difficult inland stations, as well as the three widely scattered coastal latecomers, even as the scientists were arriving. The northern summer and fall would be frantic.[2]

If Antarctica's natural menace was not daunting enough, the scope and details of the Navy's IGY assignment were. As the task-force plan put the obvious, "There are no facilities, equipment or supplies now existing on the Antarctic continent available for use in this construction program." Every-thing—*every* thing—would have to be hauled in. Besides food, fuel, clothing, and shelter, the Navy would have to provide air operations for reconnais-sance, search and rescue, and transport. That meant both compacted-snow and ice runways, ground-control approach (GCA) equipment, navigational aids, ground support, and fuel storage. The Navy would furnish communica-tions systems to connect all ship, air, and ground operations and Antarctica with the United States. It would build and maintain repair shops, garages, laundry and sanitation facilities, powerhouses and generators, science struc-tures, photo-processing laboratories, and dog kennels. It would make possible long-distance tractor-train and airdrop operations to supply the interior bases.[3]

Dufek, promoted to rear admiral, was a good choice to lead the huge, complex Antarctic operation even though he professed to prefer "warm sandy beaches." In early 1940, on naval duty on the *Bear*, he had famously earned Admiral Byrd's disgust for responding to the explorer's expectant gesture toward the awesome Barrier with "[i]t's a hell of a lot of ice, but what good is it?" But having now been on four north- and south-polar cruises, he sought the new assignment, probably his last, and had Byrd's endorsement for it. Once more, the Navy named Byrd officer-in-charge of U.S. Antarctic Programs. Frail and clearly unwell, Byrd was to "maintain effective monitorship" over the political, scientific, and operational aspects of the endeavor. John Hanessian Jr., head of the IGY Antarctic program, perceptively judged Byrd "a perfect enigma." He had "no operational command," yet was "impossible to neglect." In truth, he had no authority over actual events, and Paul Siple, among others, would find this twilight time one of "small discourtesies" and humiliations for the declining hero. Dufek had to deliver the mission and rightly took charge, but "Byrd's boys" thought there were times when a show of deference would have cost little. The admirals themselves seemed to interact with reasonable harmony, but "friction" persisted between their rival staffs.[4]

Within a month, Dufek called a meeting at the Pentagon of naval opera-tions officers who might be helpful to the unfolding Antarctic plans. Before it was over he appointed his first staff officer, Cmdr. Edward Ward, a pilot who had grown up idolizing Byrd. Ward had flown in the Arctic in the early 1950s with Project Ski-jump and was thrilled for a chance to go south. He spent the next summer recruiting and organizing staff in sweltering offices in Washington, D.C.'s Old Post Office Building before becoming the acting commanding officer of the new polar air squadron, headquartered at the Patuxent River Naval Air Station in Maryland, about seventy miles southeast on Chesapeake Bay. Actual building of the bases in Antarctica would fall to the Navy's construction battalions (CBs), called Seabees. They were based in Davisville, Rhode Island, on Narragansett Bay, where all materiel would be gathered. Preparations would proceed simultaneously at all three locations.[5]

In December 1954 Dufek dispatched the hurriedly readied icebreaker USS *Atka* on a five-month reconnaissance voyage to investigate pack-ice conditions and explore the Antarctic coast for possible IGY base sites. The ship negotiated the Ross Sea ice without undue difficulty, but the Bay of Whales, intended site for the fifth Little America, was gone. When Siple first saw it as a boy scout in 1928, the bight was about twenty miles wide and ten to fifteen miles deep. The bay ice within offered firm mooring, and the slope created as the floating ice shelf pushed around the grounded obstacle of Roosevelt Island made a usable access ramp. But by 1947 the advancing ice walls of the two capes were closing on each other, and, as Siple had predicted, they had now collided. Parts of the drifted-over Little America IV tent camp could be seen sticking out of the ice face, about to calve off. The *Atka* searched for a new site, finding a possibility about thirty miles eastward in Kainan Bay. This was a "tension" bay, formed by the widening of the ice shelf in its outward movement, unlike the "compression" formation of the Bay of Whales. But with either ice-shelf location in a dynamic state and snow-compacted runways likely unsuitable for heavy aircraft, Dufek decided to move the all-important logistics base to McMurdo Sound, about 400 miles to the west—a major change in plans. *Atka* continued eastward, rounding the Antarctic Peninsula to search for sites in the Weddell Sea area, but, after losing a propeller to thick ice, Dufek gave up and sailed for home.[6]

A handful of civilian and military scientists aboard the *Atka*, including IGY representative George Toney, managed to conduct "limited" observations, but they would significantly inform both the scientific and logistical efforts to come. Their upper-air and wind soundings, along with hourly observations of surface conditions, increased meteorological understanding for future weather prediction. The pits they dug to measure snow temperature, density, and structure would benefit IGY construction decisions. Measurements of seawater and the ocean floor improved nautical charts of the little-known area. Seismic soundings began the process of determining the thickness of the ice shelf and where it became grounded. All of these efforts offered practice in IGY techniques and served the political need to "do something" to sustain popular interest in the IGY.[7]

In January 1955, proud of his creativity, Dufek proposed the code name Operation Deepfreeze for the Navy's IGY role. (The name would be changed to Deep Freeze in late 1956 when the Amana food-freezer company complained of copyright infringement.) The admiral concentrated on assembling his Washington staff first, eventually forty-one officers and ninety-one men, most of whom would accompany him on Deep Freeze I.[8] He chose "cool-headed" four-time polar veteran Capt. Gerald Ketchum as his deputy task-force commander, in charge of overall administration and icebreaker operations. The herculean, pivotal job of logistics took a captain's rank, but Dufek wanted Lt. Cmdr. Donald Kent, whose success at getting things done he had personally witnessed, as his "no excuses" chief supply officer. He named Cmdr. Herbert Whitney, a reserve officer of the Navy's Civil Engineer Corps, to head the construction effort. "Eternally optimistic" Lt. Cmdr. John Mirabito, once an aspiring professional baseball player, became staff aerologist for the critical air operations. Dufek, who could be both stubborn and overly reliant on old buddies, applied his weight to give "Trigger" Hawkes command of the air squadron. But Hawkes was technically ineligible, having elected to give up line-officer status to become an engineering specialist. Even an admiral could not change those rules. He did, however, succeed in getting Cmdr. Hawkes, soon a captain, assigned to the task force.[9]

Paul Siple was detailed from his Army research position to Dufek's staff in 1955 as TF 43 director of scientific projects. In reality, he would promote what was called the National Program—activities in support of national interests and U.S. "rights," as outlined in National Security Council policy. Thus, while the task force fulfilled its command responsibility to meet IGY logistics needs, Rear Adm. R. E. Rose, a member of the Operations Coordinating Board Antarctic Working Group, also pushed scientific research to "arrive at a dependable appraisal of [Antarctica's] military worth." He had in mind "yet undiscovered strategic materials"; others anticipated a permanent presence and territorial claims. So there would be aerial exploration and mapping, primarily, but also oceanography, radio-wave propagation studies, polar clothing research, and other work for various armed-service units. These were quite apart from IGY intent.[10]

At the same time, Siple was a prominent member of the U.S. National Committee for the IGY and its Antarctic Committee. He probably expected, with the justification of long experience, to be named IGY chief scientist for

Antarctica. But his split loyalties likely factored into his being passed over, and his repeated invoking of "security" constraints to avoid discussing potential linkages between the National Program and the IGY further frustrated IGY leaders. Furthermore, Siple was Byrd's "personal deputy." He soon exhausted himself trying to serve many masters. During the frenzied months before deployment, he often rushed from one of a half-dozen simultaneous meetings to the next, undoubtedly reducing his effectiveness at each. Meteorologist Morton Rubin, reporting to Wexler after his polar summer in Deep Freeze I, opined that Siple, "by sticking close to Adm. B[,] did justice neither to T Force 43 or to IGY."[11]

As it happened, the entire National Program fell under the budget ax in early 1956. The Navy said it could not afford the $58 million estimated for south-polar operations. Eisenhower, committed to the IGY, countered by proposing to cut any non-IGY Antarctic program unless the scientists "requested" it. According to Wexler, "Hanessian and his two boys, [George] Toney and [Harry] Francis," cranked out a complete, justified logistics budget in thirty-six hours. The president cut it to $22 million. Lost were the "political" elements (mapping, geology—both exploitable for claims making) that Antarctic Committee chair Laurence Gould would later call "inconsistent with the world-wide agreement." The fact that the Soviets had proposed cooperative mapping alone made the State Department suspicious. The goals of the National Program remained in the directives for Deep Freeze I but were dropped, at least officially, thereafter.[12]

As logistics planning proceeded in Washington, the Task Force 43 Operations Division got to work in Davisville. There, the Navy's Mobile Construction Battalion (Special) Detachment One, or MCB (Spec), established in February 1955, set up to bring forth two Antarctic stations in Deep Freeze I. To Richard Bowers, then a Navy lieutenant, junior grade, in the Civil Engineer Corps, who would assume charge of building both the McMurdo and South Pole bases, Davisville was "a madhouse": "We had about six months to learn what we were supposed to know about where we were going, to order all the equipment and material to get there, and to put it on the right ships." About 20,000 "measurement tons" of material had to be ordered, received, listed, packed, marked, and prepared for loading. Polar cold and the long logistics line multiplied difficulty. The differing engineering requirements for construction on shelf ice at Little America and volcanic permafrost at McMurdo meant dual preparations and training for the small, thinly spread force. Indeed, the battalion had to be split, with half for each base, which meant additional administrative work, not to mention that "every box of nails, every load of fuel and every container of spare parts had to be divided for shipment" and then further subdivided to separate out what would end up at Pole and Byrd stations.[13]

Moreover, there were, in Bowers's words, "a lot of fingers in the soup: scientists, military, government agencies." For example, specialists at the Navy's Bureau of Yards and Docks drew up the site plans and ordered the appropriate types of buildings, but many of these also needed the sign-off of scientists who, overall, had little experience in structural design and were still pulling together their own programs. They did know, however, that they needed certain types of towers for tracking weather balloons, others for observing aurorae, and entirely nonmagnetic buildings to house their geomagnetics instruments, which meant brass hardware and special nonmagnetic electric heaters. Neither side understood fully the other's categorization of materials or assumptions about specific financial responsibilities. Dufek and Gould exchanged carefully controlled words over the latter.[14]

Money was a continuing problem, even with the president's interest and Congress's fervor to best the Communists. Navy money came from the budgets of its pertinent bureaus and the contingency fund of the Office of the Secretary of Defense. But the initial, January 1955, Deep Freeze budget quickly proved inadequate; its $4.8 million grew to $9.1 million and soon beyond that. With the procurement of several large items requiring long lead time, the secretary authorized the Navy Department to spend $2.5 million prior to the new money's actual availability, to be repaid with a reduced budget the next year. However, when expenses continued to mount, this reduction was waived. As it happened, fiscal 1956 funds for supplies came in small increments and not until after 1 July 1955, adding to the Davisville frenzy. The "great bulk" of material arrived between mid-September and mid-October, neither comfortably early nor in a steady flow. Having to justify purchases by brand name, even when one brand's specifications were known to be superior (for example, Easy washing machines' lowest water usage), consumed more time and patience. Even worse for overburdened supply officer Kent, the requirements kept changing. The Navy's mid-June decision, based on the *Atka* report, to build at McMurdo Sound almost doubled the scope of ship operations, base construction, and logistical support. And the IGY leaders were still negotiating for the final three stations. Fortunately, Kent was never stopped by a "no."[15]

The planned scale and location of the IGY stations demanded heavy equipment. The behemoths of Antarctic motive power would be 35-ton Caterpillar D-8 tractors, intended principally for inland tractor-train operations but also for general transport and snow moving on base. Their customized low-ground-pressure treads reportedly "reduce[d] the weight per square inch on the snow to less than that of an average man on skis." There were also smaller D-4 and D-2 "Cats," some of the former equipped with fork lifts and booms for materials handling. "Wanigans" (shelters mounted on sleds) would provide movable messing and berthing facilities on the trail. Army Weasels and larger Tucker Sno-Cats were tracked personnel carriers, the latter to be used primarily by IGY traverse parties. Most of this equipment was based on cold-weather specifications developed over many years by the Army in Greenland and the Navy at its Arctic laboratory in Point Barrow, Alaska. Much was of World War II vintage.[16]

To learn how to assemble, operate, maintain, and repair their equipment, Seabees fanned out across the country for special training. Chief Warrant Officer Victor Young, who would lead the Byrd tractor train, went with others to observe and learn at the Caterpillar Tractor Company in Peoria, Illinois. There, he recalled, workers took "a basic D-8 Cat with some bells and whistles," such as a closed, heated cab, and widened the tracks to fifty-four inches (from the usual twenty-two) to obtain low ground pressure. Increasing the track width, however, without also strengthening adjacent components spelled trouble, but this did not show up until later. When the vehicles arrived in Davisville, they had to be tested and "winterized" for –70°F. One D-2 tractor, padded and palleted, was parachuted from an aircraft over a nearby field to see if it could survive a fall onto the polar plateau, essential if the pole station was to be built by airdrop. It did. Other Seabees took training in fuel handling at Camp Lejeune, North Carolina, and still others went to Fort Belvoir, Virginia, to learn demolition techniques suitable for ice, snow, and permafrost conditions. Some learned how to install complex radar equipment in Los Angeles and to fabricate wanigans and snow-compaction gear at Port Hueneme, California. Some attended schools for fire fighting and washing-machine repair. A few were "briefly deployed" to Thule, Greenland, to observe SIPRE tractor-train operations and Arctic construction techniques, such as snow compacting for airstrips, but almost no one received polar survival training. There was no time. Wartime duty in Alaska made do for some.[17]

By construction battalion standards, Young recalled, it was "absolutely essential that every gasket head was tightened, every heater was installed, every generator was functioning properly, and everything was in working order" before departure. But such requirements fell to the crunch in Davisville. There were times when over half the Seabees were off somewhere for training. Those remaining had no time to test every item, "and that caught up with us later," recalled Bowers, incredulous still that Commander Whitney had "refused to allow us to check out the electrical generators prior to loading." At the time, Young confided to his diary, "Exec says generators will not be tested. . . . Believe this to be wrong and told him so." Sure enough, they had faulty control systems and could never be properly paralleled in service, which frustrated both scientists attempting sensitive measurements and electricians struggling to ensure life-sustaining power.[18]

Planners of crucial shelter knew the frozen desert offered only ice to build with. Tents and then crude but warm and easily built Jamesway huts would do at first. But the "permanent" buildings (actually designed to last only through the IGY) had to be well insulated and rugged enough to withstand violent winds and heavy snow loads. Limited time, challenging logistics, difficult terrain, and harsh climate also dictated that all buildings be fast and simple to erect, with maximum interchangeability of parts. Excepting a few variations for special purposes, the Navy settled on the versatile, boxlike Clements huts, designed and prefabricated by a Connecticut company of that name. Floors, walls, and ceilings/roofs alike were made of double 4- by 8-foot plywood panels separated by 4 inches of Fiberglas insulation and fitted together tongue-in-groove. Hammered-on metal clamps secured the panels to each other. They could carry 125 pounds of snow per square foot. Inside surfaces of reflective aluminum reduced heat loss. The survival of bundles of panels dropped by parachute over Rhode Island fields assured their durability.[19]

Bowers and a dozen Seabees spent July 1955 at the Detroit arsenal, refrigerated to –90°F, where in fan-driven "winds" averaging 12 miles per hour they built a 20- by 40-foot Clements hut to test the building's suitability along with their own techniques, clothing, and endurance. They learned that metal clips and flexible gasket material failed at extreme temperatures, that splines improperly positioned at the factory had to be retrofitted on-site, and that cold metal roof trusses shrank too much to hold in their pockets in the panels. The job took ninety man-hours, with fifty more for meals and rest. The men would work faster on the ice.[20]

Proper clothing for polar survival was a matter both quantitative and qualitative. The Deep Freeze pioneers would venture to the high latitudes with the best cold-weather gear the Army, Navy, and Air Force had to offer, although Siple had to fight for specific types of hand wear, for example, with Navy logisticians who did not appreciate that the leather gloves handy for summer work, when dexterity was important, would have to give way to wool-lined leather mitts in below-freezing weather and to unwieldy but warm fur-backed "bearpaws" in extreme cold. Thin, knit "contact gloves" were necessary to keep bare hands from freezing to cold metal when small parts had to be manipulated. Construction crews would learn to prefer Army gear to the Navy's shipboard issue, although the latter's waffle-weave underwear seemed the universal choice. Layers (as many as six) would mean comfort in varying temperature and wind conditions, but full outdoor dress could weigh more than thirty pounds. Wisely, parkas of several bright colors replaced standard olive drab. They were more visible from afar, helped identify the wearer, improved photogenics, and lifted morale. Numerous experimental articles of clothing would also be sent to Antarctica, including a few misguided choices such as lens-less goggles, bizarre in concept and disastrous in use, and pointed-toe ski boots that Wilkes scientific leader Willis Tressler later deplored to the point of hoping "the designer of these miserable things freezes both his feet sometime."[21]

Along with clothing came cold-weather advice: wear sunglasses outdoors always, even on overcast days; use Chapstick liberally; watch companions for the telltale white spots of frostbite. Shoes and not-too-many socks "must not be tight": "If you wear 9's but 10's feel so good you always buy 11's, your antarctic footwear should be 12's and 13's to allow motion of the toes and to give sufficient insulation." *Life* reporter Mary Cadwalader, carried away by such admonitions, wrote that task-force members would need defenses against "temperatures which could get so low that the bones in an unprotected nose would break if a man walked too rapidly," revealing in its gullibility much about contemporary awe and ignorance of the Antarctic.[22]

Navy logisticians had, of course, developed over the years lists and formulas by which to calculate amounts and types of all kinds of supplies needed for specified missions, numbers of persons, and periods of time. But Antarctica in Operation Deep Freeze was fundamentally different, beyond not being a military action in the normal sense. There would be no running to the corner store for something left behind. So the level of detail was staggering. Kent reminded himself of Amundsen's rueful admission that he had brought every conceivable necessity on his meticulously planned expedition—except snow shovels—and worked even harder to forget nothing. Dale Powell remembered meeting with other radiomen in Davisville and surveying the room to list every item in it that they might need—from the receivers and resistors of their own trade to pencils and paper clips. But somehow they all overlooked so obvious an item as a table to put the equipment on. The Seabees scrounged scrap lumber to make one, and all was well except for the embarrassment. Dr. Edward Ehrlich and his hospital corpsman Kenneth Aldrich resorted to walking through the Newport medical supply depot to use the contents of the bins as tangible reminders. Might they need this drug, that instrument?[23]

The construction battalion, the air squadron, and the IGY National Committee all submitted their own supplies lists to go down on the first ships, as did the Air Force for its South Pole airdrops. Polar-experienced logistics officers allowed "liberal contingencies" and redundancies that would ordinarily be unthinkably extravagant (two years' worth of food and fuel, spare generators) to provide a crucial cushion of security for the real, if unlikely, possibility of ice conditions preventing resupply. The shipping documents today fill nine records boxes at the National Archives, interestingly preserved in the files of the National Science Foundation, not the Navy. For example, one October 1955 purple *Ditto* list of canned goods for the South Pole read: 10 cases Peas, sweet (48 cans per case; can size: #303); 20 cases Potatoes, white; 5 cases Beets, whole. Every list included unit and total weight, unit and total "cube."[24]

Other lists included such disparate but essential items as spare radio tubes, tent poles, desk calendars, IGY forms, slide rules, dynamometer spare parts, and "cookies, creamed"[?]. Still others detailed 2 cartons Milky Ways, 20 thimbles, 12 ice pitons, 3 Chrysler engines, 72 cans pound cake, 25 lbs twine, and 18 pr butt hinges 1½" x 1½" steel, zinc coated. There were copious amounts of photographic film, dog food, and "small arms, small arms ammunition and other explosives required for ground forces during occupancy of Antarctic stations." For storage of fuel and other petroleum products, the Navy acquired a Marine Corps 350,000-gallon "assault fuel farm," including several miles of hose, pumps, and flexible rubber fuel tanks holding from 3,000 to 10,000 gallons of aviation gasoline or diesel fuel. For some, the order for refrigerators ("reefers") seemed a joke, but they were essential for preserving food while crossing the tropical latitudes, allowing the purchase of fresh meat and produce in New Zealand, and safely thawing frozen items in the South.[25]

Byrd expedition veteran Sigmund Gutenko, working in a Baltimore bakery, prepared 9,000 bars of pemmican for emergency rations, each fifteen-ounce, 2,600-calorie bar about the size of a pound of butter. Gutenko used twenty-six ingredients and a secret recipe that little resembled the traditional distasteful American Indian mix of buffalo meat, fat, and berries, but the men would not eat it anyway. Seabee cook Stanley Povilaitis vowed not to use it except under duress. No matter if "fixed as a stew, soup, or pie, it's still pemmican," he said of the concentrated, high-protein, high-fat nonperishable food that was usually shredded and cooked in water to a thick porridge called "hoosh." Trail party leader Jack Bursey, recalling pemmican as the dietary mainstay of his earlier polar ventures with Byrd, publicly downed some to support present use but later admitted, "I showed a little more gusto to establish my point than my palate felt in eating it." "The boys," he wrote, "held their noses and said I could have it." The next year the Navy quietly noted that "the DEEP FREEZE I survival ration utilizing Coman-Gutenko 'pemmican' was replaced with the Army ski-troop ration modified to provide in ounces: meatbar 16, starch and carbohydrates 17½, cocoa and chocolate 5, dried fruit 1½, dehydrated flavors and drinks 2¼, and heat tablets, vitamins, matches, toilet paper, water bag and chewing gum 2¾." This 5,700-calorie ration, with packaging, weighed 45 ounces per man per day.[26]

Medical and dental care was another concern. Those heading south would be healthy, physically fit, and mostly young, but the Antarctic was a hostile environment, much of the work both strenuous and potentially dangerous. So both bases were assigned an infirmary, a medical officer, and two hospital corpsmen. The larger McMurdo would also have a dentist. Ehrlich, Little America's physician, was on his own to deal with tooth problems, and he would ever regret having to pull teeth (fortunately few) he knew could have been saved by someone more practiced in the art. Sent to Bethesda Naval Hospital for cold-weather medical training (there was no real program), he began to get "very, very urgent" telephone calls from Chief Petty Officer Aldrich who was struggling with the medical logistics in Davisville, where he lacked the rank to get attention. So Lt. (jg) Ehrlich got himself and his "stripe-and-a-half" transferred to Newport Naval Hospital, where he could practice additional general and orthopedic surgery and other skills that might be useful in polar circumstances while applying what pressure he could to acquire more adequate equipment and supplies.

Aldrich was indeed growing frantic because virtually no medical supplies were being provided. The task-force flight surgeon had put together what was essentially a "first-aid kit for a Seabee battalion that ordinarily would be operating with medical backup." There was little besides bandages for Operation Deep Freeze, which would be thousands of miles and months of dark isolation from the nearest proper medical facility. Aldrich finally screwed up his courage for "the biggest battle of my career" and talked his way into the office of someone with authority at the Bureau of Medicine and Surgery in Brooklyn, where he discovered that BuMed had the once-classified Deep Freeze papers still secreted in a safe. Once that information saw daylight, Aldrich got the purchase authority he needed within three hours. The medical officer and corpsman, both fondly called "Doc," tried to anticipate their most likely medical problems—broken bones, burns, and frostbite, they decided. They had to consider their polar resources. Would they have running water? No. Electricity? Yes. Their autoclave for sterilizing surgical instruments would be Coleman-fired. "It looked like a locomotive," Ehrlich recalled. Aldrich, working the Navy system, got the small proposed sick bay transformed into a full dispensary. For two years' worth of supplies and equipment he spent $26,084.21.[27]

One of Ehrlich's greatest concerns was the staggering amount of "medicinal" alcohol the flight surgeon had ordered—"twenty thousand two-ounce bottles of medicinal Coronet brandy and a thousand bottles [fifths] of the Navy pharmacopeia bourbon, which was called Old Methusalem, and also fifty five-gallon drums of alcohol," which quantities he accurately remembered forty years later. He had no problem with moderate recreational imbibing (despite contrary Navy regulations), but there was simply "no medicinal justification" for it, and he felt "there were expectations that had been planted that alcohol was going to flow freely" on the ice, almost "some kind of sub rosa inducement." Controlling the liquor supply would be a reluctant responsibility for Ehrlich, who drank nothing stronger than "pop" that year to be ready for any medical emergency and to avoid having anyone think he was abusing his access. Aldrich appropriated four abandoned ammunition cases to ship the "truckloads" of liquor that came in—huge "steel lockers with the doors welded shut." But he also used some of this stash as barter for materials or work he needed done. "You could move the world with that stuff," he chortled.[28]

Also, there were dogs. Many in the modern mechanized Navy heaped scorn on Byrd's insistence on bringing sled dogs, but this was one time the old school prevailed—likely a concession for many other denials. (Dufek, though, cut the recommended four teams by half.) Inspired since childhood by the great explorers' stories and now willing to do anything to see Antarctica, Ensign David Baker spent the fall of 1955 at the Chinook Kennels in Wonalancet, New Hampshire, learning how to drive and maintain the two eleven-dog teams and eight spares. Air Force dog trainers Henrick "Dutch" Dolleman, United States Antarctic Service veteran, and Tom McEvoy, an experienced Arctic dog driver, took on the practical education of recent Ivy League graduates Baker and Lt. (jg) Jack Tuck. "School" consisted of running a team of dogs hitched to a stripped jeep frame along old logging roads on days brilliant with fall foliage. Dogs, of course, could not pull like tractors. They were justified by their rescue potential in areas where aircraft could not land, so the dog drivers also had to learn to parachute, although Tuck broke a leg on his first practice jump and did not qualify. The admiral grumbled that "this special rescue insurance [never used] cost roughly $40,000." The dogs, in fact, earned their keep primarily as lively diversions for the men. They lent an "air of romance." For the reflective Baker, they imparted a keen sense of polar life in the past.[29]

By late summer cargo began pouring into Davisville from all over the country by truck, train, commercial aircraft, and Navy barge. Seeking efficiency in the Antarctic, supply crews organized and segregated it all by unit, class or category of material, and ultimate destination. Every item was coded by color: blue for Little America, brown for Byrd Station, yellow for McMurdo, orange for the Pole. Thus material marked with orange went first to McMurdo, as did goods intended for the Pole auxiliary base, coded green. Red denoted everything needed by the Little America trail party charged with finding a safe oversnow route to Byrd. Black alerted the loaders to cargo for the site-survey party and aviation personnel arriving at McMurdo in December 1955. (Since ships could not penetrate the pack ice until well into summer, having a full season to establish Byrd and Pole meant all goods for those stations had to go down in Deep Freeze I.) Boxes, barrels and drums, bundles and bales, and unpackaged items all had their own specified sizes and patterns of markings. Letters identified the class of material: from A, equipment for off-loading ships; F, building materials; and G, communications gear; to N, trail rations, and Q, general stores. Numerical suffixes indicated multiples of a particular type.[30]

Everything had to be loaded before the end of October so the ships could sail in early November. The plan was to load last the cargo needed first, but necessarily long lead times on some items, ever-changing materials requirements, and unanticipated near-catastrophes intervened. Panic over a strike at Canada's deHavilland Aircraft Company, which manufactured the Otters ordered for midrange Antarctic air-transport duty, was averted when the Royal Canadian Air Force lent some of its own planes. A strike at the Caterpillar Company proved mercifully short. Floods washed out a railroad trestle in Connecticut and "sent a freight car full of roof trusses into a ravine." Fortunately, replacements could be found for the half that were destroyed. When the USS *Wyandot* arrived in early October for loading, scarcely 50 percent of the required cargo was on hand. So orderly procedures were impossible, with obvious costs in heavy workloads, double handling, and "not a little confusion." During the peak period, forklifts destined for the Antarctic were pressed into service in Davisville. Some late-arriving cargo had to be reshipped to Norfolk to catch late-leaving ships, and an additional twenty-seven tons were sent by air to intercept the ships in New Zealand. Seven ships eventually got loaded, none of them optimally for off-loading. "It seemed like an act of God that all of the material ordered actually reached the Antarctic at all," the Seabees' official report conceded. Perhaps it was small wonder that Antarctic unpackers discovered a few absurdities: recreational fishing gear at frozen, inland Byrd Station, 100 boxes of rubber bands at Ellsworth, "1 pump, breast" at Wilkes. "From the vantage point of a decade," task-force historian Henry Dater wrote in 1966, "it can be seen how brilliant and sound the planning was. At the time it seemed to have a distinctly 'iffy' quality."[31]

All of the 1,800 military men who participated in Deep Freeze I were, as were their successors, volunteers. They stepped forward to fulfill childhood dreams born of thrilling explorer tales, to be part of a unique technical and physical challenge, to leave their footprints where no human had walked before, to save money (though anticipated hardship bonuses would not materialize), to escape unhappy professional or personal situations, to see the world, or simply to serve the time, which "all counted for twenty" (years of military service, the price of retirement). Ed Ehrlich graduated from medical school at twenty-three but was undecided about career direction. Draft-leery, he joined the Naval Reserves and was called up. When he mentioned that the AllNav (Navy message to all ships, stations, and squadrons) about Antarctica looked "kind of interesting," his captain goaded him to seize the opportunity—accept the risks and not weasel out with a recitation of practical excuses. Dick Bowers saw in the brand-new Antarctic-bound Seabee battalion "a chance of a lifetime." Robert Chaudoin, a yeoman at the Pentagon, had hoped to go to Paris next, but, his enthusiasm undimmed after forty years, he exclaimed, "Oh, it's an *adVENture*! My God! To go someplace you've never been before, like *that*?" On the other hand, surveyor George Moss, chief petty officer, claimed he "was volunteered," his shore duty canceled when the commanding officer found he was one of very few who had received Arctic survival training on an earlier assignment. Newly married, he was not anxious to go.[32]

The Navy officers who would winter over, many astonishingly young, were taking on responsibility that had no practical backing during long months of isolation. Lt. Cmdr. David Canham Jr., officer-in-charge at the McMurdo Air Operations Facility, was among the more mature. He was thirty-five, with a wife and family. His executive officer, Lieut. James Bergstrom, was twenty-six and single. Construction engineer Bowers was only twenty-eight. Dog handler Tuck was twenty-four on taking charge of the naval support contingent at the South Pole when no one was certain that life could be sustained there, while Baker, also McMurdo's communications officer, was even younger. Lieut. Brian Dalton, medical officer at Byrd and also its military leader, had become a doctor in his native Ireland and was in the United States for additional medical study when drafted in 1956. About ten days later he impulsively raised his hand to volunteer for the Antarctic. Somewhat taken aback at being accepted, he had virtually no experience with the U.S. Navy, American culture, or leadership. He read some books and relied on common sense, he said later.[33]

Wise officers knew enough to rely on the judgment and experience of their warrant officers and chief petty officers, who "really ran the Navy," and there were many in Deep Freeze, such as Young and Aldrich and Moss, who superbly knew their jobs, their men, and the system. The other enlistees were often young, a few still in their teens, but they brought specific essential skills and Seabee "can do" spirit. Chosen to ensure the right mix of ranks and rates (technical specialties) and stable, agreeable personalities, all the selected volunteers underwent physical and psychological examinations of the type given to submariners, whose claustrophobic living conditions offered the closest analogy. Some scoffed at the tests' lack of rigor (Dalton, who had to ensure the mental as well as physical well-being of his charges, alone among them was not tested at all), but surprisingly few misfits were passed through. Fortunately, there were thousands of candidates to choose from.[34]

The science side lagged behind. It had more time, but anxiety ran high. Although many eager young graduates were signing up, Paul Siple, who chaired the Antarctic Committee's personnel selection subcommittee, was finding it surprisingly difficult to recruit scientific station leaders. Whatever lure IGY leadership in the Antarctic offered, established scientists were reluctant to leave their professional and personal lives for the long, arduous tour when more lowly researchers could gather the field data for them to analyze later for publication and credit in the comfort of their home offices. Some also resisted sharing authority with Navy officers.[35]

Antarctic science planners also stressed over the Navy's commitment and reliability, doubting the prospects for Deep Freeze II even before DF I put to sea. Hanessian, who in Wexler's opinion tended to "build molehills into mountains" but was also a sharp-eyed, useful worrywart, served as a liaison between IGY and Navy logistics. After a fall visit to Davisville, he brought home fears that Byrd Station would not be built within 300 miles of its planned site and charges that the Navy had "relegated" scientific work to "a very secondary position" in Deep Freeze I. Each concern had some basis in fact—and, from the Navy's point of view, justification. Paul Humphrey, a Weather Bureau meteorologist who would summer in Antarctica in 1956–1957, also fretted about IGY-Navy coordination. Too much was "slipping through the cracks," he wrote. How much of the 20,000 pounds of scientific equipment that should not be airdropped could the Navy land at the Pole? How many electrical outlets could project leaders count on? Who would furnish reference books, nonfiction, fiction?[36]

In September the IGY sent George Toney to Davisville to oversee the receiving and processing of scientific cargo—1,731 pieces, 252,998 pounds, 14,362 cubic feet of it—by far the most for meteorology. He found it frustrating that he had to warn careless senders to pack a "standby" substitute separately from the primary item lest both be lost if a container failed and that some apathetic cargo handlers required "constant vigilance." But he doggedly repacked and reinforced, liberally stamped "Do Not Airdrop," and applied countless gummed "Fragile" labels. There would still be some damage, of course. He warmly complimented Navy staff, and Wexler complimented his "fine job—even lugging crates," but that was Toney's style.[37]

Their nervousness implacable, IGY planners insisted on sending science people south on Deep Freeze I, which was strictly a Navy operation. "HO [Odishaw] wants a senior IGY rep on flagship to be close to Admiral Dufek and keep IGY in picture with Navy and press representatives," Wexler wrote in late September. E. E. Goodale, later serving the IGY in Christchurch, and Kendall Moulton, heading for McMurdo, would accompany Byrd and Dufek on the *Glacier*. Meteorologist Morton Rubin would join the *Arneb* to summer at McMurdo, working with Mirabito to set up the Weather Central program to be installed at Little America for the IGY. Chesney ("Chet") Twombly and Howard Wessbecher would winter over, at Little America and McMurdo, respectively, to "safeguard IGY interests," including 150,000 pounds of IGY equipment. All from the U.S. Weather Bureau, these men would also assist the Navy's aerology efforts. Wexler wanted a scientist on the main construction train to Byrd Station, too, and was unhappy with the Navy's curt response that "each [IGY] man will replace a construction man," surely a legitimate objection.[38]

Two critical components of Operation Deep Freeze remained to be readied—air and sea transport. As soon as Wilkins and Byrd had proved the feasibility of flying over Antarctica, no one would think of operating there without aircraft. On 17 January 1955 the Navy established Air Development Squadron SIX (VX-6). Named by Ward, the V stood for fixed-wing-heavier-than-air, the X for experimental, which certainly fit this "totally different" context. This was the sixth VX squadron at that time. Ward would have liked to command VX-6, but after all appeals for a waiver for Hawkes failed, Cmdr. Gordon Ebbe, his "great, close personal friend," got the job. Ebbe had flown in the Arctic, and he knew how to measure ice thickness and select landing sites on ice. Ward became operations officer at "Pax" River. While providing limited base-building support, VX-6 aircraft were primarily intended to fly long-range exploratory missions, per the ambitions of the still fiscally alive National Program.[39]

Around 4,000 volunteers applied for the 53 VX-6 officer billets and 260 enlisted specialties to be filled. Ward laid the eager response to the lure of adventure, and that was indeed the case with numerous pilots, including Lt. Cmdr. Gus Shinn, the first man selected for Deep Freeze I and the only one with Highjump experience. Admiral Byrd, his hero, inspired Lieut. Robert Paul ("Bob") Streich, who brought photomapping experience and survival training in Alaska to the new venue. One of the most colorful to sign on was Cmdr. Earl ("Bloss") Hedblom, as VX-6 flight surgeon. Ward at first thought, "Is this guy for real?" But he soon found in the blustery, comedic outdoorsman an understanding, stabilizing influence on the ice. Canham, meeting Hedblom aboard ship, judged him "somewhat of a buffoon" but also wrote, "Doc is sharp—keen insight and interest in human nature."[40]

"When it came to equipment, there was just so much that was available," Ward recalled. There was no time or budget to order new aircraft, so he had to rely on the existing inventory—World War II planes with suitable range and carrying capacity that could be made reliable in cold weather. That first year they came in twos, he said quoting maintenance officer Cmdr. Rudy Weigand—like Noah's Ark: two four-engine, wheeled R5Ds (Skymasters), for long-range photographic missions over "trackless" Antarctica; two four-engine, ski-equipped P2Vs (Neptunes), which boasted speed and long range; two twin-engine, ski-equipped R4Ds (Skytrains, also called Dakotas and Gooney Birds); and two twin-engine, triphibian UF-1 Grumman Albatrosses, operable from land, sea, or ice.

Trying several types would demonstrate which aircraft were best suited to Antarctic service. Ward knew from experience that the trusty R4D (equivalent of the civilian DC-3) "lent itself well to being ski equipped," and there were "a few skis kicking around in warehouses." "An abundance" of older R4s were being replaced. One new airplane, the small single-engine DeHavilland UC-1 (Otter) on fixed skis, with its thousand-mile range and thousand-pound load capacity, would prove "a real winner down there." Four disassembled and crated Otters were transported by ship, along with three helicopters (HO4S-3s). The helos, lashed down on deck, would first star in air reconnaissance through the pack ice. Aircraft assigned to Antarctica were simply written off the books, Ward said. The Navy did not expect to see them returned, which spoke to the understood hazards of the mission and perhaps explained the reliance on old, well-used craft. None of these Navy planes could manage the massive air-drops needed to establish a station at the Pole, however. It would take R4Ds, for example, with their five-ton load maximum, around 150 round trips from McMurdo—prohibitively costly in both time and fuel. So in Deep Freeze II, Dufek would call upon the Air Force and its huge cargo planes, the wheels-only C-124 Globemasters.[41]

Squadron members spent the summer and fall of 1955 preparing and test-ing their assortment of planes for polar deployment. Some of this work was done at Jacksonville Naval Air Station, Florida, where ground crews installed skis, high-capacity cabin heaters, and an extra fuel tank in each fuselage to double the normal capacity. They painted exteriors in high-visibility colors and put in special compasses, radio antennae, and other cold-weather in-strumentation, as well as jet-assisted takeoff apparatus. They added trimetrogon cameras for aerial mapping and extra-large side cabin windows for general photography. Ward believed all the aircraft could fly the 2,230 miles from Christchurch to McMurdo, although the range of the R4Ds and Albatrosses was so marginal that they had to take a circuitous island-hopping route even to Hawaii. Not making it south himself until Deep Freeze II, Ward oversaw the move of the Patuxent River detachment in 1956 to Quonset Point, Rhode Is-land, next door to the Seabee base at Davisville.[42]

Finally, seven ships would transport the 1,800 men of Deep Freeze I. Three were icebreakers. The USS *Glacier,* with ten diesel-electric engines, eight-inch steel plate, and 30,000 horsepower, was the country's largest, most powerful icebreaker, fresh from its May 1955 commissioning in the Pascagoula, Missis-sippi, shipyards. The six-engine USS *Edisto* was recalled from northern duty along the DEW Line for the Antarctic mission. The Coast Guard's USCGC *Eastwind* came on a bit later. Three ice-strengthened cargo ships—the USS *Arneb* (Dufek's flagship until he transferred to the *Glacier* upon reaching the pack ice), the USS *Wyandot,* and the USNS *Greenville Victory* (another later addi-tion)—and the tanker USS *Nespelen* completed the complement. Two smaller yard oilers (YOGs 34 and 70), normally used in ports to transfer fuel from shore to ships, would be towed south and then frozen into the ice at McMurdo

Icebreaker Eastwind *towing YOG-34 through Ross Sea pack ice, with helicopter scouting ice conditions, Deep Freeze I. Painting by Cmdr. Standish Backus. Courtesy, U.S. Navy Art Collection.*

Sound. Military vessels, they all carried deck guns, although anticipated "enemy forces" were, happily, "none." Certain others would view them with testy suspicion, however.[43]

The icebreakers were loaded first to sail first so they could plow the polar ice and lead the thinner-skinned vessels through. The *Glacier* left Davisville on 19 October 1955 for Norfolk. *Edisto* departed from its home port of Boston on Sunday, 30 October, after an open house at which the press was reportedly "by far" more interested in the dogs than in the humans. The *Arneb* then loaded its cargo, departing from Davisville on 10 November to call at Norfolk, as did most of the others. There, *Wyandot* also took aboard 2,500 pounds of philatelic mail for Antarctic cancellation. Wherever it took place, leave taking for the long absence was poignant and gray, both for those breaking away from last kisses and those without someone at the pier or waiting back home. For those left behind, it was undoubtedly harder.[44]

When *Arneb* and *Wyandot*, loaded to the top decks, cast off from the Norfolk pier on 14 November 1955, marking the official departure of the little fleet, the similarly burdened icebreakers had been at sea for two weeks. The *Eastwind* and *Greenville Victory* would follow. Lt. Cmdr. Canham, traveling on the *Wyandot* to McMurdo, began a detailed personal diary with the farewell ceremonies. "Dress blues were most uncomfortable," he wrote, describing the day as "warm as midsummer." At 1500 hours [3 P.M.] the "parade of admirals" began, led by remarks from Byrd and Dufek. Gould hailed the IGY as the "most comprehensive study of man's physical environment ever undertaken," the "most ambitious program in international scientific cooperation ever attempted." Stylistically written to be read by others, Canham's diary reported that "as the last 'Godspeed and good luck' was aired, the band struck up 'Auld Lang Syne'—our lines were cleared and at 1630 we were actually underway in the channel." The *Wyandot*, built in 1942, was on its first trip to Antarctic waters, "just as it was the first trip for most of us," wrote diarist Charlie Bevilacqua, a Seabee builder chief assigned to a canvas bunk and locker on the second deck.[45]

On board the various ships were meteorologists and oceanographers, providing important navigational and hydrographic information en route and beginning some of the scientific work of the IGY. Oceanographer William Littlewood, a civilian with the Navy's Hydrographic Office on the *Edisto*, for example, made physical, chemical, and biological observations of seawater, ocean bottom, and ice over time, space, and descending depths. Altogether, six Deep Freeze I ships made depth soundings along 205,000 miles of ship tracks separated by five miles to create or correct the sparse nautical charts of southern polar waters. The *Arneb* also had a cosmic ray laboratory rigged on the fantail. These science programs, a "secondary mission" of the task force, were pursued as time and conditions permitted, but generally the ship captains, who could use many of the findings, did their best to be accommodating.[46]

Others aboard included more than a dozen members of the press representing the *New York Times*, Walt Disney Productions, the Associated Press, *National Geographic* and *Life* magazines, the National Broadcasting Company, the United Press, and three Japanese news services. World War II combat artist Cmdr. Standish Backus, USNR, and civilian artist Robert Charles Haun also participated, creating a Deep Freeze I gallery of lasting value. In the international spirit of the IGY, the State Department invited representatives from the other countries planning Antarctic stations to accompany this first U.S. expedition, and six responded positively: Chile, Argentina, Britain, New Zealand, France, and Australia.[47]

Lest anyone forget the political reality of the day, *New York Times* journalist Walter Sullivan, home from the *Atka* voyage, wrote a long Sunday article on 3 April 1955. Capturing the ambitious scope and mounting excitement of the forthcoming IGY, he also declared that "any nation that sends an expedition to the Antarctic has a political motive as well." America's no-claim policy was "only a temporary position," he wrote, as if authoritatively, citing the informal claims of American explorers made with implicit encouragement from Washington. The United States could hardly "stand idly by" while others carved up the continent, which might hold "fabulous resources hidden in its mountains or under its icecap."[48]

Byrd, too, was a nationalist first. In a *Times* interview just before his departure for the ice, he saluted the IGY's "pure science" global goals but went on to emphasize that use of the data and the "fact of occupancy" would have "far-reaching strategic, political and possibly economic ramifications." He correctly foresaw permanent villages resulting from the IGY and incorrectly speculated that distant, unpopulated Antarctica might be used for testing nuclear weapons. Earlier, surely he knew impractically, he had suggested it could become a "deep freeze" for agricultural surpluses. Ever nudging, the admiral noted "with a smile" that "the nation hasn't claimed this million square miles that I explored, so I guess I own it until it does."[49]

But official policy kept the IGY apart from politics. Diplomatic constraints, in fact, reached down to the enlisted ranks. On approaching Port Lyttelton, Bevilacqua wrote, all hands heard a lecture reminding them that McMurdo Sound was claimed by England [*sic*; actually New Zealand], while the United States claimed no area and recognized no country's claims. "We were asked to conduct ourselves properly while ashore in New Zealand, to make no comments of US claims and to avoid all arguments on the subject. I guess there is more to it than the average person realizes," he decided.[50]

The second day out, *Edisto* shipped a sea so heavy it broke a window on a tractor lashed to the deck. Fortunately, perhaps wondrously, this was its only weather damage on the entire trip. By contrast, the southerly voyage of the later-leaving cargo ships began with balmy days, "kind and gentle" seas. Oppressive heat soon followed as the Panama Canal was transited and the equator neared. As the ships crossed it, dozens of young sailors wrote their longest, most vivid entries to describe the slimy initiation ceremony by which they were transformed from innocent "polliwogs" to experienced "shellbacks." On the *Wyandot* this occurred a day late to allow for the proper celebration of Thanksgiving. Oddly, the air was chilly. Bevilacqua recorded ten pages of gross details, only to admit that "it probably took only 5 minutes for the entire process, it seemed more like 5 hours before you were thru." David Grisez, machinery repairman 3rd class, summed it up tersely: "I'm a Shellback now and have a sore behind to prove it. Got beat, painted, dusted, smeared with grease, chased thru garbage and dunked in water." Most of the initiates took it with good humor.[51]

Days of turbulent seas only made worse what for some was already rough sailing. The twenty-five men on YOG-34 had a wild ride at the end of a rope behind the *Glacier*. "When there are swells, the Pacific comes crashing over the bow like the proverbial tons of bricks. The ocean then treats the YOG as though she were a cake of soap," reported its commander, Lt. (jg) Jehu ("Dusty") Blades of Baltimore, a VX-6 helicopter pilot who did not even know a YOG was a ship until he volunteered to lead it. None of his Seabee crew knew ship handling either. Blades bought a book on seamanship and got patient advice from Capt. Eugene ("Pat") Maher, skipper of the *Glacier* and a former Arctic colleague. Capable of eight knots on its own, YOG-34 was towed at fourteen to save its fuel and maintain convoy speed. For recreation and target practice, crew members fired rifles at garbage thrown over the icebreaker's side, neither activity legal today. From New Zealand, Blades followed the *Eastwind* south, but under "Yogi's" own power.[52]

Everyone's fondest memory of the voyage centered on the extraordinarily hospitable welcome they received in New Zealand when the ships docked at Port Lyttelton and passengers debarked to beautiful nearby Christchurch, still the U.S. point of departure for the Antarctic. "Everyone fell in love," sighed *Arneb* navigator Cliff Bekkedahl, recalling the freely affectionate young women. "Not all of it stuck," but a few plunged into engagements during their brief stays. The *Glacier* was the first to leave this last port of call, on 10 December, eager to make headway through the pack ice. All the ships departed to cheering throngs and "much whistle tooting." Within days the weather changed precipitously. "The seas are rising—coming over the starboard quarter steadily and the skies are sullen and threatening. Temperature dropping steadily and sundown was not until 2150," wrote Canham three days out. By the 20th, "[N]ight comes no more—mere twilight now throughout the late and early hours." Two days after that it was "as bright at midnight as it was at noon—a great help for our lookouts."[53]

Bosun's Mate Clinton Davis, who boarded the brand-new *Glacier* in Mississippi for a record eight-year run, had a hard time getting used to the rolling ride of the round-bottomed vessel designed to ride up on thick ice. "You know, you'd wobble a little" walking, he said; sometimes he had to strap himself into his bunk. Farther south, gale-force winds in the notoriously choppy Southern Ocean tossed *Glacier* about "like a toy." "Trays of food went flying, typewriter carriages got stuck in one place and the portholes looked like washing machine windows as the ship rolled," wrote Bernard Kalb for the *New York Times*.

Admiral Byrd cut up his face when his cabin chair snapped its chain and flung him into a bulkhead. Once into pack ice, no one could sleep as the ice-breaker thunderously slammed against the ice, scraped up onto it, and broke through with a heavy settling or rocked with the heeling tanks to seek release from temporary immobilization. It could sound like a subway with express trains rushing by on either side, recalled Capt. Philip Porter, who skippered the *Glacier* just after the IGY. "After awhile, you'd get used to it," recalled Davis, although Porter said simply that "sometimes everybody falls down." "Dental practice is extremely difficult on an icebreaker," the ship's 1957–1958 report noted dryly.[54]

The *Glacier* took only thirty-six hours to transit the unusually light, "not particularly consolidated" pack of late 1955. Seabees helicoptered from the ship to mark off a runway on frozen McMurdo Sound for the VX-6 aircraft waiting at Christchurch's Wigram Air Force Base. Not far from Hut Point on Ross Island, about thirty-five miles from where the *Glacier* waited, they found flat ice at least seven feet thick, with a three-inch cover of snow to assist braking and hinder skidding. Ample for two heavy Skymasters, it was "a beauty of an ice runway," Ebbe proclaimed. "The [red] flags and poles lining both sides of the strip looked like two rows of birthday candles stuck in a white cake as big as Manhattan," wrote Kalb who viewed it from the air a few days later.[55]

These first flights from New Zealand to Antarctica were historic—and uncertain. There was no scrap of solid ground en route on which to land; over much of the way the frigid sea was overlain with pack ice often pressure-driven into a jumbled mass. The frigid air could produce sudden surprises. So Dufek picketed four of his ships 250 miles apart along the flight path, the meridian 170° East, to provide weather and navigational information and the best possible chance of rescue should a plane go down. When Mirabito pronounced the weather outlook acceptable, Dufek directed the eight aircraft to take off. (A month later, Rubin would report to Odishaw that the Navy aerologist was "making forecasts on no data, but having luck so far. He has self-confidence which is a good trait.") Thirty-knot headwinds forced the slower Albatrosses and R4Ds back to Wigram. The latter got as far as Station C, nearly the point of no return (where fuel becomes insufficient to return to the point of departure). Refused permission to try landing at Cape Adare in conditions unknown, the pilots turned around—"under protest." Some would return. The UC-1s would never see the ice; the R4s would become Antarctic work-horses. After fourteen grueling hours in the air, the other four aircraft, the P2Vs and R5Ds, landed at McMurdo on 20 December 1955, completing the first nonstop air link between Antarctica and civilization.[56]

Icebreaker Glacier *leading convoy of ships through Ross Sea pack ice, December 1955. Official* *U.S. Navy photograph. Courtesy, Al Raithel Jr.*

The next day the ships rendezvoused near Scott Island, which poked above the ice-choked water around 300 miles off Cape Adare. To Bevilacqua it was "a towering bleak, black rock jutting out of the sea. A lonely and scary looking place in this fog." Here they took their places in close caravan behind the sturdy *Glacier* for transit of the pack ice. The sailors spent Christmas in the ice near the end of their 10,000-mile journey. On the 26th they cleared the pack, observing in the distance the magnificent 12,500-foot cone of volcanic Mount Erebus, quietly wreathed in steam. They photographed comical, curious Adélie penguins and shapeless sluglike seals. They grew subdued in the vastness of the silent, white world, unable to articulate the "lonely feeling." The more aesthetic among them marveled at the astonishing palette of colors the angled sun splashed over mountains and ice. And then there was work to do.[57]

CHAPTER THREE

GAINING A FOOTHOLD
Operations Base at McMurdo Sound

*I try being kind to the old pros, [but] our
dogs live on diesel fuel.*

—Charles M. Slaton, CMC USN, 1956[1]

The McMurdo-bound Seabees of Operation Deep Freeze I, with little
to go on beyond accounts of the Scott and Shackleton expeditions,
sketchy Highjump records, and their own mindful preparation, would
have to build a base where nearly a hundred men—far more than
ever before—could winter over in safety and relative comfort. They
would have to make it possible to land heavy, wheeled cargo planes
if there was to be a U.S. IGY station at the South Pole. And, given the
brevity of summer and the press of the IGY calendar, they would have
to meticulously plan every detail of Deep Freeze II operations for the
Pole, knowing that weather and other unknowns could, and probably would, bollix their best efforts.

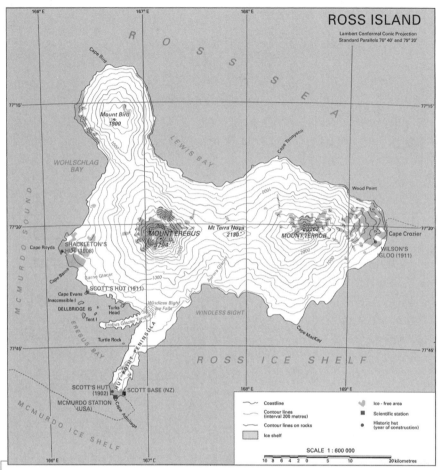

Ross Island, the site of historical expeditions, the home of McMurdo (United States) and Scott Base (New Zealand) during the IGY, and today the hub of U.S. and international scientific activity. Antarctic Information Map. Courtesy, the International Antarctic Centre, Christchurch, New Zealand.

For weeks, one thing after another went wrong. The icebreaker *Edisto* entered McMurdo Sound on 20 December 1955, but heavy ice stopped it more than forty miles north of its destination—Hut Point, a narrow finger of frozen volcanic rubble off Cape Armitage at the southern extremity of Ross Island. Onboard were members of the advance party, led by Lieut. James Bergstrom, officer-in-charge, and Lt. (jg) Richard Bowers, engineer in charge of base construction. Their job was to support incoming aircraft, erect a temporary tent camp, and lay out a permanent base site. Depositing them and their gear on the ice, the *Edisto* turned back to lead the incoming cargo ships through the pack ice. Tractor trains set off as soon as they could be assembled in the unaccustomed cold—the beginning of a ceaseless hauling operation. As Bowers reported, "Within a day, personnel were scattered . . . all along the forty-five mile trail" of "questionable" bay ice. Nature's winds, currents, tides, and seasonal warming would soon dissipate this ice, which the icebreaker could now scarcely budge. Communication among the scattering forces was erratic and unreliable, compounding the inevitable confusion.[2]

Later that first fine day the four aircraft still inbound successfully landed—fortunately, not needing much ground support, for the just-arrived advance party had little to give. The plane crews elected to live in their aircraft rather than join the others in their flimsier tents. Having no aviation gasoline for their own reconnaissance mission until it arrived by ship, they did at intervals operate their radios as a base-ships relay until more powerful radios could be installed ashore. It was a frustrating time for the restless flyers. The *Nespelen* was eventually moored against the ice, but fuel transfer by helicopter proved so laborious that the P2V pilots landed their planes on the rough snow-covered ice alongside the tanker, filled up, and ferried gas back to the wheeled R5Ds. By New Year's Day an auxiliary airstrip laid out beside the *Nespelen* served all aircraft, although, for safety, not more than two at once.[3]

On the 22nd, Bowers and others boarded a newly reassembled Otter to fly from the ice edge to Hut Point with a relief crew for the first tractor train. Immediately after takeoff, a little south of Cape Bird on the northern tip of Ross Island, the plane crashed on the ice—a total loss. Several were injured, two seriously. Bowers picked himself up, went on with his work, and characteristically put the incident behind him, but VX-6's Commander Gordon Ebbe called an Aircraft Accident Investigation Board, which later laid the blame entirely to pilot error. Cmdr. Ed Ward, the senior investigator, recalled that the pilot was unqualified to fly the plane and had airily taken possession of the left-hand seat on the basis of rank and prestige. He was Capt. "Trigger" Hawkes, Dufek's senior air adviser. Lieut. Eric Weiland, the intended flyer, fully qualified but junior and unaware, understandably did not question Hawkes's status. Hawkes had incorrectly set the trim tabs, one error the forgiving little aircraft could not overcome. "The crash brought all progress and movement to a halt" as crew members struggled to settle the injured in tents. They marked an emergency landing strip, unfortunately separated from the crash site by pressure ridges, which meant pulling sledge stretchers on foot. Lt. Cmdr. Jack Torbert flew his P2V in (on fuel remaining after the long flight from New Zealand) to

Wheels-only R5D and dog team on ice of McMurdo Sound. The dogs' chief contribution was to entertain, not haul loaded sleds. Photo by John R. Swadener. Courtesy, Marc Swadener.

bring the injured to Hut Point for interim care. The *Edisto*, just under way in the ice convoy, was ordered back to retrieve them.[4]

By 23 December a flock of tents was huddled around Scott's 1902 storage hut on Hut Point, their residents perhaps absorbing a sense of fortitude from the historic weather-bleached, fifty-year-old plank structure. That day the men of the advance party gave up trail rations to enjoy their first prepared meal in the mess tent—bacon and eggs. In time for dinner came the dog drivers and teams, who had been en route from the ship for four days. They had made seventeen miles the first day over the fairly smooth new sea ice. But the rafted older ice had been heavy going. "The dogs had not been exercised—nor had we—for fifty-plus days, so they pretty well crapped out on us. We ended up doing a lot of pulling and pushing," driver Dave Baker remembered. Unlike in Byrd's day, the dogs "were never of any real value in cargo hauling."[5]

Just about then, a blizzard pinned a tractor group down at the ice edge for sixteen hours. Fortunately, the six men had tents, provisions, and occasional radio contact with Hut Point. "We were kidding about having a white Christmas Eve and were planning to sing carols tonight," the ever-cheerful twenty-something yeoman Bob Chaudoin told Saul Pett of the Associated Press. Someone on the *Edisto*, arriving toward the end of the storm, saw the boom of a very

The Seabees' first tent camp huddled around Scott's 1902 storage hut. Mount Discovery looms across McMurdo Sound. Official U.S. Navy photograph. Courtesy, Ed Anderson.

close tractor in a momentary lull in the swirl and sent out rescuers, who finally "just about stumbled" onto their unseen tents.[6]

Conditions were scarier for Seabee commander Herb Whitney who, with Vic Young, George Moss, and construction mechanic Willie Burleson, set out by Weasel on Christmas Day with timbers to bridge a crack in the ice twenty miles out. From there they would proceed to the ice edge to board ship for Little America. But they encountered a "whiteout"—a condition where snow and an overcast sky reflect light back and forth until contrasts and shadows vanish, leaving no horizon or visible surface features. Its effect was "like marching into a milky white wall," wrote Laurence Gould of the phenomenon after his 1929 sledging expedition. Perspective was lost: "I once saw a huge rock exposure ahead of me on the homeward trail; it turned out to be old dog droppings." Balance also went awry in the "opaque white gloom." Unable to see a companion skiing ahead, Gould would "suddenly discover that he was thirty or forty degrees up in the air, or so it seemed." Despite their extra caution, the Seabees' Weasel fell into a snow-covered crack. It stuck at an angle between the ice edges, but as frigid water bubbled up through the floorboards, "I guess you know we bailed the hell out of that thing!" recalled Young later. As winds were gusting to seventy miles an hour, the four knew help could not reach them.

They improvised a tent from a parachute, and that "one piece of silk between us and the wind saved our lives." Twenty-six hours later the weather cleared, and a search helicopter found them, cold but unharmed. Crews quickly learned to carry survival gear and a radio for any trip beyond camp. Chief construction mechanic Charles ("Slats") Slaton retrieved the Weasel on New Year's Day.[7]

By 26 December the cargo ships had reached the ice edge, but Hut Point was still forty miles away. Capt. Gerald Ketchum, in charge of McMurdo operations, sent Lt. Cmdr. David Canham to mark a suitable trail across the ice for tractor trains, but the base officer-in-charge found it impossible to avoid crossing dangerous leads. Ketchum grew increasingly anxious in the passing days of the short season as unloading fell further behind and ice conditions worsened. He wanted his ships safely northbound by mid-February, summer's end. On 2 January 1956 he and a small helicopter party investigated the feasibility of establishing the base at either Cape Royds, where Shackleton had wintered in 1908, or the nearer Cape Evans, home of Scott's last expedition. Royds's limited water was contaminated by a nearby penguin rookery, and it was clearly too small. Evans's size was only "minimally acceptable," but Ketchum recommended it and Admiral Dufek radioed his concurrence. This meant finding a new tractor trail across the ice, a new site survey, more bridges across increasing and widening cracks, and "bitter disappointment." Morale began to crumble.[8]

Then, on Friday, 6 January 1956, Deep Freeze I witnessed its first tragedy. Young third-class driver Richard T. Williams and his thirty-five-ton D-8 tractor broke through the ice just after crossing a bridge over a seven-foot crack. When Chief Slaton turned in at 0200 hours, he had reported that the ice sagged as the D-8 approached the bridged area. Canham sent builder chief Milton Wise out with a work party to throw a new bridge over a new crossing site. As Canham later reconstructed it, Wise had marked a new location, but "Willy" and others suggested testing the old bridge first. Since a D-2 had been safely driven across, Wise finally agreed. As Williams got the tractor up on the bridge, Wise saw it sag and waved the driver back. But Williams "barreled forward," bouncing hard off the ten-inch drop at the far end, and when he was fifteen or twenty feet beyond the bridge "the ice collapsed." The tractor was gone in a moment. Its door and hatch were open. Someone saw Williams partway out, but either an obstacle or the cold arrested him. Standing there, horrified, was builder Charlie Bevilacqua, who remembered stripping off his heavy clothing and scrambling out onto the broken ice to pitch chunks aside, heedlessly struggling to enlarge the hole so Williams could resurface. "But he never came up. Only a seat and gas can came to the top." Bevilacqua was treated for frostbite and sedated, as were other distraught bystanders. Before Dufek left at the end of the season, he agreed to Chaplain Condit's suggestion that the McMurdo base be called Williams Air Operating Facility. Later, Williams's name was applied only to the airfield, as it still is.[9]

The accident cast a pall over the fledgling expedition. Some crew members asked to be removed from the winter-over list, but, Canham noted, "the majority are just that much more determined to carry out our job." "Can't see sticking Wise for anything," Canham wrote the next day after a board of investigation had met. He hoped they would not make this "excellent worker and fine team man" the goat for the Antarctic's treachery and a boy's impetuousness." The case was closed on a technicality, but Wise, deeply shaken and blamed by some, went home after the summer.[10]

Canham was at his best in such a situation. His men—like Chaudoin, who became a lifelong admirer and friend—found him always fair, concerned, and ready to listen. He had a keen sense of the mission and of command responsibility. He was hardworking (having to be put to bed occasionally for exhaustion), impatient with inefficiency, and thorough to the point of persnickety. "He really had his head screwed on right. I can't fault him for anything he ever did down there," Chaudoin reminisced. Machinery repairman Dave Grisez called him "my hero." For the chaplain, Canham was a "born leader," the "spark behind every activity." He sang in the choir, participated in entertainments. He encouraged church attendance, "clean speech, clean habits, and set the example for everyone." The CO, with his "tremendous insight" about people, was, to Bergstrom, "the round peg in the round hole."

However, Canham could also be supercilious, self-righteous, and sarcastic. His private journal reveals a striking and characteristic contemptuousness of superior officers' personal shortcomings and their "giving orders without knowing what was going on." En route, "ridiculous" new orders (because light pack ice was reported) for immediate departure from Christchurch—where life was rich—left him livid for weeks. He called Ketchum a "stupid ass," VX-6 planning "infantile." When he discovered that a few Seabees were trying to make some home brew, he was most peeved with his young officers Baker and Tuck, who "knew of it but hadn't thought it necessary to rpt to Jim or I—when will they grow up!" According to chief storekeeper William Hess, Canham ragged a few of the hardworking enlisted men: "He didn't want to give them an inch." This no doubt included Hess. But virtually everyone linked his decisive, caring leadership to the success of the operation. Dufek, at least once on the receiving end of Canham's judgmentalism, honored him later with a Legion of Merit.[11]

The day before the fatality and just in time, the *Glacier* returned to McMurdo Sound from Little America. In its absence, the *Edisto* and *Eastwind* had together broken ten miles of ice, but now, in thirty hours' ramming, *Glacier* cut the distance to Hut Point to seven miles, where the harder, thicker, safer old sea ice began. (It stopped short, apparently just, of destroying the ice runway five miles from camp.) That quickly, Hut Point became a feasible base site. Ketchum called off the Cape Evans effort. Unloading the ships became a round-the-clock race against the calendar and the restless ice. Crews worked twelve-hours-on/twelve-off shifts—although many put in far more in the continuous daylight. Tractor trains lumbered back and forth between the base and the new ice edge. There they took their loads from the icebreakers, which after disgorging their own were relaying material from the cargo ships still twenty-five miles distant. The latter dared not chance their thinner skins against the jagged ice lining the narrow channel. Thus almost everything had to be handled a fatiguing, frustrating three times. But at last useful progress could be seen, and spirits rose. The *Glacier* "was our salvation," Bowers declared.[12]

During this period one of Dave Baker's assignments was to drill ice corings along the transit route to assure safe thickness. One day, as his Weasel neared the moored ships, he observed a softball game in progress on the ice. Apparently the ships' skippers had declared a brief holiday routine to reward the crews' extraordinary efforts, and one ship had challenged another "in the American tradition." Soon, two or three dozen Adélie penguins tobogganed over on their bellies, probably from the rookery at Cape Royds. On arrival, they stood up and, as if knowingly, "aligned themselves with the sailors along the first- and third-base lines. It was clear that they were fans of the game," Baker mused, "since they understood the strategy from the start. When someone struck out or drove a base hit into center field or caught a fly ball for the out, they joined in the celebration by squawking and flapping their flippers in unison with the sailor spectators."[13]

Mostly, the work was endless. Even when whiteouts and blizzards let them be, tractor operations were hampered by limited resources. Only eight rated drivers were available, while at least twelve were needed per shift so that two per vehicle could spell each other. So others were pressed into service, eventually becoming reasonably proficient, although, as officially reported, "the learning states were difficult on both men and equipment." The equipment itself was insufficient. The one remaining D-8 could be used only on old sea ice nine or more feet thick, although the two D-4s could pull two ten-ton sleds fully loaded "under the worst trail conditions" over thinner, "very soft" new ice. The eight small D-2s worked near the ships, moving loaded sleds away from the ice edge and empty ones in. The tractors all broke down repeatedly under the heavy loads, difficult terrain, and inexpert handling. Mechanics cruised the trails in Weasels, performing almost miraculous repairs in the field. The D-2's tracks proved too wide, and the four bolts holding each pad were constantly breaking, Slaton remembered: "We used all the bolts that we had, and we had a world of spare ones." He finally flew back to New Zealand, where he "must've got two ton of track bolts" from the local Caterpillar dealer. Later, he had the tracks cut back to a more standard measurement, which better suited McMurdo's mostly gravelly surface.[14]

Communication was critical and no ordinary challenge. Radioman Tom ("Monty") Montgomery remembered living in a tent for weeks, struggling with variable success to maintain contact with the ships and between work parties. By the Seabees' report, "The single radioman on duty spent over half of his time trying to maintain the power source, fuel the stove, or keep the tent from blowing down." Yeoman Chaudoin, with his packing-crate desk and Remington typewriter, shared the radio tent, helping to hang onto it during the frequent "humongous" winds. At first Montgomery used an AN/GRC-9 ("Angry 9"), a fairly primitive, low-power device that required two operators—one to crank the handles (like pumping a bicycle) to generate the electricity, the other to key the message. A more adequately powered TBW-5 transmitter was working sporadically by Christmas Day, but not until 4 February did the Seabees get the communications building built around McMurdo's three large transmitters. Then they struggled in high winds to anchor fourteen poles into the frozen ground for the rhombic antennas, whose individual units would point toward specified U.S. and international receiving stations. The radio system became fully operational the day the last ships departed.[15]

On 12 January 1956 workers began grading the permanent campsite across Winter Quarters Bay from Hut Point, no small matter in the granite-like permafrost, and receiving material into the permanent supply dump. By the 17th they had accumulated enough to begin erecting the first structures' foundations. With most of the crew still laboriously commuting from the ship and tent life uncomfortable and inefficient for the rest, this was a landmark day. Completing the shell of the first 20- by 48-foot building on the 20th, two dozen exhausted Seabees "found immediate berthing accommodations within it," although the hut was slated for ultimate service as the library and ship's store. Two days later two more prefabricated Clements huts became a temporary mess hall (later the medical and administration building) and a barracks. On

Modular Clements huts under construction at Naval Air Operations Facility, McMurdo. The Seabees worked fast and efficiently, but salvaging or cleaning up debris were not priorities. Official U.S. Navy photograph. NARA II, RG 313, Records of Photography Officer DF 55–69, Box 1.

23 January, a month after the tent galley served its first meal, the camp enjoyed "a special steak dinner" to celebrate completion of the first permanent building and to honor "the outstanding job that all hands were performing." Father Condit brought his accordion and a pair of enlisted musicians from the *Wyandot*, a gift of music. After dinner, two cans of beer per person accompanied McMurdo's first movie. The sound track failed, but that seemed "not to stem the enthusiasm of watching Jane Russell." By then, 144 men were living in camp, most still in tents.[16]

Every day's efforts made the base more livable. On the 24th the snow melter produced the first 600 gallons of water, and welders completed fuel tanks for the powerhouse. The next day workers completed another storage building and the grading and demolition for a quarter-million-gallon aviation-gasoline storage tank. A 100-kilowatt generator went online to power the entire base, supplanting a 30-kilowatt unit that had earlier driven only the communications equipment. By 5 February, thirteen completed building shells had heat. Interior carpentry, electrical wiring, and plumbing soon followed. Four days later the base boasted its first heated head (Navy parlance for toilet facility) and its permanent mess hall. Moving the ship's store stock to a Quonset hut added coveted barracks space. In a week the *Nespelen* left, emptied of its aviation gasoline (AvGas), which went to permanent storage, and automotive gasoline (MoGas), to 10,000-gallon temporary rubber tanks. Visitors included Admirals Byrd and Dufek and Captain Ketchum, civilian scientists, numerous members of the press (whom the Seabees professed to scorn), and "hundreds of tourists on half-day trips from the ships."[17]

The four VX-6 aircraft had already departed for New Zealand on 18 January. Despite dissatisfaction with the early "lack of organization" and fuel, the pilots and crews managed a series of spectacular long-range flights—for exploring, photoreconnaissance, and mapping. Between 2 and 13 January they covered the Weddell Sea area, much of East Antarctica, the South Magnetic Pole, and parts of Marie Byrd Land (to help find a tractor route), also fulfilling their sub rosa claim-supporting mission. On one flight, Commander Ebbe flew Admiral Byrd, with Paul Siple and Disney photographer Elmo Jones aboard, on his third pass over the South Pole, although bad weather forbade their intended flyover of the remotest point—the Pole of Inaccessibility—which another crew later reached. Then, with the sea ice deteriorating, the flying season had to end. Enjoying tailwinds, the P2Vs and R5Ds made an eleven-hour safe return to Christchurch. Canham assumed operational control of the remaining two Otters and the helicopter.[18]

As the almost frenzied off-loading continued, Ketchum proposed to simply dump the cargo on the ice to make the earliest possible getaway, but supply chief Bill Hess insisted, with Canham's backing, that incoming supplies be placed straightaway in permanent, safe, orderly storage. He would not be hurried by working more people than he could control or having supplies arrive too fast to keep track of. If he was going to have to help dig them out, he wanted to know where they were. "And I never lost anything," he remembered proudly. The ship crews chafed, of course, feeling their vulnerability in the ice growing daily. Finally, on 13 February, with off-loading more or less completed except for what might come on the icebreakers' final calls, workers assumed a somewhat more normal single work schedule, 0600 to 1800 hours. The *Wyandot* had departed for the States on the 12th, the *Arneb* and *Greenville Victory* earlier, but the remaining ships' off-loading crews were now assigned to camp construction for one last push to have at least the shells of all winter buildings up before the last vessel headed north. On the 25th most of the last tents came down, and the next day, a Sunday, the bone-weary men enjoyed their first half-holiday and the tantalizing aroma of McMurdo's first baked bread wafting from the galley. Leap-year day, 29 February 1956, saw all nonwintering personnel board the *Eastwind* to go home. By then, twenty-eight buildings dotted the sloping landscape.[19]

For their part, the icebreakers had been shuttling continually between the two Ross Sea stations and New Zealand, where they refueled, took on mail and supplies including fresh foods, and underwent repairs. They also brought in the two YOGs left behind earlier at Port Lyttelton. The *Glacier* plowed a path into the ice on the far side of Hut Point, where in early March it took a round-the-clock effort at minus ten degrees in fifty-knot winds to anchor the oilers for freezing in. The Seabees' report noted, "Demolition charges, tractors, and brute force were all expended in large quantities." Finally secure, they became an instant fuel farm. The icebreaker also broke out a large area in Winter Quarters Bay, worrying Bowers who would need solid, stable ice for runways come spring.[20]

On 2 March, when the *Glacier* tied up for its last visit, Canham called a half-holiday so everyone could read and answer precious mail. The moment of truth arrived. On the morning of 9 March 1956, Admiral Dufek led a brief farewell ceremony in which he told those wintering over how proud he was "that so much had been accomplished in so short a time." The *Eastwind* and then the *Glacier* "took departure," leaving ninety-three souls on their own to face the long, dark night. "This was rather an awesome thought for most everyone," remembered Chaudoin, "but also a relief not to have all of the other people around. Sort of like company overstaying their welcome."[21]

That evening Canham instituted the first weekly all-hands meeting in the mess hall to discuss camp affairs. There was plenty left to do, including much interior finishing work—laying linoleum, erecting partitions, hooking up warm water in the heads—some of which would wait until after darkness fell. Besides everyday basics like the laundry, there were the aircraft maintenance

YOGs 34 and 70 moored along the outer side of Hut Point, becoming instant fuel farms for McMurdo's first winter. Courtesy, photographer David Grisez.

shop, welding shop, mechanics' garage, helicopter hangar, inflation shelter (for filling weather balloons with hydrogen), parachute-rigging loft (a 30- by 100-foot Quonset hut for preparing the South Pole materiel), Dogheim (dog quarters), and the public-address and fire-alarm systems to be made usable. It was news on 3 April that builders had started foundation work for "the LAST Quonset Hut." As it grew colder, workers' patience and skill were tested. They paid with frostbite as they learned to work fast with small parts to get their thick, warm mitts back on and to plan for two hours of pre-warming before trying to fly the helicopter (though in mid-April delaminating blades grounded it). The generators remained irksome, and on 4 April Canham set up a permanent watch of electricians and utilities men. On the 6th he wrote, "We used suggestions received from LA [Little America's chief electrician William Stroup] and finally phased our two generators—the procedure was one which factory reps at Davisville had instructed our personnel not to do under any circumstances." So at last, two generators could be used during peak periods, 0600 to 2130, then one shut down for the rest of the night. But unreliable governors permitted wide variations in the frequencies generated, so the individual units could never be confidently paralleled.[22]

It remained a "constant struggle by too few men in meager facilities to keep working equipment operational under the most adverse circumstances." All maintenance was done outdoors until the garage shell was completed on 13 February, although workers toted a portable Polar Field Repair Kit (in a wanigan), which kept tools and parts handy and offered some respite from the cold. Every unit had been taxed in the summer rush, so it was not surprising that when the last ship left, all four Cary-lifts were down, as was every tractor but one. Only three Weasels, of an original eight, were still running. Then runway preparations began, and in late July the garage went on a twenty-four-hour schedule to support that effort. Even one of the cooks and a chief bosun's mate helped out in the garage during peak periods, and the four rated drivers largely maintained their own equipment. But the five mechanics, men in related specialties (rates), and their assorted assistants were pushed to their limits to nurse along the equally overworked machines.[23]

On 12 March, Canham gave Chaplain Condit permission to construct a chapel (not in the Deep Freeze plans), but it seems that Father John had been planning and pilfering for one for some time. As the sympathetic but wary Canham wrote, "He is most anxious for a beautiful chapel—that's wonderful but [I] have to hold him in close check as he often 'borrows' much material and manpower from other jobs without checking with anyone." Indeed, workers drifted over, materials miraculously accumulated, and "Quonset spares" grew into the first church in Antarctica, the Chapel of the Snows. Bob Chaudoin painted murals for it—one for Protestants, one for Catholics, he remembered. Eventually, the chapel would sport a picket fence and a belfrey, complete with a bell "procured" from one of the frozen-in YOGs. Condit conducted the first services there on 6 May 1956. He had already baptized Chief Slaton, on Christmas Eve on the *Wyandot*, and there would be several others, recalled VX-6 line chief Michael Baronick, who was one of them. Father Condit became so aggressive in his proselytizing that he had to be told to back off. With special dispensation he conducted Protestant services, too, claiming attendance of "never less than a third" of the base population every Sunday.[24]

The handsome, extroverted Condit was an extraordinary character. He organized a forty-voice glee club aboard ship and a well-rehearsed church choir at McMurdo. An accomplished pianist, accordionist, and singer, he wrote and presented monthly theatricals starring each barracks in turn, beginning with the officers. On 14 April they staged a "wake" for actress Grace Kelly just before her marriage to Prince Rainier of Monaco, followed by a ceremony in which "Grace," six-foot-six, bearded Jack Tuck, looking "quite attractive," Grisez recalled, in his "off-the-shoulder white parachute gown," was wed to

Father John Condit (with accordion) and cook Ray Spiers entertain McMurdo's winterers with an Old West show. Official U.S. Navy photograph. Courtesy, James Bergstrom.

the shorter "prince," IGY representative Howie Wessbecher. Condit "married them right out of his little chaplain's book and they are still married," Grisez chuckled years later. The priest costumed the cast from bolts of fabric, wigs, and other stage paraphernalia he had brought south. Condit made an outstanding

Members of the wedding—"Grace Kelly's Wedding," produced by Father Condit, Deep Freeze I. Official U.S. Navy photograph. Courtesy, James Bergstrom.

contribution to camp morale. But he also used a "sharp" and "very profane tongue at times," reprobated slackers, and once insulted a Seabee by telling another that his Saint Christopher medal had been the gift of a whore. He drank—at least once sufficiently to regret it. The morning after the midwinter party, when no one appeared for church, he feared he had disgraced himself. Baker made him feel better with the simple truth that it was not Sunday. In September a vexed Canham wrote that Condit had "caused intense hatred among about a dozen or so of my men." Everyone had something to say about Father Condit.[25]

Antarctic life gradually settled into a relatively predictable routine, but the base was not without problems. Despite the overall hardiness of the population, Dr. Isaac ("Ike") Taylor had a few serious medical challenges that unrelievable isolation did not help. Just three weeks after the last ships left, an "emotionally upset" cook second-class was admitted to sick bay under twenty-four-hour surveillance. He had been a ship's cook, a last-minute replacement on the winter-over list when one of the screened cooks had to be medically evacuated. Taylor shared the patient's unstable condition with all hands so they could try to "assist in his recovery," but that would not occur on the ice. Chaudoin remembered that the troubled man would do things like "unscrew all the light bulbs except the one by the piano and pretend he was Liberace." By midwinter the doctor considered him a "chronic schizophrenic," and he was confined in a specially built, mattress-lined room unless others were close by. He got away once during the long night. Worried searchers found him in the chapel, "sitting in front of the altar completely naked going through this book telling God which ones had misbehaved." It was "funny, but sad, too," mused Chaudoin. Besides the medical and administrative burden of his care, the remaining cooks had to fill the gap he left in the kitchen. He went out on the first plane in the spring. The men later heard that he eventually improved.[26]

Stabilizing McMurdo's buildings against high winds became a key task as the autumn days shortened, and on the afternoon of 17 April Jim Bergstrom was on the roof of the BOQ (Bachelor Officers' Quarters) helping to secure tie-downs (cables strung over the roof and anchored in the ground on either side). In the absence of a ladder for disembarking, the tall Dick Bowers offered his shoulders. But Bergstrom's boots caught in Bowers's mitten straps as he prepared to jump down, and he pitched forward. Throwing up his arms to protect his face from the rough, hard ground, he took the impact with his elbows and shattered them both—the right one in nineteen places. Communications officer Baker marveled at how Doc Taylor, wisely seeking guidance from Bethesda Naval Hospital in Maryland, meticulously plotted the position, size, and orientation of each misplaced bone chip on a grid, then translated this information into a pages-long alphanumeric message for transmittal by radio. The struggling polar physician manipulated the bones as best he could (the X-ray machine soon failed) and cast the left arm straight, the right at a right angle. If it came to that, the arm would be more useful frozen bent than fully extended. Bergstrom remained on the sick list for eighty days but retained his unflappable humor and was soon working at what he could. Although he did not regain full use of either arm, he was doing calisthenics and playing pingpong with Canham by the end of June.[27]

The doctor himself was not entirely well. The Navy reported that he "suffered the first of his paroxsymal auricular fibrillation attacks" on 5 May, which unsettled many in the camp until a medical corpsmen got Dr. Ehrlich at Little America on the radio, who agreed with Taylor and assured the others that the "fairly easily treated" arrhythmia was not a heart attack. Taylor "was confined to bed for some sixteen hours but insisted on rising then." The log reported his having "another heart attack" on 12 November, but again he contended that he would be all right with twelve hours' rest.[28]

Personal time gradually increased as autumn advanced. On Easter Sunday, 1 April 1956, several adventurers climbed Observation Hill before breakfast to "catch the sun's first rays," and seventy-two attended church. That afternoon many enjoyed skiing and hiking, although the granular snow "really tore up the skis." A daily newspaper, *AirOpFacts*, appeared that day, soon becoming a more manageable weekly *Antarctic Bulletin*. By late April, with no sun but "gray twilight" for about four and a half hours each day, McMurdo personnel were working an eight-hour day, with two half-days and Sundays off—a schedule Canham thought would make the winter weeks go faster. He replaced an equal-liquor-ration policy with an open bar at the Saturday happy hours and found the consumption rate lower, morale higher. Birthday cakes for each month's celebrants had begun in March; the "comm[unication] gang" delivered McMurdo's first, perhaps only, singing telegram to Ike Taylor on his birthday in mid-June. On 1 May McMurdo made its first voice contact with the United States by amateur radio. From then on favorable conditions (no aurora, for example, or high winds to make static) and the assistance of stateside "ham" radio operators permitted conversations with home about four nights a week. The radiomen rotated contacts by turns through the camp. Weather Bureau meteorologist Wessbecher, one of the two wintering civilians, and Navy aerographers began formal weather studies, circulating their results by radio with Australian, Russian, and French Antarctic stations.[29]

In mid-May, Canham dignified the little town with some names. He called the administration/sick-bay building Dufek Hall, the library/office building Nimitz Hall. Continuing the naval theme, the two main parallel streets became Burke Boulevard and Forrestal Avenue. Radford Road, perpendicular to these, connected with Byrd Highway, the road to Hut Point. The effect on these honorees of having McMurdo's final thoroughfare, at Radford's other end, dubbed Honeybucket Lane (down which human waste was carried to the ice edge in trust of summer's melting) is not recorded. Today's more numerous dirt streets are without pattern; five come together at one point, necessitating a stop sign. Only one has a name, Beaker Street (slang for scientist). It runs by the Crary laboratory. The Deep Freeze I occupants named their own quarters, too: Ye Olde Sack Inn (officers), New Wellington (chief petty officers), Beverly-Hilton, Hotel Temporary, and Suite Sixteen (enlisted men).[30]

The passing of Midwinter on 22 June was a traditional Antarctic milestone. Half of the dark period was now over. "A slight pink tinge" appeared for a time on the northern horizon, a weak promise of returning daylight. Canham and Taylor "did a mecca to Scott's cross" on Observation Hill. There was sufficient moonlight to see Mount Erebus and its sister, Mount Terror, on Ross Island, as well as Mount Discovery and the Royal Society Range across the sound; its light "gave a soft but eerie sheen to the snow and ice and our camp was beautiful to behold," wrote Canham. In fact, during the winter, when there was a moon and the sky was clear, the moon stayed visible all day, tracing a slow. canted circle in the sky. Lacking skis but not spirit, the two officers made their steep descent in one swoop—like Shackleton, Worsley, and Crean on South Georgia in 1916—on the seats of their thick pants.[31]

McMurdo's cooks "went all out" that night to prepare a special celebratory Italian dinner, complete with checkered tablecloths and candlelight. Father Condit contributed some of his altar wine for each table, and he and Wessbecher on their accordions and drummer John Tallon, aviation machinist mate, provided music during the meal. It was Friday, so Canham kept to schedule and held a short all-hands meeting, but after that was a movie followed by a "lengthy Happy Hour featuring Doc Taylor's and [medical corpsman Floyd] Woody's Whiteout Cocktail—190 proof grain alcohol cut with orange and grapefruit juices." Twenty-five gallons of this potent nectar and twelve cases of beer disappeared before the revelry ended at 0300. Wary as always when liquor flowed, Canham was relieved to write that "most all hands were exceedingly well mannered." He did record two brief fights—the first of the year, and "may they be the last." McMurdo Station received and answered midwinter greetings from Dufek, Byrd, and several counterpart bases around the continent.[32]

By then, the primary work of the winter—preparing for the building of South Pole Station—was well under way. Lieutenant Bowers, officer-in-charge of Pole construction, had long been observing the wintering party, evaluating personal strengths and weaknesses, and making sure of including all the needed trades among the chosen crew. After the first selection meeting in the library on 26 March, thirty names appeared on his list, later pared to twenty-four. Canham was not named, but by his own account he expected to spend a month at 90° South. He did not—but he was "magnificent" about giving Bowers every man he wanted, even though McMurdo operations would be hampered by the temporary loss of key people. Bowers then approached each individual. A few declined to go. There was, after all, "an element of risk," he recalled in typical understatement. The men "weren't concerned too much about the cold," he said, but transport was a worry. They knew they would have to "depend entirely" on aircraft, and no plane had ever landed at the Pole. "And we really weren't sure that if the plane[s] landed there, they were going to get off." Bowers had "no problem at all" if someone did not want to go. But "in most every case" they did, many of them eager.[33]

Bowers made one person in each rating responsible for coordinating with McMurdo's supply chief to identify and assemble all the necessary materials, equipment, tools, and supplies his group would need to do its job. They made lists on index cards, arranging them in priority order for the sequential airdrops. Then each item, large and small, had to be packaged according to these priorities, color-coded, numbered, and labeled so that "as it came out of the airplane, we knew exactly what was coming and where we should put it." Finally, the crews brought all the crates and boxes to the parachute loft where three wintering Air Force specialists packed them on pallets and harnessed them to parachutes. The painstaking, detailed process took months; a minor forgetfulness could set off major consequences. The Seabees also worked with Wessbecher to make sure all the IGY equipment was properly readied for airlifting to the Pole and that items that could not be airdropped were packed separately for later landing.[34]

Bowers had spent many hours consulting with Paul Siple on requirements for the Pole while the latter was at McMurdo the first summer. Dr. Siple had some "definite ideas," on which, fortunately, the two had a "good meeting of the minds." He strongly urged, for example, that all roofs be at the same level to minimize drifting, lest snow soon cover and weigh down their flat tops. On the relatively snowless permafrost at McMurdo, building heights were no problem and little considered; Bowers accepted the warning to think differently on the ice cap. Siple also wanted an emergency camp to guard against the fearsome danger of fire and a system of interconnecting tunnels. They were good ideas, Bowers thought, and added, "hey, we weren't going to argue with him. He'd been there seven [sic] times and he knew more than we did."[35]

Bowers's careful planning took a blow when he learned that the roof and floor trusses for the South Pole buildings were too long to be dropped from a C-124 cargo bay. They would all have to be cut in half. He lamented to Whitney by radio in April, "It will mean a lot of work here drilling almost 10,000 holes, matched properly, and will amount to placing over 10,000 bolts at the Pole Station" using splice plates. He did not need to mention that this would be done out in the unprotected cold of the polar plateau. It took until 20 July to cut all the trusses and punch 72 holes in each. Later, Bowers would discover that the holes in the splice plates received from the manufacturer in the spring were not all evenly spaced like the ones made in the trusses at McMurdo, which would mean more work and frustration.[36]

Finally, Bowers had to plan for the unthinkable. His doubts about constructing South Pole Station numbered only one, but it was the big one—getting there. If a plane crashed or if it landed but could not take off, what then? He knew "Scott and his people manhauled sleds all over the polar plateau," so he decided that his group could, too. He organized his crew into six four-man, self-sufficient survival teams—small enough for versatility, large enough to optimize man-hauling ability even allowing for the incapacitation of one team member. He assigned each team two fiberglass banana sleds with skis, harnesses, tent, sleeping bags, Primus stove, portable radio and other survival gear, and enough food to last about fifteen days. Bowers explained, "The idea was that if we had to walk out, we would walk back toward the Beardmore Glacier to a place where an airplane could land, and if we needed more food, we could have it dropped to us." While Bowers was dead earnest in his worst-case planning, many of the Pole-bound seemed to mentally avoid the subject. Did construction mechanic John Randall worry? "Not when you're twenty years old. You're not smart enough to worry, really." Radioman Montgomery just kept "faith in Uncle Sammy's ability" to "send somebody in and get us out." Chief Slaton took the training, even learned grid navigation, but he bluntly "told Mr. Bowers and Mr. Canham that if I'm out there and an airplane crashes that I'm in, I'll still be there when they find the airplane." He vowed to stay where the food was and where "somebody knows that you're there."[37]

It was one of cold-weather mountaineer Dave Baker's jobs to organize and run survival training for the Pole crews. Indoor school began in June with twice-weekly lessons on the use of survival equipment and radio (the "Angry 9"), navigation, first-aid techniques, trail-ration preparation, care of clothing, and polar history and geography—what little was known. Each person learned the rudiments at least of two other ratings to ensure that every specialty had backup. Yeoman Chaudoin, for example, mastered enough radio and aerology to take a valid weather report, code it, and radio it back to McMurdo. Dr. Taylor gave lectures on the basics of treating the most likely medical problems, such as frostbite and altitude sickness, and Jack Tuck and Air Force Arctic expert Dutch Dolleman talked about dog handling. The Seabees test-packed their sleds. Then each team went out on at least one overnight camping trip—to use and test the survival gear and to train and condition for both Pole construction and hiking out. They practiced handling the dogs and sleds, each taking his own specialized equipment—photographer Bill Bristol, for example, took his cameras. Chaudoin, ever the enthusiast, thought the experience was "neat."

Camping out with man-hauled equipment and individual professional gear was a survival exercise for South Pole construction crews. Courtesy, photographer Robert Chaudoin.

His team hauled their sleds several miles across the ice and set up camp, tried the radio, and pretended to eat "that pemmican which tastes, oh, God-awful." Actually, "we would talk the cook out of some cans of tuna fish," he admitted, but Randall, who took his field training from Dolleman, found the greasy pemmican palatable if doctored up with a little lemon powder. Bowers called the outdoor work a break, "sort of like going off to New York for the weekend."[38]

For Baker, though, it was sometimes hard work persuading the campers to do the wise and safe thing—for example, taking their clothes off before crawling into a sleeping bag in a tent at forty-five below zero. That counterintuitive idea was "not something that's terribly appealing to most people," he admitted, so he had to use miserable personal experience as well as principles of physics to convince them that the only way to warm a cold bag was with body heat. Thus the less there is between body and bag, the better. Randall remembered well Dolleman's lesson that "jumping into a sleeping bag with your clothes on" was "a good way to freeze to death." Dolleman reminded them that if they worked, they sweated, dampening their underwear. If they slept in that underwear, their body heat would drive the moisture into their sleeping bags. Over time, ice crystals would build up, robbing the bag of its insulating qualities. Dolleman proved the point by having his team remove their inner bags and turn them inside out every morning. After they froze, they would shake them, and if there was moisture "you [could] actually see the ice crystals come out of it." While "it was rough getting up," Randall gained confidence that he "could survive because I listened to what the guy was telling me. And it makes sense."[39]

Canham, from the start disdainful of the dogs, tended to disparage Baker's efforts, privately deriding his "adolescent" ways, but he appreciated the substance and results of the program. For his part, Baker found the Pole crews highly motivated and bright, "the best of the best," but he also acknowledged "initial skepticism" toward some of the "theories," such as the effects of wind chill and tricks like first putting a little water in the snow-melting vessel to hasten the process and avoid burning out the bottom of the pot. He had to remind campers that although the roaring Primus stove could warm a tent to near comfort absent a strong wind, its purpose was cooking, not heating. It was not practical to carry enough fuel to use the stove for warmth, and the possibility of fire or carbon-monoxide poisoning could not be chanced. Such training exercises picked up as spring came and continued until 10 October. Survival training is still required for Antarctic field parties. That it is irreverently called Happy Camper School does not lessen the purpose or value of the experience.[40]

On 13 September, Baker, Bowers, and builder Richard Prescott went out with a dog team for field training near Scott's hut at Cape Evans, also used by Shackleton's 1914–1916 Ross Sea party supporting his presumed transcontinental trek. The second day out, the year's most ferocious blizzard hit. Worried that the seventy-knot winds might shred their tent, someone remembered an old Ponting photograph that showed a narrow window under the eaves above the attached pony shed, now completely obscured by drifted snow. They climbed onto the roof, chipped away with their ice axes where they thought the window should be, and there it was. Lowering himself in headfirst, Baker saw in the light coming over his shoulder a scene "that looked as if someone had stepped out just a few minutes before, and if we waited around . . . they'd be back." Cups of frozen cocoa, crackers, and jam littered the table. Dirty dishes in the sink and sweaters and dog harnesses carelessly hung on hooks gave evidence of the hurried departure of Shackleton's men when their relief ship finally arrived, perilously late in the season. For Baker, steeped in the old explorers' stories, it was a spiritual moment. "I had a feeling that I had really entered some kind of sanctuary," an emotion intensified by "the recognition that we had found a place that . . . could be a sanctuary to *us*." And it was.

While the trio sent up a green (all-is-well) signal flare on the 16th, they did not make it back to McMurdo until the afternoon of the 17th, just before the storm renewed its fury.[41]

No amount of South Pole planning or training would matter, however, if the cavernous, wheeled Air Force cargo planes could not land and take off at McMurdo for their historic airdrops on the high plateau. That made building a runway on the ice for the C-124s a primary preoccupation of the winter night, and as if his hands were not already full, this responsibility also fell to Bowers. Beginning in March, at first by helicopter and then after dark by Weasel or dog sled, teams went out periodically to survey suitable runway sites within a logistically feasible five-mile radius of camp. They made ice borings, noted cracks and snow cover, factored in likely wind conditions, and estimated safe distances from Observation Hill.[42]

Canham tended to focus his forays to the north of the Deep Freeze I off-loading site (Site Charlie), where the new sea ice was smoother, but Bowers was obsessed with keeping the runway as far south as possible to ensure thicker, more stable ice. Indeed, the previous season's sea ice had nearly all gone out, and little new ice had formed well into April. (By late July it was freezing at a rate of three to four inches a week, and by spring it would be acceptably thick, but winter calculations did not promise this and Bowers remained leery.) On the other hand, Site Alfa, on old sea ice just two miles from camp and safely ten to twelve feet thick, tended to be rougher and carried a deep, hard, dense snow cover that Bowers did not believe could be removed with available equipment, manpower, and time. Of course, no one could predict what tides, currents, storm swells, pressures of the advancing ice shelf, winds, and weather would do to their best-laid plans. The men quickly dismissed a third site, Bravo. It offered thick, rough, blue ice with little snow cover but was dangerously layered and thus weak, even if flooded. Time and conditions, naturally, prevented a thorough investigation of the entire area.[43]

During June and early July, Bowers experimented with snow-compaction techniques that had proved workable for runways in the Arctic, although no one at McMurdo had any experience with this type of construction and no one anywhere had successfully used it for anything as heavy as a C-124. He tried using a slurry of snow and saltwater mixed in a Pulvamixer as a construction material, hoping to form a hard, dense mat on the ice beneath, but he could not add water evenly enough to obtain a uniform cellular structure. A brief attempt to flood and compact the snow prior to mixing did not work either; there was too much snow. Other methods also disappointed. While the snow got harder, perhaps hard enough to handle an R4D, possibly an R5D, nothing they tried made it hard enough to support a wheeled Globemaster. It was a tense and discouraging time for Bowers, who realized that time for further experimenting was gone but still believed snow removal was beyond their capabilities.[44]

Chief Slaton had charge of actual runway construction, and by mid-June his crews had flagged a tentative airstrip following the prevailing direction of the sastrugi (wind-sculpted snow "dunes") and were struggling to build a safe road to it—which meant filling in myriad cracks and leads that crossed the proposed route. The Seabees bulldozed snow to fill the openings, then pumped in saltwater to make a "sort of snow mud," which soon froze. They could fill somewhat more than two cracks a day, but it was cold work, made colder by the men getting soaked with spray from the difficult-to-control high-pressure nozzle. Equipment broke down daily. "Slats and his boys," the mechanics and drivers, were working two twelve-hour shifts a day, much of it on equipment repair. The heavily used Cats, punished by the cold and the hard, uneven surface at McMurdo, were "in pretty bad shape." Breakage from metal fatigue became a plague. Overhauls were proving almost tantamount to rebuilding. The mechanics cannibalized wrecked equipment to keep other units running. Time marched on. Although Bowers told Whitney on 19 July that he remained convinced that with the right equipment and enough time they could build a snow and water runway directly on the ice or snow, they clearly had neither.[45]

In Canham's mind, the time for "drastic changes" had arrived. Bowers was, he wrote, an "outstanding" engineering officer, "one in a thousand," but he had never worked in ice and snow. Canham was ready to abandon snow compaction, which was "known from the first to be impracticable for the C-124!" On 17 July, after witnessing field tests of the tractors' snow-pushing capability (D-2: "not much"; D-8: "she can really push that stuff!"), he thought only one option remained, however unappealing: they would have to plow away the snow—almost fifty inches over sixteen feet of ice—at the nearest and only feasible location, Site Alfa. "I more or less had to tell Dick to drop everything else and concentrate on an *ice* runway," he penned. Then, "Dick is convinced we cannot remove the snow cover from Site Alfa—as this appears to be our only hope for an ice runway here (Dick can offer nothing) I don't agree with him—time shall tell." (Canham would return to this entry on 23 October to gloat, "We actually removed it three times in the period.") At the time he noted, officially and privately, with a grittiness bordering on desperation, that this was the "only possible way and further dallying will eliminate the possibility of ever getting the C-124's into this area this year." Almost thirty years after the fact, he would admit that, having done no "refined calculations," he had "no justification" for insisting they could do it—"other than being the C.O." It was a leadership moment. A decision had to be made, and he made it. His show of certainty, felt or not, surely prodded his charges to greater effort.[46]

Bowers drew up a runway construction plan on 19 July 1956 reflecting the latest discussions. They would attempt to remove the snow to complete an airstrip 6,000 feet by 200 feet by 15 October, Admiral Dufek's target date for the first VX-6 fly-ins. This was a reduction from "an idealistic stateside size" of 8,100 feet by 300 feet, but even then, by Bowers's careful computations—factoring in equipment availability and maintenance (breakdowns were inevitable), manpower, and weather—he judged completion in time to be "extremely questionable." He agreed there was no other alternative, which he wrote privately as well, but he also felt it "necessary" to convey a "pessimistic attitude" to the task force. Canham must have appreciated that Bowers's reasoning was solid, for as the grateful engineer put it, he "turned the camp upside down and inside out to focus every resource on the project."[47]

Indeed, Canham, Bowers, and Bergstrom lost no time in reorganizing the entire base for a three-month "all-out assault" on the runway. Plowing around the clock would require a minimum of twenty-seven people, including drivers, mechanics, and other skilled artisans, each on a twelve-hour shift. They, of course, had to be freed of all other duties. Subtracting them, plus the essential cooks, aerologists, radio operators (who volunteered to assume the fire and security watches), and powerhouse watch-standers, significantly reduced those available for all the other tasks of maintaining the base. Many enlisted would have to work outside their rates. There would be two, not three, mess cooks (those doing the galley scut work, including dishwashing and clearing tables). Further, in a jolting breach of protocol, the leaders decided that all available officers and chief petty officers would take their turns at mess cooking. That included Canham, who did, however, instruct the radio operators that "no word is to be passed back" to the States about this—"for unless the whole story is told the wrong conclusions can easily be reached." Everyone was henceforth on a six-day week; runway work on Sunday would be curtailed only enough to allow those workers two of every three Sundays off. "We all realize the significance of the South Pole Station," Canham reported to Whitney, "not to us, but the whole of the United States. . . . That is what we came down to do." Further, he wrote, unless Dufek himself said otherwise,

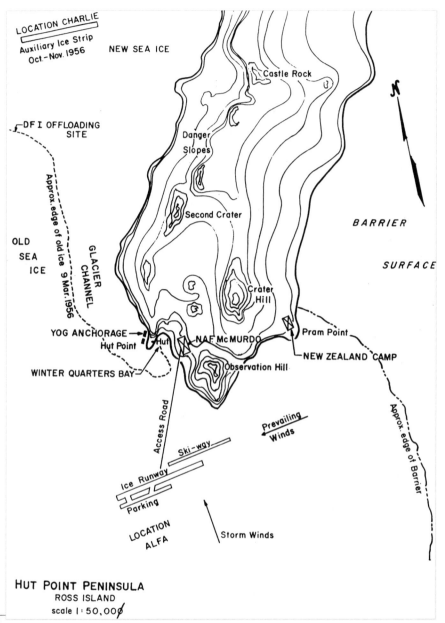

Hut Point Peninsula on Ross Island showing potential ice-runway sites. U.S. Navy, MCB (Special), Report DF I and II, vol. V, McMurdo, D-TWO-1-1.

there would be no outgoing messages "about the probability of our not getting the runway done."[48]

The telling limitation, however, was not personnel but motive power. According to the log, there was a "staggering amount of snow to remove with the limited equipment"—only one D-8 and a few operable D-2s, at best three at a time. "We envy you the number of D-8s over at Little America," Canham confessed to Whitney, but those temporarily underused machines might as well have been in Peoria. He also wondered, futilely, if "any piece of snow removal equipment" could be airdropped to him in September. He worried about fuel and requested supplemental supplies by the first ship. The D-8 used 160 gallons the first day, about 60 gallons more than it took to run the entire camp's utilities. Still, Slaton, remembering his work in northern Alaska, told the drivers never to shut off an engine on the ice. Restarting one "stone-cold" would take upward of forty-five minutes, even with aircraft preheaters and an auxiliary "pony" engine. Bowers calculated and recalculated the volume of snow versus amount of time, but the unknowns could only be guessed at. He remained pessimistic, but "maybe with God and a long handled spoon we may get the job done. We'll certainly try."[49]

Construction mechanic and sometime driver John Randall thought later that "we were damn lucky we got it done, really." As to how, "You don't try to push all [the snow] off at one time," he explained. "You push a slot the width of the blade and you just keep backing up and take another pass, keep your blade full. And then you move over and leave about three foot between it so that way you don't have the material rolling out the edge of your bulldozer blade. And then your smaller tractor will come by and clean up that little berm you left." With "slot dozing," "you can move a lot more material a lot faster." The fact was, that was the only way the D-2s, which were "just too light for the job," could help. The D-8, with D-2 backup, could move about 150 feet by 3 feet by 200 feet per 12-hour shift (3,500 yards), Bowers—feeling better—wrote on 31 July. If the men could manage 5,000 yards per 24-hour day, they could clear the ice, though not finish the surface, in a month. The ice was proving rougher than anticipated, though, and the weight of the flanking windrows of plowed snow created a crown down the centerline that invited lengthwise cracking and thwarted flooding efforts, which were soon abandoned with (dashed) hopes for resumption at the end. The crews tried to make the snowbanks as low and wide as possible to reduce this deflection, drifting, and risk to aircraft wings. But the dynamic ice would crack anyway—sometimes with a report like a rifle shot—as the forces of wind, waves, and tides also ate away the sea ice from underneath. Later calculations would show that between 22 July and

Plowing McMurdo's ice runway was dark, cold, scary work. The tiny D-2 could only clean up after the D-8's passes through the hard, deep snow. Courtesy, photographer David Grisez.

15 October, workers put in 8,873 hours of direct runway labor, not counting those in base support such as mechanics and steelworkers.[50]

The work of snow removal was exhausting, cold (extremely cold, even with a heated four-bunk wanigan beside the runway for warmth and rest following an hour's driving), and scary. "It was really tough on those kids," Slaton recalled, "out there operating that equipment twelve hours a day," most of it during the dark winter night—in July incessantly stormy, with sixty- and seventy-knot winds and runway temperatures consistently around twenty degrees colder than the low of –38°F in camp. "You can't see and you don't know if you're going to break through the ice. I had to tell them all the time, 'The ice is twenty-four foot thick. You're not going to break it.'" But Slaton understood and probably felt their fear; they were "just a good bunch of children." (The gruff and outspoken but sympathetic chief was, at the time, thirty-seven, an "old man. Some of them called me Pappy.") As it was, they kept both doors and the escape hatch open. They longed for warmth but for safety even more. Bowers, who remembered running the heavy D-8 over new sea ice the previous summer as "probably as frightening as anything I've ever done," told them to stop and take a boring any time they had a doubt. Indeed, the D-8 did break through some previously flooded but unevenly frozen ice on the new airstrip—an unnerving moment for everyone who remembered January's fatal accident.[51]

August saw fewer (though severe) blizzards, more fog, more mirages in the lengthening hours of twilight, and colder temperatures (–69°F at the airstrip on the 8th). The McMurdo log began to note the "strain of prolonged absence from normal living" and the need to accept "constant outside work at better than –60°F as 'routine.'" Canham wrote privately, after recording a series of minor brawls, that "the sunlight's return will be a good thing for all hands." Runway workers first witnessed the reappearing sun on the 22nd for about an hour midday and were "noticeably spurred" by its "mental warmth." Those in camp had to content themselves with seeing rays "touching" Crater and Observation hills, but within a few days "almost everyone" had climbed one of the ridges to bathe in the rewarded hope. The sun, wrote Canham, "joined a full moon which by itself cast a great deal of light." (Obscured by clouds, it had "factually" risen two days before anyone saw it.) There began to be less "Big Eye," the persistent insomnia that had plagued many during the dark months. By the end of the month crews, who could now see what they were doing, had 6,000 feet of runway ice cleared and were plowing the 2,000- by 300-foot parking lot, including a 500-foot turning circle. Flooding, to build up and smooth the surface, resumed—all this "in spite of an appalling number of mechanical breakdowns."[52]

In September it was warmer, as high as +16°F (low –32), with more snowfall and "almost constant blizzardy conditions." Then, on the 15th the wildest storm of the year, the one that trapped Baker's camping party, hit Ross Island. Visibility dropped to a few feet as heavy snow fell and winds up to seventy knots howled for two days, let up for a day, and returned on the 18th to their top ferocity. High drifts buried McMurdo, but it was the utter destruction of the ice runway that imprinted this storm on the souls of the exhausted Seabees. The airstrip was "just about done," remembered Randall, and the blizzard "filled the whole thing up again." They would have to start over. They had less than one thin month to have it ready. The Air Force planes had already left the States for New Zealand. After a disheartening assessment, Canham and Bowers gathered their resolve and called everyone into the mess hall where they explained that it would be "more expedient" to build a new runway parallel to the old one than to "try to recoup" the obliterated strip. Drifts had filled it beyond use, but the adjacent parking area on the lee side remained relatively clear. So they decided to "abandon the first runway, relegating to it the job of acting as a snow fence for the new strip, which was to be built by extending the parking area." That expensive "snow fence" would do the job, however, unlike the four different types (one made from burlap earmarked for covering tunnels at the Pole) that Canham had earlier ordered built. All had proved "worthless" in the first stiff wind.

In a special SITREP (situation report) to the admiral on the 18th, Canham estimated that it would take three weeks of good conditions to clear the new accumulation. But the next day, in bright sunshine and "balmy" temperatures (a "high of plus nine"), the "runway crews turned to with renewed vigor." They had a chance, they thought, with "a decent break in the weather." It held—enough. They did it. The new strip was rough but usable. The D-8's tracks ground down some of the worst ridges, but flooding plans were abandoned when time gave out. The centerline crown and gravity diverted the water from where it was most needed anyway, and the men also found that as the salt leached out from the repeated applications of seawater, "layers of weakness" formed such that the top layers of ice peeled off under load. In keeping with initial plans, now emphasized in the desperate last days, crews also managed to prepare an alternate, actually smoother, runway on seventy-three-inch-thick new sea ice under a light snow burden, about five miles from Hut Point, for use by ski-equipped aircraft or in emergencies. But it was too far away to be practical and too thin for lengthy parking of the heavy C-124s. Indeed, this runway would break up and be gone by late January.[53]

During this last surge of superhuman effort, the worn transmission of the overworked D-8, dubbed "Pogo," finally gave way. As Slaton remembered it, the "kid" who was to drive had not let the engine heat up enough after standing for several hours, and the reversing gear and parts of other gears broke off as he tried to engage the still-frozen transmission. There were no spares: "Whoever decided how many parts we should take didn't think about transmissions, I guess." He and machinists Harold Lundy and Dave Grisez welded and "ground those gears back to shape" and had the Cat back together by 28 September. "She was still going when I left there," Slats remembered, rightfully proud. "Everyone" knew "this standard piece of equipment single handedly was responsible for the successful construction of the ice runway," without which there could be no South Pole Station. But that took nothing from the human triumph of those who planned, improvised, froze their noses, and ate their despair to get the job done.[54]

At this same frenzied time, the winterers were realizing that their tours were nearly over. They lived for going home even as they hustled to ready everything for what lay ahead. Those not out on the runway or on outdoor field training built and furnished huts and VIP quarters for temporary summer newcomers. The Seabees' Report continued, "Volunteer crews held spring housecleaning field days during off hours." They made street signs, swabbed down floors, and generally spruced up the town. Others raced to complete Pole airdrop preparations, including the endless paperwork that would attend shipping 500 tons of materiel by air.[55]

On 8 October, Chaplain Condit organized a group to erect a memorial on Arrival Heights to the drowned Williams. It was a stone grotto containing a "large concrete statue of 'Our Lady of the Snows'" to remind future visitors "that we did not forget the sacrifice of one of our shipmates who will stay forever." Protestant Canham privately preferred a cross, which "could have served all [sic] religions and [upon which] the names of those who are taken here in the future could be inscribed readily." But if, as the priest assured him, Williams's family would be comforted, "then it shall be done." Forty years later, Bevilacqua arranged for the installation at the site of a large bronze plaque commemorating the young driver and all others who had died in Antarctica, replacing a wooden marker long gone. Grisez played "Taps" at the first dedication and again when he returned as a summer machinist in 1995–1996, though a more practiced bugler did the ceremonial honors.[56]

In hauling twenty tons of rocks up the steep hill, Condit's cairn team succeeded in breaking the tracks on both a D-2 and the last operating D-4. An unhappy Canham forbade the chaplain further use of any tractor until replacements arrived, "as this unfortunate incident will probably delay the setting up of the GCA [ground-control approach] crew at the runway." But the next day the latter got their radar unit, control tower gear, and a thirty-kilowatt generator to the airstrip and worked "well into the night" to make it operational by 14 October. Using the GCA equipment to plot the horizontal (directional) and vertical (glide-slope) angles and feeding this information continuously to the incoming aircraft, the GCA operator could coach a pilot to hone or correct his approach in thick weather. The directional headings were reliable, but with no planes for good-weather test flights (McMurdo's Otters having been dispatched to Little America—see Chapter 4), it was not possible to test or calibrate the glide-slope instrumentation.[57]

In other preparations for the flying season, aviation chief John Dore's line-maintenance crews moved over a hundred JATO units and firefighting equipment to the runway area, broke out skis to install on the incoming R4Ds, and readied Herman Nelson aircraft heaters. Others set up refueling equipment nearby. Just before the expected fly-in, workers placed red flags every seventy-five feet along the rough, cobblestone-like runway and numbered flags indicating distance remaining. They marked the centerline with strips of Day-Glo tape and the approach end with empty fuel drums arranged in an arrow pattern followed by a horizontal line to show the start of the runway proper. The strip had 5,350 feet cleared of snow by 14 October, but crews were still pushing for 6,000 feet because the R5Ds had no reverse pitch for stopping quickly. They made 5,600 feet by the first landing, 5,800 feet by 19 October.[58]

Monday, 15 October 1956, "one of the most beautiful we have had," turned into a "day of disappointment" when Admiral Dufek did not appear. He finally arrived at 0735 hours on the 17th in a Skymaster (R5D) piloted by Lt. Cmdr. Hank Jorda. In clear skies, Jorda landed on his first approach, stopping with 2,400 feet of cleared ice to spare. McMurdo's Deep Freeze I veterans greeted the admiral with a big "Welcome" sign, but they were more interested in the 500 pounds of mail he brought. Dufek was impressed by the amount of work they had done and their amazingly high morale. He found McMurdo humming along in good order, ready to be the administrative and logistics center of the U.S. IGY in the Antarctic.[59]

There was little time to think of such things, however, because six more aircraft were soon in the air from New Zealand. As misfortune would have it, they were all past the point of no return when the weather at McMurdo began to deteriorate. On 18 October, with a 300-foot ceiling and poor visibility of two miles, GCA operator Jim Bergstrom, a pilot but an admitted "rookie" on GCA, prepared to guide in the first plane, a P2V flown by Lieut. David Carey, while the more experienced John McCoy, air controlman first class, focused on the radar screen. Without being able to provide a reliable glide slope, Bergstrom suggested three successively lower passes over the runway, which the pilot declined. He told the tower he would conduct a low-visibility approach and began a climbing right turn. However, Carey's approach was too far left of the centerline as he pulled up for a wave-off with landing gear down. Apparently attempting to keep the runway in sight, he banked too steeply, his right wing down. "Within a matter of seconds" the plane smashed nose and wing into the ice, breaking apart as it cartwheeled crazily.

To the horrified Bergstrom the accident looked like pilot error. Perhaps Carey had not been "a hundred percent on the gauges" (flying by instrument while the copilot watched the runway, according to accepted procedure in a right-hand turn) and did not realize he was losing altitude. Still, the conscientious officer would wonder if he might have done something to bring that P2V in safely, even speculating whether driving a tractor down the centerline might have given them more confidence in the GCA equipment. (The next year New

Zealand planes at Scott Base would help test the glide-slope readings.) The board of investigation that met on 2 November found no misconduct. The pilot, flying probably no higher than 300 feet, had no visible horizon during the low-visibility approach. That plus a faulty gyro could have added "a confusion factor at the most critical time." Radioman Richard Lewis, a survivor, later recalled a "tremendous shudder" that gave him a sense that Carey had lost control and was trying desperate measures. The pilot and two others, radioman Charles Miller and engineer Marion Marze, were killed instantly. Capt. Rayburn Hudman, a Marine parachutist, died on a table in the makeshift library-surgical unit several hours later of shock and internal bleeding, perhaps exacerbated by the hour it took to get him by open sled into camp. The other four were seriously to critically injured. Dr. Taylor and Dr. Walker ("Bucky") Harris, the VX-6 flight surgeon who had just arrived with the admiral (in Hudman's originally assigned seat), worked all day on the survivors, who were later evacuated to Christchurch by C-124. All eventually recovered.[60]

Meanwhile, exhausted pilot Ed Ward was just behind the Neptune in his Skymaster. His fourteen-hour flight had already had too many anxious moments. One engine began early to use too much fuel, and both headwinds and ominously thick ice buildup on the wings slowed the overloaded plane, which made completing the distance increasingly dicey. Radio communication with the other planes suddenly failed. The crew saw why when they cleared the iced windshield: "Great tongues of fire swept across the heavens"—the awesome aurora australis, known to wreak havoc with radio transmission. Half an hour after passing the point of no return, calculations showed navigator Dick Swadener that they would arrive at McMurdo with "dry tanks." Ward contemplated a controlled landing on whatever ice field he could find, as he had done in the Arctic—if he could get as far as Cape Adare. Then, in the tenth hour, engine number four backfired and shot out flames. They "feathered" it (shut it down), and the fire mercifully flickered out. Knowing they would not make it on three engines, Ward "defied every safety procedure in the book" and ordered the engine restarted. It coughed, then whirred normally.

The end of Ward's flight was as surreal as the rest of it. As the R5D approached McMurdo, requesting a "straight-in" landing because of the fuel emergency, there was visibility of a tenth of a mile in blowing snow, ceiling indefinite, crosswinds of twenty knots gusting to thirty-five. But the P2V had missed its approach and was coming around, a procedure Ward knew would take about six gas-guzzling minutes. He looped in a holding pattern, apparently near enough to Mount Erebus to shake up a reporter aboard. Finally given permission to land, Ward came in "on the gauges" until copilot Hank

Hansen cried, "There it is!" They were less than fifty feet above the runway. Safe at last on the ground, he glimpsed through a momentary break in the squalling snow the bright red tail of Carey's plane—and sickened as the comprehension washed over him that the rest of it was not there.[61]

Over the next several hours the four R4Ds, which had taken off from the more southerly New Zealand airfield at Dunedin to stretch their marginal range, all landed safely in "progressively worse" weather. Lieut. Harvey Speed, piloting one of them, reversed course to connect with the trailing Lt. Cmdr. Gus Shinn, who had lost control of his gyrocompass. Speed navigated the rest of the way for both of them—a selfless act that cost him potentially critical fuel. The last R4D, with Lt. Cmdr. Roy Curtis at the controls, touched down in a whiteout after "a beautiful GCA run." Within a few days the planes were fitted with their skis, ready for duty on the ice. The residents dove into the crate of lettuce and tomatoes one of the plane crews had thoughtfully brought—their first fresh vegetables in ten months. Among the arriving passengers were John Hanessian, head of the IGY Antarctic staff; Paul Siple, scientific leader for the South Pole; and several members of the press. No longer was McMurdo just a naval base. Operation Deep Freeze II had begun.[62]

Despite being bracketed by tragedies, Deep Freeze I had been a success at McMurdo. The men had survived wintering over in remarkably good condition overall. They had triumphed over the weather, the ice, and their inexperience to establish a viable community, build an ice runway, and prepare to build and work at the South Pole. But they were not the only American pioneers in Antarctica. Four hundred miles to the east, the Seabees at Little America V were living out their own dramas in a parallel Deep Freeze I mission.

LITTLE AMERICA V
Science Flagship on the Ice Shelf

All you can see is big white and that's it.
That was Little America.

—YNC Richard Lucier, 1955[1]

The Navy's simultaneous task in Operation Deep Freeze I was to establish and make ready the IGY's headquarters science station on the edge of the vast Ross Ice Shelf. This was Little America V, already named to honor the legacy of America's polar hero Richard E. Byrd. Before the scientists arrived, key tasks were to map a safe route deep into the interior for Byrd Station and to prepare the massive tractor trains (called heavy swings) that would haul in every pipe and plank to build the station with in Deep Freeze II.

The day after Christmas 1955 the ships of Task Force 43 split, and the *Glacier, Greenville Victory,* and *Arneb* turned east along the titanic ice barrier to locate a site for the new Little America. They reached

Byrd's Bay of Whales on 28 December, finding it nearly gone, as the *Atka* had reported the previous year. There was no suitable approach onto the ice shelf. Byrd made a nostalgic pilgrimage by helicopter to the site of two of his former bases, now buried one atop the other near the cliff edge and marked only by the chair-high tops of once-seventy-foot radio towers. Clearly, this historic location would not do for the IGY.[2]

After further investigation Admiral Dufek settled on Kainan Bay, about thirty miles farther east, although he would have preferred Okuma Bay, another sixty miles beyond, with its teeming wildlife and scenic Rockefeller Mountains. But there was no access ramp in the sparkling 120-foot-high, sheer ice cliff forming the bay, and the area was heavily crevassed and unstable. Kainan Bay, named for a ship of Choku Shirase's 1911–1912 Japanese expedition, had no particular merits except a natural (albeit crevassed) snow ramp, but it would serve. As determined by the Reverend Daniel Linehan, a Jesuit seismologist aboard from Boston College, the ice shelf, floating over 1,500 feet of water, was 600 to 800 feet thick. The relentless forces of glaciers pushing down from the ice cap and its own accumulating weight perpetuated the outward movement of the snow-covered ice tongue, such that in a year Little America V would likely be a quarter-mile north of its founding location—latitude 78° 11' South, longitude 162° 11' West. And sooner or later it would calve off as part of an iceberg, eventually sinking to the bottom of a warmer sea to the north. The "always strange" cries and groans of the advancing ice both rattled and amused the young Seabees. "Look, it's not me," summering electrician Ken Waldron advised a companion one day when, hearing a sudden unfamiliar r-r-rip, both looked up. "Well, it's not me either!" came the retort.[3]

Action began immediately. The *Glacier* bashed out a slip in the bay ice lining the five- by four-mile, horseshoe-shaped bay. Crews dug pits in the ice and buried "deadmen" for mooring the two cargo ships. These were thick planks around which the men wrapped heavy wire straps with a loop that extended above the ice surface. When the holes were filled with snow, flooded, and frozen, the loops could securely hold the ships' lines. Thus would water come to be called "Antarctic concrete." Cmdr. Herbert Whitney made Chief Warrant Officer Vic Young Little America's operations officer ("I'll give you a letter later," he said). That put Young in charge of both moving cargo off the ships, starting on 29 December in two twelve-hour shifts per day, and building the base.[4]

Whitney would have known that Young was a good choice. The two were "old shipmates," having served together in the Philippines, Alaska, and stateside. Young had joined the Seabee Reserves after World War II because he liked

Mooring cargo ship USS Arneb *to bay ice using "deadmen," Deep Freeze I. Painting by Robert Charles Haun. Courtesy, U.S. Navy Art Collection.*

the work and the attitude of a construction battalion blacksmith he met on Guadalcanal. Long intrigued by the last continent, having "read about everything that Admiral Byrd had ever written," he called to volunteer for Deep Freeze in 1955. Whitney answered the phone and, delighted, dispatched Young almost overnight to Davisville with orders to organize the Little America advance party. This would include the reconnaissance party charged to blaze a tractor trail to 80° South, 120° West, in Marie Byrd Land, where Byrd Station would be built in the summer of 1956–1957. It was "a lot of head work." Now on the ice, Young knew there would be "no sleep."[5]

First, there were crevasses to find, fill (or bridge), and mark to make a safe trail from the ship to the campsite on the ice shelf, about four miles inland—that is, south. On New Year's Eve Young worked at this until 0600 hours into 1956, illustrating both the possibility in the twenty-four-hour daylight and the race against time and fickle weather. All hands had already turned to off-loading, beginning with the aircraft, then all equipment that could move something

Off-loading Arneb *onto bay ice in Kainan Bay. A sudden breakup of the ice precipitated an all-hands, seventy-two-hour scramble to move temporarily stored supplies up onto the ice shelf (in distance) before it went out completely. Painting by Robert Charles Haun. Courtesy, U.S. Navy Art Collection.*

else, then emergency supplies for shore parties. Since the "haul road" was still unfinished and equipment was also needed at the construction site, Young sought to expedite the off-loading by establishing a temporary supply dump on the bay ice. Lieut. Donald Mehaffey, the supply officer, and Capt. Charles ("Tommy") Thomas, Dufek's chief of staff ("Coast Guard type, ice expert") who was in command at Kainan Bay after Dufek left for McMurdo, worriedly agreed that everything not needed immediately up on the barrier for base construction would go first to this dump, 1.9 miles from the ships. Ever-alert hospital corpsman Ken Aldrich, however, not wanting liquid medicines to freeze, judiciously distributed some of his potent "bartering material" to ensure that medical supplies were moved directly to the base. A sick-bay tent soon appeared, identified by a sign that read "Sick call during daylight hours only!" Mehaffey, in his Mobile Construction Battalion (MCB) (Special) report, called supplies handling "initially an orderly operation."[6]

Orderliness was short-lived. What looked like a good idea on paper, wrote Cmdr. Paul Frazier, task-force ship operations officer, soon proved "foolish" and costly. "All hell broke loose" beginning on 16 January when, with warm summer temperatures and swelling waves from distant storms, the bay ice started to break up—dramatically—as Thomas had predicted. *Greenville Victory,* just emptied of cargo and reloaded with equipment urgently needed at McMurdo, cleared. But a frenzied unloading of *Arneb* from three holds at once had to be halted as the ice began to go. "It was as if a giant invisible robot applied a giant invisible crowbar to the countless acres of smooth bay ice, then heaved for all he was worth," recorded one overcharged but not inaccurate Navy writer. All hands, not excepting officers and journalists, joined in a frantic, thankfully successful seventy-two-hour dash to move everything up to the campsite. By 21 January the bay ice was "completely cracked up." Young saw floating slabs twenty feet thick: "A person must see it to believe it could happen. Nature sure is something." As he later remembered it, about two days after they completed the transfer the bay was "just water." Frazier said it was four hours. There would have been no winter at Little America had these supplies, including most of the food, blown north.[7]

That was only "the beginning of our undoing," wrote Mehaffey. Young had managed to get a permanent supply dump laid out on the barrier, rolled but not graded. Given the intent to move cargo in only as needed, its total space was inadequate. Tractors and sleds were too few and needed everywhere at once. Many items too heavy to be unloaded by hand were just pushed off the sleds. If a D-4 with forklift was not readily available, crates, boxes, and barrels remained where they fell, helter-skelter. Worse, as contents were needed, workers would search for and break open the containers, increasing the jumble and "rendering impossible any accurate accountability." The fastidious Mehaffey watched helplessly as the "beautiful supply dump" he had so carefully drawn up at Davisville, all color-coded and "laid out in perfect coordinates and all that type of thing," disintegrated in the mad scramble: "Supplies were all over the place in absolutely no system about it at all." He had "quite an out" with Frazier, he remembered. "I could see his problem, but he didn't see my problem, and we came practically to physical blows." Frazier later lamented ever building a supply dump on the sea ice "when the barrier was only a mile or so further from the ships. But we did, and we paid dearly for our mistake."[8]

"Our constant prayer was that a bad storm would not materialize before an opportunity presented itself to get this mess into some semblance of order," Mehaffey wrote later. Fortunately, chief commissaryman William McInvale got the food organized and stored in "a very orderly fashion" next to the galley:

"We always knew where all the food was. For sure we were going to eat." But it was not until March that Mehaffey and two storekeepers managed to locate, stack together, and inventory all the general stores and help the equipment officers do the same with their materials. According to Mehaffey's report, VX-6 personnel apparently managed less well in gathering their scattered cargo, and supply workers were deeply offended later when their incoming commanding officer, who reportedly knew the circumstances, "came forth with uncalled for derogatory comments on the supply situation." Blizzards blew in and much materiel was "irretrievably lost," although, generously outfitted for two years, Little America lacked nothing essential. Mehaffey was never able to complete a thorough inventory or site layout, but he had the foresight to obtain large aerial photographs of the supply dump before it got too dark or the snow too deep. Using coordinates marked with bamboo poles, he could suggest with some certainty where workers should dig among the drifts that grew to sixteen feet. Sometimes they had to dig twice, sometimes they found empty boxes, but "we found something of everything. I'm sure we left a lot down there too." Unloading would always be a rush, but in succeeding years there would be more and better materials handling equipment, fewer supplies to be handled all at once, and the benefit of experience to go on.[9]

Base construction also had to begin without delay to give the shore crews shelter and ensure that the camp would be self-sustaining by the time the ships left. On 4 January 1956, when Dufek and Byrd led a ceremony to commission Little America V, nothing permanent was yet standing. Saul Pett reported for the Associated Press that "only three tents and assorted orange-colored tractor vehicles were on the scene. It looked like the last tiny outpost of civilization in a white infinity." On a clear day, though, Kainan Bay could be seen to the north, and that view factored in the site selection as a psychological reprieve from the "gently rolling desert of endless snow."[10] The next day Young began the first building of an eventual sixteen Clements huts, two scientific towers, and miscellaneous shops and tunnels that would extend outward along either side of a long tunnel that soon acquired the name Main Street. It was a barracks, followed by the mess hall and galley.

Construction was straightforward, thanks to detailed planning and prefabrication, if not simple in the frigid barrens. After selecting the campsite, Young would "get a Cat up there and level off the area and stake out where the buildings are going to go." Next came the foundation—two level, parallel rows of timbers resembling railroad ties for a double-track line, but closely spaced. Two long, heavy, timber stringers went next, one down the middle of each row of "ties." Atop and perpendicular to the stringers were floor trusses 4 feet

First Clements hut under construction at Little America V. Painting by Robert Charles Haun. Courtesy, U.S. Navy Art Collection.

apart, each a lattice of connecting triangles for strength and stiffness. The air spaces also kept the underlying snow and ice from melting. (The powerhouse floor trusses were 1 foot apart to support the weight of the heavy generators, and the garage used 8-inch by 8-inch by 20-foot timbers instead of trusses.)

After that, the prefabricated deck panels, wall panels, roof trusses, and flat-roof panels could be sequentially erected and clipped together in a day or two. With the exception of those containing doors or windows (only overhead ones at snowy Little America), the panels were (at least theoretically) identical. The finished boxes' international-orange exteriors presented a striking contrast against the dazzling white snow; their aluminum interior finishes reflected heat back in. Two-by-four framing covered first with chicken wire and then burlap made tunnels and covered storage areas when snow drifted around them. The last structure—the last outdoor work—was the recreation building, completed on 15 April. This amenity was not part of the official plan for the base, so when the Seabees discovered that the normal foundation materials were gone, they built it on freight pallets, also "borrowing" some building panels from a hut intended for Byrd Station. It would house a library of books and records, game room with ping-pong and pool tables, altar and chairs for church services, movie theater, and a bar.[11]

For almost three weeks, two twelve-hour shifts ensured continuous construction. Many put in far more time. On 10 January the admiral declared a holiday, with free beer and seal steaks for the tired men. By the 16th, eight buildings dotted the snow and everybody switched to one shift, 0800 to 2000 hours, except when crises arose. As soon as the buildings' shells were up— and often before if something large or heavy such as a cookstove or generator needed to be installed—electricians, utilities men, and carpenters stepped in to wire, heat, plumb, and partition the spaces. As at McMurdo, the supposedly self-regulating generators could not control an unbalanced load. It was "just an engineering flaw in the design," said chief electrician Bill Stroup, and "they never did correct it," even after "a lot of correspondence back and forth with Caterpillar" and the company's dispatching of an engineer in Deep Freeze II. To plant each pole for the antenna farm, the men dug a hole in the snow, secured the pole to a shipping pallet to increase the load-bearing surface, placed the inverted "T" in the hole, and then alternately added snow and water. The quickly freezing mixture built up until it was deep enough to support the pole—they hoped. "We're trusting ourselves after we used snow and water to put this pole in place to go climb that?" wondered Waldron. It was rock-hard.[12]

All this time Young had also been struggling to get the trail party off to seek a safe passage onto the West Antarctic plateau for the proposed station 650 miles inland, and just two and a half weeks after coming ashore he succeeded. On 14 January 1956, Lt. Cmdr. Jacob ("Jack") Bursey of the Coast Guard Reserves set out with six men in two Sno-Cats and a Weasel. Hand-picked by Dufek for this hazardous task, Bursey was a veteran of two Byrd expeditions— the source of his strength and his weakness. His polar-exploring credentials included leadership of a 1,200-mile dogsled traverse from Little America III into Marie Byrd Land in 1940. He knew this landscape if anyone did. But his mental and emotional focus on dogs dangerously dated his expertise. He wrote in 1957, with remarkable naïveté (or evasion, given events), "The heavy mechanical equipment of modern exploration added more to the human risk and increased the dangers of the Antarctic. When we used dog teams, we had many narrow escapes and many dogs died for man; but we all came home alive." True, but the scale and distance of Deep Freeze plans exceeded the capability of any number of dogs. Young could see that "this guy had no idea about equipment," so he made sure men like construction driver Alvah ("Big Ed") Edwards and surveyor chief George Moss, strong and trained in Arctic survival, went along. The others were driver Roland Levesque, radioman Raymond Dube, photographer Chester Stevens, and mechanic Charles Wedemeyer. The plain-spoken Moss, who was operations chief for Little America as well as the trail party's navigator, thought Bursey was more interested in having his picture taken than in knowing the men, even their names. His approach was "forty years too late."[13]

With Bursey in front on skis as the cameras clicked, the diesel-powered party moved out across the ice shelf toward Prestrud Inlet, named by Amundsen for his exploring-party leader. On the third day toward this proposed gateway to the Rockefeller Plateau of Marie Byrd Land, they encountered the first "hundreds" of crevasses, but with aerial reconnaissance by Little America's one working Otter, backtracking, detouring, and safe crossing of what appeared to be minor crevasses, they eventually ascended the plateau. The trailblazers, after twenty days, were 381 miles from base (having driven 460 actual miles). Commander Whitney radioed that approximately 400 miles inland would do for Byrd Station; they had gone far enough. He ordered them to leave their vehicles and fly back to Little America.[14]

On 3 February Lieut. Robert Paul ("Bob") Streich, pilot, along with Lt. Cmdr. Glen Lathrop in the right seat, airplane crew chief John Floyd, and Disney photographer Lloyd Beebe, flew the Otter out to ferry Bursey's party home. But the single-engine aircraft could not manage all eleven passengers plus their gear, so Bursey told Moss, Levesque, Edwards, and Stevens to pack, keeping the mechanic and radioman (both of whom could drive—a premonition, he wrote), along with Beebe, for the second airlift. Hours later the plane had not shown up again, either at Little America or the trailhead. Whitney ordered Bursey to drive the vehicles back along the outbound trail to search for the obviously downed Otter. He was to establish a temporary base at Cache 4, about 200 miles out, to assist a search plane on its way from McMurdo via ship.

During this time Vic Young had been juggling base construction with building messing and berthing wanigans so he could travel along Bursey's Byrd trail to cache fuel for next summer's tractor trains. He had eighty-five fuel drums stacked on each of eight sleds, wanting to leave by 4 February while the weather was still tolerable. Loaded D-8s would gulp two to four gallons per mile. If the heavy swings had to carry all their fuel with them, there would be little capacity left for hauling Byrd's building materials and supplies. But when it became clear that the Otter must have crashed, Young got orders to assemble a search-and-rescue team and "run the trail to Byrd," which everyone hoped the plane would have followed. About 220 miles from Little America, Young's Weasel party met Bursey's. Neither had seen the Otter. They waited five days at Cache 4 before receiving orders to return to base. Along Bursey's marked route, Young had been noticing "little indentations" and did not like what he was seeing.[15]

What happened to the Otter and the men aboard is a story of Antarctic weather folded into leadership, fortitude, judgment overruling established wisdom, all-out effort, ancillary disaster, and luck—bad and good.[16] The over-loaded plane, with its three VX-6 crew members and four trail party passengers, had difficulty taking off, according to chief Moss, and soon encountered whiteout conditions. "We were in the soup for a couple of hours," pilot Streich recalled. Then the plane's wings began to ice up in freakish freezing rain, and with that added burden he was unable to maintain altitude. Streich turned around to return to the trail party. He knew he was in a mountainous area, the Rockefeller Range he thought, but he could not see. "We're gonna hit!" he shouted suddenly, and in a "microsecond," with nose high, speed slow in strong headwinds, he plowed into a peak at full throttle. The aircraft continued to skid on its belly up the slope, oddly—luckily—sticking fast where it came to rest. Just below, a sizable crevasse gaped. Steep slopes fell away a few yards off on either side. The relatively gentle impact bent the propeller, pushed the engine askew, and forced the landing gear up through the fuselage. The impact threw Streich into the yoke, knocking him unconscious for a few minutes and cutting his chin. No one else was injured beyond bruises.

Fearing fire, the seven rushed outside, then focused more deliberately on staying alive. The survival gear aboard the Otter was designed for the plane's crew—food for three men for seven days (now, perhaps, three days for seven men), one banana sled, a Primus stove with five gallons of kerosene, two pairs of skis, a parachute, two mountain tents, blankets, shovel, mountain ax, climbing rope, and a Bible. They all had sleeping bags with air mattresses and adequate clothing. In continuing zero visibility the men crafted a shelter by digging under one wing and building up walls with snow blocks, parachutes, and airplane parts. Four slept there, three in the plane. The Otter's batteries went dead, but they did have a "Gibson Girl," a hand-cranked radio transmitter that automatically sends a distress message. "You don't know whether you're getting out," said Moss, who strung an antenna onto a couple of ski poles. Cranking that "coffee grinder" was hard work, so they reduced trans-

Whiteout conditions caused by light reflected between snow and an overcast sky until contrasts and shadows vanish. Fortunately, this aircraft landed safely. Photograph by John R. Swadener. Courtesy, Marc Swadener.

mission time after the first day to five minutes an hour. (They were heard faintly in Little America and on some ships but without sufficient signal to locate them.) On the third day, in clearer skies, Moss set up his theodolite to take a series of sun lines and determined that they had come down in the Alexandra Range on the Edward VII Peninsula. They were 60 discouraging miles off the tractor trail, about 110 miles east-southeast of Little America, 50 miles from Okuma Bay.

"We've got to get out of here," declared Moss, who quickly became the group's de facto leader. This opinion flew in the face of accepted survival doctrine. The plane would be more easily spotted than they would. It offered shelter. Remaining quiet would conserve their energy. But Moss knew they had just crashed Little America's only aircraft, and a massive search was beyond the helicopter's range. (He could not know, of course, that extraordinary lengths were being taken to bring in search planes from elsewhere.) Moving was something to do, a way to avoid panic. He also knew they needed food—soon—and had earlier seen plentiful seals at Okuma Bay. Moss's memory forty years later that they had no food ("None. Zero.") except a huge bottle of vitamins his wife, Eunice, a nurse, had packed for him suggests how meager their rations felt. In fact, the men had carefully measured and divided what they had to last fourteen hungry days. Lathrop's logbook showed a calculated per-person diet based on two ounces of pemmican (twelve would be the normal amount) or a third of a can of oatmeal on alternating days. With one of these, there would be a trail biscuit, a candy bar, and three Hexavitamins. Every other day everyone would get one dried prune or a taste (half an ounce) of sugar. Total calories: 1,018 with pemmican (which two of the men could not get down, even in extremis), 776 with oatmeal. Three, even four, thousand was the recommended Antarctic caloric intake. "We're going to Okuma Bay," said Moss.

On the fourth day, the little party set out walking toward the coast. Streich and Floyd, on skis, went ahead breaking a trail. Moss and Edwards devised a makeshift rope harness and did most of the man-hauling of the sled with their supplies. The going was mostly uphill until the last. The snow was soft enough to increase the effort—"like walking on a mattress," said Moss. "You'd sink down a little bit." They rigged up a "paratepee" (tent) from the parachute, melted snow for water. They carried extra socks for frequent changes. On the seventh day, 9 February 1956, unknown to the plodders, an Otter brought from McMurdo sighted the remarkably intact plane on an uncharted, 2,700-foot mountaintop. Medical officer Ed Ehrlich, who was aboard the poorly functioning helicopter (its rotor kept losing hydraulic fluid) that then flew out and landed near the silent aircraft, heard the pilot marvel, "How the hell could anybody put an airplane down on top of a promontory just like that?" There were no signs of life, but the helo followed the departing footprints. Ehrlich recalled, "Eventually there we saw them trekking along," still at a "brisk pace," less than ten miles from Okuma Bay. "I don't think they heard us until we were right upon them, and man, they were pretty happy to see us."

In a rush of hope or avoidance, Ehrlich had decided not to bring "any real medical equipment" and "didn't feel like" toting body bags, so he stuffed his pockets with "some booze and some chocolate bars." "I kissed him," remembered Moss. Ehrlich remembered it, too. The survivors were in remarkably good condition, complaining of little besides sore calves. If some had doubts, "Big Ed and I knew we were going to make it," Moss said. "We had to." Levesque, though, who seemed "more spent emotionally and physically" than the others, decided not to winter over. Lathrop's name did not appear on the winter list either.

The story, to be complete, must note the heroic efforts made to bring airpower to bear on the rescue effort. Twice a McMurdo-based Otter attempted to fly to Little America but had to turn back in foul weather. Dufek ordered the

Eastwind to transport it and a helicopter to the ice shelf. Slightly damaged on unloading, this plane presented itself to pick up the uncritical survivors with what Moss called an "orange crate" patching its wingtip. When the weather continued unflyable, the admiral shipped a second Otter east aboard the *Glacier*. Its cargo sling broke during unloading (just after the rescue), and it fell to the ice, destroyed. Meanwhile, Captain Hawkes had wired an offer to send a long-range P2V, just back from the ice at Patuxent River, to join in the search. Bending credulity, that plane lost both engines and crashed en route in the jungles of Venezuela. Astonishingly, no one suffered serious injury, but one crew member, Marine Capt. Ray Hudman, returning a few months later, would not be so lucky again.

Wrenching moments were not over for Little America. CWO Young, still out on the trail, met up with an abandoned outbound tractor train on 12 February, with orders to unload the diesel fuel at Cache 2, about a hundred miles out, and return to base. On the 15th he wrote, "Some birthday. We are stopped dead in a raging blizzard." Heat failed in the sleeping wanigan. Fortunately, first-class construction mechanic Willie Burleson, "a good man to have with you," fixed the radiator leak and got it going again. (McMurdo's chief Slaton, who had recruited Burleson for his own team, never forgave Whitney for stealing him away.) They got back on the 18th and prepared to leave again on another cache-laying expedition, to Mile 250. The Otter rescue effort had cost precious time in the waning sunlight. "It is going to be very cold and nasty this trip," Young wrote, "and I expect it may be dark before we are back." The second train left on the 27th, with eight men, five D-8s each pulling two Otaco bobsleds, and one Sno-Cat. The train carried 528 drums of fuel, food, spare parts, and messing and berthing wanigans. Almost immediately roiling storms caught them. Just after midnight there was such "snow, wind & desolation as I have never seen before." The men repeatedly had to stop when they could not see the trail; to move again meant first digging out the drifted-in vehicles.[17]

On 2 March the tractor train encountered crevasses, unmarked. They would have to be "very careful," Young wrote. "Don't trust trail marked by Bursey." The next day lead tractor driver Max Kiel got hung up straddling a crevasse. It took three D-8s to pull his free. A wary Young set off with Burleson on snowshoes with probes and explosives to reconnoiter ahead. They uncovered five crevasses "in a distance of ¼ mile in this supposedly safe trail." Then, on the 5th, while they were gone, the worst occurred: "Today is a sad day for us all. We lost Max Kiel when his tractor dropped a distance of 75 feet down a crevasse crushing him in the cab." Kiel had been pushing snow into one crevasse and was backing away when he and his heavy D-8 fell backward into another.

Another driver, James ("Tex") Gardiner, was lowered immediately into the abyss to pull him free, but all he saw was part of an arm extending from the cab. As the ponderous weight and momentum of the plunging machine forced it deep into the narrow, unyielding ice walls, "it just squashed the cab right down to the floorboards." Because of a faulty oscillator, it was almost twelve hours before Young could make radio contact with Little America for medical help. He said simply, "Send the chaplain." Little America's Protestant cleric, Peter Bol, arrived the next day by Weasel. He conducted funeral services at the site, and then the somber party turned the train around to unload the fuel at the closer Cache 2 and return to base. Unnerved, feeling more unsafe than ever, the men drove the Cats using reins, as with a horse; that is, they attached ropes to the controlling levers so they could walk alongside. The trip had been a waste and a tragedy.[18]

When Young got back on the 10th, Dufek was waiting for him on the *Glacier*. The admiral assured him he had done everything right and asked if he wanted to go home. The home-loving warrant officer replied, "No, I don't want to go home. I want somebody down here that's going to be able to do something about getting us a trail. This Prestrud Inlet is no good. We've got to find another place. There must be one someplace." Dufek promised to work on it when he got back to Washington. A shower aboard, with "clean long handles" and socks donated by shipmates, and mail from home helped lift Young's leaden spirits. Dufek took a last walk around the base before he and the icebreaker departed for the winter. The grieving sailors asked that Kiel be memorialized, and on the spot he agreed to the naming of the Max Kiel Airfield, Little America, Antarctica. Dufek later ruefully admitted that Bursey had been a "mistake."[19]

The seventy-three wintering-over souls watched the darkness lengthen day by day with darkened hearts. The camp was in "good shape" for winter, but the entombment of the likeable "Fat Max" sent already-poor morale plummeting. The accident, on the heels of the plane crash, also threatened the viability of Byrd Station. Bursey's trail was a killer. To locate, develop, and mark a new one during the same season the heavy swings had to supply the base and Seabees build it would be pushing capability and luck to the edge. Was there a passable route? Would there be time? Could the U.S. IGY have a presence in Marie Byrd Land? Not least, fear spread reluctance among the men to work out on the treacherous ice. A number of the designated Byrd builders came to Ehrlich with reservations about risking their lives for a mission whose need they did not see. He had to talk to them "like a Navy guy," he recalled, reminding those who were "in for twenty [years]" what they had signed up for. "As a tax-payer," he told them, "and as a civilian [draftee], I would be pretty disappointed thinking that when you guys are put in a situation where you have to do a job, because it's dangerous, that you won't do it." It was a mark of the trust he had established that he could be so blunt and keep them confiding in him. Then, "Well, Doc, would you go out there?" It seemed less a trap than a plea. Ehrlich said if that was judged his duty he would go, but the task force shot back, "Under no circumstances!" Unpracticed in the required trail skills, the doctor allowed—forty years later—a soft "whew."[20]

Unfortunately, camp leadership was weak at the top, and, as Ehrlich aptly put it, "morale is very much a leadership responsibility." Whitney, as commanding officer of the MCB (Special), was the highest-ranking American wintering over on the continent. By age he was "a little removed" from the others—actually, quite a lot. The men found him indecisive, self-protective, not one in command. When Kiel was killed, for example, "the first thing that Whitney said was 'You guys don't have to go out there again. It's too dangerous.'" Ehrlich saw a decent person but a "void." "He was afraid of his own shadow," was Aldrich's less-kind assessment. "He never made an important decision" and was "pretty well under the influence a lot of the time down there." Yet he went to bed early, leaving others to police revelers' overindulgences.[21]

Whitney scheduled more-or-less daily radio conferences with McMurdo's Canham to discuss a host of concerns, from task-force orders to flight pay for pilots grounded by the dark season. The senior officer tried to assert his status, but U.S. action in Antarctica clearly centered at McMurdo. Canham, the stronger leader, seemed to have little difficulty getting Whitney to back down from a difference of opinion and, when not exasperated beyond humor, to perversely enjoy it. Whitney, for example, decreed that he finalize all outgoing messages. So Canham would send, say, McMurdo's list of needs for the spring fly-in to Little America. Whitney would incorporate it into his own list and return it for transmission to the States, since the main radio equipment was at McMurdo. In respectful phrases Canham made this process sound as wasteful and silly as it was. Whitney, outplayed, gave Canham his own authority.

At the same time Whitney was sometimes more casual about rules than the by-the-book Canham. One day he suggested that they begin canceling the vast amount of South Pole philatelic mail at McMurdo, as he was doing with mail addressed to Byrd Station. No one, including faraway superiors, would know the difference, he said. Canham was shocked, as was Bob Chaudoin, the appointed Pole postal clerk, at this "direct violation of federal regulations."

The Pole crew, for certain, would have their hands full without that time-consuming burden, and Whitney probably expected thanks. Canham replied stiffly that they would "go ahead—if you so direct." Made to look foolish again (he could not order anything illegal), Whitney said no more, and Chaudoin canceled the South Pole mail at the Pole. Toward the end of winter Canham confided to his diary: "With daylight W is beginning to feel his oats again—I shall never be happier than to depart from under his jurisdiction. Basically a nice gent—he has little or [no] admin. or navy organizational experience and is given to moods and pettiness—seems to harbor a strong feeling of jealousy toward anyone that obtains credit but himself."[22]

Canham's actual counterpart at Little America was Lt. Cmdr. Robert Graham, like himself both a pilot (heading the local air group) and the officer-in-charge. But Graham rarely had much to do with anyone; no one at either base gave him much thought as a leader. Moss dismissed him with "he slept all day." Neither he nor Whitney kept a station log. And the Calvinist chaplain, Peter Bol, contributed little despite sincere effort. For one thing, remembered Aldrich, his office was where he slept, and "there's nobody going to walk into the officers' quarters and going way in the back end to talk to this guy." Even fellow officer Mehaffey "very seldom ever saw him, and yet he only lived two little cubbyholes down from me." The "staid and sober Dutchman" suffered, even in his own mind it seemed, from inevitable comparisons with his charismatic counterpart at McMurdo. His attempts at jokes fell flat. He would lift and hug and toss the "little guys," who were repelled, not amused. They largely avoided him and his religious services. He was Dufek's other acknowledged "mistake." Bursey, who truly belonged to another era, could claim little regard, especially after the trail tragedy, although Aldrich agreeably listened to his polar stories when the older man needed someone to talk to.[23]

As it happened, Little America was blessed with a wealth of natural leaders who stepped up informally to fill the vacuum. Individuals like Chief Warrant Officer Vic Young and Chief Petty Officer George Moss took on the toughest field missions and rose to their responsibilities, remembered Ehrlich. They knew their jobs, did them well, knew and respected their men's capabilities, and worked side by side with them, inspiring both confidence and respect. Another leader was chief electrician Bill Stroup, whom Ehrlich never saw "with a downcast face or really ragging at the guys." Chief Aldrich, medical corpsman, "transmitted" the impression that the sick bay would offer "emotional asylum" for anyone feeling the need to come by. These individuals would later name each other as the linchpins of the camp, all "pulling their load." Indeed, by all accounts the Deep Freeze I sailors at both bases represented an extraordinary array of talent, leadership, and commitment that they admired and appreciated in each other ever after.[24]

One leader the men particularly credited was Dr. Ehrlich. The medical officer was young and thinly experienced for the job, but he brought gifts of good judgment, approachability, and respect for his limitations. Not overly busy given Little Americans' general robustness, he treated minor complaints, performed four elective circumcisions, regretfully pulled half a dozen teeth, and dealt with a few "severe anxiety reactions." But one early day a man came in with a "bellyache"—tenderness in the right lower quadrant, somewhat elevated white count, slight temperature. Ehrlich suspected appendicitis. The pain persisted for five days, the white count rising. The doctor reluctantly decided he had better operate, a daunting prospect: "You have to start by autoclaving your instruments—it was a long day—doing the spinal, getting the patient draped and all of that stuff, and then going ahead and doing the appendectomy." The anesthetic began to wear off. Aldrich said he had "goofed" in administering it, but they did not learn until later that the powder (to be mixed with water) should not have been frozen; they had to finish with ether. The patient's muscles became tense, and it took "a lot of physical effort" to sew him up, not to mention great care to place each stitch to ensure closure and proper healing. Afterward Ehrlich had to "nurse the guy" and even see to the laundry. "It was a normal appendix, by the way," he admitted. The Seabee probably had a viral gastroenteritis of some sort.

Both patient and surgical team (also including surgical technician Donald Watson, HM2) came through, but the physician remembered the event as a scary experience. He understood his leadership role to require not just saving the one patient but also retaining the confidence of all the others. If he did not feel like "the complete Mayo Clinic" of popular expectation, he knew he needed to conceal his uncertainties under a veneer of calm, optimistic competence. By all accounts, he did it well. Aldrich repeatedly called Doc Ehrlich a man of knowledge, skills, and courage, "the man everyone turned to when the going got rough." He "had the respect of every man in the outfit."[25]

Two civilians wintered over at Little America. One was Lloyd Beebe, a gifted photographer from Walt Disney Studios and an outdoorsman of vast experience. Strong and able, he willingly braved hostile conditions for his own work and that of others. Like his Disney counterpart Elmo Jones at McMurdo, he produced outstanding still pictures and films that, when televised back home, greatly enhanced awareness and understanding of the IGY and the U.S. role in Antarctica. The second civilian was meteorologist Chesney ("Chet") Twombly, who looked out for the interests of the IGY. He was an amiable and willing worker who, having served several winters at isolated Arctic outposts with the U.S. Weather Bureau, was steeped in polar lore. Ehrlich, who sometimes helped him with a meteorite-counting experiment, found him a "good-natured, decent, bright fellow" who made no demands.[26]

But Twombly was discouraged as he wrote IGY chief scientist Wexler a five-page report on 9 March 1956 for posting via the *Glacier* at summer's end. While all the main buildings were up, none of the special science structures were. The Navy was occupying the building designated for Weather Central. Station plans put Little America's rawin tower at the wrong end of the meteorological building; at Byrd the tangle of wires and aerials planned over the met office would interfere with radiosonde reception. While Twombly appreciated the Navy's "great care" in accounting for all IGY containers and preventing damage in handling during off-loading, when their "orderly caching" was obviously impossible, he found no one very interested in the "safety of the cargo as a whole." So, "almost wholly by hand and without assistance" he had segregated, cached, and flagged both stations' IGY material for winter storage. His Weather Bureau supervisor Ernest Wood, compiling IGY field reports, wrote that several high-ranking officers showed a "lack of sympathy" for the IGY. He named Captain Ketchum, VX-6's Captain Douglas Cordiner, and Commander Whitney, thus criticizing sea-, air-, and land-based support.

In mid-February Twombly had written disconsolately to U.S. National Committee representative Ernest Wood, "I feel like leaving." The worst of his dejection could be traced to pessimism over Byrd Station. In March, when he reported that the Byrd trail project had been halted for the season, far short of its goal, he thought it "most likely" would "have to be abandoned." Army Arctic expert Silas Bowling was saying it would take three years to find, blast, and fill every crevasse to make a safe trail. Whitney, "evasive," anticipated but one tractor train for materials transport. With Young estimating the maximum payload for a train at about 210 tons, Twombly had "little room for hope that the station can be carried by tractor train next year, beyond 100 miles." Air Force airdrops would be critical. He was not sure the Navy had ever seriously expected to meet the original objective. Science seemed a low priority.[27]

All in all, IGY prospects might seem iffy. But Twombly's frustration, while understandable at this apparent nadir of fortunes, was not entirely justified. The IGY was more than a year off. The Navy rightly concentrated on getting the bases built first. Worries about ice damage to the ships, aircraft losses, and the never-distant approach of winter fairly trumped attention to science at that early point. In fact, the rawin tower was under construction by late February, the inflation shelter was up before dark, and the first weather balloon was released with good results on 10 April 1956. Two seasons later Harry Francis, then IGY administrator at Little America, would note that "the [science] cargo has been unloaded in a record operation that was really very finely executed." Caching, by category, was 90 percent completed by Christmas, with only two misplaced boxes. About six weeks later he reported, "We have received the most magnificent support imaginable." Francis did not hesitate to note shortcomings but also recognized that the IGY had its own "large and important logistics responsibility that no one can do for us as well as we could do it ourselves." Moreover, Capt. Eugene ("Pat") Maher, wintering-over commanding officer of the Navy contingent in 1958, Francis wrote, "is wholeheartedly interested in seeing the program fully carried out." Differing personalities aside, some of these changes in perception had to reflect an evolution in operating conditions that came with time and experience.[28]

Forwarding Twombly's missives to Hugh Odishaw at IGY headquarters, Wexler noted that the IGY representative at McMurdo, Kendall Moulton, had experienced similar frustration over a lack of help and interest in handling IGY equipment and supplies—"undoubtedly one of the prime reasons" he had decided after he got there not to winter over. Whether because of having to "push IGY crates around himself," as Wexler grumbled to his diary, or for the "personal reasons" he himself offered, Moulton created problems for IGY planners by going home. (He would later fulfill many polar assignments.) He did write an optimistic status report (helpful leaders, general order, South Pole cache complete) in late February for his replacement, meteorologist Howard Wessbecher, just back from work in the Arctic. Wessbecher seemed equally satisfied as he later reviewed the year, outlining a pattern of organization, cooperation, and time for significant scientific progress. Still, IGY leaders would continue to press the Navy, especially on its commitment to Byrd Station at the agreed location, and doubts persisted.[29]

Winter came to the station on floating ice. On 25 April Little Americans saw the sun for the last time, although three hours of twilight tarried (diminishing to complete darkness by 5 May). That month it snowed fourteen inches, and temperatures dipped to the minus forties, then the minus fifties. Between February and November about 170 inches of snow would fall, blow, and accumulate

Little America V already drifting in, April 1956. Winter snows will bury the station. Official U.S. Navy photograph. Courtesy, Al Raithel Jr.

around the station—a great deal more in this ocean-front area than in the dry interior. Winds kept the flat roofs remarkably clear for a time, but drifts settled against the walls and the sides of the tunnels, which, as intended, provided insulation and cut fuel consumption. As for living on a dynamic ice shelf, "every now and then you'd be sleeping," remembered yeoman Dick Lucier, and "you'd hear this sound like a crack or a rumble and you'd think, oh, are we going or are we staying? Then the next morning you knew you weren't going anywhere so that was it." After a while, he decided "we were good and safe up there."[30]

All that snow provided unlimited water at the expense of hauling it in from a clean, off-limits "snow mine" half a mile from camp and shoveling it into melter tanks. Generator exhaust—or, in the galley, hot water—circulating through pipes in the tanks offered "free" heat for melting. Two men per four-hour shift, on a continuous fire watch, kept the heaters' fuel tanks and the three snow melters filled. They learned that a cubic foot of packed snow weighing about 26.5 pounds would yield around 3 gallons of water. The base used about 2,300 gallons of water a day, or 30 gallons per person. Heads were constructed over twenty-five-foot holes in the ice, made deeper by warm wash-water drainage. Icy drafts "definitely prevented any time being lost by person-nel lingering."[31]

The winterers made it through the dark night with neither the highs of McMurdo's ribald theatricals nor the lows of its mental illness and never-ending runway plowing. Overall, the group proved "very stable." There were no serious disciplinary actions and no serious health problems beyond the one case of pseudo-appendicitis. Dr. Ehrlich found the worst physical distress from the profound cold not outdoors, where everyone had warm clothing and could come back inside to warm up, but in the extreme dryness of the heated indoor air. For those who were busy, the time passed quickly. Chief Moss, for example, cut teammates' hair and operated the ham radio, which gave him the bonus of frequent contact with his wife. Ehrlich and chief Aldrich, both fondly called Doc, shared a keenness for building model airplanes, chuckling over having gotten their kits safely south by labeling them "Fragile, Delicate Medi-cal Gear." Some recreational gear was in short supply, however, and when summer personnel flooded in, increasing the camp population from 73 to 240, the recreation building had to be converted to a barracks and there was no place for that many more people to go for fun. Worse, sharing cots in shifts, or "hot-bunking," became a detested necessity.[32]

Little America's food was outstanding, all agreed, although as Vic Young lamented in July, "Sure do miss a good green salad with oil & vinegar & a little garlic on it." Calories, nutrition, and taste scored high all year. An "open re-frigerator" policy, wherein anyone could, and commonly did, "raid the ice box" for leftovers or snacks, contributed to good morale as well as midwinter weight gain for many. The cooks, led by chief McInvale, were generously sup-plied, beyond the absence of fresh fruits and vegetables, and were both compe-tent and imaginative. They offered frequent steaks, avoided repetitiveness with varied recipes, and were "terrific bakers." Delicacies like brandied sweet rolls and strawberry shortcake made surprise appearances.[33]

By early August there was light on the northern horizon for a few hours. Young, who had marveled—almost embarrassed by his feelings—at the "harsh . . . different beauty" of crystal-clear moonlit winter nights, now wrote, "It sure feels good. . . . The sky looks just like a sunrise, all red and gold, then it fades to a gray." The 20th saw "Old Glory" and human spirits raised in honor of the returning sun, although that day "it was not visible through a wall of ice fog." By then, physical and mental efforts focused on the upcoming tractor-train operations. It was still cold; temperatures generally ranged in the minus forties to minus sixties, with an August low of –74°F. Winds, once sixty knots, made it effectively colder. But many were glad to be outdoors again in some daylight, and officer-in-charge Young believed they would be ready for Byrd Station on time without having to resort to a seven-day workweek. He put some personnel to work repairing and improving vehicles, which had taken a beating in long hours on the hard sastrugi. Others prepared the airfield and repaired the road to the ice edge.

As had Bowers at McMurdo, Young had already selected his construction crew for Byrd Station, headed by Lloyd ("Hammer") Hon, lead builder; Stroup, chief electrician; Will Beckett, lead utilities man; and Burleson, mechanic for the powerhouse generators. Later he stated, "I think the world of those men. They really did a job." Young gave each leader a set of Byrd blueprints and instructions to identify and assemble the right amount of every possible material they might need. Calculating (or guessing from their experience) the safety of redundancy versus the cost (in weight or volume) of every spare part was serious business. Their task was greatly complicated by first having to dig out the Byrd-coded boxes. After finding what they needed, the Seabees then repacked everything according to building site and order of use and loaded the big sleds on the principle of last on–first off. "We have [the components for] 2 bldgs loaded on the sleds now and are making good progress," wrote Young on 15 September, in the same entry in which he recorded the "good news" that the incoming planes had left the United States.[34]

The summer season got off to a rocky start, however, with the jolting news of the P2V crash at McMurdo. More personally, Little Americans pined for their mail on those planes. A week later they were still waiting, as the aircraft at McMurdo were diverted to more pressing duties. Young wrote, "All hands in camp very bitter over the mail situation." No one wanted to work. Bitter himself, he noted that the Air Force had "spanned the 2300 mile gap between NZ and McMurdo with their C-124s, but the Navy can't seem to close the gap between McMurdo and Little America & that is only 450 miles." Prolonging their psychological isolation, even for a few days, seemed poor thanks for a long and difficult job done well.[35]

The mail did finally come, and so did the eleven members of the Army Transportation Corps' trail reconnaissance party. The Byrd Station tractor train and construction crew were prepared to go. The first summer's snow runway for ski-equipped aircraft was re-smoothed and marked, all its electronic and navigational equipment in place. The seven men with aviation ratings were ready for the summer's flying.[36]

The Navy had met its Deep Freeze I objectives. The two beachhead bases were functioning. But five more IGY stations plus an auxiliary base at Beardmore

Glacier would somehow have to be built during the brief summer of 1956–1957, and no one knew for certain that the chosen sites were even reachable. The defensive tone of Task Force 43's final report implicitly acknowledged the sting of criticism, no doubt from the scientific community, for its insufficient reconnoitering. Such projects were understood to be on an "if operations permit" basis, the report huffed. If some were "not fully pursued," it was because ships, men, or aircraft were needed elsewhere or there were other "exigencies inherent in Polar operations." Fulfilling the "basic mission" had to come first.[37] It would be up to Operation Deep Freeze II to prove the Navy's mettle. The scientists expected to begin their work on 1 July 1957, half a year away.

CHAPTER FIVE

MARIE BYRD LAND
Crevasse Junction, Privation Station

*Ned made a pair of leather moccasins tonight out of a
do-it-yourself kit. That's what Byrd Station is by the way—
a do-it-yourself kit with only half the pieces which
never seem to fit each other.*

—Vernon Anderson, 1957[1]

As winter began in April 1956 for the 166 souls left in Antarctica,
Admiral Dufek returned to Washington to prepare for "our biggest
year, our roughest mission." Operation Deep Freeze II would involve
twelve ships and 3,400 men, almost twice as many of each as the
year before. Attention went first to the intimidating inland sites. For
Byrd Station to rise above the ice plain of Marie Byrd Land during
the short season of sunlight, the entire camp would have to be
hauled overland nearly 650 miles, crevasses or no. Yet to be found
was a route safe for a train pulled by thirty-five-ton tractors. Yet to
be accomplished was all of the transport, construction, and hook-
up of the station even as the scientists were arriving. Not every-

thing would get there. Byrd residents would end up doing a lot of doing without.[2]

With the exception of Richard Byrd's winter alone at Advance Base, 100 miles out on the Ross Ice Shelf, no one had ever lived for any length of time in the interior of the polar continent. The logistics line was simply too long and fragile, the perils too great. So Navy officers, sobered by Bursey's misjudgments and the scope, risks, and circumscribed time frame of their task, could beg forbearance for suggesting that Byrd Station be built somewhere along the trail already marked. But since gaining knowledge of the distant vastness was precisely the attraction, IGY planners, just as understandably, decried any such degradation of the scientific effort and insisted on latitude 80° South, longitude 120° West as a vital link in a north-south global chain of stations. This locus of intense auroras and purported "pressure surges" cried for investigation, and over-snow traverse parties, Byrd leader George Toney wrote, needed a "staging point in the heart of the ice cap" for their seismic, magnetic, gravity, and glaciological studies. Of course, foreign policy interests also championed the original "American sector" site—to bolster the U.S. basis for a claim there should circumstances warrant making one. In fact, the Navy had no wish to fail in this highly visible, politically charged mission. The doubts and caveats seemed designed to diminish expectations so that any degree of success could be deemed a victory. Byrd expedition veteran and IGY representative E. E. Goodale did offer some hope to Odishaw, along with pessimism, when he wrote in November 1956 that by early aerial reconnaissance, chances for a safe trail looked "very doubtful." But, he believed, Dufek would "do his damndest to get the station in as planned."[3]

Dufek did. To start with, he made good on his promise to train-leader Vic Young to get help in finding a way through the deadly crevasses. He assigned Cmdr. Paul Frazier, one of his most trusted officers, to head the effort. To make up time and improve the odds, he turned to experts from the Army Transportation Corps, who had developed crevasse techniques on the Greenland ice cap. One was a twenty-four-year-old lieutenant, Philip M. Smith. After earning his master's degree in geology from Ohio State University, he maneuvered to fulfill his military requirement in Greenland, where the Army was constructing ice runways, "cities" in ice caverns, and the DEW Line—all aimed at thwarting Soviet attack across the North Pole. A mountaineer and spelunker, Smith quickly specialized in working through crevasse systems. One snowstormy summer day in 1956 he received a message from the admiral, which had gone up the Navy's chain of command, over to the Army's, and down the analogous long line to Smith in his remote Weasel. Dufek had heard of his expertise and wanted him to work in Antarctica along with two Army majors, Merle ("Skip") Dawson and Palle Mogensen—neither of whom had crevasse experience—and three Army enlisted men.[4]

On the spot, which was characteristic of his decision-making style, Smith radioed back that he would do it. "Well," he said, remembering his instant analysis, "I still had Army time to do, and it was a challenge." He had heard about Kiel's accident and the difficulties of building the Byrd trail. He knew about the IGY and was thinking about a career in glaciology, so he was intellectually intrigued as well. Back in Thule, he wired Dufek saying he wanted to bring a crevasse detector. He knew this experimental device was "marginally effective," more reliable in wet snow than dry but better than not having one. He asked the Navy to send two electronics technicians to Greenland for training. He would then choose one, who would ride with him in the lead trail vehicle to manage the instrument. "Now, I just did all of this, you see. Here I was, an Army lieutenant . . . sending messages back and forth to a Navy admiral telling him what I thought he ought to do." But Dufek liked the brash young officer's confident forthrightness, and the two would develop a warm and fruitful relationship.[5]

After some late-summer planning with Task Force 43, the Army contingent flew to the ice to be there as early in the new season as possible, although the numerous stopovers necessary at that time took several days. They arrived on 25 October 1956 with four crevasse detectors.[6] Almost immediately, they began a systematic air reconnaissance to locate the best breakthrough corridor to West Antarctica's Rockefeller Plateau. First, a VX-6 pilot would fly one or more of the Army officers out in an R4D to scan the entire margin of the ice shelf, siting and photographing telltale depressions in the snow that warned of bridged crevasses. They followed these sorties with shorter-range, lower-altitude flights by Otter and then close-in work by helicopter, all put at their disposal by Dufek. The Army experts decided on a route somewhat west and south of Bursey's where, Smith recalled, there was a "very tough but comparatively short set of crevasse problems to deal with." Anywhere was a gamble, but here there were no mountains to interfere with air support, and beyond "this one horrendous spot" there appeared to be "clear sailing" all the way to Byrd. But the crevasse belt was fearsome. They were estimating thirty-two crevasses in a seven-mile stretch. In fact, there were more than that, and still more were discovered as the crossings proceeded.[7]

Dawson's trail party departed from Little America on 5 November 1956—six Army and five Navy men in two Weasels, two D-8s, and one Sno-Cat. The vehicles pulled eight sleds, one with a messing wanigan and two with unheated four-bunk sleeping wanigans. When there were visitors, which was often, they all hot-bunked. Coming and going were plane crews, VIPs like Dufek and Frazier, and reporters and photographers from the *New York Times*, NBC-TV, and Disney. With their 5,000 pounds of rations (10 pounds each per day), they also carried 2,400 pounds of explosives for blowing open crevasses and 1,500 trail flags on bamboo poles. Even with air support to augment their supplies, they hauled heavy quantities of diesel fuel, "MoGas," and white gas, along with drums of lubricating oil and antifreeze. Knowing progress would be excruciatingly slow once they reached the crevasse zone, the party traveled at maximum speed at first, averaging 3.5 miles per hour. One day they made 40 miles along what they were soon calling Army-Navy Drive. Every 20 miles they stopped to build a twelve-foot snow cairn topped with a spent fuel drum to guide incoming aircraft. Periodically, they dug pits to analyze the snow. By mile 171, with Lieut. Harvey Speed flying Otter reconnaissance, they were seeing large and complex crevasse and pressure systems. Air support increased, including an assigned helicopter flown by Marine lieutenant Leroy ("Pete") Kenney and an Air Force C-124 piloted by Lt. Col. C. J. Ellen to airdrop diesel fuel.[8]

After more than a week of searching in fan-shaped patterns by land and air between miles 171 and 194 for a suitable point of penetration, the Army-Navy team identified, according to Smith, a "possible gateway with a narrow lane leading through the belt parallel to the crevasse system." They set up a base camp at mile 183.5 and began the "long, hard process of literally by brute force" creating a safe trail through the treacherous seven miles. They might not have been pleased to know that back in Washington, chief scientist Harry Wexler, understandably anxious for the IGY but ignorant of local conditions, was impatiently writing (fortunately, only to himself), "They go forward, then backwards, then sideways. I can't understand why they went so far south of last year's route." Between 19 November and 3 December, after the detected fissures were marked (using the helicopter's shadow to pinpoint the spot to flag), demolition and dozing teams—using one Weasel and one bladed D-8—probed, blasted, filled, leveled, marked, and tested the trail, the latter by rein-controlled tractor. They used some 800 pounds of dynamite per mile and pushed enormous quantities of snow into the blown-out maws (in one seven-hour period 105,000 cubic yards), constantly worrying about the D-8's position lest it unwittingly slide into a hole.[9]

Two miles of "lane distance made good" bespoke an excellent day; often there was none if major demolition was required. All along, Smith would rappel into the crevasses, seeking technical understanding of their structure and direction before they took any action. At the last, with only a few spare feet of maneuvering room for the heavy equipment, limited safe snow to "borrow," and time running out as two crevasse systems converged, they were forced to abandon the "doctrine" of "right-angle crossing." At Smith's suggestion, the team blew open the worst, most complex crevasses, partially filled them with snow (what time and material would allow), and dozed them as smooth as possible to create a trail twelve feet below grade, essentially along their new bottoms.[10]

In the end, between miles 183.5 and 190.9, sometimes called Crevasse Junction, the team built a trail that was about 35 feet wide at its narrowest, its direction "constantly weaving" to follow the path of least resistance. They marked the safe passageway with such a profusion of colored flags that they dubbed the place "Fashion Lane," a name later made official. On 28 November Young flew out to observe the last of the trail-laying operations. He did not later remember this preview, designed for reassurance, but he had confidence in "Smitty's" approach: "I knew he wasn't grabbing something out of the air. He had been down there looking around, and he had a darn good idea of just what this whole seven-mile stretch was. I learned a long time ago . . . to have trust in some people, and in some people you don't have it." By 3 December the Army-Navy group and all their equipment were safely on the plateau. Finding no new crevasses and surfaces that ranged from "soft, powdery" snow to "hard[,] crusty" sastrugi, they made as much as 45 miles a day. The team reached and marked 80° South, 120° West on 18 December. They had come 646.5 statute miles and climbed gradually on the ice sheet to an altitude of 5,100 feet, nearly a mile above sea level. "No one who has not had a glimpse of the kind of terrain traveled can properly evaluate this feat," a task-force writer asserted. Crary, writing from Little America, called it "a tremendous job" done "with little fanfare." After a flag-raising ceremony the next day, filmed by NBC, the trailblazers declared "mission accomplished" and headed back to Kainan Bay.[11]

As soon as Dawson radioed "Trail across crevasse area now ready for heavy sled movement," Young and his Seabees set out from Little America. "The Admiral gave us a good send-off," he wrote on departure day, 5 December, "with pictures and speeches" and a flag for the proud leader to raise at Byrd Station. Of Little America's original ten D-8s, one had been lost with Kiel, two were with the trailblazers, and one had to stay in camp. So the heavy swing consisted of six, each pulling two Otaco sleds, which were rated to carry twenty tons but were mostly loaded to twenty-five. Young also had a Weasel, for his own faster movement along the train, and eighteen men, whose dual charge was to deliver the supplies and build the station. Young divided the group into two twelve-hour shifts, a "Port" watch that would be on from 0700 to 1900 and a "Starboard" watch, 1900 to 0700. They would stop for an hour to change crews. The men "going off were off," free to eat and sleep. Those coming on would eat, fuel the tractors, and check out whatever needed tending. In a jolting wanigan, Ray Mishler, the tireless cook, prepared breakfast and dinner simultaneously for the outgoing and incoming crews, as well as bag lunches at noon and midnight. For all this he earned his own bed. The others endured hot-bunking. After a few shakedown days, the swing began making what became a normal pace of about three miles an hour. If this was not a lot faster than Scott had traveled man-hauling, the loads were incomparably greater, the pace sustained. The train took nine or ten hours to go twenty miles, stopping at fuel caches every forty miles or so and consuming about 2.8 gallons of diesel fuel per mile. (On the lighter return trip it would average fifty-five miles a day, burning about 2.1 gallons of fuel per mile.)[12]

On 8 December Dufek ordered Smith to leave his trail party, now devouring miles on the ice plateau, and return to Fashion Lane to escort the tractor train through. To abandon his mission, now within reach, was "heart-breaking," although it later opened other doors, Smith said, and "of course it was the right thing to do in terms of the enterprise." He knew like no one else the terrain of those seven miles while also knowing that "knew" was "something of an overstatement," given that already "the effects of glacial motion had begun to make minor changes." He also realized that appearances would not inspire courage among Navy men who were "still absolutely spooked" about crevasses. After all the dynamiting and snow moving, the area was blackened, churned into chaos; it "literally looked like a war zone." Deadly chasms still flanked the twisting trail. Dr. Ehrlich, who had heard the fears, noted that when it came time, everyone went without objection, which he attributed to good leadership. Young saw "not even the slightest bit of reluctance about doing anything." His men were "just outstanding," the "kind of people that you like to have with you." Likely, the picture was painted more vividly for Smith, to spur his willingness. Likely, the bravado among the Seabees masked considerable internal anxiety.[13]

The tractor train arrived at the crevasse zone on 9 December; soon an R4D landed with Frazier and Smith. After briefings and reconnaissance by Weasel, Smith and Young started the first tractor and one sled over at 0645, followed by the Weasel. Smith, who sat with the driver, guided him along: "Okay, now when we go another twenty-five feet, you have to make a hard turn here, so we've got to go a little bit this way over to the edge, but this is exactly as far as

The first tractor train en route from Little America, with all materials, equipment, supplies, and crew to build Byrd Station, December 1956. Official U.S. Navy photograph, by Calvin Larsen. Courtesy, Byrd Polar Research Center Archives.

you can move. You cannot go any further to the right because we don't know about whether that's safe over there or not." They safely gained the plateau two and a half hours later and returned with the tractor, to start another sled over after an interval of eight hours to allow the "nervous snow a chance to settle." Gradually, they shortened the wait to four hours without mishap, although Bill Stroup remembered getting out three or four times to walk behind the rein-driven tractor when he crossed. On the 11th, when only the wanigan sleds were left on the ice-shelf side, "we opened a crevasse in the trail we had been running over." The next day they decided to proceed anyway, "passing the crevasse on the side. The sleeping wanigan opened another crack further up the trail, however [we] brought the messing wanigan over anyway and it made it safely." By 0830 the train was all on the plateau. "I don't believe another sled would have made it," the exhausted, relieved train leader wrote.[14]

Once beyond harm on the Rockefeller Plateau, the heavy swing rumbled on, deafening the white silence. By then the crew members (only half of them experienced mechanics or drivers) were more skilled at operating the equipment and progress was smoother, although breakdowns still visited the train. These were overcome with a mix of air and base support, ingenuity, and improvisation.

For example, the very next day the train ground to a halt when a pushrod in one of the D-8s snapped. The loss of a pushrod, which properly times fuel injection, meant losing the power of that cylinder—too great a sacrifice for the heavy work. A three-day blizzard at Little America prevented resupply by air. Memories vary, but according to newly arrived Calvin Larsen, photographer chief, when the Seabee mechanics removed the broken pushrod and threw the pieces off into the snow, he dug them out "'cause I wasn't unacquainted with pushrods." He had watched his father make new ones for the farm tractor back in Montana. But they needed a suitable material. Stroup said it was Willie Burleson who homed in on the steel rod mounted around the top of the cookstove, as on a ship to keep pots from sliding off in the swells. It seemed about the right diameter. Larsen and driver Elliott Moore sawed out a length of it, welded on the usable ends of the broken part, and "after a lot of pounding, we had ourselves a pushrod." (The day was so "warm" some worked stripped to their waists; it was ten degrees, but sunny and windless.) In about five hours the train was under way. "Mishler was having a fit," Young later laughed, but replacing the purloined piece of pot guard with some wire kept the pots aboard.[15]

Confidence grew that the ponderous orange caravan would make it. Further out on the ice sheet the snow became harder and crustier, the equipment sank less deep, and the drivers could sometimes shift out of third gear into fourth. Sastrugi made for a punishing ride in the Weasel, but the heavy tractors just smashed the ridges down. The Navy's ski-equipped aircraft continued to ferry fuel out to the train, and the Air Force airdropped three loads of it (thirty tons) nearer the station. After the swing made sixty-three miles one day, Young confided to his diary that they should make it to Byrd Station before Christmas. It had been a "long hard trip. Have excellent crew or trip not possible," he wrote in grateful tribute. On the 21st Young's train met Dawson's homebound one, but both were eager to push on and did not tarry. Young reportedly radioed to Frazier, "Met band of nomads." Then: "On 23 Dec at 1400 [construction mechanic Willis] Clem and I planted a 2 x 4 timber at a point 80°S 120°W as sighted in by Ch. Moss. Distance from LAS #5 is 645.6 miles. The longest trek by the largest tractor train in the history of the Antarctic & perhaps the Arctic for all I know has come to a successful ending."[16]

Such private exaltations aside, the Seabees took little time to celebrate their achievement of so challenging a goal. Young's next sentence read: "Commenced construction of the Meteorology Bldg at 1600." At 2205 pilot Speed landed his R4D on the snow and dropped off ten additional construction workers. By midnight the shell of this largest building was up—a place to sleep. By the next evening utilities man Willie Beckett had his crew installing ducts and pipes. "Everyone working together wonderful smooth operation," Young wrote on Christmas Eve in his generous spirit and run-on style. On Christmas Day, a "regular working day," Lloyd Hon's builders completed the deck of the garage/powerhouse and the shell of the galley and mess hall, where chief Stroup and the electricians got started immediately. The crews took time for "turkey and trimmings," which Mishler prepared in the wanigan ("quite a feat"), and went back to work. By the next day they had the generators in place and were erecting the garage wall panels around them.

It was no accident that Byrd Station materialized so quickly on the snowscape. At Little America, construction of one 20- by 48-foot building had taken about eighty man-hours. But an aggravating amount of that time had gone to searching for the right materials. So when the packing was done for Byrd, Young directed that the numbered sleds, each with its own manifest, be loaded by building. Materials needed first were put on last, to be used immediately without intermediate handling. On arrival, he halted the train just beyond the surveyed site to leave the snow surface undisturbed and minimize the need for grading, another lesson learned in Deep Freeze I and reemphasized by Stroup. "When we pull a sled up alongside [the building site]," Young reviewed, "off comes the wood for the foundations, and the floor trusses and panels, and when the sled is empty, part of the building is up. When the next sled is empty, the whole building is up maybe." Construction was so tightly organized that the crew setting roof trusses worked only one panel (four feet) behind those putting up wall panels and one panel ahead of the roof-panel crew. Excepting the oil burners that were "still sitting in New Zealand," so that Herman Nelson heaters had to warm the snow in the galley melter, everything needed was remarkably at hand. Young's assessment: "It worked perfectly."[17]

On the 27th, when drivers steered the empty tractor train back into the ruts of Army-Navy Drive, northbound, those remaining had their first hot meal in the galley. The last building, the head, went up on the 29th, and everyone began looking forward to his first shower in three weeks. After "a little party," with homemade brandied eggnog that "wasn't bad" to celebrate the holiday, Young commissioned the station on New Year's Day 1957. At seventeen degrees, it was a beautiful warm, clear, sunny day. In another two days, with the four buildings completed, effort went to such tasks as erecting antennae, installing interior partitions, and preparing a snow runway. Most storage was still outdoors, unprotected except by parachutes. Fifteen tons of food and the dozen scientists and eleven Navy support personnel who would winter over began to arrive by air. Young flew out with the last of the Deep Freeze I personnel on 23 January, after several days of weather delays.[18]

———

But the life-sustaining capacity of this tiny outpost was clearly marginal at best, never mind its scientific potential. Food, fuel, and shelter were all still inadequate for safety or comfort. None of the scientific structures had been built, nor was most of the scientific apparatus on-site. George Toney's appointment as the station's scientific leader was not made public until Christmas Eve, the day after base construction started. For a time it seemed that Byrd might have to be abandoned. Antarctica's IGY Big Three—Gould, Wexler, and Crary—having just arrived at Little America, huddled daily to devise strategies to ensure the station's viability. They were relieved, task-force historian Henry Dater wrote, when Dufek "decided to gamble on getting another tractor train through with additional buildings and supplies" in the narrowing window of summer. Wexler calculated the likely weather and remaining daylight to prepare a feasibility study and justification for a third heavy swing that season, but for the Navy the main question mark was available personnel. Taking no chances, Toney led other IGY-ers through two all-nighters to hustle their scientific cargo to the sled-loading area to be first on the second train. Wexler, though "thoroughly chilled," found the experience "most exhilarating."[19]

Air support was another source of anxiety. They all knew Dufek had asked the Air Force to airdrop additional fuel and food at Byrd, but the ice runway at McMurdo had deteriorated so badly that the big planes had (temporarily, everyone hoped) flown back to New Zealand. And they still had highest-priority Pole supplies to deliver. The IGY leaders requested six R4D flights, which they thought could supply everything critical except the fuel. Lt. Cmdr. Eddie Frankiewicz, senior VX-6 pilot, offered two flights. Experienced crews were leaving, he argued and, Wexler groused, he "insisted on going through his usual pessimistic account of flying conditions in and out of Byrd Station." But Dufek himself had sarcastically "complimented" Wexler on his "choice of 80°S, 120°W." It had, he said, the worst flying weather in the Antarctic. (Indeed, there were only eighty clear days all year.) The VX-6 flew the seven remaining IGY scientists to Byrd on 2 February, but on the 4th Wexler was still worried that they would all have to come out with the tractor train. Speed endeared himself to Wexler by flying additional scientific gear and food out to be loaded onto the en route sleds. Further, the air squadron's pitifully undersized helicopter and Otters valiantly flew as far as they respectively could to cache fuel drums along the trail; R4D crews hand-pumped 20,000 additional gallons of diesel fuel from cabin tanks into rubber bladders left in the snow at Mile 240.[20]

Wexler's diary reports that Dufek finally told the IGY leaders that if the C-124s could not return to the ice, only twelve people could winter over at Byrd. They glumly prepared a list, heavy on scientists. Then the admiral changed his mind; it would be "all or none," he wrote to Gould, who immediately appealed. This news was a "bombshell" to Wexler. "We're fighting for the life of Byrd Station," he recorded, distraught, on 1 February. The two sides, both under enormous pressure, might as well have been speaking different languages. The Navy's caution sounded like a lack of commitment to the scientists, who in their zealousness seemed to the military—which was responsible for their well-being—ungrateful and unrealistic about their sustainability. In fact, the two sides' respective drives to succeed were equally compelling and largely overlapping. They certainly shared the conviction that if the Soviets were in the game—and in the polar regions they held the advantage in experience and capability—the Americans must both play and win. Besides the national prestige at stake, in those days of superheated Cold War rhetoric, any potential tip in the balance of power threatened national security. Nor was it a contradiction to note, as President Eisenhower repeatedly did, that the IGY was an opportunity for international cooperation and harmony. It was unthinkable for the United States not to lead the way.[21]

The second heavy swing pushed off for Byrd on 29 January 1957, led by Lieut. Robert K. White. Its seven D-8 tractors pulled fourteen sleds loaded with about 220 tons of material, including the bulk of the scientific equipment and the structures to house it plus "limited" food and fuel. They made the round-trip in a month "with no unusual incidents," although they, too, suffered at first from "lack of driver technique." The party found the less-than-three-month-old trail flags torn and almost too sun-bleached to be seen. Fortunately, the cairn barrel markers were securely frozen in and plainly visible, as Gould observed when he flew out to inspect the train. Smith, with Major Mogensen, again guided the tractors with one sled at a time through Fashion Lane, which showed in places the ill effects of added traffic and six inches of powdery new snow. The crew blasted and filled new crevasses parallel to the trail and redozed and remarked the entire fissure-streaked passage. All got safely through, and the train arrived at Byrd on 12 February.[22]

Meanwhile, the worried admiral had called in from Greenland Dr. Andrew Assur, a SIPRE ice expert. McMurdo's runway conditions also stranded Assur in New Zealand, but he advised by radio based on SITREPs sent him daily. They told how heavy use, warm temperatures (up to the plus forties), and solar heat acting on accumulating dirt and debris had made deep potholes in Williams Field. Assur outlined a procedure of repeatedly draining and filling melt holes with an aggregate of compacted snow, ice chips, and freshwater (which froze at a higher temperature than seawater). With this method and, finally, colder weather, McMurdo crews managed to restore the runway. The first C-124s reappeared on 9 February. After completing most of the Pole drops, the Globemasters made seventeen more supply flights to Byrd between 18 and 23 February—enough to ensure survival over the winter despite frequent losses from various parachute failures and high winds. The last airlift was delayed when an engine caught fire; the crew had to jettison their cargo on the ice shelf so they could limp back to McMurdo.[23]

Byrd Station could certainly have used more airdrops, but the limited number of aircraft and the vagaries of weather and runway conditions made additional flights too risky. As it was, aviation crews worked long hours in the air and on the ground. It was a given that the planes would be flying beyond their specified weight limits. If Byrd was relatively neglected by air, it did have the tractor trail, however slow and dangerous. There was no such alternative for the South Pole, separated from the ice shelf by high mountains. For his dual approach, Smith thought Dufek was "a good strategist and a good tactician." But Dufek's priority rankled those struggling in and for West Antarctica. Both scientists and sailors resented Pole as the "political and glamor base," asserted Byrd radioman William Lowe years later. Besides being the focus of rivalry with the Soviets, Pole also enjoyed "Dr. Siple's political clout." But Byrd was "more valuable from a scientific standpoint," insisted nonscientist Lowe, obviously reflecting local chauvinism. In any case, McMurdo probably could not have supported many more heavy wheeled aircraft on the decay-prone ice even had more been available.[24]

While all the alternative scenarios absorbed and distressed the planners, those out in Marie Byrd Land dug in to prepare for a brutal winter. Whether scientist or Seabee ("the distinction meant little" in those frantic first months), all hands turned to upon the arrival of the second supply train, which, after two days of hasty unloading, departed back to the coast to beat the darkness. The winterers had been "sleeping in every odd corner of the met-radio building and the mess hall," wrote Toney, newly flown in, so it was not difficult to inspire labor for hauling in supplies or for construction, which proceeded simultaneously. With "inexperience but ingenuity," they built first the science building, to sleep nine and provide work space for several disciplines. Then came the weather-balloon inflation shelter, with a separate shed for manufacturing the highly explosive hydrogen gas, and the more complicated geomagnetism buildings, which had to be entirely free of magnetic materials. Geophysicist Charles Bentley remembered that the panels arrived with standard steel nails, which would have "interfered drastically" with the sensitive instruments' operation. So they had to pull out every nail and rebuild the panels with nonmagnetic fasteners, which, anticipating repairs, fortunately they had. Bentley learned later that their special panels, distinctly labeled, had gone to routine use at Little America, and someone had then casually re-marked ordinary panels for shipment to Byrd.

The men installed the rawinsonde (radio-sounding) antenna dome on the roof of the meteorology building so that the legs provided for it could be used as the aurora tower, for which no materials ever arrived. The tower would raise the small aurora-observation building above and partly "astraddle" the science building. Aurora physicist Daniel Hale drew up a design for the converted frame, but the bolt holes in the aluminum legs would not line up, which required some dismantling to drill them larger, for a sloppier but workable fit. The wall panels then had to be "muscled" up onto the platform built on the legs, the plastic observation domes installed, and access hatches lined up with the dormitory beneath. The scientists were becoming anxious about the looming start of the IGY. By then, it was also fifty below and growing dark. "It was a real hairy experience up on top of 2 ladders in a 50 mph wind and blizzard," wrote glaciologist Vern Anderson. Everyone got frostbite, especially Toney, who did not like to wear a face mask. But as a "reward" for helping, the enthusiastic Bentley remembered, they all got to help stand aurora watches, "which is fun." If it was not cloudy, there was always some kind of auroral activity, sometimes spectacular.[25]

Byrd's residents spent much of March and April on the critical task of getting all their supplies—fuel drums, food, and equipment—under cover in a tunnel system connecting the now-five main buildings. They advanced the clock two hours to better use existing daylight; the summer sun set for good on 21 April, having increasingly dipped below the horizon since 22 February. They were plagued by shortages, often absences, of essential materials. So without adequate lumber, they innovatively welded empty oil drums together to fashion vertical columns as a tunnel framework. Across these they laid "a miscellaneous lot" of scrap lumber, twisted roof trusses, water pipe. This, Toney wrote, they covered with chicken wire, "the only ingredient of the original recipe for tunnels" that was delivered in quantity, and overlaid the whole with used parachutes. Concern for collapse increased with the snow load, but "judicious shoring" preserved the makeshift system, more or less, until it could be rebuilt the following summer.[26]

Anderson found a stringent situation upon his later arrival: "Boy, everything fouled up. No wiring for electricity (not enough), no tools, light bulbs, only 1 movie projector bulb. No spares of anything. No glaciology stuff (thermistors especially)." He learned that some of "the guys" were planning to propose to the station leaders that a Sno-Cat be driven back to Little America to bring out "this much needed stuff. Wow!!! (No beer here and that's one reason for this proposal I believe.) Well, we really gave that idea an emphatic NO. We'd ruin the vehicles—1200 more miles! Impossible!" But he joined in trying to "think of a way to let them know how desperate we are." Talking to Crary by radio about their just-completed inbound traverse gave the scientists a chance to relay the urgency of Byrd's need for another airlift, especially for certain scientific equipment without which "every field of study will be seriously curtailed." They also obtained Crary's agreement that the Sno-Cats must not be commandeered. "I've been thinking of the idea of using parachutes for bed linen," Anderson wrote on 1 March, "which is about all we have enough of." Confirming that he did so, on 1 June he recorded, "I changed sheets today—cut up a piece of parachute for a new clean one and threw the other away. How's that for extravagance?" On 23 July he took another.[27]

Like much else at Byrd, caches for emergency supplies in case of fire were rather ad hoc, as dictated by available time and materials. Everyone stored a bag of extra clothing over the winter in the traverse Sno-Cats, which were parked some distance from camp, as was a sled holding backup rations and medical supplies. Each pair of buildings and the several fuel dumps were separated by "enormous drifts of snow" so that one disaster would not doom the station. Fire extinguishers and radios were scattered about the camp. The main food cache they judged only "remotely combustible." There were no fires, but one day they came frighteningly close. Dr. Dalton, the medical officer, improperly lit a laboratory spirit lamp, "and the next minute the whole thing had exploded in flames." Knowing the "terror of buildings burning in polar conditions," he "just picked the thing up and ran outside and threw it in the snow," at the cost of second-degree burns on his hands. With his detailed instructions, starting with "in my right trouser pocket you'll find a set of keys [to the medical locker under his bed]," a civilian dressed the wounds and administered a painkilling shot, and Dalton recovered to care again for others. For Toney, the greatest danger was exposure from becoming disoriented in a blizzard during the long night. Indeed, more than once, Dalton remembered, "somebody did get lost and was lucky enough to find their way back to the station, because by then we were all underground, and this was like trying to find a rabbit hole on a dark night." So rope lifelines led to the entrances, and he wanted everyone present at meals so he could count heads.[28]

For Byrd's first winter, utility spoke louder than aesthetics, nicety bowed to necessity. The pioneers could manage without paint, and unfinished plywood floors would do, but when unstable line voltage caused the last movie-projector bulb to burn out in early March, crisis loomed. Spare lamps arrived from Little America on 7 March, the last flight of the season, to rescue the long year's chief entertainment—an enormous relief for Toney. But he would not dwell on privation. Nor would Bentley: "Well, hardship meant that our pool table didn't get out there, our ping-pong table didn't get out there, we were low on brandy and hard liquor, the beer froze. But that's not hardship. We had plenty to eat, we had good food, we had a warm place to live, we didn't have to work very hard." Assistant glaciologist Mario Giovinetto did not recall want except to joke about it. Even after eight persons lost two each of their four airdropped bags of personal clothing in a parachute mishap, there was plenty of warm, durable military clothing to meet the "then unknown rigors of winter in the interior"—a mark of the Navy's "solicitude" for their welfare, Toney wrote. Ping-pong and pool tables were eventually found, had there been room to set them up. Most of the library books, however, did not arrive until the following October.[29]

Some worried about shortages of food, although the reach of that adversity depended upon who told the story. Monotony, not lack of nutrition, was a fairer complaint. Toney scoffed, "If you have to use Spam instead of fresh frozen roast beef, is that a shortage?" (He slipped on his example; beef was all they had.) Byrd had started off with lobster, chicken, and rabbit. "When it wound down, we had a lot of hamburger, a lot of stew beef, and no variety, and it would get a little dull after a while," he allowed. "But there was no danger of starving, never that." Anderson, who in mid-September declared himself not yet tired of it, a month later recorded, "Roast beef and more roast beef, ugh!" Toney insisted that it was not scarcity but compassion for the overworked cook, Robert Marsh, that, after the strenuous outdoor work ceased for the winter, led the station to go on two meals a day—breakfast at 0930 and dinner at 1630. An informal coffee break at one o'clock, with an aromatic array of Marsh's bakery treats, "came to be an anticipated institution each day." He had his work cut out as the choicer meats and fresh-frozen vegetables ran out one by one. Worse, among many items reported by the Navy as inadequately or never supplied were staples as important as "canned tomatoes, catsup, spices, garlic, vinegar, olive oil, corn starch, shrimp, and cheese." The doctor offered the indefatigable improviser, sick-bay acetic acid solution, to dilute for vinegar in macaroni salads, but tomatoes, say, were harder to conjure. He testified that health did not suffer from the meal curtailment, and in fact many individuals gained weight over the winter, a few up to twenty or thirty pounds. Three meals a day returned with daylight and increased activity.[30]

One acknowledged deficit was alcohol, which was in such short supply that the winter's beer was rationed to ten cans per man, as one sailor reportedly learned too late after consuming his entire allotment one early Saturday night. There was even less hard liquor. It said something about relative yearnings that by midwinter the collection of pinups adorning the mess hall walls was overtaken by magazine advertisements for whiskey. Dalton doled out a mellowing of dreadful Old Methusalem and medicinal brandy on special occasions. Hidden away in the garage, one Seabee set up a still, using, "I suppose raisins or something," thought Toney, but he had little success and the leaders did not bother him about it. This might have been electronics technician Walton ("Denny") Welch who, as Lowe remembered, made a batch of something, drank it all himself, and the next day—"paralyzed" on one side—could not get out of his bunk. "It would've been wonderful if we'd had about a hundred times more beer than we had," Toney reflected later. At year's end, just before "the full flurry of summer activity," the Byrd men of Deep Freeze II would indulge in their first real party, ostensibly a housewarming for a new building brought in by the first spring tractor train. Punch spiked to high potency with medicinal alcohol, along with beer, freshly arrived and "provided unstintingly," spurred "toasting and speech-making" and reunited and re-energized the long-thirsty group. Teetotaler Anderson muttered, "Boy is this camp stinko."[31] Could it be that in the scientists' push to load their supplies first on the second tractor train, beer was among the camp supplies left in the snow at Little America?

As the winter's dark deepened, the spartan conditions, close quarters, and long isolation—with poor and unevenly available radio communications—challenged peaceable communal life, although Dalton saw a unifying effect in the shared straits. Even with the station's ragged state, he wrote in his official report, "the majority still felt a strong determination to complete the year." What might have become a clash of cultures between the science and military groups mostly did not, although he recalled that mealtime and social groupings tended to form along educational lines, which created similar segregation. There were tensions, of course, sometimes serious "frictions and antagonisms." Toney, looking back, found it "remarkable" that while there had been "some very hot-tempered persons and very sensitive persons" and even one, apparently suffering from power envy, who "did what he could to disrupt the harmony" and make his own job difficult, there was "never a physical dispute." Lowe recalled general concord among the Navy men and between civilians and Seabees but "considerable ego clashes amongst the scientists." Of an unnamed two, "we had fears concerning a killing—that's no joke." No one else hinted at such animosity. Yet, the leaders agreed, a few who lacked "zest for the assignment" or were temperamentally "ill-suited" had some negative impact on the group as a whole.[32]

Bentley led others in crediting the success of the threadbare year to the camp's leadership. While innocent of polar experience, command experience, and, at the time, even American experience, officer-in-charge Brian Dalton was a "bright, sensible guy"—if not a sensible, or even defensible, choice on the Navy's part. If the Irish-born physician was a "fish out of water," he was, in Toney's words, witty, energetic, and fair-minded. "And George Toney was an even brighter, more sensible, dynamic guy," in Bentley's view. The two men saw to it that everyone participated, especially in the camp dog work. Besides his polar experience, even temper, good humor, and ability to resolve problems and diffuse tense situations "fairly, without much ado," Toney earned his persuasive force in significant measure by always being the first one there to do any job, including scrubbing the latrine. For Giovinetto, there was "a great humanity about him."[33]

Toney, alone in the final reports of the IGY scientific leaders, named and described the functions, ancillary duties, and voluntary contributions of all twenty-three Byrd citizens. So we learn, for example, that Jack Penrod, builder third class, was the camp carpenter and official postal clerk who "turned out creditable menus on occasion." Ionospheric physicist Virgil Barden, from the National Bureau of Standards, endeared himself to station mates by bringing an NBS shortwave radio rig. He became "the principal link between the wintering party and their families and friends on the outside." Weather Bureau meteorologist Robert Johns set up his first office in the latrine when the crowded station offered no other space. Toney did not mention that Johns was the only American of color to winter over anywhere in Antarctica during the IGY but admired how he had gone directly to a similar IGY post on an ice island north of Alaska and mourned that he died there of a pulmonary infection. Copies of correspondence to Johns's mother told of his work on South Pacific islands, as well as in both polar regions, and confirmed the high regard of his fellows. To Toney's credit, his generous prose does not betray which one of the station's inhabitants was so personally "aggravating."[34]

Toney also highlighted the "five winters and ten summers at high north-ern or southern latitudes" previously achieved by Byrd's firsters. Several would devote their futures to polar research. Two elected to spend a second winter without ever leaving the ice. Argentine-born glaciologist Mario Giovinetto would spend his second summer on an ice-deformation study near Roosevelt Island on the Ross Ice Shelf and then move to the South Pole for 1958. Seis-mologist Charlie Bentley would stay at Byrd to do another traverse, his third, during the summer of 1958–1959. Not initially planning to remain, he was held by "excitement about the work, plus a feeling that I wasn't going to have another chance. It was now or never," he thought—erroneously, as it turned out. Antarctic science would continue, and it would become his "main life's work." He would lead six traverses over the years and spend eighteen sum-mers on the ice. Besides Johns, four others would later return to polar work, two of them over winters.[35]

However the austere winter of 1957 had gone, on 30 August the sun rose momentarily, centered in a pink glow to the north. Dan Hale invited Dalton to "observe this exciting spectacle" from the warmth of the aurora tower, and over the next few days just about everyone betrayed his "exhilaration" in shoot-ing dozens of rolls of film at the distant light on the horizon. Such was the power of "this deeply primitive experience." Now that the year was drawing to a close, Byrd meteorologists could say that weather in the heart of Marie Byrd Land characteristically featured high winds, radical temperature changes, and almost continuous heavy, blowing snow. The lowest temperature in 1957 was −70.4°F in June, the high a warm 39.9° in December, with an annual mean of −17.7°. Winds, usually from the north or north-northeast, averaged 16.6 knots for the year, although the strongest gusts were 72 knots. The sun had shown in clear skies just over 20 percent of the time.[36]

Spring brought the usual digging out and camp repairs. It also brought the arrival, on 22 October, of the first of two tractor trains with much of the materiel so far done without. Air Force C-124s made thirty-three airdrops, delivering almost 430 tons of fuel and supplies between 18 October and 4 December. To land an R4D on Byrd's packed-snow runway marked only with an arrow of fuel drums, with radio contact but no ground-control approach and only one low-frequency homing beacon, was a test of pilot skill and grit. Maintenance and repair of the primitive airstrip consisted only of running a D-8 up and down its length to break down sastrugi. With no aircraft-fueling facilities, incoming planes had to carry enough gas and JATO to make it back to Little America.[37]

During the first week of November, two R4Ds landed relief personnel and naval inspection parties. Deep Freeze III commanding officer, Capt. Pat Maher, and Task Force 43 medical officer, Capt. Earl Hedblom, accompanied by reporters, had come to investigate Byrd's alleged privation. Dalton suspected that Wesley Morris, meteorologist and would-be scientific leader who had left on an early flight, had "painted a very black picture of life at Byrd Station." But radioman Bill Lowe also had access and hoped he was responsible for alerting the press to the realities. For him it had been "a very rough year with many shortages." In his memory, which confirmed Wexler's anxious tone, it had come "almost to a decision to pull us back to LA and put max effort into establishing Pole. Our scientists put up such a ruckus that Byrd stayed—but we did not get everything we were planned to have." Lowe would not have minded scarcity so much if the Navy, meaning the admiral and his staff, "had acknowledged this and given us a pat on the back—instead they tried to cover it up." When the word got out, the Navy "looked for a scapegoat and our OiC Dr. Brian Dalton found himself close to a court martial." Dalton remembered that Maher and Hedblom indicated on leaving that he would receive a commendation. (The reporters, by their questioning, were "mostly on the wrong scent," he thought, apparently confusing Byrd's problems with quite different unhappiness at Ellsworth. See chapters following.) Dufek soon arrived with his own entourage, "clearly in a bad mood." Dalton never got his medal. It would seem that if Lowe exaggerated Dufek's attitude, he had the sense of it right.[38]

By early December 1957 all the Deep Freeze III reliefs had arrived, and the DF II personnel departed. The second year, according to Bentley, was incomparably easier and smoother. The heavy construction was done (although new barracks and recreation buildings were erected, and extensive repairs were already needed because of the poorly supplied initial work and the punishment of heavy, wind-whipped snows). Now supplies were ample. With a large, conveniently placed fuel storage tank, refills could be fewer and at chosen times, with much less digging. The food cache was enlarged and improved. (Lieut. Peter Ruseski, officer-in-charge, was appalled to find grease, garbage, and signs of "occasional urination" in the old cache—not to be allowed on his watch, he vowed. Surely Lieutenant Dalton "was not aware" of this "cesspool.") A rotary-beam antenna and high-power equipment improved amateur radio performance, and just about everyone could make a weekly outside contact. There were paint and linoleum to improve the interior ambience, judo and dancing lessons, and weekly worship services led by the chief petty officer,

N. L. Carney, in one of his many contributions. The enthusiastic new scientific leader, Stephen Barnes, wrote of his coming that "truthfully, Byrd Station looked very desolate from the air." But "what an accomplishment it had been to establish the station, to improve the facility, to set up the scientific gear, and to begin gathering scientific data prior to our arrival!" Full of admiration for his predecessors, he concluded, "It is redundant to indicate that work accomplished at this location is performed under adverse climatic conditions."[39]

As Bentley put it, by the second year "even the nominal hardships were gone. We did have a pool table, we did have ping-pong tables, we had unfrozen beer, there was liquor besides Old Methusalem." There was little to build. "And another reason that things ran particularly smoothly was that there was a Navy chief there. Chiefs are what really make the Navy go." They were "of them [the men] but still with some charge over them." Chief Carney, with his "effervescent spirit, humor, and overall appreciation of station objectives," got along "marvelously" with the other enlisted men and with Ruseski, who was more of a "hard-nosed," military type. Everything worked better with a "proper type of command system." (By Deep Freeze IV, the task force was recommending that a "well-qualified CPO" be assigned to any station whose medical officer was its only officer.) But, insisted Bentley, "I didn't feel we had a bad time the first winter anyway. I certainly didn't." Still, there was "all the difference in the world" stepping in to a "running operation where things are already pretty smooth."[40]

For all that, beleaguered Byrd could claim a landmark scientific achievement months before the IGY officially began. Making their way to Marie Byrd Land in early 1957 in three Sno-Cats, Byrd's last-arriving scientists, led by Bentley and Anderson, completed the IGY's first over-snow traverse, from Little America along Army-Navy Drive. Taking glaciological and seismic measurements en route, they learned a fundamental truth about the polar continent: contrary to the beliefs of earlier explorers, who thought relatively thin ice followed the contours of a mountainous land, they found that beneath them the ice sheet of West Antarctica extended 1,000 to 1,500 meters below sea level. "In other words, if we took all the ice away, there'd be open ocean" with scattered islands. This was a "startling" discovery for Bentley; "it took quite a lot of experimentation before I actually came to believe my own results." Washington staff did not believe it. When Toney reported the traversers' findings that ice thickness under Byrd was "over 3000 meters" (about 10,000 feet; the station's elevation was just above half that), Hanessian appended "[this sounds questionable]." But Crary stood by his charges' calculations, and they were right.[41] In a few weeks' time, a few young scientists had significantly advanced the world's frontier of knowledge. And they were just beginning.

C H A P T E R   S I X

SOUTH POLE
Dropped From the Sky

Lower and lower goes the sun at the South Pole, day by day. The last ski plane will soon land. When it leaves, taking with it our last letters home . . . we shall be isolated and alone at the bottom of the world, tucked in for the six-month night. So, we'll see you in the morning.

—Paul A. Siple[1]

All of the U.S. IGY stations came forth on a barren landscape, but nowhere was the frigid void more profound than at the South Pole. About 850 miles south of the staging area at McMurdo, at an elevation of nearly two miles, with towering, glaciated mountains en route, South Pole Station could realistically be established only by air in the time available. But the heavy Air Force cargo planes could only land on wheels, which ruled out coming down on the snow of the polar plateau. Airdrops, even of tractors, offered the only hope. Only personnel and delicate equipment would, with luck, be landed on skis by the Navy's smaller aircraft. In a concentrated feat of retrieving materiel raining from the sky interlaced with the exhausting, clumsy

153

Air Force C-124 disgorging a tractor at McMurdo Sound. This front-loading design could not accommodate skis for landing on snow. Courtesy, photographer David Grisez.

steps of building in extreme cold, the Seabees pounded the little settlement into existence. Then the ice runway at McMurdo gave out.

In mid-October 1956 Admiral Dufek, back at McMurdo for the season, listened, impressed, to the nearly completed plans for winning the geographic pole, where only ten pairs of human footprints had ever disturbed the snow. Lieut. (jg) Richard Bowers, "a lanky fellow with a scraggly beard" who, wrote Walter Sullivan, "seemed the kind of practical, commonsense man who would build a community at the South Pole if anyone could," reviewed the meticulous preparations—construction plans, materials assembly and packing, delivery priorities, and personnel training. Toward Bowers's goal that his Pole construction crew know what to expect at 90° South, there were only two firsthand accounts to draw from, both forty-five years old. No doubt many of the present pioneers still thrilled, as they had as boys, to Scott's epic of "'nerve' and will and imagination" in the face of hardship and hard luck—what cultural historian Francis Spufford called his "moral triumph over the snows," wrested from his failure to achieve the real objective. But the Seabees hearkened to the Amundsen model, one in which intensive study, calculation, and practice would forestall "luck" and make success look easier than it was. Now, as he conferred with the incoming aviation, scientific, and naval leaders,

Bowers was pleased with the smooth integration of their respective roles and grateful for Dufek's assurances that the Pole was the top priority of Deep Freeze II.[2]

The first of the eight promised C-124s (Globemasters) of the 63rd Troop Carrier Wing (Heavy), 18th Air Force, flew in from New Zealand early Sunday morning, 21 October 1956. They would always take off from Christchurch in the evening to use celestial navigation as far as possible, recalled Maj. Herbert Levack, pilot and operations officer. Chosen for their range and capacity, these "freight cars that fly somewhat like airplanes" would rotate in and out of McMurdo, with four kept on the ice at once. Before beginning their South Pole (and Byrd) airdrops, each made six "round-robin flights" to Christchurch to bring in urgently needed supplies, equipment, and seasonal workers to handle McMurdo's increased summer needs and replace the construction crew going to the Pole. The planes also ferried out the year's casualties, including the recent P2V crash victims.[3]

Landings would ever be tricky. The airstrip was, Dufek wired Maj. Gen. Chester McCarty, 18th Air Force commander, "as good as conditions warrant," but he promised to "expend every effort" to grind down the worst humps and bumps "soonest." Fliers could expect fourteen-foot thickness but must "adhere rigidly" to outline markings and flags to avoid the flanking drifts and the nearby 740-foot Observation Hill. Base commander Canham recorded only that incoming pilots called the ice runway "excellent." Most of them used only about 3,000 feet of it. On the 22nd, however, a Globemaster landed "a little bit long." The pilot threw the props into reverse, but the forward wheel collapsed and the plane skidded on its nose, damaging three propellers and the main support bulkheads. Happily, there were no injuries or losses aboard, but another aircraft was on its way, past the point of no return. Ground crews had to work feverishly to remove the crippled plane from the active runway before the new one arrived. Task unit commander Col. Horace Crosswell liked the smoother surface of the alternate runway on newer ice, but, as he recognized, it was only seventy-eight inches thick and presented refueling difficulties.[4]

The arriving aircraft obviously enabled but also complicated operations. As they disgorged new personnel along with their cargo, McMurdo's population quickly doubled. At the peak in mid-November, there were 360 souls in camp. Some, like *National Geographic* photographer David Boyer, had to sleep in the chapel, some in tents, and "the feeding situation [was] almost out of control," despite running each meal in three shifts. Within the first few days, 95 percent of the men had come down with colds, no doubt introduced by the tenderfeet. As characteristically occurred in polar communities, the wintering veterans, eager as they were to see new faces and contemplate going home, had mixed feelings about the arrivals. Their acquired sense of superiority and territoriality showed in log observations like "The day's temperatures of plus ten and minus six were quite mild for camp personnel, but the majority of the newcomers could be easily pointed out for one could not see any part of their body other than clothes."[5]

Still haunted by fears, however irrational and contrary to agreement in Paris, that the Soviets would claim the South Pole by getting there first, the admiral was eager to get going. The day after his arrival, even while struggling with the aftermath of the P2V crash, Dufek and Bowers set Pole fly-in plans in place. An R5D would orbit the Pole to determine its position. Then an R4D would make an initial landing, which should, they hoped, be within a mile of the pole. Upon proving the possibility of takeoff from the ice plateau (VX-6 pilot Eddie Frankiewicz had test-lifted an R4D off the ground at 10,300 feet in Greenland with the aid of JATO), the advance party would land and take sun lines to perfect their position. Airdrops could then begin immediately and the rest of the construction crew brought in. "The Admiral gave full support to every phase," Bowers wrote in his official log, including his requests for a dog team to accompany the advance party and a quick-to-build construction camp: "He is particularly anxious to put some sort of structures up as soon as possible, in order to get our bid in for that location." For himself, Bowers felt there was "little room for tent life during an all out construction effort in cold weather." His crews could better endure "long and arduous work days" if they had a place to warm up periodically, relax at day's end, and sleep in comfort. Dufek wanted to make a trial Pole landing himself as soon as possible. "This would presumably stop the Russians," reiterated Bowers, whose several similar entries made clear the admiral's preoccupation. He put his men on twelve-hour alert on 30 October.[6]

First, however, all the aircraft had other essential tasks to do. While two R4Ds went to support the Byrd trail party, two others were charged to help establish a temporary "auxiliary" station on the ice shelf at the foot of the Queen Maud Mountains where the polar ice cap flowed around the restraining peaks in great frozen rivers. Here, ski-equipped aircraft returning from 90° South could refuel. While R4Ds had the range for a round-trip, they could more easily take off light in the cold, thin polar atmosphere. Named in advance for the massive Beardmore Glacier that Shackleton and then Scott had painfully climbed in their quests for the Pole nearly a half-century earlier, the base would also provide weather reports, relay communications, and lead search-and-rescue efforts should that need arise.[7] Capt. Douglas Cordiner, VX-6 commanding officer, flew reconnaissance flights on 24 and 25 October. A few days later, when the intended VX-6 lieutenant became ill, Canham assigned the capable Michael Baronick, the aviation line chief who had gathered and crated most of the Beardmore materiel, to set up and run the one-hut, two-tent (for storage and the generator) summer camp.

Because of weather and aircraft mechanical problems, only four men—Baronick, builder Richard Prescott, photographer Ronald Hill, and radioman John Zegers—were landed to build the isolated post. "It broke our hearts to leave those guys there; we just had to push them out the door with their gear and take off," said Frankiewicz. Their hut, having been built once in McMurdo's aviation hangar, went together "right on the money," Baronick remembered. But the main radio was still not operating, and when expected reinforcements had not arrived in three more days, he got out the hand-cranked "Angry-9" and raised McMurdo. There was palpable relief at the other end. Rescue parties had searched for the men, feared lost, but in fact, because "your compass has a hell of a deviation" near the magnetic pole, they had been dropped off at the foot of the Liv Glacier instead, more than 160 miles from their destination. A C-124 airdropped AvGas and other supplies at Beardmore on the 30th and then flew on to reconnoiter the South Pole. Trigger Hawkes radioed Dufek that they found "very rough surface conditions" on the plateau and CAVU (ceiling and visibility unlimited) aloft. Hawkes had already calculated, from the depth of Scott's footprints and his estimated weight in full gear in the famous 1912 photograph, that the snow at the Pole would support the ski-distributed weight of a fully loaded R4D.[8]

Dufek decided that 31 October 1956 would be the day to try a Pole landing. By his own account, he had offered the flight to his old friend Hawkes, "undoubtedly the most experienced and best qualified" pilot in Antarctic flying. But Hawkes, with "modesty and fairness," deferred to Lt. Cmdr. Conrad ("Gus") Shinn of "the younger generation," retaining the right-hand, copilot's, seat for himself. These two men selected the rest of the crew: Lt. J. R. ("Dick") Swadener, navigator; aviation machinist's mate John Strider, plane captain and mechanic; and aviation electronics technician William Cumbie, radioman. Dufek and Cordiner would ride as "observers," an insult to the air squadron commander's position and experience that would remain unforgiven. Denying Cordiner his rightful place in the cockpit "couldn't be justified," in Shinn's view, "and nobody tried to justify it."[9]

Beardmore Auxiliary Station being established as a weather and radio relay station and emergency landing site for Pole-bound flights. Note rough surface. This camp was actually located near the Liv Glacier, not the Beardmore. Courtesy, photographer James Waldron.

Dufek had "emphatically stated" that only Navy personnel would accompany this flight, Bowers wrote on the big day. That, in turn, affronted Paul Siple (for not the first or last time). Byrd had asked that Siple be included in the first Pole landing, but his language had been imprecise and Dufek claimed to have honored the request by sending Siple on the first C-124 flyover of the Pole on 26 October with General McCarty, in company with forty others including eight reporters. The flight was historic in that it performed the first South Pole airdrop—10,000 pounds of fuel oil and a "grasshopper," a six-week, battery-operated automatic weather station (that failed to work). Siple dismissed the eighteen oil drums as a "token salute to the future station," but it was a significant test for the experts who had developed the techniques and the packers, riggers, and drop masters who executed them. The Air Force had proved to its satisfaction, prior to any Navy landing, that it could support the mission.[10]

Later, Siple said no more about the snub but pointedly noted that no one aboard was "hardened" for the extreme weather (which Shinn readily confirmed) or scientifically minded enough to so much as "dig a hole in the ice and take the temperature." This simple act, he wrote, would have helped the scientists estimate what the winter might bring to those who would live there (though it would later take him hours to dig a pit deep enough to obtain meaningful data). Several IGY leaders were complaining that a practice landing had not been made during Deep Freeze I. Meteorologist Morton Rubin had reported back to IGY staff in January 1956 from McMurdo that "both Byrd and Siple felt that the Task Force had let IGY down," that Pole Station might be "in jeopardy." Rubin added that Dufek had promised a polar landing (or at least one at comparable altitude) that season following higher-priority reconnaissance flights but also said, "We must be practical; if we can't land at the Pole we will put the base a few hundred miles away"—another hedging of bets that only raised more doubts among the anxious IGY planners.[11]

As pilot Shinn remembered it, there had been no word on when the Pole-landing flight would take place when he went to bed late on the 30th, "bushed, tired to death" after a long day supporting the set-up of Beardmore Station. "About two or three in the morning" someone came in to say " 'You're going to South Pole at 0800' or something." Shinn thought it was a "whiskey decision, but we dragged our butts down to the ice that morning and took off." In observance of the historic occasion, Shinn took a shower but did not otherwise agonize over it beyond his usual careful preparation. Later, he could suggest only that the admiral's motive for secrecy was that he did not want Siple, of the "Byrd faction," on that plane to share the glory. Shinn thought neither Siple nor the press knew about the flight. But reporters and photographers did ride the wheeled R5D and C-124 that accompanied the ski-landing *Que Sera Sera*, and Bill Hartigan of NBC had arranged for Hawkes to use his cameras from the R4D. Shinn assumed the escort planes served only publicity, but they were prepared to help with navigation and drop survival gear to the seven if stranded—a strategy he thought almost laughable. As it happened, the R5D developed engine trouble and had to turn back, to keen disappointment onboard.[12]

By now, numerous planes had flown over the Pole, so getting there was not the Hobson's choice of gas or food that faced Byrd in 1929. It was the landing—with all the risks of a first in an environment unpredictable, though surely hostile. As Shinn clarified, "Oh, you're going to land once you put the gear down. You don't have enough power to stay in the air. . . . But the problem was, can you get off?" It was a beautiful day, the sun too brilliant to look into. The hours droned by over the flat expanses of ice shelf and ice plateau separated by a labored climb up the hundred-mile-long Beardmore Glacier. At last, after "flying a box" over the Pole to verify their position, the pilot made three successively lower passes and touched down. Despite "moderately rough" sastrugi, Shinn kept control, to the relief of the crash-helmeted passengers. He kept the engines running as Strider pinned the landing gear and rigged the ladder for Dufek and the others. They stepped out into the limitless dazzle of white, jolted as if by a body blow as the cold shocked their faces and lungs. The air blowing around them at just under ten knots was at –58° Fahrenheit. At an elevation of 9,300 feet, it was thin as well as frigid. Panting, gasping, they struggled to plant an American flag, put up radar reflectors to guide future aircraft, and photograph themselves. (The newsreel-type movie camera and several others froze.) Numb and frostbitten after forty-nine minutes, Dufek ordered, "Let's get the hell out of here."[13]

Everyone gratefully trooped back aboard and got strapped in for the real test. Shinn could not see a thing as he prepared for takeoff: "Everything iced up; we were engulfed in a cloud of ice." It was "really tricky. You'd never want to do it again." The vacuum-tube instruments in the cockpit were sluggish from the cold, so "you couldn't get a dependable reading on anything." Shinn knew that if the hydraulic systems froze, he would not be able to get the flaps up. He revved the engines, but the chilling Dakota, with insufficient power in the oxygen-poor air, stuck where it was on the dry, granular surface. He fired four JATO bottles, getting a power burst of an extra engine running wide open during their thirty-second burn. As Dufek wrote, the plane "shuddered, but did not move." After another four JATOs the aircraft "rocked—and moved forward—slowly." Then another four, and the last three. The plane bounced over the sastrugi and "staggered" into the air at sixty knots—barely flying speed. Shinn said that when "you push full throttle and nothing happens, you just start punching off the JATO till you fire them all."

Shinn compared this instrument operation with taking off from a carrier, "right out into the dark, nothing. You fly air speed and attitude. No big deal as long as you've got the air speed." They had "not much, but enough." As to options if they were still on the snow once the JATO was spent, "I don't think I thought about it." But "everything was critical in that day. Attitude and altitude and airspeed, weight and balance. We hardly stayed in the air." Those

*Admiral Dufek (left) with Captain Hawkes at the South Pole, first landing 31 October 1956,
−58°F. Still in crash helmet, worn by all for the uncertain landing, Dufek is carrying the ice ax
it took to plant the flag in the hard sastrugi. The R4D's engines were kept running, but even
with JATO, takeoff was marginal. Photograph by John R. Swadener. Courtesy, Marc Swadener.*

circling in the Globemaster saw only a huge cloud of billowing snow streaked
with smoke and flame (from the firing JATOs) and feared an explosion. Shinn,
who credited his competence and confidence to good training and experience,
thought later that it had been foolhardy to attempt the landing when it was
still so cold and the men so unacclimatized, but he would go on to make
numerous successful Pole landings.[14]

Dufek rejoiced that no Communist flag greeted the Americans' arrival at
the Pole, but he returned from his harsh exposure ill with pneumonia and
decreed that station building be delayed until the weather warmed up—at
least a week or two. "Disturbed" by this decision, Wexler cabled him "urging
quick resumption of plans." Bowers, who wrote in the log that he expected
Pole construction to begin "tomorrow or the day following," was shocked, his
crews crestfallen, almost insulted at the admiral's insinuation that they were
not up to the challenge after their long months of preparation and training.
Dufek's staff centered their concerns on aircraft performance in extreme cold,
but Bowers still felt stung: "Why say the men cannot work at minus fifty degrees? We can. It is the equipment that failed." Then, on 4 November, "the

props were kicked out from under the Pole Station personnel as everything came to a screeching halt." The Air Force took all its planes, the ailing admiral, and four Pole crew members (apparently selected by lot, no one in the advance party) back to New Zealand, the latter for "ten days R&R." The rest of the camp, blurted the steady Bowers, "immediately fell apart at the seams." Conferring before Dufek's departure, Bowers focused on the collapse of morale. His men could prevail over the cold and altitude, he insisted, and "walk out with the dogs if necessary." Reemphasizing potential mechanical, not human, deficiencies, Dufek regretted not including the advance party on the first flight. But his position was neither frivolously taken nor unreasonable. And he knew where the blame for disaster would lie.[15]

Bowers determined to make the most of the delay, including a rest for the "keyed up" Seabees. In "low gear" they reviewed every detail, deciding, for example, that if any one of the three initial planes—the two R4Ds carrying the advance party and the supporting C-124—was turned back, the rest would go on: "It is imperative that we get a foot in the door." While the order of the early supply flights "must be rigidly adhered to," Bowers thought the others could be more loosely dictated within general priorities to "fill up the odd spaces" and allow the most efficient use of weight and volume. He gave that decision-making authority to chief Bill Hess at McMurdo, who would not hesitate to inform even the admiral once of the flight order of loaded planes after a white-out lifted. By 6 November, though, frustration had again set in, as Siple (who titled his chapter on these weeks "Waiting at the Altar") relayed rumors that the task force might try to locate Pole Station somewhere farther north and that VX-6 might not have enough planes to support the operation. Bowers felt better when Frankiewicz told him the aircraft would be available by the 15th, after supplying essential aviation gasoline to Beardmore.[16]

Members of the advance party were told on 12 November to load the aircraft on Wednesday, the 14th. As they met on Tuesday to "thoroughly" check their equipment, Bowers found morale "growing rapidly." Perhaps betraying his own inner turmoil, though, he noted that "the atmosphere was pleasant, but behind each person's face existed a downright apprehensiveness." They were going to spend two months as no one had before, "erecting a camp at that Godforsaken place." Still, they were ready and determined: "None of them have stars in their eyes." But the Pole builders did not fly on the 15th—or the 16th, 17th, or 18th. Atmospheric conditions had caused a communications blackout. "The delays are cutting the construction time down to nothing," Bowers fretted, knowing that after mid-January the weather was likely to worsen rapidly.[17]

About this time, perhaps unaware of the imminent flight plans or not trusting them, meteorologist Wexler applied "some rough temperature calculations" for the ice plateau to his worries about South Pole prospects. Factoring incoming solar radiation and outgoing terrestrial radiation from the snow, he figured that from Dufek's 31 October temperature of –58°F it would take about two months of maximum sunshine to reach a temperature of –4°, but after the summer solstice, with the sun descending, it would take only one month for the temperature to return to that low. Wexler implored IGY executive Hugh Odishaw to use these numbers to "urge Admiral Dufek to start his pole station operations as quickly as possible so that construction can be completed and scientists and their instruments installed before *really low* temperatures appear." Of course, his calculations could have been "greatly improved" had Dufek taken a meteorologist on his Pole landing.[18]

Finally, at 1700 hours on Monday, 19 November 1956, the two overloaded R4Ds took off for the Pole with their eight passengers, eleven dogs, and survival cargo. Dufek, just back from Christchurch, flew with Colonel Crosswell in the accompanying C-124, which carried the first load to be airdropped—a Weasel, POL (petroleum, oil, lubricants), rations, sleds, and other basics. As the aircraft began their forty-five-minute climb up the awesome Beardmore Glacier, sucking twice the normal amount of AvGas, tributary glaciers on either side loomed above the relatively low-flying planes. Bowers noted that the dogs "behaved well" but "showed a little discomfort" on the long, "breathtaking" ascent to 10,000 feet. He did not comment on the men's reactions but betrayed his own. Observing below the wild jumble of yawning crevasses, "just as Scott reported," he penned, "How Scott made it manhauling is hard to imagine. Literally, it looks as if it would be impossible." Could he make it?[19]

Not long after midnight on Tuesday the 20th the two planes bounced in, discharging their contents among the sastrugi while their engines whirred. "Working in the prop wash was one cold experience," Bowers remembered. The R4Ds had to "blast off with all of their JATO to get moving again" but were quickly gone. The moving dots on the snow watched them disappear with private thoughts, then quickly got to work pitching the tents, retrieving the dropped gear, and trying to figure out where they were. Using a precision theodolite to take a series of sun lines, Bowers learned they were eight miles from the Pole, which confirmed the difficulty of navigating at the extreme latitude. They would have felt better about this distance had they not just discovered that the transmission housing of the dropped Weasel had cracked; the oil had leaked out, and the batteries were inoperative. They went to bed in the sunlight "exhausted, some with minor cases of frostbite." It was a beautiful, bright day, twenty-nine below with light winds.[20]

The next day began at six when Herb Levack's Globemaster appeared overhead to drop the requested Weasel repair parts, which Bowers gratefully recorded as "an excellent example of the cooperation rendered." Then, at about 0800 they heard a thunderous rumble and felt a "tremor so great that all personnel sprang from their tents thinking that the C-124 had crash landed adjacent to the camp." But outside there were only "miles and miles of nothing." Siple later explained that the "snowquake" was caused by surface snow dropping into hollow layers underneath. Levack had gone on to the actual Pole to drop fuel and lumber, the latter by intentional free-fall. Perhaps the concussion of its hitting the snow had created the collapse, which then propagated outward like dominoes. "Underneath me is caving in? Forget this!" thought radioman Monty Montgomery. It was an unnerving start to a venture of sufficient anxiety without surprises.[21]

But everyone kept going. Dog handler Jack Tuck, Montgomery, and aerographer Jerry Nolen harnessed up the animals and took off to retrieve the drops. Unfortunately, by some mistake the replacement batteries had fallen free; their impact made a crater almost six feet deep. Only one of the four was still usable after the men dug them out. Mechanic John Randall worked all afternoon out in the open to install the new transmission, but they still could not drive the Weasel without more batteries. So on 22 November, Bowers, Tuck, photographer Bill Bristol, and radioman Dale Powell got up at 0115 for a "jaunt" to true 90° South—the one time the dogs would earn their seal meat, pulling about 900 pounds of gear. For the four humans it was a "grueling" hike, which they completed at about 1100. The snow had been "beastly soft," making it difficult to walk, and they all suffered headaches and breathlessness from the lack of oxygen. Bowers was eager to get there because more airdrops and more builders were due by 1700. He wanted them landing at the Pole, not eight miles away. Some cargo arrived, but no personnel came that day or, thanks to bad weather, the next two. The advance party set up their tents and flagged the dropped cargo but could do little more until the Weasel and more workers arrived. They did find some "goodies"—hamburger, apricots, juices, and crackers—which they "put to good use."[22]

Finally, on Sunday, 25 November, two C-124s flew over with more deliveries, including Weasel batteries and Air Force technical sergeant Richard Patton, who parachuted in at the eight-mile camp. Bowers tried to discourage this

The first tent camp at the South Pole, a tiny, fragile outpost on the vast polar plateau. The tethered dog team observes the advance party's activity. Photo by Donald Scott. Courtesy, David Grisez.

unnecessary risk, but Patton, dressed in "all the clothing he could pile on himself," jumped anyway. He carried Bowers's supplies card file (duplicating sets maintained by the Air Force load planners and chief Hess) to coordinate the airdrops from the Pole drop zone. Competent and willing, he would also work to reduce parachute malfunctioning. It was –25°F when Patton left the aircraft at 1,500 feet by "nylon elevator," but he landed without mishap and drove in to the Pole with Montgomery, Randall, Nolen, and hospital corpsman Floyd Woody in the resuscitated Weasel. They arrived at about 2200.[23]

By then the construction camp materials had been dropped, and ten more Seabees were on their way. Landing at about half past midnight, the builders immediately turned to on the first 32- by 16-foot Jamesway. "Tired as we were and cold," wrote newly arrived Charlie Bevilacqua, builder chief, and "starving to death for some air," as Slats Slaton, chief mechanic, put it, they kept working until the hut was "up and a stove in. So our first nite at the Pole we had a fairly warm and comfortable place to live." "It was a wonderful feeling to show some progress," wrote Bowers, seeing some payoff for all the prior effort. Completing the hut by 0800, the crew, now numbering nineteen, had breakfast and "turned in for a well deserved rest." By 1300 some of them were up: "It was too hot to sleep in the Jamesway, which is ironic to say the least." Outside it was about thirty-five below zero.[24]

Construction gradually became more efficient, although Bowers had to remind his workers, "even as good as they are," to have patience and respect for the harsh environment. The Seabees put up a tool tent and a two-hole-head tent (which they called the "Blue Grotto" for the intense color of the snow beneath the fabric canopy—so beautiful they took pictures). Nolen began systematic weather observations, and Slaton, Bowers's "straw boss," and his crew endlessly retrieved airdrops. An eagerly awaited D-2 tractor floated down under an umbrella of four huge parachutes on the 27th, landing unhurt on its side. This vehicle, saltwater damaged after being left in an ice crack at McMurdo, had been written off and stripped for parts. But during the winter Slaton essentially rebuilt it, prominently lettering across its back "THE WILLIAM JOSEPH," his youngest child's name. If he was not retrieving drops or grading a construction site, Slats could invariably be found on the D-2 smoothing the primitive airstrip ("Ike's Pike") with a drag fashioned from a drop platform. Getting home to his family was much on the mind of this tireless Seabee who had made his own way in the world from age ten. The men soon finished another, larger Jamesway, into which all but Bowers moved. They partitioned the first hut to provide quarters for Bowers and Siple, the rest to become the radio shack, medical office, mess hall, and galley. Everyone was now settled in "comfortable spaces." "Morale was so high" Bowers wrote on the 27th, that "each washed and had a beer or so."[25]

Siple flew in on 1 December, followed by the last five construction crew members. Tuck, whom Bowers described as "quiet, introspective, smart, highly motivated," had agreed to winter over as Pole's military leader. He returned to McMurdo for a bit of relaxation before hunkering down. Although it was "very warm—only 15° below at noon" according to Bevilacqua, the day was overcast, poor for flying. Both R4s "had to be talked down a good part of the way, using the VHF homer." Siple was glad to be there at last after a week of weather postponements or "boomerangs," when flying conditions deteriorated after takeoff. He had wanted to accompany the advance party, but Bowers insisted he wait until they had established adequate temporary housing—a solicitousness that made Siple feel like a "delicate fossil." Indeed, Bowers took seriously the welfare of the famous polar leader twenty years his senior, and Siple endured being mother-henned with good grace. The two formed a warm bond of respect for each other's expertise. Soon Siple began to dig a deep pit to take snow temperatures at descending levels. Calculating from these, he (correctly) predicted winter temperatures of minus 100 degrees Fahrenheit.[26]

Laying floor panels atop close-spaced foundation timbers for South Pole garage. The below-grade foundation will keep all rooflines at the same level, which Paul Siple correctly predicted would forestall heavy drifting. Photo by Richard Prescott. Courtesy, David Grisez.

With the construction camp completed, the workers tackled the permanent station. They excavated enough snow (about two and a half feet for the powerhouse) to keep all the rooftops level, as Siple had requested. He believed the same blizzards that would likely bury the station to the "eaves" would blow the unvarying roofs clear. (In spring's returning sunlight, he would smugly observe "virtually no snow on the flat roof of the camp proper.") Then came a slow period waiting for building materials, especially the first-needed foundation lumber and floor trusses, punctuated with other disappointments and uncertainties. It was glum news at the Pole, for example, when two Globemasters within three days misjudged their landings at McMurdo and suffered for it; one was "a definite strike." Bowers worried whether the Air Force would continue the drops. "This wreckage represents a lot of cold cash," he wrote on 30 November. Meanwhile, critical materials "streamed in"—that is, their parachutes failed to open. Or the quick-release mechanism intended to disengage the chute from its pallet when hitting the ground (so the load would not blow away) tripped high in the air instead. Such free-falling pallets slammed into the snow with enormous, often destructive force. Siple lamented the loss of a set of irreplaceable, never-found encyclopedias and the year's supply of tomato

An airdrop of fuel, four drums per parachute, over the South Pole. Crews are preparing to splice trusses that had to be cut in two to exit a C-124's dropwell. Official U.S. Navy photograph. MCB (Special), Report DF I & II, vol. VI.

juice that, sans parachute, spattered blood-red over the snow. Airdropped scientific gear also took its share of stream-in damage.[27]

Crew members salvaged what they could, Bowers radioed McMurdo for replacements (playing havoc with Hess's prior delivery priorities), and they all made do, working around missing items or cobbling substitutes. Bevilacqua, for example, used broken panels and even cardboard to insulate the floor of the garage-powerhouse building. His crew cut the shroud lines off parachutes to use the nylon for tunnel covers. "The big white ones cost $1200, and the green ones $800 each," he noted, impressed. "They are costing Uncle [Sam] plenty because they are all over the place."[28] Twice, during communication blackouts—another recurring problem—Hess boarded the C-124 and flew with the goods so he could confer with Bowers while circling overhead. All the rest of the lumber—24,000 pounds—arrived on three Globemasters on 5 December, but two bundles of roof trusses streamed in, destroying fifteen. "This will hurt us," wrote Bowers, who knew they had only fifty-six. But, he gamely decided,

"We can get along with thirty-eight plus or minus." They could frame some of the roofs with timbers. Bolting the halved trusses back together was clumsy work with either frozen or clumsily mittened fingers, but an assembly line of sorts made it go faster. Hess liked to say in adversity, "Let's do it the Seabee way," meaning whatever ingenious jury-rigging offered itself. "I have a lot of respect for those Seabees, I really do," said Hess, who was not one of them.[29]

If even the calm Bowers found it "somewhat discouraging" when on some days stream-ins seemed to outnumber properly parachuted bundles, no one faulted the skill or diligence of the Air Force. The 63rd Troop Carrier Wing was selected for its Arctic experience. Pilot Levack, like others, had flown C-124s along the DEW Line. Flight crews were practiced in high-altitude, low-temperature drops with different weights and parachute types. But there was no book to go by for the massive scale of the South Pole operation and the significantly colder temperatures. For example, no one had anticipated the heavy contrails that formed on nearly every pass over the Pole, which severely reduced visibility for the drops and took a relatively long time to disperse in the generally light winds. Arctic flyers knew grid navigation but also had to learn the southern sky for their long over-sea flights and to use "every possible method" of navigation—celestial, radar, sextant, and dead reckoning.[30]

At McMurdo, the Air Force made every hour of the short, split season count. Everyone put in twelve to fourteen hours a day, seven days a week—fliers during the day, maintenance workers at night. The aerial-port personnel worked around the clock in shifts, reloading the Globemasters as soon as they returned, for takeoff again the following morning. Using two heavy-duty sewing machines and "a vast quantity" of heavy nylon webbing, they modified parachutes and rigging to meet on-the-spot needs. Crews reinforced drop platforms for heavy, critical items like generators and vehicles. They saved materials by clustering smaller or lighter loads under a single parachute but added ribbon chutes to pallets of fuel drums after too many broke open on impact after a free fall or got buried—up to twelve feet deep. Experience taught them to band bulk lumber by size rather than weight and in relatively small units for successful free fall (though they broke apart anyway, "scattering all over the place").[31]

At the Pole, Bowers fit construction around the airdrops. With the season short and the weather always iffy, he wanted the planes flying whenever conditions allowed it: "If we knew there was a plane in the air, we were up to receive it, drag the airdropped material off the drop zone, and while we were up we'd build something. And then when we got real tired, we'd go to sleep," to start over when the next plane came, usually in the early afternoon. If there was no flying, the Pole crew might get "maybe twelve, twenty-four hours straight construction." At other times "we'd go maybe a day or two where we would do nothing but handle material." This flexible system worked well—until the ice runway on McMurdo Sound fell victim to dangerous melt holes in mid-December (see Chapter 5). With just over half the job done (about 400 tons of materials, supplies, and fuel dropped in forty-two sorties), the C-124s had no choice but to evacuate to New Zealand to await safer ice. They also needed more fuel, still en route on the *Nespelen*.[32]

Fortunately, materials and supplies were sufficient for the moment, and the construction crews were, in fact, exceeding their self-imposed deadlines. Siple was impressed with the "CB's." The half-dozen builders, he wrote, "could prepare the foundation and assemble a whole building in approximately two days." On their heels came the utility group to install the stoves, ductwork, plumbing, and electrical circuits. Meanwhile, "a small hardy team of four men and the D-2 tractor and Weasel did all of the drop retrieving and snaking the items into position for the builders." By Siple's account, between 3 December, when the first foundations were laid, and the 15th, the shells of the garage, head, mess hall, science building, and inflation shelter were up and the generators installed. Within another ten days the superstructures for the rawin-sonde dome and aurora tower were built, as were the major fuel caches and tunnel system, and the first eight builders were gone.[33]

Siple's miscellaneous fourth group "handled food service, radio, meteorology, first aid and photography." Montgomery and Powell spent days digging holes to anchor the rhombic antennas. "We'd dig, eat, sleep, go back and dig, eat, sleep. That's awful hard snow," Montgomery recalled. "You didn't do a lot of playing in the Pole." Until the radio setup was completed (on the 18th), they kept four schedules a day with McMurdo on the Angry-9. Woody did the cranking so Montgomery could key the messages. When the main Navy transmitter streamed in, the Collins ham radio gear was a godsend. Better yet, they could use voice. On 2 December Montgomery contacted McMurdo "QSA-5," Bowers's log noted—radio lingo for loud and clear, strong and reliable. It made everyone "feel great," and except for needing to adjust the carburetor of the four-kilowatt generator, Pole had a good communication system. Monty beamed: "You've got the whole world. It's all yours, you know?"[34]

On 6 December Captain Cordiner landed a P2V at the Pole with some cargo too delicate for airdrop. But he was unable to take off again, and the eight-person crew spent the night—and then another when the plane crew found a frozen fuel pump in an engine. Cordiner slept in "VIP quarters" (Bowers and Siple's space), while the others bedded down in the newly completed and heated head. Even with sixteen bottles of JATO, the plane had a "very hair-raising run down the full length of the two-mile runway" before getting airborne. The P2V, in Bowers's mind, was "overrated."[35]

The longer stay did give Bowers and Cordiner an opportunity to consult on plans. They decided to begin delivery of the remaining non-airdrop material and the wintering personnel by 20 December—by R4D, Bowers pointedly noted. To conserve flights, each return trip would carry out a few construction workers. (This plan was delayed until the 25th, however, when the Dakotas were pressed into desperately needed support of Byrd Station.) Cordiner wanted all hands back at McMurdo by 15 January, which would not displease the hardworking builders who by Bowers's calculations would be a proud month ahead of their estimated schedule. Of course, that could not include the additional barracks building Siple had fought for; its ship had not yet arrived at McMurdo. The industrious Slaton lost no time in grading and stacking fuel barrels so the tunnels could be built around them.[36]

On 13 December, Bowers called a happy hour: "The men have worked unceasingly since their arrival and deserve this small break in routine." Siple recorded another, perhaps more urgent, reason for the time-out. Rumor (untrue) had it that the Deep Freeze I veterans at McMurdo would fly out by C-124, but the Pole workers would come out too late to take advantage of this speedier transportation home. Morale sank accordingly. The next day Bowers "regarded as sort of a partial holiday." No planes were scheduled, and altitude-exacerbated effects of the partying were widely felt. Still, by day's end electricians had finished wiring the mess hall, builders had completed the inflation shelter and science building, and utilities men had heated it and connected the snowmelter in the powerhouse to the newly installed generator's exhaust. Nolen, with yeoman Bob Chaudoin's help, had sent up the first weather balloon on the 10th; Chaudoin, with Nolen's help, began canceling the nine bags of philatelic mail. Some remaining tasks, such as interior finishing and materials storage, might be better left to the station's long-term inhabitants anyway, so Bowers pushed to get as much outside work finished as possible. When word came that there was enough AvGas for two more airdrops, Bowers made a careful list of needs, but what came on the first flight was so ample that he canceled the second, deferring to Byrd's more critical need for fuel.[37]

On the 14th, as his contribution to morale, Siple saw to the erection of the South Pole flagpole on the roof of the garage. The IGY's Howie Wessbecher at McMurdo had charge of producing the bamboo pole ("my only claim to fame down there"). He selected a straight length, painted it barbershop style as directed, and made a collar at the top to which Siple could attach a sixteen-inch mirrored glass ball he had purchased in New Zealand. Before the pole was whisked off to the plane, just about everybody, including the admiral, autographed it "for good luck." Oddly, the well-photographed pole was a spiral of black and orange, not Dufek's vision of red and white candy stripes (as often symbolized the North Pole). For that, Bevilacqua would blithely take credit, having made sure that only those paints were at hand. Orange and black were the colors of his high school in Woburn, Massachusetts—a private triumph. Siple hoped the silvery ball, glinting in the sun, might beckon airborne visitors as well as cheer those in camp. On the 20th, Bowers organized a ceremony to transfer the flag from the first hastily erected flagpole to this one. A group photo also marked this event, the first time they had all gathered in one place.[38]

Siple, who for a month was the only scientist and civilian at the South Pole, felt like the outsider he was. The Navy men's jargon and insider jokes were "bewildering," their language "absolutely unprintable." He watched the construction with a mix of fascination, admiration, and horror. When an expected box of plumbing joints could not be found, the utilities men completed the head using "makeshift" fittings and plenty of brazing; no one enjoying his first shower criticized the aesthetics. Lacking a crane for lifting heavy roof panels, a D-2 driver merely pushed a snow ramp up the side of the hut; when the job was done, he bulldozed it away. "These Navy men, mostly Seabees, could certainly make the chips fly," Siple wrote approvingly for *National Geographic*. "But," he lamented in the next breath, "the chips lay where they fell." Mindful of the Seabees' work conditions and harsh deadlines, he still abhorred their careless wastefulness. Seeing a potential use for "every chunk of wood, every stitch of canvas, every length of wire," he followed the workers around to collect, sort, and store their freely tossed debris. He ended up with a sizable stash. His scavenging amused the men, but, commenting later, Bowers called Siple "not overly fastidious" but simply opposed to waste, as "any prudent person in the Antarctic" would be. Over at Byrd lived at least one Siple soulmate. "They're wasting a lot of what could be valuable stuff by burning scrap and garbage," wrote Vern Anderson. "As I see it, everything we have out here is potentially usable for our survival, wood, insulation, crates, drums, rags, parachutes, and harnesses—all the ordinary junk."[39]

With three planes expected on 24 December to evacuate the first crew members, Bowers decided to celebrate Christmas on the 23rd, with holiday routine on Christmas Eve. A well-lubricated party lasted until 0800. They had a tree, and Chaudoin remembered singing carols around the kitchen stove as if it were a fireplace. On the eve, Montgomery raised radio amateurs in New Jersey and New York, the first stateside connections from Pole. That afternoon a P2V and two R4Ds arrived, delivering nondrop IGY gear (there was no room for passengers). Eight construction workers flew out. Christmas Day, with everyone back at work, brought the worst storm yet—persistent, northerly winds with light snow all day—though "nothing compared to the blizzards experienced in McMurdo." Bevilacqua recorded a "beautiful sight"—a "rainbow around the sun with two arms sticking out and big glow on horizon." Siple called this spectacular double halo his Christmas present. Bowers, Slaton, and Bristol talked to their wives by ham radio, gifts of great meaning. Others relayed hamgrams. (A few days later, in an oddity of polar communication, the Pole radiomen, who had been unable to work McMurdo, sent their messages via ham Jules Madey, who could read both stations from New Jersey.)[40]

Memories vary on the date, but probably on the early Christmas, with the strain of the unremitting work beginning to tell, a small group of besotted Seabees staggered into the mess hall to continue their holiday celebrating—at three in the morning. Bowers, with Siple asleep at the other end of the small Jamesway, asked them to lower their voices. Slaton exploded. Where else could they go for recreation, why didn't the officers sleep someplace else? he bellowed in "good old Seabee language." The disrespectfulness of the outburst forced the young officer to consider sending his chief out on the next plane. Slaton was scheduled for early departure anyway, by Canham's request, but this would have been an ignominious end to a stellar performance. To his credit, the blustery Slats appeared in the morning with a forthright apology. Bowers, relieved, showed the leadership and grace to accept it fully. By then the frank, honest mechanic "felt pretty lousy" about the incident, though he allowed that he would have said the same thing—more politely—had he been sober.[41]

Throughout this period Bowers had been taking sun lines—about 120 altogether—to refine his location of the Geographic South Pole. On 23 December he towed a small plywood "house" built on an airdrop platform to where he thought the Pole was, about 0.4 miles from the station at 125° Grid East. But this structure would require several more moves, puzzling Bowers. He finally discovered an eyepiece mounted slightly askew, but there were many corrections to make for factors such as altitude, pressure, and temperature that also could have affected precision. On New Year's Day 1957, Tuck placed in this "observation shack" a time capsule provided by the city of Peoria, Illinois, home of the Caterpillar Company. The capsule, to be opened in the year 2000,[42] was a cylinder for a D-8. Bowers hoped the stars of the winter night would give a more accurate fix, and Siple and Tuck did take a series of star shots using a

South Pole Station, nearly completed. The tunnels, to be covered with chicken wire, then burlap, will enclose and bisect the camp, providing storage for fuel and other supplies and protected passage for humans. The empty space, center-left, will hold a late-ordered Clements hut, yet to arrive. Note the level rooflines. Courtesy, photographer Donald Scott.

precision theodolite during May and June, but they too had difficulties with accuracy. No matter how carefully they tried to shelter and steady the instrument, vibrations, winds, fluctuating temperatures, and a "very complex thermal path" distorted their readings. Palle Mogensen, scientific leader in 1958, took his own star shots with different findings, and both Siple and Tuck later independently revisited their data and methodologies, with still different conclusions. Today, Global Positioning tells us exactly where the Geographic South Pole is, although its marker migrates with the moving ice sheet.[43]

On 29 December 1956, after being lost in the air for more than two hours, the first eight wintering people arrived, including Lieut. Howard Taylor III, medical officer, and Tuck, officer-in-charge, returning with Bravo, a sled-dog pup born at McMurdo. Intended as a camp pet, Bravo would ever be Jack's dog. Unknown at the time, these would be the last arrivals for many unsettling weeks. The next day their departing counterparts briefed them, Bowers having carefully retained representatives of every trade—except for the single electrician Harold McCrillis, who would board the return flight. Thus, for young incoming electrician Ken Waldron, called "Junior," the transition was necessarily "instant." He remembered having perhaps thirty minutes with McCrillis, who told the gasping newcomer, "Don't talk. Listen. You need to breathe. He told me what he thought I should know and what he thought I could hear" in that interval. The arrivals were briefed on immediate expectations (snowmelter duty, for example) and set about creating their own interior spaces. Chester ("Chet") Segers, the new cook, prepared his first meal in the permanent galley on 2 January 1957.[44]

Bowers left with the last seven builders on 4 January 1957, after a ceremony in which he handed over the station to Tuck's keeping. The young engineer had had a "very satisfying" experience, beginning with the respect and attention the admiral himself had accorded his judgment. In forty-five days of a planned sixty, all involved had gotten in and out without loss or injury and completed their job. "We had time to throw away," Slaton "gloated," equally proud. The team had constructed seven major buildings, with an extensive labyrinth of burlap-covered tunnels connecting and enclosing them all. They had been lucky, too; the weather had been remarkably fine. Having anticipated working at −35°F routinely, they found that to be the low instead. One day the temperature rose to zero; the average was about −5°. Relatively few days had been blustery or unclear. Bowers thought the men worked more efficiently at the Pole than at the warmer but windier McMurdo. Still, no one would ever fathom how chief Slaton could stay out all day with only a sweater over his underwear and shirt while everyone else huddled in their parkas. Bowers later emphasized, in acknowledging the "motley appearance" of his comfortable crew, that "what is correct in clothing for one man is not correct for another," apparently having had to argue against enforced uniformity.[45]

Admiral Dufek rattled the nine new Pole pioneers (Siple still another minority "civilian" in another "too Navy" society) by decreeing that no more personnel would be brought in until enough food and fuel were on hand to last a full year. In fact, the passengers aboard the just-arrived planes had had to disembark, replaced with eight tons of edibles. As always, Dufek focused on the establishment and safe maintenance of the base. Worrying about its functioning as a science station could come later, in his view, and he made IGY equipment, except that to be built in by the Seabees, the "last categories of priority." Back at McMurdo, Wessbecher unhappily revisited his lists of science materials to adjust his priorities for worst cases. On 6 January 1957 Dufek tried to ease IGY anxieties by inviting Wessbecher to dinner. He emphasized the Air Force's commitment to completing the airdrops and promised that VX-6 would carry what food, people, and equipment it could. Wessbecher pressed for a pledge that VX-6 would fly until all ten tons of the supplies essential for a full science program were delivered, but that was asking too much. The next day Dufek lunched with Canham and Bowers, reiterating in the name of safety his focus on food first, then men, for Pole—and after that the same for Byrd. Only if the C-124s could return—because only they could deliver fuel in essential quantity—would he then approve equipment and construction material to support the science programs, followed by additional fuel and food to stock a two-year supply at each base.[46]

Somehow, three more scientists found passage. Weather Bureau meteorologist Edwin Flowers and his assistant, John Guerrero, an "aloha-shirted" electronics maintenance specialist, landed on the 7th, and National Bureau of Standards ionospheric physicist and magnetic observer Willi Hough came in on the 8th, making a total of eight military men and four civilians. The new men, with Siple, fretted over the fate of their IGY studies and tried to reorganize themselves to cover the basics, but they knew they could not possibly manage a full scientific program. Still, the fragility of their situation obvious, they uncomplainingly gave half of each day to heavy camp labor, despite prior understandings to the contrary and their keenness to delve into their own projects. In the latter they gladly accepted the assistance of Dr. Taylor, for a science team of five. Tuck organized the Navy contingent for general construction, tractor driving and bulldozing, food service, utilities, and radio and called everyone's cooperation "nothing less than outstanding in all respects."[47]

An anxious month later, Wexler, the scientists' unwavering champion, seized on the lopsided makeup of the Pole contingent and the possibility of no more Air Force supply missions to urge Dufek to authorize one more R4D flight—to bring in the remaining IGY people and evacuate a like number of Navy support personnel so the food supply would suffice. It did not come to that. On 9 February an ecstatic Wexler learned that a Globemaster was on its way from Harewood and, better yet, that it would load immediately to take off for the Pole. What was more, Dufek, "in a good humor" over ice-expert Assur's good work on the runway and the obligingly colder weather, invited him and Gould to accompany the flight. On the 11th, Pole meteorologists began making official surface weather observations, another source of gratification for the exhausted, exuberant scientific leader.[48]

Less than two weeks of nonstop flying finally assured the futures of both inland stations. Three and occasionally four airdrops a day became the norm at Pole, in addition to as many as five daily at Byrd. They were not without problems. The first C-124 over the Pole on 10 February brought precious personal mail, Siple wrote, but heavy film also in the mailbag tore it open and scattered the contents over "at least a square mile of the landscape." The men scurried after it for hours. Later, construction materials for Siple's awaited barracks building (to replace one Jamesway) were dropped in. But the parachute with the trusses did not disengage and, billowing in a brisk wind, kept on going along the ground. It was soon lost in a "murky ice fog." Following the path of the heavy load through the snow was easy, but Tuck and Hough had to give chase for twenty-five miles before their Weasel caught up with the wayward bundle. By the time the drops ended on 21 February, Pole had received 250 additional barrels of diesel fuel, a third thirty-kilowatt generator (an emergency spare), more food, and the critical science equipment. In sixty-four sorties from McMurdo to Pole, the Air Force delivered altogether more than 730 tons of cargo in almost a thousand bundles (Byrd received 230 tons in eighteen trips, mostly fuel, and Beardmore got 27 tons). The Air Force claimed that 94 percent of the total tonnage was recovered on the ground, a remarkable accomplishment given all the stream-in losses.[49]

In the end—far more than Byrd Station—Pole got what it needed, although it, too, had to make do sometimes with scrap lumber, "minimal construction methods," and improvisation. Siple's want list was relatively short and noncritical. A variety of small-scale stocks of plastics and metals and electronic components would have been handy for "instrument building and general gadgeteering." He would have liked, for example, to make an automatic time-lapse attachment for the IGY movie camera to study snow drifting and crystal growth. There were too few typewriters and only one electric calculator after the first one, marked "hand-carry only," streamed in. Siple came to yearn for a sewing machine, especially to fabricate items from the parachute nylon he had salvaged. (The next winter radioman Stanley Greenwood, presumably machine equipped, would earn the nickname "Betsy" for sewing parachutes into curtains to give the movie screen a theater-like atmosphere.)[50]

On 12 February 1957, at last trusting the station's viability, Dufek sent in a ski plane with the remaining five IGY scientists, Navy builder Thomas Osborne, and a young construction mechanic, Melvin Havener, to replace a re-injured Seabee. South Pole finally had its full complement—eighteen men and one dog. The scientists were four meteorologists and one each for seismology, ionospheric physics, glaciology, and aurora and airglow observation, plus Siple. The newcomers brought the news that on 23 January the military and scientific brass—Dufek, Gould, Wexler, Crary, senior wintering naval officer Capt.

E. W. Dickey, Byrd by long message, and others—had gathered at McMurdo, attended by Marines in full (not winter-worthy) dress, to dedicate the South Pole station. They named it Amundsen-Scott South Pole Station to honor the Americans' only predecessors at that singular spot. No one at Pole was invited to participate in this event, not even by radio. No one even knew it was occurring. The rudeness, the "ignominy," flabbergasted Siple. In fact, those who were living the test were not officially notified—by the Navy, the IGY, or anyone else—until nine months later when, on 26 October 1957, Lieut. Vernon Houk, the incoming Navy leader and medical officer, arrived with documentation. "It was nice to know that President Eisenhower and others wished us well for the past winter night," Siple wrote, with understandable acid. According to the Navy report, Tuck expressed a similar sense of insult.[51]

Back in Washington, the name of the station had remained up in the air almost to the last minute. Some of the affected nations' diplomats (New Zealand's embassy was mistakenly not officially contacted) seemed less than keen on the choice, but apparently they worked it out. The State Department arranged for Norwegian and British representatives to attend the ceremony. In any case, Wexler knew at least by the 18th via Gould that the Pole's dedication "may be held at McMurdo" (and Byrd's at Little America) "because of possible difficulty in returning from the S[outh] P[ole]." If the venue made sense, the lack of communication and courtesy did not. It appears the harried, overworked leaders simply dropped the ball. No one ever explained the oversight.[52]

There was little time for sulking at 90° South, however. After the airdrops concluded, Pole's pioneers knew they had a scant month to get "buttoned up" for winter. Winds were already stronger, temperatures colder—from –30° progressively down to –60°F. All hands turned to on the supplemental barracks building. The mostly amateur crew got it built in two days, taking frequent turns inside to warm up, and quickly divided up the personal spaces. Pole's inhabitants would enjoy ample elbow room. They added sections of the now-dismantled Jamesway to the original one to create a "community sitting room." Responding to Siple's enduring concern for fire, the men moved the remainder of the large Jamesway 200 feet upwind from camp, where they re-erected it as an emergency shelter. Filled with extra sleeping bags, cots, clothing (some left behind for that purpose by the departing construction workers), a stove and fuel, and concentrated foods, the shelter could have kept them alive "(most uncomfortably)" for several months. In fact, at least twice, heater malfunctions ignited small fires, but fortunately they were doused by nearby dry-powder extinguishers and quick thinking. The men also finished the aurora tower and rawinsonde dome, barely before dark.[53]

Dignitaries line up to speak at the dedication of Amundsen-Scott South Pole Station at McMurdo, 23 January 1957. Official U.S. Navy photograph. Mogensen, SSLR, Pole 1958.

In early February Siple, Taylor, and the IGY men present began hand digging a 1,000-foot tunnel, using the cut-and-cover method, to connect the camp to the seismic and geomagnetic pits. Their boards for supports were not long enough for the desired height, so they tried a snow-compaction technique developed by the Army in Greenland to build up footings using the snow already dug out. South Pole snow was too loose and dry to make a snowball, but if colder snow two to three feet below the surface was mixed with warmer surface snow and tramped down, the layers would "cement together" to "amazing hardness." In a day, the banks they built up, against forms made of old boxes, were hard enough to walk on. They then set in vertical two-by-fours to create a uniform height with the buildings and built overhead support of scrap lumber covered with burlap. Observing the success of this approach and the D-2's difficulty dragging the runway smooth after the winter's sastrugi hardened, Tuck would recommend future use of snow compaction on the Pole runway.[54]

Toward late March, when the ailing D-2 could no longer be coaxed out into the deepening cold to gather snow for melting, Siple suggested digging a snow mine—a tunnel high and wide enough to work in that would function both as a source of clean water and a deep pit for glaciological studies. Everyone took at least one two-hour shift in the snow mine every week, where the temperature hovered at around –60°F. By the following November they would dig, at an 18-degree slope, 90 feet down and 270 feet forward through ice so increasingly hard it had to be chopped with an Alpine ax. Using a coal scoop they loaded the ice chips into salvaged parachute bags and thence onto plastic sleds. Mechanic Havener devised a winch from odd parts to bring the snow sleds to the surface, while electrician Waldron lighted the long passage, using coffee cans for junction boxes when regulation supplies ran out. The wire became so stiff and brittle in the cold that he had to prefabricate the connections and cut manageable sections in the garage. Chopping and moving about 600 pounds of ice an hour each, the men would eventually haul out an estimated 10,000 to 15,000 cubic feet of snow, which yielded 50,000 to 75,000 gallons of water. Today, a well drilled deep into the ice supplies the South Pole with nearly effortless water. At depth, a hot-water drill melted an initial bulb of water, which is contained, insulated, and kept pure by the surrounding ice. Circulating exhaust heat from the power plant keeps the water liquid, and pumps bring it to the surface as needed. But showers are still limited to two minutes twice a week.[55]

As night grew imminent, Siple received a personal blow, learning that Richard Byrd, his mentor and lifelong friend, had died on 12 March 1957. He lowered the battered flag to half-staff, where it remained until taken down at sunset on 23 March for the long winter. The following Sunday he led a memorial service for Byrd, the station's first religious observance. With a hint of bitterness, Siple would note on 26 July that Admiral Dufek had been appointed officer-in-charge of the Antarctic Projects Office, making clear that Byrd's position had been primarily titular. Moreover, he, as Byrd's deputy, received not a single official communication about the appointment. It was a difficult time. The sun spiraled slowly downward. For days before it finally disappeared "you could see the sun just sort of rolling around the horizon," recalled Arlo Landolt, aurora observer. Then, as the earth's atmosphere refracted the sunlight, it would appear above the horizon a while longer—and even after that, because of valleys between far-distant mountains, a spike of light would now and then appear in the sky. After sundown there would still be twilight for several weeks, but it grew so bitter that no one wanted to be outdoors. By 23 April full darkness had descended, to last four months.[56]

Indoors, everyone had jobs to do, and routine slowly developed. The scientists wrestled their apparatus into shape, and the Navy men struggled to keep ahead of the inevitable problems of station maintenance while also assisting the science efforts. For example, it was proving a challenge to keep the three Plexiglas domes in the aurora tower from frosting up and obscuring these light shows of the polar night, which were spectacular by mid-April. When the temperature differential between the domes' inner and outer surfaces could be 150 degrees, it would take two energy-costly heaters and six fans to deny the frost a berth. In the late fall months, the combination of being productively busy but no longer pressured and out in the cold kept morale high. So did a few zanier pursuits. Siple twice tried hydroponic gardening, but "a dense growth of fungus" made short work of his quickly sprouted seeds. Doc Taylor invented a Rube Goldberg-esque "insomnia-meter" to record sleepers' movements, which surely kept them awake. Ed ("Moose") Remington, deeply committed to natural resources, puckishly organized a South Pole chapter of the Izaak Walton League to look after local flora and fauna, a commitment that would not overburden its members. Then midwinter came and went, with the usual gastronomical indulgence and relief that the ordeal by dark was half over. "June was ushered out and official IGY ushered in by a fantastic dull-red aurora that glowed like a luminous red fog about us," Siple noted on the 30th.[57]

Weather phenomena could be counted on to stimulate more than the four meteorologists. While snowfall was uncommon, showers of minute ice crystals frequently created a magical sparkle in the air. Winter winds were stronger and more persistent than in summer, but the worst gusts were "only" forty-seven knots—relatively benign for the polar continent. In the wee hours of 12

May the thermometer dipped below minus one hundred (–100.4°F) for the first time; the men ran outside to *feel* it. A total eclipse of the moon stirred excitement on the 14th. Everyone trooped out again in late August, Siple wrote, at –90°, to photograph a "picture book crescent moon just above Venus." Indeed, when it was already excruciatingly cold, it was disappointing when the mercury did not go below the hundred mark. It was far more satisfying and hardly more uncomfortable to break a record than hover near it. On 18 September, a few days before sunrise (in fact, they saw the sun, just below the horizon, in mirage), came the year's coldest day, a world record to that date: –102.1°F. By comparison, the following year twice boasted a low of –101.7°F (19 June and 19 September) and a balmy high of +5.5° (12 January), although the thermometer stayed above zero for only six hours all year. Sunrise was, of course, a major moment of any Antarctic year, nowhere more than at Pole where the winter night lasted six long months. Benjamin Remington, who wintered over in 1959, having also wintered at Little America in 1957, recalled the "fantastic feeling" of having the sun up (once up, staying up, spiraling ever higher until midsummer). Beyond euphoria, there was an "indescribable" something "deep within you." Nothing else would change much at Pole for awhile, "but, just to have the sun, you know it's there and it did come back and boy, the world was right, I'm telling you."[58]

Siple and Tuck and the other leaders of the Station Council—scientists Flowers and Hough and Dr. Taylor—made a concerted effort to keep the isolated group engaged and content. One conspicuous success was the production of a yearbook, the "first book written and 'published'" at the South Pole. This warm and informative record of the lives and work of the first year's citizens featured portrait photographs of them all. The alert, mostly broadly smiling faces show young men proud to be where they were. Each contributed a one- to three-page autobiography, including Bravo, who recorded his lineage, favorite modes of mischief, and shortcomings of "the Boss" (Tuck). The men's stories, many of them humorous, revealed widely varying backgrounds. Some were farm boys who had gone to one-room country schools, one grew up in New York City, and two had enjoyed Ivy League educations. Military service had already played a large part in many of their lives, including the civilians. Two planned to complete their careers in the Navy. Five anticipated graduate school, two hoped for college. Two-thirds of the group were in their twenties; Siple, at forty-eight, had twelve years on his nearest contemporary. Nine of the men had fathered a total of seventeen children, including McPherson's four. Half were single, two divorced. Five, including Siple, came with previous polar experience, the others all in the North.

The yearbook also included layman's explanations of each of the scientific programs—what they were trying to accomplish, why the work mattered. The scientists discussed their respective instruments, procedures, and problems and acknowledged those who had helped. Glaciologist Remington, for example, paid tribute to the snow-mine diggers who enabled him to photograph inch-thick slices from snow blocks cut in descending sequence to give a "picture story of the ages spent in building the polar plateau." Each Navy man correspondingly shared what he did. Waldron described the usefulness of by-product heat from the generators, which melted snow, dried clothes, heated nearby buildings, and warmed bodies—those of machines and their own. The seventy-page record closed with a list of forty-four U.S. amateur radio operators who had provided "faithful and friendly aid" in connecting them with their families. The self-styled "Pole-cats" showed they cared about one another. Many said so, and they all included their stateside addresses, some with invitations to visit.

The yearbook and the time it took to assemble it demonstrated and undoubtedly strengthened the bonds binding this unique group; the leaders were wise to encourage the effort. Siple noted in his "Historic Forward" that he had previously met only four of these IGY participants and did not know most of the rest even by name—a recipe for trouble, according to conventional polar wisdom. Yet this was "undoubtedly the most pleasant and smoothest" of his four winter nights on the ice. Tuck agreed. In his Deep Freeze report he pronounced the first winter "highly successful," thanks to the excellent cooperation between the scientific and military communities. The inevitable "rough spots" had been fewer than expected, none serious or long-lasting. They seemed a good group with good leadership. Although both the younger Tuck and the long-experienced Siple had resisted dual command, they had worked exceptionally well together. Moreover, they encouraged the others to do the same, and "almost without exception" they had.[59]

As the sun lightened the sky, even before it was visible, the winterers quickened their pace in anticipation of the coming transition. News came on 11 September that the U.S. Navy had reestablished the Beardmore facility, key to landing Pole flights. A "misshapen" sun rose fully on 22 September, and the next day everyone gathered to raise the flag and celebrate one more solar victory. Within the station Segers impressed Siple by getting the food supply "in perfect shape" for his relief, "without even a suggestion from Tuck." The scientists' lectures became summaries of their year's work and were taped to facilitate final report writing. In early October Siple and Tuck took time to place empty fuel barrels in a 200-foot circle around the South Pole, to include any presumed error and spin-pole motion. On that windy, –70° day, "the boys" sent out coffee to warm them, but their beards were so iced up they could not get a cup to their lips to drink it. They heard that Admiral Dufek had arrived at McMurdo on the 12th.[60]

Five days later the mail finally arrived, and morale soared. Everyone started packing amid a "burst of beard shaving." On 26 October the first plane landed, piloted by Cmdr. Vernon Coley, the new VX-6 commanding officer. Also aboard were the plane crew, five Navy reliefs led by officer-in-charge Houk, and a few others including the first two members of the press to reach the Pole, Tom Abercrombie of *National Geographic* and Oregon newspaper reporter Rolo Crick, who had won their places by lot. Those not wintering over planned to stay an hour and a half. But it was almost sixty below when the P2V landed, and its starboard engine blew an oil gasket during an attempted warmup for takeoff.

The hosts scrambled to find beds for the sixteen marooned visitors, even using the emergency Jamesway. As day after day passed, the veterans began calling their guests "The Men Who Came to Dinner," after the title of a film that expressed their ambivalence. As Landolt put it years later, innocent questions and suggestions felt like criticism, and "our family, everything was changed, broken, *everything* . . . then, by golly, you knew it was time to go home." In fact, the plane and most of its passengers would be grounded for six weeks awaiting an engine change. The newcomers brought welcome fresh milk, salad vegetables, ham, eggs, and fruit but also colds, which quickly spread through the entire station despite hurriedly administered flu shots. Water grew short, especially with few healthy hands to help in the snow mine. The new arrivals worked as willingly as they could, but besides being sick they lacked the endurance of those with a year's acclimatization. At least the overlap period gave those departing time to orient and train their counterparts, which had not been possible for everyone a year earlier.[61]

Airdrops began, but the first ones did not include spare parts for the needy Weasel and D-2, which were essential for hauling materials in from the drop zone. So Havener and the new chief mechanic, Gerald DuBois, cannibalized the spare generator and got the tractor running. On 10 November a C-124 dropped a new D-2, which proved a spectacular disaster. First came the blade on its own pallet to reduce the weight of the tractor. Inexplicably, the packers had also loaded on, but not fastened down, the disassembled steel tractor treads—two-foot-long plates weighing twenty-five pounds apiece. They came loose and fell free, like bright orange "confetti." Everyone scrambled to retrieve these critical components—no easy task, especially if they sliced into the snow instead of landing flat. While the men were still digging, the tractor on its platform spilled out of the Globemaster's dropwell, about 2,000 feet overhead. Tumbling instead of falling straight, it cut through the shroud lines of its three 100-foot parachutes and hit the snow at full velocity "like an exploding bomb." One flying crash pad hit Flowers's head, fortunately breaking only a tooth. At the bottom of a crater 10 feet deep, the wildly churned-up snow gave no evidence of the tractor. Days of digging finally revealed the mangled wreckage, beyond any hope of salvage. (Later, another D-2 and a Weasel landed successfully.)[62]

Dufek ordered three Pole veterans to come out on the first R4D, which would fly as soon as the temperature rose to –50°F. That aircraft took off from McMurdo on 7 November, but halfway up the Beardmore Glacier an engine failed, which necessitated not only returning to the Beardmore auxiliary camp (now confusingly called Liv Station) but also jettisoning the cargo, including tools and parts for repairing the stranded P2V. Finally, as their replacements arrived, small groups of winterers departed—a bittersweet time. Cliff Dickey walked out to take a photograph of the tiny, now nearly buried outpost. Carefully including his footprints in the frame, he thrilled to think he was probably the first human in history to stand where he stood, overcome by the thought that he had spent a year at the South Pole. Palle Mogensen, Siple's relief, arrived on 20 November, and Jack Tuck left while half a dozen members of Congress flew over the Pole, signaling its future as a permanent U.S. base. Tuck had sadly left Bravo behind, thinking he would be happier where he had always been, but Mogensen and Houk wanted their own puppy, so Bravo flew out with Siple on the 30th.[63]

All in all, it had been a rewarding year, but the scientists, having endured the long winter, wanted to stay the summer to continue the work they had "come to the ends of the world" to do. The weather was "perfect" at last, sunny and less than twenty below. They resented being pushed out by interlopers who did not understand or appreciate their important work or the culture they had created. During this period of fragile emotions, a "well-meaning" IGY project director sent a message cautioning Willi Hough, "as he would a child," to remember to leave behind all IGY-owned books and scientific material. This "unfortunately worded" message precipitated one of the worst morale crises of the year. Angry and protective of his young charges, Siple wrote to Odishaw that those at home had "no comprehension that these dedicated boys here have given a year of their life for science." They were not just "hirelings for masterminds at home."[64]

Siple knew it would be a long time before the maiden year's scientific results were fully understood, but other achievements perhaps rightly eclipsed science for now. He topped his list with the technological triumph of building a viable community at the bottom of the world. (Dufek might have added the political and emotional coup of getting the United States there first.) This bold, even "reckless," endeavor had required "thousands of people" and a hefty price tag. Waldron, appreciative, remembered Siple's calculation that it cost "a million dollars for putting each one of us at Pole Station." The risks to life had been "uncommon," but thanks to good preparation and mindfulness of lessons learned the hard way by their few predecessors, they had known a "relatively comfortable" year, despite an average temperature of –55°F and six months of darkness. And they had made a solid start on the IGY—as were their counterparts around the continent, including those at three more far-flung sites whose origins were as shaky as their own.[65]

CHAPTER SEVEN

THE GAP STATIONS
Hallett, Wilkes, and Ellsworth

*It's just so fantastically beautiful and pure, and no
sign of humanity—we are the only living
things around that are human.*

—Gilbert Dewart, 1957[1]

The remaining three U.S. scientific stations appeared rather belatedly
in IGY planning for the Antarctic. Widely scattered along the coastline of the polar continent—Cape Adare, the Knox Coast, and the
Weddell Sea—they were all justified by the desire to fill geographical
"gaps" in scientific coverage, although political considerations did
not escape organizers' minds. All three were established by icebreakers escorting thin-skinned cargo ships that incurred severe, even
threatening ice damage in the process. Finding a suitable, approach-
able landing site proved a sobering challenge for all three, and alternative choices were required. Summer's clock nearly ran out on them,
especially the latter two. None kept the name it started with.

Hallett Station was the smallest U.S. IGY enterprise; only fourteen would winter over the first year. Tucked in the shadow of the majestic Admiralty Range, it was beautifully sited. "Of all the magnificent and other-worldly vistas to be viewed in the Antarctic, there is little doubt that Cape Hallett is the most breathtaking," wrote Cmdr. Price Lewis Jr., Deep Freeze IV skipper of the icebreaker *Staten Island*. What became Hallett was the last American, and the only shared, scientific station to emerge in the planning. The subject first came up at the Second Antarctic Conference in Brussels in September 1955 when President Georges Laclavère asked the United States and New Zealand to consider jointly running a station at Cape Adare, the northwestern-most point of land defining the Ross Sea. The two parties agreed, confirming their final cooperative arrangements following the Third Antarctic Conference in Paris in August 1956.[2]

Both countries stood to gain from this unique bilateral arrangement. The Americans were eager to build an emergency airstrip at this closest landfall from New Zealand, and cooperation would reinforce acceptance of U.S. intrusion in the Ross Sea Dependency, New Zealand's claimed sector (although the United States pointedly declined to recognize any such rights and New Zealand was the least assertive claimant). New Zealand would get another Antarctic station to its credit, with someone else furnishing the bulk of the money, materiel, personnel, and logistical support—all much needed given the small nation's limited resources. Here was, wrote historian G. E. Fogg, a "not-too-expensive and face-saving way both of making some assertion of its sovereignty and meeting its obligations both to the Trans-Antarctic Expedition [see Chapter 8] and IGY."[3]

To promote goodwill and the mutual benefit on his way south in Deep Freeze I, Admiral Byrd made a show of expressing U.S. appreciation for ongoing use of staging facilities in Christchurch and of seeking indulgence for the U.S. presence at McMurdo. He promised the prime minister American generosity in turn. Admiral Dufek would earn gratitude and affection among New Zealanders for his personal role in providing material assistance and promoting cordial relationships, which that country's IGY leaders want remembered today. In October 1956 the U.S. National Committee for the IGY sent McMurdo-bound staffer John Hanessian Jr. to Wellington and Christchurch for numerous counterpart planning meetings, which further smoothed the way for future dealings. The group members began working out details of data collection, analysis, dissemination, and ultimate disposition of the permanent records. They also productively discussed personnel selection, joint public relations, and administrative relationships for the Cape Adare station, whose site would be especially important for surface and high-altitude meteorological observations.[4]

Meanwhile, just after the Brussels conference and almost a year before the scientific community completed its plans, the U.S. Navy had hastily assembled in Davisville a survey unit, Detachment G of the MCB (Special), to accompany the soon-departing Operation Deep Freeze I. The last of its orders was to locate and survey a possible site at Cape Adare for a small weather base and an "auxiliary airstrip on land, snow or ice." After seeking, without success, a site for a permanent runway on land at Cape Royds, whose apparent volcanic soil proved only a thin layer over solid ice, and the Taylor Dry Valley, which was too narrow for safe maneuvering, the detachment split in early February 1956. One unit deployed on the *Edisto* to examine the station potential of Cape Adare. (The Knox-Weddell unit proceeded west on the *Glacier* on a similar mission, as discussed later in the chapter.)[5]

On 6 February 1956 the *Edisto* anchored amid drifting icebergs in Cape Adare's Robertson Bay, surrounded by "jagged cliffs that rose straight from the sea." The large, inadequately sounded bay spelled danger for ship movement, so "Det Golf's" Cmdr. John Koleszar and representatives of the *Edisto*, Task Force 43, Air Force, Smithsonian Institution, Hydrographic Office, press, and IGY boarded an LCVP (personnel landing craft) and a Greenland Cruiser (double-prowed surveying vessel) to explore the coast. After four hours in wind-driven water that encased them in frozen spray and rolled their small boats like icebreakers at sea, they had to return to the ship without finding any place to land. A few days later a similar group attempted to go ashore where the northern party of Scott's last expedition had wintered, not far from Borchgrevink's first-ever wintering quarters of 1899, now in ruins. But their motorized whaleboat broached on the beach, throwing everyone into the frigid water. Unable to refloat the boat, the officers finally took shelter in the 1911 hut, building a fire from wood and coal left at the two historic sites. After they dried out, a few of the men were rescued by helicopter, but the rest had to trust an exposed rubber life raft when rotor problems grounded the aircraft.[6]

With Cape Adare thus unwelcoming, the *Edisto* proceeded southward along the coast for sixty miles, finding promise at Cape Hallett, named by Capt. James Ross for his purser on the *Erebus*. Dodging icebergs, the same officers landed safely on 11 February on a small teardrop-shaped spit of land (later called Seabee Hook) that was almost cut off by a frozen lagoon at the base of the rugged cape. Setting out on a calm, clear day under a "blazing" sun, the surveying party scarcely had time to lay out a baseline before a sudden, furious snowstorm sent them scurrying back to the ship. Others managed to leave a cache of emergency supplies. An attempted landing by LCVP on Svend Føyn, in the offshore Possession Islands, also met with a broaching and (with no helicopter) a cold, precarious night on the beach. IGY meteorologist Morton Rubin remembered that "no food had been brought. No radio. No tent. No water. Nothing." With no fire or means of making one, all they could do for warmth was keep walking, according to Koleszar. Antarctica's lesson on carrying survival gear—always, everywhere—was well learned, but little else was. On this paltry information the decisions for base building in Deep Freeze II had to be made. Before leaving Cape Hallett, "[T]he Commanding Officer claimed the area ["Edisto Acres" in the ship's report] for subdivision into lots for all present. Ample evidence of the claim was left." It was "just a little fun thing," laughed oceanographer Bill Littlewood, who "owns" one of the lots. But the impulse to acquire U.S. territory had obviously not abated.[7]

The nine ships returning to the Ross Sea for Deep Freeze II rendezvoused in mid-December 1956 at the edge of the pack ice, where the Coast Guard icebreaker *Northwind*, escorting the *Arneb*, peeled off, bound for Cape Hallett. There, at latitude 72° 18' South, longitude 170° 19' East, Seabees were to construct the IGY station still called Adare before the ships moved on to establish the Knox Coast base. But as Wilkes Station scientific leader Carl Eklund wrote to his wife, Harriet, from the *Northwind* on 19 December, "Just as we were about to move in—whambo—a message from Dufek saying proceed immediately to McMurdo Sound . . . to bring them *our* two D-8 tractors." While sympathetic with the need for heavy equipment to rebuild McMurdo's failing ice runway, Eklund (less than accurately) opined to Odishaw in Washington that "it appeared to me that priority for establishment of the South Pole Station had been placed far in excess of the situation that existed, since most of the drops had been completed." Understandably protective of his own program, he complained, through his friend and task-unit commander Capt. Tommy Thomas, to the admiral as well. The delay would probably cost them ten days to two weeks, he chafed, although the Antarctic veteran had to admit to looking forward to seeing Mount Erebus and getting mail. With heavy fog and strong currents choking their previous channel through the pack, the ships did not reach McMurdo until 23 December. They stayed until the 27th, the *Northwind* helping to ferry in cargo from ships moored farther out in the sound.[8]

Arriving back at Cape Hallett on the 29th, officers and scientists went ashore and agreed that the low-level but protected point identified a year earlier would do for the station site. However, they found the open land overtaken by a vast Adélie penguin rookery—at least 200,000 birds (half a million by some estimates). The Deep Freeze I visitors, arriving just two weeks later in the season, had encountered only a few molting Adélies, and a light snow cover apparently masked their occupation. Without hesitation, the Wilkes-bound scientists, led by ornithologist Eklund, simply "relocated" several thousand of the small, comical creatures to make space for construction, "carrying the half grown young and herding the protesting adults" beyond the base site. To keep them there, they built a fence of mosquito netting conveniently (if inexplicably) found onboard. The penguins' overpowering odor remained, however, and Eklund thought "no one should ever begrudge the 'hardship' pay earned by the Adare Station group! One has only to visit a penguin rookery to appreciate this!"[9]

Although he had anticipated off-loading from ship to shore across the sea ice, Lieut. Raymond Loomis, engineer and officer-in-charge of the construction detail, found the route riddled with grounded ice, melt holes, and pressure ridges. It would not support heavy vehicles. So he settled on using the *Arneb*'s six LCMs (amphibious landing craft). The *Northwind* broke the ice as close in to the beach as it could, and a detachment of underwater demolitionists prepared to blast out the rest.[10]

A ferocious storm on New Year's Eve interrupted this work and soon threatened the entire operation. The *Arneb* found itself pinched between the fast ice (affixed to shore) to which it had been moored and "huge masses" of pack ice grinding northward "under the influence of the northerly current, an ebbing tide, and southwesterly wind," the task force reported. "Fighting desperately" to guide the cargo ship into the lee of the cape, the icebreaker took ice damage to its starboard propeller, with a loss of power and progress toward the more vulnerable vessel. Around midnight, *Northwind* reached *Arneb*, relieving the pressure just as the latter's frame was beginning to buckle. Amid growing fears of engine-room flooding, Wilkes-bound Navy photographer Paul Noonan overheard the captain conferring with the "exec" about abandoning ship. It was "taking on tremendous amounts of water." In his pictures of the all-out pumping effort, it looked "like a waterfall going over the side." (The hull ruptures and wrinkles would prove patchable, although seawater damaged some goods in deep holds.) The next day the icebreaker narrowly rescued the *Arneb* from colliding with one of several huge grounded bergs set free by the storm, while back in Washington, IGY staff learned of these perils with fears for the two U.S. science efforts bound to these ships. And so it went until 3 January, when the weather finally moderated.[11]

But the ill winds had blown some good. The gale had pushed enough ice out of the bay to enable the ships to stand into safe open water. The *Northwind* broke out the remaining fast ice to within a few hundred yards of shore, and the demolition unit completed the job, allowing the LCMs a clear channel to

Hallett Station showing boat landing ramp (center foreground) and the "penguin-proof" fence made of fuel barrels. Official U.S. Navy photograph. Courtesy, Al Raithel Jr.

bring construction equipment and material in as far as grounded ice that could support vehicular traffic. Also gone in the wind, however, was the flimsy fence, and about half of the displaced penguins had returned. This time the Seabees built a more sturdy enclosure of two-by-twelve timbers laid on edge two high and secured by stakes; again they evicted the natives. Finally, though, to return the borrowed timber to the ship, they made a barrier of closely spaced fuel drums. That was not entirely penguin-proof either. By 1960 the fences were gone, and the penguins were allowed to "walk among us," Hallett's scientific leader Robert Thomson remembered. One day that October the men heard a tapping at the door. Thomson opened it to face three Adélies, who walked in, waddled around squawking conversationally at their astonished hosts, and after awhile stood politely by the door to take their leave. Was this a social call? A scouting of the camp before the rest of the colony returned a few days later?[12]

For a week, with help from ships' crews, cargo streamed off the *Arneb*, pulled to the shore supply dump from the landing craft with Traxcavators (track-mounted front-end loaders) towing either Athey wagons (maneuverable dump trailers on tracks) or higher-capacity rubber-tired trailers. Either worked well on Hallett's mostly bare, rocky volcanic ground. Loading the trailers right into the LCMs for direct hauling away from the beach avoided additional handling, although it took care to unload everything for Adare but nothing intended for the Knox Coast. Helped by lessons learned in Deep Freeze I, the work went smoothly, although the supply dump soon had to be moved to higher ground when high tides and wave action began to carry off stray boxes. By 9 January 1957, with crews working "twelve on/twelve off," supplies were organized, basic structures up, and communications working. Unlike the quickly buried camps on snow that had to make do with skylights, the citizens of Hallett would enjoy windows in their huts. Remarkably, they would withstand winds of 114 miles an hour without even becoming pitted from airborne volcanic gravel. But wind-driven snow would enter through the tiniest pinholes and "persist for days."[13]

The ships departed early on 10 January, leaving Loomis and about thirty Seabees to finish the base. By the time the *Atka* picked them up on 12 February, they had completed four main buildings to provide for berthing and medical care, cooking and messing, meteorology and communications, power generation, vehicle maintenance, and science. Assorted smaller units housed the latrine, spare generator, hydrogen generator, balloon-inflation shelter, darkroom, radio homer, and refrigerator. In addition, there were a seismometer hut, two non-ferrous huts for geomagnetic measurements, a rawin dome, and an aurora tower—all familiar IGY structures. Space would always be a premium at Hallett, however, inspiring ongoing new construction and reconfiguring of existing forms. The Seabees also laid the foundation for a small building in which to produce and store water, which the wintering party could complete from spare Clements panels. It was already clear that obtaining water would be a challenge. Snow cover, the usual polar source of supply, was neither continuous nor clean at Hallett thanks to relatively mild weather and the resident wildlife. At first, meltwater from a glacier about a mile away promised water for the hauling, so crews set up a catch basin and piped the water downslope to a tank on an Athey wagon for transport to storage tanks. But that system depended on above-freezing temperatures, so for winter two evaporators were set up in the water building for fairly reliable melting and purifying of sea or glacial ice.[14]

A brief commissioning ceremony on 9 January left Lieut. Juan Tur, medical officer, in charge of the wintering Seabees and Dr. James Shear, a University of Kentucky professor of geography with a master's degree in meteorology, the

Displaced Adélie penguins in their rookery just outside Hallett Station. Rounded Jamesway huts in left distance, flat-topped Clements huts to right. Official U.S. Navy photograph. Courtesy, Al Raithel Jr.

leader of the other three scientists, all New Zealanders. If the second year's experience was valid for the first, the fact that the tiny outpost was international was "hardly ever thought of." When the Yanks and Kiwis talked about differences, "this was all done in much the same manner as if we had been two states in the U.S," wrote the 1958 scientific leader Kenneth Salmon, a British-born New Zealander trained as an electrical engineer. Shear maintained that morale remained high, but he did note "a distinct feeling on the part of a minority that we were a forgotten group and one or two uttered the sentiment quite frequently." Hallett issued only two press releases all year, though, Shear reported, citing that "not much happens in a small station." Perhaps it might have sent more reminders of its presence. "Irascibility," unsurprisingly, increased during bad weather, especially high winds. In June the station endured a two-week blizzard, fortunately its only long one all winter. At this relatively northern latitude, the dark period lasted only from mid-May through mid-July. The year's temperatures ranged from a December high of +40°F to an August low of –44°F.[15]

Hallett might have been a little too small to be fully effective, both in physical plant and manpower. The scientific leader had no desk space of his own. The galley and mess hall (doubling as the movie theater), official communications and ham shack, and weather office shared one building, with the attendant cooking odors, noise, and confusion. When the latrine proved too crowded to house either a chute for the snowmelter or the darkroom, the latter went to a corner of the science building, which in turn bumped science space already crowded because the three other scientists moved in there to "relieve congestion in the barracks." And the lone radioman, who had to do everything done in teams elsewhere, was clearly overburdened. The station's name was not officially changed from Adare to Hallett until May 1957, the brink of the IGY. G. W. Markham, secretary of the NZ IGY, kept dallying, lukewarm to a U.S. proposal of Ross Station (too British, too much used) and unsure if "any useful purpose would be served," but Dufek became insistent on avoiding geographical confusion at least.[16]

While a chief purpose of Hallett Station was to maintain an emergency runway for incoming flights, the airstrip Loomis, initially surveyed on the ice of Moubray Bay, was never used. By 19 January 1957 seaward ice movement rendered it unsafe. The following October, however, resident Seabees laid out another, six miles from camp, and on 1 November the first R4D (of an eventual five) followed the oil-drum markings and landed safely, bringing fresh produce and mail. On this plane was Kim Lett, a construction driver who, after wintering at Little America, volunteered for the earliest intracontinental flight (3 September) to help plow McMurdo's ice runway and was now bringing hydraulic equipment to help repair a tractor and remain as summer help. With no coring capability at Hallett, no one knew exactly how thick the snow-free bay ice was, but what worried the young Seabee was its wind-polished slickness. He had to scramble for his crampons just to remain upright. The plane, too, had about "zero braking traction." Later, as Lt. Cmdr. Harvey Speed— "probably the premier flyer that we had down there"—fought to take off, he would, with great difficulty, line up the aircraft with the runway, but the brisk wind would "swing him right on by the nose." After several tries, "as they swung through, when they hit the direction he wanted to go, they fired the JATO bottles, and that straightened him out and away they went." Later visitors to the Hallett hamlet included press from McMurdo, Admiral Dufek with New Zealand IGY representatives, and polar-flying pioneer Sir Hubert Wilkins, who came in mid-December with an eight-man New Zealand geological survey party. By late December the runway was thought unsafe except for emergencies; its useful season would be short.[17]

The following spring, however, saw more than enough aircraft excitement. On 9 October 1958 the stir over the arrival of the season's first penguin was "completely eclipsed" by the emergency landing of an R4D because of sudden blizzard conditions at McMurdo. And shortly after that, four C-124s returning from Pole and Byrd airdrops were similarly diverted northward, the radar and lights of the R4D helping guide them all in safely. Fortunately, Hallett's sea-ice runway, marked only a few days earlier, offered 8,000 feet of clear ice in any direction. As Salmon wrote, they suddenly had "something like 65 people to feed and accommodate (as against our normal 16), nevertheless, they were all fixed up, although some had to sleep in some peculiar places." The euphoria of being "on the map at last" was cruelly burst just one week later when a Globemaster en route to McMurdo from Christchurch slammed into a mountainside thirty-five miles to the north while descending to airdrop supplies and mail. Six aboard were killed. When the weather finally cleared, helicopters flew in from McMurdo to effect a difficult rescue of the seven survivors. Investigators later blamed the crash on inadequate maps and navigation error caused by receiving false radar returns. But all this was yet to come.[18]

The ships departing from Cape Hallett on 10 January 1957 did not, in fact, proceed toward Wilkes Land as scheduled; rather, the admiral ordered them once again to McMurdo. Eklund was "about fit to be tied!"—over the "navy in general, and Admiral Dufek in particular." "This time," he wrote his "Dearest," "he has to 'inspect' the *Arneb* before deciding whether it is fit to continue around to Knox Coast! That's only another 800 miles out of our way." Two days later, able to count and band a large number of skuas en route—a good start on the dissertation he hoped his year would yield—the usually upbeat leader was more himself. But Eklund was not alone in his worries. "We were getting afraid," remembered Wilkes-bound seismologist Gilbert Dewart. All the "back and forth" and helping at Hallett was eating time they needed to build their own station and prepare their scientific programs, "and of course we had no idea what we'd encounter when we got over to *our* sector." At McMurdo, crews heeled the *Arneb* over by swinging heavy equipment over the opposite side, to bring the makeshift repairs done at Hallett above the waterline. Dufek then permitted the *Arneb* to go on but ordered the damaged *Northwind* to Christchurch for a new propeller. However, with Ross Sea operations nearly finished, he assigned the *Glacier* to the Knox Coast task group as a "substitute" and added the *Greenville Victory* after crews from the detoured ships helped off-load its McMurdo cargo. So in the end it was a larger, more robust flotilla that cast off to the north and, beyond Cape Adare, westward to East Antarctica, bound for the coast south of Australia.[19]

But troubles and delays were not over. After breaking a path through the pack for the northbound cargo ships on the 15th, the *Glacier* reversed direction to escort the *Curtiss,* with its southbound IGY leaders and wintering scientists. In transferring mail and cargo between ships, the icebreaker's last working helicopter "flipped into the sea" when it struck the bow of the *Curtiss* during an up-swell. The pilots were rescued but not the helo, which meant there would be no air reconnaissance for the work ahead. The task group rejoined on the 22nd but first had to rendezvous with the *Kista Dan*—an Australian-chartered Danish ship—to transfer fuel, some Australian scientists, and American polar meteorologist Glenn Dyer of the U.S. Weather Bureau, who was accompanying the Australians to Mawson Station.[20]

Finally, the trio of ships could target its own destination, Vincennes Bay, named for Charles Wilkes's expedition flagship, which had explored the coast along what was now known as Wilkes Land. After Operation Windmill's scouting, the *Atka* had cruised nearby in early 1955 and filed a reasonably favorable report. And the fact that the Soviets had planted their large Mirny Station (over ninety winterers) 500 miles farther west made the site a compelling political choice. The Russians, too, wanted their history remembered; *Mirnyy,*[21] the name of a ship of Bellingshausen's 1819–1821 expedition, meant "peaceful," if wary westerners knew or appreciated it.[22]

When the second unit of the Deep Freeze I Seabee survey team aboard the *Glacier* arrived to assess the area the previous autumn, in March 1956, the Soviet station had been officially running for a month. After being turned away by impassable ice in numerous locations, the icebreaker had nosed into a low spot on the ice barrier a few miles east of the Windmill Islands (actually along the Budd Coast, not the intended Knox Coast), on the bay's western flank. Following reconnaissance by air, Cmdr. A. F. Meeks, the unit's officer-in-charge, along with various scientists, set out on 19 March by LCVP and Greenland Cruiser to survey a tentatively identified station site. Civil engineer Lynn Cavendish took off with a ground survey party of three enlisted men—surveyors C. D. ("Bob") Hadley and T. W. Maines and demolitionist J. W. Herald—to lay out an access route along the rim of the clear blue-ice barrier.[23]

Almost before the men in the three scattered groups noticed a gray cloud approaching along the horizon, they were hit with a blizzard of such sudden fury that within minutes visibility fell to near zero in swirling, stinging snow. The ship was clocking sixty-knot winds. The two small craft made it back to the *Glacier* with great difficulty in heavy seas, Meeks first heading the Greenland Cruiser toward the barrier to try to locate the stranded surveyors. It bumped the shelf, getting pelted and nearly swamped by dislodged ice. Expecting to be soon met by the boats, the quartet on foot carried no survival gear. They did have among them a length of rope, two sets of crampons, and two ice axes. After a few minutes huddling around the surveying transit, they groped their way to a rocky moraine about 500 feet downslope, thinking to build a temporary shelter. But the rocks were too large and frozen in. There was no suitable snow for snow blocks. The glacial ice was too hard to work. After about an hour, growing stiff and frostbitten as they cowered in the lee of boulders, Cavendish realized they had to do something. The storm had lost none of its violence. It might last for days.

He decided to try for the *Glacier*, their only hope, about two miles away. While they could occasionally catch a hazy glimpse of the barrier, they knew there were two steep dips in it between them and the ship, so they could not just follow the ice edge. The four roped up and pushed into a wind they could barely stand against, heading first straight up to reach the ridge beyond the danger spots. Then they turned toward where they hoped the ship lay. But they had misjudged and were not high enough. The slope fell away and they with it, "sliding and tumbling toward the bay below"—about 300 feet before Cavendish managed to plant his ice ax firmly enough to hold himself and Maines, who crashed into him. Hadley, with the other ax, finally stopped himself and Herald. "I think we all had visions of splashing into the icy water," Cavendish said later. Helpless to stand or even crawl on the slick ice, they resorted to inching themselves up on their backsides, pulling against their embedded axes. At last they got to more level footing and, crossing a ridge, caught brief sight of the ship, about three-quarters of a mile away and "far below." Eventually, they could faintly hear the ship's horn, which had long been blasting signals to them, and finally they climbed aboard to wild cheering. Bruised and frostbitten, their clothes frozen, they were "in good spirits again" after some medicinal brandy and a hot shower. In the official report "the three seabees agreed, 'It was Cavendish in front and God behind' which got them safely back to the *Glacier*." Cavendish wrote later that day, "The men were superb." Within half an hour of the fortunate four's arrival the icebreaker pushed off, bound for Atka Bay and its Weddell Sea mission. Incredibly, Wilkes's inhabitants a year later would find the abandoned transit, still standing where they left it.[24]

Returning now to Vincennes Bay in Deep Freeze II to build the Wilkes Land station, the *Glacier* and two cargo ships struggled against some of the thickest pack ice, clogged with icebergs, that Eklund had ever seen. Dewart remembered fearing "iceberg alley," not so much in terms of danger as delay, even as he was proudly conscious of heading for "American turf"—where Americans had been before, "albeit a long time before." Four times this most muscular U.S. icebreaker had to retreat and try another approach. Once in to the coast, Eklund found shore conditions—unstable shelf ice, lack of solid rock—so unsatisfactory that he "refused to set our station there." Finally, 29 January became their "big day," though not an easy one. As he described it in a letter home, a cold ten-knot wind coated their Greenland Cruiser with ice and ripped down its aerial, cutting contact with the *Glacier*, which thought they were lost: "And how our small boat pitched! . . . Anyhoo—we traveled the entire length of the Windmill Is. group and what terrain it is. Reminds me of the islands off the coast of Greenland. Not a single site did we find until the very last 'island.'" It was actually the unmapped but promising Clark Peninsula—a "lucky break" after hours of discouraging search. The next day *Glacier* escorted its two charges to an open-water anchorage near the base site. *Greenville Victory* managed without mishap, but the less-ice-worthy *Arneb* sustained yet more damage.[25]

What came to be called Wilkes Station, on a low, rocky point at the west end of Clark Peninsula, was the northernmost U.S. IGY station. Located at latitude 66° 15' S, longitude 110° 31' E, it was just outside the Antarctic Circle. There would be no long winter night. Dewart remembered "one day of the year in which the sun comes right down to the horizon and then circles all the way around. And then in the middle of winter, you have one day of the year in which it just pokes up above the horizon and then goes back down again, and then you don't see it for twenty-three-and-a-half-hours." Favorable latitude plus the proximity of open water during the summer months made it also the warmest station. The first year's high temperature, in December, was a balmy +43°F; the lowest, in July, −27°F. The winter average was a fraction of a degree above zero. Wilkes enjoyed what were "almost seasons," remembered Noonan. You'd be "out there in just your thermal underwear top sweating if you were doing physical work. . . . If the sun was out and there was no wind, you'd be hot." Indeed, one of the more vexing mild-weather problems at Wilkes was endlessly leaky roofs. Meteorologist Rudolf Honkala, who first viewed the station area as a desolate, sterile "landscape from the moon," was amazed to begin noticing a richness and variety of living things around him—mosses, numerous types of birds, and seals.[26]

On 31 January 1957 shore operations began—first by blasting a ramp into a twelve-foot-high ice foot and rock-hard permafrost to allow off-loading of construction material by amphibious landing craft. Tractors then hauled everything to the base site. By 5 February Eklund was enthusiastic. "The camp is coming along swell," he wrote home. "It's *really* a good site for all our disciplines. Besides which, we're on a point overlooking the ocean, with hundreds of grounded icebergs, the ice cap, and islands. Three buildings are up and we should be moving in within 10 days." Walter Sullivan of the *New York Times* and Bill Hartigan of NBC News were writing features on his work: "It's fun, Honey." On the 13th he continued, "This is a really plush base. I've never seen anything like the equipment and buildings. Asphalt tile floors, seven Weasels, four big D-4 tractors, automatic washing machines, over 200 movies—there's no comparison between it and the East Base [where he wintered in 1940 with the U.S. Antarctic Service Expedition] as far as facilities are concerned." Moreover, "everything to the north and east of us—for the next 50 miles—is unmapped and unnamed." He would make thoughtful and generous use of that opportune fact.[27]

With assistance from ships' work parties, the Seabee crew under Cmdr. James Hiegel, construction engineer, "made amazing progress, without commotion and seemingly without effort," wrote Dufek's scribe. The familiar basics of the station, toward an eventual nineteen versatile Clements-panel buildings plus several Jamesways, were essentially up in an astonishing fifteen days. (Forty-seven had been originally allotted.) On that subject, however, Eklund cast a somewhat different light: "It irritates me no end" that the builders set "some sort of a world's record for building a base in a hurry," when it meant "they goof off and leave us with lots of work still to do." He was particularly annoyed with Capt. Gerald Ketchum, the task-group commander, whom he considered indifferent to the IGY. For example, Ketchum had said they did not need snow tunnels, "as if he knew anything about it." Eklund declared he would not accept the station for the IGY without them. He got some tunnels, or at least permission to build some, though the station would not be fully enclosed for another year. He had to fight for a darkroom to house the seismologist's galvanometers, too, "which some damned fool left out of the blueprints." But these were "minor skirmishes."[28]

On 16 February, scarcely two weeks after their arrival, Ketchum commissioned the base, turning it over to naval officer-in-charge Lieut. (jg) Donald Burnett, with Carl Eklund in charge of the scientists and the scientific program. The twenty-seven to remain on the rocks threw a party. While Eklund expected "little work and many headaches in the morning," he knew everyone

Wilkes Station was built on bedrock. Two IGY structures common to all science stations are the rounded Rawin Dome, used to track weather balloons, and the raised boxlike Aurora Tower with its Plexiglas viewing domes. Official U.S. Navy photograph, by Paul Noonan. Eklund, SSLR, Wilkes 1957.

had "worked hard—particularly our navy boys—and they deserve a celebration." He joined them. "Then we're on our own, and I'm glad," he said, echoing a common sentiment among would-be winterers. On the 17th the ship formation retraced its track through much-loosened and easily traversed pack ice, a relief for Ketchum in the darkening days. Once beyond the ice the task group disbanded, each ship going its own way.[29]

At Wilkes the seventeen Navy men and ten scientists worked eighteen-hour days, seven days a week, to be ready to meet winter and the IGY. Before attending to his lower-priority photography setup, Burnett charged Noonan to "straighten out" the "mess" left in the staging area after the hurried offloading, the urgency of which became obvious after the first snowstorm. He spent weeks brushing snow from pallets and crates to identify their contents, then directing two Seabees on D-4s with forklifts to move them to organized, retrievable storage—still "just on the ice, but we knew what was where." Except for a "dangerously marginal supply of electric light bulbs," they had plenty. Noonan, in turn, drove a tractor, did some welding (having had a little training in trade school), and learned a little carpentry. Under builder George Magee's guidance, he built most of his photo lab himself, "which was fine. It was a good experience." Finally, he helped the scientists who recorded their work on film. Noonan's willingness to work where needed seemed typical and was perhaps an important explanation of the station's success. Scientists offered their "common labor," too; it was an "all-hands operation." Wilkes would be a happy camp.[30]

A typical IGY station, Wilkes was also in many ways unique. It was the only one besides McMurdo that had a team of dogs. Eklund, a veteran of old-school exploring, requested dogs and knew how to handle them. The team of eight, later augmented with pups born in camp, was never used on the inland ice cap, but Eklund and others would take them on exploring and biological treks along the shore where the ice was unreliable for heavier tractors. Mostly the dogs became pets, greatly enjoyed. Dewart, who also learned to drive them, would take two or three of his favorites out for a run around the base almost daily "just for exercise," even in the near-darkness of midwinter.[31] Wilkes, alone, had no airfield, no air support at all. "We were waiting for our ship to come in; that was it," said Dewart, adding, "if the ships got there." Keenly aware of the uncertainties of their coming, they knew they might have to do a second year on their own, "[s]o in a sense, this drew us together." No air support also meant no visitors, no press, no VIPs coming for inspection tours. That was a plus and a minus. The isolation was long and complete, but no outsiders were interfering with their work and routines either. If Wilkes lacked airpower, it did enjoy sea power. Left with a fourteen-foot plywood boat and a five-horsepower outboard motor, various teams plied the open coastal waters to explore the Windmill Islands. Later a snowstorm buried the craft, and a tractor inadvertently ran over it. So the men attached the motor to a rubber life raft, which served well until a windstorm ripped it apart. The Seabees finally cobbled together a "catamaran"—two rows of five heavy-rubber gasoline drums, inflated and bolted together end to end with iron pipes. Fitted with a boxlike platform and powered by the trusty outboard, "this 'boat' far surpassed our expectations as to seaworthiness," Eklund wrote. They used it to "carry out glaciological, geological, biological, and mapping work from one end of the island chain to the other," their longest "ocean voyage" one of forty-three miles.[32]

By lucky happenstance, Wilkes had a sizable meltwater pond several hundred yards above the camp, which for months provided freshwater for only the labor of pumping it into a 300-gallon tank and hauling it to the station. When the pond froze, the men built a two-panel Jamesway on the ice, which they heated with an oil stove to keep the water beneath it liquid for use. Unfortunately, the hut caught fire and burned, and its fiberglass insulation polluted the water. After that, when seawater-distillation units proved labor-intensive to use, they melted snow with relative ease in a 750-gallon "asphalt cooker," which in another environment would have been used for tarring roads.[33]

Finally, on the Australian coast like Mawson's "home of the blizzard," Wilkes could claim the most capriciously violent weather of the U.S. IGY stations. On thirteen days in August 1957 winds exceeded fifty knots. Subject to both katabatic winds sweeping off the ice cap and cyclonic storms along the coast, Wilkes endured sudden blizzards of surpassing ferocity every few weeks during the winter. The barometric pressure would sometimes drop vertically as a storm approached. It could be calm, according to weatherman Honkala, and "you could see the wind driving the snow south of us coming off the Vanderford Glacier into Vincennes Bay" as the gravity-fed katabatics flowed like water toward them. Dewart agreed: "You'd see all the snow coming up, just rising up over the ice cap, and then you could see it coming towards you and coming towards you, and then it would hit you at about eighty miles an hour, and all of a sudden everything would be covered by blowing snow." In addition to windchill, frostbite, and visibility so poor that no one could go outdoors without a buddy, flying objects were a danger. (Once, in 1962, after just such a tempest, an Australian meteorologist reported to Bob Thomson, then Wilkes scientific leader, "Well, it's gone. I can't find it anywhere." An entire building had simply disappeared.) Afterward, lamenting their scarcity of tunnels, the Wilkes men would dig in to shovel the drifts—and shovel and shovel. But Dewart also remembered beneficent "periods of beautiful dry, warm days, very, very still."[34]

The seventh American IGY station was to be at the edge of the Weddell Sea, originally set for Vahsel Bay. In 1823, a year of rare ice-free conditions, Capt. James Weddell, in the employ of the British whaling firm Samuel Enderby and Sons, had penetrated the sea now bearing his name to latitude 74° South. But for 130 years afterward no one had been able to duplicate his farthest south. Thwarting access was the Weddell Sea gyre, a product of wind patterns and currents created as the prevailing easterlies bumped against the mountainous Antarctic Peninsula and were deflected northward and around, setting in motion a clockwise spiral that prevented seasonal ice escape. This phenomenon clogged the sea with old pack ice that ground together under "relentless and ruthless pressures" and jammed it against the peninsula's eastern edge. Such were the conditions that destroyed Nordenskjöld's *Antarctica* in 1903 and Shackleton's *Endurance* in 1915 and would sober later venturers to the frozen ocean. Vivian Fuchs and members of the Commonwealth Trans-Antarctic Expedition on the *Theron* were stuck in the Weddell gyre for three weeks in late 1955, although the year before that the Argentines had succeeded in putting in their General Belgrano Station, twenty-two miles still further west.[35]

The U.S. Weddell Sea station, eventually named for American explorer Lincoln Ellsworth, was the only one not approached from New Zealand, thus effectively the most remote. Its early story is largely one of getting there. In fact, in the early-1956 budget squeeze, Dufek had, according to Crary, suggested eliminating this base in that the Russians were safely distant, the nearby British (not mentioning the Argentines) were friendly, and the cost of two supporting ships for an entire summer was too high. In March 1956 he had halted the *Glacier*'s efforts to reconnoiter the Weddell coast because of bad ice and worsening weather. Firm IGY plans probably salvaged any Navy program in the area, but there was apparently less resolve and no head start on locating a base site on the South American (Atlantic Ocean) side of the continent.[36]

The Navy named Capt. Edwin McDonald, Operation Highjump veteran, as commander of Task Group 43.7 in charge of the two ships assigned to Ellsworth's establishment—the icebreaker *Staten Island* (AGB-5) and the cargo vessel *Wyandot*. The ships departed from Seattle and Davisville on 3 and 9 November 1956, respectively, and met in Panama to sail together down the west coast of South America. They put in at Valparaiso, Chile, where Capt. Finn Ronne, USNR, Ellsworth Station's military and scientific leader, came aboard. IGY seismologist John Behrendt found him short, balding, clean-shaven, "fastidious" as to his person, and "physically vigorous": "At first acquaintance he was quite charming, with a pleasant Norwegian accent and an engaging personality. Smart, ambitious—a self-made man," at fifty-seven he was "by far the oldest of our wintering group." This was to be Ronne's fourth Antarctic winter. He was clearly the expert among ice novices. But the polar explorer also had his own agenda, and it was quite apart from IGY goals.[37]

After negotiating Chile's "picturesque but tortuous" Inland Passage (to avoid the angry seas of the "roaring 40s") and experiencing a final taste of civilization at Punta Arenas, McDonald led the ships across the notoriously rough Drake Passage (not unduly so that year), then braved the ice-racked Weddell. Because effects of the gyre and katabatic winds off the ice cap had never allowed penetration directly from the north, he chose to approach from

Cape Norvegia at the eastern end of the sea, where the pack was likely the lightest and the prevailing southerly winds sometimes created a narrow channel between the shelf and the sea ice. He would then follow the ice shelf southwesterly to the IGY-chosen destination of Cape Adams on the Bowman Peninsula, at the southeastern base of the Antarctic Peninsula. That was also Captain Ronne's personal choice, where he hoped to map further landmarks in an area he had flown over on his 1946–1948 private expedition. This was "old home-town territory to me," he wrote. It was slow going through the heavy pack ice for the relatively light, 1940s-vintage Wind Class icebreaker, worse when winds and currents forced ice floes together into overriding rafts or vertical hummocks and pressure ridges. When in the occasional polynya (small "lake" of open water within the pack) oceanographers won a stop to study ice, water, and bottom characteristics, the eager young scientists and impatient sailors grew restless at the lack of movement.[38]

The ships spent clear, cold, sunshiny Christmas Day stuck in the ice, still nearly a thousand miles from their goal. Ice had ripped a seam in the *Wyandot*, with a loss of 9,000 gallons of fuel, and damaged all four blades of its single screw, crippling speed. After being beset for about five days, the ships managed to move again, and by 28 December they were inside the pack in open water, cruising westerly along the Filchner Ice Shelf. Behrendt (as did others) noted in his journal their proximity to where both the *Deutschland*, Filchner's German expedition ship in 1912, and Shackleton's *Endurance* in 1915 had become frozen in, but with the confidence of youth and trust in modern technology he was "not too worried." Forty years later he would acknowledge that "we 'scientists' should have been more concerned." The ship captains were less naive. Cmdr. James Elliott on the *Staten Island* reported "interminable, frightening days" as floes thickened and broken ice rapidly refroze. *Wyandot* skipper Capt. Francis Gambacorta, "almost always the most even tempered, unflappable Italian" VX-6 pilot Conrad Jaburg had ever met, was growing genuinely fearful of the "ever present" ice, "which at any moment could ensnare, crush and destroy this ship." He could see that the icebreaker "could hardly take care of herself" but hoped it might serve as a "refuge for the shipwrecked." Jaburg, standing deck watches with the captain, wrote, "Our hull has taken an awful beating from the ice and we don't know just how much more pounding she'll take."[39]

By New Year's Day they were beset again, this time for eleven increasingly tense days while leaked oil and jettisoned garbage sullied the pristine icescape—such dumping then accepted practice. "We were isolated in a pack larger than Texas," Ronne's autobiography would read. He and McDonald flew in to pay courtesy calls at General Belgrano and Britain's Shackleton Station on New Year's Eve, but among the rest, boredom and uncertainty fed wild rumors. "Morale is lower than a snake's belly," Jaburg penned. On 11 January the ice unaccountably opened up, but a serious rupture of the *Wyandot*'s hull required lying to in a polynya for all-night temporary repairs. While workers were belayed to weld a plate over the breach in the listing ship, a small pod of killer whales swam ominously close, but the summoned rifleman did not have to shoot. A few days later one blade of the icebreaker's port screw sheared off completely, rendering it inoperable, and before it was over the crankshaft of its number two engine broke in three places. On the 15th the *Wyandot* suffered further damage to its screw, and pumps were having difficulty with a new portside rupture.[40]

At this time reconnoitering helicopters reported two huge icebergs, each more than twenty-five miles long, blocking the way ahead. By a long detour they would eventually get past, but the admiral, across the continent and increasingly nervous about completing the mission, began firing off a stream of messages to the Weddell Sea group—which the young scientists and officers lounging in the wardroom monitored with keen interest, if not official approval. Behrendt copied them out. On 11 January Dufek told them to build the base at the "nearest available site." In fact, they had just seen a manageably low spot in the ice shelf near Gould Bay, but McDonald was then making good time in open water. Expecting to reach Cape Adams within thirty-six hours, he requested permission to proceed. By the 15th he was close enough for helicopter reconnaissance, as Behrendt wrote, but it was clear even from the ships that the ice shelf was "about 120 ft high, which is about 90 ft too high for unloading." Firing deck guns at the barrier to create a slope had no appreciable effect—"like the beak of a bird trying to chip a diamond," wrote Ronne. They had to turn back. "So near and yet so far," sighed Behrendt. Frustrated at retreating, Jaburg took some comfort from having penetrated 325 miles farther into the southwestern Weddell Sea than anyone before them. The task force claimed its charting of these previously unknown lands and waters as "a notable Antarctic 'first.'"[41]

That same day, 15 January, Dufek reminded the skippers that "time is running out," that safety of ships and men must be kept "uppermost." "My commitment to USNC-IGY was 'operationally feasible,'" Dufek went on. "There was no promise to put [the station] at Bowman Peninsula or any other specific location." A few hours later, underscoring his point, he directed them, apparently with the concurrence of Antarctic Committee chair Gould, to "select a suitable site easily accessible to you now and build the base." The disappointed Ronne made Dufek's decision—governance "from afar" without first-hand knowledge of conditions—sound capricious and arbitrary: "When the ships were within 16 miles of our original destination of Bowman Peninsula, we were directed to retreat to the Gould Bay area." He did not mention the inaccessible barrier. Lt. Cmdr. Henry ("Hank") Stephens, engineer in charge of constructing Ellsworth Station, later bristled at what he called Ronne's "personal publicity purposes." Hardly arbitrary, "any messages that Dufek sent would have been based on Capt Mc's recommendation and he was doing everything possible to try to get the Station at Cape Adams," despite the inherently problematic ice-flow patterns. McDonald kept his exposed words carefully neutral: "Only influenced by advantages which would accrue by locating station on land at maximum distance from other IGY stations," he answered Dufek. Since the Bowman Peninsula had proved "not feasible," they were "with clear conscience . . . directing our search back to the eastward."[42]

The frustrated Ronne appealed to Gould, then on the *Curtiss* in the Ross Sea, and asked the Ellsworth scientists to join in. He proposed a smaller base but as far west as possible for maximum IGY advantage; there would be little value in duplicating work others were already doing farther east, he argued. "Negative," replied Dufek. "Select suitable site and build that base as planned. Gould Bay acceptable if suitable." Then, having effected the turnaround, never favoring the risks of reduced manpower, and wishing perhaps to quash what was beginning to sound like panic, he added, "You don't have to leave by 15 February. I will tell you when to leave." The day before he had radioed: "You have plenty of time . . . take it easy. I departed Atka Bay last spring on *Glacier* on 31 March." (But Atka Bay was beyond the Weddell Sea's punishing pressure ice.) Ronne duly cited Dufek's apparent flip-flops. On 23 January, when Dufek ordered the station built at 20° East, a wave of scientific protest crested (although the desperate Gambacorta thought the decision "wise"). Three days later Dufek directed them to 41° West, making it likely that the previous, odd and anomalous, order was transmitted in error. Back in Washington the excitable Hanessian urged Odishaw to "speak up—soon" through Gould, the Central Intelligence Agency, and Byrd's office to gain a "contradiction of Adm. Dufek's precise orders." In his mind, "[T]o retreat out of the Weddell Sea will materially reduce the value of an IGY station in that area."[43]

Once again, all sides pressed their own valid concerns. Ronne, having doggedly promoted himself for years, wanted to explore. The scientists and their IGY backers wanted a virgin field to study. Stephens wanted time for his Seabees to complete their construction project. Gambacorta and Elliott, not to mention McDonald, wanted their ships safely north before ice trapped or destroyed them, a threat growing daily. And Dufek, conscious of his legacy as well as his immediate responsibility, had to want it all. Overall, he showed a keen grasp of the mission and its implications, a determined commitment to it, and a canny sense of appropriate priority at any given time in the face of unending and conflicting pressures.

On their re-traced track the ships again encountered the massive bergs, this time with ice floes blown thick against them. After a third, five-day, entrapment, which in total resulted in the loss of almost four critical weeks, they were, wrote Jaburg, "damn near where we were for ten days around New Years." Behrendt observed darkly on the 25th that "the open water is freezing over every night now, and today it didn't melt." Finally, on 26 January, the casually profane pilot continued, "Well, we're here, wherever the hell 'here' is." "Here" was 77° 41' South, 42° 07' West, about twenty miles east of Gould Bay, in a small inlet called Bahia Chica, just 500 yards east of the site bypassed earlier in the month. Here, once the *Staten Island* cleared the edge of hummocked fast ice, the low ice shelf seaward from icebound Berkner Island permitted off-loading onto a gradual slope. (Behrendt said later that a high melt rate beneath the cantilevered ice front caused it to slump there.) The station would be built about two miles inland on floating ice 860 feet thick. It was about thirty-five miles west of Argentina's Weddell Sea station and about fifty miles west of Britain's, both countries similarly taking advantage of the access but also marking their claims to the same land. Expecting to be living on land, Jaburg found the site "the most desolate spot imaginable with unrelieved snow as far as the eye can see." But widespread relief greeted the fact that the decision had been made at last. By then, "[N]o one was about to quibble with this location," wrote Behrendt. "It's not so much where you *want* to put the base," Littlewood emphasized, "it's where you are *able* to put the base."[44]

"No one needed to be told that base construction must be rushed," wrote Gambacorta as he offered all possible ship resources to the task. The Seabees had counted on fifty days to complete the station; now they had scarcely two weeks. Unloading began on 27 January—by all hands, including ships' crews, who sometimes had to wait for their replacements in order to share short supplies of cold-weather clothing. "Everybody pitched in," confirmed Littlewood, who released his own oceanographic team and "pounded some nails" himself. Scientists helped dig pits for "deadmen," and those with mountaineering experience probed for what proved to be only minor crevasses along the trail from ship to base. Engineer and geologist Nolan Aughenbaugh, with two or three Seabee assistants, surveyed the campsite. Within two days Stephens had eighteen Jamesways up and the permanent base begun. On 3 February

The cargo ship Wyandot *(left) and icebreaker* Staten Island *are moored to a low spot on the Filchner Ice Shelf for off-loading. The joined trail leads to Ellsworth Station, about two miles inland. The pack ice (lower left) has drifted north, leaving open water near shore, which is common in summer. Official U.S. Navy photograph. NARA II, RG 313, Records of Photography Officer DF 55–69, Box 9.*

Behrendt, who had been working on a barracks foundation, was "amazed at the vast amount of materiel that has come off that ship. It has piled up over acres of 'ground.' There are streets laid out, and tractors are constantly moving things around.... In spite of various difficulties, building is proceeding a little ahead of schedule."[45]

The hurry both invited and magnified problems. One day during unloading a D-4 dropped over the ice edge when a large piece of the shelf gave way. Fortunately, a floe wedged between the shelf and the ship held the tractor at water level, and both it and the driver were rescued unharmed. After that the men stood cold watches at shipside. As the ice-shelf surface continued to deteriorate under the heavy use, unloading necessarily became uneven, forcing construction to proceed according to availability of materials, not priority. So, for example, Seabees "robbed" recreation-building panels to build other structures.

*Ellsworth Station under construction, February 1957. Upper right: the Seabees' construc-
tion camp of Jamesway huts; lower right: stacked fuel drums; left: permanent station of
Clements huts in various stages of construction; upper left: supply dump in organized rows.
Official U.S. Navy photograph. Courtesy, Al Raithel Jr.*

Another vexation was finding all the interior panels a half-inch too long to
install, a prefabrication error that meant cutting each one to length on the job.
While normally minor details, they were "time consuming when time did not
exist," wrote Stephens in his official report. Builders found the antenna wire
just two days before ship departure but still managed to almost complete the
rhombic antenna system.[46]

A major problem for Stephens was Ellsworth's leader. While still aboard
ship, Captain Ronne had demanded he rearrange the camp layout. He refused, explaining that with his crews trained for the published layout and the
materials packed accordingly, changes would create chaos. "The prime motivation was so he could have his private toilet facilities," Stephens later growled.
Ronne would write officially that radio lead-in wires "crossed over the camp
site in all directions," interfering with weather-balloon launches, but, know-

ing this, the construction officer made "no effort" to "correct the situation." (Several stations faced this same problem and managed it in some way, as Ellsworth would by installing side doors in the inflation shelter so balloons could be carried away from the wires before release.) On the ice, Ronne tried to order changes while the construction officer slept, which provoked an explosive confrontation. After the exhausted Seabees left, Ronne apparently sent out a message saying that Stephens's "slow construction and the aimless wandering of the Task Group would prevent him from meeting his objectives." Wintering mechanic Walter Davis recalled Ronne writing of the construction crew "sitting in the chow hall drinking coffee. I guess he came there at the wrong time because they worked their butts off." Stephens was irate enough to pursue legal action, "but the Navy asked me not to . . . give him the publicity."[47]

On Sunday, 10 February 1957, a blowy, snowy day with a low-pressure area moving in, McDonald called a conference to announce that because of the poor weather and closing pack ice, construction personnel would have to be evacuated no later than noon the next day—or else winter over. What had been scheduled as the first nonworking day suddenly became a round-the-clock, all-hands construction effort. The *Wyandot* hurriedly cast off at 2200 hours, which, Jaburg noted, "put a hell of a damper on the [afternoon's] beer bust." To leave Ellsworth in the best shape possible, Stephens and half of his ninety-one Seabees and three officers worked thirty-six hours straight (the rest put in twenty-four hours). When he finally got to remove his socks, "I could just peel the skin off my feet," Stephens recalled later. By the time of *Staten Island*'s departure on the 11th, after McDonald's commissioning ceremonies left Ronne in charge, Stephens considered the base 90 percent finished. Those left behind would understandably question that figure, although all nineteen of the camp's basic structures had been built in those sixteen days and the generators were in place and running. The winterers, of course, would have to complete many jobs, outdoors and in, but the builders had every right to feel pride and satisfaction.[48]

As it turned out, neither ship had undue difficulty threading through the pack ice on the northbound journey. Some of Ellsworth's scientists muttered over the Navy's precipitous departure when there was still so much work to do, a complaint much muted, if present at all, in accounts of other stations. But the record shows them giving their time and muscle to get the base winterworthy even as they preferentially attended to their own disciplinary tasks. Pilot Jaburg, "sorry to see that last physical link with civilization go," was clear that everyone had contributed. "We all turned to in earnest today," he wrote on 12 February. "All 39 of us here are concerned with only two things, and those are getting the camp livable, and moving the tons of supplies and equipment into the burlap and chicken wire, wood framework tunnels which we are constructing to connect the main buildings. We do this so that when the snow comes these things won't be covered up and lost. It's a monumental task and we're in a big hurry." "All of us working steadily," he continued the next day, one in which he "lucked out," assigned to drive a D-4 Cat to move supplies. For two more days he helped build tunnels, "pounding and sawing right along with the Seabee builders," soon deciding that "I enjoy constructing things." The following week: "No rest for the wicked. Pushing crates around by hand, backbreaking but necessary." For all that, Jaburg gave his top priority to aviation matters and, like others, his personal space.[49]

One contrary note came from the hardworking Aughenbaugh, who confided to his diary on 13 February, just two days after the ships departed, "A couple of the men's attitudes and actions [on helping to prepare the base] surprised me." He cited "only [chief meteorologist] Jerry Fierle and [ionosphere assistant Donald] Skidmore [as] giving full effort—others more concerned with tidying up their own quarters and rooms. Morale not too high for this early. More cooperation needed between all." Later he would clarify that "two or three" were "not pulling their weight." So perhaps some of the IGY group did not help themselves get off on the right foot with their leader. That was unfortunate. Aughenbaugh continued: "Finn Ronne has made himself anything but beneficial to base. Wants all kinds of special favors and does *no* work. He made himself a nuisance during construction of camp to Cmdr. Stephens. Now acts like a dictator."[50]

Unlike Wilkes and Hallett, the remote Ellsworth Station had its own VX-6 squadron of three Otters (one left crated as a spare) and a helicopter, to be flown by three pilots and supported by eight enlisted men. By 2 February the "airdales" had the planes reassembled (wings and tails were crated separately) and in the air. Only Jaburg was qualified to fly both fixed- and rotary-wing aircraft, though with thin helo experience he lamented having no backup. He was enthusiastic about the Canadian-made Otter, "a wonderful airplane for a mission such as this." It could carry "ten passengers and a crate of oranges 1,000 miles at about 110 knots." He found its single, 700-horsepower radial engine efficient in the dense, cold air. It was "very easy to fly and seems born to operate in the ski equipped configuration." The helicopter, a Sikorsky HO4S-3, was designed to carry nine passengers 400 miles at 70 knots with a similar engine, but Jaburg quickly learned that flying it would be more problematic. Both the engine and the main transmission had to be preheated at least an hour before starting because the nine-foot hose distance between the

Herman-Nelson heater and the engine meant great heat loss and inefficiency. Frustratingly, inexplicably, the machine rested on four wheels, not skids, which typically broke through the snow crust at different rates on landing.[51]

By late February, as the sinking sun began dipping below the horizon for gradually lengthening nights, Ellsworth's scientists grew increasingly anxious. Only four months remained before the start of the IGY, and there were still science structures to build, apparatus to assemble and test. Aurora observer McKim Malville remembered "a very intense feeling of worry that I couldn't get stuff done in time." But on the 15th, when Behrendt helped Malville move some panels for his geomagnetism building, the captain "bawled us out" for not doing station work. So they resumed tunnel construction and other chores. By the 25th, Behrendt and science leader Ed Thiel returned to setting up their glaciology-seismology laboratory and began fieldwork to measure shelf-ice thickness. Again, in early March Ronne insisted that all scientists "go back on camp work." They decided as a group to refuse "because our programs were too far behind already." He could not force them all, they thought. "Fortunately, Carl Eklund saved our science," a grateful Behrendt added later. Eklund had sent out a science SITREP showing that at Wilkes Station "they are really doing work there. Glaciology is especially far ahead. They obviously have been working full time on their programs since they landed (even later than us)." The competitive Ronne, who was also fond of Eklund, his former traverse colleague, sent Ellsworth's scientists to do science. They would be ready for winter and the IGY.[52]

By April the outside work was more or less finished, the station was fully operative, and scientific instruments were mostly functioning—but, unfortunately, discord was already a way of life at Ellsworth. After the 26th it would be dark until sunrise in mid-August. The intense work schedule had been cut back and days became more routine, but, as happened everywhere, time and tedium grew. None of this helped as Ronne's need for power and controlling management methods increasingly frustrated and angered the station's residents. "Mark my words," predicted Jaburg at the end of the month, with the long winter night scarcely begun, "the place is going to blow sky high one of these days, owing to the captain's inability to lead and handle men, and his tendency to blow petty things up to tremendous proportions."[53]

So what made Ellsworth unique was broadly shared animosity toward the leader, who seemed daily to make things worse. The captain tried to impose a highly stratified social system, for example. He decreed that the five naval officers and nine scientists (accorded officer status by IGY-Navy agreement) would have a separate seating for dinner, where they were served at table. The twenty-five enlisted men would help themselves, cafeteria style—which everyone else, including the admiral, did everywhere else in American Antarctica. While Ronne's style was standard shipboard procedure and had Scott's precedent on the ice, emphasizing class distinctions in a small science camp was a recipe for resentment. Later, when he became angry at the "IGY men" and arbitrarily demoted them to "men," it left the captain, physician Clinton Smith, and the three pilots to dine in awkward, silent splendor while the thirty-four others lined up to "feed" on the round stools of the enlisted. "How ridiculous," said Jaburg, one of the five. Aughenbaugh, once an enlisted Marine, pronounced the new arrangement "great—the food hot and feelings running good between all concerned." Malville agreed on the "happier scene" once the scientists had overcome their "initial outrage at having been rejected by the Captain as dining companions." Ronne expected an escort to his special seat at the nightly movies and everyone, including civilians, to stand at attention when he entered the room. (Aughenbaugh took to arriving late.) He lectured Jaburg and fellow pilot William Sumrall on "fraternizing with the men (bull sessions and beer drinking). It seems that it is O.K. to shovel snow and work shoulder to shoulder with them, but we can't talk to them." It felt like a military school. Unfortunately, this approach achieved neither harmony nor order.[54]

As for the purpose of Ellsworth Station, Captain Ronne acted more like the IGY was an add-on to his program and not the other way around. His attitude seemed reminiscent of Byrd's as he hitched his second expedition onto the publicity and resources of the Second International Polar Year in 1932. With the abundance of evidence in Navy records of Ronne's stubborn persistence (his own description) in pursuing further expeditionary support, it is easy to understand and even sympathize with his thinking. Moreover, with some justification given his three previous winterings and extensive fieldwork—Antarctic experience the Ellsworth scientists were collectively innocent of—he "assumed," in Behrendt's words, that "he could tell scientists how to do their work." At the least, he might have reasonably expected some deference.[55]

Rather, the effects of Ronne's private agenda, added to those of his personality, produced festering tension. He both derided the scientists' efforts and tried to control them. "He keeps talking our chances of success down and enlarges on our ineptness and inexperience," wrote the junior seismologist on 9 July, and Ronne's own *Antarctic Command*, published in 1961, confirms the extent to which he did so. Three weeks later the sympathetic Jaburg noted that the scientists were "being thwarted at every turn by his [the captain's] interference, even to the extent that, I believe, their scientific programs are suffering."

In early October, in the same frame of mind, he wrote that Lt. Cmdr. Charles ("Mac") McCarthy, officer-in-charge of VX-6, had flown Ronne south to investigate a badly crevassed area the summer traverse party would have to cross: "He goes on these hops and won't let these poor damn scientists who are actually going to have to make the traverse go along on the flights also." Jaburg believed this was because their leader was "afraid that they might find something or do something that he didn't do." Again, Ronne's own words prove the truth of the thought. Discovery was "the explorer's incentive," he wrote, a few pages after defending his reconnaissance flights to "find the trail" for the scientists who were "untrained in the techniques of aerial observation, even under the best of conditions. Truly, it would be a waste of time to cart the civilians back and forth." At such cross-purposes did Ellsworth's IGY program move forward.[56]

Thus, with all their similarities and differences, the six U.S. science stations and the logistics base in Antarctica were in place on time for the IGY, if only just. All of them had challenged the last ounce of their founders' skill, experience, endurance, and creativity under conditions both brutal and unpredictable. The ice had spoken its own mind seven different ways. While the stations reflected their unique settings, their international-orange Clements huts, construction Jamesways left for storage or emergency shelter, fuel farms, and land and air vehicular support bore the resemblances of kinship. The seven resident "families," of greatly varying sizes, shared common tasks and experiences but created communities distinctly their own. The Navy had delivered what it promised and would continue to provide the support services required for life and work on the frigid, indifferent ice. The Air Force and the Army had come through with essential equipment and expertise. The IGY leaders had their people, programs, and apparatus poised to proceed. As each participant worried over his own risks, Admiral Dufek carried the burden for all the stations—five new ones in Deep Freeze II. It was already an extraordinary achievement. Greater would come. The story now belongs to the seekers who came to take the measure of "the last place on earth."

CHAPTER EIGHT

ON THE EVE
People, Preparations, Policies

*As I stood out on the stern of the ship at midnight a couple
nights ago, and the sun was shining over the icebergs and pack
ice and on the side of the beautiful, high, rugged Victoria
Range, I couldn't imagine myself being any place but here. That
may sound strange to you, Sweetie, but I just couldn't imagine
my being out of this big show.*

—Carl Eklund, 1956[1]

As Antarctica's Scientific Age was about to begin, IGY program leaders in Washington were still working frantically. They well knew
that Deep Freeze II represented the last chance for everything and
everybody going to the Antarctic. The fiscal 1957 supplemental budget, which would fund about half of the U.S. IGY, was still awash in
the legislative process, and more than half of the scientific bases
were not yet so much as sited with certainty—a burning concern but
one out of their control. Many scientists were still to be chosen, and
they all had to be equipped, trained, and transported during the austral summer of 1956–1957 to have their programs up and running by
1 July 1957. There were still internal and international policy issues

to settle, relationships to define and cultivate among the participating countries, and, even now, Antarctica's future to consider amid fears of the Cold War.

Topping many anxieties for the American IGY organizers throughout 1956 was the still-incomplete roster of scientific station leaders. These all-important individuals would have to shepherd their respective programs to fulfillment and inspire harmony among their human charges, both vital roles. But in IGY minds, they also had to be "well-seasoned people who can command the respect of the Navy contingent at each site, establishing a position of *dominance* [emphasis added] by their maturity and experience," Odishaw had written to Gould in April, as the command-structure negotiations warily continued. Further, unless key decisions were made soon, "we may not be able to assume our proper leadership in the Antarctic."[2]

Antarctic science leaders Wexler and Crary met with Gould in his polar-expedition–decorated Carleton College office in mid-June 1956 to consider leader choices. As Crary recollected, one was Finn Ronne, who was, with some pull from Senator Francis Case of South Dakota, still pursuing government funding for his own expedition but had now persuaded the Navy to name him military leader of the Weddell Sea IGY station. He had then approached Odishaw and Crary about the scientific leadership; he was, wrote Crary, "reluctant to take one position without having the other." Gould attested to his exploring ability and geographical contributions along the Antarctic Peninsula and, without further ado, called Ronne with an offer. Wexler wrote of his "excellent record at stimulating scientific work" and concluded, "I think we're lucky to get Finn." Ronne would get both titles at the station of his choice.[3]

Carl Eklund, a U.S. Fish and Wildlife Service ornithologist who had wintered at East Base with the U.S. Antarctic Service, was an easy selection for Wilkes Station. His condition—to work on his own biological problem—they readily agreed to, despite the IGY's geophysics focus. But after that it was not so easy. Wexler's diary reveals chase after chase of eminent polar personages, only to have them decline or be deflected for one reason or another. Alton Wade, with two Byrd Antarctic expeditions to his credit, and E. E. ("Eddie") Goodale, decorated both for his dog driving with Byrd in 1928 and later for Arctic weather expertise, were listed for Byrd and Little America stations, respectively, but both eventually declined. Worried about finding an academic meteorologist of "sufficient caliber" to head the joint effort at Cape Adare, Wexler eventually persuaded Dr. James Shear of the University of Kentucky to sign on. Gould, Odishaw, the Defense Department, and Byrd had all been leaning on Paul Siple for the scientific leadership of South Pole Station; indeed, for many others, like Crary, he was the "obvious choice." But Siple demurred over objections to dual command as well as for professional and family reasons. Calling himself "virtually drafted," he finally agreed in August 1956. (Said Bowers, who had conferred at length with Siple at McMurdo in late 1955, "He gave me every reason to believe that I would be working with him the next year at the Pole.")[4]

In October Ronne recommended Per Stoen, a fellow Norwegian and a "good survival man with Greenland experience," for Byrd Station after Wade withdrew and Norman Vaughan, another Byrd dog driver, declined. Stoen seemed a good choice. But a month later he pulled out, then re-accepted, then reported what Wexler called an "ancient diabetic condition," to which neither the IGY nor the Navy objected. The ships of Deep Freeze II were already at sea. On 17 December an exasperated Wexler "popped the question" to George Toney of the IGY staff and "said farewell to Stoen" on implied medical grounds. As for Toney, Wexler had written in September that "Bert [Crary] suggested Geo Toney for B[yrd] S[tation] leader—a suggestion I made months ago only to have Odishaw and Hanessian turn it down on grounds of need for his services and his disinclination to go." Toney, who "never did know what happened," was not, in fact, unwilling. "Miserable" as a high-school English teacher, happier as an Arctic weather observer, he came to the United States National Committee (USNC)-IGY on "loan from the Weather Bureau." Having sailed on the *Atka* for the IGY and served three Arctic expeditions, he had twenty-seven months of polar experience to his credit and expertise in polar logistics. Toney, indeed missed in Washington, would prove an excellent Antarctic leader.[5]

Scientific leadership at Little America remained undecided as well, although this situation was somewhat less urgent given Crary's posting there as resident chief scientist (and head of the U.S. glaciology program). By his own self-deprecating pen, there were others on the list but in the end the job "went to Crary by default." Wexler privately confessed "misgivings" about his colleague's ability to run the largest science station: "diplomacy, tact, sensitivity, etc not of highest." Crary might have smiled wryly reading such comments as he struggled to transcribe the often undecipherable longhand of Wexler's journal after the latter's untimely death a few years later. In truth, eager young scientists flocked to the ice precisely to follow this "demigod of polar geophysics," said geophysics professor emeritus Charles Bentley who, when awarded an endowed chair at the University of Wisconsin, named it for Crary. As a graduate student at Columbia, Bentley had heard about "this fantastic guy, Bert Crary, who was up in the Arctic and doing all these wonderful things," and he thrilled to be part of his Antarctic entourage, even at a distance. When he died in 1987, Gordon Robin of the Scott Polar Research Institute in Cambridge, England, eulogized Crary as "a modest but natural leader whose standing among his contemporaries could be compared with that of Shackleton." After two winters and three summers at Little America leading U.S. IGY science efforts, Crary would complete his career at the National Science Foundation (NSF) as chief scientist of the United States Antarctic Research Program.[6]

An additional position, sensitive and important, would have to be filled if there was to be an exchange of meteorologists with the Soviet Union's polar team, as proposed at the First Antarctic Conference. In late February 1956 the National Academy of Sciences (NAS) sent its heavy hitters—USNC chair Joseph Kaplan, IGY executive director Hugh Odishaw, and Wallace Atwood, head of the NAS Office of International Relations—to the State Department to urge approval of the Weather Central concept. Weather was a common interest and Weather Central was a uniquely international project, they argued, its data to be provided by all and shared immediately with all. Besides promoting the "cooperative tradition of science," an exchange of personnel could afford a "very unusual opportunity to evaluate the knowledge and technical ability of the Soviet meteorologists." That is, the IGY spirit could well serve foreign policy objectives. As to security, weather data would not be classified (although the visitors agreed to confer with the Defense Department before proceeding), and politically the issue seemed fairly benign. A plus was the "one-shot" nature of the IGY, while denying participation could create "embarrassment"—a minus. When State agreed, provided there was an equal exchange, Wexler proudly noted that the emphasis on reciprocity was just what he had "employed at Brussels last September."[7]

Wexler and others met with the Soviets, including Beloussov and Alexander Treshnikov, the incoming leader of the USSR Antarctic operation, at the Third Antarctic Conference in August 1956 to finalize details of exchanging a Russian meteorologist at Little America for an American at Mirny. The Americans were impressed, perhaps unexpectedly, with the quality and quantity of their counterparts' scientific progress to date, especially their weather effort. Under an "established professor," Mirny had twelve "synopticians" and assistants to run its synoptic program and altogether fifty meteorologists on the continent. "They turn out 100 univ. trained mets [meteorologists] each year," Wexler penned in his diary.[8]

Wexler hoped his outgoing, personable Weather Bureau colleague Gordon Cartwright, chief of the Division of Operations and Stations, would agree to winter over at Mirny. Cartwright was astonished by the offer: "Well, first of all, I don't know anything about the Antarctic. Secondly, I don't speak Russian," he protested. Wexler, undissuaded, suggested he could learn both. Cartwright quickly embraced the idea, "and the next thing I knew, I was in a Russian language class with an ancient White Russian colonel who, not knowing where I was going, warned me very carefully not to get involved with the Russian women!" But a month later the arrangements seemed mired in bureaucratic sloughs, apparently on both sides. Wexler submitted a $28,000 budget for Cartwright in an effort to move the process along. In early October he wrote, "No news yet from USSR re Cartwright but he will apply for visa to USSR— probably can't get there by Oct 15th now [the Soviets' original date for joining the expedition in Moscow]. Hope they're not backing out." Three weeks later, "[S]till no word from USSR re GDC [Cartwright]."[9]

On 17 November Wexler pressed a reluctant Odishaw to cable Beloussov that it was "imperative for planning purposes that we know by 1 Dec whether this will be acted on. If response is negative, we propose assigning another met to occupy space now reserved for Soviet met." Besides, if not for Mirny, Wexler wanted Cartwright, an "excellent leader," for Little America. The message was sent, and finally, in early December, Beloussov cabled instructions for Cartwright to board the *Kooperatsiya* at Capetown by 15 December. Meanwhile, until the U.S. technical system was in place, the Soviets proposed taking over Weather Central operations at Mirny, where they had "highly skilled mets and powerful radio." "Their attitude is certainly aggressive," muttered Wexler, "hardly one to inspire trust in their motives."[10]

The United States in due course agreed to receive Vladimir Rastorguev, a thirty-one-year-old Russian meteorologist, at Little America. The Soviets had wanted to send two, but the Americans felt justified in accepting only one wintering "guest participant" per country on the grounds of limited space. Rastorguev would prove a "very well educated man" and an able meteorologist, according to fellow "met" Ben Remington who worked with the station's regular weather observers. He was "one heck of a good guy. Very humorous type. Always had a quip or a joke." Construction driver Kim Lett remembered singing with him in a quartet at Saturday-night parties. While attention focused on the Russians, Wexler was taken aback to receive word in late April 1956 "from an Argentine Vice-Admiral telling us they have selected a met for WX [Weather] Central and telling us—not asking—that he will go there!" (Presumption was apparently not intended.) José Alvarez, a Navy lieutenant commander, duly arrived on the *Curtiss* along with Rastorguev and the majority of the American scientists on 30 January 1957. "You couldn't get to know Jose," Remington said. He was "very quiet." To Weather Bureau meteorologist Morton Rubin, though, who became a close friend, Alvarez was a "very fine man, very conscientious." Altogether, six people were assigned to Weather Central that year under meteorologist-in-charge W. B. ("Bill") Moreland. Rubin and E. G. Edie from New Zealand departed after the season, and South Africa's Harry Van Loon, who had worked with Rubin in his own country, participated the following summer.[11]

Wexler fretted over finding room for so many "foreigners," but, as it happened, the civilian population at Little America V during the first IGY winter would also include Herfried Hoinkes, an Austrian micrometeorologist; aurora and airglow specialist Peter Schoeck of Germany, then living in Minneapolis; and Danish ionospheric physicist Hans Bengaard. For micrometeorologist Paul Dalrymple, the "truly international" flavor was "one of the beautiful things about Little America" in the "*International* Geophysical Year." The second year the Weather Central staff of eight, under the leadership of T. I. ("Tom") Gray, would include Pavel ("Paul") Astapenko of the Soviet Union, whom IGY representative Goodale, on first meeting, called "anxious to be friendly." Speaking "better English than Vladimir," he was at first "more reserved and not quite as affable." He, too, would become well regarded. The others from abroad were Jean Alt of France, Keith Morley of Australia, and Argentina's Lieut. Alberto Arruiz. All those from countries below the equator would, of course, bring a more direct familiarity to the work than their northern counterparts.[12]

Meanwhile, Rubin had the task of securing a second-year replacement for Cartwright at Mirny, and finding someone who was both well qualified and wanting to go was proving difficult. In the end he decided the person who best met both tests was himself. He had extensive experience in Southern Hemisphere weather analysis, having worked in Peru, Chile, and the Union of South Africa. He also had, tucked away for inspiration, the memory of a day in 1938 when as a young man he got to deliver a mercurial barometer to a meteorologist leaving for Antarctica with Byrd. The excitement at the ship in the Philadelphia Navy Yard, the cacophony of sled dogs, the welter of equipment "sort of stayed in my mind somehow, that that would be a great thing to do." For all exchange scientists the experience would be that of a lifetime, the value of their personal diplomacy in a tense world beyond measure. The *Times*'s Walter Sullivan, eyewitness to much of the IGY, wrote in 1959 that "nothing could have done more to allay fears and suspicions than this exchange." G. E. Fogg, historian of Antarctic science, said the same thing in almost the same words.[13]

What the U.S. IGY Antarctic program would have done without the U.S. Weather Bureau is difficult to imagine. F. W. Reichelderfer, chief of the bureau, was extremely generous, the agency's obvious interest in Antarctic weather notwithstanding. He stripped his own staff for the IGY: Wexler to be chief scientist for Antarctica; Goodale, of Byrd's first expedition, to sail on the *Glacier* in Deep Freeze I and later to represent the U.S. Antarctic program in Christchurch; Ernest Wood, who had served on Ronne's private expedition, to represent the IGY in Antarctica during Deep Freeze I; Paul Humphrey and Kendall Moulton to summer on the ice to oversee IGY preparations, followed by Chesney Twombly and Howard Wessbecher to winter over at Little America and McMurdo, respectively, for the same purpose; Toney to the IGY staff, then Byrd Station leadership; Cartwright, and then Rubin, to live among the Russians. Several of these men and others served on the U.S. IGY meteorology technical panel. Reichelderfer favored inviting "one and all" to participate in Weather Central, despite the costs. The Weather Bureau housed the headquarters office for IGY meteorology. Its Polar Office, headed by J. Glenn Dyer, who had been on the U.S. Antarctic Service Expedition and would summer at Australia's Mawson Station, contracted with the IGY to develop engineering plans for the Antarctic stations and arranged to procure $20,000 worth of general office equipment and supplies, including clothing the Navy could not provide. When Hoinkes arrived in the United States, the Weather Bureau, part of the Commerce Department, helped clear his IGY equipment through Customs as its own.[14]

Another still-incomplete list was the one naming the scientific contingent, although as 1956 advanced the slots began to fill. The impelling call to the ice came from many sources. Some scientists were recruited by the project leaders appointed by each USNC technical panel of experts. Mentors made the difference for many. Nolan Aughenbaugh, a civil engineer, took graduate courses in glacial geology at the University of Michigan from IGY glaciology project leader James Zumberge—and "fell in love." Graduate student Charles ("Buck") Wilson got his Antarctic impulse from none other than Sydney Chapman, godfather of the IGY, who then directed the University of Alaska's Geophysical Institute. Kim Malville, president of the Caltech Alpine Club, was "fascinated by that kind of landscape" and well-read in the "history and romance" of the polar heroes. So a professor's nudge toward the polar south "was a very, very inspired suggestion." Byrd Station's second scientific leader, Stephen Barnes, who had installed and operated ionospheric equipment on tropical Pacific islands and in Alaska, made his connection through his amateur radio hobby. A talk with a scientist at Pole, coupled with his preference for active outdoor work, made a year in Antarctica seem like "a real adventure," so he applied for a position.[15]

Like other pioneers in other times, some were pulled by the thrill and significance of being first. Long interested in other venues of exploration, Gil Dewart unexpectedly found his frontier at the bottom of the globe, where "uncertain dashes" still bounded parts of the last continent. "Nothing was there! ... The emptiness that shouted 'Unexplored!' was soon drawing me toward it like an irresistibly gravitating mass," he wrote. Like other high-latitude explorers before them, some responded in their imaginations to idealized heroism. John Behrendt had "romanticized Antarctic exploration since childhood," so while he gave science and obtaining a PhD as his purpose, he later admitted that the "romance/adventure part" was what "really drew" him to the ice. The lure of science captured others. Crary fit that category. So did physicist Willi Hough, for whom the possibility of investigating the ionosphere over the South Pole made him feel that "for the first time since college" he was, professionally, "on the right road for life." Whatever else it was, the IGY in Antarctica, with the intrinsic glamour of an international effort to amass knowledge of great significance, the sublime riskiness inherent in penetrating the last geographical unknown on earth, and the laudatory publicity that attended it all, represented a privileged opportunity that no one failed to grasp. The scientists knew they would be making history, and that would mean both recognition and future opportunity that would visit few generations of young scholars at the beginning of their careers.[16]

Like their Navy mates, most of the American IGY scientists who volunteered for Antarctica were young, relatively inexperienced, and junior in their respective professions. Behrendt remembered being rejected originally for these reasons, but when "more renowned university scientists refused to go down for a year and a half," the IGY "ended up getting stuck with the people who [George] Woollard and [Maurice] Ewing and Crary selected in the first place." The "Old Boys Network" worked, he said, for the fledgling geophysicists. Wexler expected that most of them would be "observers and not professionals capable of doing research" (an underestimation of many). Arlo Landolt, aurora observer at Pole Station, a college graduate at nineteen and one semester away from a master's degree in astronomy, was all of twenty-one years old. Malville, his counterpart at Ellsworth, with his brand-new physics degree, was just twenty-two. Most were in their mid-twenties, some of the more senior discipline leaders in their thirties. Crary, in his mid-forties, was somewhat unusual, although with his prodigious energy and output it is unlikely that anyone thought of him as old. Siple, at forty-eight, on the other hand, seemed a father figure to many of his charges at Pole. Chief meteorologist Ed Flowers called him "an icon." The scientists tended to be single, although twenty-seven-year old ionospheric physics assistant Don Skidmore's fifth child was born while he was at Ellsworth.[17]

Despite the brevity of their careers, a significant number of the south-bound scientists had worked in northern polar regions—Alaska or arctic Canada, often with military connections. Bentley devoted two seasons on the Greenland ice cap to developing seismic techniques in specific preparation for the IGY in Antarctica. Crary systematized that idea, arranging with SIPRE for many glaciologists and seismologists to train there in the northern summer of 1956. According to State Department IGY records, the United States proposed to offer cold-weather training in the Thule defense area of Greenland (apparently without much discussion with mother country Denmark, offending the latter) for "ten to twenty-five" IGY glaciologists from several countries. SIPRE, a military organization, not the chair of the IGY Committee on Glaciology, would issue this invitation, Secretary of State John Foster Dulles secretly explained to the American ambassador in Copenhagen, so that "iron curtain countries" could be excluded—an action that bespoke Cold War reality even as it violated the cooperative spirit of the IGY.[18]

The IGY project leaders also provided technical training for their scientists, such as in maintenance and repair of scientific apparatus. Crary, for example, set up a schedule for glaciology-seismology-gravimetry personnel to receive training in Tucker Sno-Cat operations from the manufacturer, surveying from the U.S. Coast and Geodetic Survey, and navigation using the Sperry gyrocompass at the Sperry Company headquarters on Long Island. He sent them to the U.S. Geological Survey for briefings on geology. Before deploying south, American Weather Central meteorologists took two-month courses in Southern Hemisphere weather analysis at the Weather Bureau offices in Washington, D.C., which for most would involve some basic differences from experiences in the Northern Hemisphere. Getting acquainted with prospective colleagues was an ancillary goal and benefit.[19]

Meanwhile, with Antarctic veteran Lloyd Berkner pressing for "indoctrination" of all IGY personnel as well as intensive cold-weather training, Wexler began planning a formal orientation program, which took place over five days in mid-October 1956 at the Seabee base in Davisville. The Rhode Island site worked well. Key wintering Navy people were already there for briefings, the scientists could see their IGY shipments being readied at dockside, and initial contacts could be made between the disparate cultures soon to be thrown together. The eager novices crowded in to absorb polar wisdom from such giants as Laurence Gould, Sir Hubert Wilkins, Albert Crary, and Finn Ronne, along with the eminent Joseph Kaplan, chair of the IGY committee. They also attended talks by discipline leaders and Deep Freeze personnel, who discussed logistics and station operations, and they gathered informally by station, discipline, and traverse. They saw historic films, learned safety procedures such as rope climbing and belaying, were briefed on nuances of international political issues, and got outfitted with six duffel bags each of cold-weather clothing (though the rangy Behrendt would complain later that the sleeves of his Army-issue field jacket were too short, his heavy bear-paw mitts too small). And they met and sized one another up—those with whom they would live and work for more than a year under conditions few could imagine.[20]

Wexler welcomed the scientists. They would, he said, build on the results of earlier explorers of "planet Earth"—with improved technologies but higher sights and greater challenges. They would work in the world's "most barren and inhospitable" environment—more difficult than space or the deepest ocean floors. The orientation effectively engendered national pride and commitment, proffered the comfort of familiarity with expectations, and encouraged team building. The program was so successful that it would be continued for many years after the IGY. Wexler followed up two weeks later with a cautionary memorandum to the stations' chief meteorologists. As they "push[ed] back the line between the known and the unknown," they would be called upon for professional opinion, he wrote. For meteorology's position and reputation, they must remember the importance of "truthful but cautious" responses on phenomena not yet understood.[21]

The incoming scientists-cum-Navy-"officers" were also briefed on naval etiquette, with its hierarchies and protocols that were quite foreign to those young civilians used to a casual, egalitarian academic life. "It is mandatory that you wear coat and tie at all times," the advance material read. As "guests" of the U.S. Navy at Davisville, they must not stray from areas of the base specified in the program. Aboard ship the social order would be even more rigid. In Military and Civilian Passenger Information issued over Admiral Dufek's signature, the scientists learned, for example, that there would be four messes—separate meal accommodations for commanding officers, officers, chief petty officers, and crew that were assigned by status and were, "in effect, clubs." The IGY men would join the Wardroom (officers') Mess, where, as guests, they were to wear attire suitable to Navy uniform (starched khakis, remembered

Behrendt) and "use decorous language." They should not sit until the presiding executive officer sat, not be late, not loiter, not put out cigarettes on dishes or deck, not discuss "women, politics, or religion"—perhaps small sacrifices for being served individually at tables adorned with white linen and silver service. Adapting naval boarding practice, the civilians were instructed to face the flag with hand over heart and request permission of the officer of the deck to board. Those having no prior experience in the armed forces would be entering a new world, just as Navy support personnel would be facing a sizable adjustment by having civilians among them.[22]

The top IGY leaders converged in New Zealand to join the Navy aircraft carrier tender USS *Curtiss* bound for Antarctica. Gould, Wexler, Crary, Toney, and SIPRE ice expert Andrew Assur went aboard at Port Lyttelton, joining thirty wintering-over scientists destined for Little America, Byrd, and the South Pole. They arrived at McMurdo in late January 1957, where they learned that landing parties at two outlying bases were still struggling to come ashore, Byrd Station's viability was iffy at best, the admiral was fretting over the unusable ice runway, and New Zealand's Scott Base was rising on the other side of Observation Hill, with Dufek's active encouragement and assistance.[23]

Over at Kainan Bay, the ships arriving for Deep Freeze II were having a rough time. Warm weather and wave action had eroded the ice edge below the waterline, leaving a gouge with a twenty- or thirty-foot projection below it that prevented the ships from tying up next to the barrier while a similar overhang threatened to calve off upon them. Twenty-year-old construction driver Kim Lett found himself on a demolition team assigned to blast away the protrusions. But before one detonation they did not get far enough back for safety, and the rotted ice began to break up with them on it. Fortunately, they were roped together and managed to scramble back onto the solid barrier just before "the whole thing turned upside down." Unfortunately, the barrier, about thirty feet high at that point, was too high for normal off-loading, so as a ship's crane raised a heavy load from a hold, it would be connected by a moving line to a crane on a D-8 tractor far back on the ice shelf, then winched up and in until it could be transferred to a sled. Thus, off-loading was slowed and, in turn, Marie Byrd Land operations delayed. The dangerousness of procedures like this were one reason for abandoning Little America at the end of the IGY, although Wexler would campaign hard to save this site of Antarctica's longest weather record.[24]

On 26 January 1957 Navy pilot Gus Shinn flew Crary, Wexler, Humphrey, and Toney—along with Capt. Willis Dickey, wintering commander of the Naval Support Unit—to Little America, which, with their arrival, became the hub of science operations. First they tended to such urgent tasks as making sure all the scientific equipment and supplies got loaded on the second Byrd tractor train. Turning to personnel matters, Crary met with crevasse expert Phil Smith, who requested work with the IGY when he got out of the Army. Crary suggested that he sign on with Zumberge's ice-deformation study near Roosevelt Island in the Bay of Whales area the following summer, and he would return to do so. But in the meantime, Gould and Wexler cornered the would-be geology doctoral student and persuaded him ("try it for six months") to work in the IGY offices in Washington. The next year's science program was "kind of behind," they pleaded, thus launching Smith on an unplanned career in science policy and leadership.[25]

Crary also sought to provide a good wintering experience for seventeen-year-old Eagle Scout Richard Chappell. Selected in a national competition like his exemplar Paul Siple, the youth had understandably asked to go to Pole, but Crary sent him to Little America for what he thought would be a more active, engaging assignment. The carefully vetted Chappell was "already qualified" to assist with almost any scientific program and should be kept busy, but Crary did not want him "taken over" just to reduce some group's work. As it happened, Crary made the scout his own chief administrative assistant when his scheduled aide, James McCoy, a former Navy pilot, photographer, and Antarctic veteran (Byrd's third expedition and Operation Highjump), was sent home after a few weeks because of a heart condition. Chappell helped on many projects, earned respect and popularity on the ice, and still chairs the Antarctic scout (now girl or boy) selection committee.[26]

Facilities remained a paramount concern. Gould, Wexler, and Crary knew that Byrd and Pole were still incomplete, barely functioning. At the three coastal stations the scientists, just then arriving with the Seabees, would start from scratch, applying themselves to the physical labor of camp construction before they could begin to set up their scientific space, equipment, and procedures. Often they built their own scientific structures. such as the geomagnetic huts, aurora towers, and rawin domes, which would not be Navy priorities as long as mess halls and latrines remained undone. Only year-old Little America was routinely running, but there, too, the scientific programs were yet to be inaugurated, with the exception of weather observation done thus far primarily by Navy aerologists with somewhat different goals. Although the magnetometer building was up, Crary had to move it, delaying the start of the LA5 geomagnetic program, because tractors feeding the too-near snowmelter unavoidably caused vibrations where it was. He found the building designated for glaciology and aurora studies occupied as a barracks. The scientists had to wait almost a month before they could modify the space for their needs and move in, so they went ahead to install and test their own spectrograph and all-sky camera in the aurora tower structure and instruments such as the gyrocompasses, sun compasses, and crevasse detectors in their Sno-Cats.[27]

Little America had its share of practical problems, too. Glaciologist Vern Anderson, who arrived with other scientists on the USS *Merrell* on 3 January, noted on the 20th that warm north winds from over the Ross Sea had brought rain to Little America. As a result, the buildings were "dripping from every seam. . . . Guys' sacks are getting soaked and a priority is on pots and pans to catch the water." Moreover, the seasonal base population was fluctuating between 180 and 245 persons, far beyond its normal capacity. Anderson avoided both the inevitable hot-bunking and a wet sack by sleeping in his traverse Sno-Cat, but others had a soggy start to their polar year. While Crary acknowledged that arriving scientific cargo had been unloaded, sorted, and stored "in extremely good order," he was disquieted that it made up the last row toward the barrier of the main cache. The ice shelf remained stable, but when heavy tractors were finally available to move the IGY material in darkening April, drifting made it difficult to find, and some never was located. A year had made a huge difference, however. Newcomers could see that they would not be pioneering in quite the same way as those in Deep Freeze I, even though conditions were still fairly primitive and ad hoc. Succeeding generations of researchers would, of course, enjoy increasing comfort and well-oiled support mechanisms.[28]

All this time the season's clock was ticking for the first Byrd over-snow traverse. Not until the *Merrell* reached the ice did the interior-bound scientists learn that a safe route through "Crevasse Junction" to Marie Byrd Land had been found, prepared, and marked; that the inland base was under cover (if minimally); and that the first tractor train had returned safely to Little America. As the traversers set about gathering up supplies and equipment for their pioneering ice study along Army-Navy Drive, they described less good order than Crary did in the barrier cache. Bentley remembered that "hundreds and hundreds of boxes" of science cargo, though nominally organized, were "just scattered all over everyplace." Then a snowfall buried them. It took a couple of weeks to find most of what was theirs and repair the inevitable damage. Observing these difficulties as well as mechanical problems in one of the Sno-Cats, Crary offered to work up the trail to the crevassed area on his own traverse the following summer, and those about to sally forth gratefully accepted.[29]

The Byrd Station traverse party pushed off from Little America on 28 January 1957, a day ahead of the second tractor train. Seismologists Bentley and Ned Ostenso, glaciologists Anderson and Mario Giovinetto, and mechanic Anthony Morency headed out across the ice shelf toward the white horizon. "This driving is just like on the seas," wrote Anderson as their three Sno-Cats rolled over the sastrugi, "rocking and pitching all over." On the fifth day they reached "Fashion Lane," with the trailblazers' flags every 120 feet and fuel drums every quarter-mile. Anderson, driving in front with Giovinetto, unhitched his sled to reconnoiter the route. "It was really exciting to be the first down the trail for a month because it was all drifted in with snow from the south and made it really bumpy. We started seeing signs of crevasses after the first mile or so, and then they were all over the place. We drove through about 6 or more and skirted the edges of a dozen more." More unnerving, "The trail was canted to the left and tended to roll the Sno-Cat over to her port side. We drove with the hatch open and my door locked open." In suspicious-looking areas they used belays. The pair reached the end, Mile 190.9, and retraced their steps, doing altimetry on the way. That same day all three Sno-Cats negotiated the danger zone safely with their loads, although "the road was so steep in spots, the sleds would slide sideways down into a bordering crevasse and we'd have to race up the trail to keep the sled from falling in."[30]

From a baseline at Mile 190.9 the glaciologists "shot in" (lined up with a sextant) large green flags they had planted at the four-, three-, two-, and one-mile marks for later observance of the relative movement between the Ross Ice Shelf and the Rockefeller Plateau, thus beginning their ice studies. "Speaking of flags," Anderson continued, "I bet we saw a thousand of them through the crevasse area today. All over the place, flag after flag." On 4 February the tractor train caught up with the scientists, who now stopped every other day to do their glaciological and seismic measurements (see Chapter 11). The next day the scientists again overtook the slower-moving train, but eventually the tractors got ahead and it was not until the 17th, at Mile 517, that the Sno-Cats met the now-northbound tractors. They brought a "beautiful bulging, fat orange mail sack," to the delight of the lovesick Anderson, who counted twenty-eight letters and three cards from his girlfriend, Carole: "Wow!" On the 27th, after a month of scientific pathfinding on the trail, the traversers arrived at Byrd—although after chronic problems en route, the balky Sno-Cat quit "with two miles to go to Byrd Station; we could see it in the distance!"[31]

Americans were not alone in working up a sweat in the cold to prepare for the IGY in Antarctica. Eleven other nations—including the seven claimant states—were pushing their IGY facilities, scientific programs, and (ostensibly set-aside) political aims forward. Where and how many Antarctic stations would finally emerge would be governed, of course, by polar unknowables. Not surprisingly, Argentina, Chile, and Great Britain were set up early at several stations apiece on the Antarctic Peninsula, where they maintained overlapping claims. Some of these were considered "permanent," long pre-dating the IGY, their scientific work not necessarily focused on the geophysical disciplines. In addition, Argentina and Britain asserted their conflicting sovereignty in the Weddell Sea area with the former's General Belgrano Station and the latter's Halley Bay, established with difficulty in late 1954 and early 1956, respectively. The British base, to be run by the Falkland Islands Dependencies Survey for the Royal Society, had been planned for Vahsel Bay, but ice conditions forced them to put it 150 miles to the east.

At about the same time, Shackleton Station—the Filchner Ice Shelf base of the Commonwealth Trans-Antarctic Expedition (TAE)—ended up about thirty-five miles east of General Belgrano after Vivian Fuchs's ship lay trapped in the ice for almost a month. The treacherous Weddell gyre again dictated the terms. An advance party soon set out about 300 miles inland to reconnoiter a route for Fuchs and establish a depot called South Ice, where three hardy souls would winter over. The TAE was technically separate from the IGY, but Fuchs encouraged a mental and emotional connection, in part by making basic scientific measurements along the way.[32]

New Zealand, besides agreeing to operate Hallett Station jointly with the United States, planned to keep five scientists at Scott Base throughout the IGY. But it was members of the TAE support party who built and first occupied that station to lay supply depots for Fuchs's group, who intended to complete Shackleton's aborted surface crossing of the continent via the South Pole. Fuchs engaged the heroic conqueror of Mount Everest, Sir Edmund Hillary, to lead a contingent southward from Scott Base, tapping Hillary's famous name to garner publicity and public and private financial support in New Zealand. (Other funding came from the United Kingdom, Australia, and Union of South Africa.) At least that is what Hillary thought. The marriage would prove difficult. Hillary found Fuchs "very rigid in his views and plans," and his more "flexible" approach led to controlled but keenly felt tension. If Hillary presumed himself a partner, he soon felt excluded from Fuchs's inner circle. Fuchs was more circumspect about their relationship, but even photographs show the distance between them.[33]

In January 1956 a three-person New Zealand reconnaissance party, led by geophysicist Trevor Hatherton, had found an acceptable campsite for Scott Base at the foot of the Ferrar Glacier, Fuchs's recommended route to the ice cap. This was Butter Point, across McMurdo Sound from the U.S. facility on Ross Island, also within the New Zealand claim. Unfortunately, while the glacier's steel-hard ice would support tractors, it was unsuitable for anticipated dog-team transport of food and equipment and had no flat surface for an airfield. The Skelton Glacier might offer a better approach, but there was no satisfactory base site nearby. In December, when it was time to build, "extremely rough" ice and a wide tide crack between the sea ice and the foot of the moraine at Butter Point thwarted off-loading by tractor. Admiral Dufek, who had shipped two Weasels and about 1,000 tons of New Zealand cargo for the TAE, suggested Pram Point, just over "the gap" from McMurdo. Hillary liked what he saw, and Dufek sent a heavy tractor and some Seabees to help bulldoze the area and otherwise lend a hand. On the east side of the sound, the new location would add about fifty miles to Hillary's distance, but they were across fairly smooth and level shelf ice. By January 1957 Hillary had trailblazing parties out, and by winter two supply depots dressed the Skelton Glacier.[34]

Australia put in two continental stations, Mawson and Vestfold Hills, on the coast of its vast claim south of the homeland, far to the west of Mawson's original camp at blizzardy Commonwealth Bay. The French, under noted explorer Paul-Émile Victor, reestablished their recently abandoned base at Pointe Géologie in Adélie Land and, from it, planned to push inland 200 miles to build Charcot Station near the peripatetic South Magnetic Pole, for coordinating meteorological and geomagnetic observations. Because "terrible" winds and a lack of landing sites prohibited air support, they would supply Charcot by trains of three Weasels and two Sno-Cats, making three round-trips each. Until his sudden death in mid-1957, Harald Sverdrup, leader of the Norwegian-British-Swedish expedition, and then director of the Norsk Polarinstitutt, headed Norway's IGY effort in Antarctica—the building of one fourteen-man coastal facility, called Norway Station, in Queen Maud Land, within its claim. Several of these countries had additional stations on various sub-Antarctic islands, and New Zealand even considered Christchurch and Invercargill part of its polar effort, as Australia similarly viewed Hobart, Tasmania.

The Union of South Africa won inclusion among the Antarctic participants with an IGY station on windy, marshy, sub-Antarctic Marion Island in the Indian Ocean's Prince Edward Islands, which, at 46°S, 38°E, seemed a stretch to qualify. It also worked on Gough Island in the Tristan da Cunhas in the South Atlantic, even farther north. South Africa had also agreed to operate a weather station on Norway's Bouvet Island, at 54°S, 6°E, but found it "too uninhabitable." Belgium put in a station, named for King Baudouin, at King Leopold III Bay along the Princess Ragnhild Coast south of Africa. Directing this group was the son of Adrien de Gerlache, leader of the *Belgica* Expedition, which, trapped in the ice, had become Antarctica's first wintering party sixty years earlier.[35]

While Japanese whaling vessels plied the waters of the Southern Ocean, that country had not sent an exploring expedition south since Shirase's in 1911–1912. Now it eagerly committed to one Antarctic IGY station, Showa Base, along the Prince Harald Coast, a few hundred miles east of the Belgians. Dufek had offered to reconnoiter the area (about 40°E longitude) for a potential site in March 1956 after leaving the Knox Coast, but heavy pack ice, fog, and storms, in addition to the lateness of the season, forced him to abandon the effort. He did not survey the Weddell Sea region for the future Ellsworth Station as planned either, for similar reasons, but he did raise the U.S. flag over two sites in Queen Maud Land, attaching a record of the U.S. presence to each flagpole in a brass capsule, as was "customary for any nation," he said. *Times* reporter Bernard Kalb typically noted that the "busy day of flag-raising may have significance in the event the United States initiates claims for Antarctic areas."[36]

The Japanese planned that forty men would summer at Showa Base in 1956–1957 and eleven would winter over, with thirty to winter in 1958. Among other programs, they proposed a 275-mile traverse inland toward the geographic pole. As it happened, their ship, the *Soya*, returning in February 1957, got caught in the ice and was forced to seek assistance from the Soviet icebreaker *Ob*. When the *Soya* sailed south again in late 1957 to bring the new wintering team, it was greatly ice-strengthened, its engine power increased; the Japanese press touted their country's scientific and technical prowess, which "will not fail." But the *Soya* was again beset, this time for six long weeks. In ceaselessly foul weather, the leaders had to abandon their plans to land the main scientific team and ask for aid. The vessel freed itself the day before the USS *Burton Island* arrived, but the latter opened a path for the ice-damaged *Soya* and helped rescue the small crew of the previous winter by air. "In Japanese fashion," expedition and government leaders "apologized to the Japanese people for the failure of the mission," U.S. embassy officials reported from Tokyo. It was a painful "loss of face" for the tradition-bound and recently humiliated Japanese. Some hoped the IGY might be extended in Antarctica so Japan could still realize its full intended contribution.[37]

The Soviets, meanwhile, were scientifically a year ahead of the Americans. Commissioning their main coastal station Mirny, on the Queen Mary Coast in Australia's claim, on 13 February 1956, concurrently with McMurdo and Little America, they lost no time beginning their scientific programs. They also quickly sent a small trail party inland about 230 miles where they built an intermediate station, Pionerskaya, at about 8,850 feet. There, five men hunkered down to be the first of the IGY era to live a full winter in the Antarctic interior. The next spring the Soviets put in Oazis, a small station in the snow-free Bunger Hills area; its Highjump discoverers had hyperbolically called it an "oasis." But their primary focus trained on establishing their two "Pole" outposts, both in the remote, "entirely unexplored" interior. Vostok Station would be 900 miles south at the South Geomagnetic Pole, that "point at which the axis of the earth's magnetic field intersects the globe." As Dewart explained it, "Because the earth is not a perfect dipole magnet, the geomagnetic pole is about six hundred miles from the true magnetic pole the compass seeks." It is of "great scientific importance in the physics of the upper atmosphere and the earth-sun relationship." The other target site was the so-called Pole of Inaccessibility, about 1,300 long, cold miles from any coast.[38]

The Soviet pioneers managed to lay an advance supply depot, called Komsomolskaya, 520 miles south, but the actual Vostok party encountered extreme weather and snow conditions and in April, with winter nigh upon them, built a temporary camp where they were, 390 miles out. They called it Vostok-1. Sullivan told the world, with more than a hint of chauvinism, that the "Soviet explorers in Antarctica have been unable to set up either of the inland stations assigned to them in time for the start of the International Geophysical Year," giving nothing for the hard-won interim locations. In October 1957 the "slow, laborious overland movement" by tractor train began again. On 16 December, after wallowing through "intractably deep and soft snow," Dewart continued, the Russians reached the geomagnetic pole and built Vostok Station at almost 11,500 frigid, oxygen-deprived feet. Eleven men wintered over. Another party struck out for the Pole of Inaccessibility but were again stopped short when the season grew late, and six wintered over at a camp they called Sovietskaya. It was close enough to their goal to make scientific observations valuable. Finally, in December 1958, one last push brought them to that logistically unfeasible pole, "whose name," Dewart wrote sympathetically, "was becoming mockingly appropriate." They stayed for two weeks, just until the IGY was officially over, then abandoned their small, never-named camp intact.[39]

The new year 1957 saw American exchange scientist Gordon Cartwright settling in at Mirny, similar to Wilkes in latitude, climate, and topography. In a letter to Odishaw in late January, he described his warm reception and good life among the Russians. "Everyone is friendly and helpful," he opened, and patient, too, as he struggled to learn their language and habits. He appreciated his "comfortable single room (not the usual arrangement) in the same apartment with most of the MET [meteorology] staff." Cartwright called the houses "simple but warm and comfortable except for the toilet arrangements!" He did not elaborate on the latter point and rather belied the former in an article he radioed to the *Washington Post* in February in which he noted the presence of "caviar, carpets, wallpaper, dial phones, fresh meat, and taped music," allowing that "caviar at breakfast is hard to face." The newcomer judged Russian clothing "excellent." Made from a variety of materials (fur, leather, down-fill), it was warm and rugged, "definitely better looking and simpler to get into" than American polar apparel: "We have nothing that compares with the excellent all-purpose fur 'shapka'" [cap].[40]

Cartwright found himself deeply impressed with his counterparts. "There is no doubt about the high caliber of scientific talent on this expedition," he informed Odishaw. Many of his comrades had served fifteen to twenty years in the Arctic and were "eager to learn of differences" in the Antarctic. They were well-read in the literature of their fields (even in other languages), confident, enthusiastic, hardworking, and willing under "rough conditions." They were mostly older, well-established professionals, family men. This was in sharp contrast with the American IGY personnel—a point also made by Cartwright's successors at Mirny, meteorologist Morton Rubin in 1958 and seismologist Gilbert Dewart in 1960. Cartwright credited this to the fact that in the USSR science was "obviously a favored profession." Polar scientists got handsome bonuses, "percentage-wise, much more than ours, I believe." Most of their equipment was "first class," although they also knew how to get along with "elementary gear." Surprisingly, they still calculated—efficiently—on the ancient abacus. One important difference he noticed was the large number of women in Russian science. They made up more than half of the scientific staff of the Soviet Institute of Geography, for example. He had met two such women, "very serious scientists." "Hundreds" of women had applied for IGY positions, eager to pursue their special projects despite hardship and absence from family. Three women were currently working on the laboratory ship *Ob*, though none were at Mirny, "contrary to information I had earlier!" It would be more than a dozen years before American women scientists would win the chance to pursue their career interests in Antarctica.[41]

Throughout this period of IGY planning and early implementation, while public rhetoric centered on science and international cooperation, strategic and political interests were never far removed. Starting in early 1956, for example, the British Commonwealth's Antarctic claimants aired their worries at the State Department. Australian ambassador Percy Spender, distressed over the distrusted Soviet Union's presence within its claim, sought regular consultations toward a "common policy of keeping watch on Soviet activity and countering Soviet penetration." Given its geographic proximity and whaling interests, South Africa admitted interest in "certain territorial rights of modest scale in Antarctica," though it professed more concern about undefined "security aspects" of Antarctic activity. The British complained about the baseless (in their view) claims of Chile and Argentina, which conflicted with their own. The United States was equally intent on advancing its interests, which had yet to be articulated. In the end, Secretary of State Dulles emphasized the importance of having a "common position without getting into quarrels among ourselves" over divergent claims policies. How that was to be achieved he did not say, and, given U.S. indecision on the issue, it is unlikely that he had a plan except to keep options open. By March, State had decided to deflect the Commonwealth countries' apparent "attempt to line us up on the British side in their territorial dispute with Chile and the Argentine" and suggested "continuing existing close bilateral relationships" as usual. State presented to each country an aide-mémoire reiterating U.S. claims policy on 29 March 1956, trusting that it would not "interfere with effective and friendly cooperation on other aspects of the Antarctic question, such as scientific investigation and exploration." As for Chile and Argentina, the State Department advised USNC-IGY leaders planning to attend the upcoming Rio Conference (Western Hemisphere regional IGY conference) in July 1956 to "grin and bear" expected "long-winded speech making" so long as the Latin Americans did not try to obtain "some kind of endorsement of their claims."[42]

National interests equally occupied the press, which reflected and fanned popular feeling about the broader significance of Antarctica in the Cold War world. *Newsweek* reported in November 1955, on the departure of the ships of Deep Freeze I, that "ostensibly, these elaborate preparations are in support of scientific programs" for the IGY. But "they also signalize some international jockeying for position on the last unknown continent." The article went on: "The prospects of transportable atomic-power plants, the promise of jet travel between Asia and South America, and the far-reaching arm of guided-missile warfare all place a remarkably high premium on 'geophysical data,'" for now Antarctica's "principal export commodity." As for U.S. "official aloofness" from making territorial claims, *Newsweek* had "little doubt" that the IGY was "but the start of a sustained and widening U.S. interest." Bernard Kalb, in one of many examples, noted somewhat more sedately in the *New York Times* in April 1956 that while obtaining scientific data was the "immediate aim" of the IGY nations, "the factors of exploration and occupancy may have important political significance in the future." The science bases might become "strategic footholds," he wrote, not far from noting that the Soviets "would not like to be forgotten if the continent should be carved up." The Russians alone had no political friends on the ice.[43]

Speaking for a vocal and apparently growing constituency, Sen. Alexander Wiley, Republican from Wisconsin, introduced a bill in Congress on 31 May 1957 to establish a Richard E. Byrd Antarctic Commission for "establishing a spearhead for a continuing Antarctic policy in the Government of the United States." Not the first such effort, Wiley's bill delivered coded pressure on the administration to press a claim, or at least act more deliberately about ensuring U.S. ascendancy, on the polar continent. This attempt to create one voice, one governmental home, for Antarctic strategic interests did not pass, nor would any like it. But when the commission concept came up in March, Wexler wondered who, with Byrd gone and Siple "locked up in the ice," could bring "enough knowledge and influence" to sway polar legislation. Lunching with Dufek on 21 March, he and Odishaw urged the admiral to "step into this vacuum because [the Defense Department] is the only government agency with no time limit on it which has been given such cognizance of the Antarctic problem." Dufek, though, seemed focused on the more immediate problem of needing to know for budget purposes if a "third year," then under discussion, "is to go in."[44]

Indeed, months before the IGY officially began, U.S. science leaders such as Wexler, Berkner, NSF director Alan Waterman, and others began pushing to continue the IGY in Antarctica beyond its 31 December 1958 expiration date. The National Academy of Sciences enthusiastically agreed, arguing that the investment in money, material, and lives begged doing so and that the "paucity of previous information" on the southern high latitudes demanded a longer period of observation to "establish the patterns of phenomena there." The subject would continue to percolate.[45]

On the evening of 30 June 1957, Greenwich Mean Time, a shower of electrons from a major solar flare two days earlier disturbed the earth's electrically charged ionosphere and magnetic field, causing massive radio blackouts—"as if to start the IGY with a bang," Sullivan wrote. That morning the IGY's first, slightly premature World Interval began, asking all field scientists to increase the frequency and intensity of their observations to fully record these dramatic phenomena. President Eisenhower took the occasion to address the nation. "July 1 marks the beginning of one of the great scientific adventures of our time—the International Geophysical Year," he began. While scientists could not anticipate all the knowledge they would acquire, it would surely "give us new understanding and new powers over the forces of nature." But "as I see it," the president continued, refreshingly free of chauvinism, the most important result of the IGY would be "the demonstration of the ability of peoples of all nations to work together harmoniously for the common good." The scientific teams in sunless Antarctica were ready.[46]

COMPREHENDING THE COLD
Antarctic Weather Quest

*That Antarctic regions are cold we have known ever since
Captain Cook's voyages of 1772–1775, but how cold they are
we still do not know today.*

—Harry Wexler and Morton Rubin, 1956[1]

Executive Director Hugh Odishaw called the International Geophysical Year (IGY) the "single most significant peaceful activity of
mankind since the Renaissance and the Copernican Revolution."
The Antarctic Committee's Laurence Gould compared it to the fif-
teenth and sixteenth centuries—history's "greatest era of geographical exploration" when European explorers "doubled the size of the
known world." Now, in the late 1950s, in a global effort of unparalleled scope and intensity, scientists were poised to "map" the earth's
physical environment. They would observe the natural phenomena
of the earth's own laboratory, as they put it, doing so simultaneously
everywhere, to multiply (not merely add up) the value of individual

efforts toward the growth of human understanding.[2]

If, as historian Stephen Pyne asserts, Antarctica is the "simplest of the world's environments," it was, on the eve of the IGY, a vast, tantalizing unknown. Eager scientists spread out over the continent were already beginning their probes. Over the course of the eighteen-month "year," they would systematically study the weather, aurora and airglow, cosmic rays, geomagnetism, ionospheric physics, glaciology, and seismology. They would also add to sparse knowledge of south-polar oceanography and hydrography. Despite political and strategic concerns (claims sensitivities, economic competitiveness) that kept geology and mapping off the list of official IGY disciplines, scientists would pursue them anyway, and they would make a significant start in the areas of non-geophysical biology, physiology, and psychology. Americans alone would produce seventeen tons of data.[3]

Introducing the proposed IGY disciplines in a speech in late 1955, Joseph Kaplan, chair of the USNC, appropriately began with the meteorology program, weather being a "global entity." The atmosphere is the "'working fluid' of an enormous heat engine driven by the sun," he, like others, explained. Large- and small-scale circulation systems transport heat (and moisture) from the tropics, discharging it in the polar regions. Scientist and writer Carl Eklund added that the "exhaust" of this engine is the earth's radiation of heat back into space. The atmosphere provides life-giving oxygen, water, and insulation against deadly solar radiation. Its vital motion—winds—cleanses, nourishes, and moderates the earth's climate. USNC-IGY spokesmen held out to the Senate Appropriations Committee in 1956 the practical promise that systematically gathering and analyzing worldwide weather data would "reveal the true three-dimensional structure of the atmosphere." That was essential for learning about basic weather patterns, not to mention improving long-range weather prediction.[4]

As early National Academy of Sciences planning documents emphasized, the air masses of the Southern Hemisphere were hardly known at the time; those of the critically important upper atmosphere, anywhere on earth in fact, were almost entirely a mystery. Little understood beyond its merciless, mercurial cold, Antarctic weather commanded attention. A vast heat sink like the Arctic but even greater, the polar continent, with all of its ice impacting the interplay between ocean and atmosphere, had to be important beyond its own margins in the "great planetary heat exchange system that is the basic cause of weather." Pyne calls the Antarctic the "cold core," the "great refrigerator" of the earth's atmosphere. It is "a region so intensely frigid that it deflects the meteorological equator of the globe northward nearly 10 degrees latitude. The

solar radiation balance is negative all year round." In sunless winter no radiation enters, while in summer most of it is reflected back into space by the snow
and ice, which are both "an outcome and a contributor to that fact." But in the
1950s scientists had little to start with. George Simpson, Scott's chief meteorologist on his last expedition, had erroneously hypothesized "pressure surges"
emanating from the interior of West Antarctica, where low-pressure systems
persisted. Canadian scientist John Murray had been "nearly right" in 1893 when
he predicted the existence (yet unseen) of a continental East Antarctica with a
permanent high-pressure zone above it. And there were the accumulated
weather records from the sprinkling of exploring expeditions over the years.[5]

To organize their study of global weather patterns, IGY planners had designated three pole-to-pole "world lines" along which to string a series of stations. Of these, the United States was most interested in the one between the
meridians 70 and 80 degrees West longitude through the Western Hemisphere
and tried to site Antarctic stations along it. Although early documents list
Little America in this sequence, at 162° West it was far off. Byrd, at 120° West,
was an admitted "dog leg" but not far in miles as the meridians converged,
and the Pole formed the exact southern terminus. Scientists would use data
from this line of stations, as well as others on the polar continent, to study
various transport problems such as heat, momentum, energy, and water vapor; the strength, location, and movement of various jet streams; the basics of
southern circulation systems; and the possible interdependence of circula-
tions in both hemispheres.[6]

In addition to its broad effect on hemispheric, if not global, climate, the
weather in Antarctica was an obvious and immediate factor in safe polar travel
and even survival, so it was no surprise that every scientific base would devote
top effort to gathering weather data. Altogether there would be more than fifty
weather-reporting stations among the twelve participating nations. As for the
U.S. commitment, "We had a million dollars in 1955 to run a meteorological
program in the Antarctic. A million dollars!" remembered the Weather Bureau's
Morton Rubin, savoring still the sense of plenty. Some Antarctic stations would
employ as many weather observers and analysts as all other scientific disciplines combined. For example, in its first year South Pole had four meteorologists among its nine scientists and five among ten the second year. At the larger
Little America there were first thirteen and then fourteen meteorologists, including the exchange "mets" of Weather Central, among the two dozen scientific staff. W. S. ("Bill") Weyant, meteorologist in charge of half of the mets
during the winter of 1958, justified that many to handle all of the routine
observations, weather-balloon launchings, and special programs. With seven,

significant data reduction could be done on-site and each person could have one day off a week—a boost for morale and productivity. Wilkes boasted among its scientific staff only one meteorologist in both IGY years, but he had the help of four Navy aerologists; a similar arrangement prevailed at Ellsworth, although station leader Finn Ronne considered the efforts of IGY meteorologist Gerald Fierle duplicative of the Navy's work under chief Walter May, aerologist, and his three enlisted assistants.[7]

To obtain a three-dimensional picture of the polar atmosphere, Antarctica's meteorologists made continuous recordings of surface temperature, humidity, air pressure, and wind—direction, velocity, and gusts. They and the Navy aerographers also noted sky cover, including the extent and type of clouds at various levels; prevailing visibility by quadrants; precipitation by type, intensity, duration, and amount; maximum and minimum temperatures every six hours; and the "state of the ground." At least this was the intent. Especially at the ice-shelf and ice-cap stations, snow swirled incessantly, obscuring visibility any time winds blew at fifteen knots or higher, which was often. The difficulty of distinguishing between drifting and falling snow made it more or less impossible to measure accumulation, although observers put out innumerable calibrated stakes and read them weekly. Pole meteorologist Floyd Johnson mounted a precipitation gauge atop the ten-foot (later thirty-foot) wind mast to compare results with another gauge at the surface. He judged that "possibly as much as" 90 percent of the snow caught in the surface device was drift. Little America did not trust its six-hourly precipitation readings either, despite using both a shielded eight-inch rain gauge and a line of accumulation stakes.[8]

Antarctica itself complicated the simplest, normally straightforward tasks. Efforts to maintain sensitive automatic recording instruments and to read others manually, even when enclosed in special shelters, were thwarted by fine drifting snow, wind, darkness, and cold. Siple noted how Pole "Met men" had to hold their breath while reading thermometers outdoors lest their exhalations blur the instruments' fine gradations or their warmth distort the readings, however minutely. They learned the hard way that, say, locating solar radiation instruments near the black barrels of the fuel storage dump skewed their measurements. Snowdrifts in the lee of parked vehicles buried them. Fine snow sifting into the instruments shorted out their electrical components. Tractor vibrations shook sensitive dial needles. The cold could incapacitate. Pole micrometeorologist Paul Dalrymple added up more than 3,000 hours colder than –70° F in 1958 and 9 hours below –100°, calculating an average sundown temperature of –74.7°F. A few times it was so cold atop his instrument tower that he became acutely nauseous, forcing him to come down and warm his hands in his armpits before climbing back up to finish the readings. As Byrd Station (and others) reported, both gathering and transmitting the twice-daily weather maps proved insurmountable challenges distressingly often because of the frequent radio blackouts, "continuous storms" of blowing snow that blocked radio reception with snow static, and occasional lack of information because of failed upper-air soundings. "Gaps of from one to twenty-five maps destroyed any possible historical sequence," Byrd's meteorologist-in-charge Wesley Morris complained. Because "the entire atmosphere is the meteorologist's laboratory," it was "relatively easy to interfere" with its "representative nature," Norman Benes, chief wintering meteorologist at Hallett in 1958, noted dryly.[9]

Twice a day the mets everywhere made upper-air observations with "radiosondes," or "rawinsondes" as they were called when tracked by radar. The suffix "sonde" means sounding; the invented prefix combined radio and wind. IGY meteorologist Howard Wessbecher, at McMurdo in Deep Freeze I, explained this "fascinating little instrument" as a group of electronic weather-recording devices connected to a battery-powered radio transmitter in "a little white box, oh, maybe twelve inches on a side and maybe eight inches tall." It was carried aloft at the end of a string attached to a large hydrogen-filled balloon. A light on the device permitted visual tracking at night. The instrument converted changing temperatures, pressure, and humidity to characteristic radio frequencies, which it read alternately and transmitted as radio signals to the ground, where they were translated into actual readings and traced on recorder paper for analysis. Each station had a plastic (so as not to absorb radio signals), onion-shaped "rawin" dome on a rooftop or tower that housed a radio receiver and an antenna to track the balloon, allowing the calculation of wind speed and direction. In their hour or so of flight, some balloons went as high as 100,000 feet, about twenty miles, yielding progressive data on these five basic weather elements. Some high-altitude weather balloons released from ships had rockets attached that would fire when the balloons reached their maximum height. These "rockoons" could go as high as fifty miles. James Van Allen and members of his university team aboard the *Glacier* in Deep Freeze III launched thirty-four of them at intervals of five degrees latitude from the tropics to the Ross Sea. The weather observers then plotted selected data on graphs, to be coded and transmitted to Weather Central or to their own air and field operations.[10]

For all their importance and ubiquitous usage since the mid-1930s—even in Antarctica since 1939–1940—launching weather balloons taxed the patience, endurance, and ingenuity of meteorologists everywhere on the polar continent. For starters, "you had to make your own gas," remembered Wessbecher. By his and other accounts, the manufacturer first donned goggles, gloves, and rubber apron. He then measured about six and a half pounds of aluminum chips (punchings and scraps from companies making things from aluminum, remembered Wilkes meteorologist Rudi Honkala) and ten pounds of caustic soda (sodium hydroxide) into a lidded five-gallon can, rolling it to mix the dry chemicals. These he poured through a fill-pipe into a pressurized reaction chamber and readied ten gallons of water to be admitted by a control valve. As the water initiated the chemical reaction, the balloon attached to a hose at the top of the apparatus would begin to expand. After about half an hour the room would be "much filled by a big floppy rubber sack full of this gas." While a safety cap on the cylinder would pop if too much pressure built up, "we usually got out of the inflation gas building while the gas was generating," recalled Wessbecher, respectful of the danger. Indeed, heat for comfort was piped in to avoid having any kind of flame nearby. The whole process was "a bit tricky," allowed Cartwright of the similar operation in the Arctic and at Mirny, because of the high flammability and explosiveness of hydrogen and the dry weather. "A spark could have been the end of things." In later years, ships delivered inert helium gas in cylinders, which made the process far easier and safer.[11]

After about an hour and a half of careful preflight preparation, observation, calculation, and inflation, the balloons were normally released from an overhead trapdoor in the small inflation shelter. But high winds made it difficult to control the rising object and its delicate instrument box. The Pole mets built eight-foot "windshields" on the north and east sides of their inflation shelter for protection against the prevailing winds, after which they missed "not a single scheduled release" for wind and almost never had to resort to a second try. At several other stations, such as at windiest Wilkes (fifty knots could be expected at least four days a month), the men added side doors, which in stormy weather gave them the disagreeable option of carrying the balloon into the blowy outdoors a hundred feet or so before letting it go—still struggling, as it slowly rose, to get the payload off without destructive bumps along the ground. Side doors had significantly mitigated the problem at Ellsworth in 1957, but by the winter of 1958 drifting snow left only the overhead doors usable, and then only with daily digging. Echoing his predecessor, scientific leader Matthew Brennan grumbled that releases had to "clear the shelter, cross the camp through the radio antenna field and clear the aurora tower. Many balloons launched successfully were lost by contact with one of these obstructions." Such wires plagued (and served) every station.[12]

Navy aerologists launching a weather balloon against a fiery sunset at McMurdo. Official U.S. Navy photograph. Courtesy, Robert Chaudoin.

The balloons, made of neoprene, introduced their own problems. Quality was variable. Some had pinhole leaks, others weak spots that bulged when inflated. Even good ones became rigid and brittle in the cold air and would not ascend to desired heights. Siple credited Pole's weathermen, though others were working on it too, with developing the technique of soaking the balloons in warm diesel oil to prolong their pliability. It was, Siple wrote, "the result of persistent efforts to try every sort of remedy." Boiling balloons was a "recognized method of conditioning," wrote chief meteorologist Edwin Flowers, but comparative tests at Pole showed an average climb of 13.8 kilometers (8.6 miles) for boiled balloons, 19.5 km (12.1 miles) for diesel-conditioned ones. Conditioning was widely adopted, although experiments at Wilkes, alternating a warm gasoline or diesel oil soak with boiling in water for five to eight minutes, resulted in an average of over 2,500 feet higher with boiled balloons. For certain, moist heat helped. Height was also enhanced by another Siple-claimed Pole invention, a steam condenser used between the hydrogen generator and the feed hose to keep water out of the balloon. Honkala built one of these at Wilkes, as did Bob Johns at Byrd. Weyant at Little America, who confirmed the readiness of mets everywhere to pool their knowledge, also noted that balloons deteriorated from age or prolonged frozen storage and urged seasonal resupply. Morris recommended bringing balloons indoors to be "conditioned inside to room temperature" at least two weeks before use and the radiosonde instruments and transmitters at least one week prior to flight.[13]

During Rubin's year at Mirny he analyzed the upper-air data that came from the Soviets' twice-daily radiosondes, making what he called a "very crude and first effort" to determine the atmospheric exchange between air over the continent and air over the surrounding ocean. He wanted to learn how much heat and moisture were being transported across these boundaries, how much was going out, and how much energy was stored in the ice to see "whether, in fact, there was some kind of [heat and mass] balance." More work needed to be done, and he looked forward to a study that would include glaciological data on ice outflow as well.[14]

During the winter of 1957 Little America housed a two-person micrometeorology program, a discipline concerned with surface and near-surface weather phenomena. Dalrymple, one member, had been keen to go to the Antarctic since his boyhood reading about Byrd: "I knew all the people in those books just like I would know people that lived in the town." University courses from an Arctic expert further inspired him to apply to Byrd for "any position" on an upcoming expedition. The admiral initially wrote a polite rejection but later astonished the young scientist with another letter inquiring if he was still interested in going south with the IGY. Was he! A civilian working with the U.S. Army, Dalrymple measured variations in temperature with copper-constantan thermocouples at thirteen levels, from 1 meter (about 3.3 feet) below the surface to 10 meters above, the latter from a 30-foot mast shared with the glaciological program. He similarly observed wind gradients with three-cup anemometers at heights from 0.5 meters to 8 meters (about 26.4 feet) above the surface. High winds and the adjacent antenna farm affected readings during radio transmitting (he discovered too late that he had no shielded cable for his instruments), but with a lot of climbing up and down, he got good temperature and wind profiles from successful readings on 100 winter days, from the last of March to mid-October.

Colleague Herfried Hoinkes from the University of Innsbruck concentrated on measuring incoming and outgoing solar radiation to obtain net radiation values, observing the movement and erosion of sastrugi, and penetrating his partner's Down East accent. The next summer the two men and their instruments transferred to the South Pole, where Dalrymple wintered over in 1958, studying the great temperature-inversion layer there. Hoinkes, who spent only the summer at 90° South, concluded that even though the Pole received the most solar energy of any place on earth, most of it was lost through reflection off the ice cover; moreover, the fine grain of the snow's top layer slowed absorption of radiant heat.[15]

Antarctica's meteorologists also did additional studies as requested and equipped by stateside institutions or suggested by their own available resources and imaginations. On their own, Hallett's weathermen buried thermohms (resistance thermometers) at 10 and 50 centimeters (4 and 20 inches) in the ground to measure soil temperatures over time, probably for the first time in Antarctica. Others at Pole used two radiometers to measure, respectively, the total amount of long-wave energy received from the sun and atmosphere and the net exchange and balance of energy between the snow and the atmosphere. At both stations scientists set out two horizontal incidence pyrheliometers, one with its sensor facing upward to measure incoming shortwave solar energy, the other facing downward to measure outbound radiation from the snow. Comparing these measurements gave the reflectivity, or albedo, of the surface. With two-cell photoelectric devices they learned the duration and percentage of sunshine per day. At Little America meteorologists collected samples of precipitation for chemical analysis at the Air Force Chemical Research Center in Massachusetts and atmospheric dust for the Scripps Institution of Oceanography in San Diego, although the latter experiment suffered from heavy concentrations of soot in the air from camp stoves and power generators.[16]

One of Honkala's "side excursions" was to study snow crystals. Having learned how to make replicas of snow crystals at New Hampshire's Mount Washington Observatory, he wished he could have spent more time at this aesthetically rewarding and scientifically engaging pursuit. He would pour onto a glass plate a small amount of a chilled solution made from a powdered polyvinyl resin dissolved in ethylene dichloride. As he exposed it to falling snow, the "very hydrophilic" liquid would quickly surround and cover each crystal, "filling all its little nooks and crannies without melting it." The solution quickly evaporated, and in a few minutes he could bring what remained inside. Under a microscope "it would look exactly like the snow crystal did when it was real." Because the character of snow crystals changes "very markedly with changes in weather" (fluctuations in temperature, the amount of water vapor in the air), a good synoptic meteorologist could tell "whether a cold front is approaching you or it's gone past you based on the type of snow crystals that are falling." Honkala also collected replicas of minute crystals of snow and ice of the type that refracted light to create unforgettable optical phenomena such as halos and sundogs.[17]

Ozone studies, of moment today as the hole in the earth's shield against ultraviolet (UV) radiation has grown, were first pursued in Antarctica by scientists of Scott's *Discovery* Expedition, although, according to Rubin, they were "crude and unsuccessful." Planning documents from the spring of 1953 show IGY leaders eager to measure total ozone using the moon or stars as a light source during the Arctic night so they could "verify the existence of the ozone 'gap' thought to exist at high latitudes after the winter solstice," followed by a sharp increase to values higher than those found in lower North American latitudes. Similar proposals were soon extended to the southern polar regions. Ozone, a form of oxygen, is made photochemically when normal oxygen molecules absorb most of the sun's harmful UV radiation in the high atmosphere. It normally settles in a thin layer between the lower and upper atmosphere, about fifteen to twenty five miles above the earth. Without sunlight, ozone slowly decays to normal oxygen, releasing energy. IGY weathermen at Little America made continuous recordings of surface ozone obtained from an air intake on the roof of the meteorology building; occasionally, when sky conditions were favorable, they also measured total ozone manually with a spectrophotometer. They were amazed to find ozone during the dark winter, since it is generated by sunlight, concluding that it must have somehow traveled there from lower latitudes. Odishaw reported about 25 percent more ozone at ground level at Little America than in New Mexico. Scientists surmised that it played an important role in upper-atmospheric circulation because of the amount of energy it absorbed and released.[18]

Little America's meteorologists, often assisted in special studies by the Weather Central mets, also measured atmospheric carbon dioxide. This minor constituent in the air was important to the earth's heat balance if, as they thought, it acted like a trap for solar radiation, "much as glass does in a greenhouse." Expanding an analogy much used today, Odishaw wrote in 1958, "Our industrial civilization burns tremendous quantities of fossil fuel each year, pouring millions of tons of carbon dioxide into the atmosphere. Most of this is absorbed by plant life and by the waters of the oceans, but there is the possibility that eventually the carbon dioxide content of the atmosphere will rise enough to affect the world's climate." The IGY scientists concluded that Antarctica had about the same concentration of carbon dioxide as parts of the world not directly subject to industrial contamination.[19]

The weathermen also conducted research on atmospheric radioactivity for the Naval Research Laboratory. With a thin-wall Geiger counter they recorded the radioactivity of outdoor air as it passed through a filter. They then placed the filter in a lead cask and re-measured for about sixteen hours to distinguish natural radioactivity from the long-half-life fission products of the new atomic age. They sent melted samples of newly fallen snow from a pan on top of the high aurora tower (to try—hopelessly in blizzards—to minimize the catch of drifting snow) to the Atomic Energy Commission for analysis of tritium and Strontium 90, both found in fallout from nuclear-bomb testing being conducted in the atmosphere. In 1960 Navy flight surgeon Capt. Earl Hedblom visited Byrd's Little America III to retrieve cans of condensed milk left behind by the winterers under Siple in 1940. This "last clean milk" was to be tested for long-lived radioisotopes to establish a baseline for pre–atomic-age radiation.[20]

Finally, the Weather Bureau later asked IGY meteorologists to be alert for any "exceptional phenomena," such as rare noctilucent and nacreous clouds. Not only were they "quite magnificent and a sight not to be forgotten," they were little known and thus of great scientific interest. Deputy Chief D. M. Little asked for photographs or sketches if possible and added, "Ingenuity and extra effort will be officially noted, and observers may be sure that their work will be appreciated." Noctilucent clouds, he explained, were luminous pearly-white or bluish night clouds in parallel streaks or waves along the northern horizon, especially during the long twilight period. Perhaps they were made up of meteoric dust. Even rarer fluffy banks of nacreous clouds were iridescent, in the pastels and glossy sheen of mother-of-pearl. Byrd Station, deep in the West Antarctic interior, in particular seemed to experience many such unusual weather conditions, including optical phenomena such as double-ringed coronas and mirages, which were also seen at Pole. In late August 1957, just before sunrise, Byrd aurora observer Dan Hale reported nacreous clouds of "great variety and richness of color"—"intense" shades of "blue, green, yellow, orange, and red."[21]

(Byrd had other "sightings" as well. Charlie Bentley remembered one unnamed weather observer who worried that the legendary "Abominable Snowmen"—Yetis—of the Himalayas might exist in the Antarctic. So his mates could not resist cutting out large "feet" from scraps of wood boards and surreptitiously planting "Yeti footprints" in the snow around the outdoor weather station. For the rest of the winter, the poor hoodwinked fellow would not go out to read his instruments without taking his revolver. Bentley laughed, remembering, but also called it "unimaginable" that "in those days we were allowed to have firearms in the Antarctic."[22])

Without question, the most ambitious and significant IGY weather effort was Harry Wexler's brainchild, the Antarctic Weather Central at Little America. In broad concept, synoptic observations (identical and simultaneous in numerous locations) would reveal relationships among local phenomena that would, in turn, inform the big picture of world weather processes. While one purpose was to provide forecasts for air and over-snow traverse operations, Rubin said the Navy aerologists, using the same information, did most of the forecasting for operations. Weather Central would concentrate on analysis, with some research. It would primarily be a clearinghouse for raw Antarctic weather data, which it would collect, screen, organize, plot on maps, code, and transmit by radio back to the reporting stations and to other weather services in the Southern Hemisphere. With its small staff, Weather Central would serve as many as fifty international weather stations in an area "almost twice that of the United States," Wexler soberly but proudly forewarned his senior meteorologists assigned to Antarctic IGY stations in late 1956. Their workload would be daunting.[23]

When Rubin returned to Washington after his first austral summer of preliminary work on the system, there was still much to do to prepare for Weather Central operations. Wexler put him in charge of organizing and training its staff, including the international participants, and supplying all their material needs—a task of several months. Returning south again for Deep Freeze II to install the people and equipment at Little America, he found slow going there. Weather Central staff took over data analysis from the Navy aerographers in late January 1957, but Rubin fretted on 5 February that Weather Central was operating "only on a minimal basis." While the well-trained personnel were responding capably to polar demands, he said, they had insufficient physical space—despite their operational priority. And the Navy radiomen could have used "fuller indoctrination" on the importance of not interfering with weather traffic except in emergencies. The IGY's Hanessian had sent a memorandum to Seabee commander Whitney in late November 1956 outlining Weather Central's requirements, including temporary housing and work facilities pending the arrival of materials for an additional barracks and an annex to the communications building, but apparently to little effect.[24]

On 21 February Crary's report to Odishaw was more upbeat. The new communications structure was "now finished and operations in the Weather Central should pick up shortly." Acknowledging that "many IGY man days seem to have been wasted," he wrote that the meteorologists had stayed busy unloading supplies and doing "many other household duties necessary in establishing a station in this remote region of the earth." To this optimist the schedule was "not far behind and progress is steady." A week later, Weather Central personnel announced they would release a broadcast schedule on 15 March, anticipating the start of forecasting analyses on 1 June. Data collection actually began on 20 May and broadcasting of weather analyses on 29 May 1957, although they were still based on incomplete data that were more than a day old. Still, improvement, "though slow, was steady," and "nearly every month" the percentage of received data increased, Crary reported. By mid-June Weather Central was receiving surface and upper-air reports from all U.S. Antarctic stations and began weekly IGYNET "skeds" (schedules) with several others. By 1 July 1957 all of the primary (mother) stations were regularly passing weather data to intermediary McMurdo, but a fully workable permanent schedule would never be devised.[25]

The Weather Central communication system was inherently complicated. The Americans maintained two separate radio networks. The Navy's system connected the six science bases with McMurdo and thence with Balboa in the Panama Canal Zone for contact with the United States. In early 1956 McMurdo was designated Communications Central (or Radio Central) for all naval support units. The Navy's lead weather unit was there, too. The other network was the IGY's international "mother-daughter" system that linked all stations to Weather Central, housed at Little America, where the command headquarters of the naval support units and the scientific headquarters also resided. All weather-related radio traffic from all U.S. and foreign Antarctic stations went first to McMurdo for collecting and relaying to Little America. In practice, this meant that all traffic entering or leaving the continent and most of it among the U.S. bases went through both stations—a wasteful duplication of handling.

Gould, Wexler, Weather Central's meteorologist-in-charge Bill Moreland, and task-force officers ventilated this matter at length in late November 1957, apparently upon the Navy's request to move Weather Central to McMurdo. Wexler's scientific heart clearly beat with Little America, though he was torn. He wanted the facility joined with what could be called Science Central but knew McMurdo's Radio Central could provide better weather-data coverage. On the 29th he wrote to Odishaw that "since data are the lifeblood of the Central, this should be the overruling consideration." Two days later he informed Gould that Captain Dickey, the new Navy commander, wanted the program out, "perhaps to get out of their hair an outfit which naturally is never satisfied with the amount of met'l data." But McMurdo had no building to spare, and the "definite desire" of incoming program head Tom Gray to stay at Little America "settled it." Weather Central did not move. Wexler asked Gould to write a letter of appreciation to Dickey and hoped for improved operations.

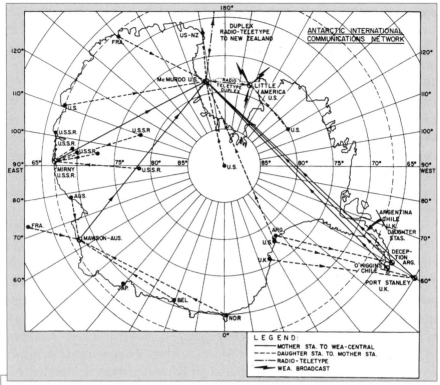

Antarctic mother-daughter weather communications network. Data were sent first to McMurdo, then retransmitted to Weather Central at Little America. NARA II, RG 307.5, Cartography Division.

A year earlier Wexler had grumbled that Hanessian was "too palsy-walsy" with the Navy, having given only a "half-hearted defense against" moving the facility to McMurdo, so the issue was long-standing.[26]

The reporting system was also complex and subject to breakdown at many points. Working like a telephone tree in reverse, the "daughter" stations, usually smaller ones, reported to a designated "mother," which then relayed the combined information to Weather Central via McMurdo. For example, McMurdo was a mother station, receiving and collating weather data from daughters Pole, Scott (New Zealand), Hallett, Wilkes, and D'Urville (France) and, via the latter, that of "granddaughter" Charcot (also France). The British station at Port Stanley in the Falkland Islands received and forwarded information from ten other compatriot units plus, for geographic convenience, the American station Ellsworth. All the Soviet stations sent their data to Mirny for further transmittal, as did Mawson (Australia) and Kerguelen Island (France). Byrd reported directly to Little America, the only mother with an only child.[27]

Weather Central also received weather data from trail parties, expedition ships, whaling vessels, aircraft, island bases, and stations in Southern Hemisphere nations. The range of their points of origin as well as distance created enduring challenges. The Union of South Africa, Chile, and Argentina maintained somewhat erratic schedules and had poor signal strength. Inadequate reports from these stations compromised the analysis of the Antarctic data. Hourly data from Canberra, Australia, by radioteletype, and Wellington, New Zealand, by code, were usually more reliable. Different stations wanting to use different radio frequencies to avoid interferences peculiar to them added further difficulties. It took some experimenting and compromising, for example, to come up with a broadcasting frequency of 6.7 megahertz that both Mirny and U.S. bases could hear. Other stations urged simultaneous transmitting on multiple frequencies for maximum reception.[28]

Antenna problems vexed Weather Central. While the system kept growing, from one transmitting and eight receiving antennae the first year to eight and fourteen, respectively, in the second, station power at Little America overall remained relatively weak. That plus the great distances demanded directional antennae, but they were limited by the placement of existing installations, such as the station's geomagnetic recorders and ionosonde transmitters. Storm-damaged antennae forced McMurdo off the air from 16 to 21 June 1957, which delayed full operation of the mother-daughter system and denied the desired month of practice before the start of the IGY. Repair and maintenance in heavy, awkward clothing in frigid temperatures (down to –70°F) and high winds (to 100 knots) were physically arduous, while coaxial cable cracked, ceramic insulators broke, and soldering was nearly impossible in the cold. Radio blackouts—at least one a month, often lasting three to five days—wreaked havoc with reporting in or out, thwarting the best efforts to provide analyses current enough to be useful. Keeping everything running depended on the "tireless ingenuity" of the wintering radiomen and electronics technicians, who necessarily "learned as they went."[29]

Manpower was another issue. According to the Navy, Weather Central operations required eight radiomen in two teams standing twelve-hour watches seven days a week. The number of any other station's daily transmissions depended on its size and staffing. A small station with a single radio operator could manage only three schedules a day; larger stations could do as many as eight. Schedules arranged to coincide as closely as possible with the synoptic map times of 0000, 0600, 1200, and 1800 hours Greenwich Mean (or "Zulu")

Time often could not be kept for myriad reasons. Leaders revised the details of traffic flow several times for efficiency, but coordination was difficult and confusion common. McMurdo itself did not have enough transmitters or personnel. Sometimes it was difficult to coordinate Weather Central and Communications Central schedules. In summer, Navy personnel at McMurdo and IGY meteorologists at Little America actually competed for data. In frustration, the Seabees' report for Deep Freeze II and III emphasized in capitals: "NEITHER STATION COULD OBTAIN ALL OF THE REQUIRED WEATHER EXPEDITIOUSLY (AND NEITHER DID) BUT WORKING TOGETHER ONE OF THEM COULD HAVE." Finally, Weather Central peak operations took five to eight hours a day, prompting the observation that it was "doubtful" if many Antarctic stations could afford the time or have a use for that much data even if they could receive them. Officials later recommended broadcasting summaries only.[30]

Because the Weather Bureau, Air Force, and Navy all used the weather information, observers recorded it on two forms, one for aviation and the other to fulfill the synoptic reporting requirements. At Little America, Weather Central analysts used the incoming information to prepare daily surface-weather charts of the Southern Hemisphere and did comparative research on consistent patterns of air movement to try to understand the influence of the polar continent on large-scale hemispheric and global circulation patterns. Of more immediate moment, they also plotted over time and vertical distance temperature, wind, and other conditions likely to affect the various geophysical disciplines and logistical operations in Antarctica. They then broadcast their "data collectives" and analyses to all interested parties four times a day around the clock. These weather broadcasts also included daily IGY advisories on special observations to be made during the next twenty-four hours, such as World Days, and the beginnings of longer World Intervals. Weather measurements everywhere were recorded on computer punch cards for further data reduction back home. Upper-air soundings, essential for forecasting, required on average about twenty cards. Navy electronics technicians produced a technological triumph on 3 June when Little America sent four Antarctic weather maps by radio facsimile to Washington for showcasing at the upcoming CSAGI conference in Paris. The task-force cruisebook bragged that these firsts were received "in excellent condition over [a distance of] 8,000 miles."[31]

In the end, despite ongoing difficulties and numerous shortcomings, the system could only be called a success. The four daily reports of fifty Antarctic weather stations would add up to at least 100,000 surface-weather observations during the IGY, more than 300,000 counting various levels of upper-air soundings. Scientifically, the pioneering program pushed back the frontiers of knowledge on Antarctic circulation patterns, including the land-ocean air exchange. "The effect of Weather Central in improving the safety and efficiency of Antarctic transportation can hardly be overestimated," wrote science historian Richard S. Lewis, citing his own flight in November 1959 on a C-124 resupply mission to the South Pole. Conditions on takeoff from McMurdo were marginal, yet on arrival the sky was clear enough to see the ring of fuel barrels circling the Pole. The successful flight "depended entirely on the accuracy of a Weather Central forecast and some additional data from the reporting network."[32]

An embodiment of international cooperation, complete with multinational staff, Weather Central helped defuse Cold War tensions and generated goodwill—indeed, lifelong friendships—across the great political divide of the time. For that alone, it was a masterful stroke. Most participants enjoyed the professional rewards of having research papers ready for publication when they left the ice. Crary made a point of noting that one of the first south-polar scientific papers of the IGY was one on Antarctic circulation jointly written by Rastorguev and Alvarez, the Soviet and Argentine guest meteorologists. There was little scientific disagreement on continuing Weather Central. Upon the close of Little America at the end of the IGY, McMurdo temporarily collected the data and relayed them to New Zealand for incorporation into the World Meteorological Organization's network until the service was taken over by the new International Antarctic Analysis Center at Melbourne in 1959. The U.S. Weather Bureau would send Tom Gray to work there as an exchange meteorologist.[33]

The Navy, meanwhile, beyond providing logistical support and assistance to civilian efforts, contributed to scientific programs on its own, as operational obligations permitted. In Admiral Dufek's not-bashful Deep Freeze III account for Gould, he noted that shipboard aerographers and those at the Liv Auxiliary Base recorded surface weather hourly and took standard synoptic observations every three hours. They also launched one or two daily radiosondes, which they summarized for inclusion in Weather Central broadcasts. Navy aerographers at McMurdo did similar weather compilation and analysis, in addition to providing forecasting for aircraft flying on the continent and between it and New Zealand. Dufek also emphasized for the record that Navy aerographers' mates had provided a "major portion" of the IGY meteorological program at Hallett, Wilkes, and Ellsworth stations.[34]

Thus, by the end of the IGY civilian and military meteorologists, Americans and others, had added greatly to world knowledge of the thermal structure, heat budget, and atmospheric circulation over Antarctica and its oceans. They came to understand the region's climate as a product of its high-latitude location, wind and storm patterns, ice-covered surrounding ocean, high thin-air elevation, and long winter night. They were able to describe the main storm tracks over the continent, normal circulation patterns, temperature ranges, and the solar radiation exchange between ice-covered earth and atmosphere. They identified, for example, a "polar vortex," similar to one over the North Pole but stronger and more persistent. Incoming warmer air from the north cooled and sank over the domed polar ice cap, flowing outward clockwise "as water flows down a slope," slowly at first, then accelerating as it funneled through the narrow mountain valleys and down the steeper coastal inclines. There, these ground-hugging katabatic winds picked up speed and could de-scend as suddenly as a flash flood and as ferociously, as Deep Freeze I ensign David Baker found out in one of his scariest experiences.[35]

Baker and three companions had taken a team of dogs out for a last run in the dusk before winter, heading southwest across frozen McMurdo Sound toward Mount Discovery. As they paused to rest the dogs six or seven miles out, they watched with alarm as the almost-still air, "in a matter of seconds," roiled into forty-mile-an-hour winds, then "sixty, seventy, eighty." As they struggled to put up their tent, "it was blowing so hard that literally we had to crawl on our stomachs." Besides fearing that their shelter might shred, Baker remembered the Scott expedition party that had gotten caught on the ice in a sudden storm; they awoke the next morning to find themselves on a detached floe drifting north. With no boats at McMurdo and the only helicopter grounded by a delaminated rotor, the imaginative young officer tried to push away thoughts of the ice breaking up under them. Fortunately for Scott's men, the wind shifted and they were able to leap from floe to floe and eventually to safety as the ice blew landward. Fortunately for Baker's party, the blizzard, after several hours, just as suddenly blew itself out. The air became "a flat calm. Absolutely not a breath of wind." The ice held.[36]

Now scientists understood both this phenomenon and the more fearsome condition that occurred when coastal cyclonic winds blowing southward and eastward from over the oceans converged with the outbound katabatics, which they did with particular fury over the edges of East Antarctica. As Australia's Mawson recorded of his two-winter expedition, 1912 and 1913, at Cape Denison, "The climate proved to be little more than one continuous blizzard the year round; a hurricane of wind roaring for weeks together, pausing for breath only at odd hours." Expedition members could not walk outdoors without crampons and "lying on the wind," while indoors they could not converse above the incessant howl. For three autumn months wind velocities *averaged* more than fifty miles per hour; on one May day a ninety-mph average was recorded.[37]

Wilkes and the French, Russian, and Australian IGY stations in the same sector also experienced these fierce and capricious winds. In July 1957 Rudi Honkala, who knew extreme weather from his work on Mount Washington, and chief electronics technician Fred Charlton had just started out by Weasel for Wilkes's ice-cap station when they were blasted by just such a sudden maelstrom. Attempting to grope their way back, they stumbled onto seismologist Gil Dewart who had gone out in another Weasel to tend instruments. Completely enveloped in swirling, shrieking white, they huddled together in one of the vehicles for a day and a half before the storm abated sufficiently for them to make the scant 3 miles back to camp. The Navy reported "almost routine" wind velocities of 100 miles per hour at Wilkes; one summer storm in 1958–1959 clocked 133 mph at its peak. Still, Dewart dismissed comparisons with Commonwealth Bay where, by Mawson's description, "[a] plunge into the writhing storm-whirl stamps upon the senses an indelible and awful impression seldom equalled in the whole gamut of natural experience."[38]

IGY scientists learned that, overall, West Antarctica—which was lower in elevation and thus less of a barrier to incoming winds from the Ross and Weddell seas—was warmer, cloudier, snowier, and stormier than its larger, higher, colder eastern counterpart where heat could more easily escape from the surface through the drier, clearer, thinner atmosphere. Rastorguev and Alvarez concluded from vertical time sections for Little America and Pole that while weather fronts penetrated deep into the interior of the continent, only the upper remnants of the most intense storm systems could "maintain their identity" all the way to the Pole. But they were strong enough to make clouds and precipitation over the polar plateau.[39]

Wexler theorized that this prevalent storm-track pattern now centered over West Antarctica would eventually reverse, as he thought it had in earlier eras. As he saw it, previous storm tracks had built up the ice in East Antarctica until it was so high (then almost three miles in places) that it deflected storms into lower West Antarctica. But eventually, deprived of its precipitation "nourishment," the eastern ice cap would shrink, as the presence of the Dry Valleys seemed to be showing, until it no longer could push away blizzards. Then the western ice cap would grow, eventually directing storm tracks and snow buildup eastward once more. Thus snow fell in one area at the expense of the other—until the heights reversed. Wexler called the phenomenon seesawing ice ages. Indeed, Byrd Station, along the route of the present Ross Sea to Weddell Sea storm track's path of least resistance, received heavy amounts of snow during the IGY. Places like the high inland Vostok got very little. Persistent low-pressure areas over both seas and persistent highs over the East Antarctic plateau, both postulated earlier and now substantiated, were also contributing factors.[40]

Meteorologists began to understand details of the cold and its effects. With the outward flow slow at first, winds deep in the interior were generally light. (Only one real storm, with thirty- to forty-knot winds, visited the South Pole during the first winter.) So the cold air coming off the cold ice did not mix much with the incoming warmer air above, creating a temperature-inversion layer during the dark period; it could be as much as fifty degrees warmer a few hundred feet above the surface than on it. Although the high latitudes received more solar heat in summer when the sun never set than warmer areas got where it did, almost all (94 percent) of that heat was reflected off the snow and re-radiated into space. Even though precipitation was meager, it accumulated because it did not melt or evaporate. Gradually, it sank and compressed under the weight of new snow, forming firn (partially compacted old granular snow) and, finally, solid ice.[41]

Temperature extremes were also instructive. Weather Central's Moreland understatedly noted as "unusual and interesting" the year's largest temperature gradient between Little America (+30°F) and the South Pole (–100°F) about 800 miles away on 11 May 1957. On 18 September that year, Vern Anderson at Byrd recorded a 100-degree difference between Pole's –102°F, then a record, and their own –2°, over a 700-mile distance. Vostok proved itself the "Pole of Cold" on 25 August 1958 at –125°F. Wexler emphasized this point at U.S. House of Representatives hearings, testifying in early 1959 that Antarctica was not uniformly "cold, snowy, and miserable," not "flat climatologically speaking." For example, the difference in winter temperatures between Wilkes Station in Antarctica's "banana belt" and the South Pole, sometimes 74 degrees, was larger than the average temperature differential between Miami Beach and the Canadian Arctic. Gould, in a written statement, cited fifty years of intermittently kept polar weather records to show a 5-degree warming at Little America during that period. Possibly just a short-term trend, he could "not refrain from noting again the significance of melting of only a few feet of ice to our coastal climates and civilization." Fossil deposits had shown that great climatic changes had taken place in the past, and they could again, cautioned Gould on a subject of growing concern today. Altogether, the IGY had enabled a "meteorological unveiling" of Antarctica, Wexler proudly concluded. He urged that the work continue.[42]

Thus was knowledge gained by Antarctica's foremost IGY effort. But weathermen were not the only scientists looking upward.

LOOKING UP
The Physics of the Atmosphere

*Geoff King and I, collaborating in attempting to correlate
ionospheric and geomagnetic activity with the aurora, produced
some very fine series of recordings which showed quite convinc-
ingly their interdependence.*

—Kenneth J. Salmon, 1958[1]

The sun—source of the earth's energy—and the little-known upper
atmosphere were the focus of IGY investigations in the interwoven
disciplines of ionospheric physics, geomagnetism (or terrestrial magnetism), cosmic rays, and the aurora. Solar disturbances are trigger-
ing forces in them all. Bursting solar flares and complex sunspots,
which follow cycles that intensify every eleven years as the sun's
magnetic field reverses itself, cause magnetic storms that interfere
with radio waves, set off auroral displays, and disturb the earth's
magnetic field—which, in turn, largely determines the paths of charged
particles entering the atmosphere. Antarctica offered the clearest view
on earth of phenomena created by these interactions, making it a

prime location for pioneering studies. The founders who timed the IGY to coincide with an active sun got their money's worth; that period was the most turbulent yet known.[2]

Meteorologists' work centered in the troposphere, up to about 5 miles above the earth at the poles (twice as high at the equator). This lowest layer of the atmosphere is where human activity resides and most weather forms and travels. Above that, up to about 40 miles, is the dry, slow-moving, fairly even-temperature stratosphere, thought to be the predictor of long-range weather. Between about 40 and 250 miles up lies the ionosphere, a region of rarified gases electrically charged (ionized) by ultraviolet radiation from the sun, which knocks out electrons from the atoms. Within the ionosphere are layers that vary in height and degree of ionization with the time of day, season, and solar cycle. Radio signals over a fairly wide frequency range reflect back from the ionized gases in the ionosphere, especially the farthest-out so-called F-layer, to make global communication possible. The troublesome inner D-layer tends to absorb shortwave radio signals during solar flares to the extent of blocking radio communications, which in Antarctica effectively shuts down aircraft operations, weather-data dissemination, official communications, and personal contacts with home. Unreliable radio, of course, puts any type of travel at risk. So understanding ionospheric properties and behavior is critical in a practical sense, as well as intrinsically interesting to science.[3]

Very little was known about the ionosphere over the Antarctic before the IGY, although during Operation Highjump scientists briefly operated an automatic sweep-frequency ionosphere sounder that measured daily echo variations in both calm and magnetically stormy weather. Until then, scientists had mostly relied on Arctic information, accumulating little by little since the Second Polar Year. Now, to be able to predict ionospheric conditions and their effect on radio transmission was an important goal of the IGY. Ionospheric physicists used ionosondes, radarlike instruments that beamed pulses of radio energy straight up into the ionosphere over a range of frequencies from about 0.5 to 20 or 25 megahertz. They photographically plotted the variation of echo-return time against frequency to determine the height at which the ionosphere reflected the signals back to earth. Analyzing these echoes, scientists deduced the radio-wave–propagating characteristics of the ionosphere, which vary in time and space.[4]

The National Bureau of Standards (NBS) supplied much of the ionospheric instrumentation, planned research, and provided many personnel—one of several cases of government-agency support of specific U.S. IGY program interests. After the IGY, the Central Radio Propagation Laboratory at NBS in

Boulder, Colorado, collected all of the ionospheric records for further analysis. Crary judged the large C-4 recorder of the ionosphere-sounding program to be the most complicated piece of scientific equipment on the ice. It was, he said, "difficult to install, to de-bug, and to maintain." But Hans Bengaard, the Dane who served as ionosphere discipline chief, having operated similar equipment in Greenland, not only made his system work at Little America but also, via radio, helped his counterparts around the continent with theirs. Ellsworth's John Brown, for example, needed that assistance when his instrument arrived without an operating manual or a wiring diagram.[5]

As South Pole ionosphere specialist Willi Hough explained it to his nontechnical wintering mates, the "monster" (on balance "fairly well behaved" despite "all the verbal abuse it received and the irritation it caused)" required 120 vacuum tubes to function. As the transmitter sent out "little bits of radio frequency energy[,] each at a different frequency," in eight fifteen-second sweeps an hour, the receiver followed along to listen after each pulse for a reflected echo. If it found one, it sent the information to a cathode-ray oscilloscope, superimposing it on a grid plotting height versus frequency. Hough's successor Charles Greene clarified that while the vertical ordinate was calibrated in kilometers, the recorder actually measured time—the difference between the transmitted pulse and received echo. Assuming constant velocity, time related directly to distance or height. Since velocity is not constant, they called the distance "virtual height." Hough explained that after he received a day's records—193 of them, called ionograms, produced on thirty-two feet of 35-millimeter film—he had to develop and "scale" them, assigning and recording numerical values for fifteen different ionospheric characteristics. If all fifteen were not there, he said, the job went a little faster, but it usually involved hours over the scaling table with its projectors and glass viewplate.[6]

One who bemoaned the secondary effects of the C-3 automatic ionosphere recorder at Pole Station was Navy electrician Ken Waldron. Those fifteen-second pulses sucked 3,000 watts from one of his struggling 30-kilowatt generators, suddenly cycling on and off every seven minutes or so. "Small generators don't like that," he well remembered, also recalling his gratitude for a week of generator training in Peoria, even though "I never in all my life thought I'd ever use what [the instructor, an electrical engineer] was saying." Waldron, like others, had difficulty paralleling his machines, which together could have more easily absorbed the jerky load. But without a solid electrical ground on the thick ice cap, there was nothing to work against when he tried to bring one onto load with the other, even after he bonded everything metal together to make a counterpoise, as taught: "As soon as a load hits, one generator's going

to pick it up faster than the other one. And as soon as it does, the other generator starts being run by this one, and that means you have a very heavy load that
can burn out the one generator." He had also been told to calculate "what kind
of horsepower you've got left" after the high elevation claimed its due. (A
diesel engine cannot develop its full power in thin air.) He figured out in
Davisville that he would get "about 24 kW out of a 30 kW generator at that
altitude. It turned out I had 22, and that 2 kW difference made a lot of difference
for us during the year." The young electrician, who "made first class" while at
Pole, would have a worrisome winter.[7]

Hough knew he would have trouble raising a proper antenna for ionospheric recording when he learned that the Air Force could not deliver the
normal 75-foot telephone-pole supports because they would not fit in the plane.
Only about a third of his promised sectional plywood mast arrived. So on a
blowy, −70° day, with the sun tickling the horizon, sturdy souls at Pole took 25
feet each from two radio masts to add them to the plywood base Bowers's
construction crew had erected. (As several hands helped raise Ellsworth's 40-
foot antenna, Con Jaburg was nearly killed when the base gave way as the
mast reached almost vertical. "About two tons of antenna hurtled to earth and
missed the cab of the Cat [the D-4 he was driving], and my head, by about three
feet," he wrote, "still shaken.") Hough got the first of his continuous records
on 10 March 1957, and after that he received records at least hourly with only
5 percent loss, a remarkable success rate similar to other ionosphere programs
around the continent.[8]

The United States sponsored 71 ionosophere programs among 253 worldwide. Six were in Antarctica, one at each science station. Given that ionization
density increases during the day (it is sunlight that breaks down and ionizes
neutral particles of the air), Pole's ionosphere observers were surprised to
learn that the free-electron concentration in the F-2-layer above them remained
high during the long polar night, in fact rising and falling diurnally as it
would elsewhere. They speculated that these particles had to be associated
with geomagnetic activity or were coming in from lighted latitudes or some
other source (which turned out to be the Van Allen Radiation Belt, discussed
later in this chapter). Using rockets to gather data, other scientists found solar
X-rays in one layer of the ionosphere, which they believed had originated in
the sun's corona. When emitted from solar flares they increased ionization in
the lower layers of the high atmosphere. As IGY teams mapped the echoes of
radio pulses reflected off the ionosphere station by station at the same time,
they developed the first "synoptic picture" of the growth and decay of ion
densities following major solar flares, which helped explain and predict dis-

ruptions of long-range shortwave radio communications. Investigators also found an ultraviolet glow that suggested an outer atmosphere of pure hydrogen as far out as halfway to the moon. This, they thought, might be caused by the effect of sunlight on non-ionized hydrogen of unknown source. Every new finding brought new questions.[9]

At Ellsworth only, the ionosphere program included the study of "whistlers," very-low-frequency radio signals that apparently are a by-product of lightning. When a bolt strikes in one hemisphere, it generates radio-frequency static that follows the earth's magnetic field far into space, then loops back into the corresponding latitude in the opposite hemisphere. Navy writers described the returning signal as a "low drugstore-cowboy whistle." According to aurora observer Kim Malville, whistlers made a "decreasing sphew, sphew, sphew" sound; some of these radio sounds earned descriptive names like "trains" and "wagon wheels." "The 'dawn chorus' was recorded almost every day during the month of August," the U.S. IGY staff reported to the international community in February 1958. Ellsworth's whistler equipment recorded its findings for correlation with those of Labrador, its conjugate point in the Northern Hemisphere. Such signals, first heard on field telephones in World War I, helped scientists determine the electron content of the atmosphere far above the ionosphere. (If space were a vacuum at that distance, the signals would not return to earth.) An IGY hypothesis suggested that solar particles arriving in the high upper atmosphere transfer energy to very-low-frequency radio waves there; the latter, thus amplified, are the radio emissions heard at ground level.[10]

In late 1958, after Scott Base unexpectedly heard whistlers, Hallett scientists built an amplifier and an antenna to try to pick up these unusual signals. On 20 December, somewhat to their astonishment, they did—and "made a tape recording of them as proof." Later, at the U.S. Eights Station, built in 1963 at the base of the Antarctic Peninsula, whistler phenomena were plentiful because its northern conjugate area was a region of high thunderstorm activity. Whistler-mode transmissions could also be readily sent from Eights thanks to the thick ice cap, which provided a low-loss support for a long horizontal transmitting antenna.[11]

Cosmic rays were addressed as an independent IGY discipline, though one interacting with and receiving data from the other studies of solar activity. In 1955 the USNC's Joseph Kaplan described cosmic "rays" as nuclear particles accelerated by the sun or other stars to "energies millions of times higher than those the best accelerators can now produce." Composed primarily of hydrogen nuclei and known since 1911 to enter the earth's atmosphere from outer space (hence the name), cosmic rays arrive at earth in a constant bombardment from every direction at tremendous energy with nearly the speed of light. "Eight or ten of these go through your body every second," cosmic ray authority Martin Pomerantz explained, although at lower latitudes all but the most energetic of these electrically charged particles (colliding, they lose electrons) are deflected by the intervening atmosphere and the earth's magnetic field. The geomagnetic equator at any given longitude is where cosmic ray intensity is lowest because the geomagnetic field is greatest, about eleven degrees off from the geographic equator. But near the geomagnetic poles the earth's magnetic lines of force, which cosmic rays follow, bend in toward the earth, allowing access to lower-energy cosmic rays—"in the billion-volt range." Here they arrive in the highest intensities on earth, making Antarctica the ideal place to study them. While their source was not known when scientists began planning the IGY, increased cosmic ray intensity during solar flares convinced researchers that they come from the sun but also from other stars and distant supernovae or even from beyond the galaxy. Cosmic ray intensity varies on an eleven-year cycle, like sunspots, but in an inverse relationship—the more sunspots, the fewer cosmic rays because during high activity, solar winds sweep outward to form a "magnetic bubble" that deflects them.[12]

In the earlier 1950s Pomerantz had pondered the effects of the earth's magnetic field on cosmic ray intensity as a function of geomagnetic latitude, then a subject of lively debate. He built a then-state-of-the-art neutron monitor to study this phenomenon, in cooperation with Swedish and Canadian colleagues, on the M/S *Lommaren*, a Swedish merchant ship sailing from Göteborg to Capetown—thus deep into both hemispheres. Over several years this pioneering effort definitively located the geomagnetic equator. A call from John Simpson, inventor of the neutron monitor and member of both the U.S. IGY Cosmic Ray Panel and the international planning committee (CSAGI), led Pomerantz to build and install one for the IGY in Thule, Greenland, not far from the Geomagnetic North Pole. He would soon make his mark on the polar south as well.[13]

Scientists from 31 nations at 195 stations worldwide studied cosmic rays during the IGY. Of the 20 U.S. stations, 2 were in the Antarctic—Wilkes and Ellsworth. Work began aboard ship, starting with experiments on the 1954–1955 reconnaissance voyage of the *Atka*. According to Walter Sullivan, who was aboard, its neutron detector showed dramatic variations in cosmic ray intensity according to latitude. These low-energy particles reached the earth in Antarctic waters at a rate of nearly 10,000 per hour, almost double that at the equator. Higher-energy mesons increased only 10 percent over that distance. The rates of both leveled off approaching the geomagnetic pole. Admiral Dufek generously routed the *Arneb* to provide hemispherical coverage of cosmic ray activity during the two succeeding Antarctic summers. Supporting these and other efforts, IGY scientists from the University of Chicago, led by Simpson, found a 40- to 45-degree westward "warp" of the inclined cosmic ray equator with respect to the geomagnetic equator—probably indicating powerful extraterrestrial magnetic fields that bend the trajectories of incoming cosmic particles.[14]

Both U.S. stations built separate buildings to house their cosmic ray equipment, since it was sensitive to background noise. Wilkes Station in 1957 had a meson telescope, consisting of several horizontal rows of glass tubes on a rack, to count (by Geiger counter) and record the changing numbers of cosmic rays hitting the earth. At first Garth Stonehocker and his assistant Robert Long, both of whom also did Wilkes's ionospheric work, thought their readings were too high, but consultations with the University of Maryland reassured them that their equipment was operating normally. The next year Dean Denison modified the scaling circuitry so the scope would count only the particles that passed through the instrument's top two trays of glass tubes, which gave more manageable numbers. Ellsworth had the only U.S. neutron monitor on the ice. Run by cosmic ray physicist Dale Reed in the IGY's second year, it acted as the terminus of a meridional chain of stations observing cosmic rays and their variation at different parts of the geomagnetic field.[15]

According to Pomerantz, a neutron monitor is a sensitive cosmic ray detector that helps scientists quantify incoming cosmic particles, especially the more sensitive lower-energy ones. It is "like a nuclear reactor in reverse," he said. The cosmic ray particles disrupt nuclei and form neutrons, which the detector can count. The structure was built up of lead "pigs" (rectangular blocks of lead) with "the hydrogenous material inside, which was wax [paraffin, later polyethylene] in cans, and then a whole layer of maybe ten centimeters or more of lead all around it and then more paraffin and that's how it went." Easier said than done, building and clamping together the 9,000-pound pile was physically demanding work. In addition, the equipment included two 1,500-pound meson telescopes and associated electronic recording apparatus.[16]

In 1959, just after the IGY ended, George Toney, then at the National Science Foundation (NSF), invited Pomerantz to install a cosmic ray station at McMurdo, as recommended by the NAS Committee on Polar Research. It would help initiate McMurdo's new science program. Delighted to complement the Thule station, Pomerantz oversaw the construction of a suitable building, copper shielded to "reduce the effect of outside stuff" such as radio interference. He hired IGY glaciologist Hugo Neuburg to install the system and winter over to run it. Neuburg, who was delayed getting under way until midwinter by late equipment arrival, punched the cosmic ray data onto paper tape that went directly to the teletype for transmittal back to the United States. On the receiving end, Pomerantz turned it over to "about five ladies" who read the tapes and did the arithmetic manually for the two stations. "Compare that with today. It's hard to believe!" he exclaimed.[17]

By the time Pomerantz was able to go south himself in November 1960, neutron monitors at Thule and McMurdo were recording the same solar event at the same time. A year or two later, when the Navy concluded that the only suitable site for its proposed nuclear-power plant was perhaps a hundred yards from the "Cos-ray" facility, Pomerantz got a new site—and a new building—on the opposite side of Observation Hill (whose mass would block errant neutrons from the reactor), where it remains today on the road to Scott Base. After overlapping operations for a time to obtain a baseline, he transferred the first facility to the South Pole in 1964 in time for the International Year of the Quiet Sun (IQSY, 1964–1966), an IGY comparative follow-on during a period of minimum solar activity. Over the years, scientists would study data on complete twenty-two-year solar cycles—the eleven-year sunspot cycle and the flipping of the direction of the sun's magnetic field and back again.[18]

IGY godfather, "rockoon" developer, rocket expert, and cosmic ray researcher James Van Allen directed work leading to one of the most exciting IGY discoveries. He designed instruments to measure cosmic ray intensity that in 1958 were carried nearly 600 miles into space by the newly developed artificial earth satellites. Expected to show increasing radioactivity as the Army's Explorer III orbiter penetrated further into space, the counts suddenly dropped to zero—a bizarre anomaly. After some initial puzzlement, his team insightfully reasoned that "a radiation count *greatly higher* than the counter's limit could paralyze it and make it register zero in reaction." Thus the radiation level was not zero but in fact suddenly, vastly increased. As Van Allen remembered it, a reporter at the news conference announcing the discovery, trying to visualize the concept, asked if this encircling radiation might be likened to a belt. The term *radiation belt* was thus born, named for Van Allen. As Carl Eklund and Joan Beckman put it in their popular history of IGY science in Antarctica, the belt was composed of "trapped, charged particles, racing in constant flight inside the earth's magnetic field till knocked out," presumably at one of the earth's two "mirror points." Here, where the ends of the radiation funnel came closest to the earth (a "mere 65 miles"), magnetic storms dislodged the ricocheting particles, releasing enough energy to trigger spectacular auroral displays.[19]

In the northern summer of 1958, the Defense Department launched a secret experiment called Argus to test the entrapment theory. Two nuclear devices were detonated over Johnston Island in the Pacific to create electrons while the rocket-borne Explorer IV satellite monitored the auroral, radio, magnetic, and electromagnetic effects. They proved to be the same effects as those of the natural Van Allen Radiation Belt. After about 100 hours the artificial radiation dissipated, the electrons lost by scattering in the atmosphere along the mirror points. Van Allen was right. While this project was non-Antarctic, its ionospheric effects were observed at Hallett Station, and its findings informed thinking on various polar phenomena. From their auroral spectra (red over Maui, Hawaii), Malville identified the explosions as hydrogen bombs.[20]

The earth's magnetic field has been used for centuries for navigation and surveying. IGY studies of this phenomenon, geomagnetism, were particularly significant in Antarctica. In addition to the South Geographic Pole (the earth's axis of rotation), the South Magnetic Pole (where the south end of a compass needle points straight down) and the South Geomagnetic Pole reside on (or near) the polar continent. The latter is a theoretical point mathematically derived from measurements of the intensity and direction of the earth's magnetic field. In simple terms, if all the earth's magnetic fields were caused by a single bar magnet through its center, the ends would be the geomagnetic poles, the axes of the earth's atmospheric magnetic field. The geomagnetic and magnetic poles would be the same were it not that the shape of the earth's magnetic field is distorted. Both of these poles drift; during the IGY they were nearly a thousand miles apart—the magnetic pole nearly at the coast, not far from France's Dumont d'Urville Station, and the other at the Soviet Union's Vostok, far into remote East Antarctica.

Ninety percent of the earth's magnetic field comes from its own ferrous molten core and is very stable, its minor variations measured in years. But IGY scientists knew from mathematical analysis of theories proposed early in the twentieth century and Van Allen's experiments in the rocket and satellite program that a smaller, rapidly moving magnetic field is generated in the upper atmosphere. These variations are measured in days and even minutes and seconds. "Here are tides, as in the sea, surging back and forth in the upper air, regularly in two tidal waves a day," wrote Eklund and Beckman. Pulled by the sun's gravity, as ocean tides are governed by the moon, these surges show marked magnetic variations daily. Solar radiation ionizes the thin gases in these upper-air magnetic tides, generating large electric currents that swirl around the earth. Violent bursts of solar radiation cause magnetic storms that are "particularly frequent and severe" at the poles, where the earth's bending magnetic field draws the solar winds in. These disturbances create both the beautiful auroras and maddening radio blackouts.[21]

Thirty countries operated 129 geomagnetic observatories pole to pole during the IGY. Thirty-one of these were American, five in Antarctica: Little America, Byrd, Pole, Hallett, and Wilkes. Ellsworth's geomagnetic program was cancelled, but when the enterprising Malville learned that a magnetometer building was being shipped anyway, he borrowed a magnetograph, built the hut, and oversaw the measurements himself. Various Antarctic nations ran 10 other programs. Many stations were set up in chains to trace and chart the complex and erratic magnetic storms. Geomagnetic observers kept a round-the-clock, two-year visual, optical, photographic, photometric, and radio watch for such disturbances—with even greater concentration and coordination during World Days, often called on short notice when magnetic storms were predicted or suddenly occurred. They compared Antarctic storms with analogous tempests in the north, concluding that most upper-atmospheric events at one pole were mirrored at the other, indeed almost simultaneously. In addition to following these fast-moving "variations," the geomagnetic observers also surveyed the polar continent's permanent ("absolute") geomagnetic field by continuous recordings to catch any changes in its direction and intensity.[22]

The U.S. geomagnetism programs were similar, in many cases run by a scientist also responsible for another discipline. Leo Davis of the U.S. Coast and Geodetic Survey installed and operated Byrd Station's geomagnetic instruments as well as its earthquake seismology equipment. He had the "most extensive real estate holdings" in the tiny camp—including two small nonferrous huts, one for measuring earth-based magnetic "absolutes," the other for upper-atmosphere "variations," as was also true at Wilkes and Little America. Byrd's program suffered from the station's overall scarcities. Snow blew in everywhere, it seemed, after the men resorted to cutting the wall panels of the variations building from twelve to seven feet to allow use of upright two-by-fours to support the roof, stretch scarce scrap lumber, and conserve heat. Finding a suitable, accessible, quiet location became impossible; the little complex was finally sited not far from the runway, since planes landed infrequently. With no materials to build a tunnel to this outpost, the men excavated a path three and a half feet deep and lined the removed snowblocks along the old surface to make snow walls six feet high, which they covered with scrap lumber and parachutes. Vern Anderson called on his snow-sculpture experience to help set the wooden piers for the "geomag shack," watering slush to freeze them into the hard snow beneath a hole cut in the floor. On these Davis built the platform to hold the instruments free from camp vibrations from whatever scraps he could salvage. The unusual length of Davis's report attests to the compensations and adjustments he had to make; improvisation carried the day.[23]

Hallett and Pole stations concentrated on measuring magnetic variations. Hallett's variograph was operating by March 1957 without undue difficulty, but in April the men had to relocate the oil-drum fence, of interfering steel, that represented their "futile effort" to lock out the penguins. The second year Geoffrey King made absolute observations once a month in addition to collecting variations data. Among their preliminary findings, Hallett scientists reported calm winter conditions but minor diurnal disturbances on summer mornings and severe but short-lived magnetic storms. (During a dramatic storm on 11 February 1958 at Wilkes, Sabastian Borrello's magnetometer measured a 15.91-degree change in magnetic declination, by far the largest that year.) Greene, who was also Pole's geomagnetician in 1958, used a typical variograph set up in a pit 500 feet from the station to record on 16-millimeter film changes in the horizontal, vertical, and declination components of the earth's magnetic field, along with the temperature and time. Geomagnetism discipline chief Ronald Viets visited from Little America in December 1957 to assist with various calibrations. He also took two observations for absolute values of the magnetic field. John Gniewek, following Viets, also set up magnetic field stations at Miles 200 and 380 along the Byrd Trail and near Little America III on the Ross Ice Shelf, as Viets had done. By then local ice movement had unleveled the piers, and Gniewek had to adjust his instruments.[24]

Geomagnetic recordings everywhere were synchronized using a chronometer driving a program clock. Collaborating with Ellsworth's ionospheric physicists, Malville ran a cable from his hut to the C-4 ionosonde to obtain accurate time signals and was "able to show the connections between powerful magnetic disturbances and the break-up of the auroral arcs when they suddenly change to brilliant, fast-moving rays."[25]

The aurora australis is "never forgotten," wrote Eklund, who had witnessed myriad dazzling displays over two Antarctic winter nights. By his description, "Giant, luminous streamers fan out across the sky in an increasing span; or the aurora may take the form of patches of light, arcs, rays, bands, or hanging draperies. The brightening streamers glow pale yellow to deep yellow, pale to brilliant red, and in hues of purple, blue, and green." The luminous arcs could sweep from the horizon "outward in progressive waves until they span large parts of the night sky, making them seem vibrant and alive," before gradually receding "like a fan closing back into its case." Stephen Pyne, who generally emphasizes the bleak, cold "reductionism" of the ice, dampens the mood by opining that the aurora is "awesome rather than beautiful," its motion "cold and mechanical." Its aesthetics, in the presence of only ice and darkness, are "magnified by the absence of competing or modulating effects." The judgment seems stingy.[26]

During the IGY, scientists were just learning that—like its northern counterpart, the aurora borealis—the aurora australis is triggered by collisions of solar winds with the earth's magnetic field such that, according to Malville, electrons and protons in the Van Allen Radiation Belt are ejected into the upper atmosphere. There they give up their energy as heat and light, the aurorae. In Pyne's analogy, "The auroral particles, a kind of magnetically directed electron beam, imprint the aurora on the polar upper atmosphere in much the same way that a television tube projects an image on its screen." The light and particular colors come from the interaction of auroral particles with the oxygen and nitrogen atoms that make up the upper atmosphere as they are excited (ionized). Scientists had learned over the years that auroral displays occur most frequently within a narrow zone lying about twenty to twenty-five degrees from the geomagnetic pole (again, where the earth's magnetic field directs most solar particles). That would put Byrd Station near the edge of the maximum auroral zone, but specific knowledge was sketchy at best. So the IGY investigators would seek to know the distance, extent, duration, direction, size, and physical properties of auroras and whether they occurred simultaneously at both poles. "These rarified regions of the high atmosphere represent a vast photochemical laboratory beyond any technical possibility of building a similar prototype on the surface of the Earth," wrote IGY planners in 1955 to justify auroral studies.[27]

The IGY established a global aurora watch, including a network of radio telescope stations, observatories, and radar and spectroscopic stations. It also engaged individual observers such as "pilots, sailors, and teachers." While forty-nine countries participated, most were in lower latitudes where auroras were seldom seen. The United States maintained thirty-nine programs, six in the Antarctic. The south-bound auroral scientists spent the northern summer of 1956 first at the Air Force Cambridge Research Center (AFCRC) at Hanscom Field, Bedford, Massachusetts, for introductory instruction and then at the University of Chicago's Yerkes Observatory near Lake Geneva, Wisconsin, to learn the nature of the auroral phenomenon from Joseph Chamberlain, in Malville's view "probably the most experienced" auroral physicist of the time.[28]

Chamberlain designed and built the spectrographs for all the scientific stations and trained the IGY recruits to use them. Made especially for the IGY to determine the elements responsible for the auroral colors, the untried equipment had to be set up and debugged in the field—an awesome challenge for the young operators who, Malville recalled, were "sort of, you know, given a handshake" and "told 'Good Luck.'" He thought later that the sophisticated equipment and ambitious research handed over to him and his equally green colleagues were "much more advanced than we deserved." "We were all called scientists," agreed Pole aurora observer Arlo Landolt, "and on some level we were, but on another level, we were all more technicians." Still, while Malville suspected, correctly, that more qualified scientists were simply unwilling to winter over in the Antarctic, "it was a wonderful gift at this time of my career to be given this opportunity." In his enthusiasm he designed his own research project to study an unusual optical effect of auroras. With some assistance at AFCRC, he assembled his own optical photometer, amplifier, receiver, and telescope to analyze the radiation of ionized sodium in the atmosphere. Sometimes, he said, in addition to the colors produced by the common atmospheric elements, a "very intense sodium glow" appeared, characteristically yellow. Working alone, he would have little time for this additional work, however.[29]

All the aurora observers had two elaborate instruments for their work. The all-sky camera, a 16-mm movie camera developed in 1946, provided a continuous image of the entire sky on clear nights—almost horizon to horizon. As Landolt explained it, light fell from the sky on a hemispheric mirror and was reflected up to a flat optical mirror above it, then back through a hole in the center of the convex mirror to the camera inside. Rather than movies, which would have consumed impracticable quantities of film, the camera made timed single exposures—about one per minute all winter in clear weather. Buck Wilson, Little America's aurora observer in 1958, eventually used his all-sky camera on the roof of his aurora tower without the Plexiglas dome. He got better images, with no adverse effects from temperatures as low as –73°F. He found that, with relatively short exposures, he could photograph the Milky Way and faint aurora even through an overcast that obscured the stars—unless there was a blizzard (when he would cover the camera with canvas) or someone forgot to turn off the outdoor lights after, say, refueling operations (an ongoing frustration). Hallett's station leader Kenneth Salmon, who also worked it in the open, pronounced the all-sky camera photographically admirable but felt that mechanically it left "much to be desired." Shutter and timing problems were common.[30]

The patrol spectrograph, Landolt said, had a fish-eye lens that automatically imaged the entire sky but only in a narrow band at once, an arc 2 degrees by 165 degrees. A grating inside the instrument dispersed the light as it entered the lens to produce, and record on special film, a spectrum of the sky. Measuring the energy spectrum of auroral particles, including infrared and ultraviolet light intensities, revealed what kinds of atoms and molecules in the atmosphere were excited by that particular bombardment. In 1958 Wilson also had a scanning spectrometer that was similar in principle to the patrol spectrograph, but, when pointed at bright aurora, it directly measured the intensity of the spectra. Unfortunately, this newly developed instrument was too complex to run in the field, especially for fledgling scientists working alone; only one aurora observer was assigned per station. When Malville completed his Antarctic tour, Chamberlain brought him back to Yerkes to figure out how to make it work—and to work within the limited environment of an aurora tower. He succeeded by midsummer 1958, just beyond the reach of the IGY's second Antarctic winter.[31]

A primary component of the aurora scientist's job was simply visual observation, to note details like auroral color, shape, and movement and record them on computer punch cards. But auroras could appear during any dark hour; a sole observer could not manage alone. Since displays tended to reach maximum intensity during the eight-hour period centered on magnetic midnight, Wilson posted himself in the tower then, although it was usually not too difficult to recruit assistance for a task so aesthetically nourishing. His report acknowledged "a great deal of help from all the Navy and IGY men as volunteer auroral observers." One assignment proved impossible, though—to draw the shape and movements of the aurora while viewing it through a clear grid. Obviously, this program was "conceived by people who'd never watched an aurora," at least not at high southern latitudes, Wilson later mused. In contrast to the quieter, more stable northern performances, these were dynamic on a grand scale, rapidly breaking up into various arcs and auroral substorms. There was "no way in the world you could ever draw what is going on." Sometimes, rarely, auroras seemed to make crackling, sparking noises, he recalled. Such sounds physically could not occur at the height of the aurora, and the speed of sound would preclude hearing them simultaneously with the visual spectacle. The phenomenon has not yet been explained.[32]

All observers witnessed awesome and scientifically interesting scenes in the night sky. Arthur Warren, aurora specialist at Ellsworth in 1958, reported a ten-hour display of rare red auroras on 8 July, with hanging arcs that changed into an "extremely bright" corona with red and white rays that lighted over 50 percent of the sky. In a 1959 paper, Malville would show that such auroras could be produced by a beam of energetic electrons that penetrate the atmosphere to 70 km (42 miles) from the earth. Peter Schoeck, at Little America in 1957, was particularly interested in the motion and symmetry of the light shows, but he observed symmetry less than 25 percent of the time, mostly near the (geomagnetic) northern horizon. Higher-altitude auroras were less likely to be symmetrical. He found that auroras generally moved clockwise, regardless of where they appeared in the sky. At Hallett, overcast precluded sightings 42 percent of the time, but on 98 percent of the clearer days, there they were. The majority approached from the northeast, but others came in at right angles to that direction, once from both directions simultaneously—a startling sight. The rarity of colored auroras disappointed Salmon, but he did note a "brilliant red glow toward the east" for about three hours after a display on 8 July. Were he and Warren observing the same event? He saw blue in the season's most impressively active aurora on 21 July—"almost certainly" caused by a form of nitrogen, in contrast to oxygen's characteristic red. And in August he reported the world's first observation of an unusual red spectral line that scientists later thought resulted from lithium atoms excited by the Argus nuclear explosions. Of course, when the long night was over, which varied by station latitude, so were auroras for the season.[33]

IGY scientists learned a great deal about the mysterious auroras, which they found to occur in the high E-layer of the ionosphere. When ionized atoms and molecules (especially of oxygen and nitrogen) revert to their normal energy states, they emit the characteristic auroral radiation. Rocket studies and laboratory experiments at Yerkes Observatory helped them conclude that electrons, not protons, are the primary source of auroral brightness and ionization. Excitation by protons caused ribbonlike auroras, but electrons were more prevalent after these patterns broke up. Since the earth's magnetic field directs most solar particles to the poles, the auroras are unsurprisingly the most active there, but the hottest region turned out to be between the magnetic and geomagnetic poles (not around the geomagnetic pole as earlier thought). Odishaw noted in *Science* magazine that mounting evidence from radar observations, polar radio data, and simultaneous flights tended to confirm earlier speculation that auroras occurred simultaneously in both polar regions and focused on conjugate points (corresponding latitudes and longitudes, north and south). By Wilson's illustration, the motion rather mimicked the mirror-image effect of fluttering butterfly wings. However, observers also found that auroras appearing simultaneously over a broad area might not look or behave the same at every observation point, perhaps reflecting local influences. The northern and southern auroral zones, too, differed in size and shape, indicating asymmetries in the earth's magnetic field. Malville, using IGY data, was the first to show the oval shape of the auroral zone in the Southern Hemisphere. One thing was certain: geomagnetic phenomena, cosmic rays, and ionospheric disturbances all related to the onset, appearance, and behavior of auroras.[34]

Listed and studied with the aurora, though with much less attention, was the phenomenon called airglow. Landolt described it as a "faint luminescence of the nighttime sky." It could contribute 25 or 30 percent of the total light present. Studies showing the presence of oxygen indicated that this light had to come from within the atmosphere, so it was not starlight, Eklund and Beckman wrote. Airglow, like the aurora, seemed to result from excitation of atoms and molecules in the ionosphere, but it remained a puzzle why the intensity and color of the light varied over the sky. U.S. rocket flights found layers of yellow sodium light at 53 miles, a green oxygen glow at 62 miles, and a red oxygen glow at 96 miles above the earth. Scientists finally agreed that the twilight glow was the "direct action of sunlight." (There should be a daytime glow, too, if it could be seen.) According to Pyne much later, solar radiation during the day breaks up atoms and molecules of oxygen and nitrogen and the hydroxyl radical in the magnetosphere (60 to 180 miles above the earth), but at night the particles recombine, liberating photons of light that together constitute airglow. If the bombardments are intense or violent, the visual effects appear as aurorae.[35]

The aurora observers were also asked to count meteors, visually and with binoculars, to try to confirm the astonishing claim of Thomas Poulter, chief scientist on Byrd's 1934 expedition, that 1,300 were once sighted and their coordinates recorded in a fifteen–hour period. (The rate during the only known southern meteor shower of the period was 5–10 per hour.) Since favorable conditions for seeing meteors coincided with good aurora viewing, this project got short shrift during the IGY, but no one came close to such a rate of sightings. Malville speculated that Poulter's observers were inspired to see fainter streaks, perhaps confusing them with physiological optical phenomena, by the incentive of "being able to work inside under relatively benign conditions." The puzzle remains. Malville later used an electromagnet to collect the first Antarctic micrometeorites. He counted these "perfectly shaped magnetic spheres" under a microscope.[36]

To close, this story must acknowledge the ultimate tool developed for IGY upper-atmospheric research. Its relationship with Antarctica was indirect and tangential but not without significance. This tool was the artificial earth-orbiting satellite, a bold extension of the balloon and rocket flights ("rockoons") that enabled scientists to measure various upper-atmosphere phenomena, processes, and events—and their altitude dependence. The IGY planners first gave voice to encouraging satellite development in a 4 October 1954 resolution at the Rome CSAGI meeting, to be able to obtain data over long periods of time and vast reaches of space. Two countries expressed interest—the United States and the Soviet Union. After formal NAS and governmental approval, Kaplan notified CSAGI president Sydney Chapman on 25 July 1955 that the United States would go forward. The USNC, he said, invited other countries to "monitor the device and make appropriate observations" of what would be "one of the great scientific achievements of our time." The public announcement cited President Eisenhower's "personal gratification that the American program will provide scientists of all nations this important and unique opportunity for the advancement of science." There was no question that the United States intended and expected to be first in space.[37]

Other leaders spoke just as confidently, but the world knows that the Russians launched Sputnik, the first space satellite, on 4 October 1957 and a second one a month later. This stunning breakthrough won hearty congratulations from their U.S. space-expert counterparts cum political adversaries, although some, such as Werner von Braun and Ernst Stuhlinger of the Army's Redstone Arsenal in Huntsville, maintained that had the United States chosen an Army Jupiter-C rocket-delivery system instead of the Navy's problem-ridden Vanguard, it could have put a satellite in space a year before it did. Army chauvinism aside, Van Allen, who designed much of the scientific payload for the early American satellites (intentionally workable with either launch system), agreed. Odishaw wired Ellsworth to request that someone record Sputnik's radio signals, and Jack Brown did so on his whistler equipment. Siple officially submitted his almost minute-by-minute notes as he monitored the orbiter's signals, or tried to, with much local interference and modest success. Many of the men on the ice asked, "What's a Sputnik" in the same voice they had queried "Elvis Who?"[38]

The "space race" came to overwhelm and overshadow the IGY, in which it was ostensibly playing a supporting role. "This intrinsically harmless act of science and engineering," wrote columnist Walt Rostow, also demonstrated Soviet military capability and was a "powerful act of psychological warfare." More positively, it provoked the administration to establish the National Aeronautics and Space Administration (NASA), increase NSF's budget from $50 million to $133 million in one year, and rain money on U.S. science for several years. Ellsworth's John Behrendt would write that Antarcticans were hardly aware of the uproar over the Soviet coup, but he felt certain that "the excellent funding available to me and all of my fellow grad students and scientists when we returned to the United States, and in the coming decades, was partially related to the US reaction to the Sputnik launch." Without a doubt it was.[39]

As for Antarctic science, the IGY disciplines (such as those described in this chapter) that were pursued on the polar continent because of the proximity of the magnetic and geomagnetic poles were precisely those seeking understanding of the nearer and more distant realms of space. Indeed, thanks to both the IGY—especially in Antarctica—and the space program, by the early 1970s upper-atmosphere expert Robert Helliwell of Stanford could report, "We now have a much clearer picture of the ways in which the sun deposits energy in the atmosphere and the resulting response of the atmosphere to this input." Moreover, the parallel malevolence of the two environments—remote, frigid, lacking resources to support life—made Antarctica seem more like space than of the earth. Indeed, investigator Jack Stuster, among others, has studied aspects of south-polar life—the effects of isolation and deprivation, leadership, medical and psychological support, food quality—for their "lessons" applicable to prolonged space travel. NASA science leaders like von Braun and Stuhlinger visited Antarctica to obtain a sense of lunar conditions. Today, IGY glaciologist Mario Giovinetto is one Antarctic scientist consulted by NASA as it plans the first peopled mission to Mars. Introduced to the world together during and because of the IGY, Antarctica and space have been broadly and intimately linked over time by science.[40]

But for all the scientists in Antarctica focused on the sky above them, others were standing on the ice pondering what lay beneath their feet.

CHAPTER ELEVEN

UNDER FOOT
Ice by the Mile

*It is really somewhat thrilling when one stops to think of it
(which we usually don't) to be seeing beautiful mountains and
climbing on rocks where no one has ever set foot.*

—John C. Behrendt, 1957[1]

What sets the Antarctic apart, of course, is the profound reality of its
ice. Vast and unrevealed, it impelled study. True, learning about ice
did not require simultaneous observation, a key IGY criterion, but it
would take concentrated, cooperative effort to make continent-wide
headway toward basic understanding. Besides, neither tantalized
researchers nor chauvinistic politicians could resist such a sublime
frontier. Teams of scientists, in winter camps and on summer traverses,
would pursue knowledge of the scope and character of the eternally
still—yet inexorably moving—continental ice sheets, including the
glaciers that flow from them as frozen rivers and the ice that spills out
into the surrounding ocean to float as ice shelves.

"Practically speaking," wrote historian Stephen Pyne, the polar continent is "constructed out of a single substance, in a single state, manifest as a single mineral." IGY scientists tingled to comprehend this one thing: its internal structure and composition, its size in area and volume, the topography of its surface and that of what lay below. Just knowing how thick it was would shed direct light on the glacial history of Antarctica, wrote geophysicist George Woollard of the University of Wisconsin, mentor to many young polar scientists. Was the ice shrinking or gaining? How much was snow accumulation offset by some form of ablation—sublimation, evaporation, meltwater runoff, wind transport, calving, or underside melting of ice shelves? How cold was the ice, and how were heat and moisture exchanged among ice, air, and sea? How heavy was the ice load, and what would that say about the strength of the earth's crust? Just how did the ice move under the forces of gravity and the stresses caused by its own geometry, the surface material over which it rode, and debris embedded within it? How would understanding the ice sheets, what Pyne called the "great archives of past climates," explain present climates and suggest future patterns?[2]

Enticing questions remained hanging from earlier explorations. One was whether Antarctica was one landmass or two, as Griffith Taylor and Raymond Priestley, geologists on Scott's last expedition, had suggested based on geological differences between the peninsular and transcontinental mountains. The rocks observed in coastal East Antarctica were predominantly Precambrian (the oldest on earth), igneous and metamorphic in origin, while rocks in West Antarctica tended to be younger and sedimentary. These early investigators also noted the embayments of the Ross and Weddell seas, which were bordered by the Transantarctic Mountains, but did not know whether they connected beneath the ice or even for certain how far the mountain chain extended. There was also the intriguing, increasingly validated theory of continental drift—that an ancestral, Southern Hemisphere supercontinent broke apart, its pieces drifting off to their present locations in sizes from Sri Lanka to South America. The proposed existence of "Gondwanaland" predated large-scale exploration of Antarctica (Taylor wrote of it), but the polar continent was clearly a central link, and the IGY was an ideal time to explore it.[3]

As Priestley and Charles Wright wrote in 1928 for the American Geographical Society, to answer such questions fully awaited "new technique or better equipment" and an "adequate scientific attack" involving "international cooperation on the grandest scale." On his first expedition, with airplanes and radio, Byrd visually investigated the West Antarctic ice cap. In 1934 his science leader Thomas Poulter measured the depth of the ice shelf and the Marie Byrd Land plateau using explosive techniques suggesting those of the IGY. For all that, Byrd wrote, "In the earth's history there is no chapter more enthralling than glaciation. It is also the blankest chapter, a glittering edifice of theories and a painful want of substantive data." Some early conclusions would prove incorrect. Scott's scientists had estimated, for example, that the ice sheet was thin, not more than about 2,000 feet thick, perhaps in a state of transition—a hypothesis strengthened by the retreat of the Ross Ice Shelf since Ross's measurements in 1842. Byrd, too, decided from air observation that since the ice of West Antarctica seemed to reveal the underlying land contours, it could not be very thick. His geologist Laurence Gould agreed, judging from the structure of the continental margin at the head of the Ross Sea. But there was really no way to ascertain ice depth over so vast a "land" with limited technologies, money, and manpower.[4]

One material assist, a scientific framework for studying the ice, was just evolving. Glaciology, the science of ice writ large, grew out of the discipline of geology, since ice was inescapable in the high mountains explored by geologists. Then, wartime interest in ice and its uses fed the formation of the British (later International) Glaciological Society in 1948, less than a decade before the IGY. In Pyne's view, it was "no accident that the exploration of Antarctica epitomized by IGY coincided with the emergence of glaciology as a distinct scientific discipline," although A. P. Crary wrote that glaciology as an IGY discipline "barely survived in the early days." He remembered that in 1953, Paul Siple had proposed instead a program of climatology based on glacial behavior (a look at global warming), but at the first international IGY meeting, Sir James Wordie (geologist on Shackleton's *Endurance*) and the NAS's Wallace Atwood, who made up the Working Group on Climates, "saved the program." That hint at tension between the two U.S. leaders goes no further, but in any event, glaciology would be a major focus in Antarctica.[5]

Scientific precedent had also just been set by the Norwegian-British-Swedish Antarctic Expedition of 1949–1952 in Queen Maud Land, an international effort whose primary purpose was to probe the mysteries of the ice. Gordon Robin, the British scientist who led this first over-snow traverse to sound the ice depth, had the latest in both scientific technologies and logistics support. Pulling wanigans ("caboose" was their term) with tracked vehicles, they were the first traveling scientific party to "sleep on spring bunks." If that was "a retrograde step to old antarctic hands," as Robin mused, the party demonstrated the feasibility of mechanized field operations and pioneered an approach that emphasized scientific results, not miles covered.[6]

Seismology, the study of earthquakes, was the other discipline brought to Antarctica during the IGY for ice research. Antarctica is seismically quiet but a good place to study earthquake belts, particularly of the Southern Hemisphere, because no intervening landmasses intercept traveling earthquake waves. Many U.S. stations and at least four others—Dumont d'Urville (France), Halley Bay (Britain), Scott (New Zealand), and Mirny (Soviet Union)—recorded seismological observations. But most polar seismologists were less interested in earthquakes per se than in what seismic waves could tell them about continental geology. So they used explosives to create seismic waves artificially, which allowed them to determine the thickness of the ice and what lay beneath it. The principle is that seismic waves travel at different known speeds through ice, water, and rock. Thus their reflections as they bounce back from these respective layers look different, revealing the composition of the substance through which they pass; the time it takes the reflection to return indicates the thickness of that substance.[7]

The scientists also used gravity meters, or gravimeters, as a supplementary way to measure ice thickness as well as the earth's gravity field, of interest in its own right. The earth's mass attracts all bodies on it. But the earth is not a perfect sphere (it flattens near the poles), its mass is not evenly distributed (ice, a less dense "rock," has less gravitational pull than the rock of a mountain), and it rotates (with less centrifugal force near the polar axes), so the pull of gravity is not everywhere the same. IGY scientists first determined the value of gravity at McMurdo Sound, calculating the natural increase from the world gravity reference point at Potsdam, and then used that value as a standard reference point for the rest of the continent.[8]

The final earth-science discipline was, logically, geology. Yet it was not included among the official IGY studies in Antarctica. Geology did not need a synoptic approach, but the planners' real reason (though little on the subject was committed to paper) seemed to be fear of loosing mineral searches that could open a rush for economic exploitation, shut down the international sharing of findings, and inflame the claims issue. Regardless, the U.S. interagency Operations Coordinating Board, responsible for "national interests" in Antarctica, was clearly interested in geology, mapping, and exploration—as, no doubt, were political forces in other countries. Antarctica put up practical hurdles to prospecting in that almost all of its rock was buried beneath ice, often at great depth. Still, in the course of other work, geologists and would-be geologists would eagerly seek exposed rock faces to identify and take specimens, all the while informally expanding geographical knowledge. Ellsworth seismologist John Behrendt ruminated at the time, "It seems rather ironic that, although geology isn't one of the fields of the IGY, we have four out of the nine scientists with geology degrees." That ratio was not atypical. Geodesy, the study of the shape and size of the earth and the exact location of points on it, did not appear on U.S. IGY discipline lists either, although mapping and other related work were quietly done.[9]

IGY science leaders concentrated first on observations the scientists could do in camp while wintering over—the cost of being in place for a full summer season in the field. Crary, who at Little America lumped the seismology, gravity, and glaciology programs together since the same team of four worked on them all, outlined a long list of winter activities. Among them were fixing the camp's elevation, studying possible bottom melting of the ice shelf in Kainan Bay, investigating area crevasses and valleys to estimate the station's life expectancy, doing shallow and deep snow-pit studies, determining gravity (including measurement of tidal periods and amplitudes from the rise and fall of the ice shelf), and seismically measuring local ice thickness. It was a heavy agenda, and, as Crary noted, for the first two months outdoors the mostly inexperienced scientists had to focus on "obtaining knowledge of working methods." The other stations conducted analogous observations where possible.[10]

The very-low-tech exercise of inspecting gradation changes on the carefully laid out snow-accumulation stakes proved a frustration everywhere. Crary blamed the greatly variable readings at Little America on its undulating topography and closeness to the sea. Eventually, the team put out more than a hundred stakes, but Crary confessed that determining a final accumulation figure "became almost entirely an exercise in statistics." Byrd glaciologists Vern Anderson and Mario Giovinetto set out only seven bamboo stakes 35 meters (115.5 feet) apart in a line running perpendicular to the prevailing wind. They read them two to five times a month from autumn through spring, but their results, too, were confusing. On one warm (−1°F), snowy May night, Anderson was "almost tempted to run out and take accumulation readings before it all blows away." At the dry South Pole, it was virtually impossible to distinguish falling from blowing snow.[11]

Measuring the movement of ice was another priority. Wilkes Station's three glaciologists, led by Richard Cameron, enjoyed the professional challenge of having the Vanderford Glacier right in their back yard. In late February 1957 they placed ice-movement stakes in its foot at what they called Site 1 (S-1), about 5.5 miles from camp. Using a nunatak as a fixed point of reference, they measured the stakes' travel with surveying equipment and calculated that the center of the glacier was moving about 1.9 meters (more than 6 feet) daily. The next year that record fell when chief glaciologist John Hollin and his assistants found the Vanderford advancing at a rate of 9 feet (2.7 meters) per day. Crary tried to calculate the absolute movement of the Ross Ice Shelf. He lowered a piece of heavy scrap metal to the bottom of the bay (about 2,000 feet down). To this anchor he attached a spring-fed cable that could be measured as it payed out with the advancing shelf. But strong current strained the wire, slackening kinked it, and finally it broke.[12]

Glaciologists augered holes to take snow temperatures at specified intervals from just below the snow surface to as far as 16 meters (53 feet) using a series of thermohm (resistance thermometer) cables and a direct-reading Wheatstone bridge (an electrical circuit used to measure the resistance of an unknown resistor by comparing it with a known standard resistance). Anderson connected his Wheatstone bridge to a selector switch housed in a snow-tight box above the surface so he could simply turn the switch through the positions of the respective thermohms. Between early May and late October about a foot of snow accumulated at Byrd, which gradually increased the instruments' depths. These snow temperatures were important data because ice is a poor conductor of heat, and at about 10 meters' (about 30 feet) depth the seasonal temperature waves damp out to within a degree of the mean annual temperature. Thus the scientists could determine a "primary climatic parameter" without long-term weather observations. Wilkes's glaciologists drilled their thermohms into the edge of the ice cap at S-1 and measured temperature differences as the ice traveled.[13]

At all stations where it was possible, glaciologists spent the winter months digging a deep pit in the hard snow, seeking in its characteristics the history of the forming ice. At intervals as they descended they measured snow temperature, density, hardness, age, and deformation. They noted snow-grain size and collected samples for tritium (from northern atomic-bomb tests), oxygen-isotope, and crystal analysis. The diggers observed the snow strata, that is, the annual layers caused by new snow piling up and compacting the older snow below. Where there was summer melting, these layers could be read like tree rings. With virtually no surface melting at the South Pole, stratigraphy was problematic, although Soviet glaciologist P. A. Shumskii showed that 2-millimeter melt crusts form as the sun's rays penetrate vertically oriented snow crystals, a "greenhouse" effect.[14]

Digging the deep pits was hard work in the frigid darkness, harder as the firn in the deepening holes grew ever denser. At Pole, glaciologist Ed Remington found that at 78 centimeters (31 inches) below the surface the snow was so hard (ramm hardness of 1200) that a ten-pound sledgehammer driving a crowbar into it bent the steel. Chief glaciologist Hugo Neuburg designed the Ellsworth pit, similar to most others, with a square opening 3 meters (10 feet) by 3 meters tapering at a 75-degree angle to 2 meters (6 feet) square at the bottom. A wire rope ladder with aluminum rungs gave access, and plywood platforms every 5 meters provided work bases and what Behrendt called "the illusion of security in climbing up and down." A single lightbulb at the bottom sufficiently illuminated the white world. To prevent drift-snow from mocking its efforts, the team raised a tent over the hole.[15]

At all stations the diggers devised some sort of mechanized pulley system for raising buckets of dug snow out of the pit, but those at the bottom went after the ice the old-fashioned way: with pickaxes. The day before midwinter, with their pit to 6.5 meters (21.5 feet), Anderson wrote, "Gosh but I really worked up a sweat today, and at 20° below." How cold it actually got in the deep pits depended on where they were. At Ellsworth, down at the digging it was about −10°F, the mean annual temperature; at Pole it was closer to −60°. Those working at the surface hauling away the excavated material also had to contend with wind and blowing snow. At Ellsworth the crew could generally work for an hour before needing the warmth of a meal or a coffee break. They made −60° the cutoff; below that they stayed indoors.[16]

By midwinter, deep-pit competition was beginning to tell. On 29 June Anderson wrote in his diary, "Well, we made 8 meters [26.4 feet] today, just." On 5 July he confided, "Mario said he and Ned [Ostenso, assistant seismologist] will dig tomorrow AM, and I'll be digging in PM with Doc [Bentley]. Hope this works out, 'cause we'll catch up a little maybe. Weddell Sea Station is 17 meters [56.1 feet] as of 1 July!" Diggers everywhere were keeping track. Behrendt also saw that SITREP. He recorded that Little America's deep pit was at 18 meters (almost 60 feet) at that time. Ellsworth was at 17, Wilkes 10 (33 feet), and Byrd 8 meters. The next day a disappointed Anderson admitted, "Two shifts of digging today and we only got about 40 cms [16 inches]. Trouble was Ned had to get used to the system." On 2 August he fretted, "Weddell Station hit 29.5 meters [97.4 feet] with their pit, which makes me look really good. Nuts!" He had already, on 17 July, decided to stop when he got to the last rung of his one cable ladder so he could take the camp's other 50-foot length along on the traverse. "We can continue deeper here by augering and studying the cores like Little America is thinking of doing," he rationalized. Still looking over his shoulder, however, he observed a few days later that Pole's diggers had hauled out 9,000 cubic feet of snow, compared with his 1,200 feet "so far." Finally, on 15 August, he declared satisfaction: "Well, a real FB [fine business: ham radio shorthand for any kind of good thing] day. We got 30 meters [99.3 feet] deep today—18 [meters (59.4 feet) of drilled core] plus the 12 meter [39.6-foot] pit and that's 100' down."[17]

Byrd's efforts gave that station a last-place finish among the American deep pits, but the glaciologists knew that SIPRE deep-core drillers were coming in the spring and would penetrate far deeper than they could by hand. They took that cue from Crary. During the winter Little America's ice team dug a pit to 20 meters (66 feet) and hand drilled another 20. While they had originally planned a 30-meter pit, Crary thought that would be an "unprofitable" use of time with SIPRE likely to send Byrd's drilling team there later. At Ellsworth the traverse seismologists helped the glaciology team haul out snow after the first few weeks of digging, and the five got their pit down to 103 feet (31 meters), then bored another 50 feet with a 3-inch drill, pulling out the drill rod every foot and a half or so to recover the core. On 28 August Behrendt bragged that their station had the "deepest pit that any of us have ever heard of and definitely the deepest at present in Antarctica." But he later had to concede being bested by Wilkes, whose diggers got 4 meters (13 feet) deeper.[18]

Wilkes Station lived on bare rock. But not far away was a relatively easy, crevasse-free ramp leading to the deep interior—an opportunity perhaps for ice-movement and deep-pit studies on the East Antarctic ice cap. (Meteorologist Rudi Honkala was also eager to do comparative weather observations away from the effects of the coast.) The decision to try it, remembered seismologist Gil Dewart, was "a matter of consensus. This was not something that was planned, it was not something the Navy had to do, it was not something that we had to do. It was something that could be done, so if it can be done, let's do it." Wilkes enjoyed plentiful supplies of spare building materials and equipment, and the scientists' enthusiasm was met by the sailors' own. The Seabees had "tremendous talent for putting things together," Dewart recalled, appreciating specifically master mechanic Bob McIntyre, carpenter George Magee, and Fred Charlton, electronics chief. And they "weren't just doing the job." They were "very much interested in what was happening." For Navy photographer Paul Noonan, going along to document the first trip inland was a highlight of the year.[19]

On 11 March 1957 leader Carl Eklund, Cameron, assistant glaciologists Olav Loken and John Molholm, Honkala, and Noonan headed out with three Weasels pulling two tons of supplies on sleds—a four-section Jamesway hut, fuel, space heater, radio transceiver, kitchen table and benches, scientific equipment, tools, food, and army cots. After eleven hours of uphill driving (to 4,200 feet) and three of construction, they had a fire lit at their satellite station (called Site 2, or S-2) 53 miles inland. Some pair or more of persons would occupy it

The deep pit at the Wilkes Icecap Station (Site 2) was, at 115 feet, the deepest dug for IGY stratigraphy studies. Official U.S. Navy photograph, by Paul Noonan. Eklund, SSLR, Wilkes 1957.

continuously from 25 April 1957 until 22 January 1958. The Navy made three additional trips to the camp by D-4 tractor to bring gasoline and diesel fuel. S-2 was a large undertaking for so small a party, Dewart said, but it was easy to get volunteer help. Ralph Glasgal, the aurora observer, for one, was glad to go up to the ice-cap station when it got too light to see auroral displays, and before long S-2 became "a little bit of a tourist site," albeit a fiercely windy one. Virtually everyone at Wilkes made at least one visit. The men came to prefer driving at night when their vehicle lights cast longer shadows, making old tracks easier to follow even in driving snow.[20]

At the ice-cap station the glaciologists dug their snow pit 35.25 meters (116 feet) deep, "the deepest such pit ever dug in Antarctica, if not in the world" and back in history to the American Revolution. An additional 85-foot core gave a stratigraphic record back to the late 1500s. They found, for example, a jump in atmospheric carbon dioxide at the time of the Industrial Revolution, a beginning perhaps of the greenhouse gases that worry environmentalists today. They also put out stakes to measure ice movement on the ice cap. Stratigraphic studies at S-2 and along the trail indicated an average annual snow accumulation of 25 inches per year.[21]

At Pole the deep pit of other stations became a sloping "hard-rock mine," doubling as a water source (see Chapter 6). In it glaciologist Ed Remington, a World War II pilot called "Moose," photographed inch-thick slices from snow blocks cut in descending sequence to provide "a picture story of the ages spent in building the polar plateau." Because at Pole it was difficult to identify layers showing annual accumulation or age, he sealed samples from all his snow slices in numbered plastic bottles for oxygen-isotope analysis back home. The next year Giovinetto had a microfiltration kit that would detect and identify microscopic particles carried in from distant disturbances such as historic volcanic eruptions. In addition to continuing Remington's studies in the snow mine, he dug eight shallow (2-meter, 6.6-foot) pits to observe differences in stratigraphic characteristics just a few meters apart.[22]

Drilling to recover ice cores from great depths for the history they secreted duly began at Byrd Station during the summer of 1957–1958 and is still an important research method. Drilling techniques had been perfected in Greenland, where SIPRE scientists bored the first 1,000-foot hole in 1956. This snow-and-ice Army research group provided most of the equipment, crew, field supervision, core analysis, and reporting for the joint IGY-SIPRE Antarctic project. Getting all twenty-six tons of equipment, including the heavy drill rig (like those used for oil), out to Byrd was a logistics triumph of its own. It arrived over two summers via Little America or McMurdo by ship, plane (C-

124 airdrops, R4D landings), and tractor train. By the time the two glaciologists, leader E. W. Marshall and Anthony Gow, flew in on Christmas Day 1957, drilling engineer Robert Patenaude, driller Jack Tedrow, and five army assistants had the mechanical problems under control and the drilling begun.[23]

The nascent technology proved remarkably effective. The gasoline-powered rotary well-drilling rig used compressed air, cooled to within a few degrees of ambient air temperature, as the drilling fluid. With practice and equipment modifications the drillers found the optimum speed of rotation of the drill string and rate of penetration (which varied with depth) to avoid setting up vibrations or breaking up the core. As the specially designed hollow drill bit bore down, it enclosed a 4-inch cylinder of ice that was brought periodically to the surface. The drillers eventually cored to 1,013 feet, recovering 98.3 percent of the ice in lengths up to 19 feet. Using a light table, the scientists could see seasonally alternating layers of coarse- and fine-grained snow but no thick ice bands that would have indicated a period of pronounced thaw. After about 400 feet the visual stratigraphy disappeared, and microscopic examination of thin sections had to wait for stateside attention. The cores went north on the *Glacier* to Boston, then by refrigerated truck to the SIPRE cold laboratory in Wilmette, Illinois, for exhaustive study. The Byrd drilling equipment returned to Little America via tractor train at the end of the season where it was used the following summer to core over 800 feet through the ice shelf near Kainan Bay.[24]

The ice cores' structure and composition—especially particles embedded in them, such as rock dust, volcanic ash, micrometeorites, and pollen—yielded an "invaluable index" of climate and precipitation over several hundred years. Completing multiple analyses, the Wilmette glaciologists concluded that the bottom layers of the Byrd ice core had fallen as snow 1,400 years earlier. They identified volcanic dust from the 1883 eruption of Indonesia's Krakatoa, finding it buried only 40 percent as deep as in Greenland (60 versus 150 feet), where snowfall was heavier. Scientists at the California Institute of Technology used the ratio of oxygen isotopes (O^{18}/O^{16}) preserved in the snow, which varies as a function of seasonal temperature, to determine annual accumulation and age of the snow—a procedure especially helpful where the layers could not be discerned visually because of scant summer melting.[25]

Meanwhile, geophysicists at stations not anticipating summer traverse programs operated seismic equipment on-site. Professors Frank Press at Caltech and Maurice Ewing at Columbia had just developed a new type of seismograph designed to pick up long-period (about 400 seconds) surface waves traveling through the earth's crust. Analysis of such waves, generated by only the largest tremors, would reveal the earth's outer structure. Dewart set up one of these seismographs at Wilkes (the first of a permanent network for continuous earthquake monitoring) right on the exposed bedrock—"that's one thing we had there at least," though vehicle vibrations and fearsome winds could not be stilled by rock bolts. Since Wilkes, itself quite aseismic, was located across the continent from the geologically active Scotia Arc leading toward South America, it could expect to receive long-period surface waves in plenty. They would describe the structure of the polar continent, if in fact it could qualify as one. And they did. Dewart's instrument monitored a powerful earthquake centered in Chile that sent waves across the intervening ocean and the breadth of Antarctica, yielding a subsurface profile of "really thick continental crust" along its path. His successor, Father Henry Birkenhauer, also recorded numerous earthquakes, most of them originating in the Pacific area, which added further proof that a true continent lay beneath them in East Antarctica.

Dewart also learned to watch for odd seismic oscillations, such as seiches—standing waves that get set up on the surface of an enclosed body of water, such as the many within the offshore Windmill Islands. Such waves introduced noise into his recordings, as did the precipitous drops in air pressure that preceded major storms. "I could tell the meteorologists exactly when the storm arrived just as well as they could with their barograph," he said. His needles would go off scale. He also noted what they came to call cryoseisms, or "ice quakes," presumably caused by ice movement such as an iceberg calving, a sudden slip of a glacier, or the opening of a crevasse.[26]

The South Pole's seismic situation was unique, wrote Siple. In the "dead center of the polar regions," it was also "on top of a mile or so of ice and snow," both of which might cushion the effects of the earthquake activity they were trying to monitor. Twenty-one-year-old Robert Benson, a math and astronomy major, tended three delicate seismometers, one oriented vertically and two horizontally at right angles to each other, hooked up to a three-component 35-mm film recorder. Benson's instruments were housed in a ten-foot pit at the end of the geomagnetism snow tunnel to avoid camp vibrations (never fully achieved) and were sheathed in aluminum foil to protect them from stray electric fields. Benson created "bedrock" for his equipment on the snow surface with a little water and the "'aid' of a –65°F. temperature." In addition to some impressive distant earthquakes, such as a big one on the Kamchatka Peninsula in eastern Siberia, Benson and his successor James Burnham recorded closer tremors, some caused perhaps by snow subsidences such as the one that unsettled Bowers's construction crew on its first morning on the plateau. All such records ended up at the Coast and Geodetic Survey in Washington for interpretation and analysis.[27]

The seismologists' instrumentation tested their grit and skill. One provocation was the delicate barrel-type galvanometer used with the film recorder. Four of the first five arrived damaged, and Benson spent hours at "many, many, many galvanometer repair attempts (conservative estimate)" trying to solder the 0.0007-inch gold thread. He finally used it all and had to set up an alternate paper recorder. The next January four new galvanometers arrived by airdrop—all broken. "It might be wiser to hand carry twice as many as one expects will be required," Burnham wrote with tense patience. Kenneth Bargh, their similarly vexed counterpart at Hallett in 1958, confirmed the helpless feeling: "While the present writer does not consider himself below average in manual dexterity or care with delicate equipment, he approaches anything concerned with these galvanometers with trepidation and as a last resort. . . . A high initial casualty rate is to be expected."[28]

Rehearsing for the summer field season, scientists at the two ice-shelf stations set off seismic explosions to measure local ice thickness. At Little America they determined the thickness of the ice in Kainan Bay, the barrier, and several valleys thereon, as well as the depth of the water and sediments in the sea floor. The outer edge of the Ross Ice Shelf measured about 660 feet (200 meters) thick. Crary also directed gravity readings every two hours for a month to measure changes in the elevation of the ice shelf with tidal movement and asked Ed Thiel's team at Ellsworth to do the same. From these firsts, they found that the shelf rose and fell twice a day with the tide, shown by relative decreases and increases of gravity, respectively. Seismic shots at Ellsworth showed the Filchner Ice Shelf to be about 700 feet (230 meters) thick, the water to sea floor about 2,500 feet (790 m) deep. The station turned out to be located over a deep trough, one first observed from water-depth measurements on the *Staten Island*. With Wilkes scientists' typical enthusiasm for expanding the planned program, they measured ice in the Windmill Islands and on the nearby shelf ice toward Cape Poinsett. In 1958 Hollin estimated that the ice from most of the Clark Peninsula had retreated about 12,000 years earlier. Freed of that load, the land had risen relative to the sea some 100 feet and was still emerging.[29]

The most glamorous ice work of the IGY was the over-snow traverse, on which "everybody" wanted to go. These expeditions were an opportunity to not only break free of the confines of camp after the long winter but also to experience,

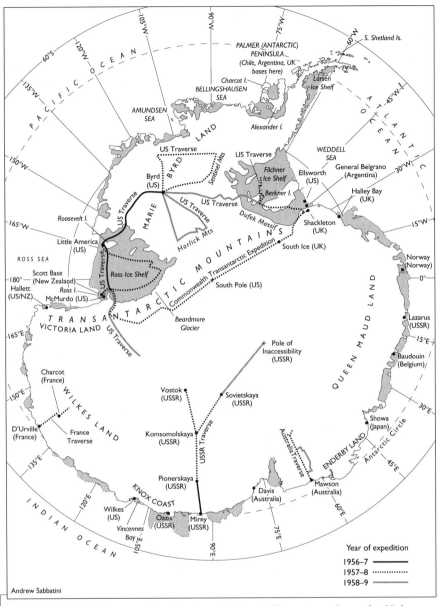

Over-snow traverse routes of the IGY. From Walter Sullivan, Assault on the Unknown *(New York: McGraw Hill, 1961), 308. Courtesy, cartographer Andrew Sabbatini. Redrawn by Bill Nelson.*

scientifically and personally, vast areas that had never known the footprint of a living thing. To keep nearly self-supporting parties out in the unknown over great distances and time demanded intensive planning and specialized procurement. In October 1955 Antarctic science leader Crary ordered eight Tucker Sno-Cats, Model 743 Freighters with 235-horsepower engines and special reinforcements. Sno-Cats were the lowest-ground-pressure vehicles at the time, exerting only three or four pounds of pressure per square inch of snow. They ran on four wide-tracked pontoons, those at the front and rear operating independently. Each was long enough to safely span a narrow crevasse. These large, high-riding boxes, costing $20,000 apiece, would serve as transport, laboratory, and living space for the traverse teams.[30]

Crary's detailed list for the first year's three proposed traverses also included sixteen 2-ton open sleds and six 1-ton sleds; 55,000 gallons of motor vehicle gasoline (a heavily loaded Sno-Cat would consume about a gallon per mile) with appropriate amounts of motor oil, grease, and antifreeze; eight wanigans (not used on the traverses); six sets of radio equipment (long-distance two-way radios and less powerful units for use within a traveling party); navigation equipment including gyroscopes, theodolites, sun compasses, and Magnesyn Compass Transmitters and Indicators; altimeters and chronometers; trail food; and other necessities such as tents, sleeping bags, air mattresses, stoves and cooking equipment, skis, snowshoes, small sleds, and trail markers. Crary added crevasse-detector units in longhand. He estimated total cost at that early date was $405,480. Of that, $23,000 would purchase explosives for seismic studies. Behrendt wrote of Ellsworth's supply: "We have 3000 lbs of Nitromon (ammonium nitrate) and 6000 lbs of Petrogel (60% nitroglycerin dynamite) and the Navy has about 20 tons of their stuff. . . . We can use all we want." Despite knowing little about the behavior of gelatinous explosives at polar temperatures, both geophysicists and Navy demolitionists became "casual" in their use. Finally, each discipline needed its own specialized equipment. Today, snowmobiles landed in the field could support much of this work, but during the IGY the heavy, bulky batteries and vacuum-tube electronic equipment required far more motive power and storage space.[31]

Winter efforts focused on preparing for and outfitting the summer traverses. The scientists checked out their vehicles and equipment, installed and tested compasses and crevasse detectors, and repacked traverse foods in ten-man-day units. They learned basic first-aid and medical techniques, such as how to splint a broken bone, treat shock, administer shots, even give blood transfusions. The station physicians assembled kits with various pain relievers, treatments

Traverse Sno-Cat outfitted with crevasse detector, pulling sled of supplies. Official U.S. Navy photograph. Courtesy, Robert Chaudoin.

for the most likely ailments such as diarrhea and toothache, bandages, antiseptics, and syringes. The traversers were entrusted with antibiotics and narcotics, including morphine, which would never be allowed today. As weather permitted, the Navy flew reconnaissance missions to scout out safe routes. In mid-April 1957 Crary took his team on a confidence- and skill-building forty-mile shakedown traverse along the Byrd Trail where temperatures dipped as low as −40°F.[32]

Navigation was an obvious concern. Charlie Bentley and the Byrd traverse team struggled to get their gyrocompass to work but did not have the right fluid to damp it properly. Common wisdom said that magnetic compasses would be unusable so near the South Magnetic Pole, but "finally it dawned on us," he recalled later, that "where we were at Byrd Station, we were actually farther from the magnetic pole than we are from the North Magnetic Pole right here in Wisconsin." They located an old tank compass, far simpler and very reliable. During the winter Bentley learned how to navigate by shooting stars with a theodolite; it was "fun," though hard on both fingers and equipment at fifty or sixty below, and the results were not too promising. But having learned the principles, "it was just a breeze" to do sunshots in the summertime. A sunshot is a measure of the elevation of the sun above the horizon, which gives one line on a plotting chart. Another angle a few hours later with the sun in a different position provides another line, and "where they cross is where you are." A third shot still later produces a little triangle ("not a point because no measurement is perfect") and further assurance of position. Only Neuburg and Aughenbaugh on the Ellsworth traverse were qualified navigators. Only Neuburg and Behrendt could receive and transmit Morse code, the latter slowly. Anderson diligently practiced code over the winter at Byrd.[33]

Traverse preparations at Ellsworth were dominated by one huge overriding problem, and it exemplified as well as any the unfortunate climate at the base. Of the several accounts of this story, the station leader's are strikingly at odds with all the others. He wrote about it in three publications. On 23 March 1957, while the scientists were out doing ice studies, they burned out the clutch in one of the Sno-Cats—"to a frazzle, that's for sure," recalled Walt Davis, the lone wintering Seabee mechanic. Captain Ronne wrote, "The seismic man who drove it [the "practically new" Sno-Cat] had gotten into the bad habit of starting off in highest gear. The clutch soon burned out." Behrendt, the inexperienced and guilty driver that day, agreed with the mechanical cause, but the blame was unjust. Early on, the scientists had found it impossible to follow the normal practice of starting in first gear and then shifting up because the tracks were too tight. So a summering Seabee chief mechanic had told them to start in the gear they planned to drive in. They did, and the strain was too much. Now they would know better, the leader snidely wrote. "Practical experience is a good teacher."[34]

There was no spare clutch. Davis, a hard and willing worker, felt "pressure from higher up" not to work on civilian equipment. Later he confessed to feeling "kind of ashamed of myself for not helping them more than I did." In fact, Behrendt, who called Davis "a really nice guy inside a gruff exterior," said he "saved our bacon on numerous occasions." Ronne suggested they have a clutch sent to McMurdo by ship and then flown over, but he knew it would arrive too late to salvage the brief field season. Maj. James Lassiter, an Air Force pilot and veteran of Ronne's private expedition, would be flying in by C-47 (R4D equivalent) to do photographic mapping missions in the spring (a classified CIA operation, Behrendt later concluded), but Ronne refused to ask him to bring a new clutch, using the excuse of excessive weight (about fifty pounds).[35]

In July, with the help of Navy radioman Chuck Forlidas, Neuburg managed a clandestine, 3 A.M. radio conversation with Byrd glaciologists Anderson and Giovinetto. He asked them to ask Crary at Little America to ask Odishaw in Washington to help get them a clutch because their communication was under "dictatorial censorship." Anderson wrote only that they "just shot the breeze and he asked a few questions about our traverse and how we're doing up here." But they must have forwarded the plea because by this roundabout route, Odishaw pressured Lassiter on behalf of the IGY. Resisting at first for the sake of his "independent" program, Lassiter finally acquiesced as a "favor." Still, on 8 September, when Lassiter asked Ronne via radio if he should bring the clutch, Neuburg and Paul Walker overheard the captain decline; the Shackleton people, he said, were "fixing everything up for us." On 5 October, three weeks before the traverse was scheduled to depart, Davis, with ruined clutch springs in hand, was allowed to fly over to the British station. From Shackleton's mechanic (who had no spare clutch either) he "got specs [specifications] on how to temper the springs" and a sample spring to bring back, but he advised the scientists to prepare two Weasels to accompany the one working Sno-Cat until Lassiter arrived with a new clutch. Ronne had also suggested Weasels but the scientists balked, knowing their unreliability in cold weather and, with higher ground pressure and smaller size, their greater vulnerability to crevasses.[36]

The determined Hugo Neuburg was not ready to give up, however. Behrendt, exultant, wrote on 8 October, "Hugo and Paul [glaciology assistant Walker] have done the impossible!" They had managed to retemper the clutch's sixteen springs in the galley stove (to its minor harm). Neuburg heated each spring, one by one, in the flames of the firebox. When it was cherry red, he quenched it in kerosene and annealed it in the oven, judging the proper amount by comparing it visually with the color of the metal in the borrowed spring. Morale among the scientists soared. "All of the credit goes to Hugo for persisting against so much discouraging advice," sang Behrendt in grateful praise. Davis called him "a remarkable man." Ronne wrote that Davis showed Neuburg how to retemper the springs but added that "there was too much work to do the IGY men's work, too." The traversers would never need the new clutch that Lassiter finally delivered; it remained at Ellsworth. Ronne wrote in his scientific-leader report that "only through the effort of the US Air Force planes when they reached the station in November with a new clutch" could the Sno-Cat be used.[37]

Sno-Cats were not the only vehicles to be readied for the traverse season. VX-6 crews began to dig out their buried aircraft in early August, as the solar glow on the horizon grew and slowly brightened. It was cold, heavy work. For six hours a day Cmdr. James Waldron and his VX-6 pilots and crews at Little America struggled to remove snow so hard-packed he feared the shovel handles would break. By the 16th it was obvious to Ellsworth pilot Con Jaburg that

Otter 671 was "one plane which will never fly again!" By his account, "Pressure of snow has compressed the fuselage until now it looks like a washboard, also the tail ski assembly has been collapsed up into the fuselage and the wing and tail surfaces are wrinkled to beat hell. All that plane will be good for will be for spare parts." The aircraft could tolerate winter cold but not harsh winds or heavy snow loads. Fortunately, Ellsworth had a still-crated spare. In September reconnaissance flights resumed, and in October so did direct traverse support.[38]

Air support was "tremendously important," said Bentley, because they could not pull more than a couple of weeks' worth of the "absolutely essential" fuel on the ground. Those aloft could spot and assess crevasses, even bridged ones in favorable sun angles, that were impossible to see at eye level. The planes would also bring a welcome diversion for the traversers who looked forward to mail, company, and treats from the base cook. R4Ds would fly fuel to the more distant points along the traverses, while the smaller Otters—with shorter range, limited carrying capacity (a few barrels, depending on distance), no radar, and only about 15 miles of radio range—replenished nearer parties. Ellsworth's traversers could not venture farther than 250 miles from camp, the Otters' limit, until Major Lassiter arrived. Little America's larger flying staff would be fully occupied supporting the Ross Ice Shelf and Marie Byrd Land traverses, as well as two Byrd tractor trains, Byrd Station itself, and miscellaneous IGY transit between Little America and McMurdo.[39]

The scientists would radio in when they needed replenishment, and the pilots would fly as soon as the weather permitted. Bentley, with the group furthest from air support, though, wondered if the idea of "resupplying the traverses, at least our traverse, hadn't really sunk in with the support people" because after calling in for fuel the first time, "we sat out there waiting and waiting and waiting." Finally, weighing whether to conserve their last few tens of gallons of gas to run the heaters or use it for science ("the weather was nice"), they took faith and burned most of it on a seismic refraction. After that one miscommunication, Bentley said "they'd be out instantly. They loved coming out to find us." Indeed they did. It was a victory to spot the tiny orange specks, although Waldron also remembered the tedium of flying long hours over a flat, featureless, white sameness, squinting into the glare. It was easy to daydream, difficult to concentrate on the mechanics of flying. When the ever-fickle weather was good, flight crews would make back-to-back trips; when it deteriorated, anxiety helped wakefulness. Most pilots had stories to tell of unplanned landings, close calls. By the end of the IGY's first summer, VX-6 crews had logged nearly a million miles carrying 2,778 passengers and 825

Navy Otter arriving to resupply Ellsworth IGY traverse. Official U.S. Navy photograph. NARA II, RG 313, Records of Photography Officer DF 55–69, Box 9.

tons of cargo in support of the scientific effort—all while perfecting their ability to get the seriously overloaded planes airborne.[40]

Three U.S. traverses were scheduled for each austral summer of the IGY, one each from Little America, Byrd, and Ellsworth. But scientists at two other stations at least also pined to rove. Eklund radioed requesting permission and air support for a traverse from Wilkes to the South Pole, about 1,700 miles distant, but McMurdo-based planes, 1,360 miles to the east, were impractically far away. "You know, you sit around during the Antarctic winter and you fantasize about all kinds of things," Dewart recalled. Wilkes scientists also drew up a more modest plan to travel south of the ice-cap station, making an angular R-shaped circuit of about 500 miles taking in Mount Long and the upper Vanderford Glacier. They had Weasels, sleds, dogs, and plentiful supplies, including food. The dreamers lined up station volunteers, both IGY and Navy, who knew a summer traverse would mean another winter on the ice because the relief ships would have come and gone by their return. It was an anguishing yet irresistible choice for some. "I mean we had families, responsibilities," explained Dewart, who was not thus obligated. Hanessian in Washington tentatively called the idea practical and scientifically valuable, but in the end the Navy balked at the added expense, and Gould and Wexler did not want to press for additional procurement when replacement costs for the planned traverses' expensive equipment would already be high. The U.S. IGY Glaciology Panel had specifically decided in August 1955 not to provide seismic sounding equipment or air support for the then newly approved station. The fantasy remained just that. In 1958–1959, though, Wilkes's glaciologists and a mechanic would make an eight-week, 400-mile traverse inland.[41]

Siple, in a SITREP in late April 1957, recommended a full-scale seismic-glaciological-gravity traverse to radiate from Pole 300 miles in several directions for the summer of Deep Freeze III. If the Navy could fly in the vehicles, instruments, and seismic personnel early in the season, he believed the station could "easily accommodate double the present population for an expanded scientific program." In his book, Siple spoke of conversations with Remington and Jack Tuck on this subject but listed more modest spokes of 50 to 100 miles. Perhaps by then they had learned that support for such a venture would not be forthcoming, although Wexler's later diary notes suggest that Siple had not really pressed his case with the IGY. (Wexler seemed interested.) In truth, the Pole scientists had no proper equipment for measuring ice thickness and could not risk their single Weasel until new vehicles arrived. Then they got word of their early evacuation. So the number of American IGY traverses remained at three.[42]

Crary's Ross Ice Shelf traverse group, the first to get under way, left Little America in three Sno-Cats on 24 October 1957. With him were glaciologists Peter Schoeck (the winter aurora observer) and Walter Boyd, both of whom had trained in Greenland in 1956; Hugh Bennett as Crary's assistant seismologist; and mechanic William Cromie, "master of all trades." By the time they returned on 13 February 1958, having made a 1,400-mile circuit of the floating and grounded shelf, the party was considerably altered. Edwin Robinson, a University of Michigan student, came on as an extra seismologist, and glaciologist Stephen ("Denny") den Hartog joined up in January. Lyle McGinnis replaced Bennett, who went out early to report on the traverse at an Antarctic symposium in Wellington in February 1958. Over the season a great deal of company also dropped in—perhaps because this was Crary's traverse as well as the most easily accessible. Guests included Sir Hubert Wilkins as well as reporters and science leaders.[43]

Soon after Crary's departure, James Zumberge of the University of Michigan led a summer field group out to study how the Ross Ice Shelf deformed as

Instruments measure crevasse movement, Ice Deformation Study, Camp Michigan, Ross Ice Shelf, 1957. NARA II, RG 401 (82), Philip M. Smith Papers, Box 1.

it flowed around Roosevelt Island and created the Bay of Whales. Phil Smith, now a civilian, brought his crevasse expertise and Mario Giovinetto his Argentine and U.S. glaciological experience (as he would again when the project resumed in 1958–1959). Topographic engineer William Austin acted as surveyor-photographer. Hauling supplies from Little America by D-8 and 20-ton sled, the team set up Camp Michigan in the heart of the disturbed area. They identified and measured three types of deformation—produced by horizontal compression, horizontal tension, or shearing action. They installed sensitive strain gauges in crevasses to measure their rates of opening, interestingly finding each rate constant although another crevasse might be opening at a different constant rate. Francis, reporting to the National Academy of Sciences from Little America on Christmas Day 1957, called Zumberge's project a "brilliant job" by a "great man" who had garnered everyone's enthusiasm and support.[44]

The Ellsworth two-Sno-Cat traverse party set out across the Filchner Ice Shelf on 28 October 1957. The group was led by Thiel, chief seismologist, and Neuburg, chief glaciologist, accompanied by Behrendt and Walker, their respective seconds, and Aughenbaugh, civil engineer and geologist who assisted both programs. Neuburg and Walker had taken a five-day training course in Sno-Cat maintenance at the Tucker factory in Medford, Oregon; with that modest preparation they made do, for this group alone included no professional mechanic. More seriously, they carried only a 7.5-watt Angry 9 transceiver for radio contact. Their communication capability was the worst of the 1957–1958 traverses, and being mostly on a thick ice shelf (a poor electrical conductor) did not help. Bentley had earlier proposed weekly radio schedules out on the ice, but with their feeble signal they were never able to connect. Weeks would go by without contact with anyone, although, ironically, they could receive broadcasts from the BBC and Moscow.[45]

On 9 December Lassiter offered the traversers a 100-watt transmitter with an auxiliary generator that had just arrived on his group's second plane, but Ronne refused to let them take Air Force equipment without Admiral Dufek's explicit approval. Pressed by Neuburg, he sniffed that early explorers had managed without radios. The field leaders, having no reliable means of communicating as they traveled beyond Otter range, consented to a Christmas rendezvous with Lassiter's C-47s, despite neither side's knowing what lay between them and the designated spot northwest of the Dufek Massif, about 250 miles away. The scientists' conclusion that their leader did not want them to be able to talk with others was reinforced, a judgment unchanged decades later. At the time, Aughenbaugh sputtered, "I want to officially note in this diary that should something happen to me and I can't get proper aid because of radio communication, I hold Finn Ronne *completely* to blame." On 29 December, when a C-47 finally arrived with fuel and food, it also brought the more powerful transmitter, with Dufek's approval—any other response as unlikely as it was unthinkable. Apparently, Ronne himself had been worried. It had been three weeks and many crevassed miles since the previous contact. Ronne was not to blame that a better radio had not been supplied, Behrendt carefully noted, but it was unconscionable when he denied them one that did become available.[46]

Ronne's original refusal put both the IGY program and five lives in jeopardy and would hardly have helped his standing as an Antarctican had something bad happened. Behrendt, looking back, realized that the captain undoubtedly wanted to lead the traverse himself and admitted that they might have benefited from his experience. But Ronne's exploratory interests clearly diverged from those of the IGY, and Thiel and Neuburg were not about to give up their assigned roles. Moreover, by then "there was too much discord to have made that a reasonable thing." Interestingly, Wexler, writing in his diary back in Washington, seemed to think Ronne *was* participating in the traverse. In late October he referred to Ronne's "impending traverse operations," a few days later worrying that his "mountain chasing" might "interfere with the planned traverse." Perhaps he misunderstood Ronne's reconnaissance flights for ground travel. In mid-December, from reading field reports, he surmised that Ronne was "out in the field and going great guns."[47]

After many mechanical delays and a false start of three miles, the Byrd traversers of 1957–1958 finally left the station on 19 November to explore the interior of Marie Byrd Land in a four-sided circuit that would clock 1,026 miles. Bentley and Ostenso did the seismic studies, while newly arrived William Long assisted Anderson in glaciology, since Giovinetto had gone with Zumberge before flying off to Pole for a second winter on the ice. Long's brother Jack was the mechanic, and aurora observer Dan Hale went along as traverse biologist and cook. They traveled in three already-named Sno-Cats. Two, like yachts, honored significant women—*Buttons* was named for mechanic Morency's daughter and *Carole* for Anderson's beloved. The seismologists, seeking to be more imaginative, or lacking female inspiration, had christened theirs *Gallirallus australis hectori* (*Hectori* for short) for a bird with "a wonderful name" that Bentley had seen pictured in New Zealand. (Crary more prosaically gave his vehicles functional descriptors: "Detector Snocat" led with its crevasse detector and gyro and sun compasses, "'Seismo' Snocat" housed the scientific instrumentation, and "Mess Cat" was the mechanic's vehicle, which also provided the cooking, eating, and main radio facilities. Ellsworth's pair suffered along as #1 Sno-Cat and #2—Behrendt later explaining that they did not need distinguishing names with only each other to call.)[48]

The traverse teams devised their own methods of travel but generally did not drive in close caravan. Keeping the Cats a few miles or an hour apart permitted later comparison of their altimeter readings, taken simultaneously with synchronized watches and radios every three miles. Altimeters measure atmospheric pressure, which changes primarily with changing weather but also with changes in elevation. Because weather would be more or less the same over the distance maintained, the separated readings would indicate altitude differences. (Ellsworth's two Sno-Cats, facing ubiquitous crevasses, stayed together.) While stopped, the scientists made limited observations such as rammsonde snow-hardness tests, magnetic and gravity readings, and sunshots for navigating. Every other day, about thirty or thirty-five miles apart, they did a full day of seismic and glaciological work, called putting in a station. The short stops were "mini-stations."[49]

With continuous daylight, the scientists tended to ignore the clock. The Ellsworth traversers, for example, lived on something close to a thirty-six-hour cycle. Intending originally to travel twelve hours, camp, and do their scientific work the next day, they instead usually ate breakfast, worked about twelve hours on science, ate another enormous meal, and then drove for about twelve hours. After being up twice around the clock they would stop, exhausted, and sleep twelve hours or more. So they "got in and out of 'day,'" but it was all the same. "Augie" ever wondered if he was eating breakfast or dinner. Antarctic travel taught patience. Many hours were spent waiting for favorable weather, fuel and other supplies, air reconnaissance, or maintaining equipment. They read a lot of books, played bridge, sometimes napped.[50]

The traverse diarists rarely missed noting the day's menu and their judgment of it. Trail food mattered. It was varied and mostly tasty. Quantities were inevitably huge, with one's own cooking better than someone else's. Behrendt—who volunteered to plan and prepare most of the food for his team—stocked, among other items, dehydrated steaks and pork chops (canned), frozen meat (stew, ground beef, tenderloin strip steaks), canned ham and Spam, instant powdered soups, dehydrated cheese, instant Carnation milk ("the best"), dried fruit, Minute Rice and potato granules, and ice cream ("plenty of Tastie Freeze"). He planned eighty days' worth of most basics including curry powder, a condiment he often liked to use—perhaps more often than appreciated. C-ration-type crackers, Army 5-in-1 rations (always including cigarettes), and "a few" emergency trail rations (featuring a pemmican-like meat bar) paid slender homage to the historic days of sledging. (Anderson wrote, "Tried the pemmican today—it will never replace food!") Compared with the weight and volume of the fuel they hauled, food was a minor factor, so, unlike the heroes, they could enjoy quantity and variety. Now the critical factor was cooking time, not weight. They always had food for an extra month, if needed.[51]

Crary's traverse suffered a near-tragedy on 31 October 1957—about forty miles and only one week out. They had just climbed over the north edge of Roosevelt Island, and the two glaciologists went to investigate an odd snow structure. Hardly beyond camp, they were neither roped nor on skis when Schoeck, a fit, macho, notoriously heavy-footed fellow, disappeared. Before Boyd lay a broken snow bridge, a gaping crevasse. By the time Crary got there, Bennett was rappelling into the gash. He found Schoeck about fifty feet down, almost buried in snow. He managed to tie a rope around the clearly injured and unconscious man, and they pulled him out with a Sno-Cat. Cromie immediately radioed Little America for imperative medical help, but he had to report that heavy overcast would make local flying marginal at best.[52]

Waldron and copilot Jack Ratzlaff lost no time getting an Otter off to give it a try. Sure enough, visibility, clear at takeoff, soon gave way to an opaque near-whiteout. Waldron asked the traverse party for a low-frequency radio signal he could home in on, and it brought them right over the camp, where he "could make out the red tractors and trailers but not much else." Cromie, crevasse minded, suggested that any landing should aim for the Sno-Cats' incoming tracks, but the pilots could not distinguish them in the milky scene. So Waldron told those on the ground to ski out along the tracks, spacing themselves about twenty-five yards apart. When they were in place and his radar altimeter indicated he was within fifty feet of the surface, he visually lined up the plane using the men as a reference for glide slope and direction: "When I was next to the man most distant from the trailers my skis dug into the snow giving me a rather hard but not damaging landing." He stopped "just feet" from the parked sleds, and they had Schoeck aboard within minutes, Waldron worrying about how their hurt passenger would manage the jolting takeoff. Although they had flown in far worse conditions and professed to view the flight as "routine," the flyers each earned the Navy's Air Medal for this rescue.[53]

Schoeck was brought to Little America for immediate care, then transferred to McMurdo and evacuated to New Zealand on 6 November. He had several broken ribs, a cracked vertebra, punctured lung, and brain concussion. Despite his pleas, the doctors forbade a return to the ice. Boyd, "thorough and meticulous," became Crary's chief glaciologist, assisted by Ed Robinson, whom Zumberge graciously lent from his own program. This "perhaps worked out better," wrote the generous Crary, who rarely dwelt on criticism but cited Schoeck as "too impatient" and likely "bored" with "tedious" data collecting. Wexler thought "Pete" a predictable casualty from his "overconfident manner," as in "going off by himself."[54]

It took the traversers thirteen days to get out of this deadly area. Despite greater care and a crevasse-detector tuneup, Crary's lead Sno-Cat slid backward into a crevasse a few days later, catching at a precarious angle. So the scientists were glad when an Otter arrived with the ice-deformation group, including Phil Smith, who agreed to help them through the danger zone. Crary could only wonder at Smith's fascination with crevasses and be grateful. He had apparently not reached the state of mind of the hero with whom he was sometimes compared. Just before Christmas 1908, bound for the Pole, Shackleton had rather cheerily written, "The usual query when one of us falls into a crevasse is: 'Have you found it?' One gets somewhat callous as regards the immediate danger, though we are always glad to meet crevasses with their coats off, that is, not hidden by the snow covering."[55]

The Ellsworth traverse, too, began in a terror of crevasses. The first hurdle was to skirt the awesome "Grand Chasm," a deadly 60-mile-long rift about 50 miles inland. Discovered the previous autumn and named by the British, "this grandfather of all crevasses" ranged from a quarter-mile to 3 miles in width and was at least 175 feet deep, extending all the way to the sea. Reconnoitering by air, Ronne had prepared a map of a safe route for the IGY team, skirting it to the east. Only one week before the start of the traverse would he take Thiel aloft for a look, though he would not take Neuburg—or Aughenbaugh, who had experience and acknowledged skill in discerning crevasses from above. By then, the latter was beyond charity: "Ronne is all out to undermine our traverse since we intend to travel in unexplored territory that he wants to *personally* explore. So he considers us a menace and rival." It did not take long for the team to encounter deep danger. Aughenbaugh growled to his diary on 3 November that they had been among crevasses for 30 miles, some of them "wide enough to drop both Sno-Cats with sleds in at the same time." The "'impossible' route that we wanted to take only had about 3–5 miles of bad crevasses to contend with and was shorter and more direct to our goal." This would have been around the west end of the Grand Chasm, a route he had identified on an "illegal" flight with VX-6 commander Mac McCarthy, later "substantiated" by the other two pilots.[56]

Ellsworth pilot William Sumrall arrived by Otter with fuel on 5 November and took everyone up for a better view of the treacherous terrain. Then, "Willie stayed with us as we drove through this area," wrote the grateful junior seismologist. "This was really wonderful for us. He kept in close radio contact and flew back and forth directing us to the right or left as required." Even when it began to cloud up, inauspicious for his return flight, Sumrall stayed: "For 10 miles and over two hours he helped us around the rift and into the clear area on the south side. After the way we stumbled around not knowing what direction to go Saturday night, we really appreciated this." By then, the team had been up for forty hours. "The adrenaline must have been flowing," Behrendt realized later. But after sleeping around the clock, they matter-of-factly got up and put in a seismic station.[57]

On 13 November, approaching the high, grounded ice of what would later be named Berkner Island (which Thiel had just seen by air), the Ellsworth team encountered another ghastly area, with crevasses running every which way. Suddenly, the sled of #1 Sno-Cat sank, almost along its long axis (the most dangerous approach), into a relatively narrow but jagged 100-foot-deep rift, pulling the tractor's rear pontoons back in with it. Roped up and belayed, Neuburg and Behrendt emptied the sled, and the team at length extricated both vehicle and trailer. Two days later VX-6 crew member Atlas Lewis, along on a reconnoitering Otter, fell unroped into a bridged crevasse. Luckily stopped in a narrow wedge only about 20 feet down, he was soon brought to safety, shaken and cold but uninjured. Shortly thereafter, the lead Sno-Cat broke through another snow bridge, luckily perpendicularly but with both sets of pontoons sharply angled down into the crevasse. Pilot Jaburg had been directing the ground travelers from the air: "The joker was, however, that I couldn't see all the crevasses, what with the new snow cover and rather poor visibility." "All this in the past mile," Behrendt told his brother via hamgram. "Don't relay this to [the] folks." On the same day, 16 November, Aughenbaugh revealed the growing anxiety: "Not too cheery of a future outlook stuck in the middle of a crevasse field with no safe way out—why does it snow." He added, "Tempers up a little among us today" and "been out in the field twenty days already and have come only 200 miles total." The weather continued to be poor. A week later they found and opened eighteen bridged crevasses within a mile and a half. "Our hope is that we can pick the thickest parts of each to drive over. I wonder how many exist that we haven't found," Behrendt worried. Finally, after two weeks' entrapment, they got through and up onto the island. "We are now for the first time on the Antarctic continent," Aughenbaugh rejoiced.[58]

The Byrd traverse party, half of whom were now experienced over-snow travelers, encountered no crevasses according to Bentley, who later admitted, "I used to believe that the crevasses were only along the margins of the ice sheet where it joins the floating ice or went around mountains or something like that. So we just drove around everywhere. Gave up worrying about cre-

Members of Ellsworth traverse party conducting stratigraphic and snow-hardness (rammsonde) measurements in the field. Official U.S. Navy photograph. NARA II, RG 313, Records of Photography Officer DF 55–69, Box 9.

vasses except for when we were right next to the mountains." They were lucky— "living in a fool's paradise" was how he put it—"because now we know that there are these huge ice streams all over the place that have thousands of crevasses. . . . But we didn't know that, so we had no crevasse problems." Actually, on 13 December Anderson dropped his left rear pontoon almost length-wise into a deep crevasse covered by a snow bridge that proved to be only 6 inches thick at its thinnest. But overall, their luck would hold.[59]

With such baptisms, the scruffy bands in their IGY Sno-Cats clattered into the white unknown to do the work they had given a winter for. During their alternating daylong stops to do scientific stations, the glaciologists dug pits 2 to 3.5 meters (6.6 to 11.6 feet) deep and drilled firn cores from their bottoms to the 10-meter level (about 33 feet). Into these they suspended thermohms over-night to record the temperature and thus determine the mean annual tempera-ture. As at base, they studied the exposed snow for its density, stratigraphy (annual layering), and grain size. At each pit site and every few miles along the trail they did rammsondes, using a device properly called a cone penetrometer that measured resistance as the force of known weights dropped a given distance around a metal rod drove it vertically into the snow. This told them the hardness of the snow, the measurement called ram hardness. Simple in concept, the process took hours.[60]

The seismologists' procedure was more involved. At each station they took reflection shots to measure the depth of the underlying snow and ice (and the water below that on ice shelves). As Bentley and Behrendt separately explained it, they arranged on the snow two 1,200-foot cables, along which twenty-four geophones (sensitive motion detectors called "jugs") were connected at 100-foot intervals. Unrolling the cables from 80-pound reels worn on their chests, the men laid out their "spread" in an L-shaped pattern. Usually at the vertex of the angle they hand-drilled a hole about 4 inches in diameter and 6 to 25 feet deep in which they shot off an explosive charge (one to five pounds of ammonium nitrate detonated with an electric blasting cap and a one-pound high-explosive primer charge). "Every now and then the silence is shattered by Charlie bellowing "QUIET!" wrote Anderson. "They can pick up footsteps on their gear so everything must be absolutely still while they do a shot and record. Then he pops up out of the Cat hatch and hollers, 'All clear,' so we can all move once again."

The geophones vibrated in response to the sound waves reflected from the point where ice met water, water met rock, or ice met rock. The vibration generated a small voltage that appropriate instruments received, amplified, and recorded on photographic paper for each of the twenty-four channels. "We could identify the reflection by noting the wave form on each channel at slightly longer times the farther the geophones were from the shot point," explained Behrendt. By knowing the velocity of sound waves in each medium, they could calculate the depths to the various reflecting materials: "Half the measured time from the shot to the recorded reflection, multiplied by the velocity of sound in the ice and snow, which we measured independently, gave the ice thickness or the combined ice and water thickness on the floating ice shelf." The procedure was similar to an echo sounder in the ocean, Bentley said, "except you have to set off an explosive charge to get enough energy into the snow."[61]

Bentley worried early on that the echoes he was seeing might be re-echoes, that is, the sound bouncing off the bottom, back to the surface, and down again, which it could do several times. If it did and they were seeing double echoes, they would be overestimating the ice thickness by a factor of two. To guard against this they tried to record both the first and second echoes. If the ice was really that thick, they would see a first echo and a second echo at twice the time. If there was nothing between them, with few disturbing noises, they

would know they were not misinterpreting the echo. Fortunately, gravity readings were showing the same results, another verification.[62]

Also at each station the seismologists shot a short refraction profile to
determine seismic-wave speed and variations of it near the surface of the ice,
which is related to how the ice density changes with depth. Long refraction
profiles covered horizontal distances of some kilometers; the seismic waves
traveled down through the ice and through layers of earth before returning at
the distant point. These required large charges (say, 250 pounds or even up to
2,000 pounds), which were buried as deep as 45 feet for the safety of the shooter
and better coupling of the energy to the snow, although no one wanted to drill
by hand any deeper than necessary. Long refractions took time and were thus
done infrequently—perhaps three times per traverse, Bentley said. Like Crary,
Ostenso, who wrote up the Byrd traverse results when Bentley stayed on the
ice, reported that record quality was governed less by the strength of the echo
than by the amount of prolonged surface noise following a shot, which interfered with the reflected arrivals. Ostenso also noted variations over time but
did not specifically tie them to seasonal temperature changes (an important
effect—colder snow increases noise), as Crary did.[63]

The seismic equipment was cumbersome and heavy (about a thousand
pounds altogether), the processes cold and messy. Each of the twenty-four
amplifiers had about ten vacuum tubes, Behrendt said. Each packaged unit,
an aluminum case of six amplifiers, weighed about 50 pounds. The control
and voltage-conversion units were just as heavy. Power for the current-sucking
vacuum tubes came from two 175-pound, 12-volt, 250-ampere-hour batteries.
A 70-pound oscillograph "camera" and photo-recording paper completed the
state-of-the-art system. The seismologists, or usually the junior member of the
team, developed the records immediately by inserting an arm through the
opaque sleeve of the miniature "darkroom" beneath the camera to catch the
emerging exposed paper in loose folds along his arm. He then sloshed the 8-
inch by 4- to 10-foot records through developing, fixing, and washing tanks, as
for ordinary film, and hung the developed records over an overhead wire to
dry if they had not already frozen. The slow, wet procedure was a recipe for
brown chemical-stained, chapped hands. Behrendt cadged surgical gloves
from Ellsworth's medical officer; Bentley remembered going through a lot of
Noxema hand cream. Data today are recorded digitally, and "it's all nice and
clean," said Bentley.[64]

Writing a year into the IGY, Woollard at Wisconsin made the point that the
seismic method was as reliable as deep drilling to determine ice depth so long
as the wave velocity in the ice was relatively constant, and it was vastly faster

and cheaper. Gravity and magnetic measurements were even faster, taking only minutes to do, but they could err as much as 20 percent and, to be useful, had to be compared with computed theoretical values based on latitude and elevation. The force of gravity increases toward the poles where the earth's radius is slightly shorter and its rotation has less centrifugal force; knowing something about the density of the underlying material increases measurement accuracy. To derive magnetic anomalies (the differences between theoretical and observed values), both diurnal and long period, it was necessary to know changes in the strength and inclination of the earth's magnetic field caused by latitude and longitude. These anomalies, which looked like topographical contour maps, were indications of estimated ice thickness. Thus the longer, more accurate seismic procedure, used every 30 to 50 miles, and the quicker gravity and magnetic readings, taken every 2 to 5 miles, together provided a remarkably true profile of the ice along the route of travel.[65]

Since the late 1960s, ground-penetrating radar has been used to measure ice thickness. Overflying aircraft send out selected-frequency radio waves that travel easily through ice; their echo is timed. Byrd expedition veteran Amory ("Bud") Waite made lateral radar tests in the snow during the IGY, and the British accidentally discovered the ice-penetrating character of radar waves, which they called radio-echo sounding, about the same time. Waite lent his radar system to Bentley to use on Roosevelt Island in 1963. A year later Bentley's team got the first radar sounding at the Pole. "To make one sounding using radar takes thirty microseconds," he marveled, comparing that with the hour or more it took to lay out the seismic spread and gather it up again for an equally accurate result. Bentley noted that gravity meters have essentially not changed since the IGY, while ice movement is now measured using GPS or satellite radar interferometry. This "really high-tech stuff" is "extremely accurate. You can detect movements of a few centimeters from a satellite. It's amazing."[66]

Crary's traverse goal for 1957–1958 was to understand the structure, composition, and behavior of the Ross Ice Shelf—that which Pyne called "a kind of crystalline exoskeleton that shapes, binds, and protects the ice continent." Scott had puzzled about the ice shelf in 1902: "This ice barrier is probably thrust off of some great body of land enveloping the South Pole. While the barrier is wearing away in front, as proven by the fact of its retreat of 30 miles in 60 years [since Ross's visit], it is being constantly fed in the rear. . . . How far off the source is, is a mystery; and when we bear in mind the scarcity of precipitation in such southern latitudes, it is almost impossible to imagine where the supply is to be found." In 1909, writing in *National Geographic*, Shackleton opined that to solve the "mystery" of the Great Ice Barrier, an expedition would have to trace the mountains forming its southern boundary. In 1935 Byrd reported, also in the *Geographic*, that the ice shelf had "moved northward considerably," 13.8 miles since 1911.[67] Crary would seek his own conclusions.

His party traveled west from Little America to Minna Bluff, which flanks Mount Discovery not far from McMurdo. There they turned south to the Beardmore Glacier, then southeast to the Liv Glacier, stopping for ice studies. Along the Queen Maud Mountains, named by Amundsen for Norway's queen, the traversers also took horizontal and vertical transit angles to provide ground control for mapping the major peaks. They then proceeded north to the barrier west of Roosevelt Island and east back to LA5, arriving on 13 February 1958. This circumnavigation showed that the Ross Ice Shelf flows around grounded ice rises (islands) in the Ross Sea, a number of them judging from hinge cracks, raised elevations, and ice-fracture patterns. Deformations predictably increased around its perimeter—where it met ice sheet, glacier, or sea ice. Unsurprisingly, the team found the ice thicker at the shelf's southern boundary (nearly 1,400 feet at the Beardmore Glacier where it joins the mainland ice sheet) than at its front at Little America (about 800 feet). It was also thicker on the eastern (Marie Byrd Land) flank than on the western (at McMurdo Sound). This led Crary to believe that Victoria Land ice flowed not to the Ross embayment but to the Pacific Ocean, which he would prove the next summer. The shelf was advancing about 5 feet per day (almost a third of a mile per year). In a January 1959 IGY Bulletin, published during his second traverse, Crary reported a record depth (4,400 feet) of sea floor beneath the Ross Ice Shelf about 90 miles south-southwest of McMurdo, again raising the possibility that a trough bisected the continent—as first postulated by Scott's scientists. With this finding, the extended trough being investigated by the Ellsworth traversers, and the deep basin measured by the Byrd team, the possibility remained that these depressions could be connected.[68]

The Ellsworth traversers of 1957–1958 investigated the Filchner Ice Shelf and the larger Ronne Ice Shelf to the west of Berkner Island, which separates them. They also aimed for a point on the proposed route of the 1958–1959 traverse from Ellsworth to Byrd to compare data. As it turned out, their track would prove rather tortuous, their intended circuit not completed. Still, all their early zigging and zagging among crevasses gave them additional opportunities to follow and measure a deep south-trending depression they had identified back in camp. Further inland the trough appeared to be a "major geologic feature," sounding typically about 3,500 feet below sea level. They called it the Crary Trough (now named for Thiel) and wondered if it went all the way to the Ross Sea but did not have time to follow it far into Ellsworth Land. The quintet ascended, mapped, and sounded ice-shrouded Berkner Island (about the size of Delaware, rising to 2,500 feet above sea level). They then traveled about 400 miles south, as far as the Pensacola Mountains, dominated on the north by the jagged, imposing Dufek Massif at the head of the ice shelf.[69]

The six "clear and sunny, very warm" days spent among these spectacular pinnacled peaks were for Aughenbaugh one sleepless, almost breathless excitement. Behind in his diary writing, chafed from walking in wet underwear, blistered from sunburn, he wrote: "I do believe I have found a geologist's dream in mountains—it has everything. What a great stroke of luck. The trip to Antarctica has sure been worth my time a hundred fold." This after months of frustration and conflict that had him earlier fearing his year would be a waste. "Put my foot on rock for the first time in over a year at 6:00 AM," he wrote on 9 December, having, with Walker, man-hauled a sled all night from the Sno-Cats' position. He privately named some knolls for family members, building a cairn to deposit the information. He recognized "lots of mineralization" on one spur, including what he thought was some high-grade ore (type unspecified). On the warmer, protected north face of the massif the awed scientists found, at 82°S, a "'dry' valley which is a wonder in itself." In it was a still more astonishing shallow pond, about 70 percent ice covered, containing "a strange pinkish plant" (algae). They saw lichens, bird tracks, and pools of meltwater in the rocks; they brought out quantities of rock specimens.[70]

On past Walker Peak, named for Paul, they found, remembered Behrendt, "a route that we could have gone on south to the South Pole. We were in the clear." The Pole was about 450 miles off, and they could have beaten both Hillary and Fuchs there. It would have been "great fun" and scientifically worthwhile. Ronne would have loved to have gone, too, Behrendt was later certain, had relations been better among them. But they believed Odishaw and Crary would think this a "stunt," and, according to Aughenbaugh, they knew that "for us to get there before [the Trans-Antarctic Expedition] would not have been what you call the best politics in the world." Besides, they still had no long-distance communication.[71]

Finally receiving the powerful Air Force radio, Ellsworth's traversers planned to proceed northwest to Mount Hassage but were told it was beyond the range of their air support. After heated argument they reluctantly turned around—to the passionate disgust of Aughenbaugh, who could not forgive giving up so close (80 miles) to their goal. Surprised to find themselves again on shelf ice, not inland plateau, they crossed the smaller, narrow Korff Island, encountering mazes of unnerving crevasse fields, mechanical breakdowns, and poor weather. They were about halfway back when they learned that Ellsworth Station's relief ships had come in and would not wait. Although the ice that summer was remarkably light, the icebreaker *Westwind* was under orders to hasten to the Bellingshausen Sea where Soviet vessels were also reportedly headed, perhaps to try for the coast and lay a claim there. In American minds that unclaimed area was American by virtue of Americans', especially Byrd's, activity there. Politics could be subdued by the IGY only so far. (As it happened, *Westwind* was unable to penetrate the ice to the Thurston Peninsula as proposed; two years later the *Glacier* would do so, but only after being beset for about two weeks.)[72]

The traverse team ran out of gas on 17 January 1958, and that afternoon two Otters flew out to pick them up. The frustrated scientists, whose truncated season ended more than a month earlier than the others', hastily packed up their scientific gear and abandoned their Sno-Cats. They had little time to brief their replacements, headed by Father Edward Bradley, a Jesuit seismologist from Xavier University in Cincinnati, and Scot glaciologist John Pirrit. The new group flew out to continue the fieldwork, planning to drive back to Ellsworth, but they, too, would have to be evacuated when it grew too cold and dangerous to try to recross the crevasses in the already-limping vehicles. In fact, they spent some worried and hungry days waiting to be picked up, not knowing that one Otter was downed—out of fuel—on the ice shelf (with an even hungrier crew) and the other damaged on the ground after landing in a whiteout a few miles from the station. Not until 10 March would everyone be safe and warm.[73]

The first Ellsworth traversers had come about 1,200 miles, wrote Behrendt. (Ronne credited them with 816.) They had made only twenty-seven stations, but given their time and troubles, that was a respectable output. They had advanced the mapping of Antarctica's ice thickness begun by the Norwegian-British-Swedish team and done important preliminary geological work in the Dufek Massif. Official IGY reports credited them with three major discoveries: that the Filchner Ice Shelf was larger (about three-fourths as large as the Ross) and extended farther inland (about 300 miles, not 50–70) than previously believed; that it was grounded on at least two islands (Berkner and Korff); and that a deep trough extended far inland.[74]

Byrd's traverse party first headed north toward the coastal mountains of the Amundsen Sea. The discovery of a rough ice-rock interface and ice thicknesses varying from 600 meters (about 2,000 feet) to 2,700 meters (nearly 9,000 feet) bespoke mountain peaks beneath their feet, all but a few below sea level—

far enough below to remain submerged even if the overlying ice were removed and the land rose to isostatic balance. They finally began sounding bedrock above sea level about 250 miles from the coast. They named a landmark peak Mount Takahe for the R4D that first resupplied them and, indirectly, for an "extinct" but recently rediscovered wingless New Zealand bird. Turning east toward the Sentinel Mountains, named from the air by Lincoln Ellsworth in the mid-1930s, they began seeing a "huge, spectacular mountain range that we didn't know was there," Bentley remembered. It was more than a hundred miles away, at least a week distant. Evidently, Ellsworth had not enjoyed clear skies because he had mapped only a few peaks. The difference was a lifetime thrill for the latter-day discoverers.[75]

On this leg of the journey, the scientists found the rock bottom smoother and as much as 200 meters (about 660 feet) below sea level. With the surface ice just over 1,500 meters (5,000 feet), that was very deep. Before they were finished they would discover ice depths of an astonishing 14,000 feet, the greatest recorded to that time. They also concluded from geological and biological evidence (comparison of more than sixty types of lichens) that the ice had once been 800 feet higher and that the Sentinels were an extension of the mountains of the Antarctic Peninsula and thus of the Andes. (However in 1961–1962 Behrendt led a traverse that found a deep trough separating these mountain groups, which proved geologically discontinuous. There could be no trough continuing to the Weddell Sea through this area.) Southwest from the Sentinels they found the rock surface rougher again, this time mostly above sea level with nunataks frequently breaking the surface. The final stretch back to Byrd was similar to the second, with deep ice and generally smooth bottom and many gravity anomalies. With so many visible mountains throughout Marie Byrd Land, "nobody suspected that there was this great lowland lying in between the mountains," Bentley recalled.[76]

The less harrowing trail life of the men from Byrd seemed almost homelike. They had a birthday party for Bentley on 23 December, complete with a candle. On the 24th Anderson "hung up a nice long wool sock." The next day he found "a candy cane and snow ball in it, and Sandy Clause had filled it up. Boy, a can of beer, cigars [he did not drink or smoke], chopsticks, toothpaste, candy, cookies, and a rotten apple." Christmas Day was beautiful on the Marie Byrd Land ice sheet, "warm enough to go around in BVDs, in fact Bill did," as they worked at their science tasks. Chaplain John Zoller arrived from Little America on a resupply plane on the 26th and, setting up an altar in the snow, led the group in religious services. "We got three sacks of mail, and I made out like a madman," crowed Anderson, who claimed a large part of it. Afterward they celebrated with gift giving. The Antarctic did show itself, of course. One day icicles on the back of Anderson's Sno-Cat formed about twenty degrees off the vertical in a stiff southeast wind. Sometimes hard, foot-high sastrugi roughed up both scientists and Sno-Cats. At other times the snow was so soft it bogged them down. They experienced the scary snow subsidences that occurred when hoarfrost layers a few years old collapsed under the weight of overlying firn.[77]

It was getting appreciably colder and dark at night when the traversers sighted a mirage of Byrd Station several hours before finally reaching it on 20 February 1958, the last field party to roll in. Most of the exhausted team left the next morning for Little America by tractor train. Anderson, who had been up for forty-one hours during and after the last push into camp, slept almost twelve hours en route despite the "sorta foul air" in the wanigans. When they reached Fashion Lane, a plane "took Ned and I and the SIPRE boys off" to fly the rest of the way to "the City." He boarded the *Glacier* on 9 March 1958, going home with marriage on his mind.[78]

The most ambitious and avidly followed traverse of 1957–1958 was that of the British Commonwealth Trans-Antarctic Expedition (TAE), brainchild of Vivian Fuchs, soon the knighted director of the British Antarctic Survey (former FIDS). Attempting to complete Shackleton's ice-foiled transcontinental quest of 1914–1916, Fuchs's party would travel by Sno-Cat and Weasel but would also keep tradition alive by using dog teams and relying on "interminable pemmican." A geologist, Fuchs planned to survey mountains en route, measure gravity, and do limited seismic soundings for ice depth and land profile— to extend the IGY coverage but also to benefit from (as well as contribute to) its global publicity. He later maintained that his primary interest was scientific, "but, of course, one had to play the adventure side" to garner public (financial) support.

The Britisher, who left Shackleton Station on the Weddell Sea on 24 November 1957, met misfortune and delay from crevasses, fuel shortages, and mechanical problems. He arrived at the South Pole on 19 January 1958. Hillary, leading the New Zealand support party from the Ross Sea side, started from Scott Base on 14 October to lay supply depots up the Skelton Glacier and out to Mile 700 on the polar plateau. Then he just kept going with his odd-looking, modified Massey-Ferguson farm tractors that offered no shelter beyond a three-sided plywood screen around the driver. Reaching the Pole on 4 January, more than two weeks before the expedition's senior leader, he caused bad feeling over his independence and breach of protocol. Flying out, then back in with Dufek to greet the TAE in ceremonial procession at 90° South, Hillary guided

Fuchs's larger vehicles down the Skelton. Fuchs and his party arrived at Scott Base, completing the 2,000-mile historic first, on 2 March 1958.[79]

Traverses from other countries that summer included the Russians' tractor trains, whose primary purpose was to establish interior bases deep in East Antarctica (see Chapter 8). Their seismic soundings en route established bedrock above sea level everywhere, generally high above—at 81° South, 65° East, almost 10,000 feet. Soviet seismologists measured ice more than 11,000 feet thick at Vostok, finding an average of 8,700 feet over their route. It was the Russians who learned to drill their shot holes 50 meters (165 feet) deep to reduce the cold-firn noise that had bedeviled the ice-measurement efforts of so many scientists, including Fuchs. The Australians and French made more modest inland traverses from their respective coastal stations in East Antarctica, a few hundred miles more or less due south. The French reported ice 9,000 feet thick in their part of Wilkes Land, somewhat east of the Americans' Wilkes Station. Altogether, these international travelers would, before the IGY was over, cover a respectably sized and broadly representative area of the polar continent and shed the light of at least preliminary understanding over it.[80]

Scientists like Crary, who wintered over twice during the IGY, agreed that the second year was easier and more relaxed. Civilian-military command had proved workable, the summer traverses had operated safely and successfully, bugs in the instruments had been worked out, the major building projects were done, and everyday living was, well, everyday. But there was much to do beyond reducing and analyzing the newly gathered field data. In conjunction with IGY and Navy leaders in Washington and on the ice, Crary would spend the winter planning the upcoming traverse routes, again from the same three bases, to build on the initial findings. Because of disappointing results from airlifted geophysical operations the first summer, he decided to work on the Victoria Land plateau in 1958–1959 rather than make another, albeit different, circuit of the ice shelf. He proposed ending up at either the Pole or Vostok Station. Having gone north from Byrd Station, Bentley now wanted to proceed south, concluding at the Pole. But the Navy in Washington, uneasy about supporting such long supply lines, countered with less far-flung alternative routes that would return to the point of origin, which the IGY and both leaders accepted. The new Ellsworth team would travel to Byrd Station. Meanwhile, Crary's change of plans meant he could not complete his promised seismic work along the Byrd Trail to Crevasse Junction in the spring, so he and four others finished that cold job from 26 March to 10 April, in the gathering dusk.[81]

Crary also plunged immediately into scientific work at Little America. On 28 February 1958, scarcely two weeks after his return, he and Denny den Hartog were working at the edge of the thirty-foot-high ice barrier trying to find a good spot for long seismic refractions to learn the thickness of ocean sediments. Suddenly, with a horrendous moan, a chunk of the ice shelf calved off.[82] The chief scientist, on it, descended into Kainan Bay "like an elevator," in C. R. Wilson's words. Fortunately for both, den Hartog stood safely back. Cautiously, he peered over the brink, searching the roiling brash for "what seemed an interminable time." At last, struggling toward light, Crary surfaced, "much to his surprise and mine." Crary lost his grip on a small bergy bit, but his companion's shouting directed him to a better floe, and he managed to clamber onto it. Den Hartog raced off in the Weasel for help. After a long, lonely silence, Crary heard noise—the station helicopter, he thought! But no. What he saw high above was a tractor with a sledload of passengers appearing to be taking pictures. Then, with wind and current driving him ever northward, they left!

Actually, beyond his line of sight the men were lowering a rubber life raft over the shelf edge, and Capt. Pat Maher, the Navy officer-in-charge, and aurora observer Buck Wilson were soon paddling through the broken ice toward him. They pulled Crary into the raft, having to "karate-chop" his frozen clothing at the joints so he could bend. The large man showed no signs of hypothermia (his body temperature was later given as "pretty low") and was completely coherent, Wilson remembered; his encasement in ice ironically offered some insulation against the wind and cold. Straining to work back toward the barrier with the wind in their faces, the rescuers answered the unpolite queries of the rescued by explaining that the helicopter was disassembled for repairs. Bespeaking a frenzied effort back at base, after an hour and a half or so, Wilson said, they heard a "lovely thwup-thwup-thwup" as the aircraft whirred into view. Maher and Wilson somehow secured Crary to the makeshift sling lowered to them, and the helo took off, dipping the poor fellow into the icy water before getting him airborne and safely, if dizzyingly, back to an awaiting Weasel and to camp. (It would have taken more precious time to reinstall the winch to raise the rescue gear.) Wilson and Maher were similarly brought ashore, including the unpleasant dunking. After a hot shower and joining a stream of well-wishers to toast his good fortune (with *his* liquor, he noted), Crary emerged from the ordeal with no apparent ill effects. Among other telegrams of good cheer, Admiral Dufek wired "Welcome to the Club." Maher and Wilson would earn Congressional Gold Medals for their rescue efforts. In the spring, Crary himself presented the Sikorsky Medal to the airmen who had reassembled the helicopter in record speed.

Crary's Victoria Land traverse left Little America on 15 October 1958. The party included both den Hartog and Wilson and, temporarily, Skip Dawson, the Army trail expert who was scouting an ice-shelf trail to McMurdo so heavy tractors could remove Little America's salvageable items after the IGY. Following Hillary's route up the Skelton Inlet and the Skelton Glacier, named for Scott's *Discovery* Expedition chief engineer and photographer, Crary compared his traverse to Scott's sledge journey in late 1902—about twenty miles north of the 1958 track, a month earlier (thus colder), and about ten days shorter. Scott and his two companions man-hauled their sleds through what he called "the most miserable place in the world" in cold, cutting wind and whiteout while the warm, protected Sno-Cat drivers fifty-five years later fussed about "not being able to drive in fourth gear."[83]

The traversers spent a month, 15 November to 15 December, in the inlet and glacier area doing detailed ice-movement and ice-depth studies, surrounded by dramatically scenic mountains. Crary and Wilson took horizontal angles between peaks on either side, then placed markers for comparison on their return to measure the flow of ice into the Ross Ice Shelf. (They would find that the central avenue of ice had advanced 16 to 18 meters [about 53 to nearly 60 feet] in two-plus months.) Using that information and the seismically determined profile of the inlet, Wilson calculated that a little less than 800 million cubic meters (just under 10 billion cubic yards) of ice flowed out of the inlet, while side-glacier and plateau-snowfield ice volume was nearly 1,000 million cubic meters (about 12 billion cubic yards). He and Crary concluded that the Skelton Inlet received little or no nourishment from the high plateau of East Antarctica, a judgment supported by a 30-mile (48-kilometer) dip in plateau elevation beyond the mountains and the presence of the Dry Valleys just to the north. Geophysicist Trevor Hatherton from Scott Base joined the traversers for the glacier and plateau studies, bringing Hillary's map up the Skelton, although neither that nor a carefully tuned crevasse detector spared them from dropping into a bridged crevasse on Thanksgiving Day. Despite careful flagging, more fissures would be accidentally discovered on the downward journey.[84]

The Sno-Cats crawled 350 nautical miles due west on the Victoria Land plateau, ending on an elevation roughly comparable to the Pole's and a scene similar to the "great plain of snow" Shackleton described on his 1908 ascent of the Beardmore Glacier more than 300 miles south. Shackleton believed the high plateau was "in all probability" a continuation of the Victoria Land plateau, and the South Pole "almost certainly" lay on it at between 10,000 and 11,000 feet. He was correct, although he had no means to verify his hunch. Crary's team saw no mountain ranges or nunataks but encountered "quite rough" sastrugi. Seismic soundings required ever-deeper holes in the extreme cold. Their deep-hole temperature measurements indicated an annual mean of –54°F, similar to Pole. They got about 300 miles from Vostok Station, but the Navy again denied permission to end the traverse there, perhaps, Wilson thought, because of increasing tensions with the Soviets elsewhere in the world at that time. The traverse returned in its own tracks to Minna Bluff, arriving at McMurdo on 31 January 1959.[85]

That same summer, 1958–1959, Bradley and Pirrit departed from Ellsworth in four new Sno-Cats with a crew of eight, including a full-time cook and mechanic, to take up the trail of the elusive transcontinental trough. Their route toward Byrd Station 1,250 miles distant, where Pirrit would winter over as scientific leader, skirted the Sentinel Mountains on the south. They found, in addition to their own collection of frightful crevasses, that the trough disappeared where the floating ice shelf joined the mainland, and the surface of both snow and rock rose more than a mile and a half—from 4,000 feet below sea level to 4,000 feet above. Soon they were traveling a mile above the sea with rock just a thousand feet beneath their feet, suggesting a buried mountain range—apparently an extension of the Sentinels, which were proving to be more extensive and massive with each new encounter. But beyond the mountains the rock floor again descended below sea level, some 6,300 feet below about 70 miles east of Byrd Station. So if Antarctica's two great embayments connected, as had been speculated for about fifty years, it had to be south of their route. The question remained.[86]

Bentley's 1958–1959 traverse, his third in as many summers, went south, his route between that of the others to the Pole-ward Horlick Mountains, named by Byrd in 1935 for one of his financial backers. The team members wanted to see if these mountains were part of the ancient Transantarctics, although vast crevasse fields blocked their approach. Here also was another opportunity to research the existence of a transcontinental trough. But they could not complete the work, having to hurry back to Byrd Station to catch a plane out if they wished to leave the ice that summer. The IGY was over and Little America was officially closing on 1 January 1959, but it was heartbreaking, and obviously contrary to expectations, to have to give up the best part of the season and curtail their planned program. (The IGY and the Navy had neglected to agree on ending dates for support. It was "our own fault," Francis admitted, for not being "precise and thorough" about their needs.) Bentley did find "a tremendous store of fossils," including a petrified tree trunk 12 feet long.[87]

Meanwhile, IGY veterans Thiel, Neuburg, and Ostenso returned to the ice for the summer to do seismic soundings across West Antarctica using an R4D for transport. They made seven landings to measure ice thickness along a 400-mile stretch of the meridian 130° West. They found the ice grounded everywhere, resting on bedrock from more than 1,600 feet below sea level to more than twice that depth. Thus there was no possible water interchange between the Ross and Weddell seas, although there could still be a "down-warped, ice-filled trough." They reported the trough as a great saddle, even though that was unapparent from the surface or even from the air at the altitudes flown at the time. Bentley, Crary, Ostenso, and Thiel would report in a joint paper after the IGY that the deep trough they had all been sounding seemed, rather, to "veer [from the Ross Sea] northwest of the Sentinel Mountains toward the Bellingshausen Sea." By then they knew that under the ice of West Antarctica was a range of mountainous islands in the north, while most of the region was a frozen sea. They believed the West Antarctic ice sheet had begun as two sheets over these mountainous areas that had merged over time and that the Ross Ice Shelf developed from its overflow.[88]

In all, U.S. traverses during the IGY covered 7,500 miles. IGY scientists together connected the Transantarctic Mountains from the Ross Sea to the Weddell. (Fuchs discovered and named the Shackleton Range and Theron Mountains beyond the U.S. Navy–named Pensacolas.) They identified the different geologic origins of the different regions of the polar continent and postulated that the continental ice sheet probably began as two (or three) that later joined. By the end of the IGY, scientists had to greatly revise upward their estimates of the amount of ice in Antarctica, to a possible volume of 8 million cubic miles. IGY glaciologists together found an average ice depth of more than 7,500 feet, almost a mile and a half—in one place in West Antarctica over two and a half miles. While they were astonished at how much of West Antarctica lay below sea level, some of that because of the great weight of the ice, they also concluded that the grounded ice sheet had decreased in thickness during the past 10,000 years, in some inland areas as much as 1,000 feet. Disagreement remained over the "ice budget" (accumulation versus ablation). The National Academy of Sciences cited estimates suggesting a "state of approximate equilibrium," but much data remained to be analyzed. It was, wrote Eklund in 1962, still too early for a definitive answer. IGY explorers in Antarctica incidentally found rock types, coal seams, petrified wood, and fossils of leaves, ferns, and bivalve shells that correlated strongly with those found in other southern continents, supporting the increasingly incontrovertible theory of continental drift. The concept is now called plate tectonics, as it is sections of the ocean floor that shift. It had to be true that the present polar continent (with its 30-million-year-old ice sheet) once, and for millions of years, boasted a temperate climate.[89]

Taking part in the scientific unveiling of Antarctica thrilled the eager investigators. "My gosh, I still look back on the excitement," remembered Bentley more than forty years later. "And you know, it wasn't just the scientific work, it was also the excitement of being out in an area that nobody had ever been before." It was the "quiet evenings" out on traverse "when all the Sno-Cats were shut down and we'd had a good bellyful of dinner, so we were warm and the day's work was done," . . . "when we listened to the silence," when "little snow crystals act like prisms" and the "whole surface sparkles" with "marvelous colors," when one could walk out in the bright sunshine ("in my biased look back" it seemed "always to be calm and sunny in the evening") and enjoy the scenery. Whether out on the ice or in camp, the experience of being there merits a look.[90]

CHAPTER TWELVE

LIFE ON THE ICE
The Experience

*I don't think you ever get over a winter in Antarctica and unless
you did winter over you don't know the Antarctic.*

—William E. Lowe, RM1, 1957[1]

However the tour went for them individually—and for most IGY participants, civilian and military, it was positive overall (at least in remembrance)—their time on the ice was a unique and powerful experience. Appreciating that they were living under conditions light years
removed from those of the historic heroes who preceded them by half
a century, they knew that they, too, were making history. It would
matter how well they met the challenges—more so when it became
clear that the International Geophysical Year would not simply go
away at the end of 1958, as originally conceived. The flavor of life at
each station was distinctly its own, yet a number of factors could be
seen to influence the overall level of contentment and productivity.

Antarcticans of the 1950s had much in common. They complained of overcrowding in summer, "tourists" who got in the way and needed special attention (especially politicians and reporters), their mates' musical tastes, the lack of fresh tomatoes, the unalterable distance between themselves and a kiss. They endured the tedium of housekeeping (even a station in a snowfield got "very dirty and dusty in no time at all"), air so dry their noses bled and fingers split, winter insomnia ("the Big Eye"), and each other's annoying little habits. They thrilled to the prolonged glories of multihued sunsets, stars so brilliant and "close" they could almost be touched, the stark grandeur and crystalline purity of their surroundings, the kept promise of sunrise after months of darkness.[2]

All in all, despite the extreme conditions that enveloped them, the IGY-era pioneers were snug—amply supplied, well fed, warm, secure from the elements—at least after they learned nature's rules. When the temperature dipped below –60°F, Pole residents had to bring the day's two barrels of fuel indoors to restore normal viscosity lest the fuel lines foul up. If they wanted to drive a nail through a 2 x 4, they would have to thaw it in the mess hall for a few days first. Until the stations became drifted in and the snow's insulation increased comfort (and reduced fuel consumption), there could be a temperature differential of fifty or sixty degrees between floor and ceiling. Few were tempted to go barefoot on floors that kept beer stored under beds ice-cold for drinking. When the beer froze, some cut the top off the can and ate it with a spoon like a slushie. At the same time, top-bunk sleepers suffered from excessive heat. Buck Wilson at Little America was one of the acclimatized outdoor workers who preferred a cooler barracks, while those who regularly stayed inside wanted it warmer. Although the Navy had installed a wire cage around the thermostat to prevent individual adjustment, he would train an infrared beam on the instrument to make the temperature register higher than it was, hoping the shiverers might think they were warm enough.[3]

The clothing supply offered plentiful personal choices from the warmest and best of each of the military services. Thermal boots kept feet so warm, even outdoors, that a Seabee medical officer felt it necessary to warn that "perspiration is just as dangerous as any other water in cold weather." Outdoor workers learned to carry extra dry socks and remove their boots occasionally to massage their feet. Frostbite, especially to the vulnerable face, was so common that it was seldom reported. As Dr. Howard Taylor at Pole explained it, an exposed nose, say, goes "cool, cold, warm, tight, hot, pings, then 'bites.'" The same sensations occurred at –100° as at –50, except that it took "a moment, not a minute." With the bragging rights of a "Polie," Taylor mused, "Why it is that around –50° the atmosphere seems to take on a warm feeling and above –30° everyone declares that 'Spring is here' is not clear." Little America's first winterers took to wearing surgical masks when it got really cold, but any face covering, including beards, would soon ice up from the moisture of breathing.[4]

Food expectedly assumed extreme importance in an environment where life's usual pleasures were few. By popular consent, the Navy sent excellent cooks to the Antarctic, where they enjoyed, and earned, high prestige in their respective communities. Chet Segers at Pole was at first embarrassed that his cakes kept falling. Finally, with the help of radio amateur Paul Blum in Syracuse, he got in touch with "Betty Crocker" at General Mills. "Some lady," Segers remembered, "went up in a plane at 10,000 feet and baked a cake." She then reported back on how much flour to add for South Pole's altitude. (Thereafter, U.S. bakers read high-altitude directions on their cake mixes, too.) He also learned to use a pressure cooker; water boiled at such a low temperature that it could otherwise take hours to cook meats and vegetables. Good food or no, Doc Taylor worried about a universal weight loss among the men. In mid-March he compiled losses ranging from 6 pounds for Arlo Landolt, who started at only 140, to Paul Siple's 39. That brought the leader down to a still-hefty 211 pounds, but for several others, losing 30 pounds from 185 or so was a significant percentage of body mass. The phenomenon was noted nowhere else, and no one gave follow-up figures that year or later. At other stations, as winter slowed physical activity the men grew paunches. At the inland, mile-high Byrd, Dr. Brian Dalton used weight gain as a rationale for cutting meals to two a day.[5]

While refrigerators were essential for the safe thawing of food (it took a week at Pole), items frozen beneath the snow would keep indefinitely. In December 1958, just before it closed, Little America's inhabitants dined on foods brought up from the long-buried Little America III, including 1938 butter and corn on the cob grown in Pennsylvania in 1937. *National Geographic* photographer David Boyer found it amusing to learn from a cook that the Navy's dieticians had "refused to allow ham and bacon to be brought down on Deep Freeze, saying it wouldn't keep. So we use the ham and bacon Admiral Byrd left here 20 years ago."[6]

At a number of IGY stations, someone tried to grow vegetables. In 1958 Hallett winterers placed a tray filled with "imported Rhode Island loam" on the roof of the science building, made a greenhouse by covering it with a plastic dome removed from the aurora tower, and set up a heater to run when the sun went down. They planted peas, broad beans, lettuce, and radishes. They all germinated, the peas and radishes grew, and everyone enjoyed fresh radishes

LIFE ON THE ICE

with Christmas dinner. Although for unstated reasons the experiment was discontinued, science leader Kenneth Salmon was convinced that vegetables could be grown in the warmer seasons with suitable equipment. Even today, even in summer, "freshies" are relatively rare. On a day with a green salad, flown in or grown in McMurdo's hydroponic farm, a joyful noise rises in the galley.[7]

Physical comfort, important as it was, could go only so far toward creating a happy polar winter, however. So the Navy worked hard to ensure that winter-overers had plenty to do in their spare time. Science leader A. P. Crary, whose diary revealed none, believed boredom reflected the person, not the locale. He alphabetically listed all the recreational opportunities at Little America—from amateur radio, bands and orchestras, and "bar-type" games (pool, ping-pong) to parties, shows and skits, and tournaments of various kinds with prizes. "Even counting the hayrides" of his youth in upstate New York, he thought the opportunities for fun on the ice compared well. All the bases were similarly equipped, although space created limitations at the smaller ones and some items never arrived, most notably at Byrd. Movies, ranging from excellent to awful, were the primary shared entertainment, offered daily at most stations with double features on weekends. By early spring, with every film seen, re-runs began, sometimes selected by ballot. Attendance flagged, but with the sun rising there was more to do.[8]

Hobby crafts included leather tooling, model making, and paint-by-number kits, although at Little America in Deep Freeze I hobby supplies were apparently so short or so unexpectedly in demand that after a while they had to be raffled. Card games like cribbage, rummy, and poker and table games such as monopoly and checkers had adherents. Scientific leader Jim Shear had a hard time drumming up interest in bridge at Hallett until the movie projector failed irreparably in July, but at Ellsworth the card game was popular, especially among the scientists. Interestingly, despite that station's chronic tension, John Behrendt, Don Skidmore, and Paul Walker played bridge with Captain Ronne on Sunday afternoons all winter. Shear wrote that the (electric) piano was little used, so there was one at that tiny outpost and presumably others. Libraries of books and records were ample and well used at all stations except Byrd, which had only a few dozen books and mostly classical music until the first tractor train of the second season. Photography, including developing personal film, was widely pursued at all stations even though camera mechanisms froze,

Despite ongoing tensions, Finn Ronne, station leader (wearing cap), played bridge with IGY scientists Behrendt, Skidmore, and Walker (left to right) on Sunday afternoons all winter. Official U.S. Navy photograph, by Walter Cox. NARA II, RG 313, Records of Photography Officer DF 55–69, Box 9.

lenses fogged, and film became brittle and broke. Weight-lifting and other gymnastic equipment provided workout opportunities. Low ceilings and constricted space discouraged, say, badminton or basketball.[9]

The outdoors beckoned hardy souls. Little Americans in 1956 "enthusiastically" played volleyball outdoors at –20°F, and other ball games drew small crowds sporadically in decent weather. For some reason there were not enough skis to go around, which was unfortunate, and Wilkes's skis arrived with no bindings. While the snow was often too granular for great skiing, there was plenty of it, and skis made walking safer in crevassed areas. At Wilkes, individuals also enjoyed fishing, skating on the meltwater pond, hiking, and seal hunting (for dog food). "Swimming was possible, but the seven of us who tried it," recalled 1958 scientific leader Willis Tressler, "only did so to become candidates for the Antarctic Swimming Club, and it could hardly be called a sport."

Any outdoor pursuit, though, whether for recreation or duty, seemed a benefit. "Frankly, I was shocked," wrote visiting chief scientist Harry Wexler in November 1957, at the wan appearance of persons who had "remained indoors tending to their tricky equipment without a break." The routine work such as plotting data had "dulled and deadened the imagination," he opined to Odishaw. Those who had to work out in the cold seemed to him "much better off." Micrometeorologist Paul Dalrymple remembered that Weather Central chief Bill Moreland "never went outside one single time during the whole winter." A "real slavedriver," Moreland kept his staff at their desks as well.[10]

Any excuse for a party helped break the monotony of the long dark months. Midwinter, on 22 June, generated the biggest celebration of the year at every station, complete with a huge, fancy meal, funny hats, and liquid spirits. It marked the halfway point of the dark period and the year on the ice. But while it seemed at that moment to be downhill from there, the men would learn that the worst weather and the worst psychological and physiological effects of winter were yet to come, usually peaking in August and September. The "Polecats," as they called themselves, threw a party at least once a month—in honor of birthdays, the full moon, even when the dog Bravo turned one. Wherever they had them (Byrd got its first two in February 1958), dogs provided warmth, affection, and entertainment.[11]

More intellectual pursuits were also available. Once he came to peace with the fact that volunteering for Antarctica meant wintering over, Ellsworth pilot Con Jaburg decided to study a foreign language and learn to play a musical instrument. Like many others with similar intentions, he did neither. He took out two Air Force college extension courses—one in sociology, the other in English literature—but they also languished. He did read heavily in the classics among the station library's holdings and would later teach literature at a community college. At Wilkes, seismologist Henry Birkenhauer taught mathematics up to introductory solid geometry, and aurora and cosmic-ray physicist Dean Denison led a class in German. At Little America, exchange meteorologists Paul Astapenko and Alberto Arruiz taught Russian and Spanish, respectively. These classes "lasted with surprising vigor," according to Crary's assistant Harry Francis, who taught history and English to the station's several foreigners. Charlie Bentley learned to play the recorder on his own at Byrd, and chief Kenneth Kent, electronics technician, brought his bagpipes to Ellsworth. At the same station, Dr. Clint Smith led a class in classical music appreciation for a small but dedicated group. Some Navy men worked on correspondence courses or otherwise prepared for promotion examinations. But more courses were sent down than were used, and of those, far fewer were completed. Many kept personal journals. What they chose to record of daily events and thoughts richly revealed themselves and their surroundings.[12]

Several stations instituted regular series of lectures during the winter to build understanding and appreciation for the mission and each other's work, as well as to impart practical information, especially in health and medicine. Siple, who liked to quantify, posited that the amount of difficulty encountered in an isolated base was apt to vary as the square of the time following midwinter. Arguments became more heated, triggered by increasingly trivial incidents or misinterpretations of words or intentions. So as many lecturers as possible were engaged to occupy minds productively and build individual self-esteem. Thus IGY scientists talked about their respective projects—how they did their work, why it was significant, how it fit into the overall IGY program. Navy personnel spoke on technical subjects, such as Jaburg's lecture at Ellsworth on how a helicopter works and Ken Waldron's at Pole on electricity. Having "never made a presentation to anybody about anything I'd ever done before," Waldron "learned a great deal from that little session." Medical officers lectured on polar medicine, including likely injuries, as training for the traverse teams, but they also spoke on topics of general concern. Pole dwellers flocked to Doc Taylor's lectures on male and female reproductive systems. After "excellent" attendance at the latter, he followed up with sessions on pregnancy and obstetrics. Siple spoke on Antarctic geography, Tuck on south-polar history.[13]

The presence and use of liquor was a significant factor in camp morale, though how was a matter of interpretation. Leaders' views on the subject varied widely. Conscientious leaders, from McMurdo's Dave Canham on, understandably dreaded events where liquor flowed freely, knowing they would have to deal with the unfortunate effects of overindulgence on some people. Others, like George Toney, would have welcomed opportunities for a mellowing now and then among his deprived charges. Bert Crary imbibed heavily himself, amazing colleagues with his ability to function at a high level despite doing so (and getting little sleep as well). Siple would have preferred to leave liquor in the States, though he acknowledged the persuasiveness of Taylor's arguments in its favor. In isolated duty, the medical officer reasoned in his report, moderate use of alcohol was "small compensation for the freedom lost in other departments." Pole observed "occasional Happy Hours" where, Siple claimed, at least a third of the attendees were teetotalers. Taylor wrote in his thoughtful report that it was "perfectly healthy for a man to get an occasional 'glow on.'"

The morale value of alcohol lay in the taste, warmth, and sense of togetherness it induced, not in getting drunk.[14]

Morale at Wilkes was "enormously aided by our adequate liquor supply," wrote medical officer Sheldon Grinnell of the first winter. "The anxiety-relieving and socializing values of alcohol are well known and were well utilized at Wilkes." Scientific leader Carl Eklund agreed, approving Dr. Grinnell's issuance of a daily two-ounce shot of brandy for anyone who wanted it. He simply left a box of the small bottles on a table in his office half an hour before dinner. The honor system worked, and the trust further built good feeling. On weekends and holidays Old Methusalem Brand Straight Bourbon Whiskey, "the world's worst bourbon," or a brandy-bourbon punch accompanied Wilkes movies, although 1,200 cases of beer proved the most popular drink. "I swear to God, old Methuselah must have made it," recalled Little America's yeoman Dick Lucier of the whiskey. "You're talking about rotgut!"[15]

Where liquor supplies were inadequate in quantity or quality, improvisation served. Exchange meteorologist Morton Rubin, sailing on the *Ob* to Mirny, marveled at the Soviet scientists' ingenuity in that regard. Aboard ship they had great quantities of alcohol for preserving animal specimens but "not the sort for drinking." So the resourceful Russians would take a large jar of plum or apricot jam, mix it half and half with the 190-proof alcohol, heat it in a flask over a Bunsen burner, and pour it through filter paper, after which "we had a beautiful liqueur to drink." At Pole in 1959 the men found that 190-proof grain alcohol from the pharmacy mixed with extract of peppermint, green food color, sugar, and water made a passable crème de menthe.[16]

Some stations were awash with liquor. In 1957 little Hallett's fourteen winterers sloshed about in 136 quarts of whiskey, 4,000 two-ounce bottles of brandy, and 15 gallons of 95-percent grain alcohol plus an unspecified amount of beer that was sold by the case. Only about a third of it was gone by the end of the year. Jaburg recorded that "through some monumental screw-up by the Navy, Ellsworth Station is the proud possessor of *3,000 double cases* of beer." That amounted to 144,000 cans, or 3,693 cans per person—10 cans per person per day, he calculated. It had to be hoped that those numbers did not reach the ears of Byrd's forced abstainers, who had to spread their 10 cans each over the entire year. At eleven cents a can and with general discontent to drown, there was high consumption at Ellsworth—too high by chief mechanic Walt Davis's standards: "It kind of got out of hand . . . overworked."[17]

One who spoke out bluntly on the subject of alcohol on the ice was Dr. Edward Ehrlich, medical officer at Little America during Deep Freeze I, who had charge of an amount of liquor he understatedly called "far in excess of

anticipated usage even with a most liberal interpretation of 'medicinal' indications." He would, "in good faith," issue recreational alcohol for the "best
welfare" of the men, but since task-force policy (Memorandum, 28 June 1955)
officially prohibited consumption, the amount sent down "could only be interpreted as intent to ignore the policy." Liquor should be either prohibited, he
opined, or conceded as recreational and dispensed under command authority,
perhaps in authorized clubs. Ehrlich particularly opposed the notion of a
"grog ration" as a "medal for heroes" who had engaged in hazardous or exposed activity. Such "rewards," inherently arbitrary as well as medically unwar-
ranted, corroded overall morale, he argued. By posted policy he provided a
brandy at every table setting a time or two per week and whiskey for punch at
the weekly Friday night party until a certain hour for general partaking.[18]

Ehrlich thought his policy fair and effective, but it ran him amok of the VX-
6 squadron that arrived in the spring. The flight crews expected special rations
for their dangerous work, arguing that their flight surgeon always supplied it.
The doctor's suggestion that they save their issued brandy for such nerve-
wracking occasions was not well received. He soon found himself sent to
McMurdo for "a little bit of rest and recreation," relieved by the VX-6 flight
surgeon. Admiral Dufek, finding Ehrlich drinking coffee in the McMurdo mess
hall early one morning, "blew his stack" at the reason he was there and sent
him back on the next plane. Dr. Ike Taylor, Ehrlich's counterpart at McMurdo,
agreed: alcohol should be available at isolated bases for morale and recreational purposes but not provided free by the command, which could seem to
"imply encouragement" for drinking. The "consent" (far from encouragement)
implied in authorized messes or clubs put the responsibility for use, financial
and behavioral, on the individual.[19]

Glaciologist Vern Anderson was not among those complaining about Byrd's
lack of liquor. On 26 May 1957 he wrote, "It's odd how guys can sit around and
keep telling taller and taller stories about how drunk they have gotten." To him
this was "typical fraternity bull, which I guess I really despise." On 6 August,
"I gave all my beer that was under my bed to Curt [utility man Brinton] today,
just to get rid of the stuff." When the second season's first tractor train arrived
on 22 October, he recorded, "Well, they're here. With 3 bags of mail for us and
lots of beer, so everyone's happy." It was the mail that excited him, not the huge
party that night. The next day he was up early getting ready for the upcoming
traverse while "the guys around here are all getting over their hangovers and
more are still carrying on with their drinking."[20]

Another who was not interested in the continuing abundance of booze at
Little America was aurora observer Wilson. He simply did not care for it, but

one night during the winter of 1958 a "big Navy chief" literally picked him up and said "here, you're going to drink this." The "torpedo juice" duly took its effect, and Wilson went off to bed, not realizing until morning what his temporary loss of lucid thought had nearly cost. A small stove heated the aurora tower, and he had opened the petcock to refill its fuel tank from the central pumping area below. In his unaccustomed fuddle he forgot to turn it off. By the time he awoke with a clearer head hours later, about 500 gallons of fuel oil had overflowed the tank, flooded the floor, and rained down through the roof of the science laboratory below, dripping on both sides of the heater there, miraculously not igniting. It took about a week to clean up the mess, but it was the narrow deliverance that got Wilson's, and no doubt everyone else's, attention. It did not enhance his appetite for alcohol or fellow feeling with sailors.[21]

Fire was, without doubt, the most fearsome threat on the ice. The Americans were relatively lucky, although a conflagration of unknown origin destroyed McMurdo's garage and its contents, including a D-8 tractor and electrical equipment, in April 1957. Fortunately, the building stood apart, and the fire did not spread. The Navy reckoned the cost at $106,000 but judged the reduced operational capability more serious. The Seabees "grumbled, groaned and swore profusely but they lost no time in starting and completing a better garage and Public Works shop." They did it "under lights" (during the winter's dark) using leftover panels that needed much adapting. Third-class construction mechanic J. A. Hrincsina later escaped with minor burns when an "empty" fifty-five-gallon drum of antifreeze exploded as he tried to cut off its top with an acetylene torch. His clothes caught fire, but he extinguished the flames by rolling in the snow. Robert Molla's burns were serious when his oil-soaked outer pants ignited while he was welding on a D-8 at Little America. Just after the IGY, in August 1960, during a howling storm (120-mile-an-hour winds), a horrific fire at Mirny claimed the lives of eight sleeping meteorologists. They "never had a chance," grieved exchange scientist Gil Dewart who helped recover the bodies. It was the "worst single disaster in the history of Antarctic expeditions," and it "cast a pall of sadness" over the rest of the experience. They never learned the cause.[22]

As with liquor, attitudes toward and the practice of religion had a great deal to do with the leanings of the leaders. Only the two largest stations had resident chaplains, and their influence stemmed from their respective personalities. McMurdo's flamboyant Father John Condit observed officially that darkness,

Looking up McMurdo's Forrestal Avenue toward the Chapel of the Snows. Spring's rising sun illuminates Observation Hill, but the rest of camp remains in twilight. Courtesy, photographer David Grisez.

loneliness, hard work, cold, close association with the same people, and "the thought that all avenues of escape were impossible" all "weighed heavily on the minds of the men." As solace, he used every means he could think of to persuade them to attend church—some of them of questionable propriety. Having the Chapel of the Snows as a designated worship hall was a plus, but he also noted approvingly that "each man took it upon himself to be a chaplain to his buddy." With less charismatic and less aggressive leadership after the first year, church attendance at McMurdo tended to decline as the year wore on.[23]

Station leaders where trained clergy were lacking took varied approaches. Those for whom religion was personally important provided spiritual leadership. Stephen Barnes, scientific leader at Byrd in 1958, offered recorded church services weekly, with the willing help, he said later, of respected Navy chief petty officer N. L. Carney, who was "extremely good with prayer." Although only about a quarter of the men attended, Barnes felt "a wholesome religious approach cannot help [but] be of definite value toward a successful operation, toward improvement of morale, and toward promoting a warmer feeling of fellowship." He led a generally contented camp. Photographer Boyer, who spent Christmas 1958 at Byrd, attended church services the next day with sixteen others (a large percentage) when McMurdo's chaplain flew in, but in his estimation religion was "a thing rather disdained in this harsh world of navy and science." On Easter the year before, in the absence of scheduled worship, Anderson took his spiritual sustenance upon himself. He stayed up all night until "sunrise" (the sun had just set for the season), writing to his sweetheart and listening to music such as the *Messiah*. In the morning he wrote, "I've just returned from my Easter sunrise service. . . . It was really inspiring out there, alone talking to God and unburdening my soul to Him."[24]

Siple encouraged weekly nondenominational Christian services at South Pole Station, finding electronics technician Cliff Dickey a willing and energetic leader in planning and delivering them. They lasted about twenty minutes, followed by a discussion—often lively—of some philosophical subject such as tolerance, goodwill, or love led by someone assigned to prepare an opening on the topic. About a dozen of the eighteen men normally attended, according to Siple, and Tuck added that the "informality" did nothing to reduce the "effectiveness" of the devotions. Over at Ellsworth, chief Walter May and physicist John Brown organized church services on the last day of March, but only six others attended, all but one (VX–6 crew member Fred Drydal) a scientist. According to Behrendt, the next week May alone represented the Navy, while seven IGY men came, "basically . . . to show support for Jack's efforts." Services continued until Easter two weeks later; there were no more. Nolan Aughenbaugh, who noted the major days of the Christian Holy Week in large letters in his journal, counted only eight again (of thirty-nine) on Easter Sunday—one time a significant turnout might be expected. Captain Ronne apparently played no part in this grassroots endeavor.[25]

At Wilkes Station, arguably the happiest group launched in Deep Freeze II, organized religious practice played a minor role at best. Photographer Paul Noonan did not remember any. That was not a problem for him, he said, and "I didn't hear anybody else consider it a problem." The official Navy report claimed services were held on Sunday evenings twice a month using the "excellent" *Minister's Handbook*, with about four men attending. However, during the second year of the IGY, Jesuit scholar Birkenhauer was there as chief seismologist and deputy station leader. Whether he was listed as chaplain in a de facto sense or by conscious decision, Wilkes managed a successful year that way as well. Weekly services continued all year, with about five Catholics at Father Birkenhauer's Mass and Denison leading five to seven Protestants in a separate gathering. During the year, Tressler noted, a chapel materialized in a corner of the science building, "nicely painted inside with stained beams, a pew, kneeling bench and prie-dieu, all carefully made by Chief [James] Lynsky, the head carpenter."[26] Thus it appears that planned religious observance was not essential to camp serenity, although when well done it seemed helpful to and appreciated by those participating. But for religion to be successful, it needed active leader support and encouragement, not necessarily by clergy.

Often, spiritual moments came unbidden, not in a built chapel but out in the vast cathedral called Antarctica. One glorious morning in 1962, on a traverse from Wilkes to Vostok, scientific leader Bob Thomson walked out a mile or two to photograph the tiny caravan against the soft pinks of clouds and limitless snow. In the stillness, as he turned to record his footprints in the scene, the "not over-religious" man "felt the touch of a hand" on his sleeve. At that moment, hundreds of miles from other humans, even removed from his teammates, he knew he was literally the "most remote person on earth," yet not alone. "I can't explain it, but there was something," he said, still feeling it after forty years. On a different kind of day, "just a terrible condition of whiteout," VX-6 pilot Eddie Frankiewicz was flying a supply mission to the Beardmore auxiliary base. He knew there were crevasses at the foot of the glacier, but "we couldn't see anything. And then I started praying real good." Miraculously, "a small patch of sunlight" appeared on the snow ahead—only that one small spot. It "lasted long enough for Gus [Shinn, in another plane] to land there and for me to land there. And then it disappeared. And I thought, 'I believe in God.'" More than half a lifetime later, unashamed tears welled as he shared the memory. The immensity, the dazzling majesty, the impenetrable mystery of the ice seem an ever-present sermon to many.[27]

The single-most-important boost to morale for Antarcticans came from short-wave radio. Mawson first introduced a primitive "wireless telegraphy" on the continent in 1912; during his second year he occasionally managed to reach Australia via a relay station on Macquarie Island. By February 1934 Byrd was able to exploit more sophisticated shortwave technology for voice broadcasts that brought Antarctica to a national radio audience. Now, during the IGY, shortwave radio was the mainstay, indeed the only means of contact with home over the long mail-less winter. Voice-to-voice communication with someone special required timing, luck, and favorable ionospheric conditions, ever problematic during this period of great solar unrest. It required people at both ends to find the right frequency to make a connection and stand by—that is, listen in—to switch the equipment from transmit mode to receive when one speaker finished and said "over." In particular, the system rested on dedicated though unofficial radio operators at the IGY stations and scores of amateur "hams" across the United States, who received and forwarded "hamgrams" (short personal telegram-like messages) and linked callers with "phone patches." (The stateside ham connected with the Antarctic caller would telephone the desired callee collect, who would pay any U.S. long-distance charges.) Such conversations were never private, of course. Even a trained radioman calling his family late at night without an intermediary knew that any ham anywhere with the inclination and equipment could listen in—which they would. Beyond basic human curiosity, Antarctica and the IGY were subjects of great contemporary interest.[28]

Byrd Station's many deprivations included some of the worst communication challenges of any Antarctic station. Not until midwinter were amateur-radio connections established with the United States, and atmospheric conditions for transmission remained erratic. Long radio blackouts were a plague because of intense geomagnetic disturbances and, secondarily, snow static caused by dry snow blowing against the antennas. From 5 January to 5 November 1957, Byrd endured 939 hours of total blackout (altogether more than five weeks around the clock and once for 141 consecutive hours, almost six days), with no signals over the entire spectrum. Consequently, phone patches were rare—only 65 all year—and, since some U.S. locations were harder to pick up than others, more difficult and expensive for some. Because Morse code was more reliably transmitted, over 1,000 hamgrams went out from Byrd, to be translated from code and typed out by the receiving U.S. ham and mailed to the addressee. Sometimes Byrd resorted to sending hamgrams "in the blind, after contact was lost," because radio signals could be heard in the United States about half an hour after they were lost in Antarctica. Sometimes reception might be fine when transmission was impossible.[29]

At most U.S. stations, each with its own call sign, anyone who could demonstrate proficiency, including knowledge of CW (Morse code, a continuous-wave signal interrupted to create dots and dashes), could operate the official radio station after hours. Whether because Antarctica was not U.S. territory, where U.S. law would apply, or because special dispensation was granted for the unique circumstances of the IGY, an amateur radio license was not required. For example, at Little America in 1957, two Navy radiomen supervised a team of up to eight IGY and Navy men who maintained continuous amateur radio operations from KC4USA when propagation conditions were favorable, usually during the night hours, Zulu time. In May the scientists won authorization to use the station equipment to discuss scientific information with counterparts across the continent, so long as they interfered minimally with morale use.[30]

After his official Navy duties were over for the day at McMurdo in Deep Freeze I, radioman "Monty" Montgomery spent hours on ham radio enabling personal calls. "We had a card system. The guys would [list the names of] their mothers or wives or whoever they wanted to talk to, and you could have five cards. One at a time we'd reach them." Since the zone of optimal reception tended to shift from west to east, they would set up the cards to start with California, and when those stations faded and dropped off they would work their way across the country. Monty would try to end up with Jules Madey in Clark, New Jersey, a teenage ham whose loyalty and long hours were legendary among lonely Antarcticans. Jules would often set up a phone patch with Monty's wife on Martha's Vineyard. Lloyd Beebe, the Disney photographer, arranged for crews at all three sites to film one of these conversations for a televised Disneyland program. One night Monty heard a distinctive voice calling KC4USV. "I knew I knew that voice. I knew I knew it, you know?" As he frantically thumbed his *Radio Amateur Callbook*, radio personality Arthur Godfrey sensed the hesitation and identified himself: "Everybody knew Arthur Godfrey in those days." Godfrey, in turn, reported on the air (heard by Lois Montgomery) that he had talked with "Monty in Antarctica"—a thrill for all.[31]

Godfrey and other famous hams such as Barry Goldwater and Art Linkletter called only occasionally, and they, like "many of the hams, content with a QSL card [a postcard verifying the contact] from the Antarctic," dropped out as time went on. Then, "the band quieted down enough to allow more satisfactory means of traffic exchange." To the gratitude of those wintering over, "it soon became apparent that certain hams in the United States were old standbys" who would invariably be there "to pass traffic or give us the latest news." Aldrich, among others, reported that in mid-1957 five local chapters of the Radio Amateurs of Greater Syracuse offered their members on a rotating watch to "keep an early morning vigil from midnight to 0400, standing by to receive and transmit messages to persons in the Antarctic," thus providing "the most private way to exchange messages with folks back home." It was a substantial commitment, and for his leadership in coordinating the effort, Paul Blum received a Navy Distinguished Public Service Award in September 1957.[32]

Blum was not alone. As the IGY neared its official completion, Executive Director Hugh Odishaw wrote to everyone connected with the Antarctic program and their families to request the names of persons deserving recognition for particular contributions to the endeavor. In his thick file of responses, the overwhelming majority began their lists with ham radio operators. One contained twenty-three such names, two of them women, all of whom would receive IGY certificates of appreciation for their support of polar morale. For "their faithful and friendly aid," the first winterers at Pole listed forty-five hams in the South Pole Yearbook. Some made list after list, attesting to their reliability and devotion.[33]

For all their good, though, radio connections were not without problems, even when atmospheric and technical conditions were met. Sometimes it seemed that certain people hogged the equipment until the signal faded. Aldrich remembered being able to talk with his wife only three times all winter. The first was just after learning of the death of his father, a blow made harsher by the unbridgeable distance. Byrd's medical officer witnessed connections made unwittingly or unavoidably at a bad time for one or the other party that left difficult issues unspoken, misunderstood, or unresolved. For example, when a spouse at home struggling with small children said something like "come home soon or don't come home," there was awkwardness and pain. And everyone in camp would know about it. Dalton wondered sometimes if "you were better off if you never had a call." For Rudi Honkala at Wilkes, the pleasure of talking with his wife, who had shared many other challenging weather-observation assignments, was overtaken afterward by the "misery of getting back into the routine." So, he admitted, he did not try to call often. Vern Anderson pursued—and won—Carole with a chaste, almost boyish ardor by any and all wireless means when letters had to wait, but less solid relationships were often impossible to maintain in absentia yet in the presence of so many third parties. Bentley remembered one hapless Byrd Seabee who wanted to call his girlfriend when his turn came. Jules got through to her and asked if she would accept the charges to talk with "John Doe" in the Antarctic. Whether misunderstanding the distance to be covered by the charge (fifteen cents) or intending her reply for what it was, she said, "No." "That was one unhappy guy"— not only rejected but humiliated for all the small community to see.[34]

At Ellsworth, communication problems were of a different sort. Only 41 Class E (personal) messages went out through the Navy the entire year, about one per person. Atmospheric conditions aside, the likely reason was the station leader's insistence on reviewing (censoring) every outgoing message, which the men greatly resented. They believed he did it to prevent them from saying anything derogatory about him or the way he ran the base. Captain Ronne also censored hamgrams, about 1,100 of which were eventually sent. Sometimes he held messages back for punishment, as he did with Aughenbaugh and Kim Malville in late July. Occasionally he tied up the circuit "for hours," sending out long, coded press releases on station activities. (The men scorned Ronne's press releases for their overblown drama, although that seemed to be the formula for publication back home, and other leaders were equally, if more tolerantly, ragged for theirs.)[35]

In June the captain ordered that a door be put on the radio shack and on it a sign that read "All Hands Keep Out." An incensed Jaburg found this "insulting as hell to the 3 officers that the sign includes, and completely unheard of." Ronne thenceforth allowed only a chosen few in the radio room, although the select individuals varied over time. The erratic Skidmore, for example, was in and out according to his current favor with the leader, although when he had access, Aughenbaugh credited him with conscientiously seeking phone patches for others. On 28 July Jaburg fumed that Ronne had had a phone patch of an hour and fifty minutes with his wife that morning, "which infuriates all the men, as they have a tough time getting to talk to their wives." "Let's face it," he said years later, "communication with the rest of the world is a very, very important thing when you're isolated." Amateur radio was their only means, and "he [Ronne] controlled that like a dictator." It was "absolutely unconscionable."[36]

The communication restrictions at Ellsworth became so onerous that the scientists finally resorted to subterfuge. On 12 September Jack Brown sent a request for supplies to Professor Millett G. Morgan at Dartmouth, chair of the IGY ionospheric physics panel, who was interested in whistlers and had been considering a visit to Ellsworth in the spring. To his radio message Brown appended, "FERVENTLY HOPE YOU CAN VISIT WITH RESUPPLY TO OBSERVE FIRST-HAND ACTIVITY HERE—INCLUDING CALIGULAS RAIN." Skidmore told the inquiring Ronne that Caligula's Rain was a dawn chorus (a phenomenon in radio physics) named for a Roman emperor, but Morgan knew of no such term. He did get the meaning, even with the carefully incorrect spelling of "reign," and did board an Ellsworth-bound ship as an IGY summer representative. As Malville remembered it, "We were just immensely amused that this was the first hint that there was a somewhat demented Roman emperor–type person who was running our base." But the situation was not so funny.[37]

Keeping the station running was essential to the pursuit of science, the point of this ambitious occupation of the polar continent. Support was the Navy's role. But given the basic inequality of their respective assignments and the social and educational differences between the civilian scientists and most of their Navy companions, this arrangement could bode trouble in a small, isolated community if not handled with tact and generosity of spirit. Getting all the work done while maintaining harmony and goodwill was a test of leadership. The approaches at America's IGY bases were varied, the results instructive.

One necessary drudgery was mess cooking—Navy parlance for kitchen scut work. At the South Pole, with only eighteen inhabitants, "the IGY personnel realized that the Station could not be maintained without their help." Siple continued, "As leaders, Jack [Lieut. Tuck] and I shared equally with all the other men in menial tasks." Mess duty there included cleaning the head and galley and taking out the garbage. In the galley it meant about an hour per meal to set up and clean up, "though more than half the time" cook Segers, having "nowhere to go anyhow," washed the dishes himself. The two leaders softened the chore by letting each mess cook choose the music played at meals during his turn. Tuck, in his official report, confirmed that Siple and the scientists gave half their time to general camp jobs. Their cooperation was "nothing less than outstanding in all respects."[38]

Other stations developed their own equitable formulas. At Wilkes, Eklund reported, all civilians "took regular turns at mess duty on Friday and Saturday evenings." Rotating through a meal at a time cut little from anyone's science program yet made a visible contribution to the tedious task. The scientists also helped on several "all-hands" work parties, took weeklong turns to maintain the recreation building and wash rooms, and cleaned their own quarters. "These duties were inconsequential," Eklund cheerfully acknowledged, "compared to the overall job of housekeeping," but the fact that they were done showed respect for the work and the Navy men who did most of it. Byrd's Navy leader Dalton wrote that during the fall he rotated mess cooking through the military personnel to allow the IGY people full-time to ready their equipment, and during the winter, when two meals were served each day, three of the more idle Navy men volunteered in turn. When they were needed again in their skill areas in the spring, the duty "reverted to all hands by daily rotation." Bentley remembered sharing in mess cooking, and "we shoveled snow for our own showers just like everybody else, and that's fair enough." The Navy men did most of the skilled work, he said, like plumbing and tractor driving, but "the really menial work that can get pretty annoying if you feel that somebody else is lording it over you, that we all shared." He credited much to the example of scientific leader George Toney, whose "first idea" was to do a job himself.[39]

Bert Crary handled the situation in his own style at Little America, where the twenty-four civilians were supported by nearly four times that many Navy personnel. When his counterpart, Capt. E. W. Dickey, commander of all naval support units in Antarctica, suggested that IGY personnel help out the "hard-pressed kitchen staff" (following an altercation between an enlisted man and a science assistant), Crary agreed that in a crisis everyone should pitch in. But he would choose which civilians could be spared from their work at a given time. (Dickey had fingered the man in the scuffle.) Moreover, in a real crisis the Navy officers as well as IGY "officers" should mess cook. Both Dalrymple and Wilson remembered Crary's amiable response as "fine, you and I will start tomorrow morning." Dickey dropped the subject. Years later Dalrymple, who wintered at two polar sites, would emphasize the "tremendous differences" station size made. At the tiny South Pole, it was obvious that everyone had to help with everything; lack of manpower was not an issue at populous Little America.[40]

Ellsworth's single leader, citing but distorting the Pole and Wilkes examples, decided to order his junior scientists to do mess cooking. As Ronne organized the task, it would require about six hours a day for two weeks and include waiting on the officers' table (the only one at any U.S. base)—a significant loss of time from the work they were sent to do. (There were twenty-nine Navy support personnel at the station, albeit some of them fully occupied with weather, radio, or cooking duties.) The scientists, like Crary, argued that as officers (the assistant scientists were GS-9s in federal-service terms, equivalent to a lieutenant) they should not be required to mess cook unless the Navy officers were. Indeed, the VX-6 personnel had little to do during the dark months when there was no flying. Jaburg himself wrote in sympathy, "I secretly agree with them that since they have been granted officer status down here, if a few get mess cooking, then all should get it including the officers. Boy has he got a mad on for the IGY people!" In his own book, *Antarctic Command*, Ronne linked imposing mess duty with the charge that the civilians had "created so much trouble and exhibited such deplorable behavior, we could not treat them as officers." On the same page he referred to the need for punishment to get results.[41]

On 11 May Ronne told Behrendt, Walker, Skidmore, and Aughenbaugh that he planned to put them on mess duty to "raise the men's morale." As for their Navy equivalents, Behrendt quoted Ronne as saying "it wouldn't look right for officers to do this kind of work." So, Behrendt continued, "we are officer status when it suits his purposes and apparently [we] lose any such rights and privileges when he wishes it." Chief seismologist and deputy scientific leader Ed Thiel demanded any such order in writing. On the 13th it came, along with the one demoting the IGY nine to the general mess with the enlisted men. Thiel and chief glaciologist Hugo Neuburg countered with a memorandum citing a Navy regulation that science observers "not be required to perform routine Naval duties" that would interfere with their work. They requested clarification by radio from Crary. Ronne, by his admission, "ignored the letter," describing the IGY staff as "uncooperative," "spoiled," "immature juveniles."[42]

Ronne further insisted that IGY personnel stand eight-hour generator watches with the enlisted, altogether placing a third of the scientific staff on camp maintenance. Jaburg wrote, "I'm *sure* the Capt. is wrong about *this* and can't understand why he would do such a thing. He knows that these people were sent down here for scientific work *only* and the Navy people are here to support the IGY not vice-versa." His next sentence: "Movie tonight was 'The Caine Mutiny' and boy what parallels with our current situation could be drawn there!"—a sentiment echoed by every other Ellsworth writer. On the 16th Thiel resigned his position as deputy leader, for whatever symbolic effect that could carry. His letter was never forwarded.[43]

On the 17th Ronne consented to consulting Crary. Although no one but Thiel was allowed in the radio room, the scientists picked up the signal on the science-building radio and managed to record and later transcribe the entire exchange. Despite reception that was, at least secondhand, sometimes poor, they all heard Crary emphasize the priority of the scientific program. In "unusual" circumstances, everyone should volunteer equally for camp work, he had said. By Ronne's account, after he gave Crary "all the facts," Thiel "made an erroneous presentation completely—which I then had to correct on the air." Aughenbaugh's fiery diary entry said that although Ronne "grabbed the mike from Ed and started his hysterical accusations and story, Ed got enough through to Crary to get him the idea and Ronne helped our cause many times by his crack-pot statements." Back at Little America, Captain Dickey, standing by unbeknownst, broke in to remind the Navy reserve captain at Ellsworth that "we are committed to supporting the IGY. This is an IGY expedition down here, and I know the Navy would never want it said we wouldn't support this operation." While he was sure officers would mess cook, if needed (notwithstanding his sparring with Crary on the subject), Dickey doubted the necessity.[44]

In his selective review Ronne did not mention Dickey in this regard. He wrote, "Crary left it to me what to do [about mess cooking], except I would have to explain upon my return if the planned IGY program suffered in any way." He had been leaving them alone, he muttered, "until the civilians had made so many infringements on law, order and some semblance of discipline that the threat of mess duty was the only means I had to bring them in line. Now,

Crary's decision made a straw out of my weak stick." The problems at Ellsworth sounded petty, beyond belief in the context of the high-minded mission. The unprivate airings both titillated and worried listeners at other stations, who could not imagine an atmosphere so unlike their own. Walker and Behrendt put in two weeks of galley duty, the latter wondering later if that amicable stint might have been why cook Ed Davis and baker Dick Grob invariably tucked in fresh breads and pies with supplies going out to their traverse.[45]

By the austral spring, when the issue rearose, Wexler in Washington was beginning to grasp the Ellsworth situation despite the hobbled communications. Hearing via Brown in a phone patch to NBS Boulder on ionosphere matters that Skidmore was being ordered to mess cook, he generously—erroneously—opined that this was "undoubtedly a result of Ronne's impending traverse operations which will leave perhaps a shortage of people at the station." But, he went on, this was a "clear violation" of the IGY-DOD agreement "regarding *equitable* distribution of housekeeping duties among *all* personnel which include officers." He was "sure," surmising correctly, that no officers, including Ronne, were washing dishes. Six days later he noted, displeased, that Malville had also been sent to the galley. "Sentenced" as a punishment for some forgotten lack of proper respect, Malville, like others, though, overcame his initial annoyance and "rather enjoyed" this opportunity to become a "member of the community." He wished, in fact, that everyone had earlier volunteered for it.[46]

But the accumulated unrest had become too obvious as information leaked through the wall of control around Ellsworth. Malville credited the visiting Professor Morgan (who had indeed reported the situation as "far worse than expected") with proposing what became a debriefing of the returning Ellsworth scientists at NAS. It was, Malville recalled, a day of "good therapy" and "healing"—their first opportunity to tell someone official of their frustrations, of the psychic costs of feeling like "outlaws." The IGY leaders were "appropriately outraged" at Ronne's lack of support for the science effort, but they seemed "most interested in just laying everything to rest." They wanted the facts but also wanted to avoid "any great embarrassing situations" that might result.[47]

Wexler's diary and actions confirm this view. He got up early on 13 February 1958 to be at Andrews Air Force Base east of Washington to greet the nine scientists as they flew in from São Paulo. Coffee and donuts at the IGY offices began the "all-Ellsworth day." (They were the only wintering group to receive such attention.) Wexler arranged for a rotation of observers, including the IGY's Odishaw and Alan Shapley, Merle Tuve of the Carnegie Institution, Weather Bureau chief F. W. Reichelderfer, and Wallace Atwood of the NAS international office. These power figures established the IGY leadership's serious view of the matter. "The competence of the fellows was established early in the game," Wexler wrote, impressed with their respective disciplines' accomplishments. In the afternoon, a more general session "gave each boy a chance to unburden at least part of the story." The "upshot," he continued, was that they would never again appoint Ronne as a scientific leader, but they "agreed not to take any action at all unless Ronne does." If he did, the USNC-IGY, not the individuals, would "fight the battle."[48]

If some, then or later, would have preferred to let the truth out to speak for itself, the overriding concern at the time was clearly to present a rosy public picture of the IGY. Attendee Pembroke Hart, a newly hired IGY program officer, wondered later what good could have come of pursuing the issue after the fact, however ill-used the scientists had been, which everyone acknowledged was true. What, in fact, could have been done? Wexler had the long session with the scientists recorded (as Behrendt and Malville remembered) so that Gould and Odishaw could hear the whole story before listening to Ronne's version, but neither tapes nor minutes survive. (Wexler's skimpy handwritten notes are essentially illegible.) Philip Mange, another IGY program officer who was aware of the proceedings but not in the room, echoed Malville in recalling an attitude of encouraging a "cathartic outpouring from their souls," followed by "lock it up and forget about it." As for tapes, he believed that if the smooth Odishaw, master of public relations, "did not think certain information would be good for posterity, it would disappear." Siple, noting "other stations" that had tried court-martial and "long-distance appeal to higher authority" to contrast the effectiveness of his "group-pressure control system," corroborated that "neither the Navy or IGY wanted the disgrace of a public hearing."[49]

The next day Wexler posted "consternation" upon learning that Ronne had never submitted to the psychiatric examination required of all winterers. In fact, the ships relieving Ellsworth in early 1958 had two Navy psychiatrists and a psychologist aboard, ostensibly to evaluate the Navy's psychological screening program and study human response to a year of polar isolation. They could have done this anywhere, but no other IGY group was targeted. The choice could scarcely have been random. Their findings, published in the *US Armed Forces Medical Journal* in 1959, named neither the station nor individuals, though it is unmistakably Ellsworth. Of course, those who were there remembered. The psychiatrists, who enjoyed a "high order of cooperation," found a mentally and emotionally normal group, although "two or three . . . might well have been eliminated as unsuitable" because of irritating or disruptive personalities. Overall, however, they judged the men tolerant of "unconventional, or even eccentric," behavior in a person who "worked hard and well and did not 'bother' anyone otherwise." The investigators concluded that the "crucial factor in understanding the dynamics of this particular group" was an "antithetical attitude" between the leader and the others that, "paradoxically," encouraged cohesiveness among the latter. Con Jaburg agreed years later: "We were able to focus all of our hate and discontent on one person." It became "more or less" a matter of "all of us against him."[50]

Ronne complained to his visiting interviewer that the "raw, bitter winds" of winter isolation "strip the veneer of civilization from men, and reduce some of them as low as one can reduce civilized beings." He faulted the selection process for giving him such a mutually uncooperative mix of sailors and civilians. He was, if so, uniquely unlucky. Malville and others noted that he had joined the ship late and made little effort to get to know them during the weeks at sea: "We were people beneath him, I think." Ronne also brought up, as he did again and again, that "the IGY personnel were being paid more than eight times the amount of some of the enlisted men"—an exaggeration of even extreme cases. To be sure, the civilians had no reason to be displeased with their remuneration, and the Navy men understandably groused about the disappearance of their anticipated hardship per diems, but not in comparison with IGY salaries, if they even knew them. Perhaps more telling was Ronne's allegation that "[e]ven I, as a captain in the Navy in charge of the station, earned less including all my allowances, than the lowest paid civilian under me." That was not true, but as early as October 1956 he had complained to Wexler that Antarctic-experienced civilian station leaders, as GS-14s with hardship allowances and overtime, would earn almost $4,000 more than he would. With Gould's support, he asked the Academy to make up the difference, which it had "no legal means" to do. The issue rankled deeply.[51]

For Wexler, the Ellsworth saga continued. The gist of the story appeared on the front page of the *Washington Post* on 10 February under the headline "Bickering Reported at Polar Base." Questioned by reporters, both Wexler and Siple untruthfully denied having heard reports of dissension, more evidence of the surpassing wish to preserve an unsullied image of the IGY. On the 21st the *Post* printed a follow-up piece in which Ronne denied (and repeated) the allegations of the first—that he had called the civilians "sissies" and "rotten eggs" and that they had called him a "martinet," one "seeking only to enhance his personal fame." Ronne also besieged Wexler over the naming of Antarctic landmarks, having heard that the Ellsworth traversers were making recommendations to the Board of Geographic Names. He insisted this was his prerogative. "He had discovered everything," wrote Wexler sarcastically of their phone discussion on 6 May. "When I suggested he might have gone through IGY channels, he exploded, saying 'What's IGY ever done for me'?" Ronne drew up a long paper outlining how the traversers could not possibly have seen anything before he did—betraying in it his intent to keep them in the dark, as several charged at the time. In the end, he offered to allow the scientists to name one feature.[52]

The Ellsworth folk later admitted that they sometimes "baited" their leader. After Ronne accused the IGY men of forming a "union" against him, Neuburg put up a sign at the deep pit that read "United Mine Workers, Weddell Local." "The Phantom" planted a "bloody" dagger in his door. A cartoon appeared on the mess hall wall featuring Ronne as an octopus beset by nine tentacles, each representing an identifiable scientist. Even at the time individuals confessed to their diaries, with some admission of pettiness, that they "were getting as bad as he was." But there was no question from what they wrote and remembered that their lives were dominated by daily dictates from and run-ins with the captain. "The guy is mad or drunk with power," Aughenbaugh confided in mid-March 1957, also admitting that "if it wasn't for him here, I sure would have a small, dull, routine diary." "Ah . . . to hell with it," Jaburg wrote in exasperation after noting that the captain had cheated at ping-pong, "this book is beginning to look as though it is Ronne's personal biography." This was true of everyone's account.[53]

As to where Ellsworth went wrong, Ronne himself provided many clues. *Antarctic Command*, his self-aggrandizing, vituperative (some said "libelous") account of that infamous year, and his later autobiography, *Antarctica, My Destiny*, brought out both his impressive polar credentials and his consuming drive to lead another Antarctic exploring expedition. It is not surprising that he latched on to the IGY as a means to his own ends—the glory of discovery— justified by offers to advance U.S. claims, continue aerial mapping, seek mineral resources, and make scientific observations. Both IGY and Navy decision makers, knowing him, might perhaps have foreseen that he would be tempted to mold the IGY agenda to his own. But the IGY was having a hard time finding experienced, willing scientific leaders, and the Navy, besides sharing his interests, seemed almost relieved for a chance to quiet his pestering. As the blunt Navy mechanic Walt Davis and many others in the field recognized, Ronne "wanted a Captain Ronne expedition, not an IGY expedition." Besides, there was just "too much horsepower" at Ellsworth, whose size merited a lieutenant or even an E-9 petty officer as officer-in-charge. (Davis, the senior enlisted man wintering at Byrd Station in 1960, by his and all other accounts, essentially ran the station and ran it well.) It was "beneath a captain's dignity to be in charge of that few men," he declared. Ronne seemed niggled by this, too.[54]

The most damaging evidence of Finn Ronne's leadership misconceptions is also provided by his own, many words. His model was the "advice" of Rear Adm. William S. Sims, who had declared in the 1920s: "Don't waste your breath on appeals to patriotism and duty. The fear of punishment and the hope of reward are the only two forces that move most men." Ronne despaired of rewarding the "already highly paid" civilians, however, and he had few means of punishment, although he did try to bring them under the Uniform Code of Military Justice. It was sad that he felt the need of either stick or carrot to lead his small cadre of eager scientists who were, in Navy man Jaburg's later assessment, "carefully chosen—very, very bright and hardworking folks" and "just super" volunteer sailors. Writing to Odishaw to recommend IGY recognition for Seabee Davis, glaciologist Paul Walker added, "Let me first state that all of the navy personnel at Ellsworth did an outstanding job." Neither group needed heavy-handed policing. As Jack Stuster, addressing qualities of leadership in his comparative study of life at the poles and in space, found, "A leader who is quick to anger or who frequently resorts to punishment in order to maintain control loses the confidence and respect of the crew," which in turn "contributes to further conflicts." As an example of negative leadership behavior, Stuster quoted a midshipman's letter describing his commanding officer: "He is . . . intoxicated with the power and rank of his situation. . . . Imagine a family where all are at variance with the father and you will know our state." The subject was Charles Wilkes of the unhappy nineteenth-century Wilkes Expedition, but the words could be read with an eerie sense of recognition in 1957.[55]

Capt. Sidney Blair, a Navy psychiatrist who screened Antarctic personnel for many years, sympathized with the challenges of military leadership at small, remote, isolated stations. These individuals had to work without such "normal leadership assets" as the power of punishment (what could be denied or imposed), the role status normally maintained by separateness (close proximity "renders informal even the most formal of hierarchies"), and the support and validation of other leaders (at best, hundreds of miles away). However, leaders who relied on the status or power of their role to deal with subordinates were "significantly impaired, and probably an inappropriate choice, for isolated and confined duty." Lieutenant Dalton, thin in the credibility that grows from experience, and having "not one CPO [chief petty officer] to assist him" at Byrd, remembered well that "you couldn't dock their pay, you couldn't put them in the brig, you couldn't ask the shore patrol to take them off your hands, you couldn't transfer them." Occasionally, he would have to "make growling remarks" about, say, the snowmelter's not being refilled: "If I catch anyone not doing this, I'm going to see they get recompense later." The inherent lameness of such threats discouraged their invocation.[56]

⎯⎯⎯⎯⎯⎯⎯⎯⎯⎯⎯⎯

The revered Siple, the idolized Crary, the admired Toney, and many others offered leadership substance and style as different as they were—yet each was effective. A particularly striking example of successful IGY leadership was that of Carl Eklund at Wilkes Station in 1957. "His goal was to make sure that all the science was done," remembered seismologist Gil Dewart. Presuming they were all dedicated, able, and reliable, he was there to remove obstructions and "make things as easy for the scientists as possible." Forthright and accessible, he was "on top of things" but "not pushy." Deputy scientific leader Rudi Honkala similarly recalled that "after he determined what abilities the individual had, he'd pretty much give you a free rein to do your job as you saw fit to do it, which in a place like that is a blessing." Dewart called Eklund a "very easygoing, lenient kind of guy who, when a decision really had to be made and the law had to be laid down, he didn't hesitate to do it." Navy photographer Paul Noonan agreed: "There were times when I could grasp that Carl was taking control of the situation. But he was very level-headed and generally easy going and a lot of fun, really. He had a great sense of humor. Of course he was very intelligent." "I don't know of anybody that didn't like Carl." With a store of OAE stories from his previous polar experience, he entertained Wilkes residents and taught them: take your survival gear, don't lay your mitts down on the snow.[57]

Moreover, said Dewart, in addition to Eklund and because of his prior experience working with the military, "we knew that we could count on the Navy people to support us because they were very well versed in what their goal was, which was to help us out, to get our program off the ground and keep things going." Lieut. (jg) Donald Burnett, officer-in-charge, was "totally cooperative," without an agenda of his own. Noonan saw Burnett as "sort of soft spoken, yet he could be firm." But he rarely had to be. The two leaders got along "wonderfully" and were a "very good combination." In his official report, Eklund hailed the Navy's "really superb job in support of the Wilkes scientific program." The scientists could thus devote "almost 100 percent" of their time to their own assignments. "Having previously wintered in Antarctica," Eklund continued, "I can appreciate what it means to be relieved of such tasks as snow shoveling, fuel and water supply, mess duty, and general work around the station." The scientists did all these things, but in small, willing doses he did not bother to note. They all also enjoyed good recreation equipment, books, dogs, liquor, trips to the Icecap Station, and "unrestricted use of the ham radio by everyone."[58]

Taking pleasure, not credit, Eklund reported, "From the beginning our men claimed Wilkes as the 'Number One Station in Antarctica,' and regardless of whether this was so or not they had the feeling it was. This kind of spirit fosters good morale." Even the "fine appearance" of the station reflected "the pride taken in it by all the men." At the end of the "marvelous" year, Eklund wrote to his wife, Harriet, "Our kids were really wonderful—and if I do say so myself, they'd do anything for the 'Eagle,' as most of them called me!" Perhaps Wilkes owed its happiness to the luck of drawing an exceptionally congenial and conscientious group of individuals. More likely, it had a great deal to do with positive leadership, where group satisfaction and success mattered more than individual ego. Far from competing with his mostly younger colleagues (he was forty-eight), Eklund reveled in their achievements and promoted their recognition. Unmentioned in his report, Eklund saw to it that everyone in camp had a nearby geographical landmark named for him. "So we all have a little piece of the Antarctic down there," said Noonan, pointing to Noonan Cove on a map of the offshore Windmill Islands that is sprinkled with the names of station mates.[59]

Ironically, Eklund remained Ronne's one true friend on the ice. The two had shared a long and productive sledging journey in 1940 from East Base on the Antarctic Peninsula, and Eklund seemed to view the senior man, about a decade older, as a mentor. In an early letter home from Wellington that bespoke each man's character, he wrote that Finn had said he should have a rubber stamp printed with his name and title, "Scientific Leader Wilkes Station, Antarctica." Eklund had demurred, but "[l]o and behold, he had one made for me and airmailed here! What a guy." Ronne had "put 'Dr.' on it" (Eklund's PhD, rewarding his IGY work on skuas, would be awarded in August 1958), so the uncomfortable recipient "cut it to make a smudge," which he stamped on his letter to verify the effect. "I'm a little sensitive about using it because it sounds a bit conceited," he wrote, admitting he had done so on some Christmas cards. He sympathized with Ronne as he fought with the admiral over siting Ellsworth Station, and when they did settle on a spot, "I must send him a congratulatory message." When his wife described Jennie Darlington's newly published *My Antarctic Honeymoon*, about her year as the second woman on the tense Ronne Antarctic Research Expedition, Eklund loyally decided that the ghostwriter "sounds like a real bitch. I haven't the slightest idea who it is—unless it's Harry [Darlington]." For his part, Ronne, so chary with praise, remembered Eklund, who died suddenly a few years later, as "the most pleasant sledging companion I ever had through more than six thousand miles of surface travel over the Antarctic." Carl was a "splendid companion," a hard worker and problem solver, a joke teller—in an "imitation Swedish accent" that greatly amused the Norwegian.[60]

Other unhappy camps, none so extreme as Ellsworth in 1957, can be named. Pole Station was less fortunate in 1958. Meteorologist Kirby Hanson, by common consent, became the real scientific leader when Palle Mogensen proved inactive, ineffective, and unpopular. Pole also saw a tense winter in 1959 when Dr. Sidney Tolchin, officer-in-charge, and Julian Posey, scientific leader, clashed in personality and authority. It did not help that by then the station was badly run down and a fuel shortage, discovered too late, prevented use of the new morale-serving chapel and recreation building. John Pirrit, 1959 science leader at Byrd, deadlocked with his Navy counterpart, Lieut. Edward Galla, the medical officer, over whether Byrd was a scientific or a naval base. It took a radio message from McMurdo to convince the officer-in-charge to accept dual command, Pirrit wrote: "To anyone who has not spent a winter at an isolated polar base, this may seem an incredibly childish way for adults to behave." It did to him, but neither man would "budge an inch." By then, the Navy was recognizing that to expect military and administrative leadership at a small station from a "customarily young, inexperienced" medical officer was illogical and unreasonable.[61]

The negative examples recall the early fears and opposition to the dual command structure, only to stand out as exceptions to the success of the compromise policy. Where it worked particularly well, the military and civilian station leaders made a conscious commitment to make the arrangement work. Like Eklund and Burnett, Stephen Barnes and Lieut. Peter Ruseski exemplified that spirit at Byrd Station in 1958. Barnes described how they called everyone together as soon as their long isolation began. Spelling out their goals, expectations, respective lines of authority, and determination to "function as a unified team," the two leaders publicly pledged to each other their "full cooperation and mutual understanding." They reminded everyone that every job, no matter how menial, was important to the mission and, thus, so was the person doing it. They urged tolerance to promote harmony, which would "greatly enhance the chances for a scientifically productive year." This they had. In several letters to Odishaw from Little America in 1958, Harry Francis saluted the Navy. Capt. Pat Maher was wholeheartedly supportive of the IGY and, thus, so were his men. He also credited "the attitude of our own personnel who have made a real effort to get to know the Navy personnel on a personal basis, officers and men." Things were so smooth that by September he almost yearned for a "hell-raiser" to "break the monotony."[62]

Thus, leaders mattered. They were, Navy and civilian, a varied lot, some more successful than others, most of them adequate at least. The most secure, enthusiastic leaders seemed to get the best individuals in their camps. Or did they inspire the best from the ones they got? Capt. Paul Nelson, a Navy social psychologist, later concluded that "esteemed" leaders during these formative years in Antarctica used a relatively democratic approach. He and others observed that they participated in group activities (including housekeeping and recreation), cared about and related to their charges as individuals, and sought their opinions in matters directly affecting them. They had the will, as well as the skill, to maintain group harmony. Stressing teamwork, they made sure a job could be done and that it got done. These leaders were adaptable, self-controlled, self-confident, alert, aggressive, and industrious. They were decisive, making technical decisions in consultation with appropriate specialists and emergency decisions "as quickly and autocratically as necessary under the circumstances." In isolated polar camps R. E. Strange found that effective leaders were able to "tolerate intimacy and status leveling without loss of authority and respect of the group" and were "self-reliant in the lonely responsibilities of command."[63]

Numerous psychologists tried over the years to anticipate what kinds of people would make the best nonleader Antarcticans. E. K. Eric Gunderson of the Naval Health Research Center, a leader in research on the behavior and selection of polar personnel, identified three behavioral factors as most central—emotional stability, ability (task motivation), and social compatibility. Noting a sharper drop in morale over the winter among military workers than among scientists, he concluded that dedication to specific work was key to contentment. Navy psychiatrists Strange and S. A. Youngman in 1971 agreed that the happiest people were those happy in their work: "A sense of usefulness and self-esteem is the single greatest factor in successful adjustment." New Zealander Bob Thomson, who led three harmonious stations for three different countries, was convinced that "the worst possible thing anywhere in the Antarctic is to have people with time on their hands." When bored or restless Navy men came to him, he would find a way to send them off with a significant job that needed doing.[64]

Early Deep Freeze leaders developed from their own observations unsurprisingly similar criteria. Dr. Ed Ehrlich, wintering at Little America in

LIFE ON THE ICE

1956, concluded that tangible reasons for being there, such as saving money or even escaping a difficult personal situation, were better predictors of emotional stability than some airy or romantic motivation like "pure adventure," since day-to-day polar life was circumscribed, tedious, and often boring. Pole's Dr. Howard Taylor in 1957 named a predilection for teamwork as the most important screening criterion, even above high motivation and a congenial personality. He found older men, ages thirty through forty-five, the most peaceable and able to endure hard work in adversity. He preferred individuals who were flexible and tractable—but not obsequious or unopinionated. Equally undesirable were dogmatic, imperious, or rigid types. When his charges resisted taking the periodic psychological tests all stations were supposed to administer (with similar results), Taylor devised his own study. Providing calendars, he asked everyone to evaluate each day and night during the month of May on a simple scale of 1 to 5 (worst to best). Thirteen participants produced an average score of 3.5, suggesting reasonable contentment. Admitting the crudeness of the instrument, Taylor saw no correlations with the weather (which "fortuitously" had the widest ranges of the year), weekends, movies, or holidays. Confirming the experts, he found satisfaction was best related to work.[65]

Coming from a different angle, Strange and Youngman named the stresses of "enforced intimacy" in a monotonous, socially deprived environment—not bitter cold or prolonged darkness—as the harshest challenge to polar adaptation. As Dr. Ehrlich put it at Little America, "Exposure to cold is temporary and intermittent and can be alleviated by proper clothing and shelter. In contrast to this, the exposure to the circumstances of isolation and confined living is continuous and inescapable." In such situations the "ability to withdraw emotionally into oneself is of great value" in the psychiatrists' view, as were a sense of humor and a sense of proportion, both of which typically drooped as winter deepened. While everybody suffered to some extent from disturbed sleep, depression, irritability, and even impaired cognition, Strange and Youngmann found it "refreshing and cheering" that in people "under real stress . . . emotional strength is indeed the human norm." New Zealand psychology professor A.J.W. Taylor went further, concluding that Antarctic isolation often produced such positive results as "a sense of personal discovery, a sense of achievement, the fulfillment of ambition, the membership of a special informal club, and the lifelong admiration of others who themselves have been unable to have the experience." Indeed, "[f]or many, wintering-over marks the beginning of a new stage of personal maturity." Siple believed Antarctica has "a profound effect on character and personality," adding that few are the same after they have been there.[66]

On the other hand, it was a hard fact that there would be no escape during the long winter if trouble came. If the power plant failed, they would soon die of the cold. If there was a fire, they would freeze without shelter or huddle for months in emergency quarters in extreme physical and psychological discomfort. If someone grew sick or was badly injured, there would be no possible evacuation until the light and warmth of spring. If they hated each other, they would still be imprisoned together for months in a tiny space. They were "men in a box," wrote Siple, anticipating the first winter at the South Pole. Two years later Tolchin wrote of the same, now much unhappier station that the average Pole temperature of almost -60°F "effectively maintained a type of oubliette [dungeon opening only at the top] whose prison yard was secured by six months of darkness." If some, like Ehrlich, could scarcely process so foreign a metaphor, others paused over the idea of Antarctica as prison. Dalton remembered getting off the plane at Byrd, where four squat orange buildings forlornly spotted a featureless white infinity, and consciously wondering if he would "survive emotionally or mentally. . . . I've got to live twelve whole months of my life in these little boxes. Can I do it? I didn't know. It concerned me. I'm sure everybody else had the same feeling to some degree, although I don't recall anyone ever telling me that." A few could not. After McMurdo's initiation with the troubled cook who had to be confined in Deep Freeze I, a dribble of evacuations for psychological reasons continued to thwart efforts to select well-balanced personnel. Little America sent three men home before winter in early 1958. A case of violent mental breakdown at Wilkes in late 1959 required a heroic rescue flight from McMurdo. Wilkes, 1,800 miles away, had no airfield.[67]

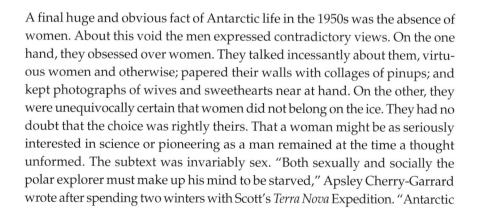

A final huge and obvious fact of Antarctic life in the 1950s was the absence of women. About this void the men expressed contradictory views. On the one hand, they obsessed over women. They talked incessantly about them, virtuous women and otherwise; papered their walls with collages of pinups; and kept photographs of wives and sweethearts near at hand. On the other, they were unequivocally certain that women did not belong on the ice. They had no doubt that the choice was rightly theirs. That a woman might be as seriously interested in science or pioneering as a man remained at the time a thought unformed. The subtext was invariably sex. "Both sexually and socially the polar explorer must make up his mind to be starved," Apsley Cherry-Garrard wrote after spending two winters with Scott's *Terra Nova* Expedition. "Antarctic work is for volunteers," Crary stated, and "deprivations are matched against gains," like money or career advancement. A man who could not give up female company for that time "would not be as apt to volunteer." Australian historian Elizabeth Chipman quoted Admiral Dufek in the *Sydney Morning Herald* on 18 September 1957 as having ruled, as if directing ship movements, that "[w]omen will not be allowed in the Antarctic until we can provide one woman for every man."[68]

Looking back, conscientious leaders such as Deep Freeze I engineering officer Dick Bowers were convinced that "women would have caused real problems in those early days," with "living conditions so primitive [and] sanitary conditions so poor." Besides the situation being difficult for women, "We had enough problems without adding sex to it." McMurdo executive officer Jim Bergstrom thought the presence of women would have made the men think they had to "watch out for the women and protect them." Dalton at Byrd in Deep Freeze II remembered realizing early on, "Thank heavens we don't [have women]." While "the sexual liberation today allows practices which would not have been available to us then," women's presence in 1957 "would not have worked. It would have been more problem than it's worth. It would have caused fights, frictions, everything. Missed them, of course."[69]

The unhappy experience of Edith Ronne and Jennie Darlington on Ronne's private expedition a decade earlier did not encourage further experimenting with mixing the sexes on the ice either, although Chipman believed this had less to do with the women's performance than the fact that governments began taking over what had been private expeditionary activity: "Governments of the 1950s did not, as a rule, seem to consider even the possibility of women taking part in their scientific expeditions." Beyond the three women scientists aboard the *Ob* that exchange meteorologist Gordon Cartwright reported and perhaps as many as a dozen female crew members on other Soviet vessels, there were no women anywhere in the Antarctic during the period.[70]

Boyer, who ghostwrote, or at least coached, some of Dufek's writing for the *National Geographic*, sent him a memorandum of thoughts for a piece on polar achievements that would appear in the October 1959 issue. Boyer encouraged the admiral to discuss women in the Antarctic: "You've always been against it, and rightly." Besides Dufek's own views, Boyer suggested one "basic" reason he had been hearing: "If women come down here, it would no longer be a place where men could go and come back from as 'heroes.' The men would resent women. They did resent even those two airline hostesses that landed for 30 minutes [at McMurdo in October 1957]. This has always been a he-man's world, with beards and toughness. Women would wreck the illusion. But they will do it one day." Dufek duly wrote that he opposed having women in Antarctica for the "simple reason that during the construction period there was no place for them." And he told how some men had avoided the comely flight attendants so they could "say that from the time they left civilization until they returned, they hadn't seen a woman!" He continued, "Eventually women will come to the Antarctic. They will prod, probe, and climb with the rest of us. They will help us open the Antarctic, as the pioneering women of early America crossed our country to open the West. We really need them." But still assuming male prerogative, he concluded, "I don't want to be the Solomon to have to decide who is to be the *first* woman to reach the South Pole." As psychologist Taylor put Boyer's explanation, "Men kept the women out because they needed to prove to themselves that they had the indomitable qualities that would enable them to triumph over deprivation and adversity." It would be nearly fifteen years after Deep Freeze I before U.S. women saw the ice in a professional capacity.[71]

So it was that Antarctica posed many paradoxes. The continent was huge, without physical fences or political barriers. The men could freely go anywhere; horizons were limitless. Yet the barren hostility of the environment restricted life to narrow confines, in winter not much beyond the station walls. They could feel isolated and alone, deprived of normal human society, especially that of their significant others. Yet they faced a lack of privacy and enforced intimacy with the same few people in the same small space day after day. When there was no word from outside support institutions, they felt abandoned: "No one cares." Yet when guidance arrived, they complained that someone who knew nothing about conditions was presuming to order them around. They yearned for new faces as well as supplies, mail, and news. Yet after the first welcome, they and their fellows, whose routines had evolved after months of living together, resented the newcomers as disrespectful, insensitive intruders. They railed against their monasticism. Yet they fought to preserve their male domain.

And despite, or perhaps because of, it all, their year in Antarctica had been an incredible experience—one known by only a handful of humans before them. Boyer mused to his family that practically everyone thought life on the ice was "entirely unnatural" and wished he were "somewhere else, almost anywhere. And yet, the strangest thing happens"—he kept meeting people he had seen there before. "What is it," he asked, that "impels men to forsake wives, children, decency, bathing facilities, and all the amenities of life to come down to a place like this and live like animals? Is that what masculinity is? To be ridiculously brave? Maybe so."[72] It was his second trip. Whatever it was, scores of veterans, IGY and Navy, would return—some of them over and over. They would have that opportunity because the IGY would not be closed out and put on a shelf. Indeed, Antarctica's future had already begun.

SCIENCE AND PEACE, CONTINUITY AND CHANGE

It was in the coldest of all the continents that there was the first memorable thaw in the cold war.

—Laurence M. Gould, 1960[1]

Science leaders pressed to continue the IGY in Antarctica, which required that the many players—with their differing issues, varying means, and complex interrelationships—agree on new organizational mechanisms. Diplomatic leaders were concluding that an internationalized Antarctica might best serve their own and others' interests. And seizing this moment could perpetuate the informal IGY moratorium on political squabbling over territorial claims even as Cold War suspicions, covered over for the IGY with wary resolve (and remarkable success), persisted. Delicate, protracted secret talks yielded the pathbreaking Antarctic Treaty of 1959, which, even with its limitations and potential pitfalls, has held and grown. The polar south continues to reveal its secrets as science programs have broadened and matured and essential support functions have evolved. The continent has become more comfortable, clean, diverse, and visited.

In early December 1956, seven months before the International Geophysical Year officially began, the United States National Committee (USNC) cabled the CSAGI (special international committee created to plan and implement the IGY) Bureau in Brussels to urge a one-year extension of the Antarctic program—to enhance the scientific and financial return on investment. Despite scientists' enthusiasm, though, the twelve participating nations divided on the issue at the Fourth Antarctic Conference in Paris in mid-June 1957. Australia stood against any pretext for lengthening Soviet occupation of its claimed territory. Britain, in support, opposed extension, as did Chile. New Zealand reserved its position pending review of current results, tying its decision to the value of the science to humanity. France and Japan tentatively approved but doubted that additional government funding would be forthcoming. The United States, USSR, Argentina, and Belgium favored carrying on. South Africa was "noncommittal." The absent Norway had earlier been negative. Yet a suggestion that convener Georges Laclavère head up Antarctic affairs after the IGY was greeted with warm applause. Then, in September, at an ad hoc Antarctic meeting in Stockholm, Mikhail Somov, who had led the Soviets' 1955–1957 Antarctic expedition, "electrified the group by calmly announcing that the USSR intended to continue all of their present and proposed stations." With that, chief scientist Harry Wexler went on, "the last bit of opposition, if there was any, collapsed."[2]

Thereupon invited by the parent International Council of Scientific Unions (ICSU) Bureau, most of the twelve states and five international scientific unions sent delegates to The Hague, Netherlands, in February 1958 to establish a Special (becoming Scientific in 1961) Committee on Antarctic Research (SCAR). Gould grandly announced "large-scale scientific operations," with South Pole the top U.S. priority. All Soviet stations would "probably continue," Somov said, later growing more expansive. Others voiced more modest, generally downsized goals; several asked for financial and logistical help. They all agreed to promote new efforts in geology, biology, cartography, physiology, and oceanography and defined Antarctica as bounded approximately by the Antarctic Convergence. They elected Laclavère president and adopted a constitution that directed SCAR to formulate and coordinate post-IGY polar science programs to be implemented, as in the IGY, by the members' national committees with government funding. They entitled countries active in polar research (and the unions) to one "permanent" scientific delegate and planned for dues (a sliding scale based on the number of wintering personnel). SCAR began in expectation that Antarctic science would enjoy a long life.[3]

In early August 1958, at the fifth CSAGI meeting in Moscow, the international community acted formally to prolong the IGY ideal, as proposed by the Soviet National Committee, whose members thirsted for prestige at home and opportunities to interact abroad. "It was more difficult, in Moscow, to get a new policy decision than to get more money for research," wrote Walter Sullivan, so the Soviets favored keeping the IGY name and organization, "whereas in Washington the reverse was true." U.S. politics decreed that the "one-shot" IGY must end as promised. Compromising, the delegates resolved to continue their respective efforts for one year, at a level of each country's choosing. They agreed to a new name, but one that suggested continuity—the International Geophysical Cooperation–1959 (IGC-59)—for what they trusted would be an interim period.[4]

Both the international enthusiasm and ambivalence were mirrored at home. Odishaw was seen as taking any opportunity to promote extension. Returning from the ice in early 1957, Gould told foreign officers and reporters in Wellington that scientific activity in Antarctica should continue for at least eighteen additional months. He emphasized not science but politics: if the USSR stayed, the United States had no choice. Robert E. Wilson of the State Department's Office of Inter-American Regional Political Affairs was aghast. Neither State nor the Operations Coordinating Board's Antarctic Working Group wanted other countries, especially the guarded claimants, thinking USNC proposals were government policy. And he was sure neither the cautious National Science Foundation (NSF) nor the lukewarm Navy would appreciate Gould's "freewheeling." His more emphatic colleague Earl Luboeansky stated that Antarctica had shown the Department of Defense a "complete lack of military significance," while parsimony described the "current temperament" of the Treasury Department and Budget Bureau. State had yet to formulate its policy, but Wilson was already thinking science should decide the issue; the Soviets would stay or go for their own reasons.[5]

A political nudge came in a January 1958 letter to the president from Congressman Oren Harris (D-Arkansas), who had just led members of the House Committee on Interstate and Foreign Commerce on an "extended study" of IGY field activities, with "special attention" to Antarctica. Deeply impressed, he urged that Antarctic research be continued—especially because intelligence reports had convinced him that "should we abandon the [South Pole] station, Russia would immediately move in." Gould, who had initially grumped about "shepherding" the politicians on their "junket," quickly changed his mind. Harris, he penned to NSF director Alan Waterman from McMurdo, "is an intelligent and perceptive man and he is seeing things right!!!" His committee could be helpful. (Today, too, work stops on the ice, mindfully if sometimes impatiently, for the education and cultivation of well-placed DVs.)[6]

In February, as SCAR first met, the National Academy of Sciences (NAS) formed a Committee on Polar Research (CPR; after 1975, the Polar Research Board) to help NSF plan post-IGY Antarctic science and to collaborate with SCAR through the NAS membership in ICSU. The committee envisioned a U.S. IGC program broadened like the one discussed abroad but found NSF, the funnel for federal funds, maddeningly dilatory. In July 1957 Odishaw had sent over an IGC program plan and a preliminary budget of $5.5 million. But repeated reminders, even reduced numbers, stirred little apparent action. Not until May 1958 did the CPR learn that Congress had approved $1 million for the 1959 program and NSF had committed another $1 million from its regular appropriation to finance specific projects. The Navy would supply all logistics needs as before, despite the exceedingly late date. Indeed, Dufek was so unclear about intentions that austral summer on the ice that he dispatched a Super Constellation to fly Phil Smith back to Washington to ascertain whether he should evacuate or resupply: "So there I was, a kind of junior officer at the Academy, being sent as an emissary by my friend Dufek to come back and try to help force a decision by explaining the fact that we could not delay much longer." Fortunately, the "excess in planning and oversupply that had gone on in Deep Freeze I, II, and III" made the added year possible.[7]

This budget did not include funds for the two remotest stations, whose long, tortuous supply lines were too expensive to sustain. The United States offered Australia the buildings and equipment if it would run Wilkes Station after the IGY. Despite the costs, Australia agreed. Anxious about its rights and interests, Australia knew it would be difficult to extract the Soviets from its claim while the Americans remained. Ellsworth was similarly transferred to Argentina. Britain dallied too long to be included in a tripartite merger of these neighboring stations. (A quirky legal problem arose. Without recognizing territorial sovereignty, there was no jurisdiction through which to act. So the receiving nations simply signed custody receipts for the property, subject to return on demand less losses from normal usage. No returns were ever made or expected.) In the IGY spirit, U.S. scientists, some of them IGY veterans, would work at both stations. Pole meteorologist Floyd Johnson wintered over with the Argentines in 1959—and, involuntarily, in 1960 when the Ellsworth relief ship, just seventy miles away, could push no closer. The meteorology building then burned, rendering the doubled tour incomparably longer.[8]

Little America, weighted with accumulating snow, was slated for closure, although Gould told Congress this was "a major disservice to science" and "unfortunate for our prestige." Wexler fought for months to save Antarctica's oldest meteorological effort, his hopes no doubt fanned by resident administrator Harry Francis's glowing monthly reports. On 26 May 1958 Francis wrote to Odishaw that another year of Navy improvements like the last "could turn this place into a resort, or near to it." By then the station boasted over sixty buildings and passageways. After roasting in the fine new sauna, three zany Little Americans went out to meet the season's first plane, at more than twenty below, wearing only their hopefully-still-steaming birthday suits. Aboard was a team of "shrinks" coming to interview them, recalled communications officer Frank Stokes, one of the "arguably deranged" greeters. "I must say that people are beginning to show signs of wear and tear down here," Francis wrote in December, not mentioning the al fresco caper, which he might equally have cited as evidence or antidote.[9]

Francis wrapped up the myriad details, arranging to ship 175,000 pounds of IGY cargo by plane, ship, or tractor train to Byrd, Pole, McMurdo, and the United States. By year's end "Little A" had begun to "disintegrate," wrote a subdued David Boyer. Apart from the "wan little electric heater" that warmed his "cubbyhole," the building was "cold as ice . . . quiet as a tomb." On 19 January 1959 the *Staten Island* evacuated the already decommissioned station. Stokes, in charge of the last ten people, turned out the lights. In the Antarctic spirit, he left emergency provisions sufficient to sustain sixteen people for a year.[10]

Despite Somov's swelling rhetoric, the Soviets cut back their expensive program too, closing down Sovietskaya, Pionerskaya, and Oazis in January 1959. The latter they turned over to Poland, but neither the relationship nor the intended Polish program proved workable. Komsomolskaya became a summer weather station and logistics base.[11]

The fiscal 1960 budget season, which would shape the future of U.S. Antarctic science, not to mention a respectable conclusion to IGC-59, was a tense repeat of the year before. Academy leaders, fearing international "embarrassment," fumed at NSF's timorous sluggishness and refusal to commit to the IGY's "integrated package" approach. Waterman called that approach a "mere continuation of data gathering" and urged NAS to get scientists to submit more research proposals. In early 1959 Odishaw sent Waterman, with one more testy USNC resolution, a copy of Soviet plans, noting without subtlety, "It appears quite certain that the USSR sees clearly the scientific importance and leadership value of a broad and comprehensive contribution to the IGC-59 world effort." But the young agency was constrained by administration policy, which directed that post-IGY activities be funded through NSF's regular programs, and by its own mission and culture of supporting individual scientists. The philosophical disagreement persisted in numerous snappish exchanges.[12]

If, indeed, "NAS-NSF relationships were at the crossroads," as CPR member Merle Tuve declared at one strained meeting, the issue was decided by the formation of the U.S. Antarctic Research Program (USARP) in March 1959 within the National Science Foundation. Headed by Antarctic program officer Thomas Jones, with Albert Crary as chief scientist, this governmental unit would coordinate all U.S. Antarctic efforts and manage their overall budget (NSF's first such experience). Generally following the agency's normal investigator-initiated funding procedures, USARP would seek the "authoritative opinion" of the NAS Committee on Polar Research on emerging research issues and, through SCAR, on international developments. The committee, first chaired by Gould, came to "assume a broad policy and advisory position," especially in long-range planning, which a politically funded agency cannot easily do. As Smith, then a USARP staffer who served as a "go-between" in transferring NAS's IGY operational functions to NSF, put it, "A long time is the life of a senator—six years." In the end, USARP oversaw a creditable U.S. IGC program, funding forty of fifty-three individual IGC proposals for about $1.8 million.[13]

In addition, USARP would arrange for ongoing logistical support from the Navy and other military services. Admiral Dufek, retiring from Operation Deep Freeze, feared putting the Foundation in charge would "prove fatal" to U.S. economic, political, and strategic interests because NSF would "neglect" these interests in its "preoccupation" with science. Perhaps that was another factor in the Navy's determination not to yield the field to others, even as it increasingly questioned the strategic value of the polar continent (though the tantalizing possibility of finding mineral resources remained).[14]

The Navy surely envisioned a long haul in Antarctica when in Deep Freeze I it began to search for a more reliable, permanent dry-land runway site. A year after the Seabees' Detachment Golf found Cape Royds and the Dry Valleys unsuitable, a small reconnaissance team helicoptered in to check out Marble Point, a small, flat, mostly snow-free finger of glacial till across McMurdo Sound from Cape Royds. In 1957–1958 Lt. Cmdr. Hank Stephens, Ellsworth's construction engineer who now commanded MCB One, returned to conduct a then-classified feasibility study. As he recalled it, this air base would have served both Deep Freeze needs and anticipated commercial flights. If viable, Marble Point would likely have supplanted McMurdo as the U.S. logistics base.[15]

Stephens's handpicked crew, military and civilian, immediately met trouble. Heavy equipment arriving by ship could not be delivered by tractor train in early summer because the bay ice had pulled away from shore, leaving a channel of open water, while pontoon barges were useless until more ice went out late in the season. So VX-6 had to deliver the seventy-five tons of equipment and supplies by air. The Seabees managed to build a rough 1,700-foot runway laid with three squarish test pads, one each of asphalt, sheet aluminum, and concrete. On 31 January 1958 an Otter carrying Dufek and Hillary made the first wheels-on-dirt landing in Antarctica. Unfortunately, a year later another Otter crashed on takeoff, killing both pilots. But Stephens's team had already recommended against Marble Point. Ship off-loading would always be problematic. Invariably, thick and hummocked ice made early re-supply, by either tractor or ship, impractical and the usable season short. Then budget support disappeared. While a later study again examined the issue and Capt. Brian Shoemaker, Deep Freeze commander in the 1980s, promoted the idea for strategic reasons, a permanent runway on land has never been built south of the Antarctic Peninsula. Today, small environmental cleanup crews are hand-removing scrap materials left from those early forays. A tiny outpost now serves as the "gas station" and hospitable lunch stop for Dry Valleys–bound helicopters.[16]

Operation Deep Freeze IV, like IGC-59, was a holding operation; but the next year, Deep Freeze 60, was anything but. The passing of the Antarctic naval command from Dufek to Admiral David Tyree in April 1959 marked the transition to a new era. Significantly, Tyree brought scientific, not polar, experience to the job. He and USARP's Jones would carry forward the example set by Dufek and Gould who, by task-force historian Henry Dater's analysis, had brought the IGY to a "triumphant conclusion," modeling how to make the awkward dual command system work with mutual respect and a "tradition of direct dealing." Tyree—in charge of eight ships, three dozen aircraft, and 3,000 men from all the military services—would, as during the IGY, transport personnel and supplies, support science in the field, maintain the four continuing U.S. stations, and look after U.S. interests, too.[17]

Repair and expansion of the weather-beaten IGY stations also signaled the Navy's long-term commitment. By 1960–1961, using an Army technique developed in Greenland, Navy crews were erecting four new structures at Byrd in long trenches they then arched over with steel to make tunnels, effectively sinking the camp below the surface so wind-driven snow would blow right over and onward. One plan for rebuilding Pole called for raising the station on stilts so snow could blow beneath it, but for the time, Dater wrote, the Navy chose a "careful program of rehabilitation." The growing McMurdo emerged as a science center in 1959 when the Navy built a laboratory, named for Carl Eklund, for research in the biological and medical sciences.[18]

The Navy's acquisition of ski-equipped C-130 Hercules turboprop cargo planes in August 1960 revolutionized Antarctic operations. The Lockheed-built "Hercs," which could land on ice or snow, abruptly ended the era of airdrops and tractor trains—which would not be missed. Besides their skis, which the front-loading C-124s could not accommodate, their speed, range, cargo capacity, reliability beyond their tested weight limits, and efficiency at cold temperatures made them ideal for Antarctic use, according to Earl ("Buz") Dryfoose, the first Navy pilot qualified in one. They flew at 30,000 feet, unlike the R4Ds that labored to clear the Beardmore Glacier by 1,000 feet en route to the polar plateau, and they made McMurdo to Pole in three hours, not eight. Their "unheard of" cockpit spaciousness made them "truly a pleasure to fly." In addition to freight, Hercs could land scientific parties in the field, complete with land vehicles and prefabricated, ski-mounted shelters. Scientists no longer had to winter over to reap a full summer season, and their range vastly expanded. These sturdy, dependable, barrel-chested aircraft, since 1962 called LC-130 (the "L" denoting the ski configuration), remain the backbone of Antarctic transport. So rugged are they that during Deep Freeze 88, Navy crews recovered one that had lain buried in "concrete-like" snow for more than fifteen years since crashing in remote East Antarctica. Originally thought beyond practical salvage, it was fully restored and still flies.[19]

Thus was the environment set for a broader Antarctic science program. In fact, little would be different except for emphasis, since a number of non-IGY fields

Author with Antarctic Deep Freeze Association partners Richard Bowers (left) and James Bergstrom at VXE-6 disestablishment ceremonies at Point Mugu, California, March 1999. This LC-130 Hercules crashed and was abandoned to the ice for years but after restoration was still flying. Courtesy, James Miller.

were already receiving small-scale, sometimes unofficial attention. Having fallen on the sword of politics during the IGY, geology now gained legitimacy, and, indeed, the suppressed minerals "rush" resumed. The CPR, meeting to plan the fiscal 1960 program, sounded as political as scientific in urging the nation "to initiate the strongest possible Antarctic geological program," especially in "those lesser known areas where original exploration was made by the U.S." While official records said nothing about mining or claims, interest in geology was unmistakably focused there. Bill Long, 1958–1959 Byrd traverse glaciologist who returned for three summers in the early 1960s with NSF grants for geological studies, later chuckled over getting blackened in the "Dirty Diamond Mine" while trying to obtain an unweathered coal sample. In fact, no economically viable minerals have yet been discovered, and international agreement now forbids their exploitation.[20]

The CSAGI delegates in Moscow also agreed to a Soviet IGC proposal to develop a uniform method of aerial photography toward compiling a single map (scale 1:3,000,000) of Antarctica. Earlier, the United States had rejected USSR-proposed aerial mapping as an IGY science in view of its "quasi-political" nature. The Soviets mapped significant areas anyway (as did others, including U.S. flyers and traversers); now this program could be done cooperatively. Gradually, the tentatively dotted coastlines would become lines and the blank interior filled in with newly named physical features and human outposts.[21]

Oceanography, though a focus of the IGY worldwide, was offshore and usually not listed among the U.S. IGY sciences in Antarctica. The icebreakers, with their own need to know the largely unplumbed Southern Ocean, fanned out to cover as much area as possible within the limits of their primary tasks and the temptations of the shortest route. The two hours required to do a "station" (the entire program conducted at one location) was time lost to ship movement, which the pressed captains were sometimes reluctant to give—especially on return voyages laughed Bill Littlewood, citing "the horse-to-the-barn factor." Dynamic sea-ice conditions thwarted the best-laid plans, while windy, icy decks threatened safety and accomplishment. Yet just during Deep Freeze III on the *Glacier* alone, Littlewood and four Navy assistants completed 35 oceanographic stations; 1,036 bathygrams using hourly drops of a bathythermograph, a device for recording temperature versus depth (actually pressure); and 1,025 surface salinity measurements. The team recorded continuous bottom profiles (by precision depth recorder), measured tidal movements, logged ice conditions and characteristics, and dredged and preserved marine fauna. They plotted current systems and refined the Convergence, calculated the water budget of the oceans, and, using radioactive isotopes from many depths, dated water masses—all work that expanded greatly in later years.[22]

The uniqueness of Antarctic wildlife invited attention to biology despite its nongeophysical nature. As early as 1956 the IGY offices began receiving a few life-science proposals, but busy staff gave them little encouragement. Carl Eklund, an exception, garnered specific approval to conduct animal research during his IGY tour at Wilkes. Most important was his distribution and life-history study of the South Polar Skua, the "real glamour bird of the south" in his proud bias. He found these "eagle[s] of Antarctica" to be fearless, graceful, clean (parasite-free), and smart enough to work in pairs to distract parent penguins while snatching their progeny. Observers from seven nations at eighteen stations helped Eklund band and track hundreds of skuas. Around animal-rich Wilkes Station, Eklund also did numerical, biological, and behavioral investigations of all four species of Antarctic seals and various nesting birds. Byrd's astonished traversers encountered the nearly fresh southerly track of a solitary penguin on New Year's Day 1958, more than 175 miles inland. They followed the tobogganing bird's belly trough, interspersed with the footprints of upright walking, measuring size and movement, but they never caught up with the confused, or reclusive, creature. William J.L. Sladen of Johns Hopkins University later identified the loner as an Adélie or possibly a rarer Chinstrap penguin.[23]

In 1957–1958 lichenologist George Llano found a remarkable array of botanical species clinging to stunted, meager life. Meltwater and dark rock or volcanic soil warmed by even a thin layer of solar radiation nourished the Lilliputian plants. On the 1,500-foot headland of Cape Hallett, he credited the powdered, updrafted guano of myriad penguins for lichen growth "luxurious out of all proportion to its surroundings." The exposed land around Wilkes Station, aided by abundant birds and the tempering effects of open sea, sported the richest vegetation overall. Byrd traverser Dan Hale collected over sixty specimens of lichens on nunatak slopes. Similarities among these and others suggested separate though similar evolutionary paths, while differences indicated unlike conditions. Distribution patterns in the Sentinel Mountains told of a once lower level of ice. Deeper inland, lichen species grew sparser and more dwarfed, as shown by Ellsworth and Byrd traverse collections at 82° and 78° South, respectively.[24]

Interest in medical research surfaced early. In 1956 Kaare Rodahl, director of research at the Air Force's Arctic Aeromedical Laboratory in Seattle, proposed to study acclimatization by looking at energy expenditure and thermal balance in cold, as measured by oxygen consumption, production and loss of body heat, thyroid function, and blood changes. At Little America physiologist Fred Milan wired up eight volunteers to record heat at various parts of their bodies, finding that at –40°F skin and hand temperatures fell steadily. Most of the medical research, however, was nonsystematic. With varying degrees of rigor, the relatively untaxed station physicians addressed concerns from diurnal rhythms to the suitability of issued clothing. Limited studies in psychology included IGY staffer William Smith's analyses of selection and performance data, group structure and dynamics, and psychiatric evaluations of wintering personnel to improve future selection criteria. After the IGY, biology, broadly defined, soon became a major polar program.[25]

Most of the IGY's geophysical sciences continued at varying levels into the new era. With ice so elemental and ubiquitous, long-distance traverses still commanded money and attention. Two U.S. traverse parties ventured forth during the IGC summer, 1959–1960. John Pirrit led one from Byrd Station north to the Amundsen Sea, where the team thrilled at viewing open blue water, and on to the Executive Committee and Hal Flood ranges for geological and geodetic studies. One day, in the quiet of walking to an outcropping, they heard a "heavy rushing noise" and were astounded to discover a "vigorous" sixty-foot waterfall. While they watched, shadows from the lowering sun crept up the slope; the gush became a trickle, then ceased. Pirrit speculated that this "most ephemeral of all falls" existed for a few hours on a few summer days when the sun's noontime heat sufficiently warmed the black rocks to liquefy the ice. The other group ascended the Skelton Glacier (finding caches left by both Hillary and Crary) and crossed the Victoria Land plateau to connect with the end point of a French traverse from Charcot Station the previous year. Crevasses prevented their intended descent through the Transantarctics, and they were evacuated by R4D—another example, in geologist John Weihaupt's mind, of the Navy's "really exceptional" support.[26]

That same summer the Russians fulfilled a long-standing goal, attaining the Geographic South Pole on 26 December 1959 by tractor train from Mirny, via Komsomolskaya and Vostok. The fifth overland party to reach the Pole, they were the first from East Antarctica. The first Americans to reach the Pole overland did so the following season, 1960–1961, from Byrd Station. Chief Walter Davis, Ellsworth mechanic who had just wintered at Byrd, accompanied Maj. Antero Havola of the Army Transportation Corps on this heaviest U.S. traverse. Arriving on 11 January 1961, they delivered two D-8 tractors to the station at Ninety South. That same year Crary returned for his final field season to lead a traverse from McMurdo to Pole—to his knowledge, becoming the first person ever to stand at both geographic poles. His eight-man crew included Sven Evteev, a Soviet exchange scientist who had served on the first Soviet IGY expedition and had just wintered at McMurdo.[27]

Indeed, SCAR leaders had agreed in Moscow to reinstate the valuable IGY international exchange program, which had lapsed in 1959, perhaps because of the late IGC planning. Crary recruited Wilkes seismologist Gil Dewart to winter over with the Soviets at Mirny in 1960. After thinking "long and hard" about the effect of another year on his career, Dewart found himself "drawn gravitationally, irresistibly" by the idea that two opposing political forces were "threatening this mutual annihilation, and here I have a chance to do something about it." After a fulfilling year on station, he accompanied a Soviet traverse to Vostok—an even exchange of experiences with his counterpart Evteev.[28]

Meanwhile, the University of Wisconsin, with its strong cadre of geophysicists headed by George Woollard, took over the traverse contract, and many traverse scientists went there to work up their data. They coordinated their work with glaciologists doing analogous analyses at Ohio State University and geomagnetists at the U.S. Coast and Geodetic Survey in Washington. They were busy. Ships returned about twenty-seven tons of scientific data, much of it on computer punchcards, to the United States. Eventually, everything would be transferred to the World Data Centers, where any scholar anywhere would have access. These centers, now nearly fifty strong around the globe, continue to receive new data. They represent a key legacy of the IGY. Fittingly, World Data Center letterhead still features the IGY logo.[29]

During the scientific transition in Antarctica, the IGY underwent several assessments. While different sources included different categories of expenditures and variously compared the numerous currencies, the world seems to have spent about a billion dollars on the IGY, "as high as $2 billion, including logistical support," wrote Harold Bullis, science and technology analyst of the Congressional Research Service. All analysts noted how little went to running the international program, including CSAGI publications and meeting costs. By the ICSU Bureau's figures, "[T]he global budget of the IGY 1957–58 amounted to the equivalent of some hundreds of millions of dollars; the annual cost of the central secretariat in Brussels, from its inception in 1953 to the end of 1958, was of the order of $50,000." Gould would later marvel that "at its peak the whole international secretariat consisted of but eight people."[30]

Congress appropriated $43.5 million for the U.S. IGY, almost half of which went to the orbiting satellite effort (offset some by agency and university contributions), according to Bullis. Before it was over, logistical support increased the U.S. outlay to about $500 million. By NAS figures of 28 May 1958, the technical programs, apart from logistics and other expenses, would cost about $18.2 million, $4.9 million in Antarctica. Of the latter, meteorology was by far the largest item at $1.2 million. Ionospheric physics, with its expensive equipment, came next at $850,000, then glaciology at $577,000. Most disciplines spent considerably less.[31]

Much of the success of the IGY must be credited to the genius, intentional or not, of its organizers. Because ICSU invited the world's scientists directly, through scientific organizations, the planning could proceed without antagonistic governments having to face one another formally, remembered Philip Mange, former member of CSAGI secretary Marcel Nicolet's staff. Likewise, since the individual programs were "national," the scientists' national committees could appeal to their respective governments to fund just their own programs (plus perhaps a little for CSAGI). The IGY had no need for an international managing body—which would never have found acceptance in those suspicious times. As Bullis put it, "The IGY was thus an international scientific enterprise, operated by scientists with the consent, cooperation, and support of their individual governments, but in effect without the direction of these governments."[32]

While no one would suggest an absence of political motivations, CSAGI maintained a firm policy of "welcoming scientific cooperation without regard to national political outlook," as Mange wrote, and Laclavère brought that leadership example to the Antarctic program. Gould recalled "a simplicity, a flexibility and freedom from political consideration hitherto unknown." Had the "apparent détente reflected in this one scientific enterprise" been "overpraised and undercriticized"? Bullis searched for criticism but found none. If Sullivan overreached in pronouncing that the IGY "marked a major turning point in history," if the Cold War would go on as before in other realms, some light had shone on a dark world. For the NAS's Atwood, science had proven itself a rare common language among humankind and shown that it "could facilitate the attainment of peaceful objectives of foreign policy."[33]

Indeed, as IGY planning revived Antarctica in political consciousness, foreign policy makers bent their antennae to its broader ramifications. Inevitably, attention centered on the chronic conundrum of territorial claims and fears of Soviet designs. In early 1957, for example, the Commonwealth claimants pressured the United States to assert a claim—to implicitly strengthen their own. Australia was especially anxious, having reluctantly "consented" to Russian IGY teams in its territory, along with homeland overflights (under rigid conditions) and ships' service calls (though not aircraft landings). "Strictly off the record," C. J. Audland of the British Embassy was even "prepared to come to some sort of an understanding" over a U.S. claim that infringed on Britain's own. But on the eve of the IGY these countries changed their minds, not wanting to contravene the spirit of the IGY or "precipitate a similar Soviet action."[34]

Having long dithered over claims, U.S. policy makers were no less discomposed than their nervous counterparts. The strict 1924 Hughes Doctrine had not deterred U.S. claims quests. Byrd's naming of Marie Byrd Land was an implicit U.S. claim, wrote Gould, who himself had left a claim cairn in the Queen Maud Mountains in 1929. Other Americans had also scattered claim sheets like confetti. None was ever officially acted upon, to Gould's lasting dismay. The building of "permanent" settlements to justify broad claims, even under Hughes's standards, motivated Roosevelt's establishment of the U.S. Antarctic Service in January 1939. In 1940, Secretary of State Cordell Hull sought to extend the Monroe Doctrine to the Pole. After the war, expanding the basis for U.S. claims persisted as a central goal of Operation Highjump and the State Department's 1948 eight-nation condominium proposal. To join the seven claimant states, State was poised to announce a sweeping U.S. claim that, ignoring the sector precedent, included basically all U.S.-explored territory. Most claimants were, not surprisingly, disinclined to support this plan, and it was moribund by the time the Soviet Union took official, negative notice of it in 1950.[35]

Even in Deep Freeze I, carrying out NSC policy trumped the Navy's command responsibility to serve the IGY in the Antarctic. That policy called for "orderly progress" toward solving territorial problems in a way that would keep the United States and friendly nations in control, providing them (only) freedom to explore, do scientific research, and access natural resources. Task Force 43 was instructed to establish "permanent stations" on the ice in support of U.S. "rights." The State Department, too, wanted the U.S. IGY program "designated in support" of permanent occupation of areas claimed or that "might later be claimed." According to treaty scholar Philip Quigg, "During 1956 and 1957 alone, the United States deposited thirty-one claims in various parts of Antarctica, including the South Pole." Members of Congress, the press, and the public demanded polar ascendancy as an earned "right" and a necessity to ward off the villainous Communists.[36]

A claim based in history on economic activity (sealing, whaling) or military expeditions (Wilkes, Highjump) or, especially, the extensive twentieth-century American explorations could scarcely be challenged. But what to claim? The wedge of Marie Byrd Land between longitudes 90° and 150° West seemed obvious; it was clearly American by argument of discovery and the only sector still unclaimed. (That would also leave nothing for the USSR to appropriate, and to the extent there was a U.S. Antarctic policy, it was to keep the Russians out.) But that wedge was comparatively small (about 20 percent of the landmass) and unapproachable by ice-choked sea. Moreover, as IGY traverse teams were proving, much of it lay below sea level.[37]

Within a flurry of conflicting policy analyses came the State Department legal office's advice at the end of 1956 to press a claim at the "earliest possible date." At an April 1957 NSC Planning Board meeting, Admiral Dufek promoted an expansive, intrusive claim, with the aim of gradually forming a condominium, while General Cutler questioned "buying a pig in a poke." Interior and NSF officers thought too little was known to make a good choice and feared a claim might "stop the flow of scientific information from the Russians which we need badly." When the idea of claiming the "American sector" and reserving unspecified rights elsewhere gained traction, Wilson wearily viewed it as "probably not more ambiguous" than another approach, perhaps "something to bargain with." But such a policy would assume the current claimants' cooperation and imply abandonment of the U.S. policy of nonrecognition. In June 1957 new National Security Policy (NSC 5715/1) called for advancing a large U.S. claim but maintaining "the utmost secrecy until IGY considerations are no longer a factor."[38]

Yet the risks lurking in claiming anything at all began to invite new kinds of questions. Was Antarctica's strategic value sufficient to justify the expense of maintaining and defending a claim? Would staking a claim that restricted other countries' rights in an area, including access, mean having to accept restricted U.S. rights elsewhere on the continent? What if the choice proved poor, that is, mineral-poor? Would a competing claim so anger the now-friendly claimant countries as to compromise their united stand against the Soviets? Would making a claim incite the Soviets to do likewise? What would a claim cost in criticism for violating the IGY freeze on political activity, not to mention to IGY spirit?[39]

An international agreement began to look both promising and timely. Smoothly continuing the peaceable IGY offered a ready context and an appealing rationale. Secretary of State Dulles called Ambassador Paul C. Daniels from retirement to head a diplomatic effort toward a treaty. Daniels boasted little Antarctic experience, but his Latin American expertise included detailed knowledge of the Anglo-Chilean-Argentine conflicts in the polar south, surely some of the prickliest challenges to be faced: Argentina harped that the British flag flew over Las Islas Malvinas (Falkland Islands on UK maps) "only through an iniquitous aggression." Chile declared its Antarctic claim a dependency of its southernmost province and a geologically proven extension of the motherland. Britain, listing but five "mutually recognized" sectors on the "present-day map," asked the International Court of Justice to arbitrate its "actively disputed" claims but knew Chile and Argentina would reject the court's jurisdiction.[40]

Daniels hoped to move quickly—before the end of the IGY and preferably before the next United Nations General Assembly—to forestall a resolution for UN control. In 1956 India had, in fact, proposed that the 11th UN General Assembly take up "the peaceful utilization of Antarctica," citing its strategic, climatic, geophysical, and economic significance to the entire world. Despite having initially proposed a UN trusteeship for Antarctica in 1948, U.S. leaders now feared that sheer numbers, sparse interest, and Communist influence would thwart favorable decision making in the global forum. Eventually, India withdrew the (likely rejected) agenda item to allow the IGY to proceed without political interference. In mid-1958 India would renew its UN proposal and once again withdraw it, this time out of respect for the treaty effort—to much relief among the Antarctic "householders."[41]

Who to include in treaty talks became a key question. The seven claimants, of course—Argentina, Australia, Chile, France, Great Britain, New Zealand, and Norway. As for the U.S. goal to exclude the Soviets, they were already in the Antarctic, working cooperatively, doing first-rate science, and planning to stay. Nothing short of force would likely dislodge them. A snub could incite them to intensify their polar activity, ratchet up political tensions, and discredit any resulting treaty—with some logic and perhaps international sympathy. The two main adversaries' positions were, in fact, similar. Neither had a claim or recognized anyone else's. Both reserved the right to make one. Both had stations in other countries' claims. If the Americans had a stronger historical record in Antarctica, the Russians brought superior infrastructure from their north-polar experience. Inviting them to the parley, as urged by the British, among others, would give them no new legal status in Antarctica; and, greatly outnumbered by friendly states, they could be more easily watched within the circle. So that unpalatable course came to seem not only more defensible but also more opportune. Far East experts urged inviting IGY-participant Japan. Marshall Green thought an Asian representative would lessen the look of a "strictly white man's club." Antarctic authority Outerbridge Horsey, posted in Tokyo, stressed the basic U.S. aim "to forget the past, to help rehabilitate [Japan] internationally"—in the interests of future policy alignment.[42]

Horsey also perceptively suggested that a logical basis for conference participation might be having an IGY station—as evidence of a legitimate interest in Antarctica, one of Daniels's criteria. Moreover, that would give the United States an undisputed place at the table without asserting a claim. The record is thin on the finalizing of this course, but South Africa could be further justified for its Southern Hemisphere proximity, and Belgium, like Japan, had a history of Antarctic exploration. And so it was that the treaty concept came to be based on the scientific cooperation of the IGY rather than "the less desirable and more controversial political basis of claims and rights." If some, incredulous, asked "why Belgium?" the unique focus on science, not politics, would prove far-sighted. The IGY criterion would also keep the group manageably small.[43]

After months of secret consultations, begun in the fall of 1957, Daniels felt emboldened to deliver, on 24 March 1958, identical aides-mémoire to the embassies of the other eleven IGY nations in the Antarctic (even though colleagues were still debating over the Russians). This document provided a framework for confidential discussions (generally, continuing them) to air each government's views "in the hope that sufficient prior agreement can be reached to justify coming out into the open with public proposals." Requesting a "flexible approach" by all, Daniels and his team listened profitably to a now-familiar litany of concerns and demands, and positive responses trickled in. The USSR never replied, so Ambassador Mikhail Menshikov was asked to call in person on 2 May, where, with an indication of the others' readiness to move forward and an attitude of trust in Soviet cooperation, Daniels handed him a formal invitation to preparatory treaty talks. That same day the other ministers got their invitations by courier. In a simultaneous press release, President Eisenhower affirmed U.S. dedication to the "principle that the vast uninhabited wastes of Antarctica shall be used only for peaceful purposes" and to the preservation of the unparalleled international cooperation demonstrated during the (yet uncompleted) IGY.[44]

Ambassador Daniels's diplomatic note, signed by Undersecretary Robert Murphy, was crafted with such care and reflection of participants' input that, as Quigg noted, nearly all of the treaty's important provisions appeared in this first open communication. The invitation pointedly mentioned the "direct and substantial rights and interests" of the United States, which it intended to reserve even as it again declined to recognize the claims of others. In such kinship with but distance from the claimants, Daniels (in silent tribute to Chile's 1948 counterproposal) posited that a treaty could be formulated without requiring any state to renounce historical rights or claims. Simply freezing the legal status quo for its duration would keep politics from hampering cooperation. The treaty would, in consonance with the ideals of the United Nations, legalize the "high principles" of freedom of scientific research and other peaceful pursuits in all of Antarctica by citizens, organizations, and governments of all countries.[45]

One by one the nations responded favorably, though not without the predictable reservations. Finally, on 2 June 1958 the Soviet Embassy sent over its affirmative reply, the last one. A working group of diplomats, sometimes referred to as the preparatory commission, first met on 13 June. Daniels sagaciously convened early sessions at the National Academy of Sciences, a nonpublic, nonpolitical, appropriately science-oriented venue. The group met in the "strictest of secrecy," making it easier to state concerns and constraints and settle differences candidly in a "quiet atmosphere" without having to posture for propaganda purposes or be second-guessed by politicians and the media. The meetings were chaired in rotation by country (alphabetically according to English), which gave the working papers, drafted as treaty articles, shared approval when put before the official delegates. Daniels would later consider these features key to the success of the preparatory work, but Alan Neidle, the U.S. team's young legal adviser, gave most of the credit to Daniels's "very old-fashioned, but very sound and excellent diplomatic manner." He had a quiet way of "drawing everybody in, getting all of the views, consulting everybody, having everybody be part of the process." It was "the best of classical diplomacy."[46]

The delicate process got off to a rocky start when the Soviet Union's Andrei Ledovski pushed to open the conference to all interested states. The others balked; only they had shown an active (financial and scientific, not merely political) interest in the Antarctic. The isolated Russians, in truth, did not force the issue beyond months of wearying repetition, but the possibility gnawed. The United States especially would never allow in any "unrecognized Communist regimes" (most notably mainland China). Among other countries (India, Italy, West Germany, Brazil) aspiring to a place, Poland actively sought inclusion and would be the first outsider to accede to the treaty, on 8 June 1961, just before it entered into force. But Poland would not meet SCAR's overwintering scientific criterion until 1977, at which time it became the first added consultative party. The IGY twelve routinely insisted that their words would "protect the interests of all other countries and peoples of the world."[47]

The preparatory group optimistically projected a signed treaty by the end of the IGY. But the formal treaty conference date of late August 1958 slipped— once, twice, then indefinitely. The Australians stated flatly that without prior agreement on basic substantive issues they "would not be present" at the conference; the Soviets insisted that all substance be postponed until the "experts" met. Britain and Australia advocated delay so the USSR could not "walk out" and bring the "question of participation" before the United Nations; Chile and Argentina, worried that UN action would interfere in their domestic affairs, wanted an early conference date. They all waited fifteen long months. During that interval the members doggedly convened every week or so—sixty times, not counting innumerable quiet side meetings of selected subgroups. Somehow, their incremental progress justified continuing the effort.[48]

By mid-April 1958 Daniels had Neidle drafting treaty articles. The budding lawyer (still in his twenties) was "pretty excited," awed, unsure. Agonizing, he finally decided the language should be plain. He began: "Antarctica

shall be used for peaceful purposes only." And the "amazing thing," he recalled forty years later with deep satisfaction, was that in all that followed,
"nobody had a suggestion to improve that sentence." Indeed, he had captured
the "soul" of the treaty. Ledovski, however, demanded an explicit prohibition
of military bases, exercises, and weapons testing. Using military logistic support for science "could not be considered as being opposed to the principle of
peaceful uses," Chile countered. Daniels said U.S. acceptance of a treaty rested
on allowing the military's "essential contribution." All this would become
Article I.[49]

Perhaps most significant, this input was both specific and substantive.
The Soviets, for months after, as before, refused to discuss anything beyond
procedural matters and treaty "principles." Did they really want a treaty? Yet,
as Daniels noted privately, they kept coming. They listened attentively. Daniels
employed the "perfect diplomatic line," Neidle observed, "which was just to
let them have their say and then to go on. And he calculated . . . correctly . . . that
they wouldn't walk out because they'd want to hear what everybody else was
saying." At first the Soviets had sat there "glum faced, silent," but around
November 1958 Daniels began to see a softening. (Khrushchev himself had
decided to "participate seriously." In his treaty study, Brian Shoemaker sensed
a mutual need to show good faith during apparent progress on nuclear-arms
limitation. Over Antarctica they could do so, "without fear of losing strategic
position.") About that same time, the working group accepted U.S. drafts of
twelve short, incomplete treaty articles as a working document.[50]

The make-or-break paragraphs were clearly those of Article IV, which addressed territorial rights. Against giving certain countries a "preferential position," Ledovski said the best way to avoid the claims problem was not to
mention it at all. Australia's Malcolm Booker, fixated on "the very obvious
fact" of Soviet presence in its claim, required words. Argentina, fearing any
treaty would be seen at home as a surrender of sovereignty, almost seemed to
hope such "fundamental differences" would doom it. The French unexpectedly fretted that suspending rights for the duration of the treaty would "create
a new status quo on its termination." To all, Daniels patiently reiterated that
no country would acquire, alter, or give up rights. Article IV would not settle
the claims issue or meddle in it; it would merely, but crucially, set it aside. At
long last the Russians yielded, persuaded that a freeze would "not contradict"
their position that claims had "no juridical significance." New Zealand's prime
minister Walter Nash, ever steadying, wrote from Wellington that to "break the
log-jam of distrust" it was "essential" to "put controversial issues of sovereignty in 'cold storage.'" So as long as the treaty lasted, "any New Zealand

claim would cease to be of practical consequence." This broad view, probably prescribed by economic circumstance, stood alone.[51]

To ensure peaceful use and prevent military activity, Daniels, in February 1959, months into the discussions, proposed an audacious enforcement scheme. What would become Article VII guaranteed "observers" (inspectors) from any participating country "complete freedom of access at any time to any or all areas of Antarctica"—all installations and equipment, and all ships and planes at points of discharging or embarking cargo or personnel, including those of nonparties. Each country would finance its own inspections and report its findings to all. State Department analysts were stunned (and suspicious) when the Soviets accepted unlimited inspection in Antarctica while refusing any inspection in the concurrent nuclear test–ban talks. But the polar continent was not homeland soil; there was no threat to military intelligence or national security. Philip Farley, special assistant for disarmament, judged the risks "tolerable": no one's movement was restricted, both sides could know what the other was up to, reciprocity would deter too many or too-nosy inspections, and military activity meriting concern (nuclear testing) could be detected by other means. Daniels admitted a lack of sanctions for violators but pointed to later articles that laid out paths for handling disputes. Despite others' disquiet, in the end this simplest of approaches would prevail. It had to be called a brilliant stroke.[52]

Related to inspection was the issue of jurisdiction—that is, whose laws applied when an Antarctican stepped over a line or was accused of doing so? Early attempts to cover everyone proved too difficult, so for now, to protect inspectors in their work, the negotiators finally agreed that observers (and accompanying staff) and scientific exchange personnel would be subject only to their own country's jurisdiction. Others, such as civilian support personnel, were left in limbo. As Daniels's assistant George Owen wrote in March, the issue bore no great political importance but was complicated legally, so trying to "thrash out a satisfactory formula at the conference" would only hold it up. Daniels included the subject in an article on administrative measures to be worked out later. It still waits. Quigg calls the issue "untidy."[53]

Another protracted controversy arose over accession—that is, whether nonparties could sign on to the treaty after ratification by the original twelve. Daniels, to avoid the risk of mischief, favored the "efficiency" of the twelve with guaranteed nondiscriminatory treatment for all. Others split in various ways, the Soviets (and less vocally the Japanese) insisting always on including any interested party. But in July, when they hinted informally that their government might accept limited accession (and had already conceded quite a lot), it became attractive to yield a little. Besides, it would be good to "eschew an exclusive 'small club' approach," which invited bad press around the world and perhaps UN intervention. Gradually, consensus gathered around the idea of limiting accession not by vote but by meeting some criterion of commitment such as fielding a wintering expedition (consistent with SCAR).[54]

Deciding exactly where the treaty applied turned out to be surprisingly unsimple. Ice masked coastal boundaries, and the legal status of ice shelves posed a unique dilemma. Such *glacies firma* were neither navigable nor "permanent." For most countries latitude 60° South offered a clear and simple delimitation, but the USSR, citing SCAR, insisted for an inexplicably long time on using the Antarctic Convergence. An appropriate boundary for science, the seasonally shifting "line" ill served a political instrument, where geographic precision mattered. Even using the fixed parallel was problematic, though, because no one wanted to (or could) provide inspection or control over that much "open" ocean. Finally, Daniels successfully suggested that the zone be set at 60° South with language stating it would not "infring[e] on the principle of freedom of the high seas." All ice shelves would be included.[55]

At last, on 26 May the working group set a formal treaty conference for 15 October 1959 in Washington. Among their Provisional Rules of Procedure, they agreed that committee decisions on drafting text would use a two-thirds rule for efficiency, but all final decisions, including ratification, would require unanimity. Of this gamble, Owen noted that if the Soviet Union did not ratify, there was little point to a treaty. Two months later the hardworking diplomats resumed their preparatory talks. Among several new faces in the reconvened group was Yuri Filippov for the Soviets, who offered a long and constructive report that moved his government nearer to the others' growing consensus. Daniels implored counterparts to seek the incomplete good within their grasp, not an impossible "eternally perfect solution."[56]

Meanwhile, internal debate flared to the last moment. While NSC policy gave as a treaty objective "freedom of scientific investigation" for anyone conforming with all treaty principles, some Far East experts wanted a footnote excepting unrecognized Communist regimes, lest the latter gain rights or "respectability." Owen (and Green) pointed out that if, outside the treaty, they someday disregarded its conditions, "we could hardly marshal world opinion or diplomatic pressure to maintain a principle from which we have deliberately excluded them." Respecting the estimable professionals who were gloomily certain that "this is never going to work," Neidle admired Daniels, who "worked very hard above my level to say this was nonsense. You just pursue your interest as you calculate it." If the United States could get the treaty it wanted, that was "in our interest." Yet just a week before the conference, he felt compelled to beg the secretary not to bow to Cold War considerations beyond Antarctica. If the Soviets reneged because of last-minute parameter changes, the onus would be on the United States. The doomsayers were somehow quieted.[57]

When the Antarctic Treaty Conference duly opened, the U.S. delegation was headed not by Daniels but by Herman Phleger, a San Francisco corporate lawyer with several years of distinguished high-level State Department service. As expected, he was elected to chair the conference, leaving Daniels to speak for the United States (in fact, more freely) in the plenary sessions. If this was a blow to his ego, Daniels gamely played the supporting role. In Neidle's mind, Ambassador Phleger brought "great brilliance and skill," the prestige of personal friendship with the late Secretary Dulles, and connections with the military establishment and Congress. Although he had the highest regard for Daniels, Neidle, who became special assistant to the chair as well as the delegation's legal adviser, thought Phleger was "able to do more." Phleger rejoiced when his equally well-connected Soviet counterpart confided, "Khrushchev has told me to make this a success."[58]

Yet the conference got off to an inauspicious start. With but an eleventh-hour warning, France moved on 20 October to delete the paragraph of Article IV that declined recognition of claims because it "implied a legal negation of France's rights." Australia choked. This provision was its (and no doubt others') sine qua non. If the treaty failed, France would bear history's blame, the shaken foreign minister Robert Casey secretly wrote to his counterpart Couve du Murville. Then Argentina proposed more restrictive language in Article II, a short commitment to scientific freedom. Unanimous approval of the peaceful-purposes Article I helped brighten the day. Without support, France would shortly come around but Argentina dug in, loath to grant any hint of legitimacy to "trespass" on its "sovereign territory." Frantic diplomatic exchanges flew between Washington and Buenos Aires. President Arturo Frondizi proved conciliatory, but the anti-Soviet Argentine press and armed forces put up "very active opposition." At last, winning words for Article II, after weeks on thin ice, were derived from an early suggestion by New Zealand: "Freedom of scientific investigation in Antarctica and cooperation toward that end, as applied during the International Geophysical Year, shall continue, subject to the provisions of the present Treaty." Somehow that minimal qualifying phrase, enshrining the emotional power of the peaceable IGY, gave Argentina sufficient political cover to accept the statement.[59]

Article III called for "international cooperation in scientific investigation," including the exchange of program information (prior to implementation), scientific personnel, and the results of work "to the greatest extent feasible and practicable"—the latter phrase Norway's compromise from an earlier "too obligatory" "shall." The wording also responded to Argentina's fallback request for "courtesy notification," though its purpose was economy and efficiency, not security. An added statement encouraged cooperation with UN agencies and other international scientific organizations. Daniels later said these first three articles proved his point that "science and international cooperation go hand in hand." They all came straight from the IGY.[60]

The critical Article IV, surviving its many challenges, stipulated that nothing in the treaty would be interpreted as renouncing one's own or recognizing another's rights, territorial claims, or basis for a claim. Nothing done would constitute a basis for asserting, supporting, or denying a claim or create any rights of sovereignty. No new claim could be made or an old one enlarged. Robert Hayton, professor of international law, in a thoughtful analysis of the treaty published before U.S. ratification, called this "sweeping" article an attempt to "be all things to all nations." He questioned its staying power amid shifting global attitudes and evolving Antarctic history. Yet "it was, without the slightest doubt, absolutely essential to a successful conclusion of the agreement." Ten years later Finn Sollie, director of Norway's Fridtjof Nansen Foundation and a specialist in international law, would write that the solution to the claims problems came "in the form of a nonsolution, a type of constructive evasion." That could be called its genius.[61]

Previously debated key provisions, such as the zone of application (Article VI) and inspection (Article VII), came to closure relatively easily. Hayton called the wide-open inspection clause "a most significant novelty." Subjecting inspectors and certain others only to the jurisdiction of their own countries (Article VIII), akin to diplomatic immunity, was "the treaty's major infringement on the 'sovereignty'" of the claimants, he thought, and "the strongest concrete stipulation in the entire agreement." What to do about "other persons" and other issues not addressed in the treaty was left to periodic consultative meetings of the treaty parties (Article IX).[62]

The delegates to these treaty meetings—representing all of the original signatories (even inactive ones, such as Belgium and Norway recently) and "active" acceding nations—would exchange information, consult on common interests, and formulate recommendations. These would become effective when approved by *all* the respective governments—thus granting a veto to any except an inactive acceding state. Chances for "expeditious agreement" on "anything but the most innocuous matters" seemed to Hayton in 1960 "rather bleak." He surmised, without access to the secret records, that some governments would not ratify without this "preservation of 'negative sovereignty.'" R. Tucker Scully, who led the U.S. treaty delegation from 1982 until 1999, stressed a saving grace—that "any or all" of the treaty rights (inspection, access for science) could be exercised regardless of whether any administrative machinery existed to facilitate them. In fact, for forty years the Antarctic Treaty would operate only through the consultative meetings, without an official secretariat.[63]

Nervousness within the State Department's European Bureau that the Soviet Union might "use one or more of its satellite countries [not subject to the treaty] to camouflage illegal activities" in Antarctica led to a U.S. proposal for a separate article that would "explicitly bind the parties not to assist nonparties in carrying on activities contrary" to treaty principles. Soviet opposition fed U.S. determination, and Article X passed, though it pressed the signatories to "exert appropriate efforts" to see that "no one" misbehaved—a more general target than the earlier accusatory focus on nonparty governments.[64]

Handling disputes (Article XI) proved a major stumbling block. The U.S. and British preference for obligatory referral to the International Court of Justice, if such informal means as mediation or negotiation failed, met with Soviet and Latin American resistance. So the delegates reluctantly, weakly, compromised: unresolved disputes would go to the court with "the consent, in each case, of all parties to the dispute." There was "not a shred of compulsory jurisdiction"—in Hayton's view the treaty's "chief disappointment."[65]

Duration and change (Article XII) saw considerable evolution. As finally agreed, the treaty could be amended at any time by unanimous agreement of the original twelve and any eligible (active) acceding parties. An amendment would enter into force upon ratification by all the governments. It would bind other acceding parties upon their ratification; not ratifying after two years would be considered withdrawal from the treaty—a possible exit strategy. The empowered parties had no way out for thirty years (early drafts said ten), but after that any party could request a review conference. Any amendments approved by a majority, including a majority of the original and active members, would go for ratification in the usual way. If they were not ratified within two years, any party could withdraw. The thirty years expired in 1991, but no one has yet called a review conference. The treaty endures.[66]

Despite earlier progress, the politically sensitive matter of accession (Article XIII) remained unresolved well into the conference. The Soviets balked at a proposal restricting accession to members of the UN and its Specialized Agencies, which, they charged, was "designed to keep out certain socialist states" (China, East Germany). Wishing, they said, to "liquidate" Cold War attitudes, the Soviets suggested a few weeks later that accession be open to UN members or those invited by unanimous consent of the contracting parties. Sensing a line in the sand, others began to relent, to save the treaty. In the end, the United States did so, too—disappointed to have made it harder for West Germany, a Specialized Agency, but relieved to have kept out the unrecognized Communist regimes. Quigg called this the treaty's "sheep and goats paragraph," which, with Article IX, clearly set up two classes of membership.[67]

At the very last arose a new issue—nuclear explosions. Sensing that action on this point could probably not be stopped, Phleger thought a separate provision (inserted as Article V, throwing off earlier numberings) that protected Argentina and Chile from atmospheric fallout "could go far" to soften their sovereignty-based objections on the still-pending Article II. He received authorization to accept such a proposal if peaceful uses of atomic energy could be permitted or if he judged the treaty could fail without it. It nearly did. As Phleger put it, Soviet ambassador Grigori Tunkin put forth language to prohibit nuclear explosions, in effect, "for all time in Antarctica no matter how desirable, unless and until there was general international agreement on the subject." In succeeding days he offered complicated alternative scenarios, interspersed with proposals to drop the subject entirely. Each met with heated opposition. In the end, a simple article banned nuclear explosions and radioactive waste disposal. A second paragraph applied the rules of any future international nuclear agreement to Antarctica. It did not prohibit peaceful, non-explosive nuclear activity—helpful to U.S. plans for a nuclear power plant at McMurdo.[68]

Finally, on 30 November, the delegates declared their work done. They set a plenary session for the following morning, 1 December 1959, eleven months after the official close of the IGY, to formalize the document and announce their achievement. Both Phleger and Daniels signed for the United States, a generous recognition of the latter's indispensable contribution.[69]

Only ratification by the twelve nations remained. In the United States, that meant garnering the approval of two-thirds of the Senate, to which Eisenhower sent the treaty with his request for "early and favorable consideration" on 15

February 1960. Senator J. William Fulbright (D-Arkansas), chair of the Committee on Foreign Relations, called hearings on 14 June. Among those testifying positively was Phleger, who emphasized the "absolutely foolproof system of unilateral inspection" and the fact that the treaty did "not relinquish in one iota any claim or basis of claim." "My profession is geology," Gould reminded the lawmakers, "and I would not give a nickel for all the mineral resources I know in Antarctica." He believed Antarctica's "most important export" for "many, many years to come" would be scientific data. "And that is terribly important indeed." Admiral Tyree, like Gould, saw the treaty as the "best possible technique" for forwarding the IGY ideal. The time for claims had passed. (Dufek apparently approved of the treaty, too, but wanted to make a claim first. No longer in charge, he did not testify.) Contrarily, Representative John Pillion (R–New York), among others, passionately deplored "our Antarctic policy of appeasement, retreat, and surrender." But on 21 June the committee voted without dissent to report the treaty favorably to the full Senate. All the relevant government agencies had cleared it, most significantly the Defense Department. The committee concluded that it served U.S. interests to treat with the Soviet Union "in an area where mutual interests appear to coincide rather than diverge." It could set an important precedent in a troubled world.[70]

Floor debate on the Antarctic Treaty opened on 8 August 1960, in a summer distracted by the quadrennial presidential conventions. It went on for three days, often to a near-empty chamber. While the Senate in the 86th Congress was strongly Democratic (65-35) and Democrats dominated the opposition, support for the treaty was bipartisan. Two senators had served on the U.S. treaty delegation, Kansas Republican Frank Carlson and Gale McGee, Democrat from Wyoming—someone's shrewd inclusion. Both emerged as treaty champions. Democrat Clair Engle of California, chair of the Committee on Interior and Insular Affairs, led the vehement floor fight against the treaty. The senators argued thus:

> GALE MCGEE (D-WY), FOR: In a world which is desperately groping for peace, a nation such as ours should be winning friends to help us lead on the road to peace. We have that opportunity now in the Antarctic where the minds of men are not frozen by habit.[71]

> CLAIR ENGLE (D-CA), AGAINST: The United States has solid claims to some 80 percent of the Antarctic. The Soviets have none. We are trading what I would call a horse for a rabbit.[72]

> HARRY BYRD (D-VA), AGAINST: [The treaty] would legalize Soviet trespass and occupancy of [areas to which they have neither rightful nor earned

access,] which might well become some of the most economically and strategically important points in the world.[73]

KENNETH KEATING (R-NY), FOR: Far from giving the Russians a chance to establish themselves further in Antarctica, the treaty would make it legally impossible for them to do so.[74]

STROM THURMOND (D-SC), AGAINST: The very fact that the Union of Soviet Socialist Republics has so willingly participated in the negotiations . . . should serve as a red flag of warning to any who appreciate the nature of the Communist ideology.[75]

THOMAS DODD (D-CT), AGAINST: Do we want to spread the disease of communism even to the penguins?[76]

FRANK CARLSON (R-KS), FOR: I wish to point out that this treaty was conceived by the United States. . . . Second, the conference which drafted it, comprising the individuals representing the 12 countries, was called at the instance of the United States. . . . Third, the treaty contained all of the provisions which the United States believed were required for the protection of our national interest.[77]

J. W. FULBRIGHT (D-AR), FOR: The demand for perfection is conducive to paralysis, not to peace.[78]

Engle's motion to delay action until after the election failed, and the votes were cast on 10 August: 66 yeas (37 Democrats, 29 Republicans), 21 nays (17 Democrats—well over half from the Old South, a number of whom, most conspicuously Thurmond, would later switch parties; 4 Republicans).[79]

Eisenhower ratified the treaty on 18 August 1960, making U.S. approval fifth in order. The first was the United Kingdom on 31 May. The Soviet Union was ninth, on 2 November. Finally, Argentina, Australia, and Chile, the most possessive claimants, all deposited their instruments of ratification with the archives of the United States, per Article XIII, on 23 June 1961. The treaty entered immediately into force. President Kennedy pronounced it a "positive step in the direction of world-wide peace."[80]

———

The Antarctic Treaty of 1959 emerged as a "limited-purpose agreement," which may have been more wise than weak. Its architects settled for what they could get—sidestepping volatile claims, ignoring controversial mineral-resource issues, and leaving jurisdictional coverage incomplete. Instead, they crafted a framework, periodic meetings of the Antarctic Treaty Consultative Parties

(ATCPs), for orderly evolution—a key to the treaty's resilience, Scully empha-sized. The ATCPs, comprising the governing body of the Antarctic Treaty Sys-tem (ATS), develop policy by consensus. The principle "if you don't ask me to say yes, I won't say no" facilitates agreement that might not be possible to reach by recorded vote. Treaty scholar M. J. Peterson, echoing Daniels, added that holding treaty meetings in secret encourages candor, helps the parties put aside contentions brewing elsewhere, and softens the voice of ideology. (Of course, secrecy also begs criticism from those outside the closed doors, which opening some sessions to nonconsultative parties and even some nongovern-mental organizations has blunted, though not eliminated.) Another strength is linking political participation to Antarctic science activity, thus ensuring interest and commitment.[81]

Some argue that inspection is the glue of the Antarctic Treaty. The United States decided early on to exercise this right—to establish the precedent of inspection to verify any treaty and to build mutual confidence in this decid-edly unusual legal instrument. Ambassador William Sebald, head of the U.S. delegation to the first treaty-specified Antarctic Treaty Consultative Meeting (ATCM) in Canberra in July 1961, emphasized U.S. intent to conduct inspec-tions as a "useful and practical" routine to ensure peaceful use. Americans, he added, would not regard another country's inspection of U.S. stations as an indication of suspicion. Inspections could well have become a minefield. As Shoemaker also wrote in 1989, they interrupt station leaders' work and expose their activities to outsiders: "Words to the contrary, it would be a relinquish-ment of sovereignty and was then, as it is today, potentially confrontational." In fact, inspection visits have unfailingly proved friendly—social events al-most for isolated stations, opportunities to receive fresh foods and send out mail, testimony to a will to make the system work. While inspectors do not pass over anything found amiss, the "main objective is being able to state that nothing is wrong."[82]

Over the years the United States has conducted the most inspections by far, although it has not been alone. Clearly mindful of nuclear-arms–control applications, President Kennedy authorized the first Antarctic inspection on 4 September 1963. But before U.S. inspectors got into the field, New Zealand sent two observers to McMurdo and then, by U.S. aircraft, to Byrd and Pole stations late in the year. They found no violations. Australia and Britain (jointly) also dispatched observers to these same stations and to Scott Base. The United States, as the first inspectee, cordially received the inspectors. In January 1964, that same season, U.S. inspectors appeared at ten stations—two each of the Soviet Union (which, to the relief of all, proved "eager to show off their base"), Britain,

Argentina, and Chile (along the disputed Antarctic Peninsula); and one each of France and New Zealand. They did not expect to find fault and did not. With these amicable firsts the treaty met its first real test. The USSR did no inspections until 1989 when it ambitiously conducted fifteen visits, two to U.S. stations.[83]

Inspections continue. Today, specialists from the Fish and Wildlife Service and the Environmental Protection Agency are as likely to staff inspection teams as the disarmament experts who monitor for military and nuclear activities, per the original intent. The costs (about $1.5 million just for icebreaker services), logistical difficulties, political considerations, and the loss to science of diverting a ship have put recent U.S. inspections on a six-year schedule, more or less. The most recent were in 1995, when the *Polar Star* nearly circumnavigated the continent to visit eight foreign stations, and 2001, when the research vessel *Laurence M. Gould* ferried two teams on an extensive peninsular inspection. They found the "letter and spirit" of the treaty "fully and uniformly demonstrated." Perhaps it is true, as Peterson argued, that as long as everyone believes the others are aboveboard, the cost of treaty compliance (doing nothing) is cheaper than cheating (for dubious benefit). The 1995 environmental inspectors found all stations struggling with waste management, especially to clean up or remove old hazardous fuel leaks. They also noted a few pets and many plants (especially tomatoes), though how big a fuss to make about such clear but minor and endearingly human winks at the ban on introducing foreign species remains a question.[84]

From the first, the consultative parties worried about protecting Antarctic animals and plants (only mentioned in the treaty as something to discuss later). They produced general Agreed Measures in 1964 and a 1972 convention to control (then-dormant) commercial sealing. Their landmark agreement was the 1980 Convention on the Conservation of Antarctic Marine Living Resources (CCAMLR), which brought scientific findings to commercial fisheries management south of the Antarctic Convergence, its ecology-based zone of application. In force by 1982, the CCAMLR defined conservation to include "rational use" and pioneered an ecosystem approach, seeking to ensure the health of both target and dependent species. Harvesting krill as a source of human, or at least animal, protein held high interest at the time. But these tiny, abounding shrimplike creatures are the linchpin of the unusually short and simple south-polar food chain. Perhaps fortunately, processing them eventually proved uneconomical. A new, rather ironic challenge is that once nearly decimated fur seals now thrive under treaty protection to the point where they threaten native plants that are also protected! The British at Signy Station in the South Orkneys installed electrified fences to separate the two.[85]

Managing mineral assets was another matter. New Zealand's Robert Thomson informally raised the issue at the 1970 treaty conference, finding only "a wish to not discuss it and the hope that such a question would go away." But, as Scully put it, belief in a "cornucopia of mineral resources down there" gained strength when scientists drilling in the Ross seabed in 1973 found traces of ethylene, which often accompanies oil deposits, and from that the U.S. Geological Survey projected significant quantities of offshore petroleum and natural gas. Extraction technologies were improving. Mineral resources appeared on ATCM agendas for twenty years thereafter. Then, non-party countries led by Malaysia in the UN demanded a share of the potential wealth, arguing that Antarctica is a "common heritage of mankind." Scholars of international law began proposing various political arrangements and distribution systems in anticipation of eventual mining. One, for example, would allocate shares of an international stock company according to a country's Antarctic exploration and investment. Quigg opined in 1983 that keeping Antarctica "permanently locked up as a scientific laboratory" was "simply not being realistic."[86]

Anxious to avoid an "unregulated 'gold rush'" that could unravel the ATS, the treaty parties began marathon negotiations that in 1988, seven years later, produced the Convention on the Regulation of Antarctic Mineral Resource Activities (CRAMRA). Congress's Office of Technology Assessment recommended U.S. ratification. But environmentalists—led by undersea explorer Jacques Cousteau, Greenpeace International, and other members of the Antarctic and Southern Ocean Coalition—seized world opinion. They charged—exaggeratedly, confrontationally, effectively—that CRAMRA's extremely tight (no adverse impact) regulations on mining, should it occur, showed an expectation, even encouragement, that it would. They also exploited the disastrous 1989 *Exxon Valdez* oil spill in Alaska and three smaller spills in Antarctic waters. France and Australia announced that they would not seek ratification. The U.S. Congress urged a new approach. The hard-won consensus disintegrated.[87]

Weary ATCP negotiators went back to the drawing board. In June 1991 in Madrid, they concluded a comprehensive Protocol on Environmental Protection to the Antarctic Treaty. President George H.W. Bush signed it. Article 7, in unqualified entirety, states: "Any activity relating to mineral resources, other than scientific research, shall be prohibited." Article 25 allows for a review conference, if requested, after fifty years from the protocol's entry into force (1997). Importantly, it requires the minerals ban to continue until and unless a new binding legal regime on that subject is in force.[88] Environmental interests won; given that no viable minerals had yet been found, no one really lost. While CRAMRA's crumbling underscored the fragility of the treaty system, the fact that the parties willingly tried again and managed to forge a new, more rigorous system of protections could only be seen as evidence of its strength and value. Treaty scholar Francisco Orrego Vicuña, though, worries that the Protocol "created a legal vacuum" that could prove dangerous *when* minerals are discovered. The subsurface issue of claims lives on.[89]

Pulling the Protocol from the ashes of CRAMRA, as well as meeting the UN's challenge, occurred as the Antarctic Treaty was approaching its potential review date of 1991—a delicate moment. It does not seem entirely coincidental or wholly science-justified that during those years large developing nations were invited to "join the club." The addition of China, India, and Brazil gave ATS representation to three-fourths of the world's people. With the exclusivity charge thus muted, the UN would have less cause to question the treaty's legitimacy. India's attitudes illustrated the lure of insidership almost as if following a script. For all its pressure in the UN during the IGY, India did not accede to the treaty until August 1983, yet it quickly won consultative status. In January 1985, at an ATS assessment workshop (held enticingly in Antarctica), Indian representatives declared, "from the perspective of a new member," that an "overhaul" of the treaty system was "neither possible nor advisable." The common-heritage principle would be best served by the unfettered pursuit of science.[90]

Overall, the ATS has worked remarkably well. It has preserved an open, demilitarized continent "as a universal laboratory for one and all." Consultative states at each other's throats otherwise (Argentina and Britain over the Falklands, the United States and the Soviet Union overall, South Africa so reviled for its racial policies that others would not meet there) have kept to purposeful discourse over the polar south. So far, the increasing numbers have not thwarted consensus. New members invited perhaps for political reasons have honored their scientific commitments. If Antarctic power is still reserved fairly narrowly, history could do worse than the example of international performance thus far shown. Beyond Antarctica, as the *New York Times* editorialized in December 1969 upon the treaty signing's tenth anniversary, "there can be little doubt that this precedent helped to create the foundations of mutual confidence on which the great diplomatic landmarks of the past decade have been based, notably the test ban treaty of 1963, the space compact of 1967, and the nuclear nonproliferation pact of 1968." In effect, the Antarctic Treaty made the polar continent a laboratory for political as well as physical science.[91]

Some treaty issues remain unresolved. While "hypothetical horribles" involving cross-national altercations "excite law professors," said Scully, various practical measures have obviated the need to anticipate every imagined jurisdictional problem. For example, NSF deputizes its leaders on the ice (at least one has made an arrest), and persons aboard ship are subject to the jurisdiction of its flag. The fact is, Antarctica has been a peaceable kingdom. Disquiet over territorial claims lingers but remains dormant. If some argue that the nonsolution of the treaty's freeze creates an "unstable equilibrium," they "miss the point." Its strength is that countries can disagree over the legal basis for activities and still permit them. It does not matter if, say, claimant Australia maintains internally that a U.S. scientist works in Wilkes Land because of its sovereign permission and the American does so in the U.S. belief that she may freely go anywhere. Both agree that she can be there. The value of the treaty must not be underplayed, Scully asserts. It underpins all Antarctic scientific activity and international interaction. If ever broken, it would be difficult indeed to replace.[92]

With science remaining the heart of human activity in the polar south, SCAR (named in CCAMLR though not in the treaty) assumed a key role. Supported by a small secretariat at the Scott Polar Research Institute in Cambridge, this nongovernmental body functions largely through working groups of scientists to develop research programs benefited by international cooperation. SCAR recommendations go to the national committees—in the United States the NAS Polar Research Board (PRB), which advises the National Science Foundation. Over his long career, Charles Bentley served on SCAR science working groups and later led an interdisciplinary Group of Specialists on Global Change and the Antarctic (GLOCHANT). As a SCAR delegate and later vice president, he was for many years an ex officio member of the PRB, chairing it during the early 1980s. Robert Thomson bridged the SCAR and ATCP communities. For fourteen years he chaired the SCAR working group on logistics, passing on vital information to the treaty parties. Now, an upgraded Standing Committee on Antarctic Logistics and Operations works within the Council of Managers of National Antarctic Programs, an "operational network among the NSFs of the world" formed in 1988 to facilitate and sometimes pool common tasks of essential science support.[93]

In the United States, Antarctic policy eventually centered in the interagency Antarctic Policy Group (APG), established by President Johnson in 1965. The assistant secretary of state for International Organization Affairs (later for Oceans, Environment and Science) chaired the APG, which included the NSF director and the secretary of defense. The U.S. Antarctic Research Program became the U.S. Antarctic Program (USAP) in 1971 when NSF assumed responsibility for all south-polar activities, including support operations. While Operation Deep Freeze continued, NSF now managed that budget and purchased the Navy's services. Phil Smith thought a prime accomplishment of that time was institutionalizing support so an "ordinary scientist" could work in the "laboratory of Antarctica" without having to be an expert in polar logistics, survival, and safety. NSF has also increasingly relied on a succession of private contractors for various kinds of support.[94]

Thomas Jones defined the USARP as encompassing "any and all sciences and studies for which Antarctica [is] a unique place to carry out such work" and not any that "could just as well be done elsewhere." Cosmic-ray physicist Martin Pomerantz recognized that 90° South is ideally suited for astronomy and solar physics research. In the late 1970s he launched the field of helioseismology, that is, study of the modes of vibration of the sun. In addition to the congenial atmospheric conditions—extremely dry, clean, clear air; relatively stable circulation patterns; limitless snow for constant background—the Pole's straddling of the earth's axis meant that "any object in the sky was always at the same altitude and it's always there, day after day." Such work has helped to monitor and predict weather conditions in space, which serves orbiting systems. Anything to do with ice was obvious. Besides the continuing IGY sciences, the dynamics of the ice sheet makes it a rich hunting ground for meteorites. Some 16,000 collected specimens offer clues about the origin of the solar system, the age of the earth, and the composition of Mars, where some meteorites are known to have originated.[95]

Antarctica also favors life-science and ecosystem research because of its harshness, remoteness, and simple food chain. Bacteria that improbably cling to life on exposed mountainsides less than 200 miles from the Pole interest those trying to contemplate life that might have once existed on Mars. Microbial processes can be studied in the lakes of the Dry Valleys without the usual effects of grazing by fish and crustaceans. Physiologists have found certain notothenid fish that survive because of organic (glycopeptide) antifreeze in their intercellular tissues and blood. While Antarctic waters teem with life (unfathomable numbers of individuals within relatively few species), scientists drilling beneath the Ross Ice Shelf in the late 1970s discovered only an "impoverished community" of fauna in the oxygen-starved, "black, ice-lidded sea." Studying the social, psychological, and physiological stresses on human life in Antarctica helps biological and medical researchers predict the health and performance of travelers in space, an even more extreme environment.[96]

As outlined by G. E. Fogg, long-term patterns and characteristics of Antarctic science have become apparent. It is, to start, remarkably holistic. Disciplinary boundaries blur. Even during the IGY it was often difficult and artificial to discuss the scientific disciplines separately. There are, Fogg wrote, close links between atmospheric physics and meteorology and also, through magnetism, with terrestrial physics. The interface between air and sea connects meteorology with oceanography, while the latter must also consider glaciology and marine biology. Polar geology incorporates both glaciology and paleontology, and paleontology merges with biology. Thus, for example, atmospheric physicists, chemists, meteorologists, and biologists all try to understand and ameliorate the increase in surface ultraviolet radiation resulting from a "hole" in the stratosphere's protective layer of ozone. Discovered in 1981 (from IGY measurements, especially at Britain's Halley Bay Station), this ozone loss is attributable to human use of chlorofluorocarbons (in refrigerants and foam plastics manufacture), which deplete atmospheric ozone. It is "far more pronounced" over Antarctic than lower latitudes. In September 2000, NASA Goddard's Total Ozone Mapping Spectrometer recorded an ozone hole three times the size of the United States. At issue is future ecosystem stability all over the world.[97]

Geological investigations through the 1960s, combined with the finding of fossilized bones of the Southern Hemisphere Mesozoic reptile Lystrosaurus near the Beardmore Glacier in 1969, helped drive acceptance of the theory that around 200 million years ago a temperate, southern supercontinent included Antarctica, tucked among present-day Africa and Madagascar, India, Australia, and South America. Called Gondwanaland, it was split apart by sea-floor spreading, as shown by studies in paleomagnetism. Antarctica drifted to its present position about 40 million years ago and acquired its current continental ice sheet 4 to 7 million years ago, burying but preserving fossil evidence of flora and fauna typical of its Gondwana neighbors. In 1981 paleontologists found a 40-million-year-old fossil jaw of an opossum on Seymour Island off the Antarctic Peninsula. A marsupial like those of North America and Australia, it could only have walked from the one landmass to the other—via Antarctica.[98]

Intentional international cooperation, another characteristic in itself, encourages a holistic, interdependent view as well—especially when working on global issues such as the environment or costly technology-driven projects such as deep-rock drilling. Thus GLOCHANT ecologists, atmospheric scientists, oceanographers, glaciologists, and geologists have studied not only temperature but also changes in sea level, ozone protection, and ice-sheet size to see if, indeed, a "systematic and unprecedented warming" is taking place and if human activity is the cause. While possibly "noticeable," Bentley thought in 2002 there is "only a very remote chance" that Antarctic ice will decrease rapidly enough to "have a dramatic effect on sea level." The recent calvings of huge icebergs seem to balance ice-shelf growth over time, he said, although the "destructive" collapses of the Larsen Ice Shelf were "almost surely due to strong warming along the Antarctic Peninsula." Global change expert Gunter Weller cited contradictory evidence over the rest of the continent—"colder and drier here, warmer and more precipitation there, disintegrating ice shelves here and thickening icecap over there." According to an NSF study, ice cores have shown a "correlation between warming and greenhouse gas increases over hundreds of thousands of years" and "markedly" higher levels of people-caused gases, such as carbon dioxide and methane, in the past 200 years.[99]

NSF's Smith, promoting internationalism, organized a joint Japan–New Zealand–U.S. Dry Valleys core-drilling project in the early post-IGY period to study past climate and area geology, and in the early 1970s a France-Australia-U.S.-USSR glaciology project focused on a million square miles of the East Antarctic ice cap. Several such programs have been sustained over many years; the recent six-nation Cape Roberts Stratigraphic Drilling Project seeks cores from beneath the sea floor aged from 30 million to 100 million years. Finally, Fogg concluded, a "powerful non-scientific factor making for the unity of Antarctic science" is the "strong bond of comradeship" that forms among those who elect to risk life and share work on the heartless ice. As Thomson described, "In Antarctica, whatever your nationality, you became an 'Antarctican.'"[100]

Antarctic science is strikingly costly. Formidable distances and hostile conditions require huge outlays for infrastructure and human support, far greater than for direct support of science. In fiscal 1997 the USAP budget was $193.5 million, of which only $30.5 million funded scientific grants. Forty-one million dollars went for direct field support and $122 million, 63 percent, for logistics and operations. Transportation is the largest single budget item. Such high costs can only be met by government funds—and that makes Antarctic science also political. "Indeed, the primary purpose of every nation's Antarctic stations is political; the science (even good science) is just an excuse for a presence on the continent," biologist David Campbell wrote in 1992. If that seems cynical, he counted twelve countries that had crowded science stations onto the unglaciated 5 percent of King George Island, where he worked. Fogg, more positively, opined that politicians "have inadvertently allowed science to become a political force and in Antarctic matters political discourse was brought to a worthy standard." Both viewpoints ring true.[101]

Antarctic science has ever and increasingly been technology dependent, another factor in cost and complexity. In 1962 Thomson led a Sno-Cat traverse from Wilkes to deep-inland Vostok Station, where no one had yet even flown. He navigated by plotting an "almost continuous" series of sunshots on graph paper. It was, understandably, "the greatest moment in my life" the day he reckoned they were within reach of their goal and he sent American meteorologist Danny Foster up through the hatch with binoculars for a look: "I waited. No sound from Danny for a while, then suddenly, 'God *damn*! I *see* something!'" It was the thin line of an antenna mast. Today, satellite-supported global-positioning computers would tell him exactly, instantly, where they were. Transistors and microchips have miniaturized and lightened electronics systems, so fieldwork can be conducted efficiently by snowmobile from portable camps set down by aircraft. Other technologies enable in situ data processing and real-time reporting to international data centers. Indeed, some scientists no longer need to go to the ice to do their polar work. (There is no longer the old political need for wide-ranging field research either, says John Behrendt: "the Cold War is over.")[102]

All these characteristics, Fogg concludes, necessarily make Antarctic science "big science." As for really big science projects, by the early 1970s the research vessel *Glomar Challenger* was drilling deep into the ocean floor as part of a massive program to collect seismic and other data in the ice-free areas over Antarctica's continental shelf. Long-term ocean drilling has contributed to understanding of climate, plate tectonics, biology, and physical oceanography. In 1976 SCAR's biology working group developed BIOMASS (Biological Investigations of Marine Antarctic Systems and Stocks), an international, multidisciplinary research program designed to understand the structure and dynamics of potential commercial resources in the Southern Ocean—especially krill. It continued until 1992. Studying the interaction of air and sea with pack ice was another huge "big-science" project best suited to cooperation among many nations. Protecting the environment requires everyone's joined effort.[103]

———————

Environmental mindfulness has a short history anywhere; in Antarctica's first half-century the concept had no meaning. Ross Island's hut dwellers of the heroic era simply tossed their trash out the window. The waste practices of

IGY personnel depended upon their station's physical setting, but it is safe to say they did not worry much about it beyond removing it from sight. At Byrd, trash was burned using old engine oil. "This technique had the double advantage," Dater wrote, "of reducing the volume and causing the remainder to sink into the snow." With human waste, in coastal areas the "honey buckets" were simply hauled to the edge of the ice periodically, to disappear with summer's melting. At stations on ice, the pioneers dug a deep pit below the latrine. The frozen ordure did not offend the senses, but the level of accumulation had to be reduced now and then. Demolitionist Charlie Wedemeyer solved the problem with explosives at Little America, a feat that immortalized him among his guffawing mates. Boyer sighed to his family in 1958 that Antarctica "is at once esthetic as a virgin waterfall in a forest and sordid as a garbage dump." But "it was a beachhead, that period of time," Smith, like others, cautioned later. "So that was the way you had to think about it. We were getting a fragile foothold on the edge of Antarctica."[104]

Gradually, environmental consciousness took root. In 1971, on the heels of the first Earth Day (22 April 1970) but twenty years before the Environmental Protocol, a special section of the *Antarctic Journal* featured environmental preservation. By then the pristine snow had known insecticides and radioactive fallout, not to mention stations' unsightly waste heaps, seeping fuel tanks, abandoned equipment, and noise pollution. A "veritable rug of litter" was forming on the ocean bottom around McMurdo, killing everything beneath it. Decomposition took years in the frigid water; plastics would last "practically forever." McMurdo put in an incinerator and sewage-treatment plant in the early 1970s, but such technologies are extremely expensive on a small scale, difficult to operate in the harsh climate, and noticeable in the fragile environment. Today most waste is "retrograded" to the United States.[105]

Happily, as the Polar Research Board concluded in 1993, there has been a "convergence of interests" among scientists, environmentalists, and the public "that looks toward a responsible stewardship of the vast antarctic land mass and its surrounding oceans." That Antarctica is an international community has made it both compelling and possible to reach broad consensus on the need to protect its vulnerable ecosystem. Scientists conduct wide-ranging environmental research, actively advise on environmental policy, and constrain themselves (as do all polar personnel) under sometimes cumbersome rules to preserve the unique environment. Today, environmental protection is second only to safety as an emphasis in polar endeavor and has become almost extreme. In 1991, as Congress debated enabling legislation for the Environmental Protocol, geologist Robert Rutford, president of the University of Texas at Dallas and then of SCAR, testified for balance. He worried that overly strict regulations on human activity might make it too difficult and expensive to do science at all. From a different perspective, Smith confessed to having "mixed feelings about cleaning McMurdo up too much." Human history there, after all, consists basically of what has been left behind: "So to have swept McMurdo sterile of almost everything that has existed over the years makes it historically a far less interesting place than if there were a few trash piles."[106]

A different kind of American polar history was made in 1962 when DePaul University biologist M. A. McWhinnie won a place on the newly launched research vessel *Eltanin* for work on marine invertebrates. Only after NSF program officers had approved the proposal did they learn that the enthusiastic, articulate Dr. McWhinnie was Mary Alice. As the first female scientist in the U.S. Antarctic Program, she made several cruises and became a world authority on krill. A few Russian women scientists (and some crew) had served aboard Soviet vessels in the IGY era, and a few more from various countries worked in or near Antarctica during the 1960s.[107]

In 1966 NSF's Jones considered positively the possibility of employing American women on land—when facilities became available. Colin Bull, the British-born director of the Institute of Polar Studies at Ohio State University (OSU) and long an advocate, assembled a team of four OSU women to conduct geological research in the Dry Valleys in 1969–1970. They all had to be women— and polar experienced(!)—he remembered NSF insisting. The quartet, led by Lois Jones, met with criticism both for the disruption of their presence and for taking too long to publish their results. Bull reckoned that "they made just about the same number of mistakes, like burning the tent, as a bunch of four neophyte males would have done. But no more, no less." He proudly claimed to have "liberated a whole continent." The next summer Irene Peden, an associate professor of engineering at the University of Washington and a polar-atmosphere scholar, became, with the nervous support of NSF and the unconcealed resistance of the Navy, the first woman scientist to work in the interior of the continent. She collected data on the lower ionosphere at a field camp near Byrd Station in late 1970, despite the fact that her equipment mysteriously never arrived. Peden went south with NSF's admonition, "If you fail, there won't be another woman on the Antarctic Continent for a generation"—a pressure she did not welcome but successfully met.[108]

When it became inevitable that women would winter over, George Llano, NSF program manager for polar biology and medicine, turned to McWhinnie. She readily signed on and suggested the cheerful, adventurous Sister Mary Odile Cahoon, her former graduate student, as a companion. (Antarctica's female pioneers could only go in pairs.) Given NSF's caution and the Navy's reluctance, it is humorous if understandable that they chose to send as firsts a "mature" woman (McWhinnie was fifty-one) and a nun. Cmdr. William Sutherland, the Navy's wintering officer-in-charge, later remarked approvingly that the men were different with women present—neater, better behaved, more civilized—an observation veterans of the 1950s returning in more recent years have also made. They were like "maiden aunts" to the young men who frequently sought their counsel, remembered Cahoon. But they went to work as well as to break barriers. In Cahoon's no-nonsense words, "If women are in science and science is in the Antarctic, then women belong there." She was proud that they "showed it could work out without any muss or fuss," but she added, "we weren't going to fail. That never occurred to either of us." Interestingly, the *Antarctic Journal,* reporting their arrival in McMurdo on 10 January 1974, made no mention of their historical significance.[109]

Today women comprise perhaps 25 or 30 percent of the U.S. Antarctic workforce, participating in all fields of science and support. But each first was hard-won. Christine Müller-Schwarze, a psychologist, arrived in October 1969 with her zoologist husband to study Adélie penguin behavior at Cape Crozier. Even being paired with a male (there were two scientific couples on Ross Island that historic summer) did not help. One "highly respected senior scientist; a family man; and one of good humor and good will" complained of her to writer Charles Neider, himself an odd duck doing book research among the scientists and servicemen: "It's no good, goddammit. She even has her own crapper." Those installing the outhouse spitefully "dedicated" it by yellowing its walls: "We stood back and aimed high. . . . No disrespect meant to the lady. I like her." Captain Shoemaker recalled that in the early 1980s "the social situation was such that women were still trying to fit into an all male environment and were trying to be as good as men or to out-do them under men's rules."[110]

Both Latin American countries used women to promote their Antarctic "rights." The wife of Chile's president became the first First Lady to visit Antarctica in 1948. In early 1978 Argentina arranged to have a baby be born there, and by the 1980s Argentine military personnel were bringing their families with them. By then, Campbell wrote, Chile, too, had at least one colony, on King George Island, with mothers and children, a hotel, and "a suburb of comfortable, rambling ranch houses with satellite TV." Utterly unprepared for

Jennie Darlington's pregnancy on Stonington Island in 1947, the frantic camp physician could think only of removing her to civilization as soon as possible—passing an opportunity to present the first-born Antarctican as a U.S. citizen. The only children ever at any U.S. station have briefly visited with tourist families.[111]

⎯⎯⎯⎯⎯⎯ ▭ ⎯⎯⎯⎯⎯⎯

Tourism little troubled the IGY pioneers, and it is not mentioned in the treaty, although many have argued that any Antarctican is at some level a tourist. Today, tens of thousands of high-paying tourists visit the polar continent each year, usually the scenic and more accessible Antarctic Peninsula. Chile's national airline flew the first paying passengers over the peninsula in December 1956 (not landing). In October 1957 a chartered PanAm flight landed at McMurdo, its two stewardesses becoming (briefly) the first women ashore there. Both Argentine and Chilean passenger ships made peninsular stops in the late 1950s. Entrepreneur Lars-Eric Lindblad, often credited with bringing the first tourists, sailed his first commercial cruise to the southern high latitudes in 1966. New Zealand ran tourist overflights for several years until 1979, when a DC-10 crashed into Mount Erebus, killing all 257 summer-clad tourists.[112]

Convinced that tourism was inevitable, Phil Smith took what he called a "very unconventional view for the NSF" in the 1960s. He believed having a policy for managing tourism was a better strategy than trying to hold it off. The Navy understandably preferred to discourage visitors, especially "adventure tourists" whose risky schemes could entail costly search and rescue. After much "back and forth" with NSF and the Navy, Smith consulted with Lindblad. He and Navy captain Price Lewis then drafted the first operational policies for the U.S. Antarctic Policy Group. In 1966 he and New Zealand's Thomson developed rules for the first large tourist cruises. Their work brought the issue to the fourth ATCM in Santiago that year and to both SCAR and treaty meetings subsequently. The treaty delegates in Oslo in 1975 produced a lengthy recommendation based on the Smith-Thomson rules that, with only minor modifications, has served since. It seeks to avoid disrupting science, to maintain the ATS, and to minimize tourists' environmental impact while encouraging their "responsible and organized" travel. In 1994 the Kyoto ATCPs put all tourism regulations into a single document legally buttressed by the Environmental Protocol.[113]

Tourists have generally been good citizens in Antarctica. They do not stay long and mostly remain aboard ship, where their effect on the terrestrial environment is insignificant, Scully said. Tour operators know it is in their interest to keep the polar continent pristine, and they even exceed environmental guidelines. Tourism researcher Peter Beck noted also that the fact that tour operators need the cooperation of treaty states for access and perhaps emergency assistance "overhangs the industry as an exceedingly credible form of implied sanction against abuse." Tour operators carry mandatory insurance to pay for any help they might need, which defrays actual costs, although time lost to regular programs cannot be recovered. The International Association of Antarctica Tour Operators and the regional Pacific Asia Travel Association have been invited to send representatives to ATCP meetings in recent years, a recognition of the importance of their understanding and goodwill. Rutford testified in 1991 that he had changed his mind about tourists: their learning about scientific research and environmental concerns was a "valuable public relations tool" for the science program.[114]

The U.S. Navy continued to support Antarctic operations for more than four decades—through Deep Freeze 97, although the parameters evolved. In an efficiency move, the Navy transferred all of its icebreakers to the Coast Guard (in the Department of Transportation) in 1965 and 1966. Last to go was the indomitable *Glacier*; it served polar duty until 1987, when hull deterioration made further ice work "imprudent." The Coast Guard commissioned two far more powerful polar-class icebreakers, the *Polar Star* in 1976 and the *Polar Sea* in 1978. Today, these ships clear Antarctic shipping lanes for incoming cargo, usually alternating by year, although difficult ice in 2001–2002 required them both. Finally, in a cost-saving measure driven by downsizing after the end of the Cold War and the desire to focus its resources on war fighting, the Navy disestablished the United States Naval Support Force, Antarctica, on 12 March 1998 at its home base, Port Hueneme, California, a few weeks after lowering the flag at Deep Freeze headquarters in Christchurch.[115]

Naval air support continued for another year. VXE-6 was disestablished in solemn and emotional ceremonies at the Naval Air Station, Point Mugu, California, on 27 March 1999. By then the Navy had completed a three-year transition of Antarctic air logistics support to the U.S. Air Force and the New York Air National Guard's 109th Airlift Wing, headquartered in Scotia, New York, which already supported military bases in Greenland and north-polar operations. A private contractor began taking over helicopter service in 1996–1997. Otters, now twin-engine, are chartered when required. DC-3s (the Navy's workhorse R4D) have been reintroduced. By its own account, in forty-four years VXE-6 logged more than 200,000 flight hours in Antarctic support, ferrying more than 195,000 passengers, 240 million pounds of dry cargo, and nearly 10 million gallons of fuel all over the continent. Flying during the winter is suspended, although a number of brave night rescues have been made, beginning in 1961 with the evacuation of a seriously ill Soviet scientist from Byrd Station. A scheduled night flight in June 1967 concluded without incident, and "winfly" (winter fly-in) in August now routinely delivers early science projects and additional support staff to help prepare for summer's busy "mainbody."[116]

If for the Navy Antarctic support was an incongruous calling, especially as the age of peace lengthened under the benign eye of the Antarctic Treaty, it did well a job no other American institution was prepared to do at all. If it simultaneously kept a Cold War ear cocked to national-security and strategic goals, it did so within the peaceable common-purpose legacy of the IGY. In 1972 Capt. Donald Mehaffey, Deep Freeze I supply officer, wrote in a Naval War College thesis that Antarctica held dubious military significance but "considerable strategic importance as a source of national prestige." Today, with the Cold War and Antarctica's military era over, civilian leaders offer "US presence" along with science and stewardship as the "principal justifications and objectives" of U.S. policy and action. They make the same point, highlighting a deep American investment in leadership on the frozen desert.[117]

Of the seven IGY "cities" the Seabees built with haste and ingenuity during Deep Freeze I and II, virtually nothing remains. Little America V was lost to the sea as the ice shelf in which it nestled advanced northward and calved off. Exactly when is not certain. According to Ted Scambos of the National Snow and Ice Data Center (NSIDC) in Boulder, Colorado, at some time in the 1960s "a berg or a couple of bergs calved off from the same area and carried all that history away." (Iceberg tracking began in the late 1970s.) This is consistent with the views of then-Lieutenant Stokes, who closed the base in January 1959. He took an aerial photograph that showed "a large, visible crevasse on the shelf cutting off LA V in a wide semi-circular arc." He believed that working crack would take the station, probably soon. By glaciologist Bert Crary's measurements, Little America had migrated about 1,400 yards northwest in a fifteen-month period during 1957 and 1958, and when the *Glacier* visited Kainan Bay in early 1960 to remove usable items from the camp, operations officer Ross Hatch saw it near the edge of the barrier, its calving looking imminent.[118]

This general agreement is sometimes confused by later writers who lumped all five Little Americas together in the Bay of Whales, but the IGY station was further east at Kainan Bay, and icebergs were later reported to contain this station when it could have been another. (By 1955 the Highjump LA IV tent camp near the ice edge was half gone, visible in the face of the barrier, but IGY men visited LA III, buried but intact from 1940.) At any rate, since the ice front is now considerably south of the latitudes of all the historic bases, they are definitely gone. The timing of the demise of Ellsworth Station is similarly uncertain, although the NSIDC cites a calving of the Filchner Ice Shelf in April 1986 that took everything north of the Grand Chasm, which would also have meant the losses of Shackleton and General Belgrano stations.[119]

Australia, faced with rebuilding the deteriorating Wilkes Station, opened a new one instead in 1969 and named it for Casey. Nearby Wilkes soon disintegrated in wind and weather. The joint operation of Hallett Station with New Zealand continued until 1964 when a disastrous fire destroyed the main science building. Americans then used it alone, only in the summer, until 1973, primarily for biology. For the unusually rich vegetation and animal life of its environs, it was designated Specially Protected Area No. 7 in 1966. In 1983 Thomson and NSF representative Kenneth Moulton agreed that Hallett's physical plant should be removed—"a pity" for Thomson, who thought Hallett was the most beautiful locale in Antarctica. One building remains as an emergency shelter; environmental cleanup continues. The new Byrd Station, built in 1961 when the first jury-rigged huts began to sag beyond repair, saw use until 1972; by then the accumulating snow load was crushing it, too. Summer field stations continue there. Several small stations have dotted the continent since the IGY to serve special research interests, later abandoned to spread resources in new directions. Among these were Siple Station at the base of the Antarctic Peninsula, the southern terminus of magnetic lines of force traveling far into space from their geomagnetic conjugate point in Quebec; Eights Station about 120 miles east-northeast of Siple, also for upper-atmosphere physics; and multipurpose Plateau Station on the high East Antarctic ice cap, the coldest and most remote U.S. outpost. Temporary camps come and go each summer.[120]

Of the originals, only Amundsen-Scott Station at the South Pole and McMurdo continue. Neither would be recognizable to IGY eyes. The first South Pole Station ("Old Pole") lies crushed and buried, without even a mound in the infinite snowscape to reveal its former life. The familiar geodesic dome station that opened in January 1975 has been outgrown and is also slowly surrendering to drift. Under construction is a two-story elevated complex designed to be jacked up in the future as snow levels slowly rise. Dick Bowers's pioneers marvel at the complexity and ambition of this third-generation undertaking while the new builders, led by NSF's Jerry Marty and Raytheon's

Carlton Walker, supported by a functioning community, stand in awe of those who started with nothing in the virgin snow. Completion of "New Pole" is scheduled for 2006–2007.[121]

McMurdo, long "the New York of the Antarctic," is by far the largest "settlement" on the continent, with a summer population of about a thousand souls. It is still the logistics hub. Ships tie up at an ice pier in Winter Quarters Bay, while planes land on one of three ice airstrips depending on the season and ice conditions. Around 200 winter over to maintain and improve the station's infrastructure, prepare for the spring influx, and pursue science. NSF's "Chalet," built in 1969–1970, is the administrative and science center. More than a dozen dormitories house a flowing crowd of scientists and support staff, who eat in pleasant, padded comfort in a light-flooded dining hall overlooking majestic pink-tinged mountains. A sprinkling of stop signs and two automatic teller machines further attest to civilized living. But sadly, except for the rebuilt Seabees Memorial on Arrival Heights, not a single identifiable structure from Deep Freeze I remains to witness the IGY builders' achievements. McMurdo's oldest existing building, an oversized Quonset hut now housing a two-lane bowling alley and, upstairs, the collections of the fledgling McMurdo Historical Society, was constructed in 1958. The oldest Clements-style building, originally a chief petty officers' club, went up in 1960. Its slightly pitched roof (to thwart the leakiness of flat ones) introduced a new design designation, T-5, and the Clements name disappeared into history.[122]

One post-IGY landmark, no longer there, was McMurdo's nuclear-power plant, the only one in Antarctic history. At a time when atomic energy seemed the wave of the future, it offered an inviting alternative to the heavy logistics demands of shipping in the fuel (more than half of all incoming freight) for generators, space heaters, and vehicles. The pressurized-water system prototype (to create steam then converted to electricity and to process potable water, another benefit) arrived on the *Arneb* in December 1961. It was small, lightweight, and modular so LC-130s could deliver the components of later units to Byrd and Pole. The plant, designated PM-3A and built about halfway up Observation Hill, delivered its first useful power to the station on 12 July 1962. It continued until September 1972 when Navy inspectors found leakage in the primary coolant piping that suggested possible corrosion stress in the reactor's pressure vessel. The Navy shut the plant down in February 1973 for a complete inspection, but in the end that high cost plus the uncertainty of its outcome led to the removal of the entire facility—including seventy metric tons of radioactive waste that was returned to Port Hueneme. Ordinary expenses also proved too high. Deep Freeze I mechanic John Randall, who wintered over at

McMurdo twice more in the 1960s as a nuclear-plant mechanic, cited the need for intensive operator training, the higher costs of building materials (they required a certificate of manufacture to guarantee specifications), and the fact that "you can operate a 350-megawatt power plant with almost the same crew size as you can a two-megawatt power plant [McMurdo's] because of their safety requirements and all that stuff."[123]

Palmer Station, on the rock of Anvers Island about halfway up the western side of the Antarctic Peninsula, is the third currently operating U.S. science station. It was built in 1965, primarily for biological research. A new, larger station was completed in 1970. North of the Antarctic Circle, Palmer operates year-round with help from both the 1992-built research icebreaker R/V *Nathaniel B. Palmer* and, since 1998, the ice-strengthened R/V *Laurence M. Gould*, which transports both researchers and supplies to the station several times a year. It also houses onboard research in marine biology, oceanography, and geophysics. Palmer joins a crowded international field of stations on the peninsula, asserting U.S. presence and perhaps a steadying hand where territorial rivalries yet persist.[124]

And so, what the Antarctic pioneers of the extraordinary 1950s wrought has endured and prospered. In 1959 Walter Sullivan wrote grandly, "It seems probable that as the world grows up economically, politically, and scientifically, there will be even more ambitious IGYs." There have been none, although a fourth International Polar Year (IPY4) is being planned for 2007–2008, the fiftieth anniversary of the IGY. The truth is, thanks to the military who provided an infrastructure and the diplomats who crafted a political peace, as well as the scientists whose appetites were only whetted, the IGY in Antarctica never ended.[125]

NOTES

ABBREVIATIONS AND SHORT FORMS USED IN NOTES

Federal records used in this study are held at the National Archives and Records Administration, Archives II facility (NARA II), in College Park, Maryland. They are designated by Record Group (RG) number.

RG 313   Records of U.S. Naval Operating Forces, Operations Plans and Reports 1955–1972, Operation Deep Freeze, I–IV. Boxes 1–28.

RG 59   Records of the U.S. State Department, CDF (Central Decimal File) 1955–1959

Boxes 1651–1656: International Organizations/Conferences VIII (399.829)

Boxes 2772–2777: Regional/Antarctica (702.022)

Many of the relevant documents of this period were originally classified Confidential or Secret. Most are now available or declassifiable.

RG 307 Records of the National Science Foundation (NSF), Office of Antarctic Programs, IGY: NAS-USNC IGY Documents 1955–1959

RG 401 Records of Gift Collections Pertaining to the Polar Regions, numbered by contributor
RG 401 (5) Carl R. Eklund papers
RG 401 (59) Laurence M. Gould papers
RG 401 (82) Philip M. Smith papers
RG 401 (124) Albert P. Crary papers

NAS-IGY Records pertaining to the IGY in the archives of the National Academy of Sciences

ADFA Antarctic Deep Freeze Association
CTF, TF Commander Task Force, Task Force
CTG, TG Commander Task Group, Task Group
DF Operation Deep Freeze (with Roman numeral or year)
GPO Government Printing Office, Washington, D.C.
McMurdo Log Narrative Log, Williams Air Operating Facility, McMurdo Sound, Antarctica, kept daily by Lcdr. D. W. Canham Jr., retyped with edits and annotations by YNC Robert L. Chaudoin
MCB (Spec) Mobile Construction Battalion (Special)
MoC Memorandum of Conversation, internal State Department record
MoM Memorandum of Meeting, State Department record
SP Log South Pole Daily Narrative, 13 October 1956–20 January 1957, by Richard A. Bowers, retyped by Chaudoin
SSLR Scientific Station Leaders Reports, for 1957–1958 and 1958–1959. Available in RG 307, Box 5.
Trans. AGU *Transactions, American Geophysical Union*
USNC-IGY United States National Committee for the International Geophysical Year
USNSFA United States Naval Support Force, Antarctica

PROLOGUE

1. [Gilbert H. Grosvenor], "An Ice Wrapped Continent," *National Geographic* 17, no. 2 (February 1907): 95. This article reviews *The Voyage of* The Discovery by Robert F. Scott.

2. U.S. Antarctic Program External Panel, *The United States in Antarctica* (Washington, D.C.: NSF, 1997), 9–16.

3. Walker Chapman, ed., *Antarctic Conquest: The Great Explorers in Their Own Words* (Indianapolis: Bobbs-Merrill, 1965), 3–4, 25–37; Kenneth J. Bertrand, *Americans in Antarctica, 1775–1948* (New York: American Geographical Society, 1971), 1.

4. Bertrand, *Americans in Antarctica*, 2–3.

5. Ibid., 77–79; Chapman, *Antarctic Conquest*, 42–60.

6. Bertrand, *Americans in Antarctica*, 4–5; Chapman, *Antarctic Conquest*, 92–105, 116–128.

7. Chapman, *Antarctic Conquest*, 114, see 106–116; Bertrand, *Americans in Antarctica*, 185 (quote), see also, chapter 10.

8. Bertrand, *Americans in Antarctica*, 148–150, 163–167 (quote on 164).

9. G. E. Fogg, *A History of Antarctic Science* (Cambridge: Cambridge University Press, 1992), 95–96.

10. Bertrand, *Americans in Antarctica*, 198–205 (quote on 203); Lisle A. Rose, *Assault on Eternity: Richard E. Byrd and the Exploration of Antarctica, 1946–1947* (Annapolis: Naval Institute Press, 1980), 10.

11. Niels H. De V. Heathcote and Angus Armitage, "The First International Polar Year (1882–1883)," International Council of Scientific Unions, Comite Spécial de l'Année Géophysique Internationale, *Annals of the International Geophysical Year, 1957–1958*, vol. 1 (London: Pergamon, 1959), 6–7.

12. Shackleton's own accounts are *The Heart of the Antarctic: The Farthest South Expedition, 1907–1909*, chapters 14–16, and *South: The Endurance Expedition* (both New York: Signet, 2000, and other editions). See Caroline Alexander, *The Endurance: Shackleton's Legendary Antarctic Expedition* (New York: Alfred A. Knopf, 2001), among other accounts.

13. See Roald Amundsen, *The South Pole: An Account of the Norwegian Antarctic Expedition in the "Fram," 1910–1912*, 2 vols., trans. A. G. Chater (London: C. Hurst, 1912); Robert Falcon Scott, *Scott's Last Expedition: The Journals* (New York: Carroll & Graf, 1996).

14. See Roland Huntford, *The Last Place on Earth* (New York: Modern Library, 1999; published as *Scott and Amundsen* by Hodder and Stoughton, 1979). Susan Solomon, in *The Coldest March: Scott's Fatal Antarctic Expedition* (New Haven: Yale University Press, 2001), compares weather data over time to show that Scott died from unusual cold, but too many poor choices seem a larger factor.

15. Shackleton's *Endurance* sailed at the outbreak of hostilities. Some close the Heroic Age with his death on South Georgia in 1922, but, practically, the difference meant little.

16. Bertrand, *Americans in Antarctica*, 285–287. Bertrand designates a Mechanical Age, beginning at the end of World War I.

17. Ibid., 275–282, 313 (quote); see also, Stephen J. Pyne, *The Ice: A Journey to Antarctica* (Seattle: University of Washington Press, 1998), 98–101.

18. Rose, *Assault on Eternity*, 20; David G. Campbell, Afterword to *Alone* by Richard E. Byrd (1938; facsimile reprint, New York: Kodansha International, 1995), 298.

19. Richard Evelyn Byrd, *Little America: Aerial Exploration in the Antarctic, the Flight to the South Pole* (New York: G. P. Putnam's Sons, 1930), 332–336, 341–342.

20. V. Laursen, "The Second International Polar Year," *Annals*, vol. 1, 216–217; Walter Sullivan, "The International Geophysical Year" [hereafter "IGY"], *International*

Conciliation, no. 521 (January 1959): 265–268; Bertrand, *Americans in Antarctica,* 313–317.

21. Byrd, *Alone,* 3–4 (quote), 15–16, 31. See also, Richard Evelyn Byrd, *Discovery: The Story of the Second Byrd Antarctic Expedition* (New York: G. P. Putnam's Sons, 1935), 225–238; Charles J.V. Murphy to Paul Dalrymple, 25 February 1981, unaccessioned research notes of Deborah Shapley for *The Seventh Continent,* NARA II.

22. William B. Allman, "Polar Star Rising," *Aviation History* (March 1999): 46–52; Walter Sullivan, *Quest for a Continent* (New York: McGraw-Hill, 1957), 101–105.

23. Bertrand, *Americans in Antarctica,* 407–409; Sullivan, *Quest,* 138–139; Finn Ronne, *Antarctica, My Destiny: A Personal History by the Last of the Great Polar Explorers* (New York: Hastings House, 1979), 94–96.

24. USAP External Panel, *The United States in Antarctica,* 21; Fogg, *History of Antarctic Science,* 157–164.

25. Jeffrey D. Myhre, *The Antarctic Treaty System: Politics, Law, and Diplomacy* (Boulder: Westview, 1986), 24; George Toney, interview with author, 28 October 1998, 5; Bertrand, *Americans in Antarctica,* 473; see also, Philip W. Quigg, *A Pole Apart: The Emerging Issue of Antarctica* (New York: McGraw-Hill, 1983), 129–130.

26. Stephen Martin, *A History of Antarctica* (n.p.: State Library of New South Wales Press, 1996), 196–198.

27. CTF 68, Army Observers' Report of Operation Highjump, September 1947, 15, RG 313, CTF 68, General Reports 1946–1947, Box 2. Myhre opined that Highjump was sited in the Antarctic "to be less provocative to the Soviets"; *Antarctic Treaty System,* 24.

28. CTF 68, Army Observers' Report, 15–16 (quote on 16). See also, U.S. Navy Antarctic Development Project 1947, Report of Operation Highjump, vol. I, 7, RG 313, TF 68, Box 1; Rose, *Assault on Eternity,* 245–246.

29. Apparently, the code name Highjump was a droll takeoff on the original designation, Operation Pole Vault, which was thought too revealing when the classified plans were in preparation. CTF 68, Army Observers' Report, 15.

30. Report, Operation Highjump, vol. I, 2; Robert D. Hayton, "The Antarctic Settlement of 1959," *American Journal of International Law* 54 (1960): 351n. See Richard E. Byrd's elliptical "Our Navy Explores Antarctica," *National Geographic* 42, no. 4 (October 1947): 429–522.

31. George Dufek, *Operation Deepfreeze* (New York: Harcourt, Brace, 1957), 6, 12; Paul Siple, *90° South: The Story of the American South Pole Conquest* (New York: G. P. Putnam's Sons, 1959), 77; Rose, *Assault on Eternity,* 95.

32. CTF 68, Army Observers' Report, 16; Rose, *Assault on Eternity,* 55.

33. Conrad "Gus" Shinn, interview with author, 11 May 1999, 6–7; Rose, *Assault on Eternity,* 53.

34. Rose, *Assault on Eternity,* 52; Bertrand, *Americans in Antarctica,* 491–492; Report, Operation Highjump, vol. II, Ship Operations, 2, 5–6.

35. Bertrand, *Americans in Antarctica,* 492–493.

36. Rose, *Assault on Eternity,* 129–132; Shinn interview, 7.

37. Dufek, *Operation Deepfreeze*, 6, 13–14; Shinn interview, 6.

38. Siple, *90° South*, 77, 79–80; Report, Operation Highjump, vol. I, Annex 2(a); Shinn interview, 4–5; Bertrand, *Americans in Antarctica*, 502–503; Dufek, *Operation Deepfreeze*, 12–22.

39. William H. Kearns Jr. [copilot of crashed PBM] and Beverley Britton, *The Silent Continent* (New York: Harper & Brothers, 1955), chapter 11; Dufek, *Operation Deepfreeze*, 25; Siple, *90° South*, 89.

40. Rose, *Assault on Eternity*, 249–250; Report, Operation Highjump, 3 vols.; Bertrand, *Americans in Antarctica*, 484–485.

41. Report, Operation Highjump, vol. II, Aviation, 71–72, 91, 160, Ship Operations, 21; vol. III.

42. Siple, *90° South*, 79–80; William J. Menster, *Strong Men South* (Dubuque: Stromen, 1949), 1–3; Report, Operation Highjump, vol. III.

43. CTF 68, Army Observers' Report, 324–326. A footnote states that the views given were those of the authors and not necessarily those of the Army, Air Force, Navy, or government agencies.

44. Ronne, *Antarctica, My Destiny*, 130. See full account in Ronne's *Antarctic Conquest: The Story of the Ronne Expedition, 1946–1948* (New York: G. P. Putnam's Sons, 1949).

45. Ronne, *Antarctica, My Destiny*, 178; Bertrand, *Americans in Antarctica*, 515–517.

46. Jennie Darlington, *My Antarctic Honeymoon: A Year at the Bottom of the World* (Garden City, NY: Doubleday, 1956), 94.

47. Ronne, *Antarctica, My Destiny*, 140 (quote), 144–145; Bertrand, *Americans in Antarctica*, 521.

48. CTF 39, Report, Second Antarctic Developments Project (1947–1948), ii, Aerology 23, Annex VI 1, RG 313, CTF 39 (Operation Windmill), Box 1; Bertrand, *Americans in Antarctica*, 533–535; Rose, *Assault on Eternity*, 252.

49. Darlington, *My Antarctic Honeymoon*, chapters 30–31; Lewis O. Smith, "'Operation Windmill': The Second Antarctic Developments Project," *Antarctic Journal* (March–April 1968): 35; Ronne, *Antarctica, My Destiny*, 177–178.

50. Untitled, undated draft press release, RG 313, CTF 66, Administrative Subject Files 1947–1949, Box 1; Concept of Operations, Highjump II, 28 December 1948 (claims posture quote); Secret Memorandum for Secretary of Defense, Antarctic Developments Project 1949–1950, undated; Ronne to Paige, 4 November 48 with attached 26 Aug 1948 proposal, RG 313, CTF 66, Staff Study Reports, Box 1.

51. Deputy Chief of Naval Operations (Operations) to CNO, Antarctic Expedition 1949–1950, Concept of Operation, 10 February 1949; H. H. McLean to OP–03, Antarctic Operation 1949–1950—Revised Study, 18 March 1949, RG 313, CTF 66, Staff Study Reports 1948–1949, Box 1; CNO to Distribution, Antarctic Developments Project 1949–1950: Cancellation of Priority, 25 August 1949; Byrd to Secretary of Defense, Importance of Operation Highjump II to Our National Security, 29 August 1949; Byrd to Johnson, 30 August 1949, RG 313, CTF 66, Administrative Subject Files 1947–1949, Box 1; Siple, *90° South*, 81.

52. Myhre, *Antarctic Treaty System*, 28–30; M. J. Peterson, *Managing the Frozen South: The Creation and Evolution of the Antarctic Treaty System* (Berkeley: University of California Press, 1988), 37–38; Quigg, *Pole Apart*, 135–136.

53. Gordon de Q. Robin, "Science and Logistics in Antarctica," in *Frozen Future: A Prophetic Report From Antarctica*, Richard S. Lewis and Philip M. Smith, eds. (New York: Quadrangle Books, 1973), 272–274.

CHAPTER 1

1. *Illustrated* (London), 27 July 1957, 26–27, cited in U.S. House, Committee on Foreign Affairs, Subcommittee on National Security Policy and Scientific Developments, "The Political Legacy of the International Geophysical Year," by Harold Bullis (Washington, D.C.: GPO, November 1973), 52.

2. James Van Allen, interview with Brian Shoemaker, 18 November 1997, 17–18. See also, James Van Allen, "Genesis of the International Geophysical Year," *Polar Times* (Spring-Summer 1998): 5. The other guests were Ernest H. Vestine, J. Wallace Joyce, and S. Fred Singer.

3. Van Allen interview, 20–21; Sullivan, "IGY," 267–268; Lloyd Berkner, Columbia University Oral History, interview with Jay Holmes, 4 June 1959, 2–3, Library of Congress, Manuscript Division, L. V. Berkner papers, Box 19; Allan A. Needell, *Science, Cold War and the American State: Lloyd V. Berkner and the Balance of Professional Ideals* ([12 countries]: Harwood, 2000), 133–135, 299–300; NAS, Antarctic Research: Elements of a Coordinated Program, 2 May 1949, reprinted for USNC-IGY, May 1954, RG 307, Box 1. See also, Albert P. Crary, "History of the International Geophysical Year," 1–2, draft manuscript courtesy of Mildred Rogers Crary.

4. Alan Shapley, interview with Brian Shoemaker, 31 January 1997; Symposium on Scientific Aspects of the International Geophysical Year, 1957–1958, 28 April 1954, *Proceedings, NAS* 40, no. 10 (October 1954); Holmes, verbatim transcript of symposium discussion, 28 April 1954, 42–43; NAS-IGY: Organization USNC, 1954.

5. Sullivan, "IGY," 270–271. See also, Harold Spencer Jones, "The Inception and Development of the International Geophysical Year," *Annals*, vol. 1, 383–413; see also, Berkner interview, 5, 9, 11–14.

6. Sullivan, "IGY," 271, 274 (quote); E. Herbays to five scientific unions, 27 November 1952, NAS-IGY: Organization USNC, 1953; Justification of Supplemental Program and Estimates FY 1956, NAS: NSF-IGY, FY56; Berkner interview, 19–26 (quote on 23).

7. Sullivan, "IGY," 273–274; Minutes, First Meeting Technical Panel on World Days and Communications USNC-IGY, 18 August 1955, NAS-IGY: Science Program World Days.

8. Sullivan, "IGY," 274–276. See also, Berkner interview, 23–26; Rudolph, MoC Bronk, Waterman et al., Satellite Launching in American Part of IGY Program, 22 March 1955, RG 59, Box 1652.

9. Organizational Structure of IGY, NAS-IGY: Organization USNC, 1957–1958; Biographical Sketch of Dr. Joseph Kaplan, of Hugh Odishaw NAS-IGY: Personnel, Antarctica; Shapley inteview.

10. Shapley interview; NAS-IGY: Background Budget Material, IGY FY 1959 Supplemental Budget, 1 June 1958; Fifth meeting USNC-IGY, 8–9 April 1954, cited in Crary, "IGY," 39–40; J. Merton England, *A Patron for Pure Science: The National Science Foundation's Formative Years, 1945–57* (Washington, D.C.: National Science Foundation, 1982), 303.

11. NAS, Roster of the US-IGY Program, 3rd ed., April 1983; Siple, *90° South,* 93–94; Atwood to Kaplan, 20 August 1953, cited in Crary, "IGY," 29.

12. Harry Wexler, Antarctic Diary, 27, 28 April, 20 May 1955, Library of Congress, Manuscript Division, Harry Wexler papers, Box 27. Albert P. Crary's extensive verbatim notes on this diary facilitated the early writing, manuscript courtesy of M. R. Crary. Crary to Folks, 30 June 1956, RG 401 (124), Box 1; *Newsweek,* 5 November 1956, 76.

13. Shapley interview; George Toney, USNC-IGY Antarctic Scientific Station Leaders Reports (SSLR), Byrd Station 1957, 1. Bound volume of all SSLRs courtesy of George Toney; they are also found at NARA II, RG 307, Box 5. See also, George J. Dufek, "Tenth Anniversary of First Landing at the South Pole," *Antarctic Journal* 1, no. 6 (November–December 1966): 267.

14. Berkner to Nicolet, 15 February 1955, cited in Crary, "IGY," 63; Chapman to Laclavère, Berkner, and Nicolet, 13 June 1955, NAS-IGY: First CSAGI Antarctic Conference Correspondence.

15. Philip Mange, phone conversation with author, 10 December 2001, and "The IGY of 1957–58, an Unprecedented Surge in International Scientific Achievement," paper delivered to the American Association for the Advancement of Science, AMSIE '97, Seattle, 17 February 1997. Mange later joined the US IGY staff. See also, Crary, "IGY," 68–69; Wexler to Odishaw, Some Impressions . . . IGY-Antarctic Conference, July 4–10, 11 July 1955, NAS-IGY: First CSAGI Antarctic Conference Correspondence.

16. Minutes, USNC-IGY Antarctic Committee Meeting, 13 October 1954, NAS-IGY: USNC Antarctic Program; Minutes, First Antarctic Conference, Paris, 6–10 July 1955, unofficial translation 5 March 1956, NAS-IGY: Delegates and Resolutions; Odishaw to U.S. Antarctic Committee, International Antarctic Conference, 24 May 1955, and Odishaw to USNC Executive Committee and Antarctic Committee, A Tentative Summary of the Antarctic Conference, 12 July 1955, NAS-IGY: First CSAGI Antarctic Conference Correspondence; Crary, "IGY," 50.

17. Minutes, First Antarctic Conference; Siple, *90° South,* 99; Wexler, diary, 8 July 1955. See also, Fogg, *History of Antarctic Science,* 173.

18. State MoC, with ambassadors of Australia, Great Britain, South Africa, and New Zealand, 9 Feb 1956, and Beam to Acting Secretary, Reply to [these countries], 9 March 1956, RG 59, Box 1651; Minutes, First Antarctic Conference; Shapley interview; Australian Embassy to Secretary of State, 2 August 1955, and reply, 11 August 1955, RG 59, Box 1652.

19. Sullivan, "IGY," 284–294; Green to McConaughy, Chinese Participation in IGY, 20 September 1956, and attachments, RG 59, Box 1651; Wallace W. Atwood Jr., "The International Geophysical Year in Retrospect," *Department of State Bulletin*, 11 May 1959, 3.

20. Wexler, diary, 7, 8 July 1955; Shapley interview; Minutes, First Antarctic Conference; Wexler to Odishaw, Report on III CSAGI Antarctic Conference, 7 August 1956, NAS-IGY: Third Antarctic Conference Correspondence; CIR 238–30-7-56, III Conference Antarctique, Report by Chairman, Antarctic Radio Transmission Working Group, NAS-IGY: Third Antarctic Conference Minutes and Resolutions; see NAS-IGY: Science Program/Weather Central LAS [Little America Station] files, including Provisional List of Antarctic IGY Radio Stations, 13 April 1956.

21. CIR 267 8/20/1956 (120), [Minutes], Third Antarctic Conference, Paris, 30 July–4 August 1956, NAS-IGY: Third Antarctic Conference, Minutes and Resolutions; Wexler to Odishaw, Some Impressions . . . [First] IGY-Antarctic Conference; Wexler to Odishaw, Report on Third CSAGI Antarctic Conference; Morton Rubin, interview with author, 24 February 2000; Wexler, diary, 8 July, 14, 15 September 1955; Bowdler to Dreier and Krieg, Briefing sessions with representatives of USNC-IGY, 19 July 1956, RG 59, Box 1652.

22. Minutes, Second Antarctic Conference, Brussels, 8–14 September 1955, NAS-IGY: Second Antarctic Conference; Wexler, diary, 11 September 1955; Edward M. d'I Ward, Memoirs: United States Navy, Deepfreeze 1 and 2, 1955–1957, Navy Task Force 43 and Air Development Squadron Six (VX-6) [privately bound, 1998], 10; Edward Ward, interview with author, 20 January 1999, 9; Dufek, *Operation Deepfreeze*, 189.

23. Kaplan cited in Crary, "IGY," 78; NSF Justification of Supplemental Program and Estimates, FY 1956, NAS-IGY: NSF-IGY FY56; Crary to Odishaw, Comparison of U.S. and USSR IGY Research, 9 July 1956, NAS-IGY: Antarctic Committee Organization.

24. Wexler to Odishaw, Report on Third CSAGI Antarctic Conference; Mirabito to Odishaw, Third Paris Antarctic Conference, 13 August 1956, NAS-IGY: Third Antarctic Conference, Correspondence; Hanessian to Odishaw, Location of Antarctic Stations, 29 July 1955, NAS-IGY: CSAGI Antarctic Stations.

25. Sullivan, "IGY," 282–283; Shapley interview; NAS-IGY, Organizational Structure of IGY, 24 April 1958, NAS-IGY: Organization USNC, 1957–1958. World Data Centers, now about four dozen strong, are still going, still sporting the IGY logo on their letterhead. Stanley Ruttenberg, telephone conversation, 12 December 2001. He was an IGY program officer.

26. *Public Papers of the Presidents, Dwight D. Eisenhower, 1954*, 25 June 1954, ¶153.

27. Minutes, First Meeting Finance Working Group USNC-IGY, 14 April 1953; Minutes, NSB, 28th meeting, 13 August 1954, Appendix 1; Waterman, Memorandum to . . . National Science Board, 25 November 1953, NAS-IGY: Organization USNC, 1953; Crary, "IGY," 22, see also, 33, 44.

28. Kaplan, Memorandum to USNC-IGY, 10 December 1953, NAS-IGY: Organization USNC, 1953; Crary, "IGY," 34–35, 43, 81.

29. NAS-IGY "Testimony" files, "Budget Hearings" and "Budget Testimony" files. Most of these formal statements are undated. England, *Patron for Pure Science*, 298.

30. Crary, "IGY," 41–42, 61–62; Minutes, USNC-IGY Antarctic Committee Meeting, 13 October 1954; Hanessian to Odishaw, NSF Representation on the OCB [Operations Coordinating Board] Antarctic Working Group, 15 February 1956, and Some Illustrations Suggestive of Pattern . . . June 1955, NAS-IGY: OCB Antarctic Group.

31. Wexler, diary, 20, 26 May, 7 July 1955; Crary, "IGY," 67, 76; Berkner cited in Needell, *Science, Cold War and the American State*, 334–335.

32. Minutes, First Meeting, Panel on Antarctic Policies of the USNC-IGY Antarctic Committee, 25 February 1955, NAS-IGY: USNC Antarctic Committee—Confidential; Paul Siple, position paper on command structure, 2 July 1956, and Antarctic Operational Command Relationships: NAS and DOD, 11 July 1956, NAS-IGY: IGY-DOD Command Structure.

33. CS to JH, [?] June 1956, NAS-IGY: IGY-DOD Command Structure; CTF-43, Operations Plan no. 1–57, Part A of Annex N: Command Structure, RG 313, Box 19.

34. Byrd to CNO (Op-33), Relationship Between Scientific and Military Personnel in the Antarctic, 20 August 1956, NAS-IGY: IGY-DOD Command Structure.

35. Quarles to Dodge, 19 March 1954; A Note on Foundation and Industry Support for the U.S. Program, May 1954, NAS-IGY: Organization USNC, 1954; Minutes, USNC-IGY Antarctic Committee Meeting, 13 October 1954.

36. Murphy to Waterman, 20 April 1954, NAS-IGY: Organization USNC, 1954; Horsey to Barbour, 7 July 1955, and Snay to Crowley, 7 September 1955, RG 59, Box 2773.

37. Raynor to Barbour and Merchant, 29 April 1955, Dearborn to Sparks, Sparks to Bishop, 19 May 1955, Crowley to distribution, with attachments, 30 September 1955, all in RG 59, Box 2773.

CHAPTER 2

1. Mary H. Cadwalader, "Operation Ante-Freeze," *Life* (21 November 1955): 63, Eunice Moss scrapbook.

2. Dufek, *Operation Deepfreeze*, 39, 41. The Navy named Task Force 43 on 1 February 1955.

3. CTF 43, DF I, Operation Plan no. 1–55, E-I-1–5, RG 313, Box 4.

4. Dufek, *Operation Deepfreeze*, 5, 11; Siple, *90° South*, 89, 119, 123; [John Hanessian Jr.], detached report, USNC-IGY Antarctic Operations, n.d. [October 1955], NAS-IGY: USNC Antarctic Committee—Confidential.

5. Ward, Memoirs, 2–4; Ward interview, 3–6, 9–12; Dufek, *Operation Deepfreeze*, 47; CTF 43, Report DF I, vol. 2, Logistics, Cargo and Supply, 445, RG 313, Box 5.

6. Dufek, *Operation Deepfreeze*, 42–44, 48; Siple, *90° South*, 40, 117; Crary, Resume of Conversation: Dr. Siple, Dr. Wexler et al., 9 November 1955, NAS-IGY: Antarctic Committee Organization.

7. USNC-IGY, "Antarctic Program" [the "Blue Book"], NAS, August 1955, 31–32, RG 307, Box 1; NSF-108, Navy Icebreaker Embarks for Antarctic Scientific Expedition, 1 December 1954, RG 307, Box 3; U.S. Antarctic Expedition 1954–1955, U.S.S. Atka (AGB-3), Appendix X to Annex A, Special Projects, NAS-IGY: Atka Voyage IGY; Minutes, USNC-IGY Antarctic Committee Meeting, 13 October 1954.

8. Operation Deep Freeze was numbered by year: Deep Freeze I (DF I), 1955–1956, the Navy's first year; DF II, 1956–1957, and DF III, 1957–1958, the bulk of the IGY; and DF IV, 1958–1959, IGY conclusion and continuation as International Geophysical Cooperation. By then, with Antarctic science clearly ongoing, the Navy dropped the Roman numerals for fiscal-year designations, beginning with DF [19]60 and continuing through DF [19]97.

9. Dufek, *Operation Deepfreeze* [retaining his format], 45–47; Peter J. Anderson, "United States Aircraft Losses in Antarctica," *Antarctic Journal* 9, no. 1 (January–February 1974): 5; Ward, Memoirs, 12–15, 41; Richard A. Bowers, e-mail correspondence with author, 28 March 2000.

10. CTF 43, Staff Instruction 1–55, 1955, 1-1, RG 313, Box 3; Defense Member OCB Antarctic Working Group to State Department Member, Proposed Reply to Senator Hickenlooper on US Interests in Antarctica, 15 March 1956, RG 59, Box 2772.

11. Wexler, diary, 15 October 1955, 7 March 1956 (citing Rubin). See also, Siple, *90° South*, 102–104.

12. Siple, *90° South*, 126–127; Wexler, diary, 28 January 1956; Laurence M. Gould, "Antarctica in World Affairs," *Headline Series*, no. 128 (New York: Foreign Policy Association, 20 March 1958), 30.

13. MCB (Spec), Report DF I and II, vol. 1, 1–3, A-ONE-1–2. Bound multivolume series courtesy of Dick Bowers; the volumes are available at NARA II, RG 313. See also, CTF 43, Report DF I, vol. 2; Richard A. Bowers, interview with author, 11 October 1998, 2–3.

14. Bowers interview, 3; Odishaw to CTF 43, 2 March 1955, and Dufek to Chairman, Antarctic Committee, 22 March 1955, NAS-IGY: Fiscal Correspondence and Policy (Planning).

15. Secretary of the Navy to Assistant Secretary of Defense (Comptroller), Revised funding requirements for Antarctic Program, 15 June 1955, NAS-IGY: Fiscal Correspondence and Policy (Planning); CTF 43, Report DF I, vol. 2, 446.

16. CTF 43, Report DF I, vol. 2, 450; Bowers interview, 3; Dufek, *Operation Deepfreeze*, 59.

17. Victor Young, interview with author, 10 May 1999, 24; Task Force 43, *Operation Deep Freeze I, 1955–56: The Chronicle of Task Force 43 and Its Service to Science in the First Phase of a Project of Four Years' Duration* [hereafter Cruisebook DF I], 24–25; MCB (Spec), Report DF I and II, vol. 1, 3–4; George Moss, interview with author, 9 February 1999, 2–3.

18. MCB (Spec), Report DF I and II, vol. 1, 4; CTF 43, Report DF I, vol. 2, 621–623; Bowers interview, 6, and e-mail, 28 March 2000; Young interview, 12; Young, diary, 8 October 1955.

19. CTF 43, Report DF I, vol. 2, 449; Cruisebook DF I, 32.

20. Richard Bowers, e-mail, 29 May 2000, citing personal records.

21. Siple, *90° South*, 104–105; Dufek, *Operation Deepfreeze*, 62; Willis Tressler, SSLR, Wilkes, 1958, 18.

22. CTF 43, DF I, Operation Plan Number 1–55, E-II-9–10, RG 313, Box 4; Cadwalader, "Operation Ante-Freeze," 64.

23. Dufek, *Operation Deepfreeze*, 56; Dale Powell, group interview with author, 8 May 1998; Edward N. Ehrlich, interview with author, 1 December 1998, 5.

24. Operation Deep Freeze Shipping Documents, 1955–1956, RG 307, Box 1.

25. CTF 43, DF I, Operation Plan Number 1–55, 2, E-1–9 (quote on E-9), RG 313, Box 4; ibid.; MCB (Spec), Report DF I and II, vol. 1, 4–5; CTF 43, Report DF I, vol. 2, 450–451.

26. Cadwalader, "Operation Ante-Freeze," 66; Bernard Kalb, "South Pole Cook Pledges Reform," *New York Times*, 4 December 1955, 21 (Pavilaitis quote); Jack Bursey, *Antarctic Night: One Man's Story of 28,224 Hours at the Bottom of the World* (New York: Rand McNally, 1957), 208–209; CTF 43, Report DF II, 61, RG 313, Box 8.

27. Ehrlich interview, 3–6; Kenneth Aldrich, interview with author, 24 September 1999, 3–5, 25; Ken Aldrich, Little America V, 1955–56 [privately bound memoir, n.d., n.p.]; Ken Aldrich, ADFA questionnaire.

28. Ehrlich interview, 4, 20–21; Aldrich interview, 6–7; MCB (Special), Report DF I and II, vol. 2, Little America, B-THREE-50.

29. David E. Baker, interview with author, 9 October 1998, 3–7, 13–14; Dufek, *Operation Deepfreeze*, 56–59.

30. CTF 43, DF I, Operation Plan Number 1–55, E-23–26; CTF 43, Report DF I, vol. 2, 460.

31. Cadwalader, "Operation Ante-Freeze," 63–64 (floods quote); CTF 43, Report DF I, vol. 2, 451–453, 459; MCB (Spec), Report DF I and II, vol. 1, 5; Henry M. Dater, "Byrd Station," unpaginated draft, 1972, courtesy of George Toney; John C. Behrendt, *Innocents on the Ice: A Memoir of Antarctic Exploration, 1957* (Niwot: University Press of Colorado, 1998), 104; Honkala to Humphrey, 15 February 1957, RG 307, Box 3; Henry M. Dater, "Organizational Developments in the United States Antarctic Program 1954–1965," *Antarctic Journal* (January–February 1966): 22.

32. Ehrlich interview, 2–3, 30 (First quote); Bowers interview, 2; Robert L. Chaudoin, interview with author, 20 January 1999, 2; Moss interview, 3–4; Moss, correspondence with author, 18 May 1998.

33. Brian Dalton, interview with author, 5 August 1999, 1–2, 18.

34. Ibid., 4–5.

35. Siple, *90° South*, 128.

36. Wexler, diary, 15 October 1955; [Hanessian], USNC-IGY Antarctic Operations, [October 1955]; Humphrey to Chief, Scientific Services Division, 18 August 1955, NAS-IGY: Antarctic Committee Organization.

37. Toney to Hanessian, IGY Staff Operations at CBC, Davisville, Rhode Island, September- November 1955, NAS-IGY: Science Program Antarctic Project Leaders 1954–1956; Wexler, diary, 1 October 1955.

38. Wexler, diary, 23 May, 3, 23 September, 29 October 1955. See also, Minutes, USNC Antarctic Committee Meeting, 14 October 1955, NAS-IGY: Antarctic Minutes of Meetings.

39. Ward interview, 10, 13; Ward, Memoirs, 15. See also, CTF, DF I, Operations Plan 1–55.

40. Ward interview, 14; Ward, Memoirs, 16–17; Shinn interview, 18–19; Robert Paul Streich, interview with Brian Shoemaker, 30 January 1997, 2–3, 12, 14; D. W. Canham Jr., diary, 6 December 1955.

41. Ward interview, 11–12; CTF 43, Report DF I, vol. 2, 443–444; Dufek, *Operation Deepfreeze*, 52; Dufek, "Tenth Anniversary of First Landing at the South Pole," 267.

42. "Jax Readies 'Deep Freeze' Aircraft," *Naval Aviation News* (December 1955): 11; Ward, Memoirs, 20–22.

43. The full designations were: Navy icebreakers USS *Glacier* (AGB-4) and USS *Edisto* (AGB-2); Coast Guard icebreaker USCGC *Eastwind* (WAGB-279); Navy cargo vessels USS *Arneb* (AKA-56), USS *Wyandot* (AKA-92), and USNS *Greenville Victory* (T-AK-236); and fuel tanker USS *Nespelen* (AOG-55). See individual ship reports, 1955–1959, RG 313.

44. Dale R. Taft, "The Glacier Poised for Polar Voyage," Providence *Evening Bulletin*, 19 October 1955; Bernard Kalb, "Antarctic Party Leaves U.S. Today," *New York Times*, 30 October 1955, 12; Dale R. Taft, "66 Volunteers Depart for Antarctica Duty" and "Seabees Sail on 'Operation Deepfreeze,'" Providence *Journal*, 11 November 1955, Moss scrapbook.

45. Canham, diary, 14 November 1955; NAS Press Release, U.S. Antarctic Science Program Revealed by Dr. L. M. Gould, 14 November 1955, RG 307, Box 3; Charles Bevilacqua, diary, 9 November 1955.

46. U.S. Navy Hydrographic Office, TR-33, Operation Deep Freeze I Technical Report, RG 313, Box 3; CTF 43, Report DF I, vols. 1 and 2, 1 October 1956, RG 313, Box 5.

47. Dufek, *Operation Deepfreeze*, 66–67.

48. Walter Sullivan, "Lure of Antarctica More Than Adventure: Science and International Politics Figure in New Byrd Expedition," *New York Times*, 3 April 1955, IV, 9.

49. Anthony J. Leviero, "Byrd Off Friday on Pole Venture," *New York Times*, 20 November 1955, 78; "Byrd Foresees Permanent Settlement on Antarctic," [uncited UP story, Washington, D.C.], Moss scrapbook.

50. Bevilacqua, diary, 7 December 1955.

51. Canham, diary, 14, 18, 24 November 1955; ibid., 25 November 1955; David Grisez, diary, 25 November 1955.

52. Bernard Kalb, "Navy 'YOG' Rolls in Pacific Swell," *New York Times*, 20 November 1955, 78; Jehu Blades, interview with Brian Shoemaker, 12 March 2000, 11–17, 24.

53. Cliff Bekkedahl, interview with Brian Shoemaker, 17 May 2001, 24; Canham, diary, 18, 20, 22 December 1955.

54. Clinton Davis, interview with author, 25 September 1999, 2–3; Bernard Kalb, "Antarctic Craft Hits Heavy Seas," *New York Times*, 13 December 1955, 2; Kalb, "Adm. Byrd Injured Slightly During Gale," *New York Times*, 15 December 1955, 10; Philip

Porter, interview with author, 25 September 1999, 17; USS *Glacier* AGB-4, Report DF III, 1957–1958, K-1.

55. Bernard Kalb, "Glacier Lays out Airstrip Atop Ice," *New York Times*, 19 December 1955, 18; Kalb, "Air Tie Advances Antarctic Tasks," *New York Times*, 22 December 1955, 25.

56. Dufek, *Operation Deepfreeze*, 82–86; Rubin to Odishaw, 28 January 1956, NAS-IGY: Draft DF I Reports; Shinn interview, 19.

57. Bevilacqua, diary, 21 December 1955; Aldrich interview, 24; Baker interview, 10–11.

CHAPTER 3

1. Charles M. Slaton, Antarctic Deep Freeze Association Questionnaire, courtesy of Richard A. Bowers.

2. Bowers interview, 7; MCB (Spec), Report DF I and II, vol. IV, McMurdo, D-ONE-6.

3. CTG 43.2, Report DF I Air Operations, 40, 191, courtesy of Al Raithel. The heavily loaded four-engine planes took off from Harewood Airport, Christchurch, not Wigram Air Force Base, because of the former's concrete runways.

4. MCB (Spec), Report DF I and II, vol. IV, D-ONE-7; CTG 43.2, Report DF I Air Operations, 190–191; Anderson, "United States Aircraft Losses in Antarctica," 6; Ward, Memoirs, 25–26. Ward gave the copilot's name as Lt. (jg) Hoffman. See also, Richard Bowers, e-mail correspondence, 13 February 2001.

5. MCB (Spec), Report DF I and II, vol. IV, D-ONE-7; Baker interview, 8, 13.

6. Saul Pett, "Six Rescued From Ice in Antarctic Blizzard," [Providence *Evening Bulletin*], [26 December 1955], Eunice Moss scrapbook; Chaudoin interview, 21–22.

7. "They 'Sweat It Out' on a Big Cake of Ice" and other articles, Providence *Evening Bulletin*, 28 December 1955, 1; Laurence McKinley Gould, *Cold: The Record of an Antarctic Sledge Journey* (Northfield, MN: Carleton College, limited edition reprint, 1984), 102, 103. See also, Byrd, *Little America*, 123; Young interview, 15–17; Young, diary, 25–26 December 1955; Moss interview, 7.

8. MCB (Spec), Report DF I and II, vol. IV, D-ONE-9–12; McMurdo Log, 2 January 1956.

9. Canham, diary, 6 January 1956; Bevilacqua, diary, 6 January 1956; Dufek, *Operation Deepfreeze*, 132.

10. Canham, diary, 7 January 1956.

11. Ibid., see 16 November to 21 December 1955, 10 April 1956; Chaudoin interview, 24–25; David Grisez, correspondence, 28 August 2002; James H. Bergstrom, interview with author, 27 October 1998, 35; Bowers interview, 34–35; MCB (Spec), Report DF I and II, vol. V, D-NINE-6; William Hess, interview with author, 29 March 1999, 13.

12. Bowers interview, 7–9; CTF 43, Report DF I, vol. 2, 456–458. Frozen seawater is called new sea ice in its first year. Old sea ice has persisted over at least one summer.

It is thicker, stands higher out of the water, and is less salty, as over time the salt leaches out. It is clearer, bluer, and, near the surface at least, potable. Terence Armstrong, Brian Roberts, and Charles Swithinbank, *Illustrated Glossary of Snow and Ice* (Cambridge: Scott Polar Research Institute, 1973), 35.

13. David Baker, e-mail correspondence, 15 September 2000.

14. MCB (Spec), Report DF I and II, vol. IV, D-ONE-18, D-TWO-66–68; Charles Slaton, interview with author, 28 March 1999, 10.

15. Thomas T. Montgomery, interview with author, 21 January 1999, 7; MCB (Spec), Report DF I and II, vol. V, D-SIX-6; Chaudoin interview, 7–8.

16. MCB (Spec), Report DF I and II, vol. IV, D-ONE-19–22.

17. Ibid., D-ONE-22–29.

18. McMurdo Log, 1, 18 January 1956; CTG 43.2, Report DF I Air Operations, 40–41, 184; Dufek, *Operation Deepfreeze*, 104–110.

19. MCB (Spec), Report DF I and II, vol. 1, A-ONE-4–5; vol. IV, D-ONE-25, -28–30; Hess interview, 7–9.

20. MCB (Spec), Report DF I and II, vol. IV, D-ONE-34; McMurdo Log, 20 February, 5–8 March 1956; Bowers, correspondence, 13 February 2001.

21. McMurdo Log, 9 March 1956, with Chaudoin's annotation.

22. Ibid., 9–24 March, 3, 6 April 1956; MCB (Spec), Report DF I and II, vol. IV, D-ONE-34, D-TWO-29; Canham, diary, 6 April 1956.

23. MCB (Spec), Report DF I and II, vol. IV, D-TWO-18–20.

24. Canham, diary, 1–11 March 1956; Chaudoin interview, 16, 35; Michael Baronick, interview with author, 21 January 1999, 28; Baker interview, 25; see also, MCB (Spec), Report DF I and II, vol. V, Chaplain's Report. McMurdo's chapel burned on 22 August 1978, a total loss. After eleven years in a "temporary" (another Quonset) chapel and another fire, workers built a third, with an organ, office space, and seating for sixty-three. This (current) white clapboard Chapel of the Snows, overlooking McMurdo Sound, was dedicated on 29 January 1989. Bill Spindler, www.southpolestation.com (accessed 30 October 2000). Spindler was Pole Station manager, 1976–1977.

25. Canham, diary, 27 November 1955, 21–25 May, 11–15 August, 11–15 September 1956; Chaudoin interview, 16–18; Bergstrom interview, 37; Baker interview, 25–26; David Grisez, interview with Lynn Lay, 22 May 2000, 13. See also, MCB (Spec), Report DF I and II, vol. V, Chaplain's Report.

26. McMurdo Log, 31 March, 6 April 1956; Canham, diary, 26–28 April 1956; Chaudoin interview, 15–16.

27. McMurdo Log, 16 April 1956; Bergstrom interview, 26–27; Baker interview, 15–16; Canham, diary, 16 April, 26–30 June 1956.

28. MCB (Spec), Report DF I and II, vol. IV, D-ONE-45; Ehrlich interview, 8; McMurdo Log, 5 May, 12 November 1956; Canham, diary, 1–5 May 1956.

29. MCB (Spec), Report DF I and II, vol. IV, D-ONE-44, -56, -59; McMurdo Log, 1 (with Chaudoin's annotation), 4, 22, 24 April 1956.

30. McMurdo Log, 16 May 1956; Canham, diary, 16–20 May 1956.

31. Canham, diary, 21–25 June 1956.

32. McMurdo Log, 22 June 1956; ibid.

33. Bowers interview, 15–16; McMurdo Log, 26 March 1956; Canham, diary, numerous entries between 6–10 May and 6–10 September 1956.

34. Bowers interview, 16–17; Air Force Task Unit 63d T. C. WG. (H), Report on Operation Deep Freeze II, 117.

35. Bowers interview, 16, 20–21; Siple, *90° South*, 165–166.

36. McMurdo Log, 17 April 1956; MCB (Spec), Report DF I and II, vol. IV, D-ONE-74.

37. Bowers interview, 23; John Randall, interview with author, 10 March 1999, 19; Montgomery interview, 27; Slaton interview, 20–21; see also, MCB (Spec), Report DF I and II, vol. VI, E-TWO-8–13.

38. Baker interview, 16–17; Canham, diary, 16–20, 26–30 June 1956; Chaudoin interview, 26, 28; Randall interview, 19; Bowers interview, 26.

39. Randall interview, 20–21; Baker interview, 16–18.

40. Baker interview, 18–22; Canham, diary, 16–20 July, 1–5 September 1956.

41. Baker interview, 30–32. Baker remembered the trio as himself, Bowers, and Tuck, but Tuck had injured his hand and stayed behind. Official sources name Prescott as the third person. Bowers interview, 26–27; McMurdo Log, 12–17 September 1956.

42. MCB (Spec), Report DF I and II, vol. IV, D-ONE-38, -50–51, -59; Canham, diary, 29 April–2 May 1956.

43. Canham, diary, 21–25 May 1956; McMurdo Log, 17, 21, 25 April 1956; Airstrip Construction Records, courtesy of Dick Bowers. These personal copies of reports and diary notes and later correspondence inform this section throughout.

44. McMurdo Log, 28 June 1956; Bowers, e-mail correspondence, 2 October 2000, 13 February 2001; MCB (Spec), Report DF I and II, vol. IV, D-ONE-67, D-TWO-42–44; Bowers, Airstrip Construction Records, see notes 15–23 July 1956.

45. McMurdo Log, 18 June, 19 July 1956; MCB (Spec), Report DF I and II, vol. IV, D-ONE-60–61.

46. Canham, diary, 1–5, 11, 15, 16, 20 July 1956; McMurdo Log, 17–19 July 1956; Bowers, Airstrip Construction Records; Canham to Dalrymple, 17 September 1984, courtesy of Kenneth Aldrich.

47. Runway Construction Plan, 19 July 1956, in Bowers, Airstrip Construction Records, 18–19 July 1956; Bowers, correspondence, 13 February 2001.

48. McMurdo Log, 19 July 1956; Canham, diary, 16–20, 21–25 July 1956.

49. McMurdo Log, 19 July, see also, 14–15, 21 August 1956; Canham, diary, 26–31 July 1956; MCB (Spec), Report DF I and II, vol. IV, D-TWO–24; Bowers, Airstrip Construction Records, equipment report, 27 July 1956.

50. Randall interview, 7–9, 13–14; McMurdo Log, 19 July, 6, 8–9 August 1956; MCB (Spec), Report DF I and II, vol. IV, D-TWO-45, -52–58; Bowers, Airstrip Construction Records, notes 31 July 1956.

51. Slaton interview, 13; MCB (Spec), Report DF I and II, vol. IV, D-ONE-64–65; Bowers, Airstrip Construction Records, construction notes 2 August 1956; Bowers interview, 43.

52. MCB (Spec), Report DF I and II, vol. IV, D-ONE-75–76, -82, -84–85; Canham, diary, 11–15, 21–25 August 1956; McMurdo Log, 20, 22, 26 August 1956; Bowers, Airstrip Construction Records, construction notes 27 August 1956.

53. MCB (Spec), Report DF I and II, vol. IV, D-TWO-46–47, -52, vol. V, D-FIVE-10–11; McMurdo Log, 15–18 September 1956; Randall interview, 8.

54. Slaton interview, 16–17; MCB (Spec), Report DF I and II, vol. IV, D-ONE-89–95, -98, D-TWO-25.

55. MCB (Spec), Report DF I and II, vol. IV, D-ONE-102; McMurdo Log, October 1956, see 15 October.

56. MCB (Spec), Report DF I and II, vol. V, D-NINE-7; Canham, diary, 25–31 August 1956; Charles A. Bevilacqua, "Our Lady of the Snows Shrine," Antarctic Deep Freeze Association reunion information, May 1998, 8–9; David Grisez, diary, 6 January 1957, and phone conversation with author, 23 April 2001.

57. MCB (Spec), Report DF I and II, vol. IV, D-ONE-100; Bergstrom interview, 22–23.

58. MCB (Spec), Report DF I and II, vol. V, D-FIVE-13; Bergstrom interview, 18–19.

59. McMurdo Log, 15, 17 October 1956.

60. Bergstrom interview, 4–5, 22–24; MCB (Spec), Report DF I and II, vol. IV, D-ONE-105–107, vol. V, D-SEVEN-31; Anderson, "United States Aircraft Losses in Antarctica," 7; Richard Lewis, conversation with author, 23 April 2003; Frank Hudman, e-mail correspondence with author, 20 August 1999, forwarding draft of Noel Gillespie, "Tragedy at McMurdo on the First Day of Operation Deep Freeze II."

61. Ward, Memoirs, 40–52; Ward interview, 18–21; Dufek, *Operation Deepfreeze*, 184–186.

62. McMurdo Log, 18 October 1956; MCB (Spec), Report DF I and II, vol. IV, D-ONE-106; Dufek, *Operation Deepfreeze*, 185–186. In Whitney's mind, Operation Deep Freeze II began on 28 October when the *Glacier* arrived at McMurdo Sound, the earliest any ship had cleared the pack ice. But the new Deep Freeze season logically got under way with the first arrivals from the States, which inevitably meant aircraft. See McMurdo Log, 27 April 1956.

CHAPTER 4

1. Richard Lucier, interview with author, 19 January 1999, 3.

2. Paul W. Frazier, *Antarctic Assault* (New York: Dodd, Mead, 1958), 87; Cruisebook DF I, 81–82; Morton Rubin, interview with Brian Shoemaker and author, 21 July 2000, 24–25; Bernard Kalb, "Byrd, 'Mayor' of Little America, Returns to His Antarctic Domain," *New York Times*, 29 December 1955, I, 7, Eunice Moss scrapbook.

3. Dufek, *Operation Deepfreeze*, 90–95; "Base Is on 2,100 Feet of Ice, Water," [Providence *Evening Bulletin*], 30 January 1956, Eunice Moss scrapbook; Kenneth Waldron, interview with author, 2 August 1999, 9.

4. Cruisebook DF I, 89; Young interview, 17.

5. Young interview, 5–7, 10–11, 13, 17.

6. Dufek, *Operation Deepfreeze*, 96–97; MCB (Spec), Report DF I and II, vol. I, A-

ONE-3; Young, diary, 30 December 1955–3 January 1956; ibid., 18; Aldrich, ADFA questionnaire; Aldrich, memoir.

7. Frazier, *Antarctic Assault,* 89–90; Cruisebook DF I, 122; Young, diary, 16–22 January 1956; Young interview, 18.

8. MCB (Spec), Report DF I and II, vol. I, A-ONE-3. This report said off-loading onto the sea ice continued for about three weeks, but Young's more immediate diary corrects this memory. Donald Mehaffey, interview with author, 30 March 1999, 12; Frazier, *Antarctic Assault,* 89.

9. MCB (Spec), Report DF I and II, vol. I, A-ONE-4; Mehaffey interview, 13.

10. [Saul Pett], "Little America Base No. 5 Dedicated," [Providence *Evening Bulletin*], 4 January 1956.

11. Young interview, 17–18; MCB (Spec), Report DF I and II, vol. II, B-TWO-1, -49, -55; "Little America V Naval Base, Antarctica, 1955–1956–1957, Welcome Aboard," mimeographed guide for summer personnel, unpaginated; Aldrich, memoir.

12. Young, diary, 4–17 January, 17 April 1956; William Stroup, interview with author, 11 May 1999, 3–4, 11–13; K. Waldron interview, 8.

13. Young interview, 15, 19; Bursey, *Antarctic Night,* 196, 229; Dater, "Byrd Station"; Moss interview, 31–32.

14. Bursey, *Antarctic Night,* chapter 3, 223; Moss interview, 15, and personal conversation.

15. Bursey, *Antarctic Night,* 224–225; Young, diary, 3–8 February 1956; Young interview, 19–20.

16. The Otter crash story (following paragraphs) is pieced together from numerous sources, including "Here is the first complete eye-witness account . . ." a transcription of untitled narrative by George Moss, n.d., courtesy of Richard Bowers; Medical Officer to Chief, Bureau of Medicine and Surgery, Intelligence Report of Survivor's Experience–Med 046, 9 March 1956, courtesy of George Moss (see also, MCB [Spec], Report DF I and II, vol. II, B-THREE-2-1–10); P. R. Streich, interview with Brian Shoemaker, 30 January 1997, 44–52; Moss interview, 15–21; Ehrlich interview, 14–17; "R.I. Seabee Describes Cheating Death by 20 Feet in Antarctica," *Providence Journal,* 12 March 1956, 1, and other national and local articles, Eunice Moss scrapbook. See also, Dufek, *Operation Deepfreeze,* 112–126.

17. Young, diary, 15 March 1956; Slaton interview, 9; [Unattributed mimeograph,] Caching Tractor Train, n.d., copy of apparently official report, courtesy of Bill Stroup.

18. Young, diary, 2–6 March 1956; Caching Tractor Train report.

19. Young, diary, 2–5, 10 March 1956; Young interview, 21–23; Victor Young, e-mail correspondence, 21 July 2000; Dufek, *Operation Deepfreeze,* 133–134; NAS-IGY: Draft minutes, NY Antarctic Conference, 19 June 1956.

20. Young, diary, 1 April 1956; Ehrlich interview, 17–18; Aldrich interview, 11. Deep Freeze II trailblazer Philip Smith confirmed the general fearfulness. Philip M. Smith, interview with author, 8 December 1998, 5.

21. Edward N. Ehrlich, ADFA questionnaire; Ehrlich interview, 27–28; Aldrich interview, 17.

22. McMurdo Log, 20 April, 1, 14 May 1956, with Chaudoin's annotation; Canham, diary, 26–31 August 1956.

23. Moss interview, 28; Ehrlich interview, 23–24; Aldrich interview, 18, 21; Mehaffey interview, 26–27.

24. Ehrlich interview, 27–28; Moss interview, 31, 33; Young interview, 41–42; Mehaffey interview, 27–30; Aldrich interview, 17–18; Aldrich, ADFA questionnaire supplement, 5.

25. Ehrlich interview, 11–13, 40, 48; MCB (Spec), Report DF I and II, vol. II, B-THREE-25–26; Aldrich, ADFA questionnaire supplement, 5; Aldrich, memoir; Aldrich interview, 9–10.

26. Ehrlich interview, 38–39. See also, Lloyd Beebe, interview with Brian Shoemaker, 21 August 2000, 4–10, 18.

27. Ernest A. Wood, Activities Report DF I, 1 June 1956, 2, 29, Annex B-2: Memos from CE Twombly, 1; Preliminary Report, 1 March 1956; Twombly to Wexler, 9 March 1956; Toney to Hanessian, Points from Rubin's communications, 16 February 1956, all in NAS-IGY: Activities Report DF I; Wood to Dyer, cover letter to Preliminary Report, DF I, 3 March 1956.

28. Little America V, "Welcome Aboard"; Francis to Jones, 25 December 1957, and Francis to Odishaw, 9 February 1958, both in NAS-IGY: IGY Field Representatives Reports.

29. Moulton to Wessbecher, Guideline for your use . . . 26 February 1956; Wessbecher to USNC-IGY, Report on IGY Activities at McMurdo . . . March 2, 1956 to January 28, 1957, NAS-IGY: Draft DF II Reports; Goodale to Wexler, 30 March 1956, NAS-IGY: Activities Report DF I; Wexler to Odishaw, Location of Byrd Land Station, 16 May 1956, Draft DF I Reports; Wexler, diary, 3 April 1956.

30. Young, diary, 25 April 1956; MCB (Spec), Report DF I and II, vol. II, B-TWO-48–49; Lucier interview, 3.

31. MCB (Spec), Report DF I and II, vol. II, B-TWO-51–52 (quote), -58, B-THREE-39.

32. Ibid., B-TWO-60, B-THREE-6, -10; Moss interview, 35; Ehrlich interview, 10.

33. Young, diary, 5 July 1956; MCB (Spec), Report DF I and II, vol. II, B-THREE-14–15; Ehrlich interview, 32–33.

34. Young interview, 24, 39; Young, diary, 24 April, 2, 20, 25 August, 4, 15 September 1956.

35. Young, diary, 25 October 1956.

36. MCB (Spec), Report DF I and II, vol. II, Air Operations.

37. TF 43, A Report Summarizing the 1955–1956 United States Antarctic Operation (Operation Deepfreeze), 10, NAS-IGY: Draft DF II Reports.

CHAPTER 5

1. Vernon Anderson, diary titled "Fire & Ice," 1 April 1957, courtesy of Carole and Suzanne Anderson.

2. Paul W. Frazier, "Across the Frozen Desert to Byrd Station," *National Geographic* 112, no. 3 (September 1957): 383.

3. Dater, "Byrd Station"; Toney, SSLR, Byrd, 1; Goodale to Odishaw, 29 November 1956, NAS- IGY: IGY Field Representatives.

4. CTF 43, Report DF II, 3, courtesy of Al Raithel Jr.; Dufek, *Operation Deepfreeze*, 162–163; Smith interview, 1–6; Dater, "Byrd Station."

5. Smith interview, 6–7.

6. Crevasse detectors consisted of four aluminum pans held on the snow surface, apart from each other, and in front of the vehicle by a timber framework. A voltage applied to the two outer pans produced a local electrical field. The inner pans picked up the current, which the driver could see, amplified, on a meter. If the pans were pushed over a bridged crevasse, the void below would change the snow's electrical conductivity, and the meter readings would suddenly decrease. Then someone would probe ahead with an aluminum rod to test the depth and strength of the snow bridge. Albert P. Crary, "On the Ice: Working on Science in the Arctic and Antarctica," 272, manuscript memoir courtesy of M. R. Crary.

7. Army-Navy Trail Party Report, 1956, 3, 5, RG 313, Box 12; Smith interview, 8–9.

8. Army-Navy Trail Party Report, 2, 6, 7, 15; Smith interview, 10; Frazier, "Across the Frozen Desert," 383–384.

9. Smith interview, 10–11; Wexler, diary, 24 November 1956; Task Force 43, Operation Deep Freeze II: The Chronicle of Task Force 43 and Its Service to Science in the Second Phase of a Project of Four Years' Duration, Joseph E. Oglesby, ed. [hereafter Cruisebook DF II], 50.

10. Army-Navy Trail Party Report, 19–23, 65; Frazier, "Across the Frozen Desert," 386, 388.

11. CTF 43, Report DF II, 4 (task force quote); Army-Navy Trail Party Report, 20–29, 57; Young interview, 28; Crary to Diana Fisher, Letter #4, 5 February 1957, RG 307, Box 3.

12. MCB (Spec), Report DF I and II, vol. III, C-9, -12; Young, diary, 4–7 December 1956; Young interview, 26; Frazier, "Across the Frozen Desert," 393. Otaco was the name of the Canadian sled manufacturer. See Fogg, *History of Antarctic Science*, 149, for comparison with Scott.

13. Smith interview, 11–12; Ehrlich interview, 18; Young interview, 28; Young, diary, 9–12 December 1956.

14. Smith interview, 12–13; Young, diary, 9–12 December 1956; Stroup interview, 23; Frazier, "Across the Frozen Desert," 393; Army-Navy Trail Party Report, 37–38.

15. Young interview, 26–27; Calvin Larsen, interview with Brian Shoemaker, 21 August 2000, 7–9; Stroup interview, 23; Frazier, "Across the Frozen Desert," 395.

16. Young, diary, 20, 22, 23 December 1956; Frazier, "Across the Frozen Desert," 398; Air Force Task Unit 63rd T. C. WG. (H), Operation Deep Freeze II, 105.

17. MCB (Spec), Report DF I and II, vol. III, C-15; Young, diary, 23, 24, 27 December 1956; Young interview, 24–25; Stroup interview, 10.

18. Young, diary, 27 December 1956–23 January 1957; MCB (Spec), Report DF I and II, vol. III, C-14–16; MCB (Spec), Report DF II and III, vol. IV, 1, RG 313, Box 16; [H. M. Dater], "Dakotas in the Antarctic: A Study in Versatility," Monograph no. 1 (Washington, D.C.: U.S. Naval Support Force, Antarctica, History and Research Division, September 1970), 7.

19. Dater, "Byrd Station"; Press Release, George Toney Appointed Byrd Station Scientific Leader in Antarctic, 24 December 1956, NAS-IGY: IGY Personnel, Antarctica; Wexler, diary, 26–30 January 1957; see also, Crary, "On the Ice," 248; Rubin, Shoemaker interview, 20–21.

20. Dater, "Byrd Station"; Wexler, diary, 24, 26, 29–30 January, 4 February 1957; Toney, SSLR, Byrd, 45; Cruisebook DF II, 60.

21. Wexler, diary, 30 January, 1 February 1957; Crary, "On the Ice," 250. See also, Papers of the Presidents, Eisenhower, 1954, ¶153, 25 June, and 1957, ¶122, 30 June.

22. Army-Navy Trail Party Report, 38–41.

23. Cruisebook DF II, 56; CTF 43, Report DF II, 2; Wexler, diary, 11 February 1957; Air Force Task Unit 63rd T. C. WG. (H), DF II, 112–113; MCB (Spec), Report DF II and III, vol. IV, 2.

24. Smith interview, 4; William E. Lowe, ADFA questionnaire, 6 April 1996.

25. Toney, SSLR, Byrd, 2–3; Toney interview, 8–9; Charles Bentley, interview with author, 2 December 1998, 9–10; Anderson, diary, 31 March 1957.

26. Toney interview, 8–9; Toney, SSLR, Byrd, 3.

27. Anderson, diary, 28 February, 1, 3 March, 1 June, 23 July 1957.

28. Toney interview, 14, 23; Dalton interview, 14, 16; Dater, "Byrd Station."

29. Toney interview, 9; Bentley interview, 12–13; Toney, SSLR, Byrd, 4; MCB (Spec), Report DF II and III, vol. IV, Recreation—3, IV-1–2; Anderson, diary, 22 March 1957; Mario Giovinetto, interview with author, 15 June 2001.

30. Toney interview, 18; Anderson, diary, 11 September, 17 October 1957; Dalton interview, 20–22; MCB (Spec), Report DF II and III, vol. IV, IV-5; Toney, SSLR, Byrd, 3.

31. Toney interview, 19–20; Dalton interview, 8–9; Toney, SSLR, Byrd, 5; Lowe, ADFA questionnaire; Anderson, diary, 13 June, 1 November 1957; see also, 13, 20 July 1957.

32. MCB (Spec), Report DF II and III, vol. IV, 2; Toney interview, 11, 20–21; Dalton interview, 12–13; Lowe, ADFA questionnaire; Toney, SSLR, Byrd, 8.

33. Bentley interview, 12, 22; Toney interview, 12, 16–17; Giovinetto interview.

34. Toney, SSLR, Byrd, 6–7; Reichelderfer to Johns, 17, 27 January 1958, NAS-IGY: Science Personnel General Correspondence, January 1958; Toney interview, 20.

35. Toney, SSLR, Byrd, 8; Bentley interview, 18; Giovinetto interview.

36. Brian Dalton, e-mail correspondence, 10 August 1999; MCB (Spec), Report DF II and III, vol. IV, II-6; Toney, SSLR, Byrd, 45.

37. Toney, SSLR, Byrd, 10–11; MCB (Spec), Report DF II and III, vol. IV, 5, V-1; Dater, "Byrd Station."

38. Dalton interview, 23; Lowe, ADFA questionnaire; Brian Dalton, e-mail correspondence, 24 August 2000.

39. Peter P. Ruseski, Operation DF III Byrd Station Log Book, 17 January 1958; Stephen Barnes, SSLR, Byrd, 1958, 1–7, 21.

40. Bentley interview, 21–22, 24; CTF 43, Report DF IV, 24.

41. Bentley interview, 3, 8; Toney, SSLR, Byrd, Appendix E, F; Hanessian to Files (528.6), Weekly Antarctic Message Report, 21 March 1957; see also 29 March and 19 April 1957, NAS-IGY: Daily and Weekly Antarctic Message Summaries, January–June 1957.

CHAPTER 6

1. Paul A. Siple, "We Are Living at the South Pole," *National Geographic* 112, no. 1 (July 1957): 34.

2. Walter Sullivan, *Assault on the Unknown: The International Geophysical Year* (New York: McGraw Hill, 1961), 302; Francis Spufford, *I May Be Some Time: Ice and the English Imagination* (New York: Picador USA, 1997), 269. See also, Huntford, *The Last Place on Earth*; Scott, *Scott's Last Expedition: The Journals*; Amundsen, *The South Pole*; SP Log, 17–20 October 1956.

3. CTF 43, Report DF II, chapter III; Herbert Levack, interview with author, 25 September 1999, 4; Jack Rice, "St. Louisan Who Parachuted at South Pole," *St. Louis Post-Dispatch*, n.d. [Spring 1957], courtesy of Al Raithel Jr.; McMurdo Log, 12 October 1957. The USAF was based at the Royal New Zealand Air Force's (RNZAF) military field at Weedons and flew from Harewood, Christchurch, commercial field. The Navy base was at RNZAF Wigram Field.

4. Dufek, *Operation Deepfreeze*, 186–187; Air Force Task Unit [AFTU], 63rd T. C. WG. (H), Report DF II, 95, 96, courtesy of Herb Levack; CTF 43, Report DF II, 19–20; McMurdo Log, 22 October 1957.

5. MCB (Spec), Report DF I and II, vol. IV, D-ONE-110, vol. V, D-SEVEN-2-1; David S. Boyer, "Year of Discovery Opens in Antarctica," *National Geographic* 112, no. 3 (September 1957): 351; McMurdo Log, 21 October 1956.

6. SP Log, 18, 20, 25 October 1956; Dufek, *Operation Deepfreeze*, 189; MCB (Spec), Report DF I and II, vol. VI, E-TWO-36.

7. The camp remained "Beardmore" during Deep Freeze II, but, oddly, the next summer when the temporary facility was built nearer the Beardmore Glacier, it was called Liv Station.

8. MCB (Spec), Report DF I and II, vol. IV, D-ONE-109–112; Baronick interview, 14–15; Dufek, *Operation Deepfreeze*, 191–192; Dufek, "Tenth Anniversary of First Landing at the South Pole," 268; Edward Frankiewicz, e-mail to Bowers, 10 February 2001.

9. Dufek, *Operation Deepfreeze*, 193–194; Shinn interview, 29–30.

10. SP Log, 31 October 1956; Bowers, correspondence with author, 13 February 2001; Maj. A. G. Thompson, "First South Pole Airdrop Mission Is Success," *Troop Courier*, Donaldson Air Force Base, SC, 30 November 1956, 3–4, courtesy of Herb Levack; Siple, *90° South*, 142, 144.

11. Siple, *90° South*, 144–145; Wexler, diary, 17 November 1956; Toney to Hanessian, Points from Rubin's Communications, 16 February 1956.

12. Shinn interview, 29–30, 33; Dufek, *Operation Deepfreeze*, 195. Dufek wrote that the Pole flight took off from McMurdo at 12:55 P.M. (1255 hours).

13. Shinn interview, 31; John Strider, interview with Brian Shoemaker, 30 October 2001, abstract; Dufek, *Operation Deepfreeze*, 198–201.

14. Shinn interview, 32–33, 39–40; Dufek, *Operation Deepfreeze*, 201–202. Shinn, and later I, counted nineteen shackles (for affixing JATOs to the fuselage) on the *Que Sera Sera*, now at the Naval Air Museum at Pensacola. Surely maximum JATOs would have been used for this risky flight, although more could have been added later. Shinn, telephone conversation, 13 March 2000.

15. Wexler, diary, 17 November 1956; SP Log, 2, 4 November 1956.

16. SP Log, 4–8, 14 November 1956; Hess interview, 20.

17. SP Log, 12–18 November 1956.

18. Wexler to Odishaw, Pole Station Operations, 15 November 1956, NAS-IGY: Antarctic Committee Organization. Wexler had learned from Finn Ronne that –40°F was the "lower limit for endurable outdoor work," but it would continue at even lower temperatures during the IGY.

19. SP Log, 19 November 1956. See also, CTF 43, Report DF II, 21.

20. SP Log, 21 November 1956; Bowers, correspondence, 13 February 2001.

21. SP Log, 21 November 1956; Siple, *90° South*, 153; Montgomery interview, 21. The Byrd traversers later had a similar, "real scary" experience. "I heard a faint roar," Vern Anderson wrote. "As we listened it grew louder and came rushing upon us. It had a definite direction, and I felt sure it was a real big wind. I actually ducked into the pit and then it hit us. 'Crack!' It sounded just like a seismic shot." Anderson, diary, 24 January 1958. Nolan Aughenbaugh and John Behrendt also set off a several-second "snow collapse" near Ellsworth. "It sure gives you a funny feeling. . . . The noise it makes is eerie and the snow actually drops beneath you." Aughenbaugh, diary, 25 September 1957.

22. SP Log, 22–24 November 1956.

23. "Sergeant Patton Is First to Jump on Deep Freeze," *Troop Courier*, 30 November 1956, 1; Rice, "St. Louisan Who Parachuted at South Pole"; Bowers, correspondence, 13 February 2001.

24. SP Log, 24–26 November 1956; Bevilacqua, diary, 25 November 1956; Slaton interview, 23.

25. SP Log, 26–27 November 1956; Bowers interview, 38; Slaton interview, 23–24; Chaudoin interview, 28; Powell, group interview.

26. SP Log, 1–December 1956; Siple, *90° South*, 149, 156; Bevilacqua, diary, 1 December 1956; Bowers interview, 30.

27. SP Log, 30 November, 4 December 1956; Siple, *90° South*, 170; Paul Siple, SSLR, South Pole, 1957, 41 (quote), 74.

28. Bevilacqua, diary, 29 November 1956. On 14 December 2001 builders of "New Pole" dug out an IGY-era parachute from under thirty feet of impacted snow.

Marty, Jensen, Walker, Smith, Wright, Spanberger to The Brave and Hearty Men . . . South Pole Station, 31 December 2001; Judy Spanberger, "Digging up Polar History," *Antarctic Sun*, 23 December 2001.

29. SP Log, 5, 9 December 1956; Hess interview, 18, 21.

30. AFTU, 63rd T. C. WG. (H), Report DF II, 4, 39–40, 115, 120.

31. Ibid., 39–40, 101, 115, Annex A, 7; Bevilacqua, diary, 6 December 1956.

32. Bowers interview, 17; AFTU, 63rd T. C. WG. (H), Report DF II, 102, 104–105; CTF 43, Report DF II, 20.

33. Siple, SSLR, Pole, 6.

34. Ibid.; Montgomery interview, 22–23; SP Log, 2 December 1956.

35. SP Log, 6–8 December 1956.

36. Ibid., 8, 11–13 December 1956.

37. Ibid., 13–15 December 1956; Siple, *90° South*, 183–184.

38. Howard Wessbecher, interview with Brian Shoemaker, 20 April 2000, 65–67; "Class of '48 Set for 50th Reunion: This Tanner Painted the South 'Pole' Black and Orange in 1956," [Woburn?, MA] *Daily Times Chronicle*, 25 September 1998, 8A; Bevilacqua interview, 27–28, qualified by later phone conversation; Siple, *90° South*, 184, 186.

39. Siple, *90° South*, 167, 176, 180–181; Siple, "We Are Living at the South Pole," 15; MCB (Spec), Report DF I and II, vol. VI, E-TWO-51; Bowers interview, 21–22; Anderson, diary, 25 March 1957.

40. SP Log, 23–25, 28 December 1956; Chaudoin interview, 32; Bevilacqua, diary, 25 December 1956; Siple, *90° South*, 186–187.

41. Slaton interview, 28–29; Bowers interview, 38–39; Siple, *90° South*, 187–188.

42. Jerry Marty, NSF's "New Pole" construction manager, still hopes to find this historic cylinder when time and resources to search for it materialize. A new time capsule was buried on 11 January 2002, its position precisely described in relation to the new elevated station. Jeff Rubin, "South Pole Buries Second Time Capsule," *Polar Times* (Spring-Summer 2002): 29.

43. SP Log, 23 December 1956–1 January 1957; Siple, *90° South*, 184–185; Siple, SSLR, Pole, 90–93; Don Guy, "South Pole Base Is Completed," *Polar Times* compilation (June 1957): 16; IGY Bulletin no. 26, *Transactions, American Geophysical Union* 40, no. 3 (September 1959): 297. A new brass marker is placed at the true geographic pole each New Year's Day.

44. Waldron interview, 19; SP Log, 29 December 1956, 2 January 1957.

45. Bowers interview, 46; Slaton interview, 26–27, 36–37; MCB (Spec), Report DF I and II, vol. VI, E-TWO-23–24, -34, -96; Siple, *90° South*, 168. Building South Pole Station earned Bowers the Moreell Medal in 1957. Named for Adm. Ben Moreell, founder of the Seabees, the award honors the year's most outstanding contribution in military engineering.

46. Siple, *90° South*, 193; SP Log, 20 October 1956, 4–7 January 1957.

47. Siple, *90° South*, 204–205; MCB (Spec), Report DF II and III, vol. VI, 4, RG 313, Box 18.

48. Wexler, diary, 4, 11 February 1957. Dufek would recommend Assur for the Navy's highest civilian decoration. See "'Ice Concrete' Expert Slated for Decoration," *Polar Times* compilation, 21; Siple, SSLR, Pole, 8.

49. MCB (Spec), Report DF II and III, vol. VI, 5; Siple, SSLR, Pole, 12–13; AFTU, 63rd T. C. WG. (H), Report DF II, 93, 110–113, Annex A, 10.

50. Siple, SSLR, Pole, 76–79; MCB (Spec), Report DF II and III, vol. VI, 7; Operation Deep Freeze Newsletter, 23 May 1958, RG 401 (5), Carl Eklund papers, Box 14.

51. Wexler, diary, 23–24 January 1957; Siple, SSLR, Pole, 12–13, 47–48; Siple, *90° South*, 228; MCB (Spec), Report DF II and III, vol. VI, 6.

52. Peavey, Memorandum for Files: South Pole Station, 31 December 1956, with addendum on same page written on or after 3 January 1957, NAS-IGY: Antarctic, Drawer 74; Wexler, diary, 20 December 1956, 18, 23–24 January 1957.

53. Siple, SSLR, Pole, 14–15, 37.

54. Ibid., 9–10; Siple, *90° South*, 214; MCB (Spec), Report DF II and III, vol. VI, 5, Air Ops 1–2, VI-4–5.

55. Siple, SSLR, Pole, 18–20, 143; Paul A. Siple, "Man's First Winter at the South Pole," *National Geographic* 112, no. 4 (April 1958): 457, 460; MCB (Spec), Report DF II and III, vol. VI, 8, VI-16; Waldron interview, 28–29; USAP External Panel, *The United States in Antarctica*, 50.

56. Siple, *90° South*, 238–239; Siple, SSLR, Pole, 16, 18, 33, 85; Arlo Landolt, interview with Brian Shoemaker, 10 April 2001, 11–12.

57. Siple, SSLR, Pole, 21, 24–25, 30–31; MCB (Spec), Report DF II and III, vol. VI, 8.

58. Siple, SSLR, Pole, 25–26, 32, 39; Palle Mogensen, SSLR, Pole, 1958, 34; MCB (Spec), Report DF II and III, vol. VI, 10, II-7–8; Siple, *90° South*, 327–328; Benjamin Remington, interview with Brian Shoemaker, 25 February 2000, 36.

59. South Pole Yearbook, 1957, courtesy of Ken Waldron; MCB (Spec), Report DF II and III, vol. VI, 1, 11.

60. Siple, SSLR, Pole, 39–45.

61. Ibid., 47–49, 89; Landolt interview, 30.

62. Siple, SSLR, Pole, 49, 51; Siple, *90° South*, 354–356.

63. Siple, SSLR, Pole, 50, 52–54; Clifford Dickey, group interview with author, 8 May 1998.

64. Siple, SSLR, Pole, 54; Wexler, diary, 28 October 1957.

65. Siple, *90° South*, 359–360; MCB (Spec), Report DF II and III, vol. VI, A.7.7. See also, Siple, "Man's First Winter at the South Pole"; Ken Waldron, correspondence, 18 April 2002.

CHAPTER 7

1. Gilbert Dewart, interview with author, 26 March 1999, 8.

2. Price Lewis Jr. Cmdr. USNR, *Rendezvous With Antarctica, 1958–59*, USS *Staten Island*, Deep Freeze IV [Cruisebook], n.p., 38.

3. Minutes, Second Antarctic Conference, Brussels, 8–14 September 1955, and Minutes, Third Antarctic Conference, Paris, 30 July–4 August 1956, NAS-IGY: IGY; Fogg, *History of Antarctic Science*, 174.

4. Wellington to Secretary of State, no. 129, 3 December 1955, RG 59, Box 1655; John Claydon (deputy commander, TAE), conversations and news clippings, January 2001, Christchurch; Sir Edmund Hillary, *View From the Summit* (London: Corgi Books, 2000), 173, 176–177, 197, 229–230; Hanessian to Odishaw, 12 October 1956, and Markham to Odishaw, 16 October 1956, NAS-IGY: New Zealand, June 1955–December 1956.

5. J. Koleszar, Detachment Golf Construction Battalion Base Unit, Davisville, RI, Narrative Report Operation Deepfreeze I (1955–1956) [hereafter Det. Golf, Report DF I], 1 May 1956, 1.

6. Ibid., 14–16; CTF 43, Report DF I, vol. I, 1 October 1956, Part H to Annex I, 94–95, RG 313, Box 4; Dale R. Taft, "Basked in Antarctic Sunshine: R. I. Seabees, Back Home, Tell Thrilling Story," *Providence Journal*, 28 March 1956. See also, William Littlewood, interview with author, 5 January 1999, 17–18.

7. "Hallett Station, Antarctica, 1956–1973," booklet at Scott Base, Antarctica, January 2001; CTF 43, Report DF I, vol. I, 94–95; Det. Golf, Report DF I, 16–17; Taft, "Basked in Antarctic Sunshine"; Rubin, Shoemaker interview, 12–13; Littlewood interview, 19–20; Guy Guthridge, "Hallett Station, Antarctica, 1956–73," *Antarctic Journal* 18, no. 4 (December 1983): 2.

8. TF 43, Report DF II, 5, 7, courtesy of Al Raithel Jr., also found in RG 313, Box 8; Eklund to [Harriet Eklund], 19 December [1956], RG 401 (5-B), Box 10; Eklund to Odishaw, 1 January 1957, NAS-IGY: Draft DF II Reports.

9. TF 43, Report DF II, 9; Eklund to Odishaw, 1 January 1957. See also, Littlewood interview, 19.

10. TF 43, Report DF II, 8; R. W. Loomis, MCB ONE, Report of Base Operations and Construction USNC/IGY Cape Adare Station, Cape Hallett, Antarctica, Operation Deepfreeze II, 29 December 1956–12 February 1957, 5, 7–10, courtesy of Joanne Loomis via Richard Bowers.

11. TF 43, Report DF II, 8–9; Loomis, MCB ONE Construction, Hallett, 9–10; Peavey to Files, Accident to the Arneb, 2 January 1957, NAS-IGY: Antarctic; Paul Noonan, interview with author, 30 December 1998, 6–7.

12. TF 43, Report DF II, 9; Loomis, MCB ONE Construction, Hallett, 10–11; Robert B. Thomson, interview with author, 27 April 1999, 11–12.

13. James Shear, SSLR, Hallett, 1957, 2–3; TF 43, Report DF II, 9; Loomis, MCB ONE Construction, Hallett, 11–13, 16, 21.

14. Shear, SSLR, Hallett, 1–2; Loomis, MCB ONE Construction, Hallett, 17–19; H. Kim Lett, interview with author, 31 December 1998, 31–32; "Hallett Station" booklet.

15. MCB (Spec), Report DF II and III, vol. VII, 5–6, table 1, II-M-1; James A. Shear Biographical Sketch, NAS-IGY: Personnel Antarctica; Kenneth Salmon, SSLR, Hallett, 1958, 5; Shear, SSLR, Hallett, 6.

16. Shear, SSLR, Hallett, 3–4; MCB (Spec), Report DF II and III, vol. VII, III-E-1; Commander, USNSFA to Chief of Naval Operations, 17 May 1957, and Markham to Odishaw, 22 May 1957, NAS-IGY: New Zealand, January 1957–February 1959.

17. MCB (Spec), Report DF II and III, vol. VII, 7–8, V-1; Loomis, MCB ONE Construction, Hallett, II-9; Lett interview, 27–30; Kim Lett, ADFA questionnaire.

18. K. J. Salmon, "Our Year at Hallett," *Antarctic* (March 1959): 13; TF 43, Report DF IV, 1958–1959, 17 June 1959, 1, RG 313, Box 26; Anderson, "United States Aircraft Losses in Antarctica," 9.

19. Eklund to [Harriet Eklund], 11, 13 January [1957]; Dewart interview, 9; TF 43, Report DF II, 9.

20. TF 43, Report DF II, 9–10; NAS, USNC-IGY Antarctic Program Report to the Fourth CSAGI Antarctic Conference, 12–15 June 1957, Paris, France, RG 307, Box 3.

21. The transliterated Russian word is variously spelled, for example, Mirnyy, Mirniy, Mirnyi. Most U.S. sources used the simpler, no-doubt oversimplified, Mirny.

22. Gilbert Dewart, *Antarctic Comrades: An American With the Russians in Antarctica* (Columbus: Ohio State University Press, 1989), 18.

23. Det. Golf, Report DF I, 18–20.

24. Lynn Cavendish, diary, 19 March 1956; Lynn Cavendish, interview with author, 9 February 1999, 15–19; ibid., 19–24.

25. Dewart interview, 9; Eklund to [Harriet Eklund], 27, 29 January 1957; TF 43, Report DF II, 10.

26. Dewart interview, 12; Noonan interview, 8, 22; MCB (Spec), Report DF II and III, vol. VIII, I-A-1, VI-A-1, RG 313, Box 18; Rudolf Honkala, interview with author, 4 August 1999, 8.

27. Eklund to [Harriet Eklund], 5, 8, 13 February 1957. For a formal positive assessment, see Eklund to Odishaw, 2 February 1957, NAS-IGY: Draft DF II Reports.

28. MCB ONE, Narrative Report, Wilkes Station DF II, in several parts, gives excellent detail on camp construction, RG 313, Box 12. See also, TF 43, Report DF II, 10; Carl Eklund, SSLR, Wilkes, 1957, 5–6; Eklund to [Harriet Eklund], 13 February, 1957.

29. TF 43, Report DF II, 10, 12; Eklund to [Harriet Eklund], 13, 15 February 1957.

30. Noonan interview, 8–11; Dewart interview, 10; MCB (Spec), Report DF II and III, vol. VIII, IV-B-1.

31. Eklund, SSLR, Wilkes, 11; Dewart interview, 13, 28.

32. Dewart interview, 31; Eklund, SSLR, Wilkes, 12.

33. Eklund, SSLR, Wilkes, 23; MCB (Spec), Report DF II and III, vol. VIII, II-D-2, VI-F-1; Noonan interview, 22–23.

34. Honkala interview, 13; Dewart interview, 11; MCB (Spec), Report DF II and III, vol. VIII, II-I-1, VI-A-1, Medical, 9; Eklund, SSLR, Wilkes, 6; Thomson interview, 27.

35. Pyne, *The Ice*, 62, 77; Sullivan, *Quest for a Continent*, 346; TG 43.6 (Weddell Sea Ship Group), Operations Order no. 1–57, DF III, A-1–3, RG 313, Box 20.

36. Crary, "IGY," 87; Bernard Kalb, "Last U.S. Ship Quits Antarctica, Ending One Phase of Expedition," *New York Times*, 31 March 1956, 1.

37. See *Staten Island* Cruise Book, "Pole to Pole," DF II, 1956–1957; Behrendt, *Innocents*, 17.

38. TF 43, Report DF II, 12–13; Behrendt, *Innocents*, 19, 24–25; Littlewood interview, 7; Conrad Jaburg, "Antarctic Odyssey" (diary), 8–9 December 1956; Finn Ronne, *Antarctic Command* (Indianapolis: Bobbs-Merrill, 1961), 16; Francis M. Gambacorta, Report USS *Wyandot*, DF II, 27 March 1957, 11–12, RG 313, Box 10.

39. Jaburg, diary, 22, 24–26, 28 December 1956; Behrendt, *Innocents*, 26, 28, 30, 37 (quote); *Staten Island* Cruisebook, 32; Gambacorta, Report *Wyandot*, DF II, 42.

40. *Staten Island* Cruisebook, 37; Gambacorta, Report *Wyandot*, DF II, 26; Behrendt, *Innocents*, 31, 34–35; Jaburg, diary, 1–11 January 1957; Ronne, *Antarctica, My Destiny*, 202.

41. TF 43, Report DF II, 13; Behrendt, *Innocents*, 34–36; Jaburg, diary, 18 January 1957; Littlewood interview, 21. The *Staten Island* Cruisebook, 36, pegged the barrier at 200 feet; Ronne, *Antarctica, My Destiny*, 203.

42. Behrendt, *Innocents*, 37–38 (Dufek cite); Jaburg, diary, 16 January 1957; Ronne, *Antarctica, My Destiny*, 202–203; Hank Stephens, e-mail to Richard Bowers, 16 October 1999, and to author, 1 November 1999. Finn Ronne, SSLR, Ellsworth, 2.

43. Ronne, *Antarctica, My Destiny*, 203; Behrendt, *Innocents*, 39–46; Minutes, First Meeting, Panel on Antarctic Policies of the USNC-IGY Antarctic Committee, 25 February 1955, NAS-IGY: USNC Antarctic Committee—Confidential; Hanessian to Peavey and Odishaw, Daily Antarctic Message Report, 23 and 24 January 1957, NAS-IGY: Daily and Weekly Antarctic Message Summaries, January–July 1957.

44. Jaburg, diary, 19–23, 26, 28 January 1957; Behrendt, *Innocents*, 46–47; John Behrendt, interview with Brian Shoemaker, 14 March 2000, 7; Littlewood interview, 22. See also, Ronne, SSLR, Ellsworth, 2.

45. Gambacorta, Report *Wyandot*, DF II, 32–33, 37; Littlewood interview, 23; Nolan Aughenbaugh, diary, 29 January–6 February 1957; Henry E. Stephens, MCB ONE, Report of Construction of Ellsworth Station, Antarctica, 25 February 1957, 7, 9, RG 313, Box 12; Behrendt, *Innocents*, 54.

46. Stephens, MCB ONE, Construction Ellsworth, 12, 15, 17, 25; Behrendt, *Innocents*, 52–53.

47. Hank Stephens, e-mail correspondence, 20 October 1999; Ronne, SSLR, Ellsworth, 5; Walter Davis, interview with author, 24 September 1999, 9.

48. MCB (Spec), Report DF II and III, vol. V, I-1, RG 313, Box 17; Stephens, MCB ONE Construction Ellsworth, 9, 18; Jaburg, diary, 10–11 February 1957; Stephens, e-mail, 1 November 1999; Ronne, SSLR, Ellsworth, 2–3.

49. Behrendt, *Innocents*, 58; Jaburg, diary, 8, 12–15, 17–24 February 1957.

50. Aughenbaugh, diary, 13 February 1957; Nolan Aughenbaugh, interview with Brian Shoemaker and author, 12 April 2001, 32.

51. Jaburg, diary, 1, 9 February 1957.

52. J. McKim Malville, interview with Brian Shoemaker, 3 October 2000, 6; Behrendt, *Innocents*, 58, 67, 69, 77.

53. MCB (Spec), Report DF II and III, vol. V, I-1; Jaburg, diary, 28 April 1957.

54. Behrendt, *Innocents*, 58–59, 258; Ronne, *Antarctic Command*, 152; Aughenbaugh, diary, 18 March, 13 May 1957; Malville interview, 7; Conrad Jaburg, interview with author, 8 May 1998, 9; Jaburg, diary, 10 March 1957.

55. Behrendt, *Innocents*, xi. See also, Ronne, *Antarctica My Destiny*, 190–196, and Operation Highjump II, RG 313, Box 1.

56. Behrendt, *Innocents*, 167; Jaburg, diary, 30 July, 3 October 1957; Jaburg interview, 9; Ronne, *Antarctic Command*, 191, 193.

CHAPTER 8

1. Eklund to [Harriet Eklund], [31 December 1956].

2. Odishaw to Gould, 4 April 1956, NAS-IGY: Antarctic Committee Organization.

3. Crary, "On the Ice," 220; Wexler, diary, 9, 15 June 1956. See also, Ronne, *Antarctica, My Destiny*, 190–195, and Ronne, *Antarctic Command*, 19–24.

4. Hanessian, Memorandum to Files, Discussion with Gould, 25 May 1956, Wexler papers, Box 28; Wexler, diary, October–November 1956; Crary, "On the Ice," 220–221; Crary, "IGY," 98; Siple, *90° South*, 129–130; South Pole Yearbook, 1957, 2; Richard Bowers, e-mail correspondence, 29 May 2000.

5. Wexler, diary, 18 September, 15, 25 October, 10, 17 November, 6, 10, 17 December 1956; Wexler to Gould, 4 September 1956, NAS-IGY: Antarctic Committee Organization; Toney interview, 3–5; USNC-IGY Press Release, George Toney Appointed Byrd Station Scientific Leader in Antarctic, 24 December 1956, NAS-IGY: IGY Personnel Antarctic.

6. Crary, "IGY," 99; Wexler, diary, 17 November 1956; Bentley interview, 24–25; Gordon de Q. Robin, Obituary, *Polar Record* 24, no. 149 (April 1988): n. p.

7. MoC, Kaplan, Atwood, Odishaw, IGY: Soviet Participation in the Weather Central . . . 24 February 1956, RG 59, Box 1652; Untitled document and Kaplan to Murphy, 15 February 1956, NAS-IGY: Science Program/Weather Central LAS; Wexler diary, 14 April 1956.

8. Wexler, diary, 1, 7 August 1956.

9. Ibid., 10, 15, 25 August, 18 September, 6, 26 October 1956; Gordon Cartwright, interview with Brian Shoemaker, 9 May 2000, 17.

10. Wexler, diary, 17, 20, 24 November, 3 December 1956.

11. Kaplan to Murphy, 15 February 1956; Remington interview, 4–5, 15; Lett interview, 35; Wexler, diary, 28 April 1956; Hanessian to Peavey and Odishaw, 5 February 1957, Daily and Weekly Antarctic Message Summaries, January–July 1957; Crary, SSLR, Little America V, 1957–1959, 19; Rubin, Shoemaker interview, 8.

12. Paul Dalrymple, interview with author, 5 August 1999, 9; Crary, SSLR, Little America, 19–20, 98; Chief Scientist to Executive Director, Antarctic Weather Central— Action Required, 24 June 1957, NAS-IGY: Science Program/Weather Central LAS; Goodale to Wexler, 28 February 1958, NAS-IGY: IGY Field Representatives, Antarctica, October 1957–February 1958.

13. Rubin, Shoemaker interview, 2 (quote), 3–7, 21; Sullivan, "IGY," 323; Fogg, *History of Antarctic Science*, 173.

14. Crary, "IGY," 96–97; Wexler, diary, 5 May 1956; Crary, "On the Ice," 228; [Hanessian], USNC-IGY Antarctic Operations, n.d. [October 1955], NAS-IGY: USNC Antarctic Committee, Confidential.

15. List: USNC Committees and Panels, NAS-IGY: Organization USNC 1953; Aughenbaugh interview, 7; C. R. Wilson, video interview with author, 19 January 2001, McMurdo Station, Antarctica, McMurdo Historical Society; Malville interview, 1; Stephen Barnes, interview with Brian Shoemaker, 13 March 2000, 9.

16. Dewart, *Antarctic Comrades*, 1–2; Behrendt, *Innocents*, ix; South Pole Yearbook, 1957, 17.

17. Behrendt interview, 3; Wexler, diary, 16 October 1956; South Pole Yearbook, 1957, 22–23; Malville interview, 1; Edwin Flowers, interview with Laura Kissel, 9 March 2000, 9; Behrendt, *Innocents*, 13, 78.

18. Bentley interview, 2–3; Crary, "On the Ice," 226; Dept of State to Amembassy Copenhagen, Training Program for International Geophysical Year at Thule, 19 April 1956, and Amembassy Copenhagen to Dept of State, no. 977, 12 June 1956, Issuance of Invitations to SIPRE Training Program at Thule, RG 59, Box 1652.

19. Crary, SSLR, Little America, 95; Crary to Antarctic Personnel, 20 September 56, NAS-IGY: Science Personnel Orientation Program, 1956–1957.

20. USNC-IGY Indoctrination Program, Davisville, Rhode Island, October 15–19, 1956, 4 October 1956, NAS-IGY: Science Personnel Orientation Program 1956–1957; Wexler, diary, 13–18 October 1956; Behrendt, *Innocents*, 53–54. See also, Crary, "IGY," 99–100.

21. Wexler, IGY Antarctic Orientation Opening Remarks, 15–19 October 1956, NAS-IGY: Science Personnel Orientation Program 1956–1957; Chief Scientist to Shear, Morris et al., 31 October 1956, NAS-IGY: Science Program/Weather Central LAS.

22. NAS-IGY: Science Personnel Orientation Program 1956–1957; CTF 43, Military and Civilian Passenger Information, DF II, NAS-IGY: Science Personnel Information; Behrendt, *Innocents*, 11.

23. Wexler, diary, 27 December 1956, January 1957.

24. Lett interview, 12–13; MCB (Spec), Report DF II and III, vol. II, 2, RG 313, Box 17.

25. Crary, "On the Ice," 247–249; Smith interview, 14–15.

26. Crary, "On the Ice," 232–233; Crary, SSLR, Little America, 4; Crary to Odishaw, IGY Letter no. 1, 21 February 1957, NAS-IGY: Draft DF II Reports; Dalrymple interview, 11.

27. Crary, SSLR, Little America, 3, 22, 46, 58; Crary to Odishaw, IGY Letter no. 1.

28. Anderson, diary, 20 January 1957; Crary, SSLR, Little America, 2; Crary to Odishaw, IGY Letter no. 1.

29. Bentley interview, 5; Anderson, diary, January 1957; Crary, "On the Ice," 249.

30. Anderson, diary, 28, 30 January, 1 February 1957.

31. Ibid., 1, 4–5, 17, 27 February 1957.

32. Antarctic Programs and Operations during the IGY, July 1956, NAS-IGY: CSAGI Antarctic Stations: Loc. and Progs. See also, Summary Description of Antarctic Programs of Other Countries, 1 February 1956, NAS-IGY: Testimony.

33. Summary Description . . . Other Countries, 1 February 1956; Amembassy London to State, no. 907, Commonwealth Trans-Antarctic Expedition, 21 October 1955, NAS-IGY: TAE; Hillary, *View From the Summit*, 163, 165; "A Talk With Sir Vivian Fuchs," in Charles Neider, *Beyond Cape Horn: Travels in the Antarctic* (San Francisco: Sierra Club Books, 1980), 257–259.

34. Hillary, *View From the Summit*, 173, 176–177; Walter Sullivan, "Ice Forces Shift in Antarctic Site,"[*New York Times*, 9 January 1957], *Polar Times* compilation, 26; Bernard Kalb, "New Zealanders Conquer Glacier," *New York Times*, 30 January 1956, 29; Antarctic Programs and Operations, July 1956; Bevilacqua interview, 29–30.

35. Antarctic Programs and Operations, July 1956; Summary Description . . . Other Countries, 1 February 1956; *Antarctic* [News Bulletin of the New Zealand Antarctic Society], untitled articles: September 1957, 179, June 1958, 257–259, September 1958, 311.

36. Bernard Kalb, "U.S. Flag Planted by Glacier Crews," 27 March 1956 (quotes); see also, Kalb, "Hunt in Antarctic for a Base Foiled," 27 March 1956, and "Last US Ship Quits Antarctica, Ending One Phase of Expedition," 31 March 1956, all in *New York Times*.

37. Amembassy Tokyo to State, no. 640, Present Status of Japan's IGY Program in Antarctica, 5 December 1957, RG 59, Box 1652; Amembassy Tokyo to State, no. 1055, Japan's IGY Program in Antarctica Suffers Severe Setback, 10 March 1958, RG 59, Box 1653; "Antarctic Ship Freed From Ice, Heads for Japan," [*New York Times*, 1 March 1957], *Polar Times* compilation, 28.

38. Dewart, *Antarctic Comrades*, 16–17; A. M. Gusev, The Advance Into the Interior of Antarctica (trans.), June 1956, NAS-IGY: USSR.

39. Dewart, *Antarctic Comrades*, 18–20; Walter Sullivan, "Antarctic Slows Russians' Effort," *New York Times*, 12 May 1957, 28.

40. Cartwright to Odishaw, 25 January 1957, NAS-IGY: Draft DF II Reports; "Red Antarctic Base Boasts Women Scientists, Caviar," *Washington Post*, 14 February 1957, NAS-IGY: Personnel, Antarctica. See also, Cartwright interview.

41. Cartwright to Odishaw, 25 January 1957. See also, Cartwright, Rubin, Dewart interviews. There was no U.S.-USSR exchange of scientists in 1959.

42. MoC, Call of Ambassadors of Australia, Great Britain et al., to Discuss the Antarctic, 9 February 1956, and Beam to Acting Secretary, 9 March 1956, RG 59, Box 1651; MoC, Blakeney, White et al., Antarctic Consultations, 29 March 1956, and Bowdler to Dreier and Krieg, Briefing Session with Representatives of USNC-IGY, 19 July 1956, RG 59, Box 1652.

43. "It's Cold Strategy," *Newsweek*, 14 November 1955, 70; Bernard Kalb, "U.S. Polar Vessel Docks in Uruguay," *New York Times*, 7 April 1956, 21.

44. "Bill Asks Antarctic Body," [*New York Times*, 31 May 1957], *Polar Times* compilation, 27; Wexler, diary, 13, 21 March 1957. Representatives William Bates (R-MA) and John Pillion (R-NY) offered similar bills in the House. See Luboeansky to Dreier, Summary of S. 2189, Bill to Promote the Increase and Diffusion of Knowledge on the Antarctic . . . , 7 June 1957, and Case to Herter, 1 July 1957, with attached article,

Thomas R. Henry, "Vistas in Science," [Washington *Evening Star*, n.d.], RG 59, Box 2773.

45. Wexler, diary, 8 December 1956; "U.S. Asks Extension of Antarctic Study," 29 June 1957, *Polar Times* compilation, 20; Sullivan, "IGY," 324.

46. Walter Sullivan, "Geophysical Year Starts," and unattributed, "President on Geophysical Year," [*New York Times*, 30 June 1957], *Polar Times* compilation, 1; Hugh Odishaw, "International Geophysical Year: A Report on the United States Program" *Science* 127, no. 3290 (17 January 1958) [hereafter "IGY"]: 115; *Public Papers of the Presidents*, Eisenhower, 1957, ¶122.

CHAPTER 9

1. Cited in Richard S. Lewis, *A Continent for Science: The Antarctic Adventure* (New York: Viking, 1965), 170.

2. Hugh Odishaw, "The Meaning of the International Geophysical Year," address at National Press Club, Washington, D.C., 4 December 1958, and Joseph Kaplan, "The International Geophysical Year," address at Wilson College, Chambersburg, Pennsylvania, 25 October 1955, in NAS-IGY: Press Releases 1955–1957, July–December 1958; Laurence M. Gould, "Emergence of Antarctica: The Mythical Land," in *Frozen Future*, 12.

3. Pyne, *The Ice*, 66, 112.

4. Kaplan, Wilson College address; Carl R. Eklund and Joan Beckman, *Antarctica: Polar Research and Discovery During the International Geophysical Year* (New York: Holt, Rinehart and Winston, 1963), 76–77; U.S. Cong., Senate, Committee on Appropriations, International Geophysical Year, Special Report by the National Academy of Sciences, 84th Cong., 2nd sess., 28 May 1956, 3.

5. NAS/NRC, USNC Proposed Program for the International Geophysical Year, March 1954, NAS-IGY: Program Proposals for IGY 1952–1953; Pyne, *The Ice*, 42–43; Lewis, *A Continent for Science*, 170.

6. NAS/NRC, USNC Proposed Program IGY, March 1954; Joseph O. Fletcher, "Polar Ice and the Global Climate Machine," in *Frozen Future*, 129–135.

7. Rubin, Shoemaker interview, 50; Crary, SSLR, Little America, 88; Eklund, SSLR, Wilkes, 1–2; Tressler, SSLR, Wilkes, 2; Ronne, SSLR, Ellsworth, 5; Eklund and Beckman, *Antarctica*, 76.

8. Salmon, SSLR, Hallett, 12–16; Siple, SSLR, Pole, 146; Crary, SSLR, Little America, 84.

9. Siple, *90° South*, 289; Siple, SSLR, Pole, 146; Dalrymple interview, 31; Hanessian to Files (528.6), Weekly Antarctic Message Report, June 28, 1957, 1 July 1957, NAS-IGY: Daily and Weekly Antarctic Message Summaries, January–July 1957; Toney, SSLR, Byrd, 39–41 (Morris cite); Salmon, SSLR, Hallett, 16 (Benes cite).

10. Eklund and Beckman, *Antarctica*, 77–81 (quote on 79); Wessbecher interview, 19–20; Dufek to Gould, 10 March 1958, NAS-IGY: Draft DF III Reports; Salmon, SSLR, Hallett, 12–13.

11. Wessbecher interview, 8–9; Ronne, *Antarctica, My Destiny*, 229; Rudolf Honkala, interview with author, 4 August 1999, 16; Hanessian to 528.6, Weekly Antarctic Message Report, June 28, 1957; Cartwright interview, 20.

12. Siple, *90° South*, 253–254; Eklund, SSLR, Wilkes, 3; Tressler, SSLR, Wilkes, 4; Wessbecher interview, 19; Ronne, SSLR, Ellsworth, 5; Brennan, SSLR, Ellsworth, 6.

13. Siple, SSLR, Pole, 60–61 (Siple quote), 146–147 (Flowers quote); Eklund, SSLR, Wilkes, 3; Toney, SSLR, Byrd, 42, 43; Crary, SSLR, Little America, 87. The mets also lofted pilot balloons ("pibals") twice daily, tracking them with theodolites to determine wind direction.

14. Rubin, Shoemaker interview, 38–39.

15. Dalrymple interview, 1–2, 8–9; Crary, SSLR, Little America, 91–93; Eklund and Beckman, *Antarctica*, 79; "The South Pole receives . . ." NAS-IGY News, 23 March 1958, USNC-IGY Press Releases, January–June 1958.

16. Salmon, SSLR, Hallett, 15; Siple, SSLR, Pole, 147; Crary, SSLR, Little America, 79–80.

17. Honkala interview, 17–18. See also, Salmon, SSLR, Hallett, 12.

18. Morton J. Rubin, "Antarctic Meteorology," in *Frozen Future*, 148; Proposed Recommendations for U.S. Participation in the Meteorological Phase of the International Geophysical Year, 27 April 1953, NAS-IGY: Program Proposals IGY 1952–1953; Eklund and Beckman, *Antarctica*, 81, 104; Odishaw, "IGY," 122.

19. Odishaw, "IGY," 122–123. See also, Crary, SSLR, Little America, 78–79, 84.

20. Crary, SSLR, Little America, 84; Wexler, diary, 28, 31 October 1957; Lewis, *A Continent for Science*, 185, 187; MCB (Special), Report DF II and III, vol. II, IV-C-5.

21. Commander, U.S. NSFA to Commanding Officers [for ships and support activities], Aerological Program for Operation Deep Freeze IV, 18 August 1958, RG 313, Box 30; Toney, SSLR, Byrd, 31 (quote), 39.

22. Bentley interview, 11.

23. Crary, SSLR, Little America, 95; Rubin, Shoemaker interview, 18; Chief Scientist to Shear, Morris et al., Suggested Procedures . . . 31 October 1956.

24. Rubin, Shoemaker interview, 8, 17–18; Rubin to Wexler, 18 March 1957, NAS-IGY: Drafts DF II Reports; Hanessian to Whitney, Establishment of IGY Antarctic Weather Central at Little America, 24 November 1956, NAS-IGY: Science Program/ Weather Central LAS.

25. Crary to Odishaw, IGY Letter no. 1; Hanessian to Peavey and Odishaw, Daily Antarctic Message Report, 5 February 1957; NAS, USNC-IGY, Antarctic Status Report no. 15, 28 February 1957; Hanessian to (528.6), Weekly Antarctic Message Report, June 7, 1957, 17 June 1957; Crary, SSLR, Little America, 3, 14. See also, monthly Antarctic Status Reports, NAS-IGY: Antarctic; MCB (Spec), Report DF II and III, vol. II, III-A-7.

26. MCB (Spec), Report DF II and III, vol. II, III-A-1–2, III-B-10–11; Wexler to Odishaw, 29 November 1957, and Wexler to Gould, 1 December 1957, in NAS-IGY: IGY Field Representatives, October 1957–February 1958; Wexler, diary, 24 November 1956.

27. MCB (Spec), Report DF II and III, vol. II, III-A-3.

28. Ibid., III-B-12, -15.

29. Ibid., III-A-5 (quote), III-D-7–8; Crary, SSLR, Little America, 96.

30. MCB (Spec), Report DF II and III, vol. II, III-A-3–4, -6, III-B-2, -6–7, -19–20; Crary, SSLR, Little America, 96–97; Task Force 43, Operation Deep Freeze III, 1957–1958: The Story of Task Force 43 and Its Service to Science in the Third—the Climax—Phase of the IGY Antarctic Program, Lt. (jg) Morton P. Beebe, ed. [hereafter Cruisebook DF III], 106.

31. Eklund and Beckman, *Antarctica*, 82; MCB (Spec), Report DF II and III, vol. II, III-B-2, -18; Crary, SSLR, Little America, 96; Salmon, SSLR, Hallett, 12–16; Cruisebook DF III, 103, 106.

32. IGY Bulletin no. 24, "Meteorological Studies in the Antarctic," *Trans. AGU* 40, no. 2 (June 1959): 191; Lewis, *A Continent for Science*, 173–174, 176.

33. V. I. Rastorguev and J. A. Alvarez, "Description of the Antarctic Circulation Observed From April to November 1957 at the IGY Antarctic Weather Central, Little America Station," *IGY World Data Center A, National Academy of Sciences, General Report Series* (Washington, D.C.: NAS, 1 November 1958); Crary, SSLR, Little America, 98 (quote); Odishaw to Robin, 23 December 1958, NAS-IGY: Science Program/Weather Central LAS.

34. Dufek to Gould, 10 March 1958, NAS-IGY: Draft DF III Reports.

35. Eklund and Beckman, *Antarctica*, 83–85.

36. Baker interview, 27–29.

37. Eklund and Beckman, *Antarctica*, 83; Douglas Mawson, *The Home of the Blizzard: A True Story of Antarctic Survival* (New York: St. Martin's Griffin, 1996), 77, 81–82, 94–95.

38. Cruisebook DF III, 89; Honkala interview, 13; Dewart interview, 11; "Trek May Keep Local Man in the Antarctic Until 1959," *Geyserville Press*, 9 August 1957, NAS-IGY: Personnel, Antarctica. Dewart's parents published this northern California newspaper. Mawson, *Home of the Blizzard*, 83.

39. Crary, SSLR, Little America, 97, citing Rastorguev and Alvarez study; IGY Bulletin no. 24, 192.

40. U.S. Cong., House, Hearings, National Science Foundation/National Academy of Sciences Report on the International Geophysical Year, 86th Cong., 1st Sess., February 1959, 119–120; Lewis, *A Continent for Science*, 182–183; IGY Bulletin no. 24, 194.

41. Siple, SSLR, Pole, 146; Eklund and Beckman, *Antarctica*, 85; House, Hearings, NSF/NAS Report on IGY, February 1959, 98.

42. Crary, SSLR, Little America, 96–97; Anderson, diary, 18 September 1957; House, Hearings, NSF/NAS Report on IGY, February 1959, 98 (Gould statement), 119. Vostok still holds Antarctica's record low temperature, −128.6°F, on 21 July 1983. See also, Eklund and Beckman, *Antarctica*, 85–86.

CHAPTER 10

1. K. J. Salmon, "Our Year at Hallett," *Antarctic* 2, no. 1 (March 1959): 14.

2. Eklund and Beckman, *Antarctica*, 88–90.

3. Ibid., 100–101.

4. Ibid., 102. [Planning document] United States National Committee for the International Geophysical Year, 10 March 1955, NAS-IGY: Organization USNC, 1955; Odishaw, "IGY," 117–118.

5. Odishaw, "IGY," 128; Crary, "On the Ice," 264–265; Ronne, SSLR, Ellsworth, 5.

6. South Pole Yearbook, 1957, 49–50 (Hough quote). See also, Siple, SSLR, Pole, 145. Pole's C-3 ionosphere recorder had somewhat less power and accuracy than the C-4; Mogensen, SSLR, Pole, 12 (Greene quote).

7. K. Waldron interview, 2, 13–15.

8. South Pole Yearbook, 1957, 49–50; Siple, *90° South*, 237; Jaburg, diary, 2 March 1957.

9. Odishaw, "IGY," 117–118; Eklund and Beckman, *Antarctica*, 106; Robert A. Helliwell, "The Upper Atmosphere as Seen From Antarctica," in *Frozen Future*, 168–169.

10. Eklund and Beckman, *Antarctica*, 107; Odishaw, "IGY," 117; Cruisebook DF III, 93–94; Malville interview, draft transcript, 18; USNC-IGY, US-IGY Antarctic Program Report . . . to the First Meeting of the Special Committee on Antarctic Research of the International Council of Scientific Unions, February 3–6, 1958, The Hague, 27 January 1958, RG 307, Box 3.

11. Salmon, "Our Year at Hallett," 13; Helliwell, "Upper Atmosphere," 171, 179.

12. Kaplan, Wilson College address; Martin Pomerantz, interview with Brian Shoemaker, 10 May 2000, 2–3; Eklund and Beckman, *Antarctica*, 109–111, 115–117; J. McKim Malville, correspondence with author, 29 January 2003.

13. Pomerantz interview, 6–8, 14; Odishaw, "IGY," 118.

14. Odishaw, "IGY," 118; Sullivan, *Quest for a Continent*, 322–323; Dufek to Gould, 10 March 1958, 5.

15. Cruisebook DF III, 87, 94; Brennan, SSLR, Ellsworth, 4–5; Eklund, SSLR, Wilkes, 4; Tressler, SSLR, Wilkes, 5.

16. Pomerantz interview, 15.

17. Ibid., 22–25.

18. Ibid., 27–30. Pomerantz chaired the U.S. IQSY (International Quiet Sun Year).

19. *James Van Allen: Flights of Discovery*, narrated by Tom Brokaw, University of Iowa, Iowa City, 2000, video courtesy of Glen Hartong; Van Allen interview, 32–34; Eklund and Beckman, *Antarctica*.

20. *James Van Allen: Flights of Discovery*; Eklund and Beckman, *Antarctica*, 113–114; Malville, correspondence, 29 January 2003.

21. Eklund and Beckman, *Antarctica*, 92–94; IGY Bulletin no. 3, *Trans. AGU*, 805–807.

22. Odishaw, "IGY," 116; Eklund and Beckman, *Antarctica*, 94–98; Wilson, video interview; IGY Bulletin no. 3, *Trans. AGU*, 807–808.

23. Toney, SSLR, Byrd, 6, 33–38 (Davis report); Anderson, diary, 1 March 1957.

24. Mogensen, SSLR, Pole, 16; Tressler, SSLR, Wilkes, 5; Shear, SSLR, Hallett, 3; Salmon, SSLR, Hallett, 47–48; Crary, SSLR, Little America, 52.

25. Malville, correspondence, 29 January 2003.

26. Eklund and Beckman, *Antarctica*, 118; Pyne, *The Ice*, 320–321.

27. Malville, correspondence, 29 January 2003; Helliwell, "Upper Atmosphere," 169–170; Pyne, *The Ice*, 319; Eklund and Beckman, *Antarctica*, 118, 123; [Planning document] USNC-IGY, 10 March 1955.

28. Eklund and Beckman, *Antarctica*, 120; Odishaw, "IGY," 116; Malville interview, 2.

29. Malville interview, 2–3; Landolt interview, 17.

30. Landolt interview, 13; J. McKim Malville, telephone conversation with author, 19 September 2002; Crary, SSLR, Little America, 25, 32, 35; Wilson, video interview; Salmon, SSLR, Hallett, 17, 19.

31. Landolt interview, 14; Malville, telephone conversation, 19 September 2002; Crary, SSLR, Little America, 39–40, 43, 45.

32. Crary, SSLR, Little America, 26, 32, 37, 39; Wilson, video interview.

33. Brennan, SSLR, Ellsworth, 4 (Warren quote); Malville, correspondence, 29 January 2003; Crary, SSLR, Little America, 28; Salmon, SSLR, Hallett, 29, 31; Salmon, "Our Year at Hallett," 13.

34. Eklund and Beckman, *Antarctica*, 122–123; Odishaw, "IGY," 116; Wilson, video interview; Malville, correspondence, 29 January 2003; Helliwell, "Upper Atmosphere," 176–177.

35. Landolt interview, 4; Eklund and Beckman, *Antarctica*, 124; Pyne, *The Ice*, 317.

36. Malville, correspondence, 29 January 2003. See also, Byrd, *Discovery*, 219.

37. Joseph Kaplan, The IGY Rocket and Satellite Program, [n.d.], NAS-IGY: Organization USNC.

38. *James Van Allen: Flights of Discovery*; Van Allen interview, 31–33. See also, Siple, SSLR, Pole, 114–139; Odishaw, "IGY," 119–120.

39. Rostow cited in Bullis, *Political Legacy of the IGY*, 38; Behrendt, *Innocents*, 242–243.

40. Helliwell, "Upper Atmosphere," 168; Pyne, *The Ice*, 110–111. See also, Jack Stuster, *Bold Endeavors: Lessons From Polar and Space Exploration* (Annapolis: Naval Institute Press, 1996); Giovinetto interview.

CHAPTER 11

1. Behrendt, *Innocents*, 357.

2. Pyne, *The Ice*, 290–291; IGY Bulletin no. 13, "Preliminary History on the Thickness of Ice in Antarctica," July 1958, *Trans. AGU* 39, no. 4 (August 1958): 772–775 (Woollard quote); C. C. Langway Jr. and B. Lyle Hansen, "Drilling Through the Ice Cap: Probing Climate for a Thousand Centuries," in *Frozen Future*, 201; Eklund and Beckman, *Antarctica*, 59.

3. Eklund and Beckman, *Antarctica*, 65; Lewis, *A Continent for Science*, 57–58. See also, Campbell Craddock, "Antarctic Geology and Gondwanaland," in *Frozen Future*, 101–121.

4. Raymond Priestley and C. S. Wright, "Some Ice Problems of Antarctica," in W.L.G. Joerg, ed., *Problems of Polar Research* ([New York]: American Geographical Society, 1928), 332, 337, cited in Pyne, *The Ice*, 282; Byrd, *Discovery*, 5–6, see also, 357–360.

5. Pyne, *The Ice*, 278; A. P. Crary, "On the Ice," 204.

6. Robin, "Science and Logistics in Antarctica," 272–273.

7. Odishaw, "IGY," 126; Eklund and Beckman, *Antarctica*, 68–70.

8. Odishaw, "IGY," 126; Eklund and Beckman, *Antarctica*, 70–71.

9. See Crary, "On the Ice," 207; Behrendt, *Innocents*, 194.

10. Crary, SSLR, Little America, 58–59.

11. Crary, "On the Ice," 256–257; Toney, SSLR, Byrd, 54–55; Anderson, diary, 14 March, 2 April, 10 May 1957.

12. Eklund, SSLR, Wilkes, 5; Tressler, SSLR, Wilkes, 7; Dewart interview, 22; Crary, SSLR, Little America, 60.

13. Anderson, diary, 27–28 April 1957; Toney, SSLR, Byrd, 54–55; IGY Bulletin no. 2, "Glaciology," *Trans. AGU* 38, no. 4 (August 1957): 631; Eklund, SSLR, Wilkes, 4–5.

14. IGY Bulletin no. 23, "Antarctic Snow Stratigraphy," May 1959, *Trans. AGU* 40, no. 2 (June 1959): 181–182.

15. Siple, SSLR, Pole, 144; Aughenbaugh, diary, 25 April–3 May 1957; Behrendt, *Innocents*, 110–112.

16. Anderson, diary, 21 June 1957; Behrendt interview, 17; Siple, *90° South*, 256.

17. Anderson, diary, 29 June, 5–6, 17 July, 2, 5, 15 August 1957; Behrendt, *Innocents*, 165.

18. Toney, SSLR, Byrd, 55; Crary, SSLR, Little America, 60; Behrendt, *Innocents*, 212.

19. Dewart interview, 23; Honkala interview, 12; Noonan interview, 14–15.

20. Eklund, SSLR, Wilkes, 10–13; Honkala interview, 11–13; Dewart interview, 21–23. The trip inland, climbing in third gear at 3 miles per hour, consumed 65 gallons of diesel fuel; the return, downhill and light in fourth gear at 7 mph, took 30 gallons.

21. Eklund, SSLR, Wilkes, 5.

22. Siple, SSLR, Pole, 143–144 (Remington quote); Mogensen, SSLR, Pole, 29.

23. Toney, SSLR, Byrd, 65–67, 69; NAS, IGY Press Release, 30 January 1958, NAS-IGY: USNC-IGY Press Releases, January–June 1958.

24. IGY Bulletin no. 16, "Deep Core Drilling Program: Byrd Station, Antarctica," *Trans. AGU* 39, no. 5 (October 1958): 1021–1023; Francis to Odishaw, n.d. [received 18 December 1958], NAS-IGY: IGY Field Representatives, March 1958–February 1959.

25. NAS, IGY Press Release, 30 January 1958, printed verbatim in *Science* 127 (14 February 1958): 331.

26. Dewart interview, 3–4, 15–18; Eklund, SSLR, Wilkes, 4, 6; Tressler, SSLR, Wilkes, 5–6.

27. Siple, *90° South*, 298; Siple, SSLR, Pole, 150–151 (Benson quote). Siple's snow-depth number was an educated guess. Though others tried, Andrei Kapitsa, Soviet geophysicist on the 1959–1960 Vostok–South Pole traverse, was the first to accurately sound the ice at the Pole. It is 2,850 meters (9,384 feet) thick, with bedrock 34 meters (112 ft) above sea level; Behrendt, *Innocents*, 390, and correspondence.

28. Siple, SSLR, Pole, 151 (Benson quote); Mogensen, SSLR, Pole, 18, 23 (Burnham quote); Salmon, SSLR, Hallett, 52 (Bargh quote).

29. Crary, SSLR, Little America, 59–60, 63; Crary, "On the Ice," 258; Behrendt, *Innocents*, 146–147, 259–260; Eklund, SSLR, Wilkes, 4–5; Tressler, SSLR, Wilkes, 6–7.

30. Crary, USNC-IGY Antarctic Traverse Logistical Requirements, 20 October 1955, NAS-IGY: Fiscal Correspondence and Policy (Planning).

31. Ibid.; Behrendt, *Innocents*, 60–61, 280. Snowmobiles, at first called motor toboggans, were introduced in Deep Freeze 61; George A. Doumani, *The Frigid Mistress: Life and Exploration in Antarctica* (Baltimore: Noble House, 1999), 166.

32. Crary, SSLR, Little America, 58–60; Barnes, SSLR, Byrd, 5–7; Behrendt, *Innocents*, 257, 273.

33. Bentley interview, 14–15, 35–36; Behrendt, *Innocents*, 280–281.

34. Ronne, *Antarctic Command*, 115, 120; Ronne, *Antarctica, My Destiny*, 209–210. See also, Ronne, SSLR, Ellsworth, 4; W. Davis interview, 5; Behrendt, *Innocents*, 55, 88.

35. W. Davis interview, 5, 13; Behrendt, *Innocents*, 43, 99–100. See also, Aughenbaugh, diary, 10, 18 April, 3 May, 31 July 1957.

36. Behrendt, *Innocents*, 169, 180–181, 219, 221–222, 241; Anderson, diary, 11 July 1957; W. Davis interview, 5; Aughenbaugh, diary, 11 July, 8 September 1957.

37. Behrendt, *Innocents*, 252, 342; W. Davis interview, 5; Ronne, *Antarctic Command*, 190; Ronne, SSLR, Ellsworth, 4. Kim Malville and Con Jaburg also corroborated details of this story.

38. James Edgar Waldron, *Flight of the Puckered Penguins*, on-line memoir, chapters 24–25, <http://www.anta.canterbury.ac.nz/resources/flight/> "published" April 1996 (accessed 3 September 1998); Jaburg, diary, 2–16 August 1957.

39. Bentley interview, 27; Waldron, *Flight of the Puckered Penguins*, chapter 19; U.S. Navy, Air Development Squadron Six [VX-6], Report DF III, 1 July 1958, 15, RG 313, Box 19.

40. Bentley interview, 27; Waldron, *Flight of the Puckered Penguins*, chapter 17; VX-6, Report DF III, 23, 31–33.

41. Sullivan, "Antarctic Slows Russians' Effort"; Dewart interview, 26–27; "Trek May Keep Local Man in the Antarctic," *Geyserville* (CA) *Press*; Hanessian to Files (528.6), Weekly Antarctic Message Reports, 7, 28 June 1957; Gould and Wexler to Odishaw, Results of Antarctic Discussions, April 22–26, 1957, 26 April 1957, NAS-IGY: Antarctic Committee Organization; Tressler, SSLR, Wilkes, 14.

42. Hanessian to Files (528.6), Weekly Antarctic Message Report, 2 May 1957; Siple, *90° South*, 341; Wexler, diary, 20 December 1957.

43. Crary, "On the Ice," 279–281; Crary, SSLR, Little America, 62.

44. IGY Bulletin no. 14, "Ross Ice Shelf Deformation Project: 1957–58," *Trans. AGU* 39, no. 4 (August 1958): 794–797; Crary, SSLR, Little America, 101–102; Francis to Jones, 25 December 1957, NAS-IGY: IGY Field Representatives, October 1957–February 1958.

45. Behrendt, *Innocents*, 93, 259, 286, 306.

46. Ibid., 2–3, 330, 342, 345, 367; Aughenbaugh, diary, 15 December 1957; Behrendt interview, 31, 34–35.

47. Behrendt interview, 25; Wexler, diary, 25, 31 October, 18 December 1957.

48. Anderson, diary, 14–19 November, early December 1957; Dater, "Byrd Station"; Toney, SSLR, Byrd, 50–51; Bentley interview, 26; Crary, "On the Ice," 271–272; Behrendt, correspondence.

49. Bentley interview, 30; Behrendt, correspondence.

50. Behrendt interview, 40; Aughenbaugh, diary, November–December 1957.

51. Behrendt, *Innocents*, 199–200, 300; Robin, "Science and Logistics in Antarctica," 278; Anderson, diary, 23 December 1957.

52. Crary, "On the Ice," 274–276.

53. Waldron, *Flight of the Puckered Penguins*, chapter 28. Ratzlaff was killed in an Otter crash on the ice a year later.

54. Crary, "On the Ice," 280–281; Wexler, diary, 1 November 1957.

55. Crary, "On the Ice," 277; Ernest Shackleton, *The Heart of the Antarctic* (New York: Signet, 2000), 220. See also, Chapman, *Antarctic Conquest*, 197.

56. John Pirrit, *Across West Antarctica* (Glasgow: John Smith & Son, 1967), 19, citing *Annals of the Association of American Geographers* 69, no. 2 (June 1959): 110–119; Aughenbaugh interview, 18, 45–46; Aughenbaugh, diary, 4–7 October, 3 November 1957. He drew page after page of detailed sketches of crevasse systems encountered.

57. Behrendt, *Innocents*, 298–299.

58. Jaburg, diary, 15 November 1957; ibid., 303, 306–311, 320; Aughenbaugh, diary, 16, 28 November 1957.

59. Bentley interview, 29; Anderson, diary, 13 December 1957.

60. Toney, SSLR, Byrd, 56; Sullivan, *Assault on the Unknown*, 322; Anderson, diary, December 1957–January 1958.

61. Behrendt, *Innocents*, 84–85, 283–285 (first quote on 285, second quote on 84); Behrendt, e-mail correspondence, 9 October 2001; Bentley interview, 31–33; Anderson, diary, 6 Februry 1957.

62. Bentley interview, 34.

63. Ibid., 33; Toney, SSLR, Byrd, 50–51; Crary, SSLR, Little America, 62; Behrendt, correspondence.

64. Behrendt, *Innocents*, 84–85, 280; Bentley interview, 15–16.

65. IGY Bulletin no. 13, 772–775.

66. Bentley interview, 16–17, 31.

67. Pyne, *The Ice*, 119; Grosvenor, "An Ice Wrapped Continent," 99, citing Scott's *Voyage of* The Discovery, vol. 2, 421; Ernest H. Shackleton, "The Heart of the Antarc-

tic," *National Geographic* 20, no. 11 (November 1909): 1007; Richard Evelyn Byrd, "Exploring the Ice Age in Antarctica," *National Geographic* 68, no. 4 (October 1935): 474.

68. Crary, SSLR, Little America, 14–16; IGY Bulletin no. 10, "IGY Antarctic Oversnow Traverses," *Trans. AGU* 39, no. 2 (April 1958): 371; IGY Bulletin no. 19, "Trans-Antarctic Trough," January 1959, *Trans. AGU* 40, no. 1 (March 1959): 48–50.

69. IGY Bulletin no. 10, 373; Behrendt, *Innocents*, 335; Lewis, *A Continent for Science*, 104, 106–107.

70. Aughenbaugh, diary, 9–14 December 1957; Behrendt, *Innocents*, 343, 352–353.

71. Behrendt interview, 33–34; Aughenbaugh interview, 44; Behrendt, *Innocents*, 358–359.

72. Aughenbaugh, diary, 5 January 1958; Ross Hatch, interview with author, 24 September 1999, 8, 14. See also, Harris to Eisenhower, 17 January 1958, NAS-IGY: Antarctic Policy.

73. Behrendt, *Innocents*, 386, 390; Pirrit, *Across West Antarctica*, 6, 8, 16–18.

74. Behrendt, *Innocents*, 384–385; IGY Bulletin no. 30, "Ice Thickness and Bottom Topography of the Filchner Ice Shelf and Along the Ellsworth-Byrd Traverse Route," *Trans. AGU* 40, no. 4 (December 1959): 424–425.

75. Toney, SSLR, Byrd, 51; Bentley interview, 17–19, 26; Lewis, *A Continent for Science*, 98–100.

76. Toney, SSLR, Byrd, 51, 58–59; IGY Bulletin no. 13, 776; Sullivan, *Assault on the Unknown*, 312; Behrendt, correspondence.

77. Anderson, diary, 23–26 December 1957, 3, 24 January 1958; IGY Bulletin no. 26, "Antarctic Notes," August 1959, *Trans. AGU* 40, no. 3 (September 1959): 298. See also, IGY Bulletin no. 22, "Wind Transport of Antarctic Snow," April 1959, *Trans. AGU* 40, no. 2 (June 1959): 162–167.

78. Anderson, diary, 20, 22, 27 February 1958.

79. Neider, *Beyond Cape Horn*, 252; Sir Vivian Fuchs, "The Crossing of Antarctica," *National Geographic* 115, no. 1 (January 1959): 37ff; Sir Vivian Fuchs and Sir Edmund Hillary, *The Crossing of Antarctica* (Boston: Little, Brown, 1958), 176, chapters 16–17, 19; Hillary, *View From the Summit*, chapters 9–10. Fuchs and Hillary, coming from opposite sides of the date line, gave dates that differ by a day.

80. IGY Bulletin no. 10, 374; IGY Bulletin no. 21, "Antarctic Notes," *Trans. AGU* 40, no. 1 (March 1959): 80. See also, U.S. Department of Commerce, "Soviet Bloc International Geophysical Year Information," weekly reports, 14 February 1958 to 2 January 1959 (translations and analyses of Soviet IGY reports); IGY Bulletin no. 27, *Trans. AGU* 40, no. 3 (September 1959): 312 (map); Behrendt, correspondence.

81. Crary, SSLR, Little America, 62; Crary, "On the Ice," 291–294; Wexler, diary, 8–20 May 1958.

82. This account is synthesized from A. P. Crary, diary, 28 February 1958, RG 401 (124); Crary, "On the Ice," 295–298; Wilson, video interview; Stephen den Hartog, quoted in Sullivan, *Assault on the Unknown*, 318; George J. Dufek, "What We've Accomplished in Antarctica," *National Geographic* 116, no. 4 (October 1959): 551, 554;

Dalrymple interview, 15–16. The helo-repair heroes were Patrick Melton and Don Foreman.

83. Crary, "On the Ice," 317–318.

84. Ibid., 311–313, 319–320; IGY Bulletin no. 27, 314–315.

85. IGY Bulletin no. 27, 313–315; Shackleton, "Heart of the Antarctic," 1003; Wilson interview.

86. IGY Bulletin no. 30, 425–426; Rev. Edward A. Bradley SJ and F. T. Turcotte, Ellsworth-Byrd Traverse, 1958–1959, NAS-IGY: DF IV Reports; Lewis, *A Continent for Science*, 111. See also, Pirrit, *Across West Antarctica*, chapter 6, although he does not detail the scientific work.

87. Lewis, *A Continent for Science*, 113–116; House, Hearings, NSF/NAS Report on IGY, February 1959, 97; Francis to Jones, 16 December 1958, and Peavey to Jones, 13 February 1959, in NAS-IGY: IGY Field Representatives, March 1958–February 1959.

88. Thiel to Field, Chairman, IGY Glaciology Panel, 2 February 1959, NAS-IGY: DF IV Reports; Lewis, *A Continent for Science*, 111–115, 117.

89. Eklund and Beckman, *Antarctica*, 63–66; Lewis, *A Continent for Science*, 57, 117–118. Numbers were variously reported and undoubtedly remained fluid. Gould told Congress in 1959 that the ice volume in Antarctica was 6.5 million cubic miles. House, Hearings, February 1959, 97; IGY Bulletin no. 10, 369–370; Behrendt, correspondence. See also, Craddock, "Antarctic Geology and Gondwanaland," 101–121.

90. Bentley interview, 18, 44.

CHAPTER 12

1. William E. Lowe, ADFA questionnaire response.

2. MCB (Spec), Report DF II and III, vol. VI, A.9.13.

3. Ibid., VI-19; Officer-in-Charge, Antarctic Support Activities, Amundsen-Scott South Pole Station, Report DF IV, unpaginated, RG 313, Box 27; Clifford Dickey, group interview with author, 8 May 1998; Wilson, video interview.

4. MCB (Spec), Report DF II and III, vol. VI, A.6.7, vol. II, Medical Enclosure, 14.

5. Ibid., vol. VI, A.1.3, IV-7, -9; Chester Segers, interview with Brian Shoemaker and author, 12 April 2001, 13–14; South Pole Yearbook, 63; Siple, *90° South*, 249; Dalton interview, 21–22.

6. Boyer to [Sharon Boyer], 12 December 1958, Antarctic correspondence courtesy of Sharon Boyer.

7. Salmon, SSLR, Hallett, 7–8. See also, Siple, *90° South*, 302, 304.

8. Crary, "On the Ice," 268–269; Siple, SSLR, Pole, 78–79. See also, SSLRs and Navy leaders' reports, Recreation.

9. MCB (Spec), Report DF I and II, vol. II, B-THREE-11; Shear, SSLR, Hallett, 6; Ronne, *Antarctic Command*, 196. See also, Behrendt, *Innocents*, diary entries 16 June–4 August 1957.

10. MCB (Spec), DF I and II, vol. II, B-THREE-11; Tressler, SSLR, Wilkes, 23; Eklund, SSLR, Wilkes, 19; Wexler to Odishaw, 29 November 1957, NAS-IGY: IGY Field Representatives, October 1957–February 1958; Dalrymple interview, 19–20.

11. Siple, *90° South*, 315; Lieut. Peter P. Ruseski, Officer-in-Charge, DF II Byrd Station Log Book, 12 February 1958, RG 313, Box 20.

12. Jaburg, diary, introduction, 4, 6, 46, 57; Tressler, SSLR, Wilkes, 24. See also, MCB (Spec) reports; Francis to Odishaw, 26 May and 31 July 1958, NAS-IGY: IGY Field Representatives, March 1958–February 1959.

13. MCB (Spec), Report DF II and III, vol. VI, Medical, 13–15, A.3.16; Siple, *90° South*, 276–277; Jaburg, diary, 9 September 1957; Jaburg interview, 14; Waldron interview, 31–32.

14. MCB (Spec), Report DF II and III, vol. VI, A.1–4.22; Siple, *90° South*, 269–270; Siple, SSLR, Pole, 85.

15. MCB (Spec), Report DF II and III, vol. VIII, Medical, 42; Eklund, SSLR, Wilkes, 21; Lucier interview, 30. The men invariably called it Old Methuselah, but a photograph of a bottle of the infamous liquor confirms Old Methusalem on the label; Cruisebook, Deep Freeze IV.

16. Rubin, Shoemaker interview, 40; OiC, South Pole Station, Report DF IV, n.p.

17. MCB (Spec), Report DF II and III, vol. VII, Medical; Jaburg, diary, 18 March 1957; W. Davis interview, 16–17.

18. MCB (Spec), Report DF I and II, vol. II, B-THREE-50–52.

19. Ehrlich interview, 20–22 (quote on 21); MCB (Spec), Report DF I and II, vol. V, D-SEVEN-37 (Taylor cite).

20. Anderson, diary, 26 May, 6 August, 22, 23 October 1957.

21. Wilson, video interview.

22. "Fire at U.S. Polar Base," *New York Times*, 30 April 1957, 15, 1; MCB (Spec), Report DF II and III, vol. III, II-F-2, VI-B-1; vol. II, 17–18, see also Medical, 8; Dewart, *Antarctic Comrades*, chapter 8.

23. MCB (Spec), Report DF I and II, vol. V, D-NINE-5 (Condit cite), DF II and III, vol. III, II-K-2.

24. Barnes interview, 16; Barnes, SSLR, Byrd, 6; Boyer to [Sharon Boyer], 30 December 1958; Anderson, diary, 19–21 April 1957.

25. Siple, *90° South*, 274; MCB (Spec), Report DF II and III, vol. VI, II-15; Behrendt, *Innocents*, 91, 98; Aughenbaugh, diary, 19, 21 April 1957.

26. Noonan interview, 27; MCB (Spec), Report DF II and III, vol. VIII, II-K-3; Tressler, SSLR, Wilkes, 24.

27. Thomson interview, 58; Edward Frankiewicz, interview with Brian Shoemaker, 23 February 2000, 12, and conversation with author, 27 March 1999.

28. Mawson, *Home of the Blizzard*, 317–319; Byrd, *Little America*, 116, 163; Byrd, *Discovery*, 98–99; Behrendt, *Innocents*, 68–69.

29. MCB (Spec), Report DF II and III, vol. IV, III-9–11. See also, Dater, "Byrd Station," later published in the *Antarctic Journal* (May–June 1975): 96–108; Toney, SSLR, Byrd, 9; Bentley interview, 22.

30. MCB (Spec), Report DF II and III, vol. II, III-B-40, -44, -51.

31. Montgomery interview, 15–16, 38. The other stations' call letters were: Byrd KC4USB, Ellsworth KC4USW, Hallett KC4USH, Pole KC4USN, Wilkes KC4USK. See CTF 43, Operation DF II, 1956–1957, Operation Order Number 1–56, M-5.

32. MCB (Spec), Report DF I and II, vol. V, D-SIX-48; Aldrich, memoir (Little America newsletter quote); MCB (Spec), Report DF II and III, vol. II, III-B-42, -47.

33. See NAS-IGY: Science Personnel General Correspondence and Returning Personnel Letters; South Pole Yearbook, 1957, 68–70.

34. Aldrich interview, 10; Dalton interview, 20–21, 33; Honkala interview, 21; Anderson, diary, see, for example, March–September 1957; Bentley interview, 22.

35. MCB (Spec), Report DF II and III, vol. V, III-1, -3. The authorship of this unusually terse, unsigned report is unclear; it may be that both Ronne, station leader, and Dr. Clinton Smith, officer-in-charge of the Seabees, wrote different sections. Both receive rather pointed criticism—perhaps from each other? Aughenbaugh, diary, 31 July 1957; Behrendt, *Innocents*, 186.

36. Jaburg, diary, 4 June, 28 July 1957; Jaburg interview, 6–7; Aughenbaugh, diary, 20 September 1957.

37. Behrendt, *Innocents*, 222; Malville interview, 18.

38. Siple, *90° South*, 262–263; MCB (Spec), Report DF II and III, vol. VI, 4, 9.

39. Eklund, SSLR, Wilkes, 20–21. Dewart and Honkala confirmed the pattern; MCB (Spec), Report DF II and III, vol. IV, IV-8 (Dalton cite); Bentley interview, 12, 22.

40. Crary, "On the Ice," 255–256; Dalrymple interview, 9, 17, 26; Wilson, video interview.

41. Behrendt, *Innocents,* 100; Jaburg, diary, 11 May 1957; Ronne, *Antarctic Command,* 150 (quote), 156.

42. Behrendt, *Innocents*, 118–121; Ronne, *Antarctic Command*, 152–154.

43. Ronne, *Antarctic Command*, 156; Jaburg, diary, 15 May 1957; Aughenbaugh, diary, 15 May 1957; Behrendt, *Innocents,* 122.

44. Behrendt, *Innocents*, 124–129; Ronne, *Antarctic Command*, 156; Aughenbaugh, diary, 17 May 1957. See also, Crary, "On the Ice," 266–267. By Crary's terse diary entry, 18 May 1957, he and Dickey just "made comments."

45. Ronne, *Antarctic Command,* 156–157; Behrendt, *Innocents,* 369.

46. Wexler, diary, 25, 31 October 1957; Malville interview, 13.

47. Malville interview, 18–19.

48. Wexler, diary, 13 February 1958.

49. Pembroke Hart, telephone conversation with author, 6 December 2001; Philip Mange, telephone conversation with author, 10 December 2001; Siple, *90° South*, 322–323; Wexler, diary and notes, 13 February 1958.

50. Wexler, diary, 14 February 1958; Charles S. Mullin Jr. and H.J.M. Connery, "Psychological Study at an Antarctic IGY Station," *US Armed Forces Medical Journal* 10, no. 3 (March 1959): 290–296. The other psychiatrist was Lieut. Fred Wouters; Jaburg interview, 9.

51. Ronne, *Antarctic Command*, 244; for pay comparisons, see 26–27, 85, 116, 153, 155; MCB (Spec), Report DF II and III, vol. V, II-E-1–2; Malville interview, 3; Gould to Odishaw, 22 October 1956, Ronne to Wexler, 23 October 1956, Kropp to Peavey, 26 October 1956, and Wexler to Ronne, 29 October 1956, all in RG 401 (59), L. M. Gould papers, Box 3. This collection contains copies of numerous Ronne letters with third parties, presumably sent by him to Gould, with whom he maintained a friendly correspondence. By Ronne's calculation, salary-plus was $9,797 for him, $13,716 for top civilian leaders. GS-9s earned $5,700 a year plus an $1,800 bonus on satisfactory completion; Behrendt, *Innocents*, 11. In 1955–1956 seamen earned a base pay of about $78 per month, an ensign $222 per month, each plus allowances; Dean Allard, correspondence with author, 6 December 2002.

52. Wexler, diary, 20 February, 6, 29 May, 18 June 1958; "Bickering Reported at Polar Base," *Washington Post*, 10 February 1958, A1, A9; Susanna McBee, "Capt. Ronne, Back From Antarctic, Denies Friction With Civilian Aides," *Washington Post*, 21 February 1958, A18; Finn Ronne, Discoveries in the Antarctic, 11 July 1958, RG 401 (59), Box 3.

53. Behrendt interview, 20; Behrendt, *Innocents*, 128, 149, 204; Aughenbaugh, diary, 18 March, 5, 21 June, 26 September 1957; Jaburg, diary, 28 April, 31 May 1957.

54. Ronne, *Antarctica, My Destiny*, 192–193. See also, Minutes, First Meeting, Panel on Antarctic Policies of the USNC-IGY Antarctic Committee, 25 February 1955, NAS-IGY: USNC Antarctic Committee—Confidential; W. Davis interview, 16, 19, 21, 24.

55. Ronne, *Antarctic Command*, 85, 150; Jaburg interview, 11; Walker to Odishaw, 15 March 1958, NAS-IGY: Returning Personnel Letters; Stuster, *Bold Endeavors*, 106, 112.

56. Stuster, *Bold Endeavors*, 96–97, 106 (Blair cite); Lowe, ADFA questionnaire; Dalton interview, 18–19.

57. Dewart interview, 13–15, 47–48; Honkala interview, 6; Noonan interview, 26.

58. Dewart interview, 38; Noonan interview, 12, 26; Eklund, SSLR, Wilkes, 20–21.

59. Eklund, SSLR, Wilkes, 21; Eklund to [Harriet Eklund], 30 January 1958, RG 401 (5), Box 10; Noonan interview, 18.

60. Eklund to [Harriet Eklund], 7 December 1956, 20, 24 January, 13 February 1957, RG 401 (5), Box 10; Ronne, *Antarctica, My Destiny*, 117, 134.

61. Dalrymple interview, 24; OiC, South Pole Station, Report DF IV, n.p.; Julian W. Posey, Report on the USARP Scientific and the Naval Support Programs at the South Pole during Deep Freeze IV, 7, and E. J. Fremouw, Report on the Aurora and Airglow Program . . . during International Geophysical Cooperation, 1959, South Pole, 26, 27, RG 307, Box 9; Pirrit, *Across West Antarctica*, 107.

62. Barnes, SSLR, Byrd, 4; Dater, "Byrd Station"; Francis to Odishaw, 23 April, 23 and 25 September 1958, IGY Field Representatives, March 1958–February 1959.

63. Stuster, *Bold Endeavors*, 9–10, 99–101 (Nelson and Strange cites).

64. Ibid., 9; E. K. Eric Gunderson, "Psychological Studies in Antarctica," in *Human Adaptability to Antarctic Conditions*, Antarctic Research Series, E. K. Eric Gunderson,

ed., vol. 22 (Washington, D.C.: American Geophysical Union, 1974), 120–121, 126; R. E. Strange and S. A. Youngman, "Emotional Aspects of Wintering Over," *Antarctic Journal* (November–December 1971): 256; Thomson interview, 6.

65. MCB (Spec), Report DF I and II, vol. II, B-THREE-8, Report DF II and III, vol. VI, A.2.18, A.1–3.21, Medical, 11, 16, A.2.2–A.3.2.

66. Strange and Youngman, "Emotional Aspects," 255–257; MCB (Spec), Report DF I and II, vol. II, B-THREE-7; A.J.W. Taylor, *Antarctic Psychology*, DSIR Bulletin no. 244 (Wellington: Science Information Publishing Centre, 1987), 25; Siple, *90° South*, 18.

67. Siple, *90° South*, 248; OiC, South Pole Station, Report DF IV, n.p.; Ehrlich interview, 30–32; Dalton interview, 24. See also, Taylor, *Antarctic Psychology*, 25; MCB (Spec), Report DF II and III, vol. II, Medical, 24; Ernest Angino, handwritten notes titled "VX-6 at its best" [October 2000], courtesy of Angino.

68. Apsley Cherry-Garrard, *The Worst Journey in the World: Antarctic 1910–1913* (London: Chatto & Windus, 1965), 576; Crary, "On the Ice," 269; Elizabeth Chipman, *Women on the Ice* (Melbourne: Melbourne University Press, 1986), 86.

69. Bowers interview, 47; Bergstrom interview, 48; Dalton interview, 24.

70. Chipman, *Women on the Ice*, 81; "Women in Antarctic," [*New York Times*, 14 February 1957], *Polar Times* compilation. Chipman wrote (p. 83) that "noted marine geologist Marie Klenova, who had long worked in the Arctic regions," came south on the *Ob* in 1955–1956, and the next year the Soviet Academy of Sciences listed two women, not three as reported in the Western press.

71. Boyer to Dufek, Memorandum, 18 November 1958; Dufek, "What We've Accomplished in Antarctica," 555; Taylor, *Antarctic Psychology*, 16.

72. Boyer to [Sharon Boyer], 10 November 1958.

EPILOGUE

1. U.S. Cong., Senate, The Antarctic Treaty, Hearings before the Committee on Foreign Relations, 86th Cong., 2d sess, 14 June 1960, 76.

2. Emmerson to State, Fourth Antarctic Conference, 17 June 1957, RG 59, Box 1652; Wexler, diary, 8 December 1956, 16 June, 6, 12 September 1957.

3. Minutes, ICSU, Special Committee on Antarctic Research, The Hague, February 3–5, 1958, 17 February 1958, Wexler to Gould, Report on First Meeting of SCAR/ICSU, 10 February 1958, and Constitution with attached Memorandum on Formation of SCAR, all in NAS-IGY: ICSU (SCAR) 1957–1959; Wexler, diary, 4–5 February 1958.

4. Sullivan, "IGY," 327; Homer E. Newell Jr., "IGY Conference in Moscow," *Science* 129 (9 January 1959): 79–80; Bullis, *Political Legacy of the IGY*, 33–34.

5. Fraleigh to State, Antarctica: US scientist discusses . . . 28 February 1957, Luboeansky to Krieg, OCB Working Group on Antarctica, 6 June 1957, and Wilson to Snow, Antarctica—Press Reports on Proposed Extension, 3 July 1957, all in RG 59, Box 1652; Wilson to Rubottom, Antarctica: Post-IGY Plans, 14 March 1957, RG 59, Box 2773.

6. Harris to Eisenhower, 17 January 1958; Gould to Waterman, NSB files, cited in England, *Patron for Pure Science*, 303.

7. NAS, Report on Status of Plans for International Program of Antarctic Research . . . with Preliminary Budget Estimates, 14 March 1958, RG 307, Box 2; Odishaw to Waterman, 10 July 1957, NAS-IGY: IGY Termination/SCAR; Odishaw to Waterman, 16 January 1958, NAS-IGY: ICSU (SCAR) 1957–1959; NAS/CPR, Revised Budget Estimates for the 1959 Antarctic Scientific Program, 1 May 1958, and Peavey to Committee on Polar Research and Panels, 23 May 1958, both in NAS-IGY: USARP FY 1959; Minutes, USNC-IGY Antarctic Project Leaders, 28 May 1958, RG 307, Box 1; Smith interview, 16–19.

8. Wilson, MoC, Antarctica: Proposed Transfer of Wilkes, 24 September 1957, Wilson to Dreier, Antarctica: Future of Weddell Sea Stations, 30 September 1957, Luboeansky, MoC, Antarctica, 15 April 1958, and Luboeansky, Memo for Files, Antarctica, 18 April 1958, all in RG 59, Box 2774; Lewis to Commonwealth NSFA, Change in Custody of Wilkes Station . . . , H. D. Davison, Confidential Narrative . . . Transfer of Custody of Ellsworth Station, 22 May 1959, both in RG 59, Box 1654; Dater, "Organizational Developments," 27; Honkala interview, 20.

9. House Hearings, NSF/NAS Report on IGY, February 1959, 4; Wexler, diary, 10 September, 9 October, 10 December 1958; Francis to Odishaw, 26 May, 16 December 1958, NAS-IGY: IGY Field Representatives, Drawer 26; Frank Stokes, e-mail to author, 29 July 2001.

10. Francis to Odishaw, n.d. [December 1958], and Francis to Jones, 16 December 1958, in NAS-IGY: Field Representatives; Boyer to [Sharon Boyer], 30 December 1958; TF 43, Report DF IV, 17 June 1959, 8, 23, RG 313, Box 26; Frank Stokes, e-mail, 28 July 2001.

11. Dewart, *Antarctic Comrades*, 20; Hayton, "Antarctic Settlement," n370.

12. Draft Minutes, Executive Session, USNC Executive Committee, 17 February 1959, Odishaw to Waterman, 29 January 1959, Waterman to Odishaw, 4 February 1959, Kaplan to Waterman, Kaplan to Bronk, 27 February 1959, and Waterman to Kaplan, 5 March 1959, all in NAS-IGY: IGY Termination, NSF.

13. Shapley to Kaplan and Odishaw, 13 March 1959, NAS-IGY: IGY Termination, NSF; Minutes, Committee on Polar Research, 1 June 1959, RG 401 (5), Box 19. Other appropriate federal agencies—Defense, Commerce, Interior, State, NASA—would provide input via the Inter-governmental Committee on Antarctic Research; Minutes, USNC Executive Committee, 4 May 1959, NAS-IGY: IGY Termination and IGC-59, Drawer 22; Smith interview, 21–22, 27 (quotes).

14. Papers of Admiral George Dufek, Part VI-I of undated [August 1959] report, Syracuse University, cited in Quigg, *Pole Apart*, 59.

15. Koleszar, Report, Detachment Golf; Bernard Kalb, "Airstrip on Land Is Antarctic Aim," *New York Times*, 29 January 1956, 31; Henry Stephens, e-mail to Richard Bowers, 16 October 1999, and to author, 2 April 2001.

16. Stephens, e-mail, 2 April 2001; Ketchum to CNSFA, Report CTG 43.4 DF III, 19 March 1958, 1, Comments and Recommendations 2, and TF 43, Report DF III, 12 June

1958, 5, 14, all in RG 313, Box 22; Brian Shoemaker, telephone conversation with author, 28 March 2001, and e-mail, 19 April 2002.

17. Dater, "Organizational Developments," 25–26. Admiral Tyree had just commanded Operation Hardtack, which conducted nuclear testing in the Pacific. Press Release, U.S. NSFA, Navy Announces Plans for Operation Deep Freeze '60, 17 August 1959, courtesy of Walter Davis.

18. Navy Announces Plans DF 60; Dater, "Organizational Developments," 28–29.

19. E. D. Dryfoose, e-mail to author, 21, 22, 24 February 2002; Navy Announces Plans DF 60; Henry M. Dater, "Aviation in the Antarctic," manuscript history of VX-6, June 1963, 19–23, 28, courtesy of Ernest Angino; Dater, "Organizational Developments," 29–30; "US Airplane Recovered From East Antarctica," *Antarctic Journal* (March–June 1987): 3–7; "Salvaged Airplane Returns to McMurdo Station," *Antarctic Journal* (June 1988): 1–3.

20. Minutes, Committee on Polar Research, 19 December 1958; William Long, interview with Karen Brewster, 28 April 2001, 57–58.

21. NAS/CPR, Revised Budget Estimates 1959, 1 May 1958, 2–3; Bullis, *Political Legacy of the IGY*, 26.

22. Littlewood interview, 12; Dufek to Gould, 10 March 1958, NAS-IGY: Draft DF III Reports; Roger Revelle, Statement before House Appropriations Committee, Subcommittee on Independent Offices, n.d., NAS-IGY: Testimony. See individual ship reports by year.

23. Eklund proposal, 11 September 1956, Eklund to [various countries], 31 October 1956 (Eklund—Skua Studies), and Sladen to Toney, 14 March 1958 (Penguin Studies), all in NAS-IGY: Special Studies; Carl Eklund job description, RG 401 (5), Box 14; Rennie Taylor, "Penguins a Pain to an Atlantian," *Atlanta Journal*, clipping attached to 15 March 1958 letter, RG 401 (5), Box 10; Eklund, SSLR, Wilkes, 15–16; Anderson, diary, 1 January 1958; Toney, SSLR, Byrd, 57.

24. "Antarctic Plant Life," IGY Bulletin no. 24, *Trans. AGU* 40, no. 2 (June 1959): 200–203; Toney, SSLR, Byrd, 57–59.

25. Minutes, Subcommittee on Stress, Committee on Psychiatry, Division of Medical Sciences NAS, 26 March 1956, Cannan to Kaplan, 4 June 1956 (NAS Advisory to IGY), unsigned notes on telephone conversation with Kaare Rodahl, 9 May 1956, Revised Human Physiology Research Program . . . 1957, n.d., Frederick A. Milan, Preliminary Report . . . Physiological Acclimatization to Cold in the Antarctic (Human Physiology), and [William M. Smith], Antarctic Psychological Research Program, draft notes, 26 March 1957 (Psychology), all in NAS-IGY: Special Studies; "Program in Biological and Medical Sciences, 1958–59," IGY Bulletin no. 18, 1219.

26. Pirrit, *Across West Antarctica*, 122, 125; John Weihaupt, interview with Brian Shoemaker, 2 October 2000, draft transcript, 25, see also, 8–18.

27. Dewart, *Antarctic Comrades*, 21; W. Davis interview, 25–27; "American Tractor Train Arrives at South Pole," *The* [New Zealand] *Press*, 12 January 1961, 6, courtesy of Davis; Crary, "On the Ice," chapter 19, esp. 338–339. Jack Long, Ed Robinson, and Mario Giovinetto were other IGY veterans on this traverse.

28. Fisher to Owen, Exchange of Personnel Programs, 26 May 1959, RG 59, Box 1654; Dewart interview, 36–37. See also, Dewart, *Antarctic Comrades*, 4–5.

29. Stanley Ruttenberg, telephone conversation with author, 12 December 2001; Philip Mange, telephone conversation with author, 10 December 2001.

30. Action Minutes, Bureau of the International Council of Scientific Unions, 1–3 April 1959, Annex B, 1, NAS-IGY: IGY Termination, ICSU 1959; Bullis, *Political Legacy of the IGY*, 2, 13; Gould, *Cold*, 200. The U.S. contribution to CSAGI overhead was about $75,000, compared with UNESCO's $85,000, the USSR's $45,000, and ICSU's $40,000.

31. Bullis, *Political Legacy of the IGY*, 14–16; USNC-IGY, Addendum to Antarctic Status Report No. 26, January 1958, NAS-IGY: Antarctic, Drawer 75. The Arctic and Antarctic program costs were similar.

32. Mange, "IGY"; Bullis, *Political Legacy of the IGY*, 12.

33. Mange, "IGY"; Gould, *Cold*, 200; Bullis, *Political Legacy of the IGY*, 2–3; Sullivan, *Assault on the Unknown*, 415; Atwood, "IGY in Retrospect," 8.

34. Horsey, MoC Spender, Blakeney, Antarctic—Soviet Request for Facilities in Australia, 13 February 1956; Wilson, MoC Audland, Antarctic Affairs, 7 February 1957; Wilson, MoC Booker, Border et al., Antarctic Claims Policy, 15 February 1957; Kavanaugh to Amembassy Canberra, 4 June 1957; Wilson, MoC White, Jeffery et al., Antarctic Claims and U.S.S.R. Plans in Antarctica, 18 June 1957; Russell to State, no. 460, Antarctic Territorial Claims, 21 June 1957, all in RG 59, Box 2773.

35. Myhre, *Antarctic Treaty System*, 24–30; Gould, "Antarctica in World Affairs," 26–30; Quigg, *Pole Apart*, 133–136.

36. CTF 43 Staff Instruction I-55, 1955, 1-1. See also, NSC 5421/1, 19 July 1954, and NSC 5528, 12 December 1955 (unapproved; Joint Chiefs of Staff gave Antarctica low priority), [State to Navy], Confidential Memorandum (quote on claim sheets), 28 July 1955, Hoover to Barbour, U.S. Antarctic Policy, 7 November 1955, with attachments, and Wilson to Dreier, Draft Antarctic Policy Review, 14 January 1957, all in RG 59, Box 2773; Quigg, *Pole Apart*, 138. See additionally, private and public correspondence in RG 59, Boxes 1653–1655, 2773, 2775; Ray Cromley, "We're Losing the Antarctic," *American Mercury* 87, no. 418 (November 1958): 5–11; Harris to Eisenhower, 17 January 1958.

37. See Crowley to Whiteman, Wilkinson et al., Antarctica, 30 September 1955, RG 59, Box 2773; Quigg, *Pole Apart*, 139.

38. Phleger to Rubottom, Review of US Claims Policy on Antarctica, 12 December 1956, Watrous to Files, Antarctic (quote on NSC Planning Board), 23 April 1957, Wilson to Dreier, Antarctic Policy Review, 14 (quote, not more ambiguous), 22 January 1957, Watrous, untitled draft secret policy review, 10 May 1957, and Rubottom to Under Secretary, Letter to Senator Francis Case on . . . Claims, 8 July 1957, all in RG 59, Box 2773.

39. Philip W. Quigg, "Antarctica: The Continuing Experiment," *Headline Series No. 273* (New York: Foreign Policy Association, March–April 1985), 14; Daniels to Under Secretary, Senator Saltonstall's Call on Friday, October 17, 1958, with attached Reasons for Not Making Territorial Claim Last May, 16 October 1958, RG 59, Box

2775. See also, Horsey to Merchant, NSC Policy Paper on Antarctica, 30 December 1955, RG 59, Box 2773.

40. Quigg, *Pole Apart*, 142; *Democracia*, cited in Buenos Aires to State, 21 April 1955, Sanders to State, Reference of Antarctic Dispute to ICJ [International Court of Justice] by UK, 16 May 1955, Sandifer to State, Argentina Rejects British Proposal for Arbitration . . . , 17 May 1955, Corrigan to Files, Chilean Antarctic: New Legislation Providing for Antarctic Administration, 23 June 1955, all in RG 59, Box 2773. Another U.S. motive was to reclaim the initiative after British internationalization proposals of October 1957; see Daniels to Under Secretary, Antarctica; Present Situation, 14 April 1958, RG 59, Box 2774.

41. Wilcox to Rubottom, Review of US Claims Policy on Antarctica, 14 December 1956, RG 59, Box 2773; MoM, 13th Antarctic Conference Preparations [hereafter ACP], 14 August 1958, RG 59, Box 1653; Dept. of State Instruction to Brussels, Buenos Aires et al., Antarctica, 19 March 1958, RG 59, Box 2774.

42. Daniels to Secretary, Antarctica, with attachments, 9 December 1957, Green to Robertson, US Policy in the Antarctic, 21 November 1957, Thompson to State, no. 316, Antarctica, 27 December 1957, and Dulles to Embassies Canberra and Wellington, Possibility of Japanese Participation . . . , attached Horsey to Green, 25 January 1958, all in RG 59, Box 2774; Quigg, *Pole Apart*, 141.

43. Horsey to Green, 25 January 1958, Dulles to Brussels, Buenos Aires et al., Antarctica, 19 March 1958, and Smith, MoC Bianchi, Silberstein et al., US Antarctic Policy (quote on IGY basis, not claims), 3 April 1958, all in RG 59, Box 2774; R. Tucker Scully, interview with author, 10 June 2002.

44. Daniels to Under Secretary, Present Situation; Elbrick to Murphy, Antarctica, 22 April 1958, attached Aide-Mémoire, 24 March 1958, RG 59, Box 2775; Daniels to internal list, Antarctica: Consultations With Other Countries, 17 March 1958, and Elbrick to Murphy, 1 May 1958, both in RG 59, Box 1653; White House, Statement by the President, 3 May 1958, and text of note, NAS-IGY: Antarctic Committee Organization.

45. Quigg, *Pole Apart*, 145; Text of diplomatic note, 2 May 1958, RG 59, Box 1653. See also, Antarctic Treaty, December 1, 1959, in US Treaties and Other International Acts Series 4780, or www.scar.org/Treaty/Treaty_Text.htm.

46. Embassy USSR, no. 15, to State, translation, 2 June 1958, and Dulles to Brussels, Buenos Aires et al., Antarctica: Status of Proposed Treaty Negotiations, 20 June 1958, both in RG 59, Box 1653; Paul C. Daniels, "The Antarctic Treaty," in *Frozen Future*, 38–39; MoM, 1st ACP, 13 June 1958, RG 59, Box 2775; Alan Neidle, interview with Brian Shoemaker, 19 July 2000, 5–6, 30.

47. MoM, 1st ACP; Luboeansky, MoC DeBenedictis, Antarctica, 5 June 1958 (quote), and Dulles to All American Diplomatic Posts, Antarctica; Considerations Relating to Participation of Countries . . . , 20 June 1958, both in RG 59, Box 1653. See also, memoranda from would-be participants, Boxes 1653, 1654, 2776.

48. Daniels, MoC Ledovski, Antarctica, 30 June 1958, and Luboeansky, Status Report on Antarctica, 24 August 1958, both in RG 59, Box 2775; MoM, 47th ACP, 26 May 1959, also 7th, 8th, 14th ACPs, 24 and 29 July, 14 August 1958, RG 59, Box 1653.

49. Daniels to Neidle, 15 April 1958, RG 59, Box 2774; Neidle interview, 4, 8; MoM, 7th ACP.

50. Owen, MoC Casey, Plimsoll et al., Antarctica, 13 October 1958, and Daniels to Murphy, Antarctica, 6 November 1958, both in RG 59, Box 2775; Neidle interview, 7–8; Brian Shoemaker, "Antarctic Treaty System Inspections: Historical Significance and Future Impact" (master's thesis, University of Cambridge, 1989), 19; MoM, 26th ACP, 18 November 1958, RG 59, Box 1653. At this time meeting documents' security classification rose from Confidential to Secret. Leaks would help no one.

51. MoM, 13th ACP; MoM, 28th ACP, 17 December 1958, MoM, 34th ACP, 10 February 1959, Daniels, Reasons for Including Article IV in the Proposed Treaty, 8 January 1959, Luboeansky to Dreier, Antarctica, 17 April 1959, and Crutcher to State, no. 733, New Zealand Approach to Antarctic Conference, 15 June 1959, all in RG 59, Box 2776; Jova, MoC Raguenet, French Position on Antarctica, 8 July 1958, RG 59, Box 1653; Owen, MoC Booker, Antarctica, 12 June 1959, RG 59, Box 1654; Thomson interview, 50.

52. Article VII, Antarctic Treaty; MoM, 34th ACP; Farley to Daniels, Antarctica Inspection, 13 April 1959, RG 59, Box 1654; Nunley to Owen, Antarctica, 24 March 1959, RG 59, Box 2776; Antarctica Conference Position Paper: Inspection, 23 September 1959, RG 59, Box 2777; Neidle interview, 16–17, 27; Shoemaker, "Antarctic Treaty System Inspections," 24–25.

53. MoM, 51st ACP, 26 August 1959, RG 59, Box 1654; Owen to Walmsley, Your Request for a Rundown . . . Preparatory Talks on Antarctica, 13 March 1959, RG 59, Box 2776; Neidle to Hager, Notes on Draft Articles, 18 September 1959, RG 59, Box 2777; Quigg, *Pole Apart*, 150.

54. Owen, MoC Casey, Plimsoll et al., Antarctica, 13 October 1958; Owen to Murphy, Policy on Antarctica, 1 April 1959, and attachments, RG 59, Box 2776; Owen to Officers Listed, Antarctic Conference, 19 June 1959, MoM, 49th ACP, 28 July 1959, and 52nd ACP, 2 September 1959, all in RG 59, Box 1654; Meeker to Murphy, Antarctica, 1 August 1959, RG 59, Box 2777.

55. Owen, MoC Casey, Plimsoll et al., Antarctica, 13 October 1958; Zone of Application of the Proposed Antarctic Treaty, paper handed Daniels by Muirhead, 15 December 1958, RG 59, Box 2775. Focusing on a "zone of application," rather than a definition, helped the negotiators find consensus. See Hayton, "Antarctic Settlement," 360; MoM, 39th ACP, 17 March 1959, RG 59, Box 2776; MoM, 50th ACP, 30 July 1959, and 55th ACP, 22 September 1959, both in RG 59, Box 1654.

56. Daniels, MoC Booker, Shimoda et al., Antarctica, 29 July 1959, Doc. 2, Provisional Rules of Procedure, 26 May 1959, and MoM, 47th ACP, 48th ACP, 23 July 1959, all in RG 59, Box 1654; Owen to Walmsley, Your Request for a Rundown . . . , 13 March 1959.

57. Green to Parsons and Bacon, Antarctic Treaty, 10 February 1959, Robertson to Acting Secretary, F[ar] E[ast] Reservations Concerning OCB Report on Antarctic Under NSC 5804/1, 13 February 1959, and Owen to Murphy, Policy on Antarctica, and attachments, 1 April 1959, all in RG 59, Box 2776; Parsons to Murphy, Amendment

of NSC Paper, 31 March 1959, RG 59, Box 1654. See also, NSC 5804/1, 8 March 1958, and NSC 5905/1, 7 April 1959; Daniels to Secretary, Policy on Antarctica, 7 October 1959, RG 59, Box 1655; Neidle interview, 10, 22.

58. See Walmsley to Acting Secretary, Chairman of the United States Delegation . . . , 5 August 1959, RG 59, Box 1654; Neidle interview, 23, 25. Christian Herter succeeded Dulles, who died on 29 May 1959.

59. Phleger, Memorandum [to Files], 12 October 1959, and "From Paris to Foreign Office, Antarctic Conference" [by hand 10/15/59], both in RG 59, Box 2777; Phleger to Secretary, 20, 21 October 1959, Beaulac to Bernbaum, 26 October 1959, Bernbaum, MoC Frondizi, Antarctic Conference, 27 October 1959, Bernbaum to State, no. 660, Argentine Opposition to Article II . . . , 29 October 1959, and Bernbaum to State, no. 718, 2 November 1959, all in RG 59, Box 1655; Phleger, Memorandum [to files], 10 November 1959, RG 59, Box 1653.

60. MoM, 32nd ACP, 27 January 1959; Daniels, "Antarctic Treaty," 40.

61. Hayton, "Antarctic Settlement," 359; Finn Sollie, "The Political Experiment in Antarctica," in *Frozen Future*, 57–58.

62. Hayton, "Antarctic Settlement," 360–362.

63. Ibid., 364; Daniels, "Antarctic Treaty," 40–41. The secretariat function has rotated, with the next host country providing arrangements, documentation, and record keeping through that meeting. The treaty parties established a permanent secretariat at Buenos Aires in September 2004; Scully interview.

64. White to Merchant, Antarctica Conference—Treatment of Non-Parties, 4 November 1959, and Long, MoC Secretary, Phleger et al., Current Status of the Antarctica Conference, 7 November 1959, both in RG 59, Box 1655.

65. Long, Current Status; Hayton, "Antarctic Settlement," 363.

66. MoM, 26th ACP, 18 November 1958, RG 59, Box 1653; Phleger to Secretary, 26 October, 2 November 1959, Phillips, MoC Rubottom, Muller et al., Negotiation of Treaty . . . 2 November 1959, and Long, Current Status, all in RG 59, Box 1655; Neidle interview, 20; Hayton, "Antarctic Settlement," 364–365.

67. Phleger to Secretary, 26 October 1959, Mein, MoC White, Conference on Antarctic Treaty, 19 November 1959, and Phleger to Merchant, Memorandum, 19 November 1959, all in RG 59, Box 1655; Phleger to Merchant, Memorandum, 20 November 1959, RG 59, Box 2777; Hayton, "Antarctic Settlement," 365; Quigg, *Pole Apart*, 149.

68. Phleger to Merchant, 17 November 1959, Phleger, Memorandum for the Secretary, 23 November 1959, Phleger to Secretary, Memorandum, 24 November 1959, Phleger to Merchant, Memorandum, 25 November 1959, and Ferguson to Satterthwaite, Antarctic Negotiations, 27 November 1959, all in RG 59, Box 1655.

69. Herter to Carlson, 30 November 1959, RG 59, Box 1655. The same day, as promised, the United States issued a joint statement with Chile and Argentina affirming that the treaty did not affect their mutual obligations under the Inter-American Treaty of Reciprocal Assistance (Rio Treaty) of 1947. This reassurance had "no legal consequence," wrote Hayton ("Antarctic Settlement," 366).

70. U.S. Cong., Senate, The Antarctic Treaty, Hearings before the Committee on Foreign Relations, 86th Cong., 2d sess, 14 June 1960, 26, 39, 40, 75; *Congressional Record*, 86th Cong., 2d sess., 1960, vol. 106, pt. 12:15981.

71. *Congressional Record*, 86th Cong., 2d sess., 1960, vol. 106, pt. 12:15989.

72. Ibid., 15981.

73. Ibid., 16067, 16068.

74. Ibid., 16054.

75. Ibid., 16051.

76. Ibid., 16065.

77. Ibid., 16102.

78. Ibid., 16046.

79. Ibid., 16114. Among the thirteen absentees rested a comfortable margin for ratification even if all 100 senators (including those of newly admitted Alaska and Hawaii) had voted.

80. John F. Kennedy, Statement by the President Upon the Entry Into Force of the Antarctic Treaty, June 23, 1961, *Public Papers of the Presidents, 1961*, ¶253. Draft articles showed the instruments of ratification to be deposited with the Secretary-General of the United Nations, but the treaty made the U.S. government the depository.

81. Scully interview; Peterson, *Managing the Frozen South*, 94. In 2001, twenty-seven countries held consultative status in the ATS; sixteen more were acceding parties.

82. Shoemaker, "Antarctic Treaty System Inspections," 27 (quote), 32–33, 46; Scully interview; Daniel Derkics, telephone and e-mail correspondence with author, April 2002.

83. Shoemaker, "Antarctic Treaty System Inspections," 37, 40–44, 47; Henry M. Dater, "The Antarctic Treaty in Action 1961–1971," *Antarctic Journal* (May–June 1971): 72.

84. U.S. Department of State and U.S. Arms Control and Disarmament Agency, Report of the United States Antarctic Inspection Team, February 9 to March 11, 1995, 1–3, CD copy courtesy of 1995 inspection team member Dan Derkics; Peterson, *Managing the Frozen South*, 221; Derkics consultations.

85. CCAMLR Articles I and II. A legally separate treaty, CCAMLR resides within the ATS. Its membership differs somewhat from the parent treaty. Scully interview; R. Tucker Scully, "The Evolution of the Antarctic Treaty System—The Institutional Perspective," in *Proceedings, Antarctic Treaty System: An Assessment*, Workshop at Beardmore South Field Camp, January 7–13, 1985 (Washington, D.C.: National Academy Press, 1986), 396–397. See also, Edwin Mickleburgh, *Beyond the Frozen Sea: Visions of Antarctica* (New York: St. Martin's, 1987), 166–169; Report, U.S. Antarctic Inspection 1995, 70.

86. Robert Thomson, "The International Background," 11–13, personal manuscript; Scully interview; Olav Schram Stokke and Davor Vidas, eds., *Governing the Antarctic: The Effectiveness and Legitimacy of the Antarctic Treaty System* (Cambridge: Cambridge University Press, 1996), 3–4; Quigg, *Pole Apart*, 205, 208.

87. U.S. Congress, Office of Technology Assessment, Polar Prospects: A Minerals Treaty for Antarctica (Washington, D.C.: GPO, September 1989), 3, 5; Scully interview; Christopher C. Joyner and Ethel R. Theis, *Eagle Over the Ice: The U.S. in the Antarctic* (Hanover, N.H.: University Press of New England, 1997), 57; Christopher C. Joyner, "The Role of Domestic Politics in Making United States Policy," in *Governing the Antarctic*, 419–421.

88. Protocol on Environmental Protection to the Antarctic Treaty, Articles 7, 25. Four annexes provide guidelines for assessing environmental impact, protecting fauna and flora, regulating waste disposal, and preventing marine pollution. A fifth, added shortly, regulated Specially Protected Areas, including sites of specific scientific, aesthetic, or historical value, and less restrictive Specially Managed Areas. H. K. Cohen, ed., *Handbook of the Antarctic Treaty System*, 9th ed., 2001, courtesy of Daniel Derkics; Scully interview.

89. Scully interiew; Christopher C. Joyner, "The Effectiveness of CRAMRA," 172–173, and Francisco Orrego Vicuña, "The Effectiveness of the Protocol on Environmental Protection to the Antarctic Treaty," 198–199, in *Governing the Antarctic*. See also, Grahame Cook, ed., *The Future of Antarctica: Exploitation Versus Preservation* (Manchester: Manchester University Press, 1990), based on papers from a conference on the eve of the Protocol.

90. Myhre, *Antarctic Treaty System*, 114–116; Quigg, "Antarctica: The Continuing Experiment," 42, 47; S. Z. Qasim and H. P. Rajan, "The Antarctic Treaty System From the Perspective of a New Member," in *ATS: An Assessment*, 372.

91. George Doumani, "Science Policy for the Antarctic," 40, cited in Bullis, *Political Legacy of the IGY*, 55; Scully interview; Quigg, "Antarctica: The Continuing Experiment," 47–51; *New York Times* cited in Gould, "Emergence of Antarctica," 28.

92. Scully interview. See also, Scully, "Evolution of the ATS," 407–408.

93. Scully, "Evolution of the ATS," 401; www.scar.org; Scully interview; Bentley interview, 37–39; Thomson interview, 50–51. See also, Rita R. Colwell, "Some Views on Antarctic Research," a review of SCAR, in Aant Elzinga, ed., *Changing Trends in Antarctic Research* (Dordrecht: Kluwer Academic Publishers, 1993), 140–149.

94. U.S. Congress, Office of Technology Assessment, Polar Prospects, 8; Smith interview, 23–24.

95. Thomas O. Jones, "Developing the US Antarctic Research Program," in *Frozen Future*, 259; Pomerantz interview, 22–24, 31; National Research Council/Polar Research Board, *Science and Stewardship in the Antarctic* (Washington, D.C.: National Academy Press, 1993), 13–15; USAP External Panel, *The United States in Antarctica*, 41, 43.

96. NRC/PRB, *Science and Stewardship*, 12–13; David G. Campbell, *The Crystal Desert: Summers in Antarctica* (Boston: Houghton Mifflin, 1992), 127, 134–135. See also, Stuster, *Bold Endeavors*.

97. Fogg, *History of Antarctic Science*, 1–4, 397, 399; "US Scientists Tackle Mystery of Seasonal Antarctic Ozone Depletion," *Antarctic Journal* (June 1988): 4; USAP External Panel, *The United States in Antarctica*, 38; Helliwell, "Upper Atmosphere," 168.

98. Campbell, *Crystal Desert*, 45–48, 52; Pyne, *The Ice*, 215–219, 276. See also, Craddock, "Antarctic Geology and Gondwanaland."

99. Bentley interview, 38–41, and e-mail correspondence, 29 October 2002; "Bipolar Order: Professor Gunter Weller Discusses Climate Change Research With Dave Norton," *Polar Times* 3, no. 1 (Spring-Summer 2002): 9; USAP External Panel, *The United States in Antarctica*, 1, 10–11.

100. Smith interview, 25, 33. See also, Philip M. Smith, "International Cooperation in Antarctica—The Next Decade," in *Frozen Future*, 90–95; USAP External Panel, *The United States in Antarctica*, 31; Fogg, *History of Antarctic Science*, 399; Thomson interview, 49.

101. USAP External Panel, *The United States in Antarctica*, 24; Campbell, *Crystal Desert*, 9; Fogg, *History of Antarctic Science*, 406.

102. Thomson interview, 30–31, 36–37; Behrendt interview, 89. See also, Report, U.S. Antarctic Inspection 1995, 2.

103. Fogg, *History of Antarctic Science*, 2, 395; Behrendt interview, 73–74; Elzinga, ed., *Changing Trends in Antarctic Research*, 24–25. See also, Smith interview, 25–26.

104. Dater, "Byrd Station"; Aldrich, looseleaf memoir; Boyer to [Sharon Boyer], 7 November 1958; Smith interview, 33.

105. Special Section: "Preserving the Environment in Antarctica," *Antarctic Journal* 6, no. 3 (May–June 1971): 49–61, see 55.

106. NRC/PRB, *Science and Stewardship*, 1–2, 17–21; U.S. Cong., House, NSF Antarctic Environment Act of 1991, Hearings before the Subcommittee on Science of the Committee on Science, Space and Technology, 102nd Cong., 1st sess., 14 May 1991, 130; Smith interview, 30.

107. Sister Mary Odile Cahoon, interview with author, 2 July 2001; Chipman, *Women on the Ice*, chapter 9.

108. Colin Bull, interview with Brian Shoemaker, 20 August 2000, 38–41; Irene C. Peden, "If You Fail, There Won't Be Another Woman . . . ," in Esther D. Rothblum, Jacqueline S. Weinstock, and Jessica F. Morris, eds., *Women in the Antarctic* (New York: Harrington Park, 1998), 17–19, 26.

109. Sister Mary Odile Cahoon, "If Women Are in Science . . . ," in *Women in the Antarctic*, 31–32; Cahoon interview; Chipman, *Women on the Ice*, 94; *Antarctic Journal* (March–April 1974): 54.

110. Charles Neider, *Edge of the World, Ross Island, Antarctica: A Personal and Historical Narrative* (Garden City, N.Y.: Doubleday, 1974), 54; Brian Shoemaker, e-mail to author, 10 July 2002.

111. Chipman, *Women on the Ice*, 80; Campbell, *Crystal Desert*, 10. Fogg, citing Chipman, says "Argentina encourages births in Antarctica for political purposes," *History of Antarctic Science*, 153; Quigg, *Pole Apart*, 117.

112. Dater, "Aviation in the Antarctic," 17; Chipman, *Women on the Ice*, 84.

113. Smith interview, 28–29; Robert Thomson to Editor, *Antarctic*, [1998], via e-mail from Richard Bowers; Richard A. Herr, "The Regulation of Antarctic Tourism: A Study in Regime Effectiveness," in *Governing the Antarctic*, 212–213.

114. Scully interview; Herr, "Effeciveness of Tourism Regulation," 210 (citing Beck), and Davor Vidas, "The Legitimacy of the Antarctic Tourism Regime," in *Governing the Antarctic*, 317; House Hearings, NSF Antarctic Environment Act of 1991, 131.

115. "Glacier Returns From Last Southern Voyage," *Antarctic Journal* (March–June 1987): 15; Donald L. Canney, "Icebreakers and the U.S. Coast Guard," www.uscg.mil/hq/g-cp/history/Icebreakers.html (accessed 12 July 2002); Richard Warchol, "Navy Comes in From Cold, Ends Antarctica Operations," *Los Angeles Times*, 13 March 1998, 3; Peter James Spielmann, "US Navy Ends Antarctica Mission After 160 Years," [New Zealand] *Standard-Times*, 21 February 1998.

116. Peter James Spielmann, "The Navy Wraps up a Long Polar Stretch," *Washington Post*, 18 February 1999, A19; John Hoshko Jr., "Night Flight to Antarctica," *Antarctic Journal* (November–December 1967): 263–264.

117. Donald C. Mehaffey, "The Strategic Importance of Antarctica" (thesis, United States Naval War College, College of Naval Warfare, 1972), 64; USAP External Panel, *The United States in Antarctica*, 1.

118. Jack Williams, "Icebergs Carried Away Antarctic History," *USA Today*, 15 May 2000, online copy (Scambos cite); Frank Stokes, e-mail to author, 29 July 2001; Crary, SSLR, Little America, 52; Ross Hatch, phone conversation with author, 30 July 2002.

119. Sullivan, *Quest for a Continent*, 303–306, photos following 192; Donna Scott, NSIDC User Services, e-mail to author, 25 and 26 September 2001; Charles Swithinbank, e-mail via John Behrendt, 9 October 2001.

120. Philip Law, "One Hundred Years of Australian Involvement in Antarctica," lecture at NSF, 11 December 2000, reprinted in the *Antarctican Society Newsletter*, vol. 00–01, no. 2 (January 2001): 8; Thomson interview, 53–54; "Hallett Station, Antarctica, 1956–1973," informational booklet, Scott Base, 2001; NSF, Facts About the United States Antarctic Program, October 1994, 4 (and earlier editions).

121. NSF, Amundsen-Scott South Pole Station information packet; conversations with named principals.

122. Author's observations and research with Ed Anderson in McMurdo building records. New Zealand is working, through the Antarctic Historical Trust, to preserve the Heroic Age huts and the original Trans-Antarctic Expedition structure at Scott Base.

123. W. G. Shafer, "Five Years of Nuclear Power at McMurdo Station," *Antarctic Journal* (March–April 1967): 38; "Navy Removing PM-3A Reactor," *Antarctic Journal* (January–February 1974): 30; "PM-3A Operations, Deep Freeze 74," *Antarctic Journal* (July–August 1974): 186–187; Randall interview, 31–37.

124. Antarctic Support Associates, Your Stay at United States Antarctic Program Stations (informational booklet for program participants), August 1998, 27–28.

125. Sullivan, "IGY," 334. The closest thing to another IGY was ICSU's International Year of the Quiet Sun (IQSY), 1964–1965, a period of minimum solar activity. It took advantage of the IGY example and remaining infrastructure.

NOTES ON SOURCES

PRIMARY SOURCES

Records of Executive Agencies

The pertinent federal records are held at the National Archives and Records Administration, National Archives II, College Park, Maryland. Significant duplication of files illustrates the interwoven nature of this story. Some documents only appear in other than the originating agency's papers.

Record Group (RG) 313, Records of U.S. Naval Operating Forces, Operations Plans and Reports 1955–1972, Operation Deep Freeze I–IV

Detailed, candid, and analytical annual reports include those of the U.S. Naval Support Force, Antarctica (Task Force Forty-Three), and subsidiary task groups, by location (e.g., TG 43.2); Mobile Construction Battalion (Special) and MCB One, by station or special assignment, such as Detachment Golf, Narrative Report of Operation Deep Freeze I, 1 May 1956, an important supplement by a Seabee reconnaissance and surveying unit; oceanography teams from the Navy Hydrographic Office; individual ships; and the Air Development Squadron SIX (VX-6). Annual Operation Orders, by task group, described anticipated conditions and actions. Deep Freeze I leaders prepared for their successors an Antarctic Manual and an Air Operations Manual for living and working safely and efficiently on the ice. Special studies evaluated, for example, experimental clothing. Several station officers-in-charge kept "official" diaries; some appear here. Lt. Cmdr. David W. Canham Jr., assisted by yeoman Robert L. Chaudoin, superbly detailed Deep Freeze I at McMurdo in the daily Narrative Log of the Williams Air Operating Facility. Lieut. (jg) Richard Bowers's South Pole Station Daily Narrative of the construction period was likewise excellent. Both were selectively reproduced in the MCB (Special) reports.

Related reports of other military services' contributions include the 18th Air Force's Report of the U.S. Air Force Tactical Air Command, 63rd Troop Carrier Wing (Heavy), for Operation Deep Freeze II (1956–1957), III, and IV, which described airdrop operations at South Pole and Byrd stations, and the Army's reports of various observers, researchers, and transportation corps units sent south. The Army-Navy Trail Party Report, 1956, detailed the work of the Greenland-trained Army crevasse experts to prepare a safe trail for heavy tractor trains from Little America to Byrd. The Navy's Byrd Trail Swing Report discussed conditions and problems met along that marked route.

Materials on the earlier Operation Highjump are filed in RG 313 under Commander, Task Force 68 (Operation Highjump) General Reports 1945–1947. These include Report, U.S. Navy Antarctic Development Project, 3 vols., 1947; Army Observers' Report of Operation Highjump, Task Force 68, 1947, probably authored by Paul Siple; and records of the much smaller Operation Windmill (TF 39, 1947–1948). Papers on the scuttled Operation Highjump II, Task Force 66, are in Administrative Subject Files 1947–1949 and Staff Study Reports 1948–1949.

Record Group 307, Records of the National Science Foundation (NSF), Office of
Antarctic Programs, NAS-USNC [National Academy of Sciences – United States
National Committee] IGY [International Geophysical Year] Documents 1955–1959

Especially helpful were budget documents, press releases, minutes of meetings of Antarctic project leaders (NAS), and correspondence from the Office of the Director, as well as fairly complete documentation of actions by NSF's counterpart agencies and institutions. Among the latter were NAS's Antarctic Research: Elements of a Coordinated Program, 2 May 1949—the first such study (reprinted for the USNC-IGY in May 1954); increasingly precise USNC-IGY program planning documents (August 1955, April 1956); and A Report on the Status of Plans for an International Program of Antarctic Research for the Year 1959 [IGC] Including a Proposed United States Program With Preliminary Budget Estimates, 14 March 1958. NSF collected the Commerce Department's mimeographed "Soviet Bloc International Geophysical Year Information," distributed weekly by subscription from February 1958 to January 1959, and it kept the Deep Freeze shipping documents that illustrated the state of preparations in 1955.

USNC-IGY Antarctic Scientific Station Leaders Reports (SSLR) became the most frequently consulted sources of basic information on the IGY in Antarctica. Following a topical formula, each revealed the personality and effectiveness of the leader and the general ambience of the camp, as well as the year's scientific challenges and accomplishments. These reports compared instructively with those of Navy leaders for the same station over the same period.

Record Group 59, Records of the State Department, Central Decimal File (CDF)
1955–1959: International Geophysical Year, Antarctica

Internal memoranda, correspondence, notes on meetings, memoranda of conversations with diplomatic visitors, policy drafts, and dispatches to and from embassies of countries active in Antarctica illustrated the State Department's struggles over many years to formulate a workable policy for Antarctica—an evolution of thinking from a fixation on territorial claims to leadership toward the Antarctic Treaty—as well as other nations' reasoning and conflicting and competing interests. Key papers were Ambassador Daniels's and others' painstaking one-on-one outreach to the other eleven participants, the U.S. aide-mémoire of March 1958, the formal invitation to negotiate in May, the informal minutes of sixty preparatory meetings spread over nearly a year and a half, and the minutes and other notes on the formal treaty conference negotiations in late 1959.

Record Group 401, National Archives Gift Collection of Materials Relating to Polar Regions

This small treasure features donated diaries, correspondence, and articles by and about numerous Antarctic pioneers of the period, such as scientific leaders Carl Eklund, Paul Siple, Laurence Gould, Philip Smith, and Albert Crary and other IGY participants.

Congressional Documents—Reports, Hearings, and Debate, Library of Congress

Key documents were: International Geophysical Year: A Special Report prepared by the National Academy of Sciences for the Senate Committee on Appropriations, Doc. no. 124, 84th Cong., 2nd sess., 28 May 1956; National Science Foundation/National Academy of Sciences Report on the International Geophysical Year, Hearings before the Subcommittee of the House Committee on Appropriations, 86th Cong., 1st sess., February 1959; and The Antarctic Treaty, Hearings before the Senate Committee on Foreign Relations, 86th Cong., 2nd sess., 14 June 1960. Later, Antarctic Minerals Policy, Hearings before [two subcommittees of] the House Committee on Science, Space, and Technology, 101st Cong., 2nd sess., 12 July 1990, and NSF Antarctic Environment Act of 1991 [to implement the Environmental Protocol], Hearings before the Subcommittee on Science of the House Committee on Science, Space, and Technology, 102nd Cong., 1st sess., 14 May 1991, proved helpful.

Senate floor debate on the Antarctic Treaty, *Congressional Record*, vol. 106, part 12, 86th Cong., 2nd sess., 8–10 August 1960, gave the flavor of contemporary political thinking. Helpful publications produced for Congress included the Congressional Research Service's *The Political Legacy of the International Geophysical Year* by Harold Bullis, for the Subcommittee on National Security Policy and Scientific Developments of the House Committee on Foreign Affairs, November 1973, and the Office of Technology Assessment's *Polar Prospects: A Minerals Treaty for Antarctica*, September 1989.

Records of the National Academy of Sciences, Archives of the National Academies, Washington, D.C.

Documentation of the role of the United States National Committee for the IGY and its Washington staff includes organizational structure and planning records; reports and meeting minutes of technical panels and committees, the USNC Executive Committee, and the Committee on Polar Research; internal memoranda; congressional testimony and speeches; personnel information;

press releases; wide-ranging correspondence; and IGY budget needs, strategies, and justifications. Other papers focused on specific science programs, including nongeophysical studies and those carried out by Navy ships and aircraft; recruitment of station scientific leaders; implementation of the international scientific exchange program; and the launching of the IGY indoctrination (orientation) program.

Interagency correspondence revealed the working relationships and recurring tensions over approach and turf with the National Science Foundation, especially over the post-IGY program, and the Navy, especially over the dual command structure. A NAS-sponsored Symposium on Scientific Aspects of the International Geophysical Year, in April 1954, helped "sell" the IGY to Congress, the press, and the public. Long, insightful letters and weekly and monthly status reports from IGY representatives in the field illuminated triumphs, cares, and needs on the ice. In Washington, John Hanessian, a detail-oriented worrier, prepared frequent summary memoranda for Hugh Odishaw and synthesized the incoming status reports, organizing them by discipline and sometimes by station.

Other correspondence, reports, and records of meetings with counterparts highlighted the international scene, such as actions of the Special Committee for the IGY (CSAGI), U.S. input to and results of the five Antarctic planning conferences in Europe (1955–1958), the formation and early progress of the Special (soon Scientific) Committee on Antarctic Research (SCAR), and the extension of the IGY program in Antarctica. USNC staff periodically updated the Antarctic programs of the other eleven participating nations, with heavy emphasis on Soviet activities.

The NAS published findings of specific IGY programs, special studies, traverses, and major political and organizational developments as thirty numbered "IGY Bulletins" in the *Transactions of the American Geophysical Union*, 1957–1959. The Committee on Polar Research produced "Science in Antarctica," NAS/NRC no. 878, 1961, conveying recent results to justify further research. The NAS later compiled a Roster of the US-IGY Program, a helpful reference for identifying personnel with their technical panels, committees, and disciplines.

HUMAN RESOURCES

Oral history interviews with persons representing diverse backgrounds, skills, and accomplishments—military officers and enlisted specialists, civilian scientists and statesmen—who personally helped build Antarctica's age of science supplemented and enriched the written record. While selective and imperfect, memories offer unique personal and experiential perspectives, yielding lively interpretations and revealing nuances of events and circumstances lost in official documentation. Listed with their latest ranks, rates, or titles (many earned after the IGY), my oral history subjects were:

Kenneth E. Aldrich, Chief Hospital Corpsman (HMC), U.S. Navy (USN) (Ret.): Seabee medical-department organizer and medical corpsman, Little America, Deep Freeze I (DF I)[1]

David E. Baker, Captain, USN (Ret.): dogsled driver, communications officer, and South Pole survival trainer, McMurdo, DF I

*Michael P. Baronick, Chief Aviation Ordnanceman (AOC), USN (Ret.): VX-6 line chief, McMurdo, and officer-in-charge, Beardmore auxiliary station, DF I–II; additional deployments through DF 60[2]

*William T. Beckett, Chief Utilityman (UTC), USN (Ret.): Seabee utilities chief, Little America and Byrd, DF I–II; three later winterings

Charles R. Bentley, PhD: two-year IGY seismologist, Byrd; leader of three (later many more) summer traverses, 1956–1959; SCAR and Polar Research Board member and leader

James H. Bergstrom, Captain, USN (Ret.): GCA [ground-controlled approach] and executive officer, McMurdo, DF I

Charles A. Bevilacqua, Chief Warrant Officer (CWO4), Civil Engineering Corps (CEC) USN (Ret.): Seabee builder chief, McMurdo and Pole, DF I–II

Richard A. Bowers, Commander, CEC USN (Ret.): construction officer in charge of building McMurdo and Pole stations, DF I–II

Sister Mary Odile Cahoon: marine biologist, one of first pair of women to winter over at McMurdo, 1974

*Lynn M. Cavendish, Captain, CEC USN (Ret.): member of Seabee survey unit, DF I; McMurdo construction officer, DF II

Robert L. Chaudoin, Chief Yeoman (YNC), USN (Ret.): yeoman, McMurdo and Pole, DF I–II

---

1. Successive Deep Freeze operations were renumbered at the start of the summer season (about October). Some wintering military men were thus active in two. IGY scientists usually arrived late in one calendar year or early in the next. After wintering and a full field season the following summer, they often departed in a third calendar year. Deployments typically lasted from fifteen to eighteen months.
2. Sadly proving the fragility of living resources, those indicated with an asterisk have died since their interviews.

Paul C. Dalrymple, PhD: micrometeorologist wintering at Little America, 1957; Pole, 1958

Brian C. Dalton, MD: medical officer and Navy officer-in-charge, Byrd, DF II

Clinton Davis, Boatswain's Mate, Second Class (BM2), USN (Ret.): bosun's mate, "plank owner," and longest-serving crew member on icebreaker *Glacier*, DF I–DF 63 (1955–1963)

Walter L. Davis, Senior Chief Construction Mechanic (CMCS), USN (Ret.): construction mechanic, Ellsworth, DF II; Byrd and Byrd-Pole traverse, DF 60–61; later winter at McMurdo

Gilbert Dewart, PhD: seismologist, Wilkes, 1957; exchange scientist, Mirny, 1960

Clifford R. Dickey Jr., Master Chief Electronics Technician (ETCM), USN (Ret.): electronics technician, Pole, DF II

Edward N. Ehrlich, MD: Navy medical officer, Little America, DF I

Mario Giovinetto, PhD: glaciologist, Byrd, 1957; Pole, 1958; Byrd trail traverse 1956–1957; Ross Ice Shelf deformation project 1957–1958 and 1958–1959; McMurdo-Pole traverse 1960–1961

Ross Hatch, Captain, USN (Ret.): *Glacier* operations officer, DF 60–61

*William T. Hess, Chief Storekeeper (SKC), USN (Ret.): storekeeper, McMurdo; Pole supplies coordinator, DF I–II

Rudolf A. Honkala: meteorologist, Wilkes, 1957; Wilkes (with Australians), 1960; Palmer, 1966

Conrad J. Jaburg, Captain, USN (Ret.): VX-6 Otter and helicopter pilot, Ellsworth, DF II–III

H. Kim Lett, Major, USAF (Ret.): Seabee equipment operator, Little America, McMurdo, and Hallett, DF II–III

Herbert Levack, Colonel, USAF (Ret.): Air Force operations officer and C-124 pilot for Pole and Byrd airdrops, DF II, IV

William H. Littlewood: civilian oceanographer with Navy Hydrographic Office on icebreakers *Edisto*, *Staten Island*, and *Glacier*, DF I, II, III, IV

Richard E. Lucier, Senior Chief Yeoman (YNCS), USN (Ret.): yeoman, Little America, DF I

Donald C. Mehaffey, Captain, USN (Ret.): supply officer, Little America, DF I

Thomas T. Montgomery, Chief Radioman (RMC), USN (Ret.): radioman, McMurdo and Pole, DF I–II

*George Moss, Lieutenant Commander, CEC USN (Ret.): operations chief, Little America; surveyor chief and navigator, tractor-trail reconnaissance party and Byrd tractor train, DF I–II

Paul F. Noonan, Senior Chief Photographer (PHCS), USN (Ret.): photographer, Wilkes, DF II; Task Force 43 staff member, DF IV

Philip W. Porter, Captain, USN (Ret.): commanding officer, *Glacier*, DF 60–61

*Dale L. Powell, Senior Chief Radioman (RMCS), USN (Ret.): radioman, McMurdo and Pole, DF I–II

*John A. Randall, Master Chief Equipmentman (EQCM), USN (Ret.): construction mechanic, McMurdo and Pole, DF I–II; nuclear-power plant operator and mechanic, DF 65, DF 68

R. Tucker Scully: retired State Department officer, longtime head of U.S. Antarctic Treaty Conference delegations, expert on oceans and fisheries

Conrad S. Shinn, Lieutenant Commander, USN (Ret.): Highjump pilot; VX-6 pilot, DF I (not making it to Antarctica), DF II (making first landing at the South Pole), DF III

*Charles M. Slaton, Chief Construction Mechanic (CMC), USN (Ret.): construction mechanic, McMurdo and Pole, DF I–II

Philip M. Smith: Army crevasse expert and Byrd Trailblazer, DF II; later with IGY staff, U.S. Antarctic Research Program (NSF), White House science office, and National Research Council

William E. Stroup, CWO4, CEC USN (Ret.): chief electrician, Little America and Byrd, DF I–II

Robert B. Thomson, Order of the British Empire (OBE): scientific leader at Hallett, Scott (two summers), and Wilkes stations, 1960–1964; director, New Zealand Antarctic Program, 1965–1988, with ongoing leadership in Antarctic Treaty Consultative Meetings and SCAR

George R. Toney, JD: IGY staff member; scientific leader, Byrd, 1957; NSF polar programs staff member

Kenneth L. Waldron, Master Chief Utilityman (UTCM), USN (Ret.): electrician, Little America, DF I; Pole, DF II

Edward M. d'I Ward, Commander, USN (Ret.): first Deep Freeze staff member; organizer and acting commander, VX-6; pilot, DF II

Charles R. Wilson, PhD: aurora observer, Little America, and traverse glaciologist, 1958–1959; a dozen seasonal returns

Victor Young, Lieutenant Commander, CEC USN (Ret.): chief warrant officer and operations officer, Little America; leader, first tractor train to Byrd, DF I–II

The tapes and transcripts of these interviews, the latter corrected, edited, and sometimes augmented by the interviewees, are held in the archives of the Byrd Polar Research Center (BPRC), the Ohio State University, Columbus. The libraries of the National Science Foundation, Arlington, Virginia, and the Scott Polar Research Institute, Cambridge, England, have copies of the transcripts for research use.

Through the BPRC's concurrent Polar Oral History Archival Program, headed by Brian Shoemaker and Raimund Goerler (see Acknowledgments), I also consulted the recollections of:

Nolan Aughenbaugh, PhD: civil engineer, surveyor, geologist, and traverse member, Ellsworth 1957–1958; Ross Ice Shelf deformation study member, 1958–1959

Stephen Barnes: ionosphere-program and scientific leader, Byrd, 1958

Lloyd Beebe: Disney photographer, Little America, DF I

John C. Behrendt, PhD: assistant seismologist and traverse member, Ellsworth, 1957–1958; later summer expedition leader, scientific consultant for Antarctic Treaty meetings

Cliff Bekkedahl, Captain, USN (Ret.): navigation officer, USS *Arneb*, DF I

Jehu Blades, Commander, USN (Ret.): naval aviator, commander of towed YOG-34, DF I; wintering officer-in-charge, McMurdo, DF 65

Colin Bull, PhD: polar scientist; director, Institute of Polar Studies, Ohio State University

Gordon Cartwright: U.S. Weather Bureau meteorologist; exchange scientist, Mirny, 1957

Edwin C. Flowers: chief meteorologist, South Pole, 1957, 1960

*Edward Frankiewicz, Commander, USN (Ret.): VX-6 pilot, DF I (not reaching Antarctica), DF II, III

Helen Gerisamou: secretary, NSF polar programs, 1959–1979

David N. Grisez: Navy Machinery Repairman First Class (MR1), McMurdo, DF I; civilian summer machinist, McMurdo, 1995–1996

Julian Gudmunson, Master Chief Builder (BUCM), USN (Ret.): builder, Little America, DF II; blaster and builder, nuclear-power plant, McMurdo, DF 61, 62; rebuilder, Pole, DF 63; in all, seven deployments

Walter Jones, Chief Equipment Operator (EOC), USN (Ret.): equipment operator, Little America and two Byrd tractor trains, DF II–III; wintering equipment operator and radioman, McMurdo, DF 64

Arlo Landolt, PhD: aurora observer, Pole, 1957

Calvin Larsen, Lieutenant Commander, USN (Ret.): chief photographer, Little America, two Byrd tractor trains, McMurdo, and Beardmore, DF II–III

William Long, PhD: glaciologist, Byrd, 1958; traverse glaciologist 1957–1958, 1958–1959; geologist, three summer traverses, early 1960s

J. McKim Malville, PhD: aurora observer, Ellsworth, 1957

Alan Neidle, JD: State Department legal adviser for Antarctic Treaty negotiations

Martin Pomerantz, PhD: cosmic-ray pioneer, builder of post-IGY cosmic-ray detector facilities at McMurdo and Pole; later South Pole astronomer and helio-seismologist

Benjamin Remington: weather observer, Little America, 1957; Pole, 1959

*Morton Rubin: Weather Bureau meteorologist who helped establish U.S. IGY weather program and Weather Central, DF I, II; exchange scientist, Mirny, 1958

Chester W. Segers, Chief Commissary Steward (CSC), USN (Ret.): cook, Pole, DF II; chief of Christchurch galley with VX-6 until DF 64

Alan H. Shapley, PhD: ionospheric physicist and vice chairman of the United States National Committee for the IGY

*Robert P. Streich, Commander, USN (Ret.): VX-6 pilot, Little America, DF I–II

John P. Strider, Chief Aviation Machinist's Mate (Reciprocating Engine Mechanic)/Air Crewman (ADRC/AC), USN (Ret.): VX-6 plane captain for first Pole landing

*James Van Allen, PhD: IGY founder; space pioneer, discoverer of the Van Allen Radiation Belt

John Weihaupt, PhD: traverse geologist, 1959–1960

Howard Wessbecher: U.S. Weather Bureau meteorologist, IGY representative, and one of two civilians wintering at McMurdo, DF I

Lloyd Berkner, proposer of the IGY concept, was interviewed by Jay Holmes, 4 June 1959, Columbia University Oral History, Library of Congress, Manuscript Division, Lloyd V. Berkner Papers, Box 19, Washington, D.C. A video interview, *James Van Allen: Flights of Discovery*, narrated by Tom Brokaw (University of Iowa: Blooming Tree Productions, 2000), gives another founder's view.

Electronic correspondence with numerous veterans of varied expertise and several Antarctic Web sites answered many specific questions.

Antarcticans have historically been faithful diary keepers. Among the many I consulted, that of Harry Wexler (Library of Congress, Manuscript Division, Harry Wexler Papers, Box 27) was exceptionally useful, thanks to both his high-level political and scientific involvement and his insightful candor. Albert Crary's voluminous verbatim notes on Wexler's journal, typed (the original was begun in nearly impenetrable longhand), greatly eased initial access. His own terse, factual diary (National Archives II, RG 401) emphasized science pursuits of the day. Navy leader Dave Canham wrote long, intense, evaluative passages in his private journal (original also in RG 401). Vern Anderson brought a love story to his diary, and Nolan Aughenbaugh expressed daily frustrations with his leader in his, along with both men's scientific and station-life commentary. Navy men Charlie Bevilacqua, Lynn Cavendish, Dave Grisez, Con Jaburg, and Vic Young also lent their diaries. Whether publicly or privately held, all of these intimate journals offered rich and revealing contemporary thought. The "South Pole Yearbook 1957," produced by the first winterers at Pole, gave a close glimpse of the volunteers, their work, and their views.

A number of Antarcticans of the IGY years wrote later of their experiences. Albert P. Crary's yet-unpublished memoir, a manuscript later titled "On the Ice: Working on Science in the Arctic and Antarctica," was a pearl, quietly conveying the scientific enthusiasm and modest but inspiring leadership his many disciples remember. James Waldron's thoughtful remembrances as a VX-6 officer and pilot appear on the Internet as "Flight of the Puckered Penguins" at <http://www.anta.canterbury.ac.nz/resources/flight/>. Edward M. de'I Ward, "Navy Task Force 43 and Air Development Squadron Six (VX-6), Deepfreeze 1 and 2, 1955–1957," and Ken Aldrich, "Little America V," were informative, informally bound memoirs shared by their authors.

PUBLISHED SOURCES FOR THE 1950s

Books and Monographs

Numerous IGY participants published their memoirs, shedding light on particular polar locales through personal experience. Paul Siple's *90° South: The Story of the American South Pole Conquest* (New York: G. P. Putnam's Sons, 1959) is a classic of the first winter at Pole. *Innocents on the Ice: A Memoir of Antarctic Exploration, 1957* (Niwot: University Press of Colorado, 1998) perceptively details John Behrendt's year at Ellsworth Station. This skillfully annotated diary offers a striking counterview to leader Finn Ronne's version of the same station the same year, *Antarctic Command* (Indianapolis: Bobbs-Merrill, 1961). Ronne's autobiography, *Antarctica, My Destiny: A Personal History by the Last of the Great Polar Explorers* (New York: Hastings House, 1979) further illuminates his personality and Ellsworth's stressful winter of 1957. His *Antarctic Conquest: The Story of the Ronne Expedition, 1946–48* (New York: Putnam's Sons, 1949) is also instructive. Glaciologist John Pirrit's modest, posthumously published *Across West Antarctica* (Glasgow: John Smith & Son, 1967) follows Behrendt's account chronologically and, in part, geographically. George Doumani stresses the human condition in the immediate post-IGY years in *The Frigid Mistress: Life and Exploration in Antarctica* (Baltimore: Noble House, 1999). *Antarctic Comrades: An American With the Russians in Antarctica*, by Gilbert Dewart (Columbus: Ohio State University Press, 1989), explores with grace and generous spirit his year, 1960, as an exchange scientist at the Soviets' Mirny Station. His recent, equally fine *Journey to the Ice Age* (n.p.: Rubei Tang, 2003) remembers his IGY year at Wilkes.

Adm. George Dufek's *Operation Deepfreeze* (New York: Harcourt, Brace, 1957) outlines the Navy's pivotal role in Deep Freeze I and II, along with something of Highjump and the United States Antarctic Service. Commander Paul W. Frazier, Task Force 43 operations officer and Dufek admirer, recalls the same period in *Antarctic Assault* (New York: Dodd, Mead, 1958). Lt. Cmdr. Jack Bursey, U.S. Coast Guard Reserve, *Antarctic Night: One Man's Story of 28,224 Hours at the Bottom of the World* (New York: Rand McNally, 1957), tellingly reveals polar expertise and interests derived from earlier times. Patrick Trese's glib *Penguins Have Square Eyes* (New York: Holt, Rinehart and Winston, 1962) offers an early overview. Lisle A. Rose's excellent *Assault on Eternity: Richard E. Byrd and the Exploration of Antarctica, 1946–47* (Annapolis: Naval Institute Press, 1980) critiques the scope and value of Operation Highjump. *The Silent Continent* by William H. Kearns Jr. and Beverley Britton (New York: Harper & Brothers, 1955) provides Kearns's eyewitness account of Highjump's tragic plane crash. Fr. William J. Menster gives a homey account of his role as Highjump's chaplain in *Strong Men South* (Dubuque, Iowa: Stromen, 1996). All predate the IGY.

Henry M. Dater, Task Force 43 historian, produced several reliable articles and brief manuscript histories, among them "Aviation in the Antarctic" (1963), a survey of VX-6, and "Dakotas in the Antarctic: A Study in Versatility" (1970), an appreciation of the trusty R4Ds. His useful review, "Organizational Developments in the United States Antarctic Program, 1954–1965," appeared in the premier issue of the *Antarctic Journal* (January-February 1966); his history of Byrd Station's first two years is found in the May-June 1974 issue. The Navy's polar expeditions were customarily commemorated with "cruisebooks." The air squadron and individual ships often had their own as well. Resembling class yearbooks in content and tone, those for Operations Deep Freeze I through

IV, under varying titles, boasted excellent photography and basic, if breezy, descriptions of operations and challenges.

Studies of the International Geophysical Year include general contemporary accounts by key players, such as Sydney Chapman's *IGY: Year of Discovery, the Story of the International Geophysical Year* (Ann Arbor: University of Michigan Press, 1959), which looks at the IGY globally through the lens of scientific learning. The Antarctic, while important, is dwarfed by the attention given earth satellites. J. Tuzo Wilson's *IGY: The Year of the New Moons* (New York: Knopf, 1961) similarly emphasizes outer space. The *New York Times*'s Walter Sullivan traveled with the Deep Freeze Navy to write the popular *Quest for a Continent* (1957) and *Assault on the Unknown: The International Geophysical Year* (1961), both from McGraw-Hill, New York. His useful review, "The International Geophysical Year," appeared in *International Conciliation* (New York: Carnegie Endowment for International Peace, January-May 1959). Wallace W. Atwood Jr.'s "The International Geophysical Year in Retrospect," Department of State Bulletin, 11 May 1959, explains the structure and workings of the International Council of Scientific Unions (the IGY's parent organization) and its international IGY planning committee (CSAGI), the national committees, and the World Data Centers. Albert P. Crary's draft "History of the International Geophysical Year" assembles a broad collection of documents, or parts thereof, with connecting commentary. With an insider's eye he had begun to mesh the confusion of simultaneous activity in many venues into an organized and valuable narrative but put it down before reaching the IGY's start date. Allan A. Needell, *Science, Cold War and the American State: Lloyd V. Berkner and the Balance of Professional Ideals* ([12 countries]: Harwood, 2000), is an excellent analysis of the background, personality, and contributions of a pivotal IGY figure.

Sir Vivian Fuchs and Sir Edmund Hillary, *The Crossing of Antarctica* (Boston: Little, Brown, 1958), tells the story of the Commonwealth Trans-Antarctic Expedition (TAE) of 1955–1958, a contemporary, technically separate venture closely tied to the IGY. Hillary offers his own perspective on the TAE experience in chapters of his memoir, *View From the Summit* (London: Corgi Books, 2000).

For IGY science, Carl Eklund and Joan Beckman, *Antarctica: Polar Research and Discovery During the IGY* (New York: Holt, Rinehart and Winston, 1963), is an engaging resource for lay readers, as is Richard S. Lewis, *A Continent for Science: The Antarctic Adventure* (New York: Viking, 1965), which explores historical bases for his theme. G. E. Fogg's scholarly *A History of Antarctic Science* (Cambridge: Cambridge University Press, 1992) considers specific sciences, especially during the IGY, and observes "persistent features" of Antarctic science. Richard S. Lewis and Philip M. Smith, eds., *Frozen Future: A Prophetic Report From Antarctica* (New York: Quadrangle Books, 1973), is a valuable collection of short pieces by important Antarctic players that examine scientific, operational, political, and diplomatic issues of the IGY era from the perspective of the early 1970s. The International Council of Scientific Unions, Comité Spécial de l'Année Géophysique Internationale, *Annals of the IGY,* were published by Pergamon Press between 1959 and 1970 to summarize Polar Year precedents, IGY activities, conferences, and research findings. Fifteen volumes appeared by late 1961.

The Antarctic Treaty inspired several helpful studies, such as Philip W. Quigg's *A Pole Apart: The Emerging Issue of Antarctica* (New York: McGraw-Hill, 1983) and his *Antarctica: The Continuing Experiment* (Headline Series no. 273, March-April 1985, for the Great Decisions Program), which look at the mix of economic, political, scientific, and environmental factors that motivated the various participants. Jeffrey D. Myhre, *The Antarctic Treaty System: Politics, Law, and Diplomacy* (Boulder: Westview, 1986), examines the diplomatic origins of the treaty and each article in turn. Writing during the decade of intense effort toward a minerals convention, neither author had access to all of the still-classified treaty-negotiation documents. M. J. Peterson, *Managing the Frozen South: The Creation and Evolution of the Antarctic Treaty System* (Berkeley: University of California Press, 1988), and Olav Schram Stokke and Davor Vidas, eds., *Governing the Antarctic: The Effectiveness and Legitimacy of the Antarctic Treaty System* (Cambridge: Cambridge University Press, 1996), look at the treaty in practice over time, touching on scientific and operational issues of the IGY as they related to policy. Stokke & Vidas also address newer concerns, such as environmentalism and tourism. Brian Shoemaker, "Antarctic Treaty System Inspections: Historical Significance and Future Impact" (master's thesis, University of Cambridge, 1989), analyzes a key provision from his perspective as a former commander of the U.S. Naval Support Force, Antarctica. The Report of the United States Antarctic Inspection, February 9 to March 11, 1995, conducted under the auspices of the U.S. State Department and Arms Control and Disarmament Agency, illuminates the inspection system and practices as a whole. A frequently updated Handbook of the Antarctic Treaty System (ATS), such as that edited by H. K. Cohen in 2001, gathers all of the agreements comprising the ATS plus ancillary documentation.

Evaluations of the Antarctic Treaty System include Robert D. Hayton's cogent analysis of anticipated strengths and weaknesses before the treaty went into force in "The Antarctic Settlement of 1959," *American Journal of Interna-*

tional Law 54, no. 2 (April 1960): 348–371, and Henry M. Dater's backward look in "The Antarctic Treaty in Action 1961–1971," *Antarctic Journal* (May-June 1971): 67–72. Ambassador Paul C. Daniels gave his uniquely germane views in *Frozen Future* (described earlier) in 1973. In January 1985 the Polar Research Board/National Research Council's Commission on Physical Sciences, Mathematics, and Resources convened an international workshop at Beardmore South Field Camp, Antarctica; its informative proceedings were published as *Antarctic Treaty System: An Assessment* (Washington, D.C.: National Academy Press, 1986).

PERIODICALS

National Geographic magazine has been presenting Antarctic discovery, exploration, and science since at least February 1907, when it reviewed Robert F. Scott's *The Voyage of 'The Discovery.'* Shackleton and Byrd both wrote for the magazine, the latter on his own expeditions and on Operation Highjump: "Our Navy Explores Antarctica" (October 1947). Several eyewitness articles highlighted the IGY: Paul A. Siple, "We Are Living at the South Pole" (July 1957); David S. Boyer, "Year of Discovery Opens in Antarctica" (September 1957); Paul W. Frazier, "Across the Frozen Desert to Byrd Station" (September 1957); and Sir Vivian Fuchs, "The Crossing of Antarctica" (January 1959). Adm. George J. Dufek, "What We've Accomplished in Antarctica" (October 1959), and Adm. David M. Tyree, "New Era in the Loneliest Continent" (February 1963), reviewed the Navy's role. With superb photographs and maps, these stories attest to contemporary awe over the unfolding of the mysterious continent.

Science, the journal of the American Association for the Advancement of Science, faithfully reported IGY events and milestones. Major articles on progress at the time included Hugh Odishaw's "International Geophysical Year: A Report on the United States Program" (vol. 127, 17 January 1958). Part II of Odishaw's report appeared on 2 January 1959. See also, Homer E. Newell Jr., "IGY Conference in Moscow: Reports on the Organizational Setup and on the Soviet Presentation of Their Rocket and Satellite Work" (vol. 129, 9 January 1959), and ongoing short pieces.

The *Antarctic Journal*, published on varying schedules by the National Science Foundation since January-February 1966 and for several years with the Department of Defense, contains a wealth of topical and historical articles. Besides those already cited are George J. Dufek, "Tenth Anniversary of First Landing at the South Pole" (November-December 1966); Kenneth J. Bertrand,

"A Look at Operation Highjump Twenty Years Later" (January-February 1967); Capt. Lewis O. Smith, USN (Ret.), "Operation Windmill: The Second Antarctic Developments Project" (March-April 1968); Peter J. Anderson, "United States Aircraft Losses in Antarctica" (January-February 1974); James H. Zumberge, "The Remains of Camp Michigan" (May-June 1974); Guy Guthridge, "Hallett Station, Antarctica, 1956–1973" (December 1983); "US Airplane Recovered From East Antarctica" (March-June 1987); and "Salvaged Airplane Returns to McMurdo" (June 1988). Short reports have appeared on Navy support activities, such as building construction, the introduction of new types of vehicles, ship and aircraft operations, nuclear-power plant construction and operation, the first winter flight to McMurdo, arriving scientists and their projects, scientific findings, international relationships, tourism, SCAR, and treaty meetings. *Antarctic*, the quarterly journal of the New Zealand Antarctic Society, provided short, useful articles on not only New Zealand activities but also those of other polar nations.

The American Polar Society's *Polar Times* frequently features historical as well as contemporary polar concerns. Issue no. 44, June 1957, reprinted a sizable collection of newspaper articles pertaining to the IGY in Antarctica. Unfortunately unprovenanced, they all appear to have been from the *New York Times;* most were dated internally and could be confirmed using the *Times* Index, itself a useful research tool. The *New York Times* kept at least two reporters in the field at the time—Sullivan and Bernard Kalb. Eunice Moss, whose husband, George Moss, was a chief petty officer in Deep Freeze I, assembled a thick scrapbook of clippings, primarily from northeastern newspapers, that I was similarly able to identify. Articles in news and feature magazines during the late 1950s bespoke popular interest in the IGY and the polar continent, for example, "U.S. Breaks Into a Frozen Continent," *Life*, 2 April 1956, 38–47, and "Compelling Continent," a cover story focused on Paul Siple, *Time*, 31 December 1956, 12–17.

HISTORICAL AND TOPICAL LITERATURE

The universe of historical writing on Antarctica is surprisingly large and fine. From Capt. James Cook, Antarctic circumnavigator of the 1770s, on, explorers inevitably wrote books to offset the high costs of their expeditions and gain future support. For an introduction, Walker Chapman offers well-selected writings, from ancient speculations about the continent's existence to voices of the IGY era, in *Antarctic Conquest: The Great Explorers in Their Own Words* (Indianapolis: Bobbs-Merrill, 1965). The most significant early American among them is Charles Wilkes, controversial naval-expedition leader and author of the five-volume *Narrative of the United States Exploring Expedition During the Years 1838, 1839, 1840, 1841, 1842* (Philadelphia: Sea & Blanchard, 1845). Chapman's *The Loneliest Continent: The Story of Antarctic Discovery* (Greenwich, Conn.: New York Graphic Society, 1964) gives a brief and generally reliable, though undocumented, overview covering the same sweeping time frame. Alan Gurney's title well describes his *Below the Convergence: Voyages Toward Antarctica, 1699–1839* (New York: Norton, 1997); the book details key navigational developments as well as geographical findings. Stephen Martin's *A History of Antarctica* (n.p.: State Library of New South Wales Press, 1996) is a general account with a foreign (Australian) point of view. U.S. activity is amply covered, although curious details and quoted passages are sometimes chosen. Foremost, indeed definitive, for U.S. involvement in the polar south is geographer Kenneth J. Bertrand's monumental *Americans in Antarctica, 1775–1948* (New York: American Geographical Society, 1971), an exhaustively detailed tracing focused on discovery and science. It ends at the doorstep of the present study.

A great body of Antarctic literature highlights the Heroic Age (1895–1922), with a plethora of books (many in multiple editions) by or about the larger-than-life expedition leaders and their "firsts." A few of the works particularly applicable to the IGY follow. Obvious inclusions are Roald Amundsen, *The South Pole: An Account of the Norwegian Antarctic Expedition in the "Fram," 1910–1912*, 2 vols., A. G. Chater, trans. (New York: New York University Press, 2001, first published 1912), and Robert Falcon Scott, *Scott's Last Expedition: The Journals* (New York: Carroll & Graf, 1996). Participant Apsley Cherry-Garrard's deep-felt *The Worst Journey in the World, Antarctic 1910–1913* (London: Chatto & Windus, 1965) describes Scott's last expedition, with poignant analysis of its undoing. Roland Huntford, in his stunning comparative biography *The Last Place on Earth* (London: Pan Books, 1985; published by Hodder and Stoughton Ltd. in 1979 as *Scott and Amundsen*), harshly judges Scott, his compatriot, while hailing the victorious Norwegian's skill and preparation. Susan Solomon, in *The Coldest March: Scott's Fatal Antarctic Expedition* (New Haven: Yale University Press, 2001), analyzes weather data over time to try to explain the Scott tragedy.

Ernest Shackleton's *The Heart of the Antarctic: The Farthest South Expedition, 1907–1909* (New York: Signet, 2000, first published in England by William Heinemann, 1909) and *South: The Endurance Expedition* (New York: Signet, 1999, 1919) recount his extraordinary attempts to pierce the continent. Huntford also admirably assesses Shackleton in *Shackleton* (New York: Carroll & Graf, 1985). As the Pole was being won and lost, Australia's Douglas Mawson led an expedition in stormy East Antarctica, immortalized in *Home of the Blizzard: A True Story of Antarctic Survival* (New York: St. Martin's Griffin, 2000).

Richard Evelyn Byrd, an American, dominated the interwar period in Antarctica. His expeditionary accounts, all published by G. P. Putnam's Sons and inhaled by many an IGY pioneer, were *Little America: Aerial Exploration in the Antarctic, the Flight to the South Pole* (1930), *Discovery: The Story of the Second Byrd Antarctic Expedition* (1935), and *Alone* (1938). Laurence McKinley Gould's *Cold: The Record of an Antarctic Sledge Journey* (Northfield, Minn.: Carleton College Limited Edition, 1984, first published 1931) is a literate account of the later Antarctic Committee chair's wintering with Byrd and leading an exploration of the Queen Maud Mountains by dogsled in 1929–1930. A scholarly biography of Byrd awaits, although one is reportedly in progress. Edwin P. Hoyt relied on secondary sources for his venerative *The Last Explorer: The Adventures of Admiral Byrd* (New York: John Day, 1968). Rose's *Assault on Eternity* offers perceptive analysis of Byrd's character and accomplishments within the scope of that study. Raimund E. Goerler, editor, presents Byrd's since-questioned North Pole flight in *To the Pole: The Diary and Notebook of Richard E. Byrd, 1925–1927* (Columbus: Ohio State University Press, 1998).

Stephen J. Pyne, *The Ice: A Journey to Antarctica* (Seattle: University of Washington Press, 1998; Iowa City: University of Iowa Press, 1986), explores the "idea" of Antarctica; he considers history (including the IGY) along with other approaches ranging from science to art to geopolitics. It is a unique and formidable work. Francis Spufford, *I May Be Some Time: Ice and the English Imagination* (New York: St. Martin's, 1997), and William E. Lenz, *The Poetics of the Antarctic: A Study in Nineteenth-Century American Cultural Perceptions* (New York: Garland, 1995), are recent intellectual studies taking a literary approach. Both focus on earlier eras, but their analyses of attitudes toward polar ice and cold, especially by those not there, are illuminating.

On issues important since the IGY, *Eagle Over the Ice: The U.S. in the Antarctic*, by Christopher C. Joyner and Ethel R. Theis (Hanover, N.H.: University Press of New England, 1997), is a policy study of U.S. goals and interests as rooted in the Antarctic Treaty. Continuing interest in the economic potential of Antarctica is shown in Neal Potter, *Natural Resource Potentials of the Antarctic* (New York: American Geographical Society, 1969), and Martijn Wilder, *Antarctica: An Economic History of the Last Continent* (Sydney: University of Sydney Department of Economic History, 1992). *The Seventh Continent: Antarctica in a Resource Age*, by Deborah Shapley (Washington, D.C.: Resources for the Future, 1985), looks at resource conservation and political issues nationally and internationally within the treaty context. A 1991 international symposium in Sweden marking the 30th anniversary of the treaty produced *Changing Trends in Antarctic Research*, Aant Elzinga, ed. (Dordrecht: Kluwer Academic Publishers, 1993). *The Future of Antarctica: Exploitation Versus Preservation*, Grahame Cook, ed. (Manchester, England: Manchester University Press, 1990), emerged from a conference exploring resource development at the University of London in the interval between the failure of the minerals convention and the success of the Environmental Protocol. The Polar Research Board/National Research Council call attention to changing environmental attitudes and suggest ways to implement the newly approved Protocol in *Science and Stewardship in the Antarctic* (Washington, D.C.: National Academy Press, 1993).

Psychologists unsurprisingly found rich research material in Antarctica. A unique spotlight on one IGY experience was Charles S. Mullin and H.J.M. Connery's "Psychological Study at an Antarctic IGY Station" (*Armed Forces Medical Journal* 10, no. 3, March 1959), which (without naming names) analyzed the difficult first winter at Ellsworth. Later studies illuminated the pioneer period as well as their own. One exemplary book is Jack Stuster, *Bold Endeavors: Lessons From Polar and Space Exploration* (Annapolis: Naval Institute Press, 1996), which looks at such issues as leadership, isolation, food, and work in Antarctica to plan for successful travel in space. New Zealand psychology professor A.J.W. Taylor, in *Antarctic Psychology* (New Zealand Department of Scientific and Industrial Research, DSIR Bulletin no. 244, 1987), studied similar issues at Scott Base. He used a prison analogy to describe polar life, especially wintering over. E. K. Eric Gunderson edited a fine and generally positive Antarctic Research Series volume, *Human Adaptability to Antarctic Conditions* (Washington, D.C.: American Geophysical Union, 1974). Navy psychologists R. E. Strange and S. A. Youngman's "Emotional Aspects of Wintering Over" (*Antarctic Journal*, November-December 1971) also stressed the importance of fulfilling work and effective leadership in isolated living.

Among the few books that focus on south-polar women is Elizabeth Chipman, *Women on the Ice: A History of Women in the Far South* (Melbourne: Melbourne University Press, 1986). Her scope is global; she offers revealing quotes from Admiral Dufek in the Australian press, although without notes. Another is Esther D. Rothblum, Jacqueline S. Weinstock, and Jessica F. Morris, eds., *Women in the Antarctic* (New York: Harrington Park, 1998), based on oral history interviews with women pioneers, explorers, scientists, and support personnel (Navy and civilian).

The post-IGY period has seen proliferating personal accounts. Charles Neider's *Edge of the World: Ross Island, Antarctica: A Personal and Historical Narrative* (Garden City, N.Y.: Doubleday, 1974) and *Beyond Cape Horn: Travels in the*

Antarctic (San Francisco: Sierra Club Books, 1980) lift too many long passages from earlier heroes, but his interviews with historic figures (Fuchs, Gould, Sir Charles Wright) add to understanding. Neider was also interesting as an early, if not the first, nonscientist to work on the ice. Edwin Mickleburgh emphasizes the Greenpeace/environmentalist perspective in *Beyond the Frozen Sea: Visions of Antarctica* (New York: St. Martin's, 1987). Robert Fox, *Antarctica and the South Atlantic: Discovery, Development and Dispute* (London: British Broadcasting Company, 1985), juxtaposes the 1982 territorial war with Argentina over the Falklands with the possible demise of the Antarctic Treaty. Marine biologist David G. Campbell's *The Crystal Desert: Summers in Antarctica* (Boston: Houghton Mifflin, 1992) is scientifically informative and beautifully written. James Gorman, in *Ocean Enough and Time: Discovering the Waters Around Antarctica* (New York: HarperCollins, 1995), contemplates the strangeness of human society at high southern latitudes. Mark A. Hinebaugh, *Flying Upside Down: True Tales of an Antarctic Pilot* (Annapolis: Naval Institute Press, 1999), suggests in personal stories the ways Antarctic flying and survival have changed and not changed over time.

Among miscellaneous reference works, the *Illustrated Glossary of Snow and Ice* by Terence Armstrong, Brian Roberts, and Charles Swithinbank (Cambridge: Scott Polar Research Institute Spec. Publ. no. 4, 1973) was frequently consulted. Though quaint and sexist to modern eyes, Anne Briscoe Pye and Nancy Shea, *The Navy Wife*, 3rd rev. ed. (New York: Harper & Brothers, 1955), colorfully articulates the Navy structure and culture of the time. Jeff Rubin, *Antarctica*, 2nd ed. (Melbourne: Lonely Planet, 2000), a travel guide, is full of useful information, both historical and contemporary. The 1979 edition of *Survival in Antarctica*, by NSF's Division of Polar Programs, used historical examples such as the Otter crash of Deep Freeze I as object lessons for staying alive in a hostile environment. Among NSF's continuing stream of publications, the U.S. Antarctic Program External Panel's "The United States in Antarctica" (Washington, D.C.: NSF, 1997) offers a concise, illustrated overview of historic and then-current program efforts and needs.

The retrospective Library of Congress *Antarctic Bibliography, 1951–1961* (Washington, D.C.: GPO, 1970), one of a series sponsored by the NSF Office of Polar Programs annually since 1988, helped direct my research, as did the annotated *United States IGY Bibliography, 1953–1960*, compiled by Frank M. Marson and Janet R. Terner for the Library of Congress, NSF, and NAS (Washington, D.C.: NAS-NRC Publ. 1087, 1963). Treaty scholar Robert D. Hayton compiled National Interests in Antarctica, an Annotated Bibliography for the U.S. Antarctic Projects Officer (Washington, D.C.: GPO, 1959).

INDEX